ENGLISH PLACE-NAME SOCIETY.   VOLUME IX

GENERAL EDITORS
A. MAWER *and* F. M. STENTON

THE
PLACE-NAMES OF DEVON

PART II

LONDON
Cambridge University Press
FETTER LANE

NEW YORK · TORONTO
BOMBAY · CALCUTTA · MADRAS
Macmillan

TOKYO
Maruzen Company Ltd.

ENGLISH PLACE-NAME SOCIETY. VOLUME IX

THE
PLACE-NAMES OF DEVON

By
J. E. B. GOVER, A. MAWER *and*
F. M. STENTON

PART II

CAMBRIDGE
AT THE UNIVERSITY PRESS
1932

All communications with regard to the
Society should be addressed to

THE HON. SECRETARY,
English Place-Name Society,
University College,
Gower Street,
W.C. 1.

ADDENDA ET CORRIGENDA

Among the chief contributors of material for the Addenda and Corrigenda printed in this volume have been:

Mr F. G. Emmison (F. G. E.),
Miss M. S. Holgate (M. S. H.),
The Rev. J. B. Johnston (J. B. J.),
Dr Sigurd Karlström (S. K.),
Mrs Rose-Troup (F. R.-T.).

If not mentioned in full, we have endeavoured to indicate their contributions by printing their initials at the end of the addenda which are due to them.

VOL. I, PART I

p. 111, l. 18. For 'Putney (Mx)' read 'Putney (Sr).'

VOL. I, PART II

p. 29, s.v. great. Delete reference to Greatham (Sx).

p. 30. hæfen should precede (ge)hæg.

p. 33, s.n. har. Mr G. M. Young calls attention to an interesting example of *Harestone* as the name of a boundary stone. In the Stanton St Bernard Charter (BCS 600) there is mention of a *gemerstan* which is still in position at the meeting place of three parishes, while the piece of down there is called *Harestone* on the 6″ O.S. map.

p. 39, s.v. hryding. Delete reference to Woodridden (Ess).

p. 49, s.n. ræge. Add 'or roe (f).' (J. B. J.).

p. 58, l. 3. Delete Strudwick (Nth).

VOL. II

p. xxvii. Add Black Prince. *Black Prince's Register* (1930–1).

p. 43, s.n. FOSCOTT. For 'Foscott (D)' read 'Foscott (O).'

p. 84, s.n. LISCOMBE. The form *Lichecumbe* in the Curia Regis Rolls for 1207 and 1208 makes the etymology suggested on page 85 exceedingly doubtful. The first element may after all be OE hlinc, with early loss of *n* from the consonant group, or possibly it is OE *lic*, 'body, corpse,' the valley being named from some unrecorded incident or practice in the past.

p. 88, s.n. NETHERWELD. Add *Netherwelde juxta Wenge* 1304 FF.

p. 95, s.n. HAWRIDGE. Add *Harugge* 1347 Black Prince.

p. 173, s.n. LOOSLEY ROW. Add *Louslerowe in parochia de Rysburgh* 1464 FF (le Neve Index).

p. 206, s.n. CHAWLEY (FM). Add *Challey in parochia de Westwycombe* 1464 FF.

p. 264, s.n. CHALVEY. For '244' read '234.'

p. 267, s.n. LOOSLEY ROW. For '174' read '173.'

p. 274. For 'Winkburn (Nth)' read 'Winkburn (Nt).'

VOL. III

p. 12, s.n. STODDEN. The Hundred-name survived as late as 1607 (*Terrier*) in *Stodden Field* in the north-west part of Pertenhall parish (cf. *Beds. Hist. Rec. Soc.* 12, 93–5).

p. 17, s.n. SHIRDON. The name survives locally in Shirdon Hall on the Kimbolton-Pertenhall boundary (F. G. E.).

p. 28, s.n. GALSEY. Delete reference to Galsworthy (D).

p. 40, ARNOE is just by *Herneho Wood* (since stubbed up) in the Tithe Award for 1839. This wood appears as *Harner Wood* (1834 O.S.). Mr Emmison in giving this information aptly suggests that as this is in a corner of the parish this points to a compound of OE hyrne and hoh, hence 'hill in the corner of the parish.' The identification with *Audenho* is doubtless incorrect.

p. 45, s.n. DILWICK. *Dilwick Lane* connects Wootton Wood End with the extreme west of Kempston West End (Wootton End Award, 1838) (F.G.E.).

p. 54, s.n. LANGNOE. This was near the boundaries of Colmworth, Roxton and Gt Barford. (*Beds. Hist. Rec. Soc.* 12, 6, 16.)

p. 59, s.n. SUDBURY. *Sudbury Meadow* is marked on the End Award (1800). It lay in the S.E. of the parish. (F.G.E.)

p. 66, s.n. REDBORNSTOKE. The Hundred meeting-place was probably in Marston Moretaine parish near the *Hundredway* of a Terrier of 1715 (*Beds. Hist. Rec. Soc.* 12, 95).

p. 109, s.n. KINWICK. For the location of this place v. *Beds. Hist. Rec. Soc.*, 5, 73.

p. 122, s.n. EDE WAY. Mr F. G. Emmison notes that this is called *Sault Waye* in a deed of 1569 at the point where Ede Way forms the parish-boundary between Leagrave and Sundon. He notes also what seems to be a further example of a *þeodweg* in *Theetsway* in Caddington, in a deed of 1650.

p. 159, s.n. STAPLEFORD. This is marked on the maps of Gordon (1736) and Bowen (1749). It lay between Copthall and Luton Hoo mansion where the present by-way between these places crosses the Lea. (F. G. E.)

p. 174, s.n. FEAKS WELL. The name survived till 1834 O.S. (F. G. E.)

p. 250, s.n. OLD WESTON. Add ref. 74 F 9.

The publication of two Bedfordshire Subsidy Lists, 1309 and 1332, in No. XVIII of the Suffolk Green Books (Bury St Edmunds, 1925) supplies information as to the origin of a good many minor Bedfordshire names either not recorded in this volume or insufficiently documented. The additional information is set forth below, grouped under hundreds and parishes.

STODDEN HUNDRED

BOLNHURST. BROOK FM. Cf. Alicia *atte Broke* (1309).

CLAPHAM. CLAPHAM GREEN. Cf. Richard *ate Grene* (1309).

OAKLEY. HILL FM. Cf. Rosia *atte Hul* (1332).

PERTENHALL. GREEN END. Cf. Joh *atte Grene* (1309). WOOD END. Cf. Ad *ate Wodende* (1309).

RISELEY. GRANGE FM. Cf. Elia *ad Grangiam* (1309). HARING'S FM. Cf. Rich *Heyroun* (1309).

WILLEY HUNDRED

BLETSOE. WHITWICK GREEN. Cf. Beatricia de *Whitewyk* (1332) taxed under the neighbouring parish of Sharnbrook.

CARLTON. BRIDGE END. Cf. Wm de *Ponte* (1309). MOORS (6″). Cf. John de *la More* (1309), Ric *atte Moer* (1332).

FELMERSHAM. MOOR END. Cf. Robt de *la Moer* (1309). PARSON'S BARN (6″) is on the border of Sharnbrook parish where a family of *Person* is assessed in 1309.

HARROLD. BROWNAGE WOLD. This was probably the home of Regin *Bronsege* (1309) and Henry *Brunshege* (1332). The new forms leave the etymology uncertain.

PAVENHAM. EAST END (6″) and WESTEND FM. Cf. Simon *Est* (1309) and Henricus *West* (ib.). HILL BARN (6″). Cf. Simon *atte Hull* (1309).

STAGSDEN. BECKS ASH SPINNEY (6″). Cf. John *Bekke* (1309).
  HILL FM. Cf. Richard *atte Hul* (1332).
  WHITE'S WOOD (6″). Cf. Cecilia and Nicholas *le Whyte* (1332).
STEVINGTON. PARK END. Cf. Hugo de *Parco* (1309).

BARFORD HUNDRED
  COLMWORTH. WESTWOOD (6″). Cf. Joh *West Wod* (1332).
  EATON SOCON. BROOK HO (6″). Cf. Hugo *ater Broke* (1309).
    COXFIELD (6″). Cf. John *Coke* (1309).
  RENHOLD. HOWBURY HALL. Cf. Robt *atte Ho* (1309).
    WATER END. Cf. Wm *atte Water* (1332).
  WILDEN. SMARTWICK. Cf. Hugo *Smart* (1309).

REDBORNSTOKE HUNDRED
  CRANFIELD. EYRESWOOD FM (6″). Cf. Willo *le Heyr* (1309), Willo *le Eyr* (1332).
  MARSTON MORETAINE. CAULCOTT. Cf. Joh de *Caldecote* (1309).
  WOOTTON. BOURNE END. Cf. Elia *atte Bourne* (1309).

WIXAMTREE HUNDRED
  SOUTHILL. FLANNELS (6″). Cf. Alicia de *Flaunuyle* (1332) in the neighbouring parish of Warden.

BIGGLESWADE HUNDRED
  SANDY. COX HILL. Cf. Henrico *le Cock* (1332).

MANSHEAD HUNDRED
  ASPLEY GUISE. WRIGHT'S SPINNEY. Cf. Wm *le Wrigthe* (1332).
  EVERSHOLT. BIRCHALL'S WOOD. Cf. (?) Ric *Brikelis* (1309).
    TYRRELL'S END. Cf. Robt *Tyrel* (1309).
    WATER END. Cf. Pho *ad aquam* (1309).
    WITS END. Cf. Rad *le Withe*, Juliana *le Wythe* (1309), i.e. (probably) 'the white.'
  HARLINGTON. GOSWELL END (6″) is probably to be associated with the family of Richard and John *le Gosele* (1309), but the relation of the forms to one another is obscure.
  STUDHAM. HILL FM. Cf. Willo *atte Hulle* (1309).
  TINGRITH. DAINTRY WOOD. Cf. Isabella de *Dauentre* (1332).
  WESTONING. SAMSHILL. (?) Cf. Reginald *Sampson* (1332).

FLITT HUNDRED
  BARTON-IN-THE-CLAY. CHURCH END. Cf. Joh *atte Chirche* (1332).
    STONLEY WOOD. Cf. Robert de *Stonle* (1332).
  CADDINGTON. CHAUL END. Cf. Joh de *Challeye* (1309), Robt *Chaleie* (1332).
  HYDE. SOMERIES CASTLE. Cf. Joh de *Somerey* (1309) from the neighbouring parish of Luton.
  LUTON. HART HILL AND LANE. Cf. Wm *Herte* (1309).
    PARK TOWN. Cf. Richard *atte Park* (1332).
    TURNER'S KNOLL. Cf. Wm *le Turnour* (1309).
  PULLOXHILL. GAGMANSBURY. Cf. John *Gageman* (1332) from the neighbouring parish of Silsoe.
  SILSOE. BRAYBURY LODGES. Cf. Matthew de *Bray* (1309).

CLIFTON HUNDRED
  ARLESEY. ETONBURY. Cf. Wm de *Etone* (1332).
  MEPPERSHALL. HOO FM. Cf. Finota *atte Hoo* (1332).
  SHILLINGTON. UPTON END. Cf. Reginald *Upmanende* (1309).

VOL. IV

p. 12, s.n. ISBOURNE. The form *Esegburna* should have been given with the date 777 (11th) as it is found not only in Harleian 4060, but also in Cotton Tiberius A 13. The second form *(Bi)esingburnan* should be dated 872 (13th) as it is found in the Cartulary of St Peter's, Gloucester. These corrected dates suggest to Dr Karlström that the first element is a river-name identical with Eisey (W), which is found as *æt Esig, Eseg* BCS 226. For the later *ing*-forms he compares the forms for Tavistock *at Tauistoce* KCD 629, *on Tæfingstoce* KCD 1334. (PN D 217.)

p. 83, s.n. BERRINGTON. Karlström (ZONF 7, 251) notes that unstressed *-e-* and *-i-* often interchange in this district as in *Bradi burne, Brade burne* BCS 356, *dunne bæce* and *dunni bæce* (Heming 246), *Alritune* (ib.) for Orleton (PN Wo 67), and suggests that this name may after all be from OE beretun, with late substitution of *ing* for *i.*

p. 116, s.n. COTHERIDGE. Karlström (ZONF 7, 252) calls attention to the locality called *on Codran* in the neighbouring parish of Leigh. He suggests that that name also underlies the DB and Surv forms of Cotheridge, and that *Coddanhrycg* is formed by dissimilation from *Codranhrycg*. The meaning of this place-name element is unknown.

p. 164, s.n. SEDGEBERROW. Karlström (ZONF 7, 252) notes that in BCS 219 *secges mere* is an alternative name for the place called *secgmere* in BCS 667. This might get over the formal difficulty, though the persistent *s* of the forms of Sedgeberrow is a little surprising, but still leaves the semantic difficulty that one can hardly have a sedge-grove.

p. 188, s.n. NAFFORD. The form *Nethford'* (1196 P) tends to confirm Ekwall's suggestion as to the etymology of this name.

p. 223, s.n. PINVIN. Add *Pendefen* 1196 P.

p. 331, s.n. BEVINGTON. The DB form *Buintun* has been omitted (S. K.). This would suggest that the pers. name in question is *Beoua* rather than *Bifa.*

p. 406, s.n. HARVINGTON (Chaddesley). For '237' read '238.'

Dr G. B. Grundy has recently completed his study of the Anglo-Saxon charters of Worcestershire (Birmingham Archæological Society, Volumes 52 and 53), and some further identifications of Worcestershire names recorded in Anglo-Saxon charters have been made by him. The most important are as follows (the references are to Parts I and II of that Study as re-printed at the Oxford University Press (1929 and 1931)):

PART I

pp. 14 and 38. SLEDGEMOOR COPPICE (6″) in Wichenford is the *secges mere* of an 8th century charter (BCS 219), and the *seges mere* of another 8th century charter (BCS 233). Dr Grundy suggests that this means 'sedge pond.'

p. 50. DILMORE LODGE in North Claines is *Dillamere* in a charter of 1038 (Earle 239). The second element is mere. The first can hardly be the plant-name *dile* as this only grows on dry pastures.

p. 83. NOSTERN WELLS PIECE, a field-name on the bounds of Elmley Castle and Netherton, is the *Nottestan* of a charter of 1042 (KCD 764). This is probably for *hnottestan*, 'the bald or bare stone.'

pp. 112–113. The field-names WINDSBRIDGE and WENSBRIDGE in Feckenham, earlier *Wynes brugge*, are the *Wines Brycge* of BCS 1006. The name denotes 'the bridge of one *Wine.*'

p. 122. The field-name WARELEY in Grimley is the *waer legan* of a charter of 816 (BCS 356), and, as noted by Grundy, the first element is the common word 'weir,' the field lying by the Severn.

PART II

p. 36. The field-name HAMSTEAD in Severnstoke is the *ham stede* of the Pershore Survey (BCS 1282).

p. 62. THURLAND FURLONG, a field-name in Tredington, is the *torde londa* of a survey of Shipston (Heming 347). The first element is probably the word *turde*, 'dung.'

VOL. V

p. 16, s.n. SKELTON. Karlström (ZONF 7, 254) suggests that in some of these Skeltons we may have OScand *skiæl*, 'division, boundary,' found in Sw *Skälby*, where it has apparently the sense of *væghaskiæl*, 'cross-roads.' Skelton near Ripon, it may be noted, is close by the Riding boundary.

p. 32, s.n. CORNBROUGH. Karlström (ZONF 7, 255) points out that it is unlikely that *cron-* for *cran-* would be found in Northern England, so that we cannot have that word in Cornbrough.

p. 111, s.n. RAVENSCAR. Delete the article on this name. The early form quoted probably refers to the lost Ravenser in the East Riding, and Ravenscar would seem to be a modern coinage.

p. 155, s.nn. MICKLEDALES, MORDALES. Karlström (ZONF 7, 256) suggests that we have ON *deld* (East Scand) or *deild*, *deilð* (West Scand) rather than the late English vulgarism.

p. 156, s.n. SALT SCAR. Karlström (ZONF 7, 256) points out that this is a rock (ON *sker*, 'skerry'). The one ME form is clearly defective.

p. 200, s.n. KILVINGTON. Karlström (ZONF 7, 256) calls attention to the fact that *Cylfantun* (BCS 553) is now Kilton (So), and is close by Kilve (So), DB *Clive*, elsewhere *Kelve*, *Kilve*, *Culve*, showing that at least in that name we have to do with a toponymic element rather than a personal one.

p. 228, s.n. THEAKSTON. Karlström (ZONF 7, 257) would prefer an ON nickname *þjokka*, as suggested for *Theokemareis* (PN NRY 84).

p. 248, s.n. AIKBER. Delete the first form, which is that of a lost place in the East Riding.

p. 344, s.n. RAINTON. For '185' read '184.'

VOL. VI

p. 22, s.n. HEYSHOTT. Add *Esshiete*, *Essyete* c. 1250 *Harl* 1708 ff. 109, 110 (M. S. H.).

p. 23, s.n. KNAPP FM. Add *Chneppe* 12th Egerton 3031, *Chneppa*, *Knappa* c. 1250 *Harl* 1708 ff. 109, 116 (M. S. H.).

p. 41, s.n. THE RAKE. A further example of this place-name element is found in Rake in Witley (Sr), the home of Richard de *Rake* in 1332 (SR). Rake lies in a shallow valley, and the reference may be to the stream which runs from Witley to Milford. We may note also Raikes Fm in Abinger (Sr) for which we have *Weste* and *Easte Rake* in 1654 (ParReg). The *s* is clearly pseudo-manorial, and the Raike is probably the well-marked valley to the south-west of the farm.

p. 51, s.n. NORTH MARDEN. Add *Normerdon'* 1207 Cur.

p. 52, s.n. LORDINGTON. Add *Herdinton'* 1196 P.

p. 53, s.n. SINGLETON. Add *Schengelton'* 1196 P.

p. 86, s.n. EASTON FM. Add *Eston'* 1207 Cur.

p. 113, s.n. VALEWOOD HO. Forms *Fellwooll* (1639), *Fellwool* (1722) from the Haslemere Parish Registers confirm the early forms for this name, but do not help us to arrive at an etymology.

p. 117, s.n. LIMBO FM. The Surrey *ate Ymphagh* is probably Emplye Barn in Bramley (6″), *Implye Lands* in 1604 (Surrey Wills).

p. 132, s.n. Dunhurst. Add *Dunhurst* 1244 Liberate Rolls.

p. 132, s.n. Gunshot. *Pokshudde* is now Puckshot in Haslemere (Sr).

p. 135, s.n. Songhurst Fm. Cf. Song Hurst in Ewhurst (Sr), the home of Wm de *Sunghurst* (1332 SR).

p. 195, s.n. Durrington. Wallenberg (KPN 239–40) makes a strong point in favour of identifying this place with *Derantun* (BCS 702) when he notes that the neighbouring manor of West Tarring belonged to Christchurch, Canterbury. One cannot accept, however, his attempt to derive the p.n. from a river Darent (cf. *Diorente* BCS 370). None of the forms of that river-name as found in Darenth (K) or Dart (D) show the same phonological development as Durrington.

p. 201 and p. xlvi, s.n. Sompting. In his volume, *Studies on English Place- and Personal Names* (pp. 84–8), Professor Ekwall deals with the history of Sompting, Sunt Fm in Shipley, Sunte Ho in Lindfield, in the light of further topographical information which the Survey was able to place at his disposal, largely through the kindness of Miss M. S. Holgate. This information showed that the element uniting these names was probably the presence of marshy land rather than anything in the nature of a hill. Sompting church is on a steep hill, but it is immediately above what must have been marshy land. Sunt Fm in Shipley lies between two streams, and the slight hill, of which mention is made in PN Sx 201, is reported by the Vicar of Shipley to be land 'as flat as a pancake.' Sunte Ho in Lindfield is on a hill, but the detailed topography as given to the Survey by Miss Holgate shows that it is a water-logged hill. She writes, 'The house stands at the end of a low ridge from which the ground slopes gently away on three sides. On the E. side the ground has been artificially levelled leaving a terrace on the east side of the house with sloping banks on N. and S. leading to a large pond which lies across the eastern boundary of the garden. The whole of this enclosed level is green and soft though this is a very dry season, and one gets the impression that the water has been pushed off into the pond. The house itself is very dry, but the surrounding meadows, especially on the north side, are full of springs, some of them full of iron. Water never alters in level in the well.' The only other Sunt of which we know is Sunt Fm in Surrey, which lies on a feeder of the Eden.

The common topographical element in these places would seem, therefore, to be something denoting marshy land, and Professor Ekwall suggests that we have here a lost OE word *sum(p)t, cognate with OHG *sunft*, 'fen, marsh.' It may be that this word has left a further trace in the common English word *sump*, hitherto supposed to be a continental loan word. An OE *sumpt* would quite naturally become *sunt*. For further details v. *loc. cit*.

VOL. VII

p. 253. Add Racks. We have on the 6″ map Great and Little Racks Wood. The 'Racks' is used locally with no addition of Great, Little or Wood (*v.* Sx NQ 3, 118), and it is suggested that the reference is to racks used for drying cloth which had been prepared at one or other of the Fulling Mills in Ardingly. Miss Holgate notes the parallel in the Rackfield in Pilton (D), which, according to Gribble's *Memorials of Barnstaple*, was 'long used for purposes of drying woollen cloth.'

p. 277, s.n. Slaugham. Add Trucker's Hatch (6″), *Tregars Hatche* (1550 Pat). (M. S. H.)

p. 305, s.n. Berth Lane. An additional form for this rarely recorded name is *the Byrte* 1575 *Add* 37688. (M. S. H.)

p. 336 n. 1. A further example of this alternative name is *Britzlegh* (1363 *Add* 20086). (M. S. H.)

p. 352, s.n. PRESS RIDGE WARREN. A 13th cent. form *presteberg* (Lambeth MSS 1212, f. 93), with marginal note in another hand *prestebrigge*, makes it clear that this name was originally *Preosta beorg*, 'Priests' hill.' For such a development cf. Weybridge (PN BedsHu 232) and *Rumbridge* (PN Sx 88). (M. S. H.)

p. 404, s.n. RIPE. Wallenberg (KPN 37 ff.) shows that the *Rhipp* of BCS 161 and 160 (an original charter) must topographically be identified with West Ripe in Lydd (K) and the adjacent East Ripe (6″) in Lydd, and Midrips in Broomhill (Sx). He suggests that the Marsh called *biscopes uuic* in the same charter may have left its trace in the Wicks in Broomhill and Wick Wall (6″) and Wick Petty Sewer (6″) in Lydd.

p. 511, s.n. CLEEVE AXE. A late trace of this word *exe* is to be found in a place called *Eaxe Lands* in Peasmarsh in a map of 1710, now in Rye Museum. (M. S. H.)

p. 519, s.n. MORGAY FM. Wallenberg (KPN 32 *n.* 2) notes a further example of this name in Morghew Fm (K) and quotes from a Kentish charter (BCS 1307) the phrase *þa geuþe Ælfeh hire morgengife æt Crægan*, i.e. 'then Ælfeh gave her (i.e. the widow of his nephew) her *morgen gife* at Cray.'

p. 523, s.n. DIXTER. Wallenberg (KPN 206–7) notes Denstroude (K), earlier *Dionsterue* al. *Dunesterue* as containing a further example of OE *stiorf* as a p.n. element, and suggests that this word may have been used of poor woodland, affording no pannage or pasturage.

p. 600, s.n. SINGLETON. For '52' read '53.'

VOL. VIII

In the Addenda for Volumes VIII and IX we are indebted to a review of Blomé's *Place-Names of North Devonshire* in ZONF 7, 257. Since Volume VIII was published we note also certain valuable notes in StudNP 2, 67–9 on the place-names of Devon, in which Dr Karlström had anticipated some of the points in our articles on Bidna (102), Countisbury (62), Lower Creedy (419), Down Fm (101), Ladford (108), Thelbridge (412), Zeal (375).

p. xxxix. Add

Black Prince   *Black Prince's Register* (1930–1)

p. xliv. Add

Visit   Visitation of manors, Dean and Chapter Archives, 1281 (*ex. inf.* Rev. E. D. Drake-Brockman).

p. li, l. 34. For '58' read '258.'

p. lv, s.n. CISSBURY. Dr W. L. Renwick points out that the form in the 1590 text of Camden is *Cis(s)bury*, and the forms in Holland's translation of Camden are *Cis(s)burie* in 1610 and *Cis(i)burie* in 1637, and that the form *Sissasbury* is from Norden's map and not from the text itself.

p. lv, l. 3 from foot. For '266' read '276.'

p. 4, s.n. DALCH. For 'Brit. *dubo*' read 'OCeltic *dubo-*.' (J. B. J.)

p. 7, l. 2. OE *grand* should be starred as hypothetical as is done by Zachrisson in his paper. (J. B. J.)

p. 13, s.n. SWINCOMBE R. For '61' read '199.'

p. 21, s.n. CALENDARHAY. For 'The *calendar*...enclosure' substitute 'This was the place of residence of the *Brethren of the Calendar* who recorded obits and other information in the Calendar of the Saints.' The editors regret the previous mis-statement of Mrs Rose-Troup's views.

p. 27, s.n. BARNSTAPLE. The form *Bardestaplensis burg* from the Exon DB should have been included. (J. B. J.)

p. 53, l. 4. For '(PN NRY 30)' read '(PN NRY 301).'

p. 55, s.n. RALEIGH. Read 'wild she-goat' or 'roe (f).' (J. B. J.)

p. 59, s.n. LEEFORD. Add *Looford, Lefford* 1355 Black Prince.

p. 84, s.n. CARTLAND. Add *Carkeland*' 1196 Cur (p).

p. 99, s.n. FRIAR'S HELE. Mr G. S. Fry notes that John *Frye* of Hele is already mentioned in a De Banco roll of 1401 and that his successor was *Gal*fridus and not *God*fridus Frye (as erroneously printed). The manor is called *Frye Hele* in Lysons and he says it is erroneously called *Hele Prior*.

p. 112, s.n. ALVERDISCOTT. *Ælfweard* is more likely than *Ælfred*. (J. B. J.)

p. 125, s.n. BICKINGTON. *bike* should be rendered 'bees' or wasps' nest,' not 'bee-hive.' (J. B. J.)

p. 158, s.n. BODGATE. The Rev. J. B. Johnston calls attention to a possible Scottish parallel, at least for the second element of this name, viz. Bathgate (Linlithgow) c. 1160 *Bathchet*, c. 1200 *Batchet*, 1316 *Bathgat*. (Mackenzie, *Scottish PN* 177, adds 1250 *Bathket*, 1275 *Bathkit*.) This suggests that British *cet* might develop to later *yate* or *gate*, and if so, the first element in Bodgate may be British *bod*, 'dwelling,' hence 'dwelling in the wood.'

p. 164, s.n. PANSON. For '81' read '781.'

p. 167, s.n. SOLLAND. For 't. Ed 6 *Rental*' read 't. Ed 3 *Ass*.' s.n. UNDERDOWN. For 't. Ed. 3 *Ass*' read 't. Ed 6 *Rental*.'

p. 177, s.n. CHURNDON. A possible parallel is to be found in Chirnside (Berwick), c. 1098 *Cirnside* (J. B. J.).

p. 192, s.n. BRIMPTS. In BCS 1214 we have the phrases *on stut þare on vppe stut*, which clearly suggests the use of OE *stut* as a hill-name.

p. 193, footnote. For '262' read '282.'

p. 213, s.n. BRENTOR. Add '*v*. Addenda lix.'

pp. 218, 221, s.nn. GULWORTHY and HATCHWOOD. Add 'the abbot's weir called *Goloworthyache*' 1354 Black Prince.

p. 223, s.n. BERE FERRERS. The Rev. J. B. Johnston suggests association with Welsh *ber*, 'pike, spit,' Irish *bir*, 'point.' If that is correct, the reference may be to the big spit of land between the Tamar and the Tavy.

pp. 226 and 268, s.nn. CUMEREW and CUMERY. The Rev. J. B. Johnston suggests that these names may be identical with Cumrew (Cu), 'valley-slope.' Cf. W *rhiw*, 'slope,' and Ekwall *Scand-Celts* 111.

p. 232, s.n. SMEARDON DOWN. A similar compound is found in Smarkham in Wonersh (Sr), the home of Thos de *Smerecombe* in 1332 (SR).

p. 240, s.n. STOKE DAMAREL parish. Add BULL POINT. Mr Bracken notes that in Carew's *Survey of Cornwall* (1769) 'There is a rock on eache side of the river, the one termed the Bull, the other the Hen—that on the Devon, this on the Cornwall side.' The name is of interest in itself and provides a parallel to the suggested interpretation of the 'Cat' element in Cattedown, Cattewater *supra* 234.

p. 249, s.n. PLASTER DOWN. Cf. Pleystowe in Capel (Sr), the home of Robert *ate Pleystowe* in 1332 (SR), and of Robert Stere of *Plestore* in 1596 (SurreyRecSoc 10, 235).

p. 260, l. 9. For '649' read '1649.'

p. 262, s.n. WINSOR. Windlesham (Sr) is seven miles south-west of Old Windsor. In view of the character of the intervening country it is probable that the same man gave his name to these two places.

p. 268, s.n. COMBE FM. Add *Comb* 1359 Black Prince.

p. 284. Add TORPEEK (6"), William *atte Torre Pik* 1362 Black Prince.

p. 285, s.n. MARRIDGE. For 'lx' read 'lix.'

p. 288, s.n. WOOD. Add 1357 *La Wode* Black Prince.

p. 298, s.n. PUDDAVEN. The Rev. J. B. Johnston suggests that the first element is OE *pāde*, 'toad,' ME *pode*.

VOL. IX

p. 346, s.n. QUEEN'S NYMPTON. Mrs Carbonell informs us that the name Queen's Nympton is quite modern. It is applied to an outlying district of South Molton, which was so named in 1900 in honour of Queen Victoria.

p. 348, s.n. GEORGE NYMPTON. Mrs Rose-Troup calls our attention to a further example of *nymet* in the words *Leofrices Cildes æt Nymeð* in Cotton Tiberius B V f. 75, an Exeter MS, wrongly printed by Kemble (KCD 1353) as *Hymed*. Napier and Stevenson, in their edition of the Crawford Charters, p. 59, wrongly refer to this as a Bath manumission, following the false lead of Thorpe.

p. 356, s.n. RIDDLECOMBE. Professor Förster's suggestion receives support from the place-name Ruddle in St Austell (Co) with early forms *Rydel* (1296 *Ass*), *Ridel* (1327 *SR* (p)), *Ridell* (1420 FF).

p. 416, n. 2. BCS 726 is a grant by Aethelstan of one hide at a place called *Munecatune* for the benefit of the monastery of St Mary and St Peter at Exeter. The charter is endorsed in 14th cent. hands '*Carta Adelstani Regis super manso quod olim vocabatur Moneketon modo tamen Exchestre pro fundacione Ecclesia,*' '*Carta Adthelstani Regis concessa Beato Petro de manso quod antiquitus vocabatur Moneketon ad monasterium quod nunc nuncupatur Exechestre,*' Hooker (*History of Exeter* 98) uses in connexion with Aethelstan the phrases '*civitatem que antiquitus monketon vocatur nunc autem Exeter*' and '*antiquitus vocatem Munketon nunc Exeter vocari voluit.*' We do not know Hooker's authority for this statement. He may have had knowledge of the endorsement of the charter and be reproducing the statement in the first of the two endorsements given above, but the endorsements themselves are inconsistent in their statement. If *Munecatun* is in or near Exeter, Mrs Rose-Troup would identify it with the Fee of St Sidwell and take *sceoca broc* to be the Shutbrook (*supra* 24), with later substitution of *t* for *c*.

p. 444, s.n. POLTIMORE. In the Cartae de Glamorgan (ed. G. T. Clarke) we have mention of more than one place bearing a name closely resembling the Devon Poltimore. The spellings are variantly *Pultimor* (the most frequent), *Poltimor* (once), *Pulthimor* (thrice), *Punthimor* (once) and *Poulzmor* (once), their dates being of the 13th and 14th centuries. Through the kindness of Mr C. A. Seyler the site of one of these places has been approximately identified, viz. the place called variously *Pultimor* and *Poulzmor*, which was in the neighbourhood of Landimore on the north coast of the Gower peninsula, on the estuary of the river Loughor. The position of the Devon and Glamorgan places is much the same, viz. on marshy ground by a river. The Glamorgan place-name must, it would seem, be in some way related to the name of this neighbouring Landimore, earlier *Landimor* or *Landymor* (*passim*), *Landemor* (twice), the forms being of the same date as those given above. The variant *d* and *t* would be explained by the lenition of *t* which would take place after the feminine *lan* (*llan*), as distinct from the masculine *pul* (*pwll*). One might suggest that in both names the nucleus was an OW *ty mōr*, 'great house,' with OW *pul*, 'pool,' prefixed in one case and OW *lan*, 'church,' in the other, hence '"pool" and "church" by the great house,' but it would seem somewhat unlikely that so rare a type of name as 'pool by the great house' would repeat itself in Devon, and it is perhaps unsafe to go further than suggest that Poltimore is in all probability a name of Celtic origin.

p. 449, s.n. SCARHILL. It is difficult to say if it is more than a coincidence that there is a place-name Scorrier in Cornwall with early forms *Scoria*, *Scorya*, from 1331 (AD iv) onwards.

pp. 485, 565, s.n. SAINTHILL. For the use of *sweynt* in a place-name, we may compare the field-name *Sweyntethornys* in Brixworth in the Cartulary of St Andrew's Northampton (14th century), meaning first, perhaps, 'swinged or beaten thorns,' and then 'scraggy thorns.'

p. 489, s.n. CHUDLEIGH. Professor Ekwall would prefer, on account of the numerous forms with double *d*, to assume a pers. name *Ciedda*, a West Saxon weak form of Anglian *Ceddi*.

p. 507, s.n. BOOHAY. Possibly a further trace of such a settlement is to be found in *Lydewicnæss infra* 590 n. 1, also on the coast.

p. 520, s.n. STAVERTON. The Rev. E. D. Drake-Brockman calls attention to the names of certain lost hamlets, *Metherell, Harradon, Hollocombe*. Unfortunately, the only one for which we have really early forms is Metherell, with the form *Mederhelle* in the Archives of the Dean and Chapter, going back to the 13th century. *Hollocombe* is first recorded as *Holcombe* in 1525.

p. 549. After Leonard Fm and Moor, insert LOCKSHALLIS FM. Karlström, in ZONF (7, 259), rightly identifies *Luttukeshel* in Dugdale v, 714 which deals with places in the neighbouring parish of Cullompton, with this place. We may add three further references, *Luttekeshel* 1291 (1408) Dartmoor, *Lottoke-shele* 1346 *Ass, Lottockyshele* 1538 *FF*. As indicated by Karlström, these provide an interesting parallel to Lutsford (PN D 75) as containing a personal name *Luttoc*.

p. 569, s.n. SILVERTON. Mrs Rose-Troup would connect this with the *sulhford* on the Exe in Brampford Speke (Crawf 2), which is mentioned also in the Stoke Canon Charter (BCS 723). This can only be true if the *tun* took its name from a well-known ford some three miles to the south.

p. 590, n. 1. *Lydewicnæss* may contain the same element noted under Boohay *supra* 507, and testify to Breton settlement.

p. 591, s.n. MOUNTAIN FM. Cf. Mountain Wood in E. Horsley (Sr), the home of Walter *ate Montagne* (1332 SR).

p. 595, s.n. SALCOMBE REGIS. The Rev. J. G. Cornish of Salcombe notes that a trace of the old royal holding may remain in the hillside and rough land, north of the Lyme Regis road, known as 'King's Down.'

p. 599, s.n. ELWILL DAIRY. In 1692, in a dispute with the lord of the manor about land here, John Elwell was stated to be a newcomer in the district, so the name is probably post-medieval in origin. (F. R.-T.)

p. 606, s.n. TIPHILL. There is a small stream in Ottery which runs at the foot of Tiphill, known as the *Teape* (F. R.-T.). Its connexion with Tiphill is obscure.

DEVON

XIV. SOUTH MOLTON HUNDRED

Moltone 1084 Geld Roll, *Mouthon* 1242 Fees 767
Sumolton 1174 P, *Sumoton* 1238 *Ass*

v. South Molton *infra* 346. The modern Hundred of South
Molton comprises also the ancient Hundreds of Molland
(*Mollande* 1084 Geld Roll), which included the parishes of
Molland and Knowstone, and North Molton (*Normoltone* 1084
Geld Roll), which included the parishes of North Molton and
Twitchen.

East Anstey

EAST ANSTEY 119 J 8

Anesti(n)ga 1086 DB, (*H*)*anestinges* 1201, 1205 FF
Anestye 1242 Fees 784, 772, *-teye* 1301 Ipm, *Estanesty* 1263
    Exon, *-tygh* 1285 FA, *Yestansty* 1343 Ipm, *Ansteycrues* 1405
    Exon

v. anstig. East and West Anstey are over a mile apart and
have no topographical feature in common. The names must
have arisen independently and since the places are situated on
hilltops the names may in each case have referred to a small
track leading up to the churches at the summit. Presumably the
second *n* in the earliest forms is due to an error of repetition.
Robert de *Cruwes* held the manor in 1285 (FA).

CHERRICOMBE (6″) is *Churecombe* 1244 *Ass* (p), *Chirkcombe*
1515–18 ECP 5, 140. No certainty is possible. OE *ciric* from
Brit *cruc*, 'hill, barrow,' is possible. Ekwall (*Studies* 53) suggest,
the possibility of a compound of cumb and OE *cierr*, 'bend.'
The valley is not, however, a particularly winding one. He
makes the same suggestion for Chercombe *infra* 462, where
the valley winds more but the forms with medial *i* and *y* are
somewhat against derivation from *cierr*.

RADNIDGE is *Rodenasse* 1285, *Rothenesse* 1292 *Ass*, *Rothenaysh*
1330 *SR* (p), *Lower Radnishe* 1619 *FF*. Possibly '*Hrōda*'s or

Hrōðá's ash,' as suggested by Blomé (67), these being pet-forms of OE names in *Hrōþ-*. *Hrōda* is recorded from Devon c. 970 as the name of a serf (BCS 1246).

BLACKERTON is *Blakedon* 1333 *SR* (p). 'Dark hill,' cf. Blagdon *supra* 126. CRUWYS BALL (6″) probably takes its name from the *Crues* family, *v. supra* 335. For *ball*, *v. supra* 211. DUNSLEY is *Donyslegh* 1333 *SR* (p), *Dounyslegh* 1345 *Ass* (p). '*Dunn*'s clearing,' *v.* leah. LISCOMBE is *Lillescomb* 1285 *Ass* (p), *Lillicomb* 1333 *SR* (p). '*Lil*'s valley,' *v.* cumb. OAK is *Oake* 1742 *Recov.* RHYLL is *Ryll al. Hill* 1756 *FF*. 'At the hill,' cf. Rill *infra* 606. SMALLACOMBE MOORS is *Smalecumb* 1278 *Ass* (p). 'Narrow cumb.' WADDICOMBE is *Wadcomb* 1330 *SR*, *Wadecomb* 1333 *SR* (p). '*Wada*'s cumb' or 'woad valley,' *v.* wad. WOODBURN is *Westwodeburn* 1292 *Ass*. *v.* Woodburn *infra* 388. YAMSON LINHAY (6″) is *Yeanston* 1649 *FF*. *v.* tun. For *Linhay*, *v. infra* 592.

West Anstey

WEST ANSTEY 119 J 7

> *Anesti(n)ga* 1086 DB
> *Anesties* 1175 P, *Westanostige* 1234 Bracton, *Westanesti* 1249 *Ass*, *-tigh* 1285 FA, *-teghe* 1308 Exon
> *Ansty-le-Moigne* 1326 Cl

'West' as opposed to East Anstey *supra* 335. Robert *Monachus* held the manor in 1175 (P). This is only a latinised form of the French family name found as *le Moyne* (1242 Fees 772), *le Moigne* (1284 FA).

GUPHILL is *Gopewell* 1281 *Ass* (p), *-wille* 1291 *Ass*. Probably '*Guppa*'s spring' as suggested by Blomé (68), *Guppa* being a pet-form of such OE pers. names as *Gūþbeald, -beorht*, through an intermediate stage **Gubba*. We may note Gupworthy (So), *Guppewurþe* 1155–8 (1334) Ch, *Gopeworthy* 1327 *SR*, as supporting the suggestion. Wallenberg (StudNP 2, 91) suggests associating the first element in Guphill with OE *gupe*, 'buttock,' but it is difficult to see how that word would explain the two recorded compounds. It may be, however, that *Guppe* is a late OE name (of the nickname type) derived from OE *gupe*.

RINGCOMBE is *Est Ringcomb juxta Westanesteye*, and must be by *Ringhendona* 1086 DB, *Ringedon* 1249 *Ass* (p) and *Westrington juxta Westanesteghe* 1291 *Ass*. The relation of these names to one another is not certain. Ringcombe is in a valley. *Ringedon* was probably the hill above it. The two names with the same first element, together with early forms *Ringhen-*, *Ringe-*, make it likely that in both cases we have to do with a pers. name *Hringa*, an unrecorded pet-form of one of the numerous OE names in *Hring-*.

COMBE, HILL, NETHERWILL, WOODLAND and YEO MILL were probably the homes of Walter *atte Comb* (1333 *SR*), Ralph *de la Hulle* (1244 *Ass*), Ricardus *Atewill* (1428 FA), i.e. 'at the spring,' Walter de *Wodelonde* (1330 *SR*) and Thomas *atte Yoo* (1333 *SR*), i.e. 'at the water,' *v. supra* 17–18.

BADLAKE is so spelt in 1765 D, *v.* lacu. SLADE is so spelt in 1765 D, *v.* slæd. TOWN FM was the home of Henry *Town* (1428 FA), *v.* tun.

Chittlehamholt

CHITTLEHAMHOLT[1] 128 B 1

> *Chitelhamholt(e)* 1288 *Ass*, 1350 Ipm, 1481 IpmR, *Chitelham Holte* 1302 Pat, *Chitilhamholte* 1310 Pat
> *Chetelham(p)holt* 1315 Ipm, 1324 Pat
> *Chetilmeholt* 1377 Orig, *Chittenholt* 1577 Saxton, *Chitteholt al. Chittlehamholt* 1708 Recov

This place-name and Chittlehampton *infra* 338 are clearly related, but topographically the places are so far apart that there can be no question of any common descriptive element. Rather we must suggest that Chittlehamholt was a forest settlement of the people at Chittlehampton and was called in the first instance *cietelhæmaholt*, *v.* Chittlehampton *infra* 338. It may be added that Chittlehamholt is on a hill and not in a cietel or hollow.

HEAD BARTON is *Heved* 1272 Ch, *Havede* 1305 Ipm, *La Hefde* 1328 FF, *Heaved* 1350 Ipm, *La Hevede* 1356 AD iv. The name is descriptive of the long narrow ridge of land between the Taw and the Mole, which at its south-eastern end broadens out into a high headland. *v.* heafod.

---

[1] A parish formed from Chittlehampton in 1885.

SNYDLES

> *Esnideleia* 1086 DB (Exon), *Smidelie* (Exch)
> *Snyddelg'* 1242 Fees 784, *Snideleg(h)* 1253 Ipm, 1278 *Ass*,
>   *Snydelegh* 1294 *Ass*
> *Sniddele* 1278 *Ass*, *Snyddelegh* 1292 Ipm, 1441 IpmR

This name looks as though it came from an OE *snida-lēage* (dat.), 'woodland of (or with) cuts or incisions,' a compound of OE *snid*, 'cut,' and leah, though no parallel for such is known.

BUTLERS, COCKRAMS and TAYLOR'S COTTAGES (all 6″) are probably to be associated with the families of Thomas *Botiller*, Robert *Cokerham* and Stephen *Taillour* (1333 *SR*).

DITCHATON WATER (6″) is *Dycham Water* 1553 Pat. FAIR OAK (6″) and PRESBURY are *Fair Oak*, *Presbury* 1765 D. SLEW (6″) is *Slo* 1240 Exon, *Slowe* 1553 Pat. 'Slough, mire.' Cf. Slew *supra* 28.

Chittlehampton

CHITTLEHAMPTON 118 J 8

> *Citremetona* 1086 DB, *Chiterhanton* 1177, 1178 P
> *Chitelimtona* 1107 (1300) Ch, *Chitelhamton(e)* 1176 P *et passim* with variant spelling *-hampton(e)*, *Chithelamton* 1249 *Ass*
> *Chitelmetun* 1219 *Ass*, *Chitelmanton* 1317 *Ass*
> *Chedelhampton'* 1242 Fees 778, *Chydelhampton* 1428 FA
> *Chetlanton* 1285 FA, *Chytlampton* 1461 Barum 2, 86
> *Chetelhampton(e)* 1296 Ipm, 1297 Pat, 1377 Orig

Chittlehampton lies in a hollow which may well have been called cietel, i.e. 'kettle.' Cf. Hellkettles (Y). The whole name was presumably *cietel-hǣma-tūn*, 'farm of the dwellers in the hollow,' *v.* hæme, tun.

BRADBURY is *Brod(e)bray* 1407 IpmR, 1523 *SR*, *Bradberie* 1621 *SR*. The farm is near the river Bray *supra* 2, and the modern form is therefore probably corrupt. 'Broad' may have the sense of 'great,' 'chief,' as in Broad Clyst, Broadhempston *infra* 573, 509, perhaps in relation to Knight's, High and South Bray *infra* and *infra* 346.

SOUTH BRAY is *Braia* 1086 DB, *Sudbray* 1242 Fees 794, *Suth-* 1261 FF, *Southbraigh* 1428 FA. From the river Bray *supra* 2.

GAMBUSTON is *Gambenston* 1481 IpmR and takes its name from the family of Galfridus *Gambun* (1238 *Ass*) and Walter *Gambon* (1330 *SR*).

HATHERCOMBE (6″) is *Heddrescumbe* 1277 *FF*, *Hordercomb* 1330 *SR* (p), *Hathercombe* 1408 IpmR. *v. s.n.* Hatherleigh *supra* 142. The second form is probably corrupt.

LERWELL

>*Luriewell* 1219 *Ass*
>*Luriwell* 1219, 1249 *Ass*, *Lurewyll*, *Lyrewelle* 1331 Ipm
>*Loriwell* 1275 RH (p), *Loryewell* 1279 Ipm (p), *Loriawill* 1333 *SR* (p)

No satisfactory suggestion can be offered for the etymology of this name.

NORTH and SOUTH NEWTON (6″) are *Neuetona* 1086 DB, *Neuton* 1198 FF, *Nyweton* 1279 Ipm.

WHITESTONE

>*Wadestan* 1086 DB, *Watestan* 1199 ChR
>*Wetestan* 1198 FF, -*ston* 1279 Ipm,*Wetteston* 1199 ChR, 1285 FA, *Wettesteston* 1244 *Ass*
>*Whetteston* 1249 FF, 1330 *SR* (p), *Whetstone* 1680 DA 38

Probably 'at the whetstone,' the modern form being corrupt. According to Mr R. P. Chope there are quarries in the neighbourhood.

ASH (6″), CLEAVE, COMBE, FORD (6″), HILLHEAD (6″), HOE[1], MOOR FM (6″), NETHERCLEAVE and WHEY FM[2] were probably the homes of John de *Aysshe* (1333 *SR*), Richard *atte Clyve* (ib.), William *atte Comb* (ib.), John *atte Forde* (1330 *SR*), John *atte Hille* (1333 *SR*), Walter *atte Hoo* (1330 *SR*), Walter de *la More* (1275 RH), Joceus *Bynytheclyve*, i.e. 'below the steep place,' (1330 *SR*) and Roger *atte Weye* (ib.). *v.* clif, hoh, mor, weg.

BIDDACOTT is *Bittecot*' 1244 *Ass* (p), *Buttecote* 1330, *Byttecote* 1333 *SR* (p). '*Bitta*'s cot(e).' BLACKMANTLE (6″) is *Black Mantle* 1765 D. BLAKEWELL is *Blakewelle* 1277 *FF*, -*wall* 1286 *Ass*, 1330 *SR* (p). 'Dark spring,' *v.* blæc, wielle. BRATTON (6″)

---

[1] *Howeford* 1553 Pat.   [2] *Way* 1523 *SR*.

is *Bratton* 1333 *SR* (p). Cf. Bratton *supra* 29. BRAY BRIDGE
is *Braybrigge* 1541 *SR*. *v.* Bray river *supra* 2. BRIGHTLEY
BARTON is *Brittelegh* 1238 *Ass*, *Brightlegh* 1339 *FF*. *v.* leah.
COLLACOTT is *Calecoth'* 1242 Fees 778, *Colecote* 1277 *FF*, *-cota*
1330 *SR* (p), *Collecot* 1492 Ipm. '*Col(l)a*'s cot(e).' COURT (6″)
is *Court* 1621 *SR*. DORRIDGE (6″) is *Thorrugg'* 1330 *SR* (p).
Possibly 'thorn ridge.' For change of *th* to *d*, *v. supra* xxxv.
EASTACOTT is *Yestecote* 1339 *FF*. 'East cot(e).' FULLABROOK is
Foulebrok 1317 *Ass* (p). 'Dirty brook,' *v.* ful. FURZE is *Furse*
1444 IpmR, 1492 Ipm. HALSWELL is *Halswill* 1333 *SR* (p).
'Hazel spring,' *v.* hæsl, wielle. HAWKRIDGE BARTON is *Hauek-
rigge* 1308 Exon, *Haukrugge* 1361 Ipm. HUDSCOTT is *Hudescote*
1281 *Ass* (p), *Hodescote* 1330 *SR* (p), *Huttyscotte* 1523 *SR*.
'*Hud(d)*'s cot(e).' LANGATON is *Langedon* 1244 *Ass*, 1330 *SR*
(p). 'Long hill,' *v.* dun. OLDRIDGE (6″) is *Olderuge* 1527 *Rental*.
SHILSTONE is *Shylston* 1524 *SR*, *Shelston* 1541 *SR*. *v.* Shilstone
infra 433. SOUTHCOTT (6″) is *Southcote* 1440 IpmR.

Knowstone

KNOWSTONE [nɑustən] 128 A 6

    Chenutdestana, Chenuestan 1086 DB

    Cnutstan 1220 FF (p), 1238 *Ass*

    Cnuston' 1242 Fees 793, *Cnouston* 1276 Ipm, *Knouston Beaupel*
       1285 FA

    Cnudstone 1243 Exon, *Cnodston* 1279 Exon, *Knotstone* 1318
       Ch, *Knoudestone* 1360 Exon

    Botreaux Molland otherwise…Knowston 1489 Ipm

'*Cnut*'s stone,' *Cnut* being a Scand pers. name more familiar
in the form *Canute*, cf. Knuston (Nth), *Cnutestone* DB, *Cnoteston*
1220 Fees. The 'stone' may have been at the place called
ROCK (6″) just east of the village. The subsoil in the parish is
rock (Kelly). Robert *Beaupel* (i.e. 'fine skin') held the manor
in 1276 (Ipm) and the family name is preserved in BEAPLE'S
BARTON, WOOD, MOOR, HILL and COMBE.

HARPSON is *Herbertyston, Herberdeston* 1270 *Ass*, *Herbyston*
1526 CtRequests, *Herberston* 1550 *AOMB*. '*Herbert*'s farm,'
v. tun. A Walter *Herbert* was one of the jurors of South
Molton Hundred in 1281 (*Ass*), and *Herberd*, a Continental pers.
name, occurs already in Devon c. 1100 (Earle 257).

WADHAM is *Wadeham* 1086 DB, *Wodham* 1244 *Ass*, *West Wadham* 1270 *Ass*, *Estwaddeham* 1278 *Ass*, *Estwadham* 1292 *Ass*. '*Wada*'s ham(m).' Alternatively the first element may possibly be OE wad, 'woad.'

FORD FM, HILL (6″), MOORTOWN and POOLE were probably the homes of William de *la Forde* (1333 *SR*), Walter de *la Hille* (ib.), Galfridus de *la More* (1238 *Ass*) and Ralph de *la Pole* (1249 *Ass*), *v.* mor, pol.

BOWDEN is *Westboghedon* 1330, *Bokadon* 1333 *SR* (p), *Westbowdon* 1461 IpmR. *v.* Bowden *supra* 37. HARES DOWN is *Haredown* 1818 *Recov.* HOLE (6″) is *La Hole* 1270 *Ass*, *v.* holh. KIDLAND is *Kydelond* 1249 *Ass*, 1333 *SR* (p), 1384 *FF*, *Kida-* 1249 *Ass* (p). '*Cyd(d)a*'s land.' LITTLE COMFORT (6″) is so spelt in 1679 *Recov.* Cf. the same name *supra* 40. LUCKETT is *Lughyngcote* 1330, *Loghyngcote* 1333 *SR* (p). '*Luh(h)a*'s cote,' *v.* ing and cf. Luffincott *supra* 152. MIDDLECOTT (6″) is so spelt 1818 *Recov.* OWLABOROUGH is *Ouleburgh* 1333 *SR* (p). 'Owl hill,' *v.* beorh. SHAPCOTT BARTON is *Shapcott* 1524 *SR* (p), *Shepcott* 1541 *SR*, 1606 *FF*. A p.n. found elsewhere in England, probably referring to a shepherd's dwelling. WHITEFIELD is *Witefel* 1238 *Ass* (p), *Whit(e)feld* 1333 *SR* (p), 1477 IpmR, *Wydefeld* 1485 Ipm. Cf. Whitefield *supra* 52.

Landkey

LANDKEY [læŋki] 118 H 7

Landechei 1166 RBE (p)
Landeg(e) c. 1225 HMC iv, 66, 1225, 1269 Exon
Landekey(e) 1225 Exon, 1346 Pat, 1428 FA
Londekey(e) 1285, 1303 FA, 1287 *Ass*, 1310 *Ass*, *Loundekeye* 1318 Ch
Lankey 1604 Cai, *Lanky* 1675 Ogilby

This is a Celtic p.n. identical with *Landighe* 1086 DB, *Landegai* 1202 P, *Landegeye* 1235 Ch, *Landeke* 1265 FF, the old name of Kea (Co). The first element is Co *lan*, 'church' (W *llan*). The second is the saint's name, *Cai* (NSB 20), preceded by the pronoun corresponding to Co *te*, 'thy,' commonly used as a term of endearment.

ACLAND BARTON is *Akkelane* 1238 *Ass*, 1330 *SR*, *Acke-* 1249 *Ass*, 1275 RH (all p), *Akelane* 1299 *Ass*. '*Acca*'s lane,' cf. Accott *infra* 351.

HARFORD is *Bradeharpeford, Little Harpeford* 1228 FF, *Hareford* 1281 *Ass* (p), *Brodehertford, Parva Herpford* 1285 FA, *Brodeher- ford juxta Barnastapel* 1318 *FF, Litelhertford* 1347 Orig. This probably has the same history as Harpford *infra* 590, the meaning bèing 'highway ford,' *v.* herepæþ. The name may have referred to a ford over the Yeo here, about half-a-mile above the main road from South Molton to Barnstaple.

PORTMORE is *Portmor(e)* 1319 DA 11, 1333 *SR* (p), 1387 IpmR. *v.* port, mor. The name refers to the flat marshy land stretching from here to Newport in Barnstaple *supra* 27.

HILL FM (6″) and PILL (6″) were the homes of Nicholas de *Hulle* (1330 *SR*) and Michael de *la Pille* (ib.). *v.* pyll.

BABLEIGH is *Babbelegh* 1306 *Ass* (p), 1330 *SR* (p). '*Babba*'s leah.' BRADNINCH is *Bryngersh* 1444, 1454, *Brynhersh* 1477 IpmR. *v.* ersc. The modern form must be due to the influence of Brad- ninch *infra* 555. HUNNACOTT is *Honnecote* 1330 *SR* (p). Pro- bably '*Hūna*'s cot(e),' *v. s.n.* Honeychurch *supra* 165. INDI- CLEAVE WOOD (6″) is *Indecleve* 1739 *FF*. 'Beyond the clif,' *v.* Indicombe *supra* 35. NEWLAND is *Newland juxta Londkey* 1480 IpmR. WESTACOTT is *Westecot(e)* 1242 Fees 784, 1303 FA, *Westecotebeaupel* 1346 Pat. The manor was held by Robert *Beaupel* in 1284 (FA). WHIDDON is *Whitton* 1333 *SR* (p). 'White farm or hill,' *v.* tun, dun. WILLESLEIGH is *Willesleg* 1219 *Ass.* Probably 'leah of (or by) the spring,' *v.* wielle. There are springs here. YOULDON is *Yoldedon* 1330 *SR* (p), *v.* Addenda, Part i, lviii.

Molland

MOLLAND 119 H 6

> *Mollanda*[1] 1086 DB, 1100–3 (1332) Ch, t. Hy 2 (1387) Pat, 1204 ChR, *Parva Mollande* 1181 P
>
> *Mouland* 1202 FF, 1212 Fees 97, 1238, 1249 *Ass*

[1] Interesting as is Wallenberg's note on Molland (*bis*) in Kent (StudNP 2, 91) coming from OE *mōr land*, the early forms of Molland and Molton forbid our taking the Kentish Molland into consideration here.

Modland (sic) 1205 FF
Mollond(e) 1238 *Ass*, 1242 Fees 783, 1274 Ipm, 1279 Exon,
-*launde* 1279 QW, *Mollond Botreaus* 1286 *Ass*

v. s.n. Mole river *supra* 10. William de *Boterell(is)* held the
manor in 1212 (Fees 97) and William de *Botereus* in 1286 (*Ass*),
the family name being preserved in Bottreaux Mill [bɔtə:z] *infra.*

BOMMERTOWN is *Bouemore* 1238 *Ass* (p), 1249 *FF*, *Boghemore*
1333 *SR* (p), *Bomore* 1523 *SR*. 'Marshy land in the curve or
bend,' *v.* mor and cf. Bowden *supra* 37. For *town*, *v. infra*
676.

CHAMPSON is *Mollaund Chaumpeus* 1281 *Ass*, *Champe(l)leston*
1281 *Ass*, 1285 FA, *Champeston* 1333 *SR*, *Champeauxton* 1422
Ass, 1428 *FF*. It represents the manor of *Mouland* held by William
and Robert de *Campellis* in 1202 (FF). In 1219 the surname is
spelt *Champell* (FF) and in 1281 *Champeus* (*Ass*). Cf. IPN 132.

GATCOMBE is *Godcumbe*, *Gadecumbe* 1238 *Ass* (both p), *Gotcumbe*
1244 *Ass* (p), *Gotecoumbe* 1335 Exmoor. OE *gātacumb*,
'goats' valley,' *v.* gat, cumb.

GOURT is *la Grutte* 1270 Exmoor (p), *la Grotte* 1333 *SR* (p). OE
greot, 'gravel,' cf. Girt *supra* 37.

HILL, LEE and STONE were probably the homes of Robert de
la Hulle (1330 *SR*), William de *Leghe* (1333 *SR*), and Roger *atte*
Stone (ib.). *v.* leah.

BEER is *Bere* 1523 *SR*. *v.* bearu. BOTTREAUX MILL, *v. s.n.*
Molland *supra*. BREMLEY is *Bromlegh* 1244 *Ass* (p), *Bremy-*
llegh 1330 *SR* (p) and BRIMBLECOMBE is *Brumelcome* 1281 *Ass*
(p), *Bremylcomb* 1330 *SR* (p). 'Bramble clearing and valley,' *v.*
bremel, leah, cumb. CUSSACOMBE COMMON is so spelt 1781
Recov. LANDCOMBE is *Langcumbe* 1270 Exmoor. 'Long valley.'
LUCKWORTHY is *Lokeworthi* 1287 *Ass* (p), 1330 *SR* (p). '*Luc(c)a*'s
worþig.' Cf. *oþ lucan weorþig* Crawf 4 (Devon). LYSHWELL is
probably identical with *Lilleshull* 1318 *Ass* (p), 1335 *FF*. '*Lil*'s
hill,' cf. Liscombe *supra* 336, about five miles distant. NEW
MOOR is *Newmoore* 1717 *Recov*. WEST PARK is *Parke* 1717
Recov. *v.* pearroc. PULWORTHY is *Poleworth(i)* 1330 *SR* (p),

1333 *SR* (p), cf. the same name *supra* 143. SMALLACOMB is
Smalecumbe 1244 *Ass*, 1249 FF. 'Narrow valley,' *v.* cumb.
WATERFORD (6″) may be the spot referred to as *apud la Watere*
(1281 *Ass*). WHITLEY (6″) is *Whetelegh* 1333 *SR* (p), 'wheat
leah.' WOODS is *Woode* 1581 *SR*.

North Molton

NORTH MOLTON 118 H 11/12

> *Nortmoltona, Normoltone* 1086 DB, *Northmolton* 1266 Pat, *et
> freq* to 1428 FA
> *Normout'* 1212 Fees 99, *Northmouton* 1220 FF
> *Nort(h)multon* 1267 Pat, 1270, 1290 Ch, 1286 *Ass*, *Nort
> Multon* 1269 Ipm
> *Moleton* 1283 Ch

> *v. s.n.* Mole river *supra* 10.

FLITTON BARTON is *Flittington* 1303 DA 11, *Fletyngton(e)* 1311
Exon, 1333 *SR*, *Fletington* 1329 DA 11, *Flityngton* 1330 *SR*,
1334 *Ass* (all p), *Flitton* 1364 Cl. This may, as suggested by
Blomé (73), be a derivative of OE fleot, 'stream,' but such a
formation with ingtun would be difficult and we should have
expected some forms in *Flut-*. Dr Ritter suggests derivation
from an OE pers. name *Flita*, 'striver,' of the nickname-type.

NADRID is *Nadreade* t. Eliz *SR* and was the home of Thomas de
Naddereheved (1330 *SR*). *v. s.n.* Nadrid Water *supra* 11. Just
to the south the 6″ map marks 'Source of Nadder water.'

RABSCOTT is *Roberdescote* 1238, 1244 *Ass* (both p), 1330 *SR*
(p), *Rapscott* 1592 *SR*. '*Robert*'s cot(e),' a post-Conquest p.n.
Cf. Rapson *supra* 119. A *Rotberd* is already found in the county
c. 1100 (Earle 257).

NORTH and SOUTH RADWORTHY

> *Raordin* 1086 DB
> *Radewrthi* 1199 ChR, *-wurth* 1234 Fees 396, *Suthradewurthi*
> 1262 FF, *-thy* 1274 *FF*, *Northradeworthy juxta Northmolton*
> 1330 *Ass*
> *Redewrth* 1199 ChR, *-wurth* 1234 Fees 396

Identical with Radworthy *supra* 60.

NORTH and SOUTH LEE[1], MARSH HO, PORTGATE CROSS (6″) and UPCOTT[1] were probably the homes of William *atte Leye* (1330 *SR*), Herbert *de la Mersa* (1238 *Ass*), John *atte Porte* (1330 *SR*), and Richard *de Uppecote* (1291 *Ass*). *v.* leah, cot(e). Portgate Cross is on the road between Nadrid and North Molton, which latter was probably the port or town referred to.

DOBB'S DOWN and PARKER'S WOOD (both 6″) are probably to be associated with the families of Robert *Dobbe* (1330 *SR*) and Edmond *Parker* (1609 *SR*).

BARHAM (6″) is *Beriham* 1330 *SR* (p), *v.* burh, ham(m). BENTWITCHEN is *Bayntwichene* 1330 *SR*, *Baintwitchin* 1581 *SR*, *Bentwichin* 1609 *SR* (p). Perhaps '*Bǣga*'s crossways,' cf. Twitchen *supra* 57. BORNACOTT is *Barnecot* 1492 Ipm. BRINSWORTHY is *Bruneswrthi* 1238 *Ass* (p), *Brinsworthie* 1581 *SR*, *Brymsworthy* t. Eliz ChancP. Probably '*Brȳni*'s worþig.' BURCOMBE is *Biricom(b)* 1275 RH, 1330 *SR* (p), *Bircumbe* 1281 *Ass* (p). *v.* burh, cumb. BUTTERY is *Buttewerthe* 1269 Exmoor (p), *Butterie Corner* 1651 Exmoor. '*Butta*'s worþig.' DARLICK is *Darlake* 1651 DA 39. *v.* lacu. EMBERCOMBE CROSS (6″) is so spelt 1748 *Recov*. EWORTHY is *Ayworthi* 1333 *SR* (p), *Ewerthie* 1609 *SR*. *v.* worþig. FYLDON is *Felleden* 1330, *Filedene* 1333 *SR* (p). *v.* Filleigh *supra* 42. NORTH HEASLEY is *Haseleg* 1249 FF (p), *Hes(e)le* 1330, 1333 *SR* (p). 'Hazel wood or clearing,' *v.* hæsl, leah. HOLDRIDGE is *Alderig* 1220 FF, *Halrugg'* 1330 *SR* (p). 'Steep ridge,' *v.* heald. HUNSTONE is *Hundeston* 1323 *Ass* (p), *Honston* 1330 *SR* (p). '*Hund*'s farm,' *v.* tun, or possibly 'hounds' stone' (OE *hunda stan*). LAMBSCOMBE is *Lomescombe* 1219 *Ass*, 1333 *SR* (p). Cf. Lamerton *supra* 149. LITCHATON is *Lycheton* 1423, *Licheton* 1448, *Lecheton* 1481 IpmR. The first element may be OE līc, 'corpse,' the whole name denoting a *līc-tūn* or burial-ground, cf. Litchdon Street *supra* 26, but no local reason for such a name is known. MILLBROOK is *Milebrok* 1281 *Ass*, 1330 *SR* (p), *Westmilbrok* 1409 IpmR. Self-explanatory. MOLLAND was the home of Thomas *de Mollond* (1330 *SR*). *v.* Mole River *supra* 10. OAKFORD is *Okeford* 1765 D. POPHAM is *Poppeton* 1330 *SR* (p), *Popton* 1607 FF, 1776 *Recov*. '*Poppa*'s farm,' *v.* tun. For the change of second element, cf. Clapham *infra* 498. SANNA-

---

[1] *Ley, Upcott* 1581 *SR*.

COTT is *Swanecote* 1238 *Ass* (p), 1313 Exon (p), *Swancote* 1490 Ipm. 'Peasants' cottage(s),' *v.* swan, cot(e). SHERRACOMBE is *Shearecombe* 1632 *Recov*, *Skirkham ridge* 1651 Exmoor. Possibly 'shire valley,' *v.* scir, cumb and Introd. xxxv. It is near the boundary line between Devon and Somerset. SHORTACOMBE is *Shortecomb(e)* 1330 *SR* (p), 1427 *Ass*. 'Short valley,' *v.* cumb. SPAN HEAD is *the Spann* 1657 Exmoor. STITCHPOOL is *Stuttespole* 1330 *SR* (p). The first element is probably a ME surname *Stut(t)*, perhaps identical with OE *stūt*, 'gnat.' For the modern form, cf. Titchberry *supra* 76. STOWFORD (6″) is *Stouford* 1291 *Ass*, 1330 *SR* (p). *v.* Stowford *supra* 41. WALSCOTT is *Wallescotte* 1524 *SR*. *v.* cot(e). Without earlier forms it is impossible to decide whether the first element is OE wealh or weall. WEST PARK is *le Westpark in Northmolton* 1464 *Cl*. WITHYGATE is *Withiyete* 1333 *SR* (p), *Wideyeate* 1408 IpmR. Self-explanatory. The ME forms show the usual Devon form *ye(a)te*. WEST YARD is *la Hurde* 1291 *Ass* (p), *Yardyate* 1613 *FF*. *v.* Yard *supra* 48.

South Molton (including *Queen's Nympton*)

SOUTH MOLTON [zaumoultən] 118 J 11

> *Sut Moltona* 1086 DB (Exon), *Sud* (Exch), *Suthmolton* 1238
>   FF, *Sud-* 1219, 1238 *Ass*, *Suthmoleston* 1244 *Ass*
> *Sumouton* 1246 Ch, *Suthmulton* 1286 *Ass*
> *Moleton* 1283 Pat, *Moulton* 1577 Saxton

> *v.* Mole River *supra* 10 and Addenda, Part ii, xiii.

NORTH and SOUTH ALLER are *Alra* 1086 DB, *Sudaure* 1242 Fees 772, *North Alre* 1326 Ipm, *Suthalre* 1279 *Ass*. 'At the alder,' *v.* alor.

DAW'S BLACKPOOL and MIDDLE and LOWER BLACKPOOL (6″) are *Blacapola* 1086 DB, *aqua de Blakepol* 1238 *Ass*. The 'water' must have been the Nadrid Water, *v. supra* 11. There was a Hugh *Daw* in the parish in 1734 (Wills).

KNIGHT'S BRAY (6″) and HIGH BRAY are probably *Estebray* 1242 Fees 772, *Estbray(e)*, *Westbray(e)* 1284, 1303 FA, *Westbrei* 1316 FA, referring to places on or near the river Bray *supra* 2.

BREMRIDGE is *Bremerigge* 1086 DB, 1219 FF, *Brimelrigge* 1186 P (p), *Bramelrugg* 1220 FF, *Bremelrygg' juxta Fillegh* 1334 *Ass.* 'Bramble ridge,' *v.* bremel.

CLATWORTHY is *Cloteworth'* 1242 Fees 772, *-thy* 1326 Ipm, *-thi* 1328 Exon, 1330 SR (p), *Clotesworthi* 1256 FF, *Clateworthy* 1281 *Ass* (p). This name seems to be identical with Clatworthy (So). The first element is OE *clāte*, 'burdock,' the second is worþig.

HACCHE is *Achia* 1086 DB, *Hach'* 1242 Fees 774, *Ha(c)ch(e)* 1244 *Ass* (p), 1285 FA, 1364 *FF* (p). *v.* hæcc.

HONITON [hʌnitən] is *Hunitona* 1086 DB, *Huniton* 1275 RH, *Honigton* 1279 *Ass*, *Honyngton* 1361 *Ass* (p), *Honyton lane* 1399 *Ct.* The early forms clearly point to 'honey farm' rather than '*Hūna's* farm,' *v.* tun and Honeychurch *supra* 165.

MEETHE is *la Methe* 1249 *Ass*, *atte Methe* 1330, 1333 *SR* (all p), *Meethe Greene* 1615 *FF.* Probably OE *mǣþ*, 'hay land,' cf. Meeth *supra* 98.

COOMBE, WEST FORD[1], GREAT HELE[1], HILL[1], MILL LANE (6″), STONE and TOWNHOUSE[2] were probably the homes of Richard de *Cumbe* (1219 FF), Jordan de *la Forde* (1270 *Ass*), Walter de *Hele* (1330 *SR*), John *atte Hille* (ib.), John *atte Mille* (ib.), Henry *atte Stone* (ib.) and William *atte Toune* (1333 *SR*). *v.* cumb, healh, tun.

CLAPWORTHY [klaperi] is *Clobworthy* 1731 *Recov.* COCKERHAM is *South Cockerham* 1792 *Recov.* There was a John *Cokeram* in South Molton in 1549 (Pat). COMBREW (6″) is *Combrew al. Cambrew* 1750 *Recov.* Cf. Cumery *supra* 268. DEERHILL (6″) is *Durrehill* 1399 *Ct.* Possibly OE *dēora hyll*, 'animals' hill.' FURZE BRAY is perhaps to be associated with the family of William de *Furse* (1324 *FF*). For the river Bray, *v. supra* 2. KINGSLAND BARTON is *Kyngeslond* 1480 DCo NQ 3, *Old Kingesland* 1609 *Recov.* The manor of South Molton was king's demesne TRE, cf. DB f. 83 *b.* LORD'S DOWN (6″) is *Lordesdoun* 1527 *Rental.* PARKHOUSE is so spelt 1750 *Recov.* SHALLOWFORD is so spelt 1748 *Recov.* SNURRIDGE is *Snerigge* 1244 *Ass* (p), 1330 *SR* (p).

---

[1] *Ford, Hele, Hyll* 1523 *SR.*
[2] *Tannehouse al. Townehouse* 1608 *Recov.*

George Nympton

GEORGE NYMPTON 128 A 2

> *Limet, Nimet* 1086 DB, *Nimet* 1249 Ipm
> *Nymet*(*h*) *Scī Georgii* 1281 *Ass*, 1291 Tax, 1308 Exon, *Nimid
> Scī Georgii* 1326 Orig, *Nymet Georgii* 1345 Exon
> *George Nemyton* 1523 *SR*

The element *Nymet* is found in (*a*) George Nympton on the Mole and Bishop's Nympton on a tributary of the Mole, and King's Nympton on a hill 1½ miles east of the Bray, (*b*) Nymet Rowland on a hill between the Taw and the Yeo, Broadnymet on the Yeo, Nymet Tracy, 1 mile east of the Yeo, Nichols Nymett, 1 mile north of the Yeo, and in Nymph and East Nymph near the source of the Yeo. Elsewhere we find *Nymet, Nymede* in Somerset charters (BCS 168) referring, as tentatively suggested by Ekwall (RN 305) and confirmed by Grundy (*Som. Arch. Soc.* 74, 62), to a stream. *Nymed* is also found in Devon charters referring (BCS 1331) to the Yeo and probably also to the same river elsewhere (BCS 1303). Apart from these names the only other known example of the element is to be found in Nymphsfield (Gl), *Nymdesfeld* BCS 535, the topography of which makes a stream-name unlikely. It is clear that the element *nymet, nymed,* found in all these names is cognate with Irish *nemed,* 'sanctuary,' and goes back to an Old British *nemeton,* found also in Lanivet (Co)[1], which apparently denotes a church (Co *lan*) on the site of an earlier heathen sanctuary. It is difficult to know just how this term came to be applied to streams in Devon or to be sure that in every case it is actually a stream-name— group (*a*) is less certain than group (*b*). Stevenson thought (*Crawford Charters* 58 ff.) that it might have been used of some large area. *v.* Addenda, Part ii, xiii.

FRENCHSTONE is *Freynston* 1270 *Ass* (p), *Frensheton* 1330 *SR* (p), 1340 *SR*, 1331 *FF*, *Frenston* 1489 Ipm and perhaps takes its name from the family of William *le Fra*(*u*)*nceis,* a juror in South Molton Hundred in 1238 and 1244 (*Ass*).

BROOMHOUSE, HAYNE (6″), HELE[2], MILL, THORNE and EAST

---

[1] *Lannived, Lanivet* 1268 Exon, *Lannyvet* 1283 FF, *Lannevet* 1298 FF.
[2] *Brode Hele* 1578 Wills.

TRAYNE were probably the homes of John de *Bromhous* (1330 *SR*), John *atte Heghes* (1330 *SR*) and John *atte Heghen* (1333 *SR*), *v.* Hayne *supra* 129, Walter de *Hele* (ib.), *v.* Hele *supra* 46, John *atte Mille* (1330 *SR*), Roger *atte Thorne* (ib.) and Jordan *atte Trewen* (ib.), i.e. 'at the trees,' *v.* Train *supra* 26.

BURY SLADE (6″) is *Buryslade* 1718 *Recov. v.* slæd. CULVERHILL (6″) is so spelt in 1723 *Recov.* 'Dove-hill.' NARRACOTT is *Northecote* 1270 *Ass*, 1330 *SR* (p). 'North cot(e),' *v.* Narracott *supra* 150.

Satterleigh and Warkleigh

SATTERLEIGH 128 A 1

> *Saterleia* 1086 DB, -*leye* 1277 *FF*, 1370 Exon, -*legh*(*e*) 1291 Tax, 1334 *SR*, 1339 Exon, *West Saterlegh* 1319 *Ass*, *Estsaterlegh* 1372 *Ass*
> *Satirleghe* 1339 Exon
> *Saturlegh* 1421 IpmR

This is possibly OE *sǣtera lēage*, 'wood' or 'clearing of the robbers,' as suggested by Blomé (75), who notes also the numerous OE compounds with *loddere*, 'beggar,' *v.* leah.

WARKLEIGH

> *Warocle* 1100–3 (1332) Ch, t. Hy 2 (1387) Pat, *Warocleia* 1204 ChR
> *Wauerkelegh'* 1242 Fees 794, *Wauerleg* 1281 *Ass*
> *Warkeleye* 1277 *FF*, -*le*(*gh*) 1326 Ipm, 1381 Exon
> *Warekelegh* 1285 FA
> *Wortly* 1675 Ogilby, *Warkleygh oth. Wortley* 1737 *Recov*

A possible parallel for the first element in this name is to be found in Warkworth (Nth), 12th cent. charter *Wauercuurt*, 1206, 1219 *FF*, t. Hy 3 *Wauercurt*, 1220 Wells *Wauerkeworthe*, 1274 Ipm *Warkewrthe*. For Warkleigh one may suggest the possibility of an OE *wǣferce*, 'spider,' derived from OE (*gange*)-*wǣfre*, 'spider,' with the same formative suffix which is found in OE *lāwerce*, 'lark,' *v.* leah.

PUGSLEY is *Poghlegh* 1303 FA, *Poggeslegh* 1330 *SR* (p), *Poggyslegh* 1346 FA, *Pogysleygh* 1428 FA. Probably '*Pocg*'s clearing,' *v.* leah. This pers. name is not on record but may be inferred from *on Pocging rode* (BCS 866).

DEASON (6″) is *Dauyston* 1330 *SR* (p). Possibly 'Davy's or David's farm,' *v.* tun, in which case the name is a ME formation. GREENDOWN is *Grenedon* 1346 FA. HAYNETOWN is *la Heyne* 1270 *Ass, atte Heghes* 1330 *SR* (p). *v.* Hayne *supra* 129. HILLTOWN is *La Helle* 1256 FF, *Hilton* 1330 *SR* (p). Self-explanatory. HIGHER and LOWER OLDRIDGE (6″) is *Holderigg* 1256 FF. PRESTON (lost) is *Prusteton* 1303, 1346, 1428 FA, 1330 *SR* (p). 'Priests' farm,' *v.* tun. SHORTRIDGE is *Scortarigga* 1282 (1328) Ch, *Schorterugg* 1306 *Ass* (p). Self-explanatory. SNAPDOWN (6″) is *Snapedon* 1330 *SR* (p), *Snapdoune* 1611 *FF. v.* Snapper *supra* 44. WATERTOWN was probably the home of Henry *atte Watere* (1330 *SR*). For *town* here and in HAYNETOWN *supra, v.infra* 676.

Swimbridge

SWIMBRIDGE 118 H 8

> *Birige* 1086 DB
> *Svimbrige* 1225 Exon, *Swymbridge* 1535 VE
> *Swynbrigge* 1274 Exon, *-brug(ge)* 1334 *SR*, 1422 Exon, *Swinebregge* 1286 *Ass*
> *Sumbridge* 1577 Saxton, *Som(e)bridge, Sonebridge* 1628 Barum 1, 61, *Symbridge* 1632 Wills

The first element is apparently to be derived from the *Sawin* (OE *Sǣwine*) who held the manor of *Birige* in 1086 (DB f. 194 b). If this is so, the stress accent must later have been shifted to the second syllable. Cf. Shrewton PN W 148, Wyrardisbury PN Bk 244; the name was then associated with the word 'swine,' common in p.n.'s. The bridge here is over a tributary of the Taw.

BROOMSCOTT is *Brunescota* t. Stephen France, *-cote* 1285 FA, *Brywenescote* 1303 FA, *Brounyscote* 1330 *SR* (p), *Brounscote* 1346 FA, *Bromescote* 1428 FA. Probably '*Brūn*'s cot(e).' The 1303 form is best considered as a blunder.

DENNINGTON is *Dynenthon'* 1242 Fees 767, *Dyneton* 1288 *Ass* (p), *Dinington* 1285 FA, *Dynyngton* 1288 *Ass*, 1303 FA, 1333 *SR* (p), *North-* 1317 *Ass, South-* 1333 *SR* (p). '*Dynna*'s farm,' *v.* ingtun. Cf. also Dinnaton *supra* 269.

ERNSBOROUGH is *Erneberg(a)* 1175 P (p), 1281 *Ass, Yhernebergh, Ernesburgh* 1244 *Ass, Yerneburg̃* 1249 *Ass* (p), *Ernesburg(h)* 1260 Exon (p), 1303 FA, *Yernes-* 1346 FA, *Yeasborough* 1667 *Recov.* 'Eagle's or eagles' hill,' *v.* earn, beorh. For the last form, cf. Yes Tor *supra* 205 and Easdon *infra* 482.

HEARSON is *Heringeston, Hiringeston* 1249 *Ass, Heryngeston* 1333 *SR* (p), *Hereston* 1501 Ipm. It probably takes its name from Walter *Hering* who held it in 1249 (*Ass* 176 m 12).

HURSCOTT is *Ihurtescota* 1155–60 HMC iv, 47, *Hertescote* 1238 *Ass* (p), 1330 *SR* (p), *-tis-* 1329 DA 11 (p), *Hurdescote* 1281 *Ass* (p), *Hurtescote* 1333 *SR* (p). '*Heort*'s cot(e),' cf. Harting (PN Sx 35) and Hartland *supra* 71.

RIVERTON is *Reveton* 1238 *Ass* (p), 1275 RH (p), *Refeton* 1244 *Ass* (p). 'The reeve's farm,' *v.* tun and cf. Rifton *infra* 393. The name has been altered to fit the position of the farm upon a stream.

STOWFORD is *Stoford* 1281 *Ass* (p), *Stafford* 1285 FA, *Staford* 1301 Ipm, *Eststoweford juxta Chitelmenton* 1317 *Ass, Stouford* 1330 *SR* (p). *v.* Stowford *supra* 41.

COOMBE[1], DEAN HEAD, HOLE[1], SMALLDON COPSE (6″), STONE and UPCOTT were probably the homes of Richard de *Cumbe* (1238 FF), Walter de *Deneheved* (1333 *SR*), Nicholas *atte Hole* (1330 *SR*), Batin de *Smaledon* (ib.), Seman *atte Stone* (ib.), William de *Uppecote* (ib.). *v.* cumb, denu, holh, dun, cot(e).

ACCOTT is *Akecot* 1238 FF, *Hakecote* 1244 FF, *Accote* 1282 FF. '*A(c)ca*'s cot(e),' cf. Acland *supra* 342, about 4 miles distant. BICKELL CROSS is *Bykehull* 1333 *SR* (p), *Bekehyll* 1541 *SR*. '*Bic(c)a*'s hill,' *v. supra* 124. BIRCH is *La Birch* 1440 IpmR. BYDOWN HOUSE is *Bydowne* 1625 *Recov* and was the home of Robert *Bydoune* (1333 *SR*). 'By the down.' CHUGGATON (6″) is *Choggaton* 1677 FF, 1739 *Recov.* The first element is probably a ME name corresponding to the present Devon surname *Chugg*, cf. Richard *Chugge* (1330 *SR*). COBBATON is *Cobetone* 1308 Exon (p), *Cobbeton* 1330 *SR* (p). '*Cobba*'s farm,' *v.* tun. FROGMORE (6″) is *Froggemere* 1340 FF. 'Frog-pool,' *v.* mere. HANNA-

---

[1] *Come, Hole* t. Eliz *SR.*

FORD is *Haneford* 1281 *Ass* (p), 1330 *SR* (p), *Hanover* 1765 D.
'Cock ford' or '*Hana*'s ford.' For the last form, *v.* Introd. xxxiv.
HUTCHERTON is *Hiccheton* 1330 *SR* (p). *v.* tun. KERSCOTT is
Karscot 1281 *Ass.* 'Cress cottage.' NEWLAND HOUSE (6″) is *la
Nywelond* 1281 *Ass.* NEWTOWN is *Neweton juxta Barnestaple*
1391 IpmR. SANDICK is *Sondholca* 1302 *Ass* (p), *-hulke* 1330 *SR*
(p), *Sandick* 1581 *SR.* *v.* Hucken Tor *supra* 244. TORDOWN is
Tredowne 1581 *SR.* This may be for ME *atter doune*, 'at the
down,' the place being on a hill-top. See further Tredown *supra*
146. WOODLAND is *La Wodelond* 1285 FA. WRIMSTONE is so
spelt in 1641 *SR.* Cf. *on wriman ford* (BCS 1312). Several stones
are marked in the neighbourhood. YARMACOTT is *Arnicott* 1556
Wills, *Yarmacott* 1643 *FF*, (*or Yarnacott*) 1749 *Recov.* We may
perhaps compare Yarnacombe *supra* 289.

Bishop's Tawton

BISHOP'S TAWTON 118 H 6

> *Tautona* 1086 DB, *Tawatonam* c. 1150 (14th) *Launceston,
> Tautone Episcopi* 1284 Exon, *Bisshopestautone* 1374 Exon,
> *Toweton Bishop* 1398 Pat, *Tawton Bushoppe* 1559 Wills

'Farm on the Taw,' *v.* tun. It was held by the bishop of
Exeter in 1086.

EMMETT is *Emytt* 1523 *SR* and was the home of Geoffrey de
Empnete (1333 *SR*). This is OE *emnet*, 'plain, level ground,'
from *emn*, *ef(e)n*, 'even, level.' There is comparatively flat land
just here.

HALMPSTONE is *Halgmerston* 1285 FA, *Halghemerstone* 1317 Exon
(p), *Halmerston* 1330 *SR* (p), *Halmeston* 1394 *Ass* (p). The early
spellings suggest a compound of OE halig, (ge)mære or mere
and stan, the meaning being either 'holy boundary-stone' or
'stone by the holy pool.' The former derivation is the more likely
since there is no pool here now and the place is only 600 yards
away from the parish boundary.

KEWSLAND is *Kiweslond* 1288 *Ass* (p), *Kyweslonde* 1333 *SR* (p).
The first element is probably the name of a medieval owner.
Wallenberg (StudNP 2, 91) compares *le Keu*, found as a pers.
name in Sx (1296 SR).

BEARA[1], BROADMOOR (6"), HALL[1], HAYNE, HERNER, HILL, HORS-
WILL LAKE, NEWHOUSE (6"), OVERTON, UPCOTT, VENN CROSS
(6"), GREAT WESTACOTT, WHITEMOOR and YEOTOWN[2] were pro-
bably the homes of Robert de *la Beare* (1281 *Ass*), Walter de
Brademor (1330 *SR*), William de *Halle* (ib.), William *atte Heghen*
(1333 *SR*), *v.* Hayne *supra* 129, Richard *atte Hurne* (1333 *SR*),
Thomas *atte Hille* (1329 *Ass*), Richard de *Horswillake* (1321
Exon), William *atte Newhous* (1374 Exon), Hugo de *Overtone*
(1330 *SR*), Thomas de *Uppecote* (ib.), Thomas de *la Fenne* (1281
Ass), William de *Westecote* (1330 *SR*), Adam de *Whitemor* (1249
Ass), and Thomas de *la Yo* (1333 *SR*). *v.* bearu, mor, heall,
hyrne, wielle, lacu, tun, cot(e), fenn and Yeo *supra* 17–18.

CHESTWOOD is so spelt 1777 *Recov.* CODDEN is *Coddeton* 1281
Ass, *Coddon* 1333 *SR*, *Coddedone* 1345 *Ass* (all p). 'Codda's farm
or hill,' *v.* tun, dun. FISHERTON is *Fissertone* 1258 Exon (p),
Fisheriston 1333 *SR* (p). 'Fisherman's farm.' The place lies by
the Taw. HEATON is *Had(d)eton* 1330, 1333 *SR* (p). 'H(e)adda's
farm,' *v.* tun. HORESTONE COTTAGES is *Horestone* 1610 *Recov.*
'Boundary stone,' *v.* har. The place is by the parish boundary.
NEWBRIDGE COTTAGE (6"). An order was made *pro reparacionem
Novi Pontis juxta Tautone* c. 1326 (Exon). LITTLE PILL is *Pylle*
1379, 1400 Exon, and was the home of Michael *atte Pille* (1333
SR). *v.* pyll. PULREW (6") was probably the home of Gilbert
atte Pole (1330 *SR*). rew is OE ræw, 'row,' cf. Rewe *infra* 445.
SHILSTONE is *Seliston* 1333 *SR* (p). *v.* Shilstone *infra* 433.
WELLESLEY is *Weleslegh* 1333 *SR* (p), *Wellislegh* 1340 *Ass* (p).
cf. Willesleigh *supra* 342. There is a spring about 300 yards away.
WOOLSTONE is *Ulveston* 1330 *SR* (p), *Olveston* 1333 *SR* (p).
Probably 'Wulf's farm,' *v.* tun, though the absence of *w* in the
early spellings favours rather the ON *Úlfr*, the name of some
Anglo-Scandinavian settler.

Twitchen

TWITCHEN 118 H 13

> *Twechon* 1442 Pat, *Twycchyn* 1524 *SR*, *Twitchen* 1609 *SR*
> *Tuchyn* 1577 Saxton
> *Twitching Common* 1679 DKR 40, 303

---

[1] *Beare, Hall* 1503 Ipm.   [2] *Yeo al. Yeo Towne* 1680 *Recov.*

This is the OE *twicene*, 'crossways,' 'place where roads meet';
four roads meet here.

BICKINGCOTT is *Bykenecote* 1244 FF, *Bykingcote* 1244 *Ass*, *Bike-
necot* 1249 *Ass*. The forms are too few for certainty. There are
other names in which -*ene*- at times appears in entirely sporadic
fashion. Professor Förster suggests OE *Biccinga cote*, 'cot(e) of
Bic(c)a's people.'

PRAUNSLEY

> *Pla(n)teleia* 1086 DB
> *Brauntesle* 1244 *Ass* (p)
> *Prantesleg* 1249 *Ass* (p)
> *Promtesle* 1330 *SR* (p), *Promptislegh* 1333 *SR* (p)
> *Prontislegh* 1427 *Ass*

This would seem to be a name of late formation in which the
first element is a pers. name of Continental origin, showing the
OHG form *Prant* of the common Germanic name *Brand*. *v.* leah.

PULHAM is *Polham* 1086 DB, 1235 FF, 1378 IpmR, *Poleham*
1303 FA. 'Ham(m) by the pool,' *v.* pol.

PULSWORTHY is so spelt 1717 *Recov* and is perhaps identical
with *Polhamford*, *Pulehamesford* 1244 *Ass* (p), *Polamesford*
1249 *Ass*. If so, it may mean 'ford belonging to Pulham'
supra. Pulsworthy is on a small stream about 1 mile away from
Pulham. For the interchange of *ford* and *worthy*, *v.* Introd.
XXXV.

BLINDWELL is *Blyndwill* 1443 IpmR. 'Hidden spring,' *v.* wielle.
There is a spring here. BURCH is *Birch* 1809 M. KERSWELL is
Carswill 1330 *SR* (p). 'Cress spring,' *v.* wielle. MARLEDGE (6")
is *Mirilynch* 1333 *SR* (p). 'Pleasant hlinc.' SUNDERCOMBE is
Sundercumb 1249 *Ass*. *sundor* in OE compounds usually has the
sense of 'private, special,' as in *sundorland, sundormǣd*. Here it
may mean 'cut off,' 'remote.' WHITCOTT is *Whetecote* 1581 *SR*,
Wheatcott 1632 *Recov*. The 16th and 17th cent. forms probably
give the correct etymology.

XV. NORTH TAWTON HUNDRED

Tauuentone 1084 Geld Roll, *Nortauton(e)* 1167, 1168 P

v. North Tawton *infra* 370. The ancient Hundred of North Tawton did not include the parish of Winkleigh which in medieval times was a hundred in itself.

Ashreigney

ASHREIGNEY [-'reini] 127 D 14

Aissa 1086 DB, *Esse* 1219 FF, *Esshereingni* 1238 *Ass*, (*Reygny*) 1283 Ipm, (*Reyny*) 1284 *Ass*, (*Regni*) 1291 Tax, (*Regnie*) 1314 Ipm, (*Regine*) 1440 IpmR, *Ringgesashe* 1306 Exon, *Regnysasshe* 1381 Exon

Rynggesasche 1312 Exon, *Ashreigney oth. Ringsaish* 1739 *Recov*

OE æsc, 'ash-tree.' The family of *Regny* are first mentioned in connexion with the place in 1219 (FF). *Rings* is merely a corruption of *Regny's*.

EAGLE DOWN is *Eggeldon* 1281 *Ass* (p), *Egeldon(e)* 1281 *Ass* (p), 1333 *SR* (p). No certainty is possible. It may be that we have OE *Ecgela*, a possible diminutive of OE names in *Ecg-*. Hence, '*Ecgela's* hill,' *v.* dun. Later, folk-etymology has been at work. Cf. Riddlecombe *infra* 356 for loss of inflexional syllable.

GOODCOTT (6″) is *Godevacota* 1086 DB (Exon), *Godeve-* (Exch), *Godeue Cote* 1245 FF, *Godecot'* 1333 *SR* (p). It takes its name from a woman *Godeva* (*-ve* Exch) who held the manor TRE. This pers. name corresponds to the OE *Gōdgiefu*, more familiar in the Latin form *Godiva*. Cf. Goodwood (PN Sx 66).

HANSFORD BARTON is *Hamtoneford* 1205 FF, 1244 *Ass*, *Hantuneford* 1219 *Ass*, *-tone-* 1238 *Ass*, *Ham(p)tenesford* 1242 Fees 773, 783, *Est-*, *West-* 1286 *Ass*, *Littlehauntesford* 1292 Ipm, *Hantesford* 1303 FA, (*Parva*) 1378 IpmR, *Little Hampteford* 1326 Ipm.

There are three Han(d)sfords in the county, all in North Tawton Hundred: this one, another in Chawleigh and another in Bondleigh. The early forms resemble one another closely and it is difficult to assign them all to the appropriate place. Indeed one cannot be sure that they are all actual place-names, for

Handsford in Chawleigh is certainly not on a *ford* at all and is most likely manorial in origin, i.e. for *Handsford's*. The early forms suggest OE *hāmtūnesford*, 'ford of (or by) the hamtun,' but the use of this latter word in Devon is extremely rare. Alternatively we might take it to be from OE *hēantūnesford*, 'ford of (or by) the high farm,' but we know of no Heanton or the like in the immediate neighbourhood. No certainty is possible.

HOOK FM is *Hoca* 1086 DB, *Hoke* 1212 FF, *Westhoke juxta Aysshereygny* 1321 *Ass. v.* hoc. It is just below a spur of land.

HIGHER and LOWER MINICLEAVE WOOD (6″) is *Meneclyf(f)* 1443 *FF*, 1503 Ipm. *v.* clif. The forms are late but it is possible that the first element is the Co *meneth*, 'hill' (**monijo*), cf. Maindea *supra* 175. The wood is on the steep slope of a hillside.

RIDDLECOMBE is *Ridelcoma* 1086 DB *et freq* to 1428 FA with variant spellings *-cumbe, -combe, Redelcumbe, Ridelecumbe* 1238 *Ass, Riddelcumbe* 1323 Cl, *Rudelcombe* 1324 Inq aqd. This may possibly be from an OE *Riddelancumb*, containing an *l*-diminutive of the recorded pers. name *Ridda*. We should have expected some forms *Ridele-*, but cf. Eagle Down *supra* 355. Professor Förster suggests that the first element may be a derivative of the Cornish word corresponding to W *rhyd*, 'ford,' *ell* being a diminutive suffix in modern Welsh. *v.* Addenda, Part ii, xiii.

DOBBS and ISAACS (6″) are to be associated with the families of Walter *Dobbe* and John *Isak* (1333 *SR*).

HAYES, MOORWATER, PITT FM[1] (6″) and WESTYARD were probably the homes of John de *la Heghen* (1333 *SR*), Walter de *la More* (ib.), William *atte Pytte* (ib.) and Arnulph *atter Westyurd* (1317 *Ass*). *v.* leah, mor, pytt, and Yard *supra* 48.

EAST and WEST ARSON is *Asseton* 1333 *SR* (p), *Arson mil al. Austyn mill, East Austyn* 1681 *Recov.* 'Ash farm' cf. Arscott *supra* 127. BEERA is *Beere* 1669 *Recov. v.* bearu. COLEHOUSE (6″) is *Cowlehouse* 1669 *Recov.* CRAWTHORNE (6″) is *Crowethorn* 1384 *FF, Crothorne* 1669 *Recov.* Self-explanatory. DENSHAM is *Densheton* 1443 *FF. v.* tun. The first element is probably a late pers. name. FURZE is (*La*) *Furse* 1356, 1504 Ipm. HOLE FM (6″) is *La*

[1] *Pytt* 1504 Ipm.

Hole 1245 FF. *v.* holh. HORRIDGE is *Horygge* 1407 Cl, 1443 *FF.* Probably 'boundary ridge,' *v.* har. It is near the parish boundary. KERSHAM BRIDGE is *Kistmelbrigg* 1345 *Ass*, *Kesmerbridg* 1669 *Recov. v. s.n.* Kismeldon Bridge *supra* 161. LAKE (6″) is *Lake* 1443 *FF. v.* lacu. LEY (6″) is *atte Leye* (nom. loc.) 1245 FF. *v.* leah. NORTHCOTT BARTON is *Northecoth'* 1242 Fees 778, *Northcote* 1378 IpmR. REDLAND is *Redisland* 1518–29 ECP 5, 369. WESTACOTT is *Westecot(e)* 1333 *SR* (p), 1397 IpmR. WOODROW is *Woderewe* 1475–85 ECP 2, 155.

Atherington

ATHERINGTON [æðriŋtən] 127 A 13

> *Hadrintone* 1272 Exon, *Adringtone* 1311 Exon
> *Atheryngton* 1298 *Ass*, 1333 *SR*, 1350 Ipm, -*ing*- 1322 Cl, *Atherington*, *Addrington* 1675 Ogilby
> *Atheligton* 1306 *Ass*

'Farm of *Ēadhere* or of *Aeþelhere*,' cf. Atherington (PN Sx 139). *v.* ingtun.

HEMMOCK (6″) was the home of Jacob de *Hemyok* (1333 *SR*). The name is probably manorial, deriving from Hemyock *infra* 616.

LANGLEY BARTON is *Langelegh* 1303 FA, 1333 *SR* (p), 1414 Exon. It was also known as *Western Langeleye next Womberleghe* (FF) and is no doubt identical with the DB manor of *Bichenel(e)ia*. *v.* leah. It is of interest to note that, according to DB, *Bicheneleia* had been added to the manor of (High) Bickington *infra* 358. There can be little doubt that they contain the same pers. name and refer to the same man. *Bickingleigh* was probably additional woodland assigned to the manor.

UMBERLEIGH HO

> *Umberleia* 1086 DB *et freq* to 1310 Ch with variant spellings Umbre- and -*leg(h)*, *Humberlegam* 1211 RBE
> *Wumberlegh* 1270 *Ass*, *Womber-* 1285 FA, 1296 Ipm, 1322 Misc, *Wymber-* 1440 IpmR, *Whomber-* 1489 Ipm

v. leah. The first element is probably a stream-name identical with Umborne *supra* 15, referring to a small tributary of the Taw here.

BREMRIDGE (6″), FORD COTTAGES (6″), KNAPP (6″), KNOWLE and WOOTTON were probably the homes of Girard de *Bremelrigge,* i.e. 'bramble ridge,' John *atte Forde,* Henry de *Knappe,* William de *Knolle* and Henry de *Wodeton* (1333 *SR*). *v.* cnæpp, cnoll, wudu, tun.

[margin handwritten note: What did they Do?]

BOREAT [bʌrjət] is *Boryate* 1333 *SR* (p), *Boryatt* 1650 *FF.* Apparently a compound of burh and geat, but there are no remains of any fort or the like here now. LITTLE WEIR is *Littlewere* 1313 Exon (p). WIXLAND is *Wykeslond* 1333 *SR* (p). Perhaps 'land of the wic or dairy farm.'

High Bickington

HIGH BICKINGTON   127 B 14

[margin handwritten arrow]

> *Bichentona* 1086 DB, *Bykanthon'* 1242 Fees 774, *Bykynton* 1373 Cl
> *Bukint(on)* 1212 Fees 96 *et passim* to 1350 Ipm, with variant spellings *Bukyng-, Buke(n)-, Estbuketon, Westbukyngton* 1356 Ipm, *Heghebuginton* 1423 IpmR

'*Beocca*'s farm,' *v.* ingtun. 'High' from its situation and to distinguish it from Bickington *supra* 124.

LITTLE SILVER is so spelt 1663 *Recov.* This is the first example of a name which is curiously common in D and part of So, occurring in the former county nine times and in the latter four times. The earliest spelling so far noted is *Lytelselver* 1449 FF (So), but the locality of this is uncertain. Of the Devon places all except one are by or very near streams and it may be that the names are in most cases of fairly recent date, the reference being to a sparkling stream. Cf. Silverbridge Lake *supra* 12, where Silver is certainly used of a stream and *Selverlake* (1342 Ipm) in Mudford Tracy (So). Little Silver in Great Torrington is some distance from a stream but no early spellings have been found and the name may be a quite recent and artificial one.

SECKINGTON is *Sakemanne(s)ton* 1301 Ipm, 1379 IpmR, *Sakmanton* 1330 *SR* (p), *Sacampton* 1477 IpmR. This name, which occurs also in Dawlish *infra* 493, suggests an OE form *sacumannes-tūn, sacumanna-tūn.* No OE word *sacumann* is known, though it is a conceivable name for someone who engages in a lawsuit, cf. ON *saka-maðr,* 'litigious person.'

South Heale[1], Lee Barton and Weirmarsh Fm were probably the homes of Robert de *la Hele* (1330 *SR*), William de *Leghe* (ib.), William de *la Were* and Richard de *la Mershe* (ib.). *v.* healh, leah, **wer.**

Bale's Ash is *Bauliesaysh* 1345 *FF*, *Balesaysch* 1501 Ipm. The first element looks like the name of a medieval owner. Bragg's Hill (6″) is to be associated with the family of John *Bragge* (1333 *SR*). Dadland is *Doddelond(e)* 1330, 1333 *SR* (p). '*Dod(d)a*'s land.' Deptford is *Depeford* 1244 FF, *Dupeford* 1333 *SR* (p). 'Deep ford.' Gratleigh is *Grat(e)clyve* 1322 *Ass*, 1333 *SR* (p), *Greteclyff* 1524 *CtWards*. 'Great slope.' There is a steep descent here to the Taw. Middlewood is so spelt in 1592 *SR*. Shuteley is *Schuttelegh* 1356 AD iv. *v.* leah. For the first element, *v.* Shute *infra* 417. It lies on a small promontory of land. Snape (6″) is *Snape* 1407 IpmR. Cf. Snapper *supra* 44. Stowford Down (6″) is *Stoford* 1609 *SR*. Cf. Stowford *supra* 41. Yelland is *Yollelonde* 1281 *Ass* (p), *Yeallelond* 1333 *SR* (p). *v.* Addenda Part i, lviii.

Bondleigh

Bondleigh 128 G 1

> *Boleneia* 1086 DB
> *Bonlege* 1205 FF, *Bonelegh* 1242 Fees 773 *et freq* to 1390 IpmR,
>   (*juxta Northtauton*) 1340 *Ass*, *Bonlegh* 1482 IpmR
> *Bondleigh al. Boneleigh* 1620 *InstPRO*

This difficult name may derive from an OE *Bolanlēage,* 'clearing of one *Bola*.' The sequence *l-n-l* would inevitably lead to difficulty and the first *l* was early lost. *v.* leah.

Clapper Bridge (6″), Heywood, Hill and Moorend were probably the homes of Matilda de *la Claper'* (1330 *SR*), Henry de *Haywode* (1333 *SR*) (*v.* (ge)hæg), Thomas de *la Hille* (ib.), and Guydo de *la More* (ib.). A clapper bridge in Devon is a bridge formed of flat stones laid across stone pillars; they are common round and on Dartmoor.

Drewsland is to be associated with the family of John *Dreu* (1333 *SR*). Lowton is *Luueton* 1333 *SR* (p), *Loveton* 1390 IpmR.

[1] *Hele* 1499 Ipm.

Probably '*Lēofa*'s farm,' *v.* tun. WESTWORTHY is *Whishworthy* t. Eliz ChancP, *Whissery* 1624 *Recov.* *v.* worþig. The first element may be OE wisce, 'damp meadowland,' etc. There is much boggy land round about.

Bow

Bow (Nymet Tracy) 128 H 3

   Limet 1086 DB

   Nymeton 1259 Ch, *Nymetbogh(e)* 1270, 1311 *Ass*, *Nimetebowe,* *Nymetbowe* 1281 *Ass*, *Nymytbowe* 1394 *Ass*

   Nemethe Tracy 1270–6 Exon, *Nymet Tracy* 1274 Ipm, *Nimia Tracy* 1326 Cl, Orig

   la Bogh 1281 *Ass* (p), *Boghe* 1343 Pat, *Chapel Sancti Martini de Bowe* 1400 Exon

   Nymettracy al. Bowe 1600 *Recov*

The 'bow' was perhaps the arched bridge over the river Yeo here, cf. PN Mx 8, PN Wo 10. Otherwise, one must take it to refer to the curving hill at this point. For *Nymet*, *v. supra* 18, 348. Oliver de *Trascy* held the manor in 1212 (Fees 99), a member of the Honour of Barnstaple. The original site of the settlement was at Nymet Tracy where the church is. Later the centre of population shifted to Bow on the main road from Exeter to Launceston.

HALSE is *Hax* 1086 DB, *Halse* 1196 P 17, 1273 *FF*, 1303 FA, *Hause* 1242 Fees 783. This place is on a definite neck or col of land dividing the Taw valley from that of the Yeo. Halse, therefore is here identical with OE *heals*, 'neck.' See further *s.n.* Halsdon *supra* 139 and Addenda Part i, lviii.

HAMPSON is *Hermaneston* 1244 *Ass*, 1303 FA, *Hermanyston* 1333 SR (p), *Hermeston* 1346 FA, *Harmiston* 1421 IpmR, -*mes*- 1563 *FF* and represents the manor of *Nimet* held by one *Hermer* in 1086 (DB f. 389b). *Hermer* is probably the Continental pers. name *Heremar* found in England in the form *Hermer*. Since all the earlier spellings, however, show medial *n*, it may be that the name contains the OE pers. name *Hereman*, the holding of the manor by one *Hermer* in 1086 being only a coincidence.

HILLERTON is (*on*) *healre dune* 739 (11th) Crawf 1, *Helleredun* 1238 *Ass* (p), *Esterhellerdon, Hildredon* 1322 *Ass*, *Helliton* 1809 M.

For this difficult name Professor Ekwall suggests the possibility of an OE *hēalre*, genitive singular of an unrecorded *hēalor* allied to OE *hēala*, 'rupture' and *hēalede*, 'hydrocelous,' denoting 'a swelling,' 'a hill.' Cf. *healre mere* BCS 1282. The phonological development is curious but there is little doubt of the identification of forms. There is still an *East* Hillerton Fm (6″).

NATSON is *Notteston'* 1242 Fees 778, 1303 FA, (*juxta Nymet Tracy*) 1364 *Ass*. '*Hnot*(*t*)'s farm,' *v.* tun and cf. Natsley *supra* 58. The fact that the manor was held by one *Notte* in 1428 (FA) may be only a coincidence.

BROWNSLAND is *Brunes-*, *Burnesland* 1201 Seld 1 (p), *Brounlond* 1410 IpmR. '*Brūn*'s land.' COXMOOR is *Cokkesmor* 1333 *SR* (p). '*Cocc*'s moor' or '*cock*'s moor,' *v.* mor. EASTERBROOK is *Estbrok* 1249 *Ass*. LANGFORD is *Langeford* 1330 *SR* (p). 'Long ford.' NYMETWOOD is *Attewode juxta Nimet Tracy* (nom. loc.) 1316 *Ass*. SPESTOS is *Spesters* 1669 FF.

Brushford

BRUSHFORD 128 F 2

> *Brisforda, Brigeforda* 1086 DB
> *Brig*(*g*)*eford*(*e*) 1219 *Ass*, 1242 Fees 787, 1244, 1249 *Ass*,
>   *Brigheford* 1242 Fees 783, *Brigford*(*e*) 1269 Exon, 1275 RH,
>   1291 Tax
> *Bryxford* 1322 *Ass* (p), 1346 FA, 1392 IpmR, *Brixford Speekes*
>   1392 Cl
> *Brushford* 1330 *SR*, *Brussheford*(*e*) 1377, 1392 Cl, 1375 *Min*
>   *Acct*, 1535 VE
> *Brishford* 1333 *SR*, *Brissheford* 1378 IpmR
> *Burshford* 1687 *Recov*

One can hardly doubt that the original form of this name was *Bridgeford*, i.e. ford with some kind of causeway laid across it, for OE **brycg** does not necessarily imply the spanning of the stream as we understand it. Later, perhaps owing to the frequent use of brushwood causeways (cf. Rice Bridge, PN Sx 258), folk-etymology seems to have been at work. Cf. Brushford (So), *Brigeford, Brucheford* 1086 DB, *Brigeford, Brugeford et freq* (13th cent.), *Brissheford* (1427 FF), *Brussheford* (1428 FA). Richard de *Espec* held the manor in 1242 (Fees).

PARTRIDGE WALLS is *Pertricheswall'* 1242 Fees 783, *-rych-* 1346 FA, *Pertrikeswall* 1303 FA, *Pertrichewolles* 1378 IpmR, *Pertriggewalles* 1394 *Ass*, *Pertryggewallis* 1493 Ipm. The first element is clearly to be connected with the bird's name, but as 'partridge's wall' is an unreasonable name we should probably assume that *Pertriche* is here a ME surname of the nickname-type. So similarly Wallenberg (StudNP 2, 91).

BATELEASE (6″) is *Baidlease* 1562 *FF*. *v.* læs. REEVE is *atte Rewe* 1394 *Ass* (p), *Westrewe* 1562 *FF*, *Reeve* 1765 D, *Rew oth. Reeve* 1797 *Recov*. *v.* ræw. For the interchange of *v* and *w*, *v. supra* xxxv.

Burrington

BURRINGTON 127 C 15

Bernurtona, Bernintona 1086 DB (Exon), *Bernintone* (Exch) *Berington* 1249 FF
Burnintone 1265 Exon *et freq* to 1303 FA with variant spellings *-nyg-, -nyng-, -nyn-, Berninton* 1306 *Ass*
Buringtune 1275 RH, *Burryngtone* 1304 Exon

'*Beorn(a)*'s farm,' *v.* ingtun. The first DB form is probably corrupt.

BRIDGE FM (6″), CLEAVE, HIGH HAYNE, HILL, SOUTHDOWN[1], TWITCHEN and UPCOTT were probably the homes of Richard *atte Brigge* (1304 *Ass*), Thomas *atte Clyve* (1333 *SR*), Richard *atte Heghen* (ib.), Claricia de *Hille* (ib.), John de *Souddon* (ib.), Adam de *la Twichene*, i.e. 'at the crossways,' *v. supra* 353, (1306 *Ass*), and Robert de *Uppecote* (1333 *SR*). *v.* clif, cot(e) and Hayne *supra* 129.

AYLESCOTT is *Aylescote* 1333 *SR* (p), 1426 IpmR. Perhaps '*Ægel*'s cot(e),' cf. Aylesbury PN Bk 145. BARNPOOL is *Barne Pole* 1550 *AOMB*. BIRCHAM (6″) is *Bircham* 1407 Cl, *Byrcheham* 1443 *FF*, 1503 Ipm. 'Birch ham(m).' BRAGGAMARSH is *Braggymersshe* 1516 *Recov* and is probably to be associated with the family of *Bragge* noted *supra* 359. CALLARD is so spelt 1616 *FF*. COMMON HEAD (6″) is *Comynhed al. Coumehed* 1544 *Deed*. GOLLAND (6″) is *Gouelond* 1333 *SR* (p), *-land* 1501 Ipm. For the first element, *v. s.n.* Goveton *supra* 318. GREAT HALFSBURY is

---

[1] *Southdon al. Sowdon* 1544 *Deed*.

Halsbury 1330 *SR* (p), *Hallesbury* 1333 *SR* (p). It lies on a spur of land between two valleys and we may have a compound of OE *heals* and burh, but *v.* Addenda, Part i, lviii. KING'S HILL is *Kyngeshill(e)* 1391 *FF*, 1547 *Deeds Enrolled, Goore al. Kingeshill* 1607 *FF*. For the alternative name, *v.* gara. LEACHLAND (6″) is *Lechelond* 1544 *Deed*. NORTHCOTE is *Northecoth'* 1242 Fees 778, *Northcote* 1303 FA, *Narracott oth. Northcott* 1759 *Recov.* PAVINGTON is *Padyngton in the parish of Boryngton* 1501 Ipm, *Padyngton* 1544 LP. Probably '*P(e)ada*'s farm,' *v.* ingtun. WEEK is *Wyke* 1269 *FF*. 'Dairy farm,' *v.* wic. WHITECLEAVE (6″) is *Wyteclyve* 1333 *SR* (p), *Whyteclyff* 1503 Ipm. *v.* clif.

Chawleigh

CHAWLEIGH 128 D 3

> *Calveleia* 1086 DB
> *Cheluelega* 1227 BM
> *Chauveleg* 1228 FF, *Chauuvelegh* 1254 Pat, *Chaveleg'* 1275 RH
> *Chalvelegh(e)* 1285 FA, 1291 Tax, 1292 Ipm, *Chalfelee* 1286 *Ass*

'Calves' clearing,' *v.* leah. Cf. Chawley (Berks) *Chaluele(ye)* 1241, 1284 *Ass*.

CHENSON FM is *Chenneston* 1242 Fees 783, 1292 Ipm, *Cheyneston* 1278 *Ass*, 1346 FA, 1378 IpmR. The place takes its name from the family of *Chenne* who held the manor in 1242 (Fees 783). In 1346 (FA) the surname is spelt *Cheygny*.

DOCKWORTHY CROSS (6″) is *Dochorda* 1086 DB, *Dockesw(o)rth(y)* 1228 FF, 1303 FA, *Dockeworth* 1242 Fees 787, 759, 1281 *Ass* (p), -*thy* 1370 *Ass*. 'Dock farm' or '*Docca*'s farm,' *v.* worþig. It may be noted that there is a place DUCKHAM in the parish, possibly for earlier Doccombe (cf. Huckham *supra* 56).

HARDING'S LEIGH (6″) is *Hardewinesl(e)gh* 1242 Fees 783, *Hardeneslegh* 1292 Ipm, *Hurdyngeslegh* 1481 IpmR. '*Heardwine*'s clearing,' *v.* leah.

FORD FM (6″), HILL, LEIGH, NETHERCOTT, SOUTHCOTT, STONE BRIDGE (6″) and UPCOTT were probably the homes of John *atte Forde* (1333 *SR*), Henry *de la Hulle* (1281 *Ass*), Adam *de Leghe*

(1333 *SR*), Symon de *Nithercote* (ib.), de *Southecote* (ib.), Robert fil. Richard de *la Stane* (1238 *Ass*) and Walter de *Uppecote* (1333 *SR*). *v.* leah, cot(e).

BURRIDGE is *Burrigge* 1333 *SR* (p). *v.* burh, hrycg. There is an ancient 'camp' here. CARPENTER'S CROSS (6″) is to be associated with the family of Philip *Carpenter* (1333 *SR*). EDWORTHY (6″) is *Yadeworth* 1333 *SR* (p), *Yeodeworthy* 1427 *Ass*. '*Ēada*'s farm,' *v.* worþig. FIDDLECOTT is *Fytelecoth*' 1242 Fees 774, *Fytlecote* 1333 *SR* (p), *Vyttelecote* 1451 IpmR. '*Fitela*'s farm,' *v.* cot(e) and cf. Fittleworth PN Sx 126. MOORTOWN is so spelt 1768 *Recov.* For *town, v. infra* 676. NUTSON is *Notyngeston* 1333 *SR* (p). The first element is probably a pers. name of ME origin. TOATLEY is *Totelegh* 1330 *SR* (p), 1394 *Ass* (p). '*Tot(t)a*'s clearing' or perhaps 'look-out clearing,' *v.* leah. Cf. Toat Hill PN Sx 161. The place commands a wide view to the west. CHAWLEIGH WEEK is *Wyk*' 1242 Fees 783, *Challeighweeke* 1612 *Recov. v.* wic. Probably the dairy farm of Chawleigh. WOOD HOUSE is so spelt 1612 *Recqv* and was perhaps the home of William *at Woode* (1428 FA).

Clannaborough

CLANNABOROUGH 128 G 4

Cloenesberga 1086 DB

Cloueneberge 1239 FF, *-burg*(*he*) 1242 Fees 783, 1291 Tax, 1334 Ch, *-birg*' 1250 Cl

This name clearly means 'cloven hill.' The reference is probably to the marked valley which runs up into the hill just west of Clannaborough village. There is a corresponding valley on the north side of the hill, so that it is divided into two well-marked halves. Cf. *la Clovenetorre* (1291 *Add*) near South Brent.

APPLEDORE is *Apledora* 1086 DB, *Apeldure* 1242 Fees 783, *Appeldore* 1346 FA, *Appuldure* 1378 IpmR. 'Apple tree,' *v.* apulder.

KIDDICOTT (6″) is *Cudingcote* 1245 FF (p), *Cudicote* 1249 *Ass* (p), '*Cud(d)a*'s cottages,' *v.* cot(e), with connective ing and common development of *u* to *i* before a dental.

THORNE is *La Thorne* 1242 Fees 783.

WALSON BARTON[1] is *Waleston(e)* 1242 Fees 783, 1303 FA, 1306, 1325 *Ass*. This represents the DB manor of *Limet* held by one *Walo* (Exch DB *Wado*) TRE, hence 'Walo's farm,' *v.* tun. For this name, *v.* Forssner 242. For *Limet, v. supra* 348.

Coldridge

COLDRIDGE 128 F 2

Colriga 1086 DB *et passim* to 1316 FA with variant spellings
   -rig(g)e, -rugge, Colriche 1328 Pat
Colleruge 1184 P (p), *Colerugge* 1317 Pat
Caulridge 1577 Saxton
Cowlridge 1675 Ogilby

For the interpretation, *v.* Collacott *supra* 50.

CHILVERTON is *Chilverton* 1281 *Ass* (p), *Chilverdon* 1333 *SR* (p). No certainty is possible, but Wallenberg (StudNP 2, 90) may be right in suggesting that the first element is OE *cilfor(lamb)*, 'ewe-lamb,' cf. dialectal '*chilver*.' Hence, 'lamb-farm.'

GILLSCOTT [gilskət] is *Gillescote* 13th Buckland, 1347 *FF*, *Gilescote* 1388 Cl. *v.* Gilscott *supra* 85. The editor of the VCH would identify this with the DB manor of *Chetellescota* held by one *Chetel* TRE (VCH i, 496), but this is stated to have been in the Hundred of Winkleigh and in any case the change from *Chetel-* to *Gill-* would be difficult to explain.

TITTERTON is *Toyterton* 1303 FA, 1540 *FF*, *Toytirton* 1346 FA, *Toiterton* 1350 Ipm. The place stands high, with a good view down the Taw and Professor Ekwall suggests that this may be from OE *tȳtera tūn*, 'farm of the watchmen,' *tȳtere* being an unrecorded derivative of OE *tȳtan*, 'to peer forth.' For the curious phonological development, cf. Loyton *infra* 536.

EAST HAWKRIDGE, SOUTH MOOR, VENN and WESTACOTT were probably the homes of Maurice de *Haukerigge*, John de *Southmor*, John de *Fenne* (1333 *SR*) and Basilia de *Westecote* (1287 *Ass*). *v.* mor, fenn, cot(e).

BANKLAND (6") is *Bank(e)lond(e)* 1501 Ipm. The place is on a hillside. The name must be of late origin as *bank* is a Scand

---

[1] This is the spelling on the old 1" map, on the 6" map, and in Kelly's directory. The latest 1" map has *Watson*, probably a mistake.

loan-word. BIRCH is *La Burch'* 1242 Fees 778, *la Birche* 13th
Buckland, *atte Birche* 1333 *SR* (p). FROGBURY is *Frog(g)ebury*
1330, 1333 *SR* (p), *Frogbur'* 1482 IpmR. The name referred
perhaps to a deserted earthwork in damp surroundings, cf. IPN
148. EAST and WEST LEIGH is *Legh'* 1242 Fees 783. *v.* leah.
MILLSOME is *Mileston* 1303 FA, 1378 IpmR, (*juxta Colrygge*)
1318 *Ass*. This may, as suggested by Blomé (62), be from OE
mylen stān, 'mill stone.' There are two quarries near by. MOOR
is *More* 1493 Ipm. *v.* mor.

Dolton

DOLTON 127 D 13

> *Dueltona, Duveltona* 1086 DB (Exon), *Oueltone* (Exch)
> *Duwelton(e)* 1217–22 HMC ix, 494, 1274 Ipm, 1292 Cl
> *Dyvilton* 1235 Cl
> *Dughelton* 1235 Pat, 1238 *Ass*, 1285 FA, 1292 Ipm, *Dughilton*
>   1339 *Ass*
> *Dueltune* 1275 RH, *-tone* 1291 Tax, 1297 Pat, *Duylton* 1315 Pat
> *Deweltone* 1279 Exon, *Deulton* 1341 Cl
> *Doghelton* 1364 *Ass*, *Dowelton* 1477 BM, *-yl-* 1535 VE,
>   *Doulton* 1675 Ogilby

The first element in this name is clearly identical with that of
the adjacent parish of Dowland *infra* 367. Since the places have
no topographical feature in common, the probability is that as in
Petherwin and Molland *supra* 158, 342, the first element is the
name of some ancient district or large area. No suggestion can
be made for the etymology apart from the fact that the first
syllable may be the British word for 'black,' cf. the early spellings
of Dawlish and Duvale *infra* 491, 531.

BUCKLAND is *Bocchelanda* 1086 DB, *Boclond White juxta Doghelton*
1364 *Ass*, *Buckeland* 1504 Ipm. *v.* bocland. Richard *le Wyte*
held the manor in 1303 (FA).

CHERUBEER

> *Churbear* 1238 *Ass*, *Churibe(a)r(e)* 1244 *Ass*, 1334, 1340 *SR*,
>   *Churebe(a)re* 1422 IpmR, 1470 Pat
> *Chyreber* 1244 *Ass*
> *Cherebe(a)r(e)* 1244 *Ass*, 1377, 1420 IpmR, *Cherybear* 1535 LP

  v. bearu. There are two tumuli on the hill above this
place. If Reichel's identification of DB *Bera* (f. 295) with

[handwritten marginal notes:] ? ever part of Honor of Okehm
cf Fees 1242, p787
(Of Reichel)
Either VCH Devon I 452 is wrong in doubting
BERA held by Richard of Baldwin as Cherrybear cherubeer
? Vapula. Inq PM 19 H VI no 40 or EPN meaning of Ber p357 "in..."

Cherubeer is correct, it is perhaps more likely, however, that the first element is OE cyrice, 'church,' than cyric from British cruc, 'barrow, hill' (cf. Ekwall Studies 41).

HALSDON HO is Halgheston 1285 Ass, 1303 FA, Halgeston 1346 FA, Halkeston 1504 Ipm, Halston 1625 Recov. Probably 'the holy stone,' though no such stone is known here. v. halig, stan.

IDDLECOTT is Edrichescote 1168 P (p), Yedescoth' 1242 Fees 778, Ediriscote 1303 FA, Edrichscot' 1330 SR (p), Hidryscote 1346 FA, Yedel(e)cote 1394 Ass, 1396 FF, Idelcote 1428 FA, Edrichecote 1440 IpmR. This place represents the manor of Duueltona held by one Edric (i.e. Ēadric) TRE (DB f. 462). The forms show common confusion of l and r.

STAFFORD BARTON is Stafort, Stadforda 1086 DB, Stouford 1333 SR (p). v. Stowford supra 41.

CHAPPLE FM, DOWN FM, HAM FM[1], HILL WOOD (6″), WESTLAKE (6″) and WOOD were probably the homes of (   )[2] atte Chapele (1330 SR), Henry de Doune (ib.), Richard de Hamme (1333 SR), William atte Hulle (ib.), Henry de Westlake (ib.) and William atte Wode (ib.). v. dun, hamm, lacu.

ASHWELL is Asshewell 1285 Ass, Aysshwyll 1443 FF. CUDWORTHY is Codeworthy 1431 IpmR, 1485 Ipm. 'Cud(d)a's farm,' v. worþig. MERAVIN (6″) is Le Mireven 1244 Ass. v. fenn and cf. Merrivale supra 247. VENTON is Fenton 1625 Recov. 'Marsh farm,' v. fenn, tun. WISTLAND (6″) is le Wystlond 1522 DA 33. WOOLRIDGE (6″) is Wollerigge 1315 Exon (p). Probably 'wolves' ridge,' cf. Woolacombe supra 54.

Dowland

DOWLAND [dɑulənd] 127 E 13

Duvelanda 1086 DB

Duhelanda 1173–5 (1329) Ch, Duelonde 1269 Exon, 1316 FA
Dugheland' 1242 Fees 778, -lond 1346 FA, Doughelonde 1291 Tax

Duuland 1266 Pat (p), Duylond 1340 SR, Doweland 1428 FA
v. Dolton supra 366.

---

[1] Lower Ham 1641 SR.   [2] Christian name illegible.

BERRY (6″) is *atte Bury* 1345 *Ass* (p), *la Bury* 1333 *SR* (p), *Bury* 1504 Ipm. *v.* burh. There are no remains here now. EASTACOTT is *Es(t)cote* 1238 *Ass* (p), 1504 Ipm. HAWKDOWN is *Hokedon* 1333 *SR* (p). *v.* hoc, dun. There is a hill here with a prominent spur. MOUSEHOLE (6″) is *Mousehole* 1330 *SR* (p). 'Mousehollow or hole,' possibly a term of contempt, *v.* holh. PEWSON BARTON is *Pustone* 1333 *SR* (p), *Puyston* 1339 *Ass*, 1504 Ipm. *v.* tun. The first element may be the ME pers. name noted under Pusehill *supra* 84. STAPLE (6″) is so spelt 1504 Ipm. *v.* stapol. The 'staple' may have been at the spot now marked Staple Cross. UPCOTT is *Uppecott* 1219 FF.

Down St Mary

DOWN ST MARY 128 G 4

Dona 1086 DB, *Doune* 1284 Exon, (*Sancte Marie*) 1394 Exon

'The hill,' *v.* dun. 'St Mary' from the dedication of the church.

CHAFFCOMBE is *Chefecoma* 1086 DB, *Chaffecomb* 1238 *Ass*, 1500 Ipm. It must be identical with Chaffcombe (So), *Caffecome* 1086 DB, *Chaffacomba* t. John (1313) Ch, *Chaffecumbe* 1235 FF, *Chefcumbe* 1252, *-combe* 1314 Ipm, and contain the same first element as Chafford Hundred (Ess), *Cesfeworda, Ceffeorda* 1086 DB, *Ceaffeworda* 1130 P. Professor Ekwall would take it to be a pers. name *Ceaffa*.

WOOLFIN is *Nimet* 1086 DB, *Numet* 1222 FF, *Merdesnymeth'* 1242 Fees 778, *Wolvysnymet* 1359 Ipm, *Wolvenymet* 1373 IpmR. *v.* George Nympton *supra* 348. The manor was held TRE by one Alward *Merta*. In 1222 (FF) it was in the possession of Gregory *Lupus* (i.e. Wolf), in 1303 (FA) of Ricardus *le Low* (OFr *lo, lou,* 'wolf'), and in 1359 (Ipm) of Walter *Wolf* or *Le Wolf*.

THORNE and YEO were probably the homes of Adam *atte Thorne* and Robert de *la Yea*, i.e. 'at the water' (1333 *SR*), *v. supra* 17–18.

BRADIFORD is *Bradeford* 1222 FF, 1242 Fees 778. 'Wide ford,' *v.* brad. ELLICOMBE is *Ellecomb* 1333 *SR* (p). '*Ella*'s combe' or possibly 'eldertree combe,' *v.* cumb, ellen. LAMMACOTT is

Lammecote 1170 (Hy 6) Oliver 302, *Lamecote* t. Ed 3 Exon. Probably 'lambs' cot(e)' with early loss of *b*. Cf. Shapcott *supra* 341. WALES is *Willes* t. Eliz ChancP.

Eggesford

EGGESFORD [egzvəd] 128 E 2

Egkeneford 1238 *Ass*, *Egeneford* 1291 Tax, *Ekenefford* 1297 Pat
Eg(g)enesford 1242 Fees 783 *et freq* to 1428 FA, (*juxta Colrygge*) 1339 *Ass*, *Egnesford* 1303 FA
Eggesford 1377 Cl, 1493 Ipm, *Egsford* 1629–51 Barum 1, 59

Probably '*Ecgen*'s ford' with continuant *cg* stopped before following *n*. Cf. Ekwall, *Studies* 8.

TRENCHARD is *Trenchard in Eggesford* 1518–29 ECP 5, 206 and is probably to be associated with the family of Antony *Trenchard* mentioned in connexion with Eggesford in 1280 (*Ass*). The more regular form would be *Trenchards*.

HAYNE is *La Heghe* 1242 Fees 783, *Heghen* 1303 FA, *Heghes* 1378 IpmR. *v.* Hayne *supra* 129. KITCHADON is *Kechedon* 1492 Ipm. The first element may be the pers. name *Cycca*, found in Kitchenham, Kitchenour (PN Sx 478, 527). Hence, '*Cycca*'s hill,' *v.* dun. LYLAND WOOD (6″) is *Leylond Wood* 1548 Pat. WOOD FM (6″) was the home of John de *la Wode* (1333 *SR*).

Lapford

LAPFORD 128 F 3

Eslapaforda 1086 DB (Exon), *Slapeforda* (Exch)
Lapeford 1107 (1300) Ch, *Lappeford(e)* 1238 *Ass*, 1285 FA,
1291 Tax, 1296 Ipm, *Lappi-* 1350 Ipm, *Loppeford* 1434 Exon
Lapford 1272 Ipm, 1303 FA, 1327 Pat

Blomé (64) interprets this name as OE *lēapa-ford*, 'ford marked by leaps,' i.e. baskets or weels for catching fish. Professor Ekwall notes the DB form with *s* and suggests the pers. name *Hlappa*. Cf. *s.n.* Lapland *supra* 300.

BURY BARTON is *Beria* 1086 DB, *Bury* 1503 Ipm. *v.* burh. This may have been some stronghold guarding the passage of the River Yeo here.

BOWERTHY is *Bowewurd* 1249 *Ass* (p), *-worth* 1285 Ipm. 'Farm by the curve,' referring to the contour of the hill here. *v.* worþig and Bowden *supra* 37. BROOMSMEAD is *Brymysmede* 1501 Ipm, *Brymesmede* 1544 LP. COBLEY is *Cob(b)eleghe* 1291 Tax, 1333 *SR* (p). '*Cobba*'s clearing,' *v.* leah. EASTINGTON is *Estyngton* 1330 *SR* (p), 1384 *FF*. It is at the east end of the parish. Cf. Sodington (PN Wo 60). EDGELEY (6″) is *Eggesle* 1262 FF. '*Ecgi*'s clearing,' *v.* leah. HOLE was the home of Richard de *la Hole* 1249 *Ass*. *v.* holh.

Nymet Rowland

NYMET ROWLAND 128 F 3

> *Limet* 1086 DB
> *Nimet Rollandi* 1242 Fees 783, *Nymet Rolaund* 1292 Ipm, *Numet Rolond* 1374 Exon, *Nemytroland* 1558 Wills

v. George Nympton *supra* 348. The distinctive manorial addition is probably to be traced to *Rolandus* de Nimet (1166 RBE).

CLEAVEANGER is *Clifhangre* 1278 *Ass*, *Clyfhang(e)re* 1281 *Ass* (p), 1333 *SR* (p). *v.* clif, hangra.

HEAL (6″) and NYMET BRIDGE were the homes of Alan *atte Hele* and John *atte Brigge* (1333 *SR*). *v.* healh.

North Tawton

NORTH TAWTON 128 H 1

> *Tawetona* 1086 DB, *Tauton* 1158 P
> *Chepin(g)tauton* 1199 FineR, 1238, 1244 *Ass*, *Chepyngtowtone* 1447 Exon
> *Nortauton* 1262 Ipm, *Northtauton* 1316 FA, *Northtaunton* 1420 IpmR

'Farm on the river Taw' (*supra* 14). 'North' or *Cheping*, 'market,' *v.* cieping, to distinguish from South Tawton *infra* 448.

BATHE BARTON is *Ba* 1281 *Ass* (p), *Bathe* 1333 *SR* (p), *Bath* 1635 *FF*. This must be the OE *bæþ*, 'bath,' cf. Bampton *infra* 530. There is a Bathe Pool close at hand. Polwhele (19) mentions it in 1790 as 'Bath Pool' in a pit in a field, 8 feet deep.

BROADNYMET is *Limet* 1086 DB, *Bradenimet*' 1242 Fees 783,

Brodenymet 1292 Ipm, (*juxta Northtauton*) 1303 *Ass. v. supra* 348. 'Broad' here probably means 'great' as in Broad Clyst, Broadhempston *infra* 573, 509, in contrast perhaps to Nichols Nymett not far off.

CROOKE is *Cruc* 1086 DB, *Cruk* 1234 Fees 400, 1242 Fees 787, (*juxta Northtauton*) 1310 *Ass*, *Cruk Burnel* 1316 FA, *Crok(e) Burnel* 1331 Ipm, 1346 FA, *Croke* 1491 Ipm. This is probably a Celtic name corresponding to W *crug*, Co *cruc*, (*croukā), 'barrow, hill.' Cf. Crook *infra* 638. Robert *Burnel* held the manor in 1234.

GREENSLADE is *Ghernesleta* 1086 DB, *Grenesland* (sic) 1198 FF, *Greneslade* 1238 *Ass* (p), 1242 Fees 783, 1344 Ipm. 'The green slæd.'

NICHOLS NYMETT is *Nimet* 1086 DB, *Nymet Nicole* 1303 FA, *Nycolesnymet* 1333 SR (p). The identity of *Nichol* is unknown. There was a '*Nicholas de la Yalelande*' in the parish in 1238, *v. infra*, but there is no mention in Fees or FA of such a man as a feudal holder in the district.

BRIDGE FM, SANDFORD, STONE, UPCOTT, WEEK, WESTACOTT and YELLAND were probably the homes of Walter *atte Brigge* (1412 *Ass*), William de *Saunforde* (1333 *SR*), William *atte Stone* (1333 *SR*), Robert de *Uppecote* (ib.), Philip de *Wike* (1275 RH), Henry de *Westecote* (1330 *SR*), Galfridus fil. Nicholas de *la Yalelande*, (1238 *Ass*), i.e. 'of the old land,' *v.* Addenda, Part i, lviii, and cot(e), wic.

BEERE is *Bere* 1238 *Ass* (p), 1242 Fees 783. *v.* bearu. HOLLA CROOKE is *Holecruke* 1238 *Ass* (p), -*crok* 1333 *SR* (p), *Holy Croke* 1491 Ipm. *v.* Crooke *supra*. The farm lies in a hollow. LARKSWORTHY (6″) is *Larkworthys* 1797 *Recov*, suggesting that the name is really manorial from a man who came from Larkworthy *supra* 128. NEWLAND (6″) is *Niwelaunde* 1242 Fees 783. SLADE is *Slade* 1563 *Deed*. *v.* slæd. STADDON is *Stoddon* 1238 *Ass* (p), 1242 Fees 787, 1330 *SR* (p). 'Stud hill,' cf. Staddon *supra* 79.

Randolph de Byr, Hundred Rolls 3 ED I = 1274 No 25 p 75.
Reginald de Bere
under nova jur

Wembworthy

WEMBWORTHY [weməri] 128 E 1

Mameorda 1086 DB
Wemeworth' 1207 Cur, *Wemmewrth'* 1242 Fees 783 *et freq* to
1333 *SR* with variant spellings -*worthi*, -*worthe*, -*worthy*,
Wemmaworth(y) 1346 FA, 1396 Exon
Wenneworth(y) 1303 FA
Weymeworthe 1309 Exon
Wembworthy 1420 Exon, *Wemry* 1629–51 Barum 1, 59

The first element here is probably *Wemma*, a pet-form of
such an OE name as *Wēnmǣr* or *Wēnmund* which, though not on
record, would be regular formations. (Cf. OGer *Wenemar*,
Wanmund.) Blomé (66) suggests a river-name *Wem*, which
Wallenberg (StudNP 2, 91) would connect with OE *wamm*,
wemm, 'stain, uncleanness,' and suggests that Wem (Sa) is
so called from its situation in marshland.

RASHLEIGH BARTON

Liega 1086 DB
Rasle 1278 Ipm *et freq* to 1505 Ipm with variant spellings
Rays(s)h(e)-, *Rassh(e)*-, *Rasch(e)*- and -*legh(e)*, *Atterashlegh*
1292 Ipm (p)

Probably 'at the ash wood or clearing,' *v.* æsc, leah, the *r* being
a remnant of the ME inflexional form *at ther*, cf. Rook *supra*
270, Rill *infra* 606.

COMBE (6″) was the home of Isabella *atte Combe* (1333 *SR*).
HEYWOOD WOOD is *Haywode* 1373 Orig. 'Enclosed wood,' *v.*
(ge)hæg. LABDON (6″) is *Lobbeton* 1330 *SR* (p), *Lobeton* 1339 *Ass.*
v. Lobb *supra* 33. SCRABBACLEAVE COTTAGE (6″) is so spelt
1787 *Recov. v.* clif. SPEKE'S CROSS is to be associated with the
family of Juliana *Speek* (1333 *SR*). UPCOTT is *Uppecote* 1330 *SR*
(p), *Upecote in Wenworthy* 1481 IpmR. WEMBWORTHY DOWN is
Down 1503 Ipm.

Winkleigh

WINKLEIGH 127 F 14/15

> *Wincheleia* 1086 DB *et passim* to 1426 IpmR with variant
> spellings *Winche-, Winke-, Wynke-* and *-legh(e), Wynkelegh
> Tracy* 1350 Ipm
> *Wenkelegh* 1282 Exon

'*Wineca*'s clearing,' v. leah. A compound of OE wincel and
leah is also possible, denoting a clearing near some nook or
corner, or notable for its nooks or corners. Henry de *Tracy* held
one fee here in 1242.

CADDITON is *Codiaton* 1330 *SR* (p), *Cadiaton* 1333 *SR* (p) and
must be associated with the family of Roger *Cadya* who was
living here in 1333 (*SR*). For *ya* v. Introd. xxxvi.

LOOSEDON BARTON

> *Lollardesdona* 1086 DB
> *Lullardeston'* 1242 Fees 778, *Lullardisdon* 1303 FA, *Lullardes-
> ton juxta Wynkelegh* 1323 *Ass*
> *Luwardeston* 1346 FA
> *Lullesdon* 1394 *Ass*, *Lollesdon* 1503 Ipm, *Lousdon al. Lulisdon*
> 1746 *FF*

The second element is either dun or tun. The first is clearly a
pers. name, probably a late OE name of Continental origin. It
may be the Middle Dutch *lollaert, lollaerd*, not hitherto recorded
earlier than c. 1300, denoting 'a mumbler,' cf. Verwijs and
Verdam *s.v.* Such a word as a nickname may have a long history
behind it. We may compare Dollaston (Pembrokeshire),
Dollardyston in 1331 (*Cymmorodorion Rec. Soc.* 7, 137), clearly
containing the name of a Flemish settler nicknamed 'dullard.'
That word is of LGer origin, v. NED, and *Dullert* is used as a
pers. name in Holland (cf. Verwijs and Verdam *s.v.*). See also
Wallenberg in StudNP (2, 97).

EAST LUXTON is *Luggeston* 1346 *Ass* (p) and may derive from the
family of Nicholas *Lug*, a juror in Winkleigh Hundred in 1238
(*Ass*).

Down Fm (6″), Heath, Hole Fm (6″), Moortown[1] (6″), Taw Green and Westwood (6″) were probably the homes of Robert *atter Doune* (1333 SR), Robert *atte Hethe* (1330 SR), Nicholas de *la Hole* (1333 SR), William de *Mora* (1244 Ass), William de *Taw*, i.e. 'by the river Taw' (1330 SR), and Walter de *Westwode* (ib.).

Babbages, Helliars and Paddons (all 6″) are probably to be associated with the families of Henry *Bobich* (1330 SR), Reginald *le Helyere* (1333 SR) and Thomas *Paddon* (t. Eliz SR).

Ashley is *Esshelegh, Asselegh* 1238 Ass, *Aysshlegh* 1330 SR (p). *v*. leah. Bitbeare is *Bittebere* 1281 Ass (p). '*Bitta*'s wood,' *v*. bearu. Birch (6″) is *la Birche* 1305 Ipm. Bransgrove is *Braundesgrove* 1339 Ass, *Brandes-* 1356 Ass, *Brounes-* 1496 Ipm. '*Brand*'s grove.' Chapple is *la Chapele, Chapell* 1256 Ass. Chapple Down (6″) is *Chappledown Mill* t. Eliz ChancP. Collacott is *Colecote* 1238 Ass (p), 1330 SR (p), *Colle-* 1275 RH (p). Cf. Collacott *supra* 50. Coulson is *Colstaton* 1330 SR (p). A Robert *Colste* occurs in the 1330 SR, but not in this part of the county. Crispin (6″) is *Cryspyndowene* 1492 FF, *Crispen al. Crewespyne* 1682 Recov. West Gosland Down (6″) is *Gosselandoune* 1448 Deed. Gray's Bridge Fm is *Grayesbridge* 1699 Recov. Heckapen is *Hakepenne* 1330 SR (p). Cf. Hackpen *infra* 538. Herdwick (6″) is *Hurdewik* 1333 SR (p). *v*. heordewic. Hollocombe is *Holecumb(e)* 1235 Cl, 1238 Ass, 1261 Cl, *Hale-* 1242 Fees 778. 'Hollow valley.' Kingsland (6″) is possibly identical with *Kayngmaneslond* 1333 SR (p). Lutehouse (6″) is *the Lutehouse* 1566 Deed. Narracott is *Nither(e)cote* 1301 Exon. 'Lower cot(e).' For the modern form, cf. Nurcott in Winsford (So), *Nithercote* 1327 SR (p). Penson is *Penstaton* 1330 SR (p). Great Pitford is *Pudeford* 1281 Ass (p), *Piteforde* 1330 SR (p), *Putteford* 1346 FA (p). Possibly '*Putta*'s ford.' For *u* > *i*, *v*. Introd. xxxiv. The earliest form is probably corrupt. Puncherdon is *Pyncheton* 1330 SR (p), *Puncheton* 1333 SR (p). Possibly '*Puneca*'s farm,' *v*. tun and cf. Pinchaford *infra* 477. Riddiford is *Radeford(e)* 1275 RH (p), 1330 SR (p). 'Red ford.' Riddistone is *Redelestun al. Ridelestun* 1204 BM, *Raddeston* 1553 Deed. Southcott is *Sudthecot'* 1242 Fees 778, *Southecote*

[1] *Moortowne* 1741 FF.

1330 *SR* (p), *Southcote juxta Wynkeleghe* 1365 *Ass.* STABDON is *Stappedon* 1333 *SR* (p), *Stapdon* 1731 *Recov.* This is probably OE *stēapandūn*, 'steep hill.' STABLE GREEN is *la Stapele juxta Wynkelegh* 1313 *Ass.* *v.* stapol. WEEK HOUSE (6″) is *Wyk Tammill* 1303 FA, *Wickehouse, Wekehouse* 1592 *SR.* *v.* wic. *Tammill* may be a scribal or transcriptional error for *Taumill*, i.e. 'mill by the river Taw.' WHEATLAND is *Whytelond* 1281 *Ass* (p). Probably the early form is the correct one. WOODTERRILL is *Woodterrell* 1727 *FF* and is to be associated with the family of Richard *Tirel* (1249 *Ass*) and Galfridus *Tyrel* (1333 *SR*).

Zeal Monachorum

ZEAL MONACHORUM[1] 128 G 3

> *Sele* 1228 FF, 1263 Ipm, 1276 Exon, *Sele Monaco'* 1275 RH, (*Monachorum*) 1309 Exon
> *Monekenesele* 1346 *Ass*

v. sele. The place corresponds to the DB manor of *Limae* (Exch *Limet*), held by the monks of Buckfast Abbey. *v.* George Nympton *supra* 348.

BARON'S WOOD is *Baronyswode* 1482 IpmR and is to be associated with the family of Robert *Baron* (1333 *SR*).

BURSTON is *Burdevileston'* 1242 Fees 783, -*vyles*- 1346 FA, *Bordevileston* 1303 FA, *Burdestone* 1329 Exon, *Bordouliston* 1362 IpmR, *Nymet Bordevyle* 1316 FA, (*juxta Nymet Tracy*) 1345 *Ass*, *Nymet Bordeville* 1410 *FF*. The first element of this name would seem to be a French pers. name *B(o)urdeville* of manorial origin, but no such name has been noted in any records relating to Devon.

LOOSEBEARE is *Losbera* 1086 DB, -*berg(am)* 1107 (1300) Ch, 1228 FF, -*bare* 1238 *Ass*, -*bere* 1291 Tax, *Loseberewe*, -*berghe* 1262, 1268 FF. The first element is OE hlose, 'pigstye.' The variants in spelling do not permit one to decide whether the second is beorg or bearu.

---

[1] Birch hesitatingly identifies this with the place called *at Seale* in BCS 968. That place is, however, coupled with *at Dunnynghefd* and the two are to be identified with Zeal and Donhead in south-east Wiltshire. No place is known in Devon which could correspond to *Dunnynghefd*.

LOWER NEWTON is *Nieutona, Newentona* 1086 DB (Exon), *Niwetone* (Exch), *Newenton* 1212 FF. Further forms are without medial *n*. 'New farm,' *v*. niwe, tun.

SERSTONE is *Serleston* 1239 FF, 1244 *Ass*, 1334 *FF*. 'Farm of *Serl(o)*' (*v*. tun), embodying a common Anglo-Norman name. Cf. Walson *supra* 365.

ALLER[1] (6″) and WEEK were probably the homes of Stephen de *Alre*, i.e. 'by the alder,' and Philip de *Wyke* (1333 *SR*). *v*. wic.

BEER LANE (6″), cf. *Berehede* 1493 Ipm. *v*. bearu. FOLDHAY is *Foldehegh'* 1242 Fees 787, *Fauldeheye* 1244 *Ass* (p), *Foldheye* 1333 *SR* (p). Probably OE *falda-(ge)hæg*, 'enclosure of (or with) folds.' NORTHWOOD is *Northwode* 1493 Ipm. NYMPHAYES (6″) [nimp-] was probably the home of Henry de *Nymetheia* of Winkleigh (1333 *SR*). *v*. (ge)hæg. For the first element, *v*. George Nympton *supra* 348.

XVI. WITHERIDGE HUNDRED

Witric, Wetrige 1084 Geld Roll
Wederige 1167 P, *Wederinge* 1168 P, *Witherigge* 1175 P
v. Witheridge *infra* 397.

Cheldon

CHELDON BARTON 128 D 3/4

Chaeledona, Chadeledona 1086 DB (Exon), *Cheledone, Cadeledone* (Exch)
Chedeladon c. 1185 Buckland, -*le*- 1238 *Ass*, -*dune* 1242 Fees 783, -*don* 1285 FA, *Estchedeldune* 1242 Fees 758, *Est Chedeledon* 1285 FA, *Cheddeledone* 1321 Exon
Chydeladon 1281 *Ass*

'*Ceadela*'s hill,' *v*. dun. Cf. Chillington *supra* 332.

MOUNTICOMBE is *Montecomb* 1330 *SR* (p), *Mountacomb* 1333 *SR* (p). Probably this name should be taken with Mounson *infra* 429 and *Muntelonde* (13th *Canonsleigh*). The names may well be of late origin and contain a ME surname *Munt* or *Munta*, deriving ultimately from the common word *munt*, 'mount.'

[1] *Aller* 1592 *SR*.

Chulmleigh

CHULMLEIGH [tʃʌmli] 128 D 2

Chalmonleuga 1086 DB (Exon), *Calmonleuga* (Exch)
Chamundesleg 1219 *Ass*, *Chaumunleg* 1228 FF, *Chaumundlegh*
1254 *Ass*
Chaumelega 1222 Bracton, *Chalmelegh* 1242 Fees 761, *Chaum-*
leghe, *Caumeleye*, *Cheaumeleghe* 1260–80 Exon
Chelmelelegh (sic) 1244 *Ass*, *Chelmelegh* 1377 Cl
Chulmeleg(h) 1274 Ipm, 1275 RH, 1281 *Ass*, 1292 Cl, 1297
Pat, *Culmeleghe* 1260–80 Exon
Chylmelegh 1281 *Ass*, 1306 *Ass*, *Chilmelegh(e)* 1308 Exon,
(*juxta Nymet Regis*) 1334 *Ass*
Chymley 1600 Cai, *Chimleigh* or *Chulmleigh* 1675 Ogilby

'*Cēolmund*'s leah.' The forms in *Chal-*, *Cham-*, *Chaum-* are
difficult, but *v.* Chelmscott (PN Bk 84).

BEALY COURT is *Baylekewrth*' 1242 Fees 783, *Bailikeworth* 1292
Ipm, *Baillekeworthy* 1307 *Ass*, *Baylekewordy* 1378 IpmR, *Bayly*
Court 1728 *FF*. If this name is old it may contain the OE pers.
name *Bǣgloc* (BCS 181), though we should have expected a
possessive *s* in that case. Cf. Bashley (Ha), *at Baglucesleia* KCD
798[1], *Bailocheslei* 1086 DB, *Ballokesle* 1271 *Ass*, *Bayllokeslee*
1314 Ipm. There are parallels, however, in Devon for the
omission of the *s*, cf. Killington, Wiverton *supra* 66, 251.

BENLEY CROSS is *Benelegh* 1242 Fees 758 (p), 1285 FA, *Binelег̄*
1249 *Ass* (p), *Buneleg(h)* 1292 Ipm, 1330 *SR* (p), *Buna-* 1333 *SR*
(p), *Bynglegh* 1378 IpmR. This is probably OE *bēona lēah*, 'bee-
frequented wood or clearing,' *v.* leah and cf. Beenleigh *supra* 299.

BUNSON is *Bonevileston(e)* 1242 Fees 783, 1292 Ipm, 1303 FA,
Boneston 1378 IpmR, *Bonston* 1503 Ipm. This is '*Bonevil(l)e*'s
farm,' a post-Conquest p.n., *v.* tun. A Ricardus de *Bonavilla*
occurs in Devon in 1166 (RBE), but the family have not been
noted in connexion with this parish in early documents.

CADBURY BARTON is *Cadebire* 1238 FF, 1242 Fees 783, *Caddebir*
1238 *Ass* (p), *Cadebury Copenere* 1303 FA. '*Cada*'s burh.'

---

[1] We owe this reference to the kindness of Professor Ekwall.

A Robert le *Copener* was one of the jurors of Witheridge Hundred in 1242 (Fees).

COLLETON BARTON is *Coleton(e)* 1242 Fees 761, 1285 FA, *Colaton* 1443 *FF*. It was held by one Roger *Cole* in 1242. This may be only a coincidence or it may be that the name *Cole* was common here as a second name a good deal earlier than 1242. On the whole evidence tends to show that second names became hereditary rather earlier than has commonly been supposed.

EAST and WEST MOLLAND (6″) is *Monalond(e)* 1330, 1333 *SR* (p), *Monelond* 1378 IpmR. The forms are too late for us to decide between a first element *mōna*, 'moon' (cf. Moonhill, PN Sx 264), or *Mōna*, a pers. name, cf. Moonhouse *supra* 190.

PYNAMEAD (6″) is *Paneʒhemede* 1308 Exon (p), *Paneghemede* 1333 *SR* (p), *Pan(n)emede* 1346, 1428 FA. The first element here is ME *paneʒ*, 'penny,' cf. *pennyland*, a common term for land valued at a penny a year. Here we have meadowland similarly valued. Cf. *Pennemade* 1387 *MinAcct* (Hackney, Mx).

SHEEPSBYRE

> *Shitelesbere* 1242 Fees 783, *Chytelesber'* 1281 *Ass* (p)
> *Chettisbeare* 1285 FA, *Schitesbere* 1303 FA, *Schettesbeare* 1415
>   *Ass*, *Scetisbere* 1481 IpmR, *Shittisbeer* 1809 M
> *Shyddesbeere* 1377 Cl, *Shiddesbeare* 1378 IpmR

The first element is probably the word *scyttels*, 'bolt, bar,' found in Sheepstor *supra* 238; the exact sense of the compound of this word and bearu must remain obscure, as one cannot know the appearance of the wood or whether it had some locked opening or the like. The modern form shows the same euphemistic corruption as Sheepstor itself.

BONDS (6″) and DOBB'S MOOR are probably to be associated with the family of John *Bonde* (1330 *SR*) and John *Dobba* (1333 *SR*).

BROOKLAND, COOMBE[1], HILL HEAD FM (6″), HOLE (6″), LAKEHEAD and LEIGH HO were probably the homes of Thomas *Brokelond* (1524 *SR*), Richard de *Cumbe* (1238 *Ass*), William *atte Hulle* (1333 *SR*), Robert de *la Hole* (1238 *Ass*), Galfridus de *Lakeheved*, i.e. 'at the stream-head' (1330 *SR*), and Osb de *la Legh* (1238 *Ass*).

[1] *Combe* 1408 IpmR.

BYCOTT is *Biacote* 1238 *Ass* (p), *Byecote* 1281 *Ass* (p), 'cot(e) in the bend or curve (OE *byge*),' cf. Huccaby *supra* 194. The place is in a fork between two streams. CUTLAND is *Cotelonde* 1330 *SR* (p), 1346 FA. *v.* cot(e). DARTRIDGE is so spelt 1765 D. DODYARD (6") is *Dodeherd* 1238 *Ass* (p). '*Dod(d)a*'s yard of land,' *v.* Yard *supra* 48. FORD FM (6") is *Ford* 1500 Ipm. GARLAND is *Gorelaunde* 1242 Fees 783, *Gorlonde* 1292 Ipm, *Goralonde* 1330 *SR* (p). 'Dirty land,' *v.* gor. OE gara, 'corner of land,' is also possible as the first element. EAST HOLLAND COTTAGES (6") is *Hulland* 1561 *FF*, *Holland* 1622 *Recov*, 1628 *Deed*. HUNTACOTT is *Huntecote* 1330 *SR* (p), 1356 *Ass*, 1378 IpmR, 1393 *FF*. 'Hunta's cot(e)' or 'huntsman's cot(e).' KEMPLAND is *Kempelond* 1377 Cl, *Kymplond* 1378 IpmR. Cf. Kimber *supra* 154. LADY WELL COTTAGES (6") mark the site of an ancient chapel and holy well referred to as *capella Sancte Marie atte Wille* 1378 Exon. NEWNHAM BARTON is *Neuham* 1238 *Ass* (p), *Nywnham by Chilmelegh* 1341 Ipm. 'New ham(m).' SPITTLE is *Le Hospital* 1242 Fees 783, *Spitele* 1346 FA, 1367 *FF*. The Knights Hospitallers owned land in Chulmleigh. STONE BARTON is *Stayne* 1242 Fees 783, *la Stane* 1249 *Ass* (p), *La Stone* 1285 FA. There is the site of an ancient castle here. The *ay*-form may show the influence of OE *stǣne*, discussed in PN Sx 292 *s.n.* Steine. THURLE is *Thrale* t. Eliz ChancP. WEEK[1] is *Wik* 1242 Fees 761, *Est-*, *Westwyke* 1378 IpmR. 'Dairy farm,' *v.* wic. WIXON may be identical with *Wizodeston* 1238 *Ass* (p). It is *Wixon* 1621 *SR*. '*Wigod*'s farm,' *v.* tun, *Wigod* being a late OE name.

Creacombe

CREACOMBE [kreikəm] 128 B 6

> *Crabecoma, Crahecoma, Crawecoma* 1086 DB (Exon), *Crawecome* (Exch), *Craucomb* 1254 *Ass*
> *Creucumbe* 1284 Exon, *Crew(e)comb(e)* 1333 *SR*, 1422 Exon
> *Croucombe* 1291 Tax, *Croucumb juxta Whytherugg'* 1303 *Ass*

> 'Crow valley,' *v.* cumb and Introd. xxxiii.

BATSWORTHY is *Bateswurth* 1249 *Ass* (p). '*Bætti*'s farm,' *v.* worþig. Cf. Battishill *supra* 177. CROWDHOLE is *Croudewall*

---

[1] EAST and WEST WEEK (6").

1330 *SR* (p). FRANKHILL is *Fraunkeille* 1270 *Ass*, *Frankehille*
1278 Exon (p). 'Franca's hill.' HORSEHAVEN is *Southhorsaven*
1609 *FF*. Probably 'horse marsh,' *v.* fenn. For the medial
syllable, *v.* Introd. xxxvi. Cf. also Cockhaven *infra* 487.

Cruwys Morchard

CRUWYS MORCHARD [kruˑz] 128 D 8

Morc(h)et, Morceth 1086 DB, *Morceth* 1242 Fees 758, 793
Cru(w)ys Morchard 1257–80 Exon, (*Cruwes*) 1301 Ipm, *Crews-
marchard* t. Jas 1 ECP, *Morcherde* 1261 Exon
Morcestr(e) Crues 1279 QW, 1284 Exon, 1291 Tax

This is a Celtic name, as first explained by Johnston, PN
England and Wales *s.n.*, the elements corresponding to W *mawr*,
(**mor*), 'great, big,' and *coed*, (**cēt*), 'wood.' Cf. also Morchard
Bishop *infra* 408. The form was later affected by the common
orceard. It is doubtful if the same wood can be referred to in the
two names, the places being about 10 miles apart. Alexander de
Crues held the manor in 1242.

GOGLAND is *Goggalond* 1330, *Goghalond* 1333 *SR* (p). The first
element may, as suggested by Blomé (114), be the dialectal word
gog, 'bog, quagmire,' the land being somewhat marshy here.
Another possibility is that the name is to be connected with the
family of William *Gogha* found in Meshaw (about 10 miles
distant but in the same Hundred) in the *SR* for 1333.

HILL FM is *Hilla* 1086 DB, *Hulle* 1228 FF, 1303 FA, (*Dacastre*)
1316 FA, *Hillakastell* 1374 IpmR. Roger de *Acastre* held the
manor in 1228.

RUCKHAM is *Rouecomma* 1086 DB, *Est Ruggescumbe* 1286 *FF*,
Roggecumbe 1311 *FF*, *Rogecome* 1389 IpmR. Probably 'Hrucga's
combe,' cf. *hrucgan cumbes ford* (Crawf 2), also in Devon.

STICKERIDGE is *Stykerugg'* 1330 *SR* (p), *Netherstekerig* 1400
IpmR, *Stykerygge* 1492 *FF*. Probably from OE *sticelan-hrycg*,
'steep ridge.' *v.* sticol.

THONGSLEIGH is *Twangeslegh'*, *Thauangeslegh'* 1242 Fees 775,
Thwange(s)legh 1242 Fees 762, 1244 *Ass* (p), 1356 *Ass*, *Thwenges-
legh* 1371 Cl. *v.* leah. The first element may be identical with

that of Tongham (Sr), *Tuangeham* 1205 ClR, *Twengham* 1235 FF, *Twangham* 1245 FF, 1299 Ipm, *Thuangham* 1341 Pat. This is probably, as suggested by Blomé (115), the word *thong* (OE *þwang*) used in the sense of a long narrow strip of land. The genitival compound offers difficulties, however, and it is possible that the name is of late origin from a ME surname *Thwang*.

YEDBURY is *Addeberia* 1086 DB, *Addebir'* 1242 Fees 762, *Yeadburi* 1334 *SR*, *Yadebury* 1389 IpmR, *Yedbury* 1428 FA, *Yaddebir'* 1275 RH, *Yhaddeburi* 1305 Ipm. '*Eadda*'s burh.'

DOWN, FURZE and MOOR were probably the homes of Thomas de *la Doune* (1279 *Ass*), Robert *atte Forse* (1333 *SR*), and Henry *atte More* (1330 *SR*). *v.* dun, mor.

CLAW (6″) is *Clawe* 1564 *Deed*. *v.* Clawton *supra* 138. It is in a river fork. COOMBE and COOMBELAND are *La Cumb* 1256 FF, *Coombland al. Combland* 1720 *Recov*. DEPTFORD is *Dupeforde* 1372 IpmR. 'Deep ford.' EDGEWORTHY is *Eggeworthe* 1281 *Ass* (p), *Egheworthi* 1333 *SR* (p), *Edgeworthy* 1703 *Recov*. '*Ecga*'s worþig.' FILK KNAPP (6″) is *Filleknap* 1333 *SR* (p). *v.* cnæpp. The first element may be the OE *filiþe* discussed *s.n.* Filleigh *supra* 42. FORD BARTON is *Forde* 1492 *FF*. FORK FM is *la Forke* 1279 *Ass* (p). It is situated in a river fork. HOOKWAY is *Hookeway* 1657 *Recov*. The farm is on a lane running up a well-marked spur of land, *v.* hoc. LUGSLAND is *Lugge(s)lond* 1270 *Ass*, 1281 *Ass* (p), *Loggeslonde* 1330 *SR* (p). Probably from a medieval owner *Lug(g)*, cf. Luxton *supra* 373. NORTHCOTE is *Northecoth'* 1242 Fees 733, 780, *Northcote juxta Cruesmorchard* 1309 *FF*. HIGHER PARK is *West Parke* 1649 *Recov*. PENNYMOOR is so spelt 1765 D. SPRINGHAY (6″) is so spelt 1683 *Deed*. STUBBORN is *Stubborne* 1683 *Deed*. This is probably a nickname for a farm difficult to work. THORN COTTAGE (6″) is *La Thorne* 1244 *Ass*. VULSCOMBE is *Vowelscombe* 1607 *FF*, *Fulscombe* 1711 DKR 41, 388. The first element is probably a pers. name, either OE *Fugol* or ME *Fow(e)l*, cf. Fulscot (Berks), *Fowelescot* 1327 *SR*. WRINGSLAND is *Wrencheslond* 1330 *SR* (p), *Winchesland* 1649 *Recov*. The first element may be the name of a medieval owner.

Mariansleigh

MARIANSLEIGH [ma·li], [mɛ·ri ænzli·] 128 A 4

    Leiga 1086 DB (Exon), *Lege* (Exch)
    Marinelegh(e) 1238 *Ass* (p) *et freq* to 1337 Exon
    Seyntemarilegh' 1242 Fees 761
    Maryonlegh, Marnelegh, Maryneslegh c. 1400 Exon
    Marle al. Marynalegh 1465 IpmR, *Marley al. Mariansleigh*
      1747 *Recov*
    Marynglegh 1541 *SR*
    Mary Annesleigh 1765 D

    v. leah. The dedication of the church is to St Mary, but there may have been an early dedication to St Marina. Cf. St Merryn (Co).

EASTACOTT (6″), MILLTOWN, SOUTHACOTT (6″), WESTACOTT and YEO BARTON[1] were probably the homes of Henry de *Estacote* (1330 *SR*), John *atte Mille* (ib.), Adam de *Southecote* (ib.), John de *Westacote* (ib.) and Gilbert de *Yea*, i.e. 'by the water,' (ib.). *v. supra* 17–18, and cot(e).

ALSWEAR is *Alzer* 1765 D. OXEN MOOR (6″) is *Yeomore al. Oxenmoore* 1675 *Recov. v.* Yeo *supra*. ROWCLIFFE (6″) is *Roweclyve* 1333 *SR* (p), *Roughcleave* 1765 D. 'Rough hillside,' *v.* clif. TIDLAKE is *Todelake* 1333 *SR* (p), *Tudlake* 1628 *Recov. v.* lacu and Tiddy Brook (*supra* 14). TRITTENCOTT is *Trutyncote* 1524 *SR, Trytencotte* 1581 *SR*. UPPACOTT is *Uppecoth'* 1242 Fees 759, *Oppecot* 1261 Exon.

Meshaw

MESHAW 128 B 4

    Mauessart 1086 DB, *Malessart* 1175 P
    Madisheue 1212 Fees 98
    Mausard(e) 1242 Fees 759, 783, 1263, 1288 Exon, 1292 Ipm,
      1346 FA, *Meusard* 1298 *Ass*
    Mausawe 1249 *Ass, Menaschaf'* 1253 Ipm, *Meus(h)aue* 1291
      Tax, 1303 FA, *Meushagh* 1307 Cl, 1316 FA, 1334, 1340 *SR*,
      -shathe 1342 Exon, 1362 *Ass, -schate* 1370 Exon, *Meweshawe*
      1468 IpmR

                   [1] *Yeo, Yoe* 1497 Ipm.

This is probably a name of Norman-French origin from NFr *mal-essart*, 'bad (unfertile) clearing' (cf. Sart *infra* 634). At a later stage owing to vocalisation of the *l* and loss of final *t* the true meaning was obscured and the name associated with OE sceaga, 'shaw.'

IRISHCOMBE FM is *Eruescoma* (sic) 1086 DB, *Yernyscombe juxta Wytherygg* 1314 *Ass*, *Irishcombe* 1738 *Recov.* 'Eagle's combe' or possibly '*Earnwīg*'s cumb,' a name which would perhaps better explain the modern trisyllabic form.

BLACKLANDS, NARRACOTT, WHITESTONE and YONDERLAKE (6″) were probably the homes of John de *Blakelonde* (1330 *SR*), William de *Northecote* (1281 *Ass*), Gervas de *Whitaston* (1333 *SR*) and William *Byundelake*, i.e. 'beyond the streamlet' (ib.). *v.* blæc, cot(e), lacu.

BROADS MOOR (6″) is *Brodemore* 1288 *Ass*. GIDLEY ARMS[1] is *Guddele* 1330 *SR* (p). '*Gydda*'s clearing,' *v.* leah. PRESCOTT (6″) is *Prestecota* 1175 P (p), *Prustecote* 1298 *Ass*. 'Priests' cot(e).'

Bishop's Nympton

BISHOP'S NYMPTON[2] 128 A 4

> *Nimeton(a)* 1086 DB, 1238 FF, *Nemetone Episcopi* 1269 Exon, *Bysshopes Nymet* 1334 *SR*, *Bishops Nymeton* 1377 Cl, *Nymet Busshop* 1557 Wills

v. George Nympton *supra* 348. The manor was held by the Bishop of Exeter in 1086.

DREWSTONE is *Thordeston* 1281 *Ass* (p), *Over Throwston* 1615 *Deed*, *Threwstone* 1703 *Recov*. Possibly '*Thorward*'s farm,' with later shifting of stress. The name is Anglo-Scandinavian. Cf. Drewston *infra* 424.

GRILSTONE

> *Gerardeston'* 1242 Fees 759, *Gireldiston* 1249 *Ass* (p)
> *Giroleston'* 1244 *Ass* (p), *Girellestone* 1261 Exon (p), *Gerelleston* 1285 FA
> *Gyrlyston* 1346 FA, *Girleston* 1359 *Ass* (p), *Grilleston* 1428 FA

[1] Now a public house. Originally a farm.
[2] Locally 'Bish' Nympton.' Cf. BISH MILL in the parish.

This is probably 'Gerard's farm,' a post-Conquest p.n. v. tun. A *Girard* is already found in Devon c. 1100 (Earle 257), but the pers. name has not been noted in connexion with Bishop's Nympton parish. For initial hard *g*, cf. Garrigill and Crosby Garrett (We), containing the same pers. name.

JOHNSTONE is *Ioneston* 1281 *Ass* (p), *Ionyston* 1333 *SR* (p), *Jonestone* 1397 *FF*, *Johnson* 1581 *SR*, 1675 Ogilby. 'John's farm,' v. tun. The p.n. must be of ME origin. Cf. Johnston (Pemb), *Villa Johannis* 1297 Dugd iv, 503, *Jonyston* 1406 EpReg. (St Davids).

KIPSCOTT is *Kippingescota* 1235 Bracton, -*coth'* 1242 Fees 759, *Kippyngescot(e)* 1281 *Ass* (p), 1316 Ipm. '*Cypping*'s cot(e),' cf. Kipscombe *supra* 31.

MUCKFORD is *Mokeford* 1249 *Ass*, 1330 *SR* (p), *Mocke-* 1333 *SR* (p), *Moggeforda* 1427 *Ass*, *Nokeworth* (sic) *in Nymet Epī* 1465 IpmR, *Mukford* 1472 IpmR. '*Moc(c)a*'s ford,' cf. Muckworthy *supra* 129. Wallenberg (StudNP 2, 95) suggests that we have in these two names the ME *muck*, but that word is of Scandinavian origin and is never used of 'dung' in the south of England.

RAWSTONE is *Raweston'* 1242 Fees 795, *Roweston* 1306 *Ass*, *Rowyston* 1333 *SR* (p) and is to be associated with *Ralph* de Nimet (1198 FF). Hence, 'Ralph's farm,' v. tun.

REACH was the home of John Aleyn *atte Reche* (1394 *Ass*). Reach is on a hillside. The interpretation of the name is obscure. For the topographical use of the term as so far observed, v. Reach (PN BedsHu 125).

TORKRIDGE (lost) is *Torkaringa*, -*rigge* 1166 RBE (p), *Turkerig* 1242 Fees 759, *Thorkerigge* 1303, *Torkerygg* 1346, *Thorkeright* 1428 FA. Blomé (17) suggests that the first element may be an old river-name identical with Turk (RN 420), but as we know nothing of the site the etymology had better remain open.

VERABY is *Farebi* 1238 *Ass* (p), *Faireby* 1249 *Ass* (p), *La Fayrebie* 1285 FA, *Veriby* or *Fairby* 1762 *Recov*. 'Fair (river) bend,' cf. Huccaby, Grammerby *supra* 194, 221.

ALLER, BRIDGE[1] (6"), LITTLE OAK (6"), EAST and WEST PORT, SLOUGH and WEEK were probably the homes of Thomas de

---

[1] *Burdge* 1570 *Deed*. For this form, cf. PN Bk xxiv.

Allere (1359 *Ass*), David *atte Brigge* (1359 *Ass*), William *atte Och* (1330 *SR*) and Henry de *Oke* (1333 *SR*), John de *Estport* (1330 *SR*) and de *Westport* (1333 *SR*), John *atte Slo* (1330 *SR*), i.e. 'at the slough,' cf. Slew *supra* 28, 338, and Michael de *Wyke* (1333 *SR*). *v.* alor, port, wic. East, West and Middle Port lie along Port Lane, with Port Cross and Porthill's Quarry on it. The use of *port* in these names is obscure. Cf. *s.n.* Doggaport *supra* 95.

AVERCOMBE is *Anecombe* (sic) 1577 Wills. BICKNOR is *Bykenore* 1311 *Ass* (p), 1330 *SR* (p). '*Bic(c)a*'s bank,' *v.* ora. See further Abbots Bickington *supra* 124. BURWELL is possibly identical with *Birifelde* 1330 *SR* (p). *v.* Introd. xxxv. GARLIFORD is *Gerlaford* 1333 *SR* (p). '*Gerla*'s ford,' cf. Guarlford (PN Wo 211). GOR-TONHILL is *Gorton* 1524, 1592 *SR*. HAYNE is *Chapelheghen* 1303 FA, *la Heghene* 1359 *Ass*. *v.* Hayne *supra* 129. HILLTOWN is *La Hulle juxta Nimeton* 1289 *Ass*. For *town*, *v. infra* 676. KERSCOTT is *Kerescote* 1238 *Ass*, *Carsecote* 1249 *Ass*, *Kirschote* 1285 FA, *Cascot Hill* 1675 Ogilby. 'Cress cottage(s).' KNOWLE (6″) was possibly the home of Alice de *Knouyll* (1330 *SR*). LIMESLAKE must be identical with *Lyoneslake in decenna de Nympton Episcopi* 1394 IpmR. MORNACOTT is *Mornecote* 1286 *Ass*, *Murnacott* 1621 Wills. RADLEY is *Radlegh* 1281 *Ass*, *Radelegh* 1429 Pat. 'Red clearing,' *v.* leah. SHEEPWASH is *Sepwasse* 1238 *Ass* (p), *Sheppe-wasshe* 1281 *Ass* (p), *Shepwash juxta Nymeton* 1303 *Ass*. SIL-COMBE CROSS is *Sylcombe* 1675 *Recov.* WATERHOUSE was probably the home of Gilbert *atte Watere* (1330 *SR*). WEBBERY is *Wibebyr'* 1249 *Ass* (p). '*Wibba*'s burh.' WELLAND is *La Wyldelond(e)* 1249 *Ass*, (*juxta Nymtone*) 1285 FF, *atte Willalond* 1330 *SR* (p). 'Wild (uncultivated) land,' cf. Willand *infra* 553. WHITECHAPEL is *La Chapele* 1242 Fees 759, *Blaunchechapele* 1281 *Ass*, *Alba Capella* 1305 Ipm, *Whitchapell* 1333 Ch, *Chapell al. Whitchapell* 1388 Fine. There was a chapel here attached to the manor of Hayne *supra*. Cf. Whitechapel (Mx).

King's Nympton

KING'S NYMPTON 128 B 2

Nimeton(a) 1086 DB, 1228 Ch, 1242 Fees 761, *Nimmeton* 1236 Cl

Kyngesnemeton 1254 *Ass, Kinges-* 1287 Cl, *Nymeton Kynges* 1281 *Ass, Nymynton Regis* 1316 Ch, *Kyngesnymyngtone* 1341 Exon, *Kingsnimpton* 1649 *Deed, Kings Nement* 1675 Ogilby

'Nymet farm,' *v. supra* 348. It was a royal manor TRE (DB f. 98).

GREAT LIGHTLEIGH is *Letlelegh infra maneriū de Nymeton* 1244 *Ass, Leightele* 1330, *Leystalegh* 1333 *SR* (p). If the earliest form is corrupt, the meaning may be 'light (bright) clearing,' *v.* leah.

SLETCHCOTT is *Sleghecote* 1330 *SR* (p), *Sletchacott* 1668 *FF*. The cottages were perhaps so called from the presence of a smithy with the blacksmith's *sledge* (OE *slecg*) or hammer. *gh* is unvoiced before following *c.*

SMITHA [smiðə] was the home of Roger de *la Forge* (1254 *Ass*), John de *la Smythe* (1311 *Ass*), and John *atter Smythe* (1330 *SR*). 'At the smithy,' cf. Smithaleigh *supra* 255.

WADDINGTON is *Wadeton* 1455 *Deed*. It is there described as land of one Walter *Wade.* Hence, '*Wade*'s farm,' *v.* tun. For the later intrusive *ing*, cf. Woodington and Murchington *infra* 396, 453.

WAMPFORD is *Wanford(e)* 1242 Fees 788, 1244 *Ass* (p), 1311 Exon (p). The first element here is probably OE *wan*, 'dark,' cf. such names as Brightford and Lightford.

SOUTH ASH (6″), CLEAVE, HEAL[1], LAKE (6″), EAST STONE (6″), WOODA[2] and YEOTOWN (6″) were probably the homes of David de *Esse* (1330 *SR*), Walter *atte Clyve* (1333 *SR*), John de *Westhele* and Philip de *Litelehele* (1330 *SR*), John *atte Lake* (1333 *SR*), Walter *atte Stone* (1330 *SR*), Henry de *la Wode* (1254 *Ass*) and Gilbert *atte Ya*, i.e. 'at the water' (1333 *SR*). *v. supra* 17–18 and clif, healh, lacu.

BEERA (6″) is *Beare* 1691 *FF*, *Bearah* 1765 D. *v.* bearu. BROOMHAM is *Bromham* 1581, 1592 *SR. v.* ham(m). COLLACOTT is *Colecote juxta Nymeton Regis* 1289 *Ass. v.* Collacott *supra* 50.

---

[1] EAST and WEST HEAL (6″).
[2] *Woode* 1581 *SR*.

HAM COTTAGES (6") is *Ham* 1675 *Recov. v.* ham(m). HIGHRIDGE
is *Yerugge* 1311 *Ass*, 1330 *SR*, *-igge* 1340 *Ass* (all p), *Iridge* 1581
SR. HUMMACOTT is perhaps identical with *Wemmecote* 1311 *Ass*
(p), *Wemma-* 1333 *SR* (p). The first element is probably the
same as in Wembworthy *supra* 372. HUXFORD is *Hokesford* 1219
Ass, *Huxford* 1289 *Ass* (p). '*Hōc*'s ford' or 'ford by the spur of
land,' *v.* hoc. KINGSTREE is *Kynestrewe* 1289 *Ass*, *Kynys-* 1330
SR (p), *Kenes-* 1443 IpmR, *Kynstruwe* 1356 *Ass*. '*Cyne*'s tree.'
The modern form may have been influenced by the parish name,
cf. Kingscombe in Linkinhorne (Co), *Kynescumbe* 1284, *Kynnes-
cume* 1317 *Ass*. LENTON is *Leynton* 1330, *Lyniton* 1333 *SR* (p).
OAKWELL is *Akewell* 1249 *Ass* (p), *Okwille* 1330 *SR* (p), 1406
IpmR. TONGUE LAKE (6") is *Tonglake* 1765 D. *v.* lacu. VENN FM
(6") is *Fenn* 1691 *Recov. v.* fenn. YELMACOTT is *Yealmacott* 1675
Recov.

Oakford

OAKFORD 128 A/B 9

Alforda (sic) 1086 DB
Acford(e) 1166 RBE (p), 1167 P (p), 1238 *Ass*, 1260 Exon,
    Hak- 1249 *Ass*
Okeford 1249 *Ass*, *Hock(e)-* 1249, 1253 Ipm, *Ocford* 1282 Ipm,
    Hokefford 1377 BM
Wocford 1559 Wardens

Self-explanatory.

BICKHAM BARTON is *Bichecoma* 1086 DB, *Bicumbe* 1228 FF, *Bike-
cumbe* 1238 *Ass* (p), *Bykecumb'* 1242 Fees 789, *Bykecombe juxta
Hocford* 1296 *Ass*. '*Bi(c)ca*'s combe,' *v.* Abbots Bickington
supra 124.

GRACESFORD (6")

Grauestine(s)ford 1238, 1244 *Ass*
Grastinisford 1311 *Ass*, *-tene(s)-* 1321 Misc
Grastingesford, *Grastyngford* 1333 *Ass*

The first element here is almost certainly a ME surname.
Were it not for the first form one might suggest some Anglo-
Norman settler from Grestain (Eure).

MILDON is *Mildedona* 1086 DB, *Middelton* 1242 Fees 759, -*don(e)* 1242 Fees 792, 1249 *Ass*, 1279 Ipm. 'Middle hill,' *v.* dun.

PINKWORTHY is *Pynkeworthy* 1281 *Ass* (p), 1501–4 ECP 4, 55, *Pinckery al. Pinckworthy* 1699 DKR 41, 167. '*Pinca*'s farm,' *v.* worþig. There was a Sewine *Pinca* in Devon c. 1100 (Earle 262).

SPURWAY BARTON

> *Espreuweia, Sprewea* 1086 DB, *Spreweye* 1242 Fees 793, 1244
> *Ass* (p), (*West-*) 1276 Ipm, *Spreyweye* 1303 FA
> *Estspirweye* 1345 *Ass*, *Estspyrwey(e)* 1370, 1427 *Ass*
> *Spryweye* 1356 Ipm, *Spurwey* 1489 Ipm

'Track or path through brushwood,' *v.* weg and cf. Sprytown *supra* 208.

EAST and WEST TAPPS is *Ausa* 1086 DB (Exon), *Ause* (Exch), *Westapse* 1242 Fees 784, *Apse* 1285 FA, *Westereapse* 1330 *SR* (p), *West Apes* 1423 IpmR. 'At the aspen,' *v.* æspe (æps). For the *t*, cf. Tuckenhay *supra* 315, or the *t* may be due to misdivision of *Eastapse, Westapse*.

VALERIDGE (6″) is *Falurigg'* 1249 *Ass*, *Falwarigge* 1285 FA, *Falwe-* 1356, 1359 *Ass*. Probably 'fallow ridge,' but the first element might be OE fealu, 'yellow, dun, dusky.'

WOODBURN is *Odeborna* 1086 DB, *Wodeburne* 1228 FF, 1242 Fees 787, *Upwodeborn* 1330 *SR* (p). 'Wood stream,' *v.* burna.

NETHERCOTT, PITT COTTAGE (6″) and WEST LAKE (6″) were probably the homes of Roger de *Nitheracote* (1333 *SR*), Simon *atte Pytte* (1356 *Ass*) and William *Bywestelake*, i.e. 'west of the streamlet' (1330 *SR*). *v.* cot(e), pytt, lacu.

BOWDENS is to be associated with the family of William *Bowdon* (1524 *SR*). HAMSLADE is so spelt 1738 *Recov. v.* slæd. HARTON (6″) is *Horton* 1249 *Ass* (p). Probably 'dirty farm,' *v.* horh, tun. HIGHLEIGH is *Heghelegh juxta Ocforde* 1325 *Ass*. 'High clearing,' *v.* heah, leah. LOOSEMOOR is *Losemore* 1249 *Ass* (p). 'Pig-stye moor,' *v.* hlose, mor. STUCKERIDGE is *Stykerugg'* 1333 *SR* (p). Cf. the same name *supra* 380. SWINEHAM is *Swindon* 1333 *SR* (p). Probably 'swine hill,' *v.* dun. UPCOTT is *Uppecote* 1249 *Ass*.

Westcott is *Westcote* 1626 *Recov.* Western is *Wasthorne* 1333 *SR* (p). 'Thornbush in the mud' (OE *wāse*). There is marshy land here.

Puddington

Puddington 128 E 7

Potitona 1086 DB, *Potinton* 1219 FF (p), 1301 BM, *Potington* 1238 *Ass*, *-tune* t. Ed 1 Ipm, *-ton* 1309 Ipm, 1316 FA, 1334 *SR*, (*al. Podyngton*) 1310 Ipm, *Potyngdone* 1291 Tax, *Pottyngton* 1303 FA

Little Putinton 1238 FF, *Putiton* 1242 Fees 793, *Putingthon'* 1242 Fees 758, *Puttyntone* 1331 Exon

Poddyngton 1281 *Ass*, *Podyngtone* 1343 Exon, *Peudyngdon* 1346, *Peutyngdon* 1428 FA

'*Putta*'s farm,' *v.* ingtun. Cf. Puddington (Ch), DB *Potitone*.

Ash was the home of John de *Aysshe* (1330 *SR*). Bamson is *Bathemyston* 1330 *SR* (p), *Batmysdon* 1333 *SR* (p), *Bampisdon in Podynton* 1460–66 ECP 1, 306. Probably '*Beaduhelm*'s farm,' *v.* tun. Coombe is *Combe* 1379 Cl. Raddiford (6") is *Radeford(e)* 1323 *Ass* (p), 1333 *SR* (p). 'Red ford.' Scotsham is *Stodesham* 1330 *SR* (p), *Scotsham* 1765 D. Smynacott is *Smythenacote* 1333 *SR* (p). *v.* Smithacott *supra* 93. Yowlestone is *Aldeston* 1279 *Ass*, *Yolleston* 1301 Ch, 1379 Cl. Probably 'old stone,' cf. Youlston *supra* 68.

Rackenford

Rackenford 128 B/C 7

Racheneforda, Litel Racheneforda 1086 DB

Racarneford(e) 1147–61 Buckland, *Rak-* 1387 Exon, *Rakerneford* 1238 FF, t. Hy 3 BM, 1285 FA, 1291 Tax, *Racrenneford* 1350 Pat

Racheneford 1204 Cur, *-kene-* 1242 Fees 784, 1267 Exon, 1303 FA, *-kenne-* 1292 Ipm, *-kenes-* 1313 Exon, *Parva Rakeneford'* 1242 Fees 761, *Rageneford* 1297 Pat

Rakereford' 1246 Cl

Rattenford, Rackingford 1628 Barum 1, 60, 62

Blomé (120) suggests that this difficult name is from OE *racuærna-ford*, 'ford of (or by) the houses by the *racu* or path.'

BACKSTONE is *Bachestane* 1086 DB, *Baggestane* 1242 Fees 759, 787, *-ston* 1285 FA, 1380 *FF*, *Bagaston* 1333 *SR* (p). Probably '*Bacga*'s stone.'

BULWORTHY is *Bolehorda* 1086 DB, *Bullewrthi* 1238 *Ass* (p), *Bulewrthy* 1238 *Ass*, *Boleworth'* 1242 Fees 781, *-thi* 1285 FA, *-thy* 1388 IpmR. 'Bull farm' or '*Bula*'s farm,' *v.* worþig, and cf. the same name *supra* 112.

CANWORTHY (6″) is *Canewurthy* 1249 *Ass* (p), *Canneworth(y)* 1327 Banco (p), 1493 Ipm, *Cannaworthi* 1330 *SR* (p), *Kanworthi* 1378 IpmR, *Cannery* 1765 D. '*Canna*'s farm,' *v.* worþig. Cf. Cannings (PN in *-ing* 69) and William *Canna* (1333 *SR*).

MOGWORTHY is *Moggeford* 1238 *Ass* (p), 1330, 1333 *SR* (p), *Muggeworth* 1244 *Ass* (p), *Mokeworth* 1424 IpmR. '*Mogga*'s ford' or 'worþig.' This pers. name is not on record, but would be related to *Mocca*, which is well evidenced. See further *s.n.* Lugworthy *supra* 180. For interchange of *ford* and *worthy*, *v.* Introd. xxxv.

SYDEHAM is *Sideham* 1086 DB *et freq* to 1267 Exon (p) with variant spelling *Syde-*. 'Broad hamm,' cf. Sydenham *supra* 200.

TIDDERSON is *Tidderedun'* 1242 Fees 758 (p), *Tidarteston* 1244 *Ass* (p), *Tyterasdon* 1270 *Ass* (p), *Tyderesdon* 1275 RH (p), *-rys-* 1412 *Ass*. '*Tidheard*'s hill,' *v.* dun.

WORTHY FM is *Ordia* 1086 DB, *Wrthi* 1242 Fees 783, *Worth* 1284, 1346 FA, *Worthi* 1330 *SR* (p). *v.* worþig.

MIDDLECOTT (6″) and THORN[1] were the homes of Thomas de *Middelcote* and John de *Thorne* (1333 *SR*). *v.* cot(e).

BLINDWELL (6″) is *Blindwell al. Benwell* 1731 *Recov*. 'Hidden spring,' cf. Blindwell *supra* 354. CRUWYSHAYE is *Crofteshaye* 1330 *SR* (p). *v.* croft, (ge)hæg. The modern form may have been influenced by the not far distant Cruwys Morchard *supra* 380. LANELAND (6″) is *Atterlane juxta West Rakerneford* (nom. loc.) 1310 *Ass*. MEADOWN is so spelt 1765 D. NUTCOTT is *Neatecote* 1310 *Ass* (p), *Neatecote* 1330, 1333 *SR* (p). The first element is probably OE *nēat*, 'cattle,' the modern form being corrupt.

---

[1] *Thorne* 1659 *Recov*.

OAKSBERRY PLANTATION (6″) is *Okespry Moore* 1627 *Deed.*
'Brushwood land dotted with oak trees,' *v.* Sprytown *supra* 208.

Romansleigh

ROMANSLEIGH (rʌmzli) 128 B 3

Liega 1086 DB
Reymundesle 1228 FF
Romundeylegh' 1242 Fees 781, *Romundeslegh(e)* 1267 *Ass et
freq* to 1406 IpmR with variant spellings -*mond*- and -*dis*-,
Romenedesleghe 1281 Exon, *Romaundesleghe* 1291 Tax, *Rode-
mondesleghe* 1326 Exon, *Romyndyslegh* 1346 FA
Rumonsleigh vulgo Rumsleigh 1765 D

v. leah. The church is dedicated to St *Rumon*, a Celtic saint,
cf. Rumonsleigh in Tavistock *supra* 220.

ODAM BARTON is *Waudam* 1242 Fees 759, *Wodham* 1242 Fees
781, 1306 *Ass* (p), 1333 *SR* (p), 1346 FA, *Wodeham* 1303 FA.
'Woad ham(m).' For loss of initial *w*, *v.* Introd. xxxv. The first
form is probably an error.

BEERA, LANGLEY and THORNDON COTTAGES (6″) were probably
the homes of Walter *atte Beare* (1333 *SR*), Richard de *Langelegh*
(1330 *SR*) and Agnes fil. Richard Godman de *Thorndon* (1329
Ass). *v.* bearu, leah, dun.

CATSHEYS LINHAYS (6″) is *Cattishayes* 1549 Pat. *v.* Hayne *supra*
129 and Linhayes *infra* 592. HORRIDGE is *Holrugg'* 1281 *Ass* (p),
Horigg' 1329 *Ass* (p), *Horugg'* 1330 *SR* (p). *v.* holh, hrycg. The
farm is by a hollow in the well-marked ridge here. KITCOTT
BARTON is *Kutecote* 1244 *Ass* (p), *Kyttecote* 1298 *Ass*, 1521
Recov, *Kyte*- 1339 *Ass* (p). 'Kite cot(e)' or '*Cȳta*'s cot(e).'
LITTLE SILVER is so spelt 1765 D. *v. supra* 358. ROADCLOSE
COPSE (6″), cf. *Redcloseleigh* 1549 Pat. ROWLEY is *Rowalegh* 1333
SR (p), *Rouwa*- 1340 *Ass* (p), *Roweleghe juxta Chalvelegh* 1431
FF, *Estrawleigh* 1549 Pat. 'Rough clearing,' *v.* ruh, leah.

Rose Ash

ROSE ASH 128 A 5

Aissa 1086 DB, *Esse* 1198 FF, 1242 Fees 759
Assherow(es) 1281 *Ass*, 1386 Cl, *Esse Ra(u)f(e)* 1319 Exon (p),
1387 Exon, 1492 Ipm, *Aysshraf* 1455 *FF*

Rowesassche 1400 Exon, *Rawysaysshe* 1438 Exon, *Raffisaisshe* 1502 ECP 4, 99, *Roseashe* 1577 Saxton

'The ash.' The family of *Radulphus*, *Ralph*, *Raf*, held the manor in 1198 (FF). '*Rose*' is a late corruption of '*Rafe's*, *Raves*, *Rawes*.' Cf. Rousdon and Rosehayne *infra* 647, 653.

CATKILL is *Westkatdehill* 1333 *SR* (p), *West Cattkill* 1725 *FF*. The material is scanty but may point to an OE *Cadecan hyll*, '*Cadeca's* hill.' Cf. Kigbeare *supra* 203.

DITCHETT is *Dichyet* 1333 *SR* (p), *Ditchet* 1789 *Recov*. The name is probably identical with Ditcheat (So), *Dichesgate*, -*yate* 842 BCS 468, *Dicesget* 1086 DB, *Dichesieta* 12th HMC x App. 3, 14, t. Hy 2 Wells i, 26. The latter is clearly a compound of OE *dic* and *geat* with reference to the Roman road from Ilchester to Bath; the significance in this case is unknown. It should be noted that there was another *dicesget* not far from this one, which is mentioned in the great Crediton Charter (BCS 1331).

YARD is *Hierda* 1086 DB, *Yerde* 1242 Fees 784, *Hyurde* 1275 RH (p), *la Yurde*, *la Yerde* 1292 Ipm, *Yurdecola juxta Nymeton Epī* 1345 *Ass*. *v*. Yard *supra* 48. The identity of *Cola* is unknown.

BEARA, HEATH (6″), MAIRE, NETHERCOTT, VENHAY DOWN, WESTACOTT and WOOD COTTAGE (6″) were probably the homes of Richard de *la Beare* (1333 *SR*), Robert *atte Hethez* (1333 *SR*), Robert *atte Mere* (ib.), Robert de *Nitheracote* (1333 *SR*), Gilbert de *Westfenheie*, i.e. 'marsh enclosure' (ib.), William de *Westacote* (ib.) and Radulphus *atte Wode* (ib.). *v*. bearu, mor, cot(e), fenn, (ge)hæg. *Mere* is probably from OE mere as the place is not on the parish boundary.

GREAT ASH MOOR is *Aishmore* 1699 *Recov*. BICKWILL (6″) is *Bikewill* 1407 IpmR. BIGBROOK (6″) is *Bickebroc* 1230 P (p), *Bykebrok* 1279 *Ass*, 1394 *FF*. '*Bic(c)a's* spring and brook,' *v*. wielle, broc. BURCOMBE is *Biricomb* 1330 *SR* (p), *Bircombe* 1384 *FF*. *v*. burh, cumb. CHERRIDGE (6″) is *Cheridge* 1576 *Deed*. DENSDON (6″) is *Denewaldesdon* 1330 *SR* (p). '*Deneweald's* hill,' *v*. dun. Cf. Densham *infra* 400. FOXCROFT (6″) is so spelt 1412 IpmR. *v*. croft. HONEY CLIFF (6″) is *Honycliffe* 1699 *Recov*. *v*. Honeychurch *supra* 165. HUNT'S COPSE (6″) is to be associated

with the family of William *Honte* (1330 *SR*). MUNSON is
Monyeston(e) 1330 *SR* (p), 1441 IpmR. The forms are insufficient
for any interpretation to be suggested. NETTLEFORD (6″) is
Notelewurthe, Netlewurth 1281 *Ass* (p), *Netelworthi* 1333 *SR* (p),
Neteleworth 1340 *SR*. 'Nettle worþ(ig).' NUTCOMBE is *Nuttecumb*
1238 FF, *Nottecombe* 1340 Pat. 'Nut combe.' OVERCOTT is so
spelt 1607 *FF*. Cf. Nethercott *supra* 392. RODSWORTHY is
Rodesworthi 1330 *SR* (p). *v.* worþig. SEVERY (6″) is so spelt
in 1675 *Recov*. SOUTH MEADOW (6″) is *Southmeade Downe*
1615 *Deed*. SWINCOMBE (6″) is *Swyncombe* 1540 *Deed*. 'Swine
valley,' *v.* cumb. WHIPPENSCOTT is *Whypmanscott* 1540 *Deed*,
Whipamscott, Whippingcott 1622 *FF*, the first element being
possibly a ME pers. name.

Stoodleigh

STOODLEIGH 128 B 9

> *Estodleia, Estolleia* 1086 DB (Exon), *Stodlei, Stollei* (Exch)
> *Stodleg(he)* 1205 FF *et passim* to 1373 Exon, *Est-, Weststod-*
> *legh* 1242 Fees 760, *Est Stodelegh* 1326 Ipm, *Stowdeleighe*
> 1550 Pat
> *Stouleghe* 1264 Exon
> *Studley* 1675 Ogilby

'Stud clearing,' *v.* stod, leah.

BLATCHWORTHY is *Blagewrthi* 1238 *Ass* (p), *Blackesworth'* 1242
Fees 760, *Blakeworth* 1242 Fees 787, *Blacchesworth(y)* 1346 FA,
1398 IpmR, *Blakchesworthy* 1428 FA. Probably '*Blæcci*'s
worþig,' cf. Blachford *supra* 269.

RIFTON is *Restona* 1086 DB, *Reft(h)on* 1198 FF, 1242 Fees 760,
Reveton(e) 1261 Exon (p), 1299 Ipm. This is probably from an
OE *(ge)rēfantūn*, 'reeve's farm,' the place being perhaps so called
because it was the residence of a reeve. Cf. Riverton *supra* 351.

THROWCOMBE is *Throucumb'* 1242 Fees 760, 774. This, as
suggested by Blomé (122), is probably a compound of OE
cumb and þruh. The latter has various senses in OE, all going
back to the idea of something hollowed out, and the term is also
found in the p.n. Througham (Gl), OE þruhham (BCS 180).
Througham lies on the edge of a well-marked hollow; in Throwcombe the reference is doubtless to the shape of the combe.

WARBRIGHTSLEIGH BARTON [warpsle, wasple]

> *Wirlbesliga* 1086 DB (Exon), *Wasberlege* (Exch)
> *Warbritteslegh'* 1237 Fees 612, *War(e)brighte(s)legh* 1242 Fees
> 787, 1276 Ipm, *Werbritteslegh* 1244 *Ass*
> *Warbesleg* 1244 *Ass*, *Warpeslay* 1577 Saxton
> *Warburghislegh* 1303 FA

'*Wǣrbeorht*'s clearing,' *v.* leah, and cf. Wapsworthy *supra* 232.

WEST WHITNOLE is *Witechenolla* 1086 DB (Exon), *Withechenolle* (Exch), *Whytecnolle* 1242 Fees 760, 787, *Wyteknoll* 1303 FA. 'White round hill,' *v.* cnoll.

ASH, DIPFORD and DOWN were probably the homes of John de *Esse*, Robert *Dupaford*, i.e. '(at the) deep ford,' and Richard *atte Doune* (1333 *SR*), *v.* dun.

BELLBROOK (6″) is *Bulbrooke* 1660 *Recov*. The earlier form is no doubt the correct one. BROADMEAD is *Brademed(e)* 1238, 1244 *Ass*. *v.* brad, mæd. CARSCOMBE is probably identical with *Cobbeliscomb* 1330, 1333 *SR* (p), *Cobbescombe* 1650 *Recov*. The first element may be the name of a medieval owner. COLEFORD is *Colford* 1330 *SR* (p). *v.* Collacott *supra* 50. STEART was the home of John fil. fabri *atte Sturte* 1333 *SR* (p). *v.* steort. There is a long narrow ridge of land here. STONELAND is so spelt 1702 *Recov* and was probably the home of Thomas *atte Stone* (1330 *SR*). WORMSWORTHY COTTAGE (6″) is *Wolmysworthi* 1333 *SR* (p). *v.* worþig. The first element is clearly a pers. name, probably either *Wulfhelm* or *Wulfmǣr*. If the latter, the usual abbreviation comma has been omitted before the *y*.

Templeton

TEMPLETON 128 D 8

> *Temple* 1238 *Ass*, 1577 Saxton
> *Templeton by Tiverton* 1335 Buckland, *Templeton* 1439 Exon

The parish is a comparatively late one centring round the Knights Templars' manor of Coombe (*infra* 395).

COLSTON BARTON is *Kolteston'* 1242 Fees 760, *Colteston* 1303 FA. '*Colt*'s farm,' *v.* tun and cf. Coulsworthy *supra* 37.

NORTH and SOUTH COOMBE

Coma 1086 DB, *Cumbe* 1238 *Ass*
Cumb Munceus 1242 Fees 773, *Combe Mounceaux* 1326 Ipm
Cumbe Templar 1281 *Ass*, *Templecombe* 1356 *Ass*, 1399 IpmR

v. cumb. William de *Moncellis* held the manor in 1242, but in 1276 (Ipm) one fee was held by the master of the Knights of the Temple.

CLEAVE[1], CROSSMOOR COTTAGE and TOWN FM (all 6″) were probably the homes of Roger Collyng *atte Clyve*, Roger *atte Crosse* and Robert *atte Toune* (1333 *SR*). *v.* clif, tun. Town Fm is in the village itself.

PARTRIDGE (6″) is *Parkerigg* 1256 FF, *-rygg'* 1270 *Ass*, *-rugg'* 1330 *SR* (p). *v.* pearroc, hrycg. STARRATON is *Staryadon* 1270 *Ass*. Possibly from OE *stæra-dūn*, 'starlings' hill.'

Thelbridge

THELBRIDGE 128 D 5

Talebrua 1086 DB (Exon), *-brige* (Exch), *Tallebrig* 1238 *Ass* (p)
Thelebrig 1242 Fees 758 *et freq* to 1328 Exon with variant spellings *-brug(ge)*, *-brigge*, *T(h)ellebrigge* 1280 Exon, 1297 Pat, *Thelbrigge* 1291 Tax
Delbridge 1577 Saxton

'Plank bridge,' *v.* þelbrycg. This must have been over the little stream about half a mile north of the church.

CHAPNER is *Chatemere* 1242 Fees 758, 773, 1303 FA, 1359 AD vi, *Chadmore* 1428 FA. '*Ceat(t)a*'s mere,' *v.* mere. The ground in the neighbourhood is marshy. For the development cf. Chapmore End (Herts), *Chattemere* 1294, 1296 *SR* (p).

CHARNAFORD FM is probably identical with *Churne* 1397 Pat, *Churne in the parish of Witherigge* 1489 Ipm, the place being just by the parish boundary. This is probably the common streamname *Churn* (*v.* Ekwall RN 78).

CURRITON is *Corre-*, *Corraton* 1330, 1333 *SR* (p). As this place is on the Dalch, a river with a Celtic name, it cannot be derived,

---

[1] *Cleyve* 1566 *Deed.*

as suggested by Blomé (124), from the old river-name *Cury*. It looks as if it might be connected with ME *curre*, 'dog,' perhaps used as a nickname. Cf. Curham *infra* 549 and Alexander *Corra* (1330 *SR*) (Devon).

HENCEFORD is *He(n)gsteford* 1281 *Ass* (p), 1285 FA, *Northengesteford* 1311 *Ass*, *Southheyngsteford juxta Wytherigge* 1322 *Ass*. 'Stallion ford,' *v.* hengest.

LEWDON (6″) is *Luedon* 1330, *Luwedon* 1333 *SR* (p). The first element is probably OE *hlēow*, 'shelter, protection,' or the corresponding adjective *hlēow* postulated in the NED as the source of the adjective *lew*, 'warm, sunny, sheltered.' Cf. also Leeford *supra* 59, and Lewdon *infra* 428. The farm lies on the slope of a down facing south.

MIDDLEWICK BARTON is *Wica* 1086 DB, *Middlewick* 1765 D. *v.* wic.

STOURTON BARTON is *Stordet(h)on* 1242 Fees 774 *et freq* to 1428 FA, *Strodeton* 1303 FA, *Sturdeston, Strotheton* 1374 IpmR, *Stourton al. Stourditon* 1687 *Recov.* This may be from OE *strōdatūn*, 'farm of the marshy places,' with common metathesis of *r*. So also Wallenberg in StudNP 2, 96.

STRETCH DOWN is *Stretthe* 1285, *Strath* 1346, *Strecche* 1428 FA, *Streccheton* 1330 *SR* (p), *Strecheston* 1359 AD vi, and is identical with *Strecchederta* 1359 AD vi. There is a long stretch of land here above the Dart river. See further Strashleigh *supra* 273.

WOODINGTON is *Hodeton* 1285 Ipm, *Odeton cum Hegsteford* 1285, *Oddeton* 1303 FA, *Odeton juxta Wytherygge* 1339 *Ass*. Probably 'Odda's farm,' *v.* tun, the later *w* being inorganic. For *ing*, cf. Waddington *supra* 386.

BATSON (6″) is *Batesdone* 1359 AD vi. '*Bætti's* hill,' *v.* dun and cf. Battishill *supra* 177. BILLHOLE is *Billihole* 1249 *Ass* (p), *Bille-* 1330 *SR* (p). '*Billa's* hollow,' *v.* holh. BUDDLESWICK is *Botheleswyk* 1317 *Ass*, *Buddlesweeke* 1730 *FF*. *v.* wic. Probably "the wic attached to (a lost) Budleigh." For the first element, *v. s.n.* Budleigh *infra* 484. HELE BARTON is *Heale Greene*, *Heale Downe* 1687 *Recov.* *v.* healh. MARCHWEEKE is *Marchwyke*

t. Eliz ChancP. *v.* wic. The first element may be OE mearc, 'boundary, border,' the place lying by the parish boundary. SHILLITON (6″) is *Shilvedon* 1359 AD vi. 'Shelving hill,' *v.* scylf, dun. HIGHER SOMERWELL is *Somerwill(e)* 1330, 1333 *SR* (p), and probably takes its name from a never-dry spring. *v.* wielle. UPCOTT is *Uppecote* 1285 FA, 1330 *SR* (p). WAY, EAST and WEST, is *Weie* 1359 AD vi and was probably the home of Walter *atte Weye* (1333 *SR*). The farms are on a main road. WESTCOTT is *West(e)cote* 1285, 1346 FA. WOODFORD is *Wodeford* 1333 *SR* (p). WOODHOUSE was probably the home of Walter *atte Wode* (1333 *SR*) and of Thomas *Wodhouse* (1428 FA).

Washford Pyne

WASHFORD PYNE 128 D/E 6

> *Wesforda, Wesfort, Wafforda* 1086 DB (Exon), *Wasforde* (Exch)
> *Wafford* 1219 FF, 1284 FA
> *Was(se)ford(e)* 1242 Fees 758, 778, 1280 Exon, *Wassheford* 1292 *Ass*, *Whasford* 1299 Ipm, *Wahsford* 1308–19 Exon
> *Wayshford, Parva Waysheford* 1316 FA, 1340 *SR*, *Waysford* 1373 Cl, *Wayssheford* 1428 FA

All the forms from DB onwards suggest that this is a compound of (ge)wæsc and ford. Herbert de *Pinu* held the manor in 1219 (FF).

BLACK DOG (hamlet) is so called from a public house here of that name. PYNE FM is *Pyne* 1650 *Recov*, taking its name from the above-mentioned family. WONHAM is *Mervell Wonham* 1569 *Deed*.

Witheridge

WITHERIDGE 128 D 6

> *Wiriga* 1086 DB, *Wyrig'* 1242 Fees 787
> *Wetherigge* 1249 *Ass*, -*rudge* 1535 VE
> *Wytherigge* 1256, 1262 FF *et passim* with variant spelling -*rugge*

It is probably unnecessary to go beyond OE *weðra-hrycg*, 'ridge of the wethers,' for this name, with the same fluctuation between forms with *e* and *i* as in Withersfield (PN Sf 30) and Weathersfield (Ess). Cf. *Wedreriga* (Exch *Wederige*), an unidentified DB manor in Plympton Hundred.

ADWORTHY is *Odeordi* 1086 DB, *Oddeworth'* 1242 Fees 761, *Oddeworthy* 1539 *Deed*, *Adworthie* 1616 *FF*. '*Odda*'s farm,' *v.* worþig. For *o* > *a* cf. Introd. xxxiv.

BETHAM is *la Bidene* 1238 *Ass*, *Bydene* 1281 *Ass*, *atte Bydena* 1333 *SR* (all p), *Betham* 1650 *FF*, *Bythen* 1902 Kelly. Identical with Bidna in Northam *supra* 102. The place is situated in a long narrow combe opening into the Dart valley.

BRADFORD BARTON is *Bradeford(a)* 1086 DB, 1242 Fees 792, *Bradeford Tracy juxta Wytherigge* 1314 *Ass*. 'Wide ford,' *v.* brad. William de *Tracy* held the manor in 1242.

DART RAFFE is *Derta* 1086 DB, *Derth'* 1242 Fees 774, 787, *Derte Rauf* 1329 *Ass*, *Dertre* 1359 AD vi and takes its name from the stream here, *supra* 5. Ralph de *Derth'* held the manor in 1242.

DRAYFORD is *Draheforda* 1086 DB, *Draiford* 1238 *Ass* (p), *FF*, *Dray-* 1242 Fees 758, 1285 FA, 1440 Exon. This is clearly a compound of OE **dræg** and ford. The sense of **dræg** is as always obscure. In this particular case it might be OE *drǣge*, 'drag-net,' from the use of such near the ford; or possibly we may have that word already used in the sense 'dray,' a use hitherto not recorded before 1369. Hence, perhaps, 'ford over which a *dray* can pass.'

FREEMANCOTT (lost) is *Fremannecoth'* 1242 Fees 758, *Freman(e)-cote* 1303, 1346, 1428 FA, 'cot(e) of the freemen.'

HEIFFERS is *Heweferse* 1238 *Ass* (p), *Heaufors* 1333 *SR* (p). The second element is clearly **fyrs**, 'furse.' Professor Ekwall suggests that the first may be OE *hīewe*, and the whole name mean 'place where furze was cut.'

EAST and WEST PILLIVEN (6″) is *Pilefen(ne)* 1238 *Ass* (p), 1269 FF (p), *Pillefenne* 1242 Fees 758 (p), 1408 IpmR, *Pyle-* 1270 *Ass* (p). This is probably from OE *Pīlan-fen,* '*Pīla*'s marshy land,' *v.* fenn, with the same pers. name as in Pilmoor (PN NRY 23). See, however, Pilemoor *infra* 420.

QUEEN DART is *Dertera* 1086 DB (Exon), *Dertre* (Exch), *Queen Dert* t. Jas 1 ECP, *Queene Darte* 1612 *FF*. It is not known what queen is referred to here.

WHEADOWN is *Wheydoune juxta Estwolryngton* 1294 *Ass*, *Weydon* 1295 *Ass*, 1333 *SR* (p). The first element may, as suggested by Professor Förster, be the OE *hwǣg*, 'whey,' but the meaning of such a compound is obscure.

DOWN, FORD DOWN, FOXDON, HOLE, NEWLAND[1] (6″), NORTH COMBE and PILEY LANE (6″) were probably the homes of Henry de *Dune* (1242 Fees 774), William *atte Forde* (1333 *SR*), William de *Voxdon* (1330 *SR*), Roger *atte Hole* (ib.), John de *Nywalond* (1333 *SR*), William de *Northacomb* (1333 *SR*) and John *atte Pile* (1330 *SR*). *v.* dun, holh and Pilemoor *infra* 420. CANNINGTON (6″) is *Canyngton* 1330 *SR* (p). 'Can(n)a's farm,' *v.* ingtun. Cf. Canworthy *supra* 390, only a few miles distant and perhaps named after the same man. ELWORTHY is *Illeworthi* 1330, *Ylla-* 1333 *SR* (p). 'Farm of *Ylla*' or '*Illa*,' *v.* worþig. GRENDON is *Grenedon* 1285 FA, *Grene-*, *Grenaduna* 1359 AD vi. 'Green down.' HORESTONE was probably the home of Gervase *atte Horeston*' 1330 *SR*. 'Boundary stone,' *v.* har, stan. The place lies by the parish boundary. NEWHOUSE is so spelt 1789 *Recov*. PULLEN'S ROW (6″) is to be associated with the family of Henry *Poulyn* (1333 *SR*). ROSE MOOR is *Rosemoore* 1652 *FF*. Cf. Rosedown *supra* 75. ROWDEN (6″) is *Rowedon* 1285 FA, *Rouwe-* 1359 AD vi, 1374 IpmR. 'Rough hill,' *v.* ruh, dun. STOCKHAM (6″) is *Stodcumbe* 1281 *Ass*. 'Stud valley,' *v.* stod, cumb. UPCOTT SQUIRE (6″) is *Uppecote* 1316 *Ass*, *Lyteluppecote* 1387 BM. WEST YEO is *Westeye juxta Wytherigge* 1283 *Ass*, *West(a)ya* 1285 FA, 1287 *Ass*, *West Yow* 1529–32 ECP 6, 16. 'West of the water,' *v.* Yeo *supra* 17–18. It lies west of Witheridge village across the river Dart.

Woolfardisworthy

WOOLFARDISWORTHY [wulzəri] 128 E/F 6

Olfaldeshodes 1086 DB (Exon), *Ulfaldeshodes* (Exch)
Wolfaresworth' 1242 Fees 758, 787, *Wlvereswurth* 1274 *FF*,
    Wolfres-, *Wolveresworthy* 1281 *Ass*

---

[1] *Westnewland* t. Eliz ChancP.

Wulfordeswurth 1244 *Ass et freq* to 1378 IpmR with variant
spellings *-dis-*, *-worthe*, *-worthy*, *Wolferdesworth(y)* 1316 FA
Wollesworthye 1577 Saxton
Woolfardisworthy oth. *Woolsworthy* 1825 *Recov*

'*Wulfheard*'s farm,' *v.* worþig and cf. the same name *supra* 80.

BRINDIFIELD is *Brendelefenne* 1330, *-la-* 1333 *SR* (p), *Brendelfen*
1429 *Deed*. It looks as if we have here an early example of the
adj. *brindle*, meaning 'striped.' That is thought to be connected
with *brinded*, earlier *brended*, 'burned.' *v.* fenn.

DENSHAM is *Dimewoldesham* (sic), *Donevoldehamme* 1086 DB,
Denewoldesham 1219 FF, 1242 Fees 760, 1330 *SR* (p). '*Dene-
weald*'s ham(m),' cf. Densdon *supra* 392 and *on denewaldes stan*
BCS 451, a Devon charter.

EMLETT

  Emhylte 1249 FF (p), *Northemhilt* 1296 *FF*, *Emylt(e)* 1340 *SR*,
    1356 AD iv, *Emilt* 1347 *FF*
  Emmehult 1249 *Ass* (p), *Embelt* 1263 Ipm

The second element in this name is probably OE *hylte*,
'wooded place,' a derivative of holt, postulated for certain names
in PN Sx xlv. One might take the first element to be OE *efn*,
'level, smooth,' but the topography is not favourable. Emlett
Hill is a fairly steep hill with South Emlett at its eastern end,
while East and West Emlett are on other hills.

HUDGERY is *Hedgeworthy* 1827 G and was probably the home of
Richard de *Herdisworthi* (1333 *SR*). It may be identical in etymology with Hardisworthy *supra* 78.

MINCHENDOWN is *Mynchenaton* 1333 *SR* (p), *Myncheton* 1423
FF, *-don* 1631 *FF*. 'Nuns' farm,' *v.* myncen, tun. It belonged
to the nuns of Polsloe Priory, representing their land in the parish
called *Munecheneland*' in 1242 (Fees 760).

EDDICOMBE (6") is *Yedcomb* 1503 Ipm. Cf. Edworthy *supra* 364,
about eight miles distant. TREE was probably the home of Adam
atte Trewe (1330 *SR*). *v.* treow.

East Worlington

EAST and WEST WORLINGTON[1] 128 D 5

Ulurintona, Olurintona, Oluridintona 1086 DB (Exon), *Ulurintone, Uluredintune* (Exch)
Wolvringt(h)on 1242 Fees 758, 774, *Wulrynton* 1249 FF, *Wulfrintone, Est Wlfrintone, West Wlfrintone* 1261 Exon, *Estwl(u)ryngtone* 1284 Exon, *Est-, Westwolryngtone* 1291 Tax, *Westwluringtone* 1286 Exon, *Estwulryngton* 1327 Banco
Este Worlington 1581 Deed

'*Wulfrēd*'s farm,' *v.* ingtun. Cf. Werrington *supra* 171, and for the modern form cf. Arlington *supra* 56.

BLAGROVE is *Blacagrava* 1086 DB, *Blakegrave* 1242 Fees 758, 787, *Blakgrove juxta Wytherigge* 1370 *Ass.* 'Dark grove,' *v.* blæc, grafa.

LUTWORTHY is *Loteworthy* 1281 *Ass* (p) and may perhaps contain a pers. name **Lutta*, the weak form of *Lutt*, discussed *supra* 75. Cf. also Lotley (So), *Lutelegh* 1327 *SR* (p), *Lutecombe* 1384 IpmR (So), Robert *Luta* 1333 *SR* (D), and Richard *Lotya* 1330 *SR* (D).

PEDLEY BARTON

Piedelega 1086 DB, *Pedeleiga* 1093 France
Piddelegh' 1242 Fees 758, 787, *Pydde-* 1330 *SR* (p), 1394 *Ass*
Peddelegh 1285 FA, 1377 Cl, *Pedlegh* 1391 IpmR

'*Pidda*'s clearing,' *v.* leah. For such a pers. name, cf. Pidborough (PN Sx 13).

RUSTON is *Rinestanedona* 1086 DB, *Ringstanesdune* 1242 Fees 761, *Ryngstaneston* 1282 Cl, *Rustisdon* 1333 *SR* (p). *v.* dun. Probably the first element is a pers. name **Hringstān*, which would be a regular formation; *hringstān*, 'circular stone' (or the like) is also possible, but no such stone has been noted here.

WILSON may be identical with *Weveston* 1238 FF, *Wened(e)ston* (sic) 1285, 1303 FA, *Wufedeston* 1333 *SR*, a manor mentioned in connexion with Worlington in FA. This must be a compound of

---

[1] Formerly two distinct parishes, now united.

OE *wēofod*, 'altar,' and stan, 'stone,' and refer to some lost sacrificial stone of pre-Saxon date.

GROVE COTTAGE (6"), HALSE (6"), STONE and THORNHAM were probably the homes of Edward de *la Grove* (1299 *Ass*), Alexander de *Halse* (1330 *SR*), German de *la Stane* (1238 *Ass*) and Robert Wyot de *Thorndon* (1330 *SR*). *v.* grafa, stan, dun. For Halse, *v.* Addenda, Part i, lviii. The place is on a neck of land.

AFFETON BARTON is *Alfeton* (sic) 1242 Fees 787, *Affeton* 1278 Exon, 1340 *Ass.* '*Æffa's* farm,' *v.* tun. Cf. Afton *infra* 505. BURROW CROSS is *la Burgh juxta Whiterugg'* 1299 *Ass. v.* beorg. There are tumuli here. COBLEY is *Cobelega* c. 1200 *St Nicholas*, *Cobbeleghe* 1352 Exon (p). '*Cobba's* clearing,' *v.* leah. Cf. Cobley *supra* 370. CUDDENHAY is *Cod(d)yngeshaye* 1330, 1333 *SR* (p). '*Cudding's* enclosure,' *v.* (ge)hæg. The name may be of ME origin. Wallenberg (StudNP 2, 96) notes that there was a Thos *Codyng* in Chittlehampton in 1428 (FA). DENERIDGE is *Den(e)rigge* 1238 *Ass* (p), 1333 *SR* (p). HENSLEY is *Hendeslegh* 1330, *Hemundeslegh* 1333 *SR* (p). '*Hēahmund's* clearing,' *v.* leah. HORSEFORD (6") is *Horsford juxta Eswolrinton* 1289 *Ass.* MOUSEBERRY is *Mousbiri* 1330 *SR* (p). 'Mouse burh,' *v.* Musbury *infra* 646. There is a tumulus here. NARRACOTT LINHAYS (6") is *Northecote* 1327 Banco 'North cot(e),' *v.* Linhayes *infra* 592. YEATHERIDGE is *Yerderighe* 1374 IpmR, *Yertherigge* 1429 *FF.* The first element may be OE erþ, ierþ, 'ploughed land, arable land.'

XVII. CREDITON HUNDRED[1]

Chridiatone, Crediatone 1084 Geld Roll, *Cridietona* 1131 P *Cridinton* 1175, *Crieton* 1181 P, *Criditon* 1238 *Ass*

v. Crediton *infra* 404.

[1] BCS 1331–3 are grants of land at a place called *Cridie* and convey the Hundred of Crediton together with Upton Pyne, Brampford Speke, Hittisleigh, Drewsteignton and part of Cheriton Bishop in the Hundred of Wonford. The details of the boundaries are worked out by Stevenson (*Crawford Charters*, pp. 46 ff.). He identifies in succession Voghays in Whitestone, the Tedburn of Tedburn St Mary's, Lilly Brook (*supra* 8), Harford in Crediton, the Crediton river Yeo, Grendon in Cheriton, the Teign, Parford and Drascombe in Drewsteignton, Hollycombe in Spreyton, Nymet (cf. George Nympton *supra* 348), the Dalch river and Binneford in Sandford.

Colebrooke

COLEBROOKE 128 H 5

Colebroc(h) t. Hy 2 HMC iv, 51 *et passim* to 1291 Tax with variant spellings *-brok, -broc*
Colbrok(e) 1280 Exon, (*juxta Crytton*) 1345 *Ass*

'Cool brook' or '*Cola*'s brook,' *v.* Collacott *supra* 50.

COPPLESTONE is (*on*) *copelan stan* 974 BCS 1303, *Copleaston* 1275 RH (p), *Copelaston* 1281 *Ass* (p), *-le-* 1294 *Ass* (p), *Coplestone* 1384 Exon. Toller (BT Supplt *s.n. copel*) suggests that we have here an OE *copel*, 'unsteady, rocking,' found also as an element in the participial adj. *coppling* used in East Anglia in the same sense. The history of that word, however, is obscure and it may be that the earliest sense recorded in the NED 'swelling upwards' is the truer one, the later one developing owing to confusion with the word *cockling* used in the same sense. There was an OE *cop(p)*, 'top, summit,' from which may have been formed an adjective *coppel*, 'peaked, rounded,' or the like, and the adjective may here be descriptive of the stone which gave its name to the place. As Copplestone is on the bounds of three parishes, the stone was very probably a boundary stone. The stone is the upright stone which still stands here, some ten feet high. It is a granite pillar brought from some distance. It may be added that there are places called Copplestone in Newton Tracy and Tiverton, but no early forms have been noted.

PASCHOE is *Pac(c)hescot(e)* 1285 FA, 1330 *SR* (p), *Pascote* 1573, *Pascow* 1615 *Deed*. '*Pæcci*'s cot(e),' cf. Patchill *supra* 211. For the modern form, cf. Kittitoe *supra* 66.

PENSTONE is *Paynistone* 1301 Exon, *-nes-* 1330 *SR* (p). '*Payn*'s farm,' a post-Conquest place-name. Cf. Penson *supra* 303.

To these may now be added Curtlake in Crediton (*infra* 405) and the association of *wealdan cumb* with Oldridge (*infra* 457). We may note further that we now have ME evidence confirming Stevenson's tentative identification of Hillerton in Bow (*supra* 360), and of *bucganford* (*v.* Budbrook *infra* 431). On the other hand, later ME evidence makes it clear that *hananford* is not Honeyford in Cheriton (*infra* 430), that *puttan stapul* is not to be associated with Puddicombe (*infra* 434), and that *wonbroc* is not Woodbrooke (*infra* 430).

TRONEY BRIDGE (6″) is *Tronabrydge al. Fursehayne* 1558 *Ct, Thorn(e)bridge* 1730 *Recov*, 1758 *FF*. Possibly the first element is OE *trēowen*, 'wooden, of wood,' from **treow**, 'tree.' The river-name Troney is a late back-formation, cf. 15 *supra*.

WHELMSTONE BARTON is *Wulmer(e)ston* 1249 *Ass, Wolmer(e)-ston(e)* 1285 FA, 1374 Exon, *Wolmeston juxta Colbrok* 1358 *FF*. '*Wulfmǣr's* tun.'

COMBE HO, FORD, GREAT HEAL, ROAD FM and WOOD FM were probably the homes of John de *Come* (1249 *Ass*), Alexander *atte Forde* (1330 *SR*), Dewdone[1] de *la Hele* (1249 *Ass*), Walter Red' *atte Rode* (1330 *SR*), and William *atte Wode* (1333 *SR*). *v.* healh, rod.

BUTSFORD BARTON (6″) is *Botesford(e)* 1263 Ipm, 1330 *SR* (p), 1330 Exon (p), *Botteford* 1356 *Ass*. '*Bott*'s ford.' COLEFORD is identical with *Colbrukeford* 1330 Exon (p), *Colbrokforde* 1333 *SR* (p). *v.* Colebrooke *supra* 403. ELLEY is *Elneye* 1292 *Ass, Eleney* 1301 Exon, *Elnhay* 1345 *Ass*. 'Eldertree enclosure,' *v.* ellen, (ge)hæg. GUSCOTTS COTTAGE (6″) is *Estgodescote juxta Colbrok* 1305 *Ass*. '*Gode*'s cot(e).' The *s* is pseudo-manorial. HOR-WELL is *Horghewill(e)* 1330 *SR* (p), 1356 *Ass* (p). 'Dirty spring,' *v.* horh, wielle. LANDSEND is *Londesend* 1466, *Londesyend juxta Criditon* 1473 IpmR. It is at the western end of the parish. PENNYLAND is *Penyland* 1553 *Ct, Penny-* 1730 *Recov*. Cf. Pyna-mead *supra* 378. STUDHAM (6″) is *Stodham* 1275 RH (p), *Stodesham* 1330 *SR* (p). 'Stud ham(m).' WOTTON is *Wu(o)deton* 1249 *Ass* (p), *Wodeton* 1275 RH (p). 'Farm by the wood.'

Crediton and Crediton Hamlets

CREDITON [kəˈrtən] 128 H 7

> *Cridie* 739 (11th) Crawf 1, *æt Cridiantune* 930 Crawf 4, *Crydiatun* 974 BCS 1303, *Cridiantun(e)* 977 (c. 1000) ASC (C), 1046 KCD 1334, *Cridian tun* 980–8 Crawf 7, (*in to*) *crydian tune* 1008–12 Crawf 10
> *Cridiensis ecclesiae* 933 BCS 694
> *Chritetona, Chrietona* 1086 DB, *Crytton* 1322 *Ass*, -*i*- 1344 *FF*

---

[1] This pers. name perhaps corresponds to Modern French *Dieudonné(e)*.

Cridentun c. 1150 William of Malmesbury, *Criditon* 1231 Cl, *Crideton* 1231 Ch, *Cridinton* 1238 *Ass*, *Crydyton*, *Cridding-ton* 1295 *Ass*, *Cridyngton* 1332 Cl *Credington* 1274 Pat, (*in veteri*) *Crediton* 1284 *Ass* *Kyrtone* 1380 Exon, *Kirton* c. 1550 Leland, *Curton* 1601 Cai, *Crediton al. Kirton* 1637 BM, *Crediton vulgo Kerton* 1675 Ogilby

'Farm on the river Creedy' (*supra* 4), *v.* tun. Originally the place took its name from the river alone.

CREEDY BRIDGE is *Cridianbrycg* 739 (11th) Crawf 1, (*æt*) *Crydan brigce* 956 (c. 1200) BCS 972, *of crydian bricge* 997 OS Facs iii, 35.

CURTLAKE COTTAGE (6") is *on cyrtlan geat* 739 (11th) Crawf 1, *Curtelhyate* 1269 FF (p), *Curtelyete* 1333 *SR* (p). '*Cyrtla*'s gate,' cf. Kirklington (PN NRY 220).

DUNSCOMBE is *Denescumb* 1242 Fees 762, 791, *Dunescumbe* 1278 Ipm, *Donescome* 1298 *Ass*, *Dynescoumbe* 1305 Ipm. '*Dynni*'s cumb.'

GUNSTONE is *Gunnareston* 1240 FF, *Gunnardeston* 1242 Fees 761, *Gunnoreston* 1244 FF, (*juxta Criditon*) 1288 *Ass*, *Gonnereston juxta Criditon* 1296 *Ass*, *Gunston* 1499 Ipm. '*Gunner*'s tun,' or possibly '*Gunwerd*'s tun.' These are Anglo-Scandinavian pers. names but the place-name probably does not go back further than the 11th or 12th cent.

HARFORD is *herepaðford* 739 (11th) Crawf 1, *Herpeforde* 1593 DA 26, 172. *v.* herepæð. There is no important road here such as is commonly found when the term herepæð is used. Almost equally obscure is the herepæð found in Harpford Fm in Langford (So), *Herpoðford* 904 BCS 610, 1065 KCD 816, *Herpeford* 1236 FF.

HOLLACOMBE is *holancumbes* (*heafod*) 930 Crawf 2, *Hollecoumbe* 1238 *Ass* (p). 'Hollow valley,' *v.* holh, cumb.

JEW'S HOLLACOMBE is *Hollecombe Jewe* 1482 IpmR and is to be associated with the family of Nicholas *le Jeu* (1333 *SR*).

KEYMELFORD is *Kemelford(e)* 1332 Inq aqd, 1598 DA 54, *Kemyl-* 1571 Wills, *Kemelford* or *Keymelford* or *Kembleford* or *Kemylford*

1754 *Recov.* If the first element is identical with that of Camel's Head *supra* 240, there is a possibility that it was an old name of the river Yeo or of one of its head streams. If this is the case, we have an example of river-worship as in Brent and Dee (Ekwall RN 51, 117).

NEOPARDY [nepədi] is *Nepewurth* 1249 *Ass* (p), *-worth(e)* 1307 Exon, 1327 Banco (p), 1333 *SR* (p), *Eastnepworthie* 1646 *Recov*, *East Neperdy* 1662 *FF*, *Neoperthey* 1777 *Recov.* The first element here is either OE *nǣp*, 'turnip,' or possibly ME *neppe*, 'catmint.'

POSBURY

Postbir' 1270 *Ass*, *-byry* 1281 *Ass* (p), *-biry* 1322 *Ass* (p)
Possebury 1276 *Ass* (p), 1499 Ipm, *-byr'* 1277 *Ass* (p)
Posbyr' 1281 *Ass* (p), *-bury* 1378 IpmR

The second element is burh referring to the ancient camp here. The first is uncertain; it may be OE *post*, 'post,' though no other such compound is known and the sense would be uncertain. More probably we have the same pers. name *Possa* which seems to be found in Poston (Sa), DB *Possethorne*, and Postwick (Nf), 1203 *Ass Possewic*.

SPENCE COMBE is *Spenceryscome* 1415 Exon. At that date Richard *Spencer* was granted a licence for an oratory here. The family however appear earlier in the person of John *Spenser* (1333 *SR*).

TROBRIDGE Ho is *Trowbregg'* 1281 *Ass* (p), *Trouburgg* 1285 FA, *-brigg* 1289 *Ass* (p), *Trobrigge* 1303 FA, *-brugge* 1400 IpmR, 1411 Exon. 'Tree bridge,' *v.* treow. The name probably referred to a felled or fallen tree used to cross the little stream here. Cf. Trowbridge (W), *Troubrug* 1212 PatR.

UTON is *Yeweton* 1285 FA, 1435 IpmR, *Jouweton* 1292 Ipm, *Iuweton juxta Cridyton* 1296 *Ass*, *Yoweton* 1334 *FF*, *Uton* 1486 Ipm. 'Farm by the river Yeo,' earlier *Eowe* (*supra* 17), *v.* tun.

VENNY TEDBURN is *Fennytetteburn(e)* 1299 *Ass*, 1311 *FF*, *Fenny Tetteborne* 1385 *FF*, *Venytedborne* 1589 *SR*. 'Tetta's stream,' *v. supra* 14. *Fenny*, i.e. marshy, to distinguish it from Tedburn St Mary *infra* 451.

WINSTOUT is *Winstowte* 1576 Wills, *-stode* 1754 *Deed* and is to be associated with Gilbert *Wynstout* (1330 *SR*). The second element may be the same as that found in Brimpts *supra* 192, for Winstout is on a steep hill. The first element is obscure, unless it be the pers. name *Wine*.

BERE, COOMBE, EASTACOTT (6"), EASTCHURCH, FORD, HOOKE, LANGRIDGE, GREAT LEIGH, MOOR, NORTHCOT COTTAGE (6"), PITT, ROCK, SHORTACOMBE, SHORTRIDGE and STOCKEYDOWN (6") were probably the homes of Osb' de *la Bere* (1249 *Ass*), Simon de *Combe* (1330 *SR*), William de *Yestecote* (1310 *Ass*), i.e. 'east cottages,' Walter *Byestecherche* (1330 *SR*), i.e. east of the church[1], Martin *atte Forde* (1244 *Ass*), William *atte Hoke* (1330 *SR*), Richard de *Langerig*' (ib.), Thomas *atte Leye* (ib.), Thomas de *la More* (1244 *Ass*), John de *Northecote* (1364 *Ass*), Walter *atte Putte* (1330 *SR*), Adam *atte Rocke* (ib.), William de *Schortecume* (1249 *Ass*), Thomas de *Shortrig*' (1330 *SR*) and John de *Stokedon* (ib.). *v.* bearu, cot(e), hoc (there is a spur of land here), lang, leah, mor, pytt, stocc, dun.

DICKERS and TAPPERS (both 6") are probably to be associated with the families of Richard *Dikere* (1330 *SR*) and Robert *Tapper* (1617 Wills).

BINNEFORD is *Bineford* 1249 *Ass* (p). This may be the same name as Binneford *infra* 411. BRADLEIGH is *Bradelegh* 1281 *Ass*, *Westbradelegh juxta Cryditon* 1314 *Ass*. 'Wide clearing,' *v.* leah. CADDIFORD is *Cadeworthi* 1238 *Ass* (p), 1330 *SR* (p), *Estkadeworthi juxta Criditon* 1322 *Ass*. '*Cada*'s worþig.' CHIDDENBROOK (6") is *Chedyngbrok* 1330 *SR* (p), *Chechyngbroke* 1499 Ipm, *Chuddenbrooke* 1598 DA 54. CROSS (6") is *la Crosse* 1333 Oliver. ELSTON is *Ayleston* 1330 *SR* (p), 1427 IpmR. Perhaps '*Ægel*'s tun.' FORDTON is *Fordeton* 1249 *Ass* (p), (*juxta Criditon*) 1289 *Ass*, *Forteton* 1256 FF, *Forton* 1675 Ogilby. *v.* tun. GOLDWELL is *Goldwill(e)* 1270 *Ass*, *Goldewille juxta Crytton* 1322 *Ass*. 'Spring by which some gold-coloured flower grows,' *v.* wielle and cf. Gullaford *infra* 521. HOLWELL (6") is *Holewelle* 1281 *Ass* (p), *Holewill juxta Cridyton* 1370 *Ass*. 'Spring in the hollow,' *v.* holh, wielle. HOOKWAY is *Hokeweye* 1210–12 RBE (p), *Hockeweye* 1262 FF (p), *Hocweye* 1285 FA, (*juxta Crydinton*) 1290 *FF*,

---

[1] The reference is to Hittisleigh church just to the west of the farm.

referring probably to the curving road here. KERSFORD is *Caresford* 1262 FF, *Carsford* 1290 *FF*, 1383 BM. 'Cress ford.' KNOWLE is *Knolle* 1281 *Ass. v.* cnoll. MOORLAKE is *Madlake oth. Marlake* 1809 *Recov. v.* lacu. PRIESTCOMBE is *Prust(e)combe* 1333 Oliver 76, 1370 *Ass, Preste-* 1335 Pat. 'Priests' combe.' A prebendal manor of Exeter Cathedral. RUDGE is *la Rigge* 1249 *Ass* (p), *Rigge* 1333 Oliver 76, *Rugge Arundell* 1485 Ipm. *v.* hrycg. Thomas *Arundell* held the manor in 1485. VINNICOMBE is *Venycomb* 1524 *SR*. 'Fenny (marshy) combe.' WESTACOTT BARTON is *Westcot* 1281 *Ass*. WESTWOOD (6″) is *Westwode* 1504–15 ECP 4, 452. WOODLAND is *la Wudelond* 1249 *Ass*. YEO (6″) is *Iowe* 1234 Fees 399, *Iwe* t. Hy 3 BM, *Yewe* 1285 FA, *Yo(u)we* 1316 Ipm, 1333 *SR* (p). YEOFORD is *Ioweford* 1242 Fees 790, *You(u)eford* 1281 *Ass*, 1334 *SR*, *Yewford* 1754 *Recov*. For these two names, *v.* River Yeo *supra* 17.

Kennerleigh

KENNERLEIGH 128 F 6

Kenewarlegh' 1219 *Ass*, *Kynwarleye* 1275 *FF*
Kinwardelegh 1244 *Ass*, *Kyn(e)warde(s)ley(e)*, *-legh* 1281 *Ass*, 1336 Ipm (p), 1497 Ipm
Kyneworthlegh 1281 *Ass*
Kynnerley 1577 Saxton, *Kenworleighe* 1609 *FF*

'*Cyneweard's* clearing,' *v.* leah. For omission of the genitival *s*, cf. Killington, Wiverton *supra* 66, 251.

DELVE'S COTTAGE (6″) is to be associated with the family of Robert *Delve* (1330 *SR*). HIGHER UPTON was the home of William de *Uppeton* (1330 *SR*). 'Higher farm,' *v.* tun. It lies above Kennerleigh.

Morchard Bishop

MORCHARD BISHOP 128 F 5

Morchet, Morceta 1086 DB, *Morchet* 1165 P, *Morchet Episcopi* 1207 ClR, 1256 *Ass*, (*in*) *bosco de Morchet* 1256 *Ass*
Morcestre 1199 FF, (*Episcopi*) 1258–74 Exon
Morcherd 1226 FF, *-cerde* 1258–74 Exon

Bisshopes Morchestre 1289 *Ass, Bisschoppesmorchard* 1311
Exon
Morchut, Marchut 1675 Ogilby

For this name, *v.* Cruwys Morchard *supra* 380. The manor
was held by the bishop of Exeter in DB. Cf. Bishop's Leigh
infra.

EASTON BARTON is *Estemeston* 1238 *Ass* (p), *Esteueneston* 1281
Ass (p), *Esteneston* 1333 *SR* (p). The forms are not sufficiently
consistent for any solution to be offered. The farm is on the west
side of the parish and not on the eastmost side.

ROLSTONE BARTON is *Rauleston* 1242 Fees 767, *Rouleston* 1269 FF,
Rolueston 1340 *SR, Roweleston juxta Morchard* 1420 IpmR. This
name is clearly of post-Conquest origin, the first element being
a Norman pers. name *Raulf* or *Rolf.* These two names are
commonly confused in ME documents. Cf. Björkmann NP 108,
113, *s.nn. Raðulf, Roðulf.*

SHOBROOKE is (*on*) *scipbroc* 739 (11th) Crawf 1, *Eschipabroca* 1086
DB (Exon), *Schipebroc* (Exch), *Sibebroc* 1219 FF, *Shipbrok* 1238
Ass, Shepbrok 1330 *SR* (p). 'Sheep brook.' The modern form
has been influenced by Shobrooke *infra* 416. There would seem
to have been alternative forms with *scip* and *scipa* (gen. pl.).

ASH, BROADRIDGE, HILL, LEIGH, LONGMARSH PLANTATION (6″),
NORTHWOOD, RUDGE[1], SLADE, UPCOTT and WEEK were probably
the homes of William de *Asshe* (1302 *Ass*), Petronilla de *Brade-
rigge* (1330 *SR*), Richard *atte Hille* (ib.), Alexandra de *Leghe* (ib.),
Peter *Langemersh* (1333 *SR*), David *Bynorthewode* (ib.), Peter
atte Rugge (1330 *SR*), Richard *atte Slade* (ib.), Richard de *Uppecote* (1304 *Ass*) and Sarra de *Wyke* (1330 *SR*). *v.* leah, hrycg,
slæd, cot(e), wic.

BIRCHENBEER COTTAGE (6″) is *Burchingbeare* 1658 *Recov.*
'Birch(en) wood,' *v.* biercen, bearu. BISHOP'S LEIGH is *Bisshopes-
leg* 1249 *Ass.* 'Bishop's leah,' *v. supra.* BROWNSTONE is
Brounyston 1330, *Brouneston* 1333 *SR* (p). '*Brūn*'s farm,' *v.* tun.
BUGBEAR MILL (6″) is *Bukbearemyll* 1502 ECP 4, 99, *v.* bearu.
BUTCOMBE (6″) is so spelt 1779 *Recov.* COLT'S HILL (6″) is *Great-*

[1] *Westrigge* 1502 ECP.

colthill 1611 *Recov.* FARTHING PARK is *Furthingparke* 1611 *Recov.* *v.* feorðung. FROST is so spelt 1701 *Recov.* KNATHORN is *Knavethorne* 1330 *SR* (p), *Knawthorne* 1710 *Recov.* 'Young man's thorntree,' *v.* Knaworthy *supra* 92. KNIGHTSTONE is *Cnizteston* 1285 FA, *Knyttheton* 1307 Ipm, *Knyghte(s)tone* 1311 Exon, 1330, *Knighteston* 1333 *SR* (p). 'Farm of the cniht' or possibly of a person so called. MIDDLECOTT is *Middlecot* 1771 *Recov.* OLDBOROUGH is *Oldburrough* 1701 *Recov.* *v.* beorg. OXENPARK is *Esteroxenparke* 1611 *Recov.* PARADISE (6″) is *Paradice* 1616 *FF.* SHARLAND (6″) is *Sherlond* 1524 *SR* (p), *Shyrlande* 1579 Wills. SOUTHCOTT is *Suhtcote* 1249 *Ass*, *Southecote* 1330 *SR* (p). *v.* cot(e). VENN is *la Fenne* 1311 Exon. *v.* fenn. WATCOMBE (6″) is so spelt 1611 *Recov.* WIGHAM is *Wygeham* 1330, *Wyggeham* 1333 *SR* (p). '*Wicga*'s ham(m).'

Newton St Cyres

NEWTON ST CYRES 128 J 8

(*æt*) *niwan tune* 1050–73 Earle, *Newentona, Niwentona* 1086 DB *Nywetone juxta Exoniam* 1264 Exon, (*Sancti Ciricii*) 1330 Exon, *Seynt Serys Newton* 1525 *Recov, Newton St Cires* 1605 Wills

'New farm,' *v.* niwe, tun. The church is dedicated to St *Ciricius.*

BIDWELL BARTON is *Bedewille, Bydewille* 1302, 1303 Exon (p), *Bidewille* 1333 *SR* (p). No certainty is possible. In Bydemill Brook (W), which is near *byde wil* (KCD 767), *byde* is a stream-name, and it may be such here. A small tributary of the Creedy flows near the farm. Bidwell (*infra* 573), however, is not on a stream, neither is Bidwell in Quantoxhead (So), *Bydewell* 1279 Ass (p), and it is possible that both names contain the element discussed under Bidna *supra* 102.

NORTON HO is (*æt*) *norðtune* 1050–73 Earle, *Northon'* 1242 Fees 793, *Northtone* 1291 Tax, *Norton juxta Shokebrok* 1339 *Ass*, (*juxta Nyweton Sci Ciricii*) 1346 *Ass.* 'North tun.' It lies north of Newton and on the borders of Shobrooke parish.

HAYNE FM, LAKE and WOODLEY were the homes of John *ate Heghen* (1301 Exon), Walter *atte Lake* (1330 *SR*) and Thomas *atte Wodelegh* (ib.). *v.* lacu, leah, and Hayne *supra* 129.

GREENLAND is *Greeneland* 1634 *FF*. HOLME is *Westhome* 1497
Ipm, *Westholme* 1722 *Recov*. It is just west of Newton village.
The modern *l* is probably incorrect. LANGFORD is *Langeford*
1330 *SR* (p), (*juxta Critton*) 1346 *Ass*, (*juxta Upton Pyn*) 1359
FF. MARSH BARTON (6″) is *Merse juxta Norton* 1294 *Ass* and was
the home of John *atte Mershe* (1330 *SR*). NORTHRIDGE is
Notterigge 1524 *SR* (p), t. Ed 6 *Rental*. Cf. Noddon *supra* 267.
SMALLBROOK is *Smalebrok* 1238 *Ass* (p), *Smalebrok Coterel juxta
Nyweton* 1311 *Ass*. 'Narrow brook,' *v.* smæl. Sampson *Coterel*
was a juror in Crediton Hundred in 1238 (*Ass*). SNAKE ASH (6″)
is so spelt 1768 *Recov*. WINSCOTT is *Wynescote* 1262 FF (p),
1303 Exon (p). '*Wine*'s cot(e).'

Sandford

SANDFORD[1] 128 G 6

   (*æt*) *sand forda* 930 Crawf 4, (*æt*) *Sandforda, Sandford* 997 OS
     Facs iii, 35, *æt Sandforda* 1008–12 Crawf 10
   Saunford 1340 Pat, *Sanford* 1675 Ogilby

'Sandy ford' (over a small tributary of the Creedy).

BINNEFORD is *Beonnan ford* 930 Crawf 4, *Bynneford* 1330 *SR*
(p). '*Beonna*'s ford.'

BRIMLEY (6″) is *bromleage* 930 Crawf 4, *Bremlegh* 1333 *SR* (p).
'Broom clearing,' *v.* leah, with later common confusion of brom
and bremel.

BROXHAM COPSE (6″) must be near the *Brocheardes hamm* of the
Crediton charter of 930 (Crawf 4). '*Brōcheard*'s ham(m).'

COMBELANCEY is *Comb* 1285 FA, *Combe Launceles* 1301 Ipm,
Comb Lancelys 1303 FA. *v.* cumb. Jocelin de *Lancel* held the
manor in 1285 (FA).

---

[1] BCS 1343 is a grant of land at Sandford. The boundaries are dealt with
by Stevenson (*Crawford Charters*, pp. 67 ff.). They are difficult to trace at all
fully because they do not correspond to the boundaries of the present parish
of Sandford except to a very limited extent. They include Hollacombe in
Crediton, Broxham, Brimley, Pidsley, Thelbridge, Henstill and Ruxford in
Sandford parish. Stevenson was probably right in suggesting that Beacon
Cross, to the north-west of Ruxford, on a prominent hill, might be identified
with *weardsetl*, 'watch-seat.' If so we have an interesting parallel to the
Hampshire Beacon Hill, earlier called *weardsetl*, cf. PN Wo 253 *s.n.* Warshill.

DOGGETSBEER (6″) is *Doggesbeare* 1650 *Recov* and is probably to be associated with the family of Walter *Doket* (1330 *SR*). *v.* bearu.

DOWRICH HO

> *Douerigge* 1238 *Ass, Est, West Dourygge* 1349 *FF, Dowrigge* 1422 IpmR
> *Duris, Douryz, Durisse* 1256 *Ass, Douriz* 1303 FA
> *Dowrish* 1330 *SR* (p), *Dowrisch* 1390 IpmR, *Dourysshe* 1483 IpmR

This was probably a stream-name, originally identical with *Doferic* (Wo), a derivative of the British *dubro-* (W *dwfr*), 'water' (cf. Ekwall RN 136, Blomé 131). The name must have been used of the stream which unites with Holly Water to form the Creedy river.

HENSTILL is (*oþ*) *henne stigele* 930 Crawf 4, (*oð*) *henne stigle* 997 OS Facs iii, 35, *Estenestil* 1249 *Ass, Hennestille* 1281 *Ass*. 'Hen-path,' *v.* stigel.

PIDSLEY is *pideres leage* 930 Crawf 4, *Pydereslegh, Pydeneslegh* 1281 *Ass, Pyderslegh* 1292 *Ass, Piddeslegh* 1483 IpmR. *v.* leah. The first element cannot be a river-name as the place is on the top of a hill. It may conceivably be the British element *Pider* noted under Petherwin *supra* 158. For such a genitival compound with a Celtic name, we may compare *Andredesleah*, the old name for the Weald. *v.* leah.

PROWSE is *Prowse al. Higher Dodridge* t. Jas 1 ECP, *Prowseland* 1638 *FF*, and is probably to be associated with the family of Walter *Prou* (1330 *SR*), *Prowse* being for *Prou's*.

RUXFORD BARTON is *hroces ford* 930 Crawf 4, *hrocesford, of hrocesforda* 997 OS Facs iii, 35, *Rokeford* 1254 BM, *Rokesford* 1403, 1437 IpmR. 'Rook's ford,' or 'ford of a man named *Hrōc*,' cf. Roxford (Herts), *Rochesforde* 1086 DB, *Rokesford* 1240 *FF*, 1248 *Ass*.

THELBRIDGE BRIDGE is *þelbrycg* 930 Crawf 4, (*oþ*) *ðel bricge*, (*of*) *þel bricge* 997 OS Facs iii, 35. 'Plank bridge,' *v.* þel.

BOROUGH, BREMRIDGE, FURZELAND, HELE HO (6″), SOUTHDOWN HILL, VENLAKE, VENN, YELLAND and YEO were probably the homes of Walter *atte Burghe* (1330 *SR*), William de *Bremelrig*, i.e. 'bramble ridge' (ib.), John de *Furslonde* (ib.), Mabilla *atte Hele* (1333 *SR*), Robert *Bysouthedon*, i.e. 'south of the down' (1330 *SR*), Johanna de *Fenlake* (ib.), William de *Fenne* (1275 RH), John de *Yolond*, i.e. 'old land' (1330 *SR*), *v*. Addenda, Part i, lviii, and Robert *atte Yo*, i.e. 'at the water' (1333 *SR*), *v. supra* 17–18. *v*. beorg, healh, fenn, lacu.

ALLER is *Alre* 1333 Oliver. 'At the alder.' ALLER DOWN is *Allerdowne* 1650 *Recov*. ASHMOOR BARN (6″) is *Ashmore* 1621 *Recov*. ASHRIDGE is *Ayssherig* 1330 *SR* (p), *Assherigge* 1390 IpmR. BAGBOROUGH is *Baggebergh* 1249 FF, -*burgh* 1330 *SR* (p). '*Bacga*'s hill,' *v*. beorg, cf. Bagborough (So), *Bacganbeorge* 904 BCS 610. BLACKMOOR COOMBE is *Blakemanescomb* 1333 *SR* (p), *Blackmans Combe* 1390 IpmR. '*Blæcman(n)*'s combe.' cf. *Blakemanneshassoc* 1219 *Ass* (D), site unknown. BURRIDGE is *Burrigg*' 1330 *SR*(p). *v*. burh, hrycg. There is no earthwork or the like here now. CLAMPITT is *Clampitts* 1749 *Recov*. 'Loamy hollow or pit.' *v*. Clampitt *infra* 431. DIRA is *Diarah* 1765 D and is probably to be associated with the family of John *Dira* (1330 *SR*). DODDRIDGE (6″) is *Doderig* 1275 RH, *Dodderigge juxta Criditon* 1356 *FF*. '*Dodda*'s ridge.' DOWNHAYNE is *Dounehayne* 1690 *Recov*. For *hayne*, *v. supra* 129. FROGMIRE is *Froggemere* 1261 Exon, 1407 *FF*, *Frogemere juxta Crydyton* 1295 *Ass*. 'Frog pool,' *v*. mere. HEATHFIELD COTTAGES (6″) is *Hetfeld* 1390 IpmR. KERSWILL COTTAGE (6″) is *Carswell* 1333 Oliver 76. 'Cress spring.' NORTH CREEDY is *Northcredy* 1604 Wills. POOL (6″) is *La Pole* 1333 Oliver 76. PRIORTON is so spelt in 1390 (IpmR). It belonged to Plympton Priory. RANSCOMBE (6″) is *Ramscombe* 1589 *SR*. STURRIDGE is *Stourugge* (possibly with *u* for *n*) 1249 *Ass* (p), *Storudge* 1608 Wills. Perhaps 'stone ridge,' cf. Storridge *supra* 310. SWANNATON is *Swaneton* 1330 *SR* (p), 1345, 1349 *Ass* (p). 'Peasants' farm,' *v*. swan, tun. WEST SANDFORD is *Westsaunford* 1347 Pat, *West Sandford* 1589 *SR*. WITHYWIND (6″) is *Witheven* 1650 *Recov*. Probably 'withy fen,' the modern form being corrupt. Cf. Introd. xxxiv–v. WOOLSGROVE is *Wolmersgrove* 1281 *Ass* (p), *Wolsgrove* 1333 Oliver 76. '*Wulfmær*'s grove.' YARMLEY is *Yarmeleg* 1270 *Ass*, *Yermelegh* 1417 *FF*. *v*. leah. The first element may be OE *earm*, 'poor, wretched.'

XVIII. WEST BUDLEIGH HUNDRED

This was originally a detached part of East Budleigh Hundred *infra* 580. It is first referred to as *hundred of Westbuddelegh* in 1333 (*SR*).

Cheriton Fitzpaine

CHERITON FITZPAINE 128 F 8

> *Cerintona* 1086 DB, *Cheriton* 1428 FA, *Cheryton Phezpayn* 1510 *Deed*, (*Fyshepyne*) 1555 *Deed*
> *Churiton(e)* 1242 Fees 775, 1291 Tax, 1303 FA, 1308, 1328 Exon, *Churitone Santone* 1274 Exon, *Churiton Fitz Payn* 1354 *FF*, *Chureton* 1346 FA
> *Chiriton* 1256 FF, (*Pagan*) 1297 Pat, (*Fitz Payn*) 1334 *SR*

'Church farm' *v.* cyric(e), tun. Cf. Cheriton *supra* 59 and Addenda, Part i, lii, *s.n.* Churchill. Roger, son of *Pagan*, held the manor in 1256 (FF) and the patron of the church was Roger filius *Pagani* in 1274 (Exon). *Santone* refers to Thomas de *Santon'* who held three parts of a fee in *Churiton* in 1242 (Fees).

BRINDIWELL is *Breydenwill, Breyndewell* 1270 *Ass, Bredenewille* 1330 *SR* (p). This is a difficult name. The first element may be OE *breden, briden, bryden,* 'made of bredes or planks,' referring to some structure round the spring, but the phonology is difficult.

CHILTON is *Cilletona* 1086 DB, *Chilleton* 1219 FF, 1333 *SR* (p). Probably '*Cilla*'s farm,' *v.* tun.

CODDIFORD is *Codaforda* 1086 DB, *Codeford* 1196 Oliver 396, 1249 *Ass, Cuddeford(e)* 1301 Ipm, 1379 IpmR. '*Codda*'s ford.'

COOMBE is *Comba* 1086 DB (Exon), *Cumbe* (Exch), *Combe* 1295 Ipm. *v.* cumb.

LOWER DUNSCOMBE (6″) is *Danescoma* 1086 DB, *Denescumbe* 1198 FF, *Dynescumbe* 1281 *Ass,* -*com* 1282 Cl, *Donescumb* 1303 FA. Probably '*Dynni*'s combe,' the DB spelling being corrupt. Cf. Dunsley in Tring (Herts), *Daneslai, Deneslai* DB, *Dynesle* 1296, 1307 *SR* and Dunscombe *supra* 405.

FORD[1], HAYNE, MARSHAY FM, STOCKADON, VENN and WOLLAND were probably the homes of Stephen *atte Forde* (1333 *SR*), Joel *atte Heghen* (1330 *SR*), Galfridus de *Mersheghes* (ib.), Robert de *Stokedon* (1281 *Ass*), Walter *atte Fenne* (1330 *SR*), Matilda *atte Willelond* (ib.), de *Wildelond* (1333 *SR*). *v.* stoc(c), dun, fenn and cf. Hayne *supra* 129, and Willand *infra* 553.

COTTON is *la Cotene* 1301 *Ass* (p), *atte Coten* 1330 *SR* (p), *la Coton* t. Ed 3 *Ass*. 'The cottages,' cf. the same name *supra* 331. DALLEYS (6″) is to be associated with the family of Richard *Daley* (1544 *SR*). FARLEIGH is *Ferlegh* 1238 *Ass* (p), *Westferlegh juxta Churiton* 1302 *Ass*. 'Bracken clearing,' *v.* fearn, leah. FURZE is *La Fursen* 1303 FA, (*atte*) 1330 *SR* (p). For the *en*, *v. supra* 130. LEY'S CROSS is *Lease* 1765 D. *v.* læs. SMITH HAYNE (6″) is *Smythsheies* 1333 *SR* (p). 'Smith's enclosures,' *v.* (ge)hæg. TRUNDLEMORE FM is *Trendelmor'* 1330 *SR* (p). *v.* trendel, mor. The name must refer to the shape of the valley here. UPCOTT BARTON is *Uppecote* 1324 *FF*, (*juxta Poghhill*) 1339 *Ass*. WELL-COOMBE is *Welcomb(e)* 1301 *Ass* (p), 1330, 1333 *SR* (p). *v.* wielle, cumb. WHITE CROSS is *Whytecrosse* 1468 IpmR.

Poughill

POUGHILL [pɑuəl] 128 E/F 7

> *Pocheella, Pochehilla* 1086 DB, *Pochelee* 1073–1103 *St Nicholas*
> *Pokehill* 1219 FF, *Pokeille* 1221, *Pochell(ee)* 1222, 1227 *St Nicholas, Pochehull* 1238 FF, 1284 *Ass*
> *Poghahille* 1238 *Ass et freq* to 1381 Exon with variant spellings *Pog(he)-, -hull(e), Poghelle* 1279 Exon
> *Pouhahille* 1238 *Ass*

'*Pohha*'s hill.' Cf. Poflet *supra* 216 and Poughill (Co), *Pochehelle* DB, *Poghehille* 1198 FF. It may be noted that the Cornish place-name is pronounced [pɔfəl].

GRANTLAND is *Granteland'* 1242 Fees 761, *Grauntelond* 1281 *Ass*, 1286 *FF* (all p). A river-name *Granta* is not out of the question, though river-names do not as a rule seem to be compounded with *land*. For Grantley (Y) and Grantham (L) Ekwall (RN 183)

---

[1] *Eastforde* 1617 Recov.

suggests the possibility of an OE pers. name. The present p.n., like many other land-compounds, may contain a ME pers. name, here the OFr *graunt*, 'great,' ModEng *Grant*.

WELSBERE BARTON is *Welesbere* 1238 *Ass*, *Wellesbyare juxta Poghehulle* 1313 *Ass*, 1317 *FF*, *-beare* 1379 IpmR. Probably 'wood by the spring,' *v*. wielle, bearu and cf. Welsford *supra* 77. There is a spring here.

CLEAVES, CROSS FM[1] (6″), MILL FM (6″), NEW HO and NEWLAND were probably the homes of Richard de *Westclyve* (1330 *SR*), William *atte Crosse* (ib.), William *atter Mille* (1333 *SR*), Thomas *atte Nywehouse* (1330 *SR*) and Roger de *Niwelond* (ib.). *v*. clif.

BABBADON (6″) is so spelt 1610 *FF*. Probably '*Babba*'s hill.' BROADRIDGE FM is *Braderig* 1242 Fees 761, 790, *-rug*' 1330 *SR* (p), *-regge* 1539 *Recov*. PENHAY is so spelt 1431, 1458 IpmR. Perhaps a compound of penn, 'pen,' and (ge)hæg. VENN CHANNING (6″) is *Fenne juxta Poghull* 1378 IpmR. *v*. fenn.

Shobrooke

SHOBROOKE 128 H 8

> (*of*) *sceoca broces* (*forda*) 938 BCS 726[2]
> *Sotebroca* 1086 DB (Exon), *-och* (Exch)
> *Sokebroc, Schokebrocke* 1260 Exon, *Shokebrok juxta Criditon* 1289 *Ass*
> *Shogbroke* 1329 Exon, 1524 *SR*, *Shogge-* 1450 Exon
> *Shackbroke* 1371 Exon, *Shabbroke* 1541 *SR*
> *Shawbrook* 1675 Ogilby, *Shobbrooke* 1694 *Recov*

OE *sceoca brōc*, 'goblin brook'; *sceoca* is a variant form of scucca.

PENNICOTT and UPPINCOTT are *Pinnecote* 1238 *Ass* (p), *Pine-* 1262 FF, *Pynne-* 1274 *FF*, 1326 Ipm, 1330 *SR* (p), *Uppynnecote* 1274 *FF*, *Uppynecot* 1323 *Ass*, *Uppynghecote* 1330 *SR* (p). '*Pinna*'s cot(e),' cf. Pennaton *supra* 291. Uppincott lies higher than Pennicott.

---

[1] *Crosse* 1543 *SR*.
[2] The identification is not certain. It occurs in the land boundaries of *muneca tun*, the site of which is not known. In any case it is probable that the names are identical. *v*. Addenda, Part ii, xiii.

WEST RADDON is *Ratdona* 1086 DB, *Raddon'* 1242 Fees 761, 793, *Reddoñ* 1257 FF, *Westraddon* 1276 Ipm. 'Red hill,' *v.* dun. 'West' as opposed to Raddon *infra* 572. Also distinguished as Raddon *Baldewyn* (1316 FA) from the family which held the manor in 1242.

SHUTE is *La Shete* 1242 Fees 762, (*juxta Shokebrok*) 1321 *Ass*, *Schete* 1295 Ipm, *La Schute* 1303 FA, *la Shute et non in la Shut' et non in la Shete* 1321 *Ass*, *Shuterychard juxta Thorverton* 1381 *Ass. v. s.n.* Shute *supra* 184. As pointed out by Blomé (109), the place lies in the south-east corner of the parish. The *Rychard* of the 1381 reference is not known. In the Assize Roll reference there was a dispute about the ownership of land in *la Shete juxta Shokebrok*, one of the parties concerned maintaining that the correct spelling of the place-name was *Shute*. This proves that in the 14th cent. the vowel was sufficiently uncertain to give ground for a dispute in a Court of Law.

WYKE is *Wica* 1086 DB, *Wyke* 1330 *SR* (p). 'Dairy farm,' *v.* wic.

HILL FM (6″), MOOR FM, WESTACOTT and WOOD FM were probably the homes of Adam *atte Hille* (1330 *SR*), William *atte More* (ib.), Jordan de *Westecote* (ib.) and Philip de *la Wode* (1359 Ipm). *v.* mor, cot(e).

DOWN FM is *Downe* t. Eliz ChancP. GREAT GUTTON is *Godeton* 1330 *SR* (p), 1353 *Ass*. '*Gōda*'s tun.' LITTLE SILVER is so spelt 1694 *Recov. v. supra* 358. REW is *Rawstokhay* 1451 IpmR, *Rewstockheye al. Rewe in parochia de Shobroke* 1582 *Deeds Enrolled. v.* ræw, stocc, (ge)hæg, hence 'wooden enclosure by the cottages.' TREW is *La Trewe* 1281 *Ass*, *Trew(e) Sancti Jacobi* 1334 *SR*, 1503 Ipm, *atte Trewe* 1330 *SR* (p), *Truwe* 1351 Pat, *Seynt Jamys Tre* 1524 *SR*. 'At the tree,' *v.* treow. The connexion with St James is unknown. YENDACOTT MANOR is *Yendecoth'* 1242 Fees 779, -*cote* 1323 *Ass*, *Jondecot* 1254 FF, *Yundecote* 1303 FA, 1330 *SR* (p), 1370 *Ass* (p), *Ende-* 1346 FA. '(Place) beyond the cot(e),' i.e. Pennicott, cf. Indicombe *supra* 35.

Stockleigh English

STOCKLEIGH ENGLISH 128 F 7

> *Estocheleia* 1086 DB (Exon), *Stochelie* (Exch), *Stockelegh* 1242
> Fees 762, *Stokeley Engles* 1268 Exon, *Stokele Engleys* 1281
> *Ass*, *Stokleyenglisch* 1390 *FF*

v. stocc, leah, and for the interpretation cf. Addenda, Part i,
liii, *s.n.* Yardley. Gilebertus *Anglicus* held the manor in
1242.

Down Fm and Piend were probably the homes of Walter *atter
Doune* (1333 *SR*) and Henry *atte Pynde* (1330 *SR*). *v.* Piend
supra 151.

Hollyford is *Holleford* 1333 *SR* (p). Probably 'ford in the
hollow.' Rookbeare is *Rokebere* 1274 *FF*, 1333 *SR* (p). 'Rook
wood,' *v.* bearu. Cf. Rockbeare *infra* 594.

Stockleigh Pomeroy

STOCKLEIGH POMEROY 128 G 8

> *Estocheleia* 1086 DB (Exon), *Stochelie* (Exch), *Stochelega*
> 1187 P, *Stokkelegh*' 1242 Fees 764
> *Stokelegh Pomeray* 1261 Exon

v. the preceding parish name. Henry de *Lapumrai* or de *la
Pumerai* held the manor in 1200 (Cur).

Strangaton (6″) is *Strangedone* 1293 Fees 1315, *Stranhedon*
1330, *Stranedon* 1333 *SR* (p). The adj. *strang*, 'strong,' can
hardly have been applied to a hill and it is probable that we have
to do with a pers. name *Stranga*. The weak adj. *stranga* may have
been used as a pers. name of the nickname type, cf. the well-
attested and early OE *Stronglic*, *Stranglic* in which the adj. in
fuller form is used as a pers. name. We may note that the adj.
tūnlic, i.e. 'rustic,' was similarly used in early days.

Coombe, Lake (6″), Wallen Barton (6″) and Lower Westwood were the homes of Radulphus de *la Cumb*' (1293 Fees
1315), Roger de *la Lake* (ib.), John de *la Walle* (ib.) and Peter
atte Wallen, i.e. 'at the walls' (1330 *SR*), cf. *supra* 130, and Henry
de *Westewode* (1293 Fees). *v.* cumb, lacu.

Upton Hellions

UPTON HELLIONS 128 G 7

Uppetone Hyliun 1270 Exon, (*Hylon(e)*) 1385, 1416 Exon, *Upton Hellyng* 1557 Wills.

v. tun. 'Up' may have reference to the place being further up stream than Crediton. For 'Hellions,' *v.* Creedy *infra*.

LOWER CREEDY

þære gyrde be cridian 1018 Crawf 4
Cridia, Creda 1086 DB, *Cridie* 1242 Fees 791, *Crye* 1242 Fees 790
Crydihelyhun 1242 Fees 762, *Cridrehellyun* 1244 FF, *Hylioun Cridia* 1303 FA
Crydie Wiger 1270 Exon, *Cridie Peyteveyn* 1305 Ipm

v. Creedy river *supra* 4, the first phrase describing a *yard* or *virga* of land on that river. In 1242 (Fees) one manor was held by Robert *le Peytevin* (i.e. of Poitou) and the other, probably the later Upton *supra*, by William de *Helihun*, a Breton name. The former manor had passed to the *Wiger* family by 1282 (Ch).

HASKE is *Hassok'* 1242 Fees 774, 1244 FF, 1302 *Ass*, (*juxta Criditon*) 1311 *Ass*, -*ek* 1244 *Ass*, -*ak* 1303 FA. OE *hassuc*, 'coarse grass,' cf. Hassocks (PN Sx 276). Cf. further Hask Barn *infra* 430, and *Hassokes*, a Northamptonshire field-name (1251 *Forest Pleas*).

MERRIFIELD is *Merifeld* 1333 *SR* (p). *v.* Merrivale *supra* 242.

Washfield

WASHFIELD 128 C 10

Wasfelta, -fella 1086 DB, *Wasfeld(e)* 1166 P, 1283 Exon, 1291 Tax, (*Magna*) 1317 *Ass*
Wassefeld 1242 Fees 762, (*Parva*) 1242 Fees 761, *Was(s)h-felde* 1316 FA, 1342 Exon, *Wayshfelde* 1329, 1354 Exon, *Wasshe-* 1351 *Ass*, *Waysche-* 1409–16 Exon
Wesfelde 1265 Exon, *Westfeld* 1283–7 Exon

OE *wæsc-feld*, 'open land by the low-lying marshland,' *v.* (ge)wæsc. The place stands high but there is flat marshy land in the Exe valley below.

ENNERLEIGH

> *Hinewelleſt* 1249 *Ass, Inwollesleghe juxta Tuvertone* 1306 *FF*
> *Innewrdeslegh* 1280 *Ass, Inwardesle* 1330 *SR* (p), *Ingwardes-*
> *legh* 1346 *FF, Inwardlegh* 1413 *Ass, Inwardly* 1626 *Recov*
> *Endwardeslegh* 1310 *Ass*

v. leah. The exact form of the pers. name is difficult to determine. Blomé suggests (107) that we have the same Anglo-
Scandinavian pers. name *Inwar* as in Inwardleigh *supra* 149.
OE *Inweald* or *Inweard* is also possible. *Inuald* is on record
in OE.

HATHERLAND is *Hederlond(e)* 1286 *Ass et freq* to 1394 *Ass,* (*juxta
Wasshefelde*) 1351 *Ass,* Hedir- 1356 *Ass. v.* Hatherleigh *supra*
142.

HUTSWELL is *Hutteshull* 1244 *Ass,* 1289 *Ass,* -*tis*- 1346 *FF,*
Hotteshulle 1311 *Ass* (p), *Hodishille* 1333 *SR* (p), *Hodeshele* 1394
Ass (p), *Hoddeshill* t. Ed 4 *Ct, Hutswell* 1613 *Recov.* It is difficult
to know whether the pers. name involved is *Hutt* or *Hudd*. For
Hutt as a pers. name, *v.* Upbury (PN BedsHu 161).

PILEMOOR is *Pylemor(e)* 1249, 1305 *Ass, Pyla*- 1345 *Ass,* 1358
IpmR, *Pila*- 1347 *FF.* It is impossible to be sure here whether
we have as a first element the gen. pl. of OE *pīl,* 'stake,' or an
OE pers. name *Pīla* (cf. Pilmoor PN NRY 23). If the former is
correct, the name would mean presumably 'swampy land indicated or marked off by stakes.' That *pīl* was used in place-names
is clear from Pile Hill (Sr), *atte Pile* 1332 *SR,* (Berks) *Pyle* 1477
AD v, from various surnames *atte Pyle* from the Subsidy Rolls
of Dorset, Wilts and Hants, and the place-names *la Pile* and
Pylelonde 13th (*Canonsleigh*).

RAMSTORLAND (6″) is *Remmest(e)urte* 1351 *Ass* (p), 1394 *Ass,*
Remsterte t. Ed 4 *Ct, Rampsterland* 1726 *Recov.* Probably
'*Hræfn*'s steort.' There is a spur of land just south-west of the
farm. The *e*-forms show that we have to do with *Hræfn* rather
than **ramm**.

WINDBOW is *Wonbogh* 1242 Fees 764, *Wenbogh* 1244 FF, 1333
SR (p), *Wonebowe* 1464 *FF, Northwonebowe* t. Ed 4 *Ct, South-*
wyndbowe 1489 *Ct.* Probably 'at the crooked curve,' *v.* woh and

s.n. Bowden *supra* 37. The *e* in some of the early spellings is probably a clerical error for *o* as is often the case in 13th cent. records. The land is much broken here.

WORTH HO is *Wrda* 1086 DB (Exon), *Worde* (Exch), *La Worth(e)* 1242 Fees 762, 1281 *Ass*, *Worthy* 1303, *Wirthe* 1316 FA, *la, atte Werthe* 1311 *Ass*, 1333 *SR* (p). *v.* worþ.

PITT[1] and SLADE[2] (6″) were the homes of Philip *atte Pytte* (1333 *SR*) and John *atte Slade* (1330 *SR*). *v.* pytt, slæd.

BADCOT (6″) is *Baddecote* 1238 *Ass* (p), *Baddescote, Baddycote, Esterebadecote* 1270 *Ass.* ' *Badda*'s cot(e).' COURTNEY is probably identical with *Corton in Waysshefyld* 1504 Ipm. It was then held by one William *Courteney*, whence probably the modern form. DRYHILL is so spelt 1606 *FF*. EMMERFORD (6″) is so spelt 1546 *Rental*. HAYDON is *Heddon(e)* 1310 *Ass* (p), 1310, 1346 *FF*, 1613 *Recov.* Possibly 'heath hill,' cf. Heddon *supra* 42. KERRIDGE COPSE (6″) is *Keaurigge* 1333 *SR* (p), 1351 *Ass* (p), *Kewerygge* 1464 *FF*. MOORHAYES is *Morheghes* 1330 *SR* (p), *Morehay* 1464 *FF*, *Moorehayes* 1620 *Recov. v.* mor, (ge)hæg. PARKHOUSE (6″) is *Pkhous* t. Ed 4 *Ct*. SELWELL is *Selewille* 1316 Exon, 1330, 1333 *SR* (all p). Possibly a compound of sele and wielle, 'spring by the hall.' STANTERTON is *Stantorr(e)* 1330, 1333 *SR* (p), *Stantern* t. Ed 4 *Ct*. Cf. Stantor *infra* 516. For the later *ton, v. infra* 676. WEBLAND is *Webbelond* 1330 *SR* (p). Possibly 'the weaver's land.'

XIX. WONFORD HUNDRED

Wenfort 1084 Geld Roll
Wunford 1131, 1167, 1187 P, 1249 *Ass*, *Wnford* 1184 P, *Wonford* 1238 *Ass*, *Wom-* 1244 *Ass*, 1275 RH, *Wone-* 1278 *Ass*
Wundeford 1168 P
Winford 1175, 1176 P, *Wynforde* 1320 Ipm, *Wymford* 1303 *Ass*, *Wineford* 1179 P

v. Wonford *infra* 441.

---

[1] *Pitte* 1587 *Deed.*   [2] *Slade* 1464 *FF.*

Alphington

ALPHINGTON 138 B 9

(*an*) *Alfintune, hundred of Alfinī* 1050–73 Earle 258
Alfinton(a) 1086 DB *et passim* to 1307 *Ass* with variant spellings
-*yn*-, *Alph*-, (*juxta Cuwyk*) 1298 *Ass*, *Alphington* 1269 FF
et passim with variant spellings *Alf*-, -*yng*-, (*juxta Exon*)
1307 *FF*
Alfinctona 1231 Bracton, -*toune* 1281 Totnes
Ealvinton 1245 HMC iv, 67
Affynton 1577 Saxton, *Affington* c. 1630 Pole, *Affin(g)ton*,
Avington 1675 Ogilby

'*Ælfa's* farm,' *v.* ingtun. Nothing further is known of the
'hundred' of Alphington.

CLAPPERBROOK (6″) is *Clapper Brooke* 1743 *Recov. v.* Clapper
Bridge *supra* 359. CUTTERIDGE is *Cotterugg'* 1281 *Ass* (p),
Coterugg' 1330 *SR* (p). '*Cotta's* ridge.' EASTWOOD is *Eastwoode*
1589 *SR*. Self-explanatory. Near by is WESTWOOD. MARSH
BARTON is *in loco qui dicitur ad Mareis* 1142 (c. 1200) ANG,
Cella de Marisco 1263–73 BM, *la Mershe* 1306 *Ass* (p). There is
flat marshy land here by the Exe.

ALDENS FM (6″), BALL'S FM (6″), MARK'S FM, SOBEY'S FM (6″)
and WEBBY'S FM are probably to be associated with the families
of Charles *Alden* (1704 Wills), John and William *Bolle* (1228 FF),
William *Markes* (1628 Wills), Stephen *Sobey* (1749 Wills) and
Samuel *Webby* (1790 Wills).

Brampford Speke

BRAMPFORD SPEKE 128 J 9

Branfort, Branfortuna, Brenfort 1086 DB (Exon), *Brenford*
(Exch)
Branford, -*fort* c. 1170 *St Nicholas, Branford'* 1242 Fees 773,
1249 *Ass*
Bramford 1194 P, *Bramford Spec* 1275 RH, 1285 FA, *Bram-*
ford Pyn 1285 FA, *Speke Bramford* 1282 Pat
Braunford(e) 1242 Fees 785, 1269 Exon, 1292 Ipm, (*Pyn*) 1303
FA, (*Speke*) 1318 Exon, 1326 Ipm
Braunford Pyn et Braunford Speek 1316 FA

This is probably a compound of OE **brame** and **ford**, hence 'ford by the bramble,' with early dissimilation of *mf* to *nf*. The manor was held by Richard de *Espec* c. 1170. In 1242 (Fees) one manor was held by the same family and another by Herbert de *Pynu*.

BERRYWELL COPSE (6″) is *Berrywill* 1782 *Recov*. PONSFORD (6″) is *Ponsfords* 1782 *Recov*, deriving probably from the family of Robert *Ponsforde* (1620 ParReg). WOODROW is *Lower Woodrow* 1782 *Recov* and was the home of Walter *de Bosco* (1230 P), and John *atte Wode* (1333 *SR*).

Bridford

BRIDFORD 138 C 6

> (*of*) *Bridaford*(*es gildscipe*) 1072–1103 Earle 265, *Brideford*(*a*)
>   1086 DB *et freq* to 1438 Exon
> *Brudeford* 1253 Ch
> *Bridford* 1285 Pat
> *Bredeforde* 1399 Exon

'Ford of the young birds' (OE *brid*(*d*)*a ford*), i.e. frequented by such, or, perhaps more probably, 'brides' ford' (OE *brȳdaford*). Cf. Breadwick and Maidenford *supra* 49, 26, and Bridwell *infra* 537, for names of the latter type and the difficulty of interpreting them precisely.

LAPLOYD BARTON [læpləd] is *Lappeflode* 1275 RH (p) *et freq* to 1333 *SR* (p), *Lapflote* 1409 Exon. For the first element, *v. s.n.* Lapland *supra* 300. The second is **flod**. There is a small stream here, now dammed up to form a reservoir.

SMITHACOTT is *Smythenecote* 1286 *Ass et freq* to 1420 *FF*, *Smythecote* 1461 IpmR. The first element is probably a late OE genitive plural of OE *smiðð*, 'smith,' hence, 'cottages of the smiths.'

HOLE, STONE, THORN (6″), VENN and WOODLANDS were probably the homes of Richard de *la Hole* (1281 *Ass*), Thomas de *Stone* (1524 *SR*), Robert de *la Thorne* (1281 *Ass*), William *atte Fenne* (1333 *SR*), and Richard de *la Wodelonde* (1281 *Ass*). *v.* **holh**, **stan**.

ASHBURY HILL (6″) is *Ayshbery hyll* 1584 *Deed*. *v.* **burh**. BEACON DOWN (6″) is *Downe* or *Beaken Downe* 1754 *Recov*. BIRCH (6″) is

Byrche in Brydeford 1482 *Deed.* BURNICOMBE is *Burnacombe* 1748 *Recov.* CLAPPERMARSH (6″) is *Clapper marsh* 1748 *Recov.* There is a bridge over the Teign here. *v.* Clapper Bridge *supra* 359. COPPLESTONE (6″) [koulstən] is *Colputston* 1333 *SR* (p). There is a rock here, but the first part of the name is uncertain. DIDWORTHY (6″) is *Didworthy in Bridford* 1598 *Deeds Enrolled, Dudworthy* or *Dydworthy* or *Diddory* 1754 *Recov.* FURZELAND is *la Furslaund* 1244 *Ass* (p). HEATH (6″) is *Heath* 1748 *Recov.* HELTOR is *Heltor* 1612 *FF. v.* torr. NEADON is *Bynethedoune* 1294 *Ass.* 'Beneath the down.' POOK'S COTTAGES (6″) are to be associated with the family of Martin *Pook* (1582 *SR*). POOLE (6″) is *Pooleland* 1712 *Recov.* SHIPPING (6″) is *Shyppen* 1584, *Shepen* 1588 *Deed.* OE *scipen,* 'shippon, cow-shed.' SWANAFORD (6″) is *Sweynaford* 1584 *Deed.* TRENCHFORD is *Trenchford* t. Eliz ChancP 2. WEEKE BARTON is *Weke* 1543, *Wyke* 1568 *Deed. v.* wic. WESTCOTT is *Wescote infra parochia de Brydforde* 1562 *FF.* 'West cot(e).' It is at the west end of the parish.

Chagford

CHAGFORD [tʃægfəd, tʃægivɔrd] 138 C 2/3

Cagefort, Kagefort 1086 DB (Exon), *Chageford* (Exch), *Kageford* 1238 *Ass, Chaggesford* 1184 P

Chageford(e) 1196 AC *et freq* to 1429 Exon, *Chaggeford(ia)* 1234 Bracton, 1261 Exon, 1281, 1319 *Ass,* 1447 Exon, *Jageford* n.d. AD vi

Chaghhford 1275 RH, 1285 FA, *Chaghford* 1297 Pat

Chakeford 1315 Exon

Geaggeford 1363 Black Prince

Chegford 1675 Ogilby

The use of the element *chag-* from an OE *ceacge,* the source of *chag,* a dialect word for broom or gorse, found in OE only in place-name compounds, is fully discussed in PN Sx 296 *s.n.* Chailey. It is found also in Chasty *supra* 147 and Jackmoor *infra* 456.

DREWSTON is *Thurwardeston* 1281 *Ass* (p), *Throwardeston* 1333 *SR* (p), *Throuston* t. Hy 6 *Ct, Throwston* 1466–83 ECP i, 365 (p), *Threwstone* 1639 *Recov, Trueston al. Dreweston al. Thurstone* 1670 *Recov.* 'Thurweard's farm,' *v.* tun. This is a late tun formation. There was a Thomas *Thorward* in the parish in 1333 (*SR*). It was probably named from an earlier member of his family. The modern form has perhaps been influenced by that of the neighbouring Drewsteignton *infra* 431.

FRENCHBEER is *Fryncepisbere* 1346 *Ass* (p), *Freinschebeare* 1504–15 ECP 4, 217. *v.* bearu. The first element is probably the name of a late medieval owner. Cf. John *Frencheyppe* (i.e. friendship) taxed under Meavy parish in 1525 (*SR*).

HOLY STREET HO is *Holesterte* 1219 *Ass*, -*sturt*(*e*) 1311 *Ass*, c. 1450 *Ct* (all p). *v.* holh, steort. There is a tail of land here in the hollow where the North and South Teign rivers join.

JURSTON [dʒesən] is *Jordaneston* 1238, 1244 *Ass*, *Jurdaneston'* 1242 Fees 786, (*juxta Northbovy*) 1314 *Ass*, *Jurdeston* 1443 *Ct*, *Jesson* 1765 D. '*Jordan*'s farm,' *v.* tun. This pers. name is of continental origin, but is found in the county already a. 1100 (Earle 260). Cf. Jordanston (Pembrokeshire), *Jordanestoun* 1325 Ipm.

KING'S OVEN (6″) is *furnum Regis* 1240 *Peramb*, Buckfast, *Kinges Oven* 1608 Dartmoor. The name refers to an ancient 'blowing house' for tin-smelting which stood here.

MIDDLECOTT is *Midelcota* 1086 DB, *Middelcote* 1238 *Ass* (p), *Myddel-* 1446 *FF*. *v.* cot(e).

RUSHFORD BARTON is *Risfort* 1086 DB, -*ford* 1242 Fees 785, *Rissheford* 1292 *Ass*, *Russhe-* 1504 Ipm. Self-explanatory.

SHAPLEY is *Escapeleia* 1086 DB (Exon), *Scapelie* (Exch), *Sepeł* 1216 ClR, *Shapelegh* 1228 Cl, *Schaplegh* 1248 Ipm. 'Sheep leah.'

SOUTH HILL is *Stouthill* 1484 *DuCo*, 1491 Dartmoor, *Southill* 1556 *DuCo*. The modern form appears to be corrupt. For the first element, *v.* Brimps *supra* 192.

STINIEL and the adjacent STINHALL (6″) are *Stenenhalle* c. 1224, *Stenehall* c. 1280 DA 25, *Stenhall* 1613 *Recov*. 'The stone hall' from the OE adj. stǣnen and heall.

TEIGNCOMBE is *Taincoma* 1086 DB, *Tengecome* 1303 FA, *Teyngcomb* 1326 Ipm, *Tyncomb* 1326 Cl, *Tinckham* 1787 *Recov*. It seems to be identical with the manor known as *South Teign* in early records (*Suthteng* 1301 Ipm, etc.). *v.* cumb. For the River Teign, *v. supra* 14.

GREATWEEK is *Wyk*(*e*) 1244 *Ass* (p), 1301 Ipm, 1432 Exon, *Brodewyk juxta Chageford* t. Ed 3 *Ass*, *Wyke Southtenge* 1342 Ch, *Greate Weeke* 1635 *FF*. *v.* wic. For 'broad' in the sense of 'great,' cf. Broad Clyst and Broadhempston *infra* 573, 509. Cf. also Great Rissington (Gl), *Braderisendon* 1220 Fees, *Risendune Magna* c. 1075 Dugdale iii, 284, 289.

YARDWORTHY is *Iadeworde* 1244 *Ass*, *Yadeworth* 1340, 1347 *SR* (all p), *Yedeworthy* 1443 *Ct*, *Yadworthy* 1664 *Recov*, *Yadrey* 1675 Ogilby. '*Ēada*'s worþig.'

NORTH and SOUTH HILL (6″), HOLE, THORN, VENN and YEO were probably the homes of John de *la Hulle* (1249 *Ass*), William *atte Hole* (1340 *SR*), Robert *atte Thorne* (1333 *SR*), Stephen de *la Fenne* (1249 *Ass*), and Walter *atte Yo*, i.e. 'at the water' (1333 *SR*), *v. supra* 17–18. *v.* holh, fenn.

BATWORTHY is *Badworthy* 1411 Dartmoor, *Badeworth*(*y*) 1412 *Ct*, t. Hy 6 *Ct*, *Badworthy al. Battery* 1696 *Recov*. '*Bada*'s worðig.' BUDA (6″) is *Boghewode* 1330 *SR* (p). 'Bow-shaped wood,' *v. supra* 37. CHAGFORD COMMON is *Meanamoore al. Comon Moore* 1738 *FF*. *v. s.n.* Manadon *supra* 246. COLLIHOLE is *Colehall*(*e*) 1330 *SR* (p), 1417 *Ct*. *v.* Collacott *supra* 50. The second element is probably heall. COOMBE is *Combe* 1390 DA 25. *v.* cumb. CORNDON is *Corndoune* 1289 *Ass* (p), *Westcorundon juxta Chaggeford* 1319 *Ass*. *v.* Corringdon *supra* 290. CROSSPARK (6″) is *Crospark* 1613 *Recov*. CULLATON (6″) is *Coletone* 1390 DA 25, *Colerewe al. Collaton* 1584 *Deed*. *v.* Collacott *supra* 50. DOGMARSH is *Dogmerssh* 1380 Pat. DOWNPARK (6″) is *Duneparke* 1542 *Deed*. *v.* pearroc. EASTON is *Shutt al. Eston* 1578 *Ct*. 'East farm,' *v.* tun. It lies east of Chagford. For the alternative name, *v.* Shute *supra* 184. GREATSTONE is *Greston* c. 1450 *Ct*. HORSELAKE is *Horslake* 1244 *Ass* (p), 1333 *SR* (p). 'Horse streamlet,' *v.* lacu. HURSTON is *Hurteston* 1340 *SR* (p), *Hurstonridge* 1731 *FF*. Either 'farm of the hart' or '*Heort*'s tun,' taking *Heort* to be a pers. name. LAKELAND (6″) is *Lakelond, Lackelond* 1578 *Ct*, *Lake al. Lakeland* 1613 *Recov*. *v.* lacu. LANGAFORD BRIDGE (6″)

is *Langforde* 1505 Ipm. 'Long ford.' MELDON HILL is *Milledone* 1393, *Middeldone* 1432 DA 25. 'Middle hill,' *v.* dun. METHERALL is *Meddelhull* 1327 DA 33, *Middel-* 1330 SR, *Midder-* 1333 SR (all p). 'Middle hill,' *v. supra* 175. NATTADON COMMON is *Nottedone* 1334 DA 25. 'Bare hill' or '*Hnotta's* hill,' *v. supra* 267. PADLEY COMMON is *Padeleghe* 1432 DA 25. '*Pada's* leah.' TEIGN MARSH (6″) is *Teingemarsh* 1696 Recov. WAYE is *Waye* 1435 DA 25, *Westway* 1504 Ipm. *v.* weg. WEDDICOTT is *Wade-cote* 1393 DA 25, 1423 IpmR, 1443 Ct (p). '*Wada's* cot(e).' WEEKBROOK COTTAGES (6″) and WEEK DOWN (6″) are *Weeke-brookes, Weekedowne* 1704 Recov. *v.* wic. WESTCOTT FM (6″) is *Westecote* 1334 DA 25. *v.* cot(e). WHITEABURY (6″) is *Whitebery* 1541 Deed, *Whittabery* 1642–9 ParlSurv. *v.* burh. WILLAND-HEAD (6″) is *Wyllenhed* 1443 Ct, *Wyllinghed* 1555 DuCo and was the home of Richard *atte Willenheade* 1333 SR. 'At the spring-head,' *v.* wielle. WITHECOMBE is *Wythicumb* 1287 Ass, *Wydecomb* 1340 SR (p), *Little Withecome* 1466–83 ECP i, 365, *Brodewethe-comb al. Great Wethecomb* 1562 Deed. *v* wiðig, cumb. For *broad* in the sense of *great,* cf. Broad Clyst *infra* 573. WOODTOWN (6″) is *Wode* 1435 DA 25. For *town,* v. *infra* 676.

Cheriton Bishop

CHERITON BISHOP 138 A 5

> *Ceritona* 1086 DB, *Cheriton(e)* 1270 Exon, *(Episcopi)* 1316 Lives, *(juxta Crokkernewell)* 1284 Ass
> *Churiton(e)* 1242 Fees 779 *et freq* to 1291 Tax, *Churyton Episcopi* 1396–1400 Exon, *Suth Churiton* 1310 Ass
> *Suthchiriton* 1314 Ass, *Chyryton* 1356 AD iv
> *Bishops Churyton* 1370 Pat, *Bisshopps Cheriton al. South Cheriton* 1675 Recov

'Church farm' *v.* cyric(e), tun, and cf. Cheriton Fitzpaine *supra* 414. One acre here was granted to the bishop of Exeter a. 1280 by Eleanor de Melewis (DA 34, 335). 'South' perhaps to distinguish from Cheriton Fitzpaine.

COXLAND is *Cockyslond* 1333 SR (p), *Cooksland* 1617 Recov and is probably to be associated with the family of Elena *Cok* (1333 SR).

CROCKERNWELL is *Crochewella* 1086 DB, *Crokkernewell* 1284 *Ass*, *-will* 1330 *SR* (p), *Crockernawitl juxta Druesteyngton* 1327 *Ass*, *Crokernewill* 1412 IpmR, *Crokkernwelle* 1491 Ipm. *v.* wielle. For the first part of the name, *v.* Crockern Tor *supra* 193. In early materials for the study of English roads such as the Gough map in the Bodleian, Crockernwell appears as a half-way house between Exeter and Okehampton and may well have been an important early settlement.

EASTON

> *Alvrikestone, Ailrichestone* 1157 RBE
> *Alricheston̄* 1158 P, 1242 Fees 779, *Alriggeston* 1275 RH, 1285 FA, *Alryscheston* 1346 FA
> *Ailricheston(a)* 1159, 1167 P, *-tun* 1212 Fees 98
> *Ayriston* 1356 AD iv, *Ayr(e)ston* c. 1450 Ct, 1524 *SR*
> *Easton oth. Eason* 1741 *Recov*

Probably '*Æþelrīc*'s farm,' though the first form suggests '*Ælfric*'s,' *v.* tun. For loss of *r* before *s*, cf. Easdon *infra* 482.

EGGBEER

> *Eighebera* 1086 DB (Exon), *Eigebere* (Exch)
> *Eggebere* 1242 Fees 785, 1270 *Ass* (p), *-byare* 1310 Exon (p), *-beare* c. 1320 Exon (p), *Eggibere* 1279 *Ass*, *Lyteleggebeare* 1441 Pat
> *Eghbeare* 1275 RH, 1285 FA
> *Eggenebere* 1303 FA

'*Ecga*'s wood,' *v.* bearu.

GRENDON is *(on) grenan dune* 739 (11th) Crawf 1, *Grendon* 1244 *Ass* (p), *Grendonhaye* 1675 *Recov*. 'Green hill,' *v.* dun.

LAMBERT is *Lantfort, Lanforda* 1086 DB, *Parva Lampford'* 1242 Fees 788, *Lampford* 1491 Ipm, *Lamford* 1275 RH, 1285 FA, 1330 *SR* (p). 'Lamb-ford.' For *þ*, cf. Lampham (PN Sx 445) and *v.* Ekwall in StudNP 1, 103.

LEWDON is *Levedon* 1288 *Ass*, 1504 Ipm, *Lywedene* 1308 Seld 17, *Lyuedon* 1330 *SR* (p), *Luwedon* 1378 IpmR. *v.* dun. This name probably has the same history as Lewdon *supra* 396, the farm lying just below a hill-top. Cf. also Libbery (PN Wo 201).

MEDLAND MANOR is *Mideland(a)* 1086 DB, 1228 FF, *Middelond* 1268 FF, 1275 RH, 1330 *SR* (p). 'Middle land.'

MOUNSON is *Muntesdon* 1302 *Ass*, *Montesdone* 1313 Exon, *Mountesdon* 1330 *SR* (all p). No OE pers. name *Munt* is on record, but the name can hardly be a compound of OE *munt*, 'hill, mountain,' and dun, for 'hill of the hill' is impossible as a place-name. The name may well be of ME origin and contain a ME surname, cf. Mounticombe *supra* 376 and Mountsland *infra* 478.

NATSON is *Gnattesdon* 1330 *SR* (p). This could mean 'hill of the gnat' (*v*. dun), but more likely the first element is a pers. name *Gnæt*, derived from the insect, cf. Gnatington (Nf), *Gnatinctone*, *Gnatingtona* 1101–19 (14th), *Gnatingetone* 12th BM, and Knettishall (Sf), *Ghenetessala* DB, *Gnateshale* 1190 P[1]. The surname *Gnatte* occurs in Wiltshire in 1333 (*SR*).

TILLERTON is *Tilledene*, *Tyliadon* 1287 *Ass*, *Tilidon* 1330 *SR* (p). Perhaps '*Til(l)a*'s hill,' *v*. dun. For *Tylia* we may perhaps compare the surname *Tylia* found in the Subsidy Roll for 1330, which is presumably a variant of *Tilla*. *v*. Introd. xxxiv.

TREABLE FM [tribəl]

> *Tryfebel* 1242 Fees 779, *Triffebel(e)* 1327 *Ass*, 1356 AD iv
> *Triffabel* 1275 RH, 1285, 1346 FA, *Tryfabell* 1425 IpmR
> *Trefelebeale* 1303 FA, *Treffebele* 1333 *SR* (p), 1499 Ipm
> *Truffebele* 1327 DA 33 (p), *-eble* 1329 *Ass* (p)
> *Trebell* 1412 IpmR, *Trebell al. Trifebell* 1561 *FF*

This name is probably Celtic, the first element being the Cornish *tre(v)*, 'homestead, village.' Professor Ekwall suggests that the second element may be a pers. name *Ebell* corresponding to the Gaulish *Epillus*.

WILSON is *Wolgareston* 1242 Fees 779, *Wolgereston* 1275 RH, 1285 FA, (*Cheriton cum*) 1428 FA, *Wolgerston* 1330 *SR* (p), *Wylgeriston* 1356 AD iv. '*Wulfgār*'s farm,' *v*. tun.

WEST BEER, CROSS (6″), FORD PARK (6″) and HOLE were probably the homes of Isabella *atte Beare* (1330 *SR*), William *atte Crosse* (ib.), Richard Dyer *atte Forde* (ib.), and John *atte Hole* (ib.). *v*. bearu, holh.

[1] *Ex inf*. Dr O. K. Schram.

BOWDEN is *Bogheton* 1333 *SR* (p), *Bowdon* 1620 *Recov. v.* Bowden *supra* 37. GORWYN is *Gorefenne* 1288 *Ass, Gorfenne* 1322 *Ass* (p), *Gorven al. Gorwin* 1696 *Deed.* 'Muddy fen,' *v.* gor, fenn and Introd. xxxiv. HALF ACRE (6″) is *Halfacre* 1620 *Recov.* HASK BARN (6″) is *Haske* t. Hy 6 IpmR and was the home of Robert *atte Haske* (1333 *SR*). Cf. Haske *supra* 419. HAYLAKE is *Heilake* 1275 RH, 1284 FA, *Hay-* 1423 IpmR. 'Streamlet by the enclosure,' *v.* (ge)hæg, lacu. HONEYFORD is *Honyworthi* 1330 *SR* (p). 'Honey farm,' *v.* worþig and cf. Butterberry *supra* 232. MEAD-WELL PLANTATION (6″) is *Medwill* 1249 *Ass.* 'Meadow spring,' *v.* wielle. MILLBALL COPSE (6″) is *Milball* 1664 *Recov.* For 'ball,' *v. supra* 211. PARTRIDGE (6″) is *Parkerugg, Pearkerugge* 1330 *SR* (p), *Parkerygge* t. Hy 6 IpmR. 'Hill marked by enclosures,' *v.* pearroc, hrycg. PITTON is *Pyteton* 1311 *Ass* (p), *Pitteton* 1314 *Ass.* 'Farm in the hollow,' *v.* tun. SPIRELAKE is *Spirlake* 1576 Wills. Possibly 'rush streamlet,' *v.* lacu and cf. Spirewell *supra* 261. STADDON is *Steddon* (sic) 1275 RH, *Stoddon* 1285 FA, 1330 *SR* (p). *v.* stod, dun. THORNE is *Thorn juxta Suth Churiton* 1310 *Ass.* WOODBROOKE is *Wodebrok* 1244 *Ass*, 1330 *SR* (p). WOODLEIGH is *Wodelegh* 1311 *Ass. v.* leah.

Christow

CHRISTOW 138 D 6/7

> *Cristinestowe* 1244 *Ass*, 1258, 1259–80 Exon, *-tein-* 1244 Fees 1386, *-ten-* 1269 Exon, 1275 RH, 1285 FA, 1291 Tax, *Cristenestou* 1259–80 Exon, *-sstouwe* 1285 FA
> *Cristowe* 1361 *Ass, Crystowe* 1535 VE, *Christow al. Christen-stow* 1618 *Deed*

The church is not dedicated to St *Christina* and we have no evidence for her cult in England, so we are probably right in taking the name as derived from OE *crīstene-stow*, 'place hallowed by Christian associations,' cf. Halstow *supra* 313.

BENNAH is to be associated with John *atte Bydene* (1333 *SR*), *atter Bydene* (1346 *Ass*). For the interpretation, *v.* Bidna *supra* 102. Bennah lies at the head of a deep valley.

CANONTEIGN HO is *Teigna* 1086 DB, *Tigneam* c. 1125 France, *Kanone Teyng* 1276 RH, *Teygne Canonicorum* 1281 *Ass.* For the river Teign, *v. supra* 14. The manor was granted to the canons of the monastery of St Mary du Val (c. 1125 France).

CLAMPITT is *La Clampitte* 1219 FF, *la Clampette* 1281 *Ass*, *atte Clampytte* 1333 *SR* (p). 'Muddy pit or hollow,' the first element being OE *clām*, 'mud, clay,' still surviving in Devon and Somerset dialectal *cloam*. Cf. Clampitt in Linkinhorne (Co), *Clompitte* 1358 FF.

KENNICK is *Kaynek, Kaynok* 1294 *Ass* (p), *Kennok* 1504 Ipm. This is probably an old stream-name, the root being identical with W *cain*, 'clear, bright, fair.' For the second element *-oc*, *v.* Ekwall RN lxxviii.

ALLER (6″), COMBE, SHUTTAMOOR, WAYE DOWN (6″)[1], and WOOD COTTAGES (6″), were probably the homes of William de *Alre* (1333 *SR*), Cecil fil. Walter de *Cumbe* (1244 *Ass*), Nicholas *atte Shute* (1333 *SR*), John Potter *att Wey* (1582 *SR*), and John *atte Wode* (1333 *SR*). *v.* alor, cumb, dun, and Shute *supra* 184, 417.

BARNE (6″) is *Barne* 1458 *FF*. BOWDEN is *Bogheton* 1333 *SR* (p). 'Farm in the bow or curve,' *v.* Bowden *supra* 37. PALE FM (6″) is *Pale* 1571 *SR*. SOUTHWOOD is *Southewode iuxta Tengebrigge* 1289 *Ass*.

Drewsteignton

DREWSTEIGNTON [-teintən] 138 B 4

> *Taintona* 1086 DB, *Teintun* 1235 BM, *-ton* 1238 *Ass*, *Teynton* 1244 FF
>
> *Teyngton Drue* 1275 RH, *Druesteynton* t. Ed 1 BM, *Druesteyngton* 1327 *Ass*, *Driuisteynton* 1342 Pat, *Drewstenton* 1623 Wills

'Farm on the river Teign' (*supra* 14), *v.* tun. *Drogo* (i.e. *Drew*) is first mentioned in connexion with the place in 1210 (RBE).

LOWER BUDBROOK (6″) is *Boggebrok* 1285 FA, 1318 Ipm, 1330 *SR* (p), (*juxta Druesteyngton*) 1327 *Ass*, *Boghebrok* 1311 Fine. This place is in the neighbourhood of *bucgan ford* (Crawf 1) and probably both the ford and the brook took their names from the

---

[1] *Wey* 1546 *SR*.

same person, named *Bucge* (f) or *Bucga* (m). Cf. Bognor (PN Sx 92).

COOMBE HALL is *Cuma* 1086 DB, *Combe-halle* 1384 Exon. *v.* cumb.

DRASCOMBE

> *Drosncumb* 739 (11th) Crawf 1, *Droscumb(e)* 1212 Fees 96, 1219 FF, Fees 264, 1274 Ipm
> *Troscumba* 1167 P
> *Drascumb* 1250 Fees 1188, *Druscombe* (sic) 1275 RH

v. cumb. The first element is OE *drosn*, 'dregs, sediment, dirt, etc.,' hence 'dirty valley.'

FINGLE, EAST and WEST (6″) (and FINGLE BRIDGE) are *Fenghyl* 1317 *Ass* (p), *Feynghel* 1330 *SR* (p), *West Fangle* 1610 *FF*, *Fingle Bridge* 1765 D. They lie along a stream and we have the same stream-name which is found in *on fengel* (BCS 724) in the land boundaries of Culmstock *infra* 612. The name is clearly English as is shown by the initial *f*. It must be a derivative of the stem *fang*, 'to hold, catch,' found in OE *fengel*, 'prince,' but its application to a stream is obscure. It might perhaps be used of a stream where there was good prospect of a catch.

FURSHAM is *Fierseham* 1086 DB, *Fursham* 1244 FF, *Forsham* 1275 RH, *Frusham* 1327 *Ass* (p). 'Furse ham(m).'

HAREPATH is *herepað* 739 (11th) Crawf 1, *Herpath(e)* 1330, 1333 *SR* (p). *v.* herepæð. The road here is the main road from Exeter to Launceston.

MARTIN is *Merton(a)* 1086 DB, 1332 *FF* (p), *Marton* 1582 *SR* (p), *Martenpark* t. Jas 1 ECP 138. Probably 'boundary farm,' *v.* (ge)mære, tun. It lies near the parish boundary. Cf. Martin (Ha), *Merton* 946 (14th) BCS 817, *Mereton* 1227 Ch, on the borders of Hants and Wilts.

PARFORD is *Paþford* 739 (11th) Crawf 1, *Patford(a)* 1086 DB, 1249 *Ass* (p), *Pafford'* 1242 Fees 769. *v.* pæþ, ford.

REDLAKE (6″) is *Attarredelake juxta Teynton* 1314 *Ass*, *Rede-*, *Rade-*, *Rydelake* 1322 *Ass*, *Ride-*, *Redelake* 1326 Orig. 'At the red streamlet,' *v.* lacu. The soil here is reddish.

SHILSTONE

Selvestan 1086 DB, 1238 *Ass* (p)
Silvestane 1242 Fees 788, *Shilveston* 1249 *Ass* (p), *Schilveston*
1303 FA
Shilston 1262 Ipm

v. scylf, stan. This must refer to the famous cromlech near by
called the Spinster's Rock. The first element in this name is
OE *scylf*, 'shelf, ledge, floor, story,' referring to the flat stone
lying on top. The probability is therefore that the compound
scylfestan denoted a cromlech in OE, though at the five other
places in the county where the p.n. occurs there are now no
remains of such.

THORNBURY is *Torneberia* 1086 DB, *Thornbyre* 1244 FF, -*bury*
1333 *SR* (p), 'burh by the thornbush.'

BURROUGH, FORD HO[1], NARRAWAY (6″), STONE FM, UNDERDOWN,
UPPERTON and VENTON were probably the homes of Walter *atte
Burgh* (1330 *SR*), Durling *atte Forde* (ib.), Nicholas *Bynorthe-
weye*, i.e. 'north of the way' (1333 *SR*), Robert de *la Stane* (1249
Ass), William *Underdoune*, i.e. 'below the down' (1296 *Ass*),
Richard *Uppeton* (1249 *Ass*), and Walter de *Fenton* (ib.). v. beorg,
uppe, tun, fenn.

BOWDEN is *Buledune* 1242 Fees 785, *Boledon* 1303 FA. 'Bull
hill,' v. dun. The name has been influenced by the numerous
Bowdens in the county. BROADMOOR HO is *Brodemore* 1589 *SR*.
CHAPPLE (6″) is *The Chapell Londe* 1502 ECP 4, 99. DREWSTON
HO is *Driweston* 1330 *SR* (p). 'Drew's farm,' v. tun. Presumably
this was the same man who gave name to the manor. FLOOD is
Flood 1589 *SR*, *Fludd* 1719 Recov. v. Fludda *infra* 471. FUR-
LONG is *Forlang* 1301 Ipm, *atte Furlong* 1329 *Ass* (p). GREAT
TREE FM (6″) is *Great-Worth al. Greatworthy* 1630 Westcote,
Greattree al. Greatworthy 1730 *Deed*. If this is a worðig name
we may compare the latest form of Trentworthy *supra* 134.
HOBHOUSE (6″) is *Hobbehouse* 1329 *Ass*, 1330 *SR* (both p).
Probably *Hobb(e)* was its medieval owner. NATTONHOLE is *Notte-
knoll* 1358, *Notnoll* 1537 *Deed*. Probably a compound of OE
hnot, 'bare, bald,' and cnoll, v. Noddon *supra* 267. PIDDLEDOWN

[1] *Ford* 1589 *SR*.

is *Piddledon* 1662 *FF*. PRESTON is *Prusteton* 1270 *Ass* (p), 1330 *SR* (p), *Prestone* 1275 RH (p). 'Priests' farm,' *v.* preost, tun. PUDDICOMBE HO is *Podecomb(e)* 1322 *Ass*, 1326 Orig (both p). '*Podda*'s valley,' *v.* cumb. TOR DOWN is *Tarrdowne* 1730 *Recov. v.* torr. For the *a*-spelling, *v.* Introd. xxxiii. WALLON is *la Walle* 1249 *Ass* (p), *Walle juxta Teynton Dru* 1310 *Ass*, *atte Wallen* 1333 *SR* (p). 'The wall(s),' cf. Pitten *supra* 263. WINSCOMBE is *Wynscombe* 1580 DA 31. Probably '*Wine*'s cumb.' WISEDÒM FM (6″) is *Wisdoms* 1464 Pat.

Dunsford

DUNSFORD 138 B 6

> *Dunnesforda, Dunesforda* 1086 DB, *Dunesford* 1238 *Ass et freq* to 1290 Pat
> *Dunisford'* 1237 Fees 612
> *Donesford(e)* 1259, 1261 Exon, 1275 RH, *Dounesford* 1275 RH

'*Dunn*'s ford' (over the Teign).

BIGPORT is *Bicport* 1175 P (p), *Bykeport* 1330 *SR* (p). '*Bicca*'s port,' though the application of the term 'port' is difficult, cf. Doggaport *supra* 95.

CLIFFORD BARTON is *Clifort, Cliforda* 1086 DB, *Clyfford* 1274 *FF* (p), 1292 Ipm, *Clyfford Corbyn* 1491 Ipm. *v.* clif. There is a steep descent here to the Teign valley. Members of the *Corbin* family are found as jurors of Wonford Hundred in the 13th cent. Assize Rolls.

GREAT FULFORD is *Folefort* 1086 DB (Exon), -*ford* (Exch), *Fuleford* 1242 Fees 785, *Fole-* 1275 RH, 1402 Exon. 'Dirty ford,' *v.* ful.

SOUTH HALSTOW is *Halestou* 1086 DB (Exon), *Alestou* (Exch), *Halestowe* 1244, 1249 *Ass, Halstowe* 1277 *Ass*, 1286 *SR, Halftouwe* (sic) 1285 FA, *Yalstowe* 1346 FA. It is doubtful if this name can mean 'holy stow,' as one would have expected to find some early spellings with medial *gh* or *w*, cf. Halstow (K), earlier *Halghsto, Halwestowe* and Halstow *supra* 313. Hastoe in Tring (Herts) has early forms *Halstowe* (1275 *FF*, 1296 *SR*) and would seem to be a compound of heall and stow (cf. Cotstow). It may be that this Halstow has the same origin. The early spellings with medial *e* offer difficulties, but cf. Halsbury *supra* 104.

MIDWINTER COTTAGE (6″) is *Mid(de)wynter* 1499 Ipm and is to be associated with the family of John de *Midwinter* (1238 *Ass*). The etymology is obscure. So, similarly, Radwinter (Ess), DB *Redewintra*, 1166 RBE *Radewinter*.

RAMRIDGE may be identical with *hrēna hricge* 11th Earle 257. If so, the meaning is 'ravens' ridge,' *v.* hræfn.

SOWTON BARTON is *Suthton* 1244 *Ass*, *Sutheton* 1277 *Ass*, 1292 Ipm, *Southeton* 1276 Ipm, 1381 Exon, *Suthinton* 1277 Ipm, *Soudthton* 1286 *SR*. 'South farm,' *v.* tun.

BROOK, HOLELAND (6″), MOOR, TOWNSEND (6″) and SOUTH ZEAL were probably the homes of Robert *atte Brok* (1333 *SR*), William *atte Hole* (1330 *SR*), Robert *atte More* (ib.), Mazelina *atte Touneshende* (13th *Canonsleigh*), and William *atte Sele* (1330 *SR*). *v.* holh, mor, sele.

FARRANTS and SCUTSHILL appear as *Ferantes* t. Hy 6 IpmR, *Brooke al. Scuttishill* t. Eliz ChancP 1 and are probably to be associated with the families of Alexander *Feraunt* (1333 *SR*) and Adam *Scut* (1377 *FF*).

BERRY BARTON is *la Byry* 13th *Canonsleigh*. BOYLAND is *Boylaunde* 1315 Exon, *-lond(e)* 1329 *Ass*, 1330 *SR* (all p). *v.* Bystock *infra* 600. BURNWELL is *Brunewell* 1244 *Ass*, *Broune-* 1275 RH (p), *Brun-* 1277 *Ass*, *Brone-* 1286 *Ass* (p), *Brounewille* 1325 *Ass*. 'Brown spring,' *v.* wielle. COLLABRIDGE is *Colebrugg'* 1330 *SR* (p). *v.* Collacott *supra* 50. CORRIDGE is *Colrugg'* 1330 *SR* (p). 'Charcoal ridge,' cf. Coleridge *supra* 227. COTLEY is *Cottelegh(e)* 1296, 1334 *Ass*. *v.* Cotleigh *infra* 625. GOATLAKE is *Gotelake* c. 1400 Exon (p). 'Goat streamlet,' *v.* lacu. HORRIDGE BARN (6″) is *Horigg(e)* 1249 *Ass* (p), 1275 RH. Probably 'dirty ridge,' *v.* horh. LANGLEY is *Langgelegh* 1316 FA. 'Long clearing,' *v.* leah. LENDON is *Lyndene* 1333 *SR* (p). 'Limetree valley' or 'flax-valley,' *v.* lind, lin, denu. LISTONDOWN BARN (6″) is *Lustenesdon* 1461 IpmR. Possibly 'Lustwine's down.' MEADHAY is *Medhay(e)* 1291 Tax, 1399 IpmR. 'Meadow (ge)hæg.' OWLHOLE (6″) is *Houleholle* 1281 *Ass* (p), *Oulehole* 1420 FF, *Owelhole* 1461 IpmR.

'Owl hollow,' *v.* holh. SMALLAKE (6″) is *Smalelake* 1238 *Ass* (p), *Smallake* 1374 *Ass.* 'Narrow streamlet,' *v.* smæl, lacu. STOR-RIDGE is *Storugge, Stonrigge* 1281 *Ass* (p). Probably 'stone ridge.' WARNSCOMBE (6″) is *Wermiscombe* 1330 *SR* (p), *Warmescombe* 1394 *Ass* (p). The first element may be a pers. name such as *Wærmōd.* WESTCOMBE was the home of Henry de *Westecomb* (1333 *SR*). This is probably for earlier *Bywestecomb,* 'west of the valley,' *v.* Introd. xxxvii. WHIDLEY HO (6″) is *Withelegh* 1289 *Ass, Wetelegh* 1330 *SR* (both p). Probably 'withy clearing,' *v.* leah.

Exeter St Davids[1]

ST DAVIDS, ST DAVIDS HILL

> (*super*) *montem S. Dauid* 1247 *St Nicholas,* 1436 DA 14, *Seynt Davys Doune* 1494 Ipm
> *capellarum Sancti Davidis...* 1270 Exon, *capella Sancti David* 1457 HMC iv, 85
> *parish of Seynt David without Northgaytt* 1538 HMC Exeter 304

DURYARD [deriəd]

> *Derard* 1146 *St Nicholas, Dereyerd* 1270 *Ass*
> *Dorerd* 1186–91 Oliver
> *Durhard* a. 1225 *St Johns, Duryerd* 1442, *Dureyourd* 1449 Deed, *Dureyerde, Duerierde* 1493 Ipm

'Animal enclosure,' *v.* deor, geard. Cf. Derriads, PN Wilts 69.

HOOPERN HO is *Hoperneslande* a. 1225 *St Johns, Hopernewode* 1462 Pat, (*la*) *Hoperne* 1535 VE, 1540 LP. The name may possibly describe an ærn or house where barrel-hoops were made. Cf. Potterne, Colerne (W) and Crockern Tor *supra* 193 for similar compounds of ærn.

BARTON PLACE is *Le Bertynhouse, Le Bertynplace* c. 1510 HMC Exeter. *v.* beretun. STREATHAM HALL is a modern house (*ex inf.* Mrs Rose-Troup).

[1] For the street-names of Exeter and for the name of the city itself, *v. supra* 20 ff.

Exeter St Leonards

St Leonards

parochia Scī Leonardi ext^a Exon 1289 *Ass, capella Sancti Leonardi* 1291 Tax, *Seyntleonardisdoune* 1501 Ipm

EXE ISLAND (6″) is *Northexhilond* 1295 Exon, *Exeylonde* 1351 *Ass,* 1355 DCo NQ 5, 174, *Exiland al. Westyate* 1479 IpmR. An island in the river Exe. LARKBEARE (6″) is *Leverkebeare* 13th HMC Exeter (p), *Lerkebeare juxta Exon'* 1321 *Ass.* 'Lark wood,' *v.* bearu. MOUNT RADFORD (6″) is *Mountradford* 1602 Moulton and is probably to be associated with the family of Nicholas *Radford*, recorder of Exeter in the 15th cent. (HMC Exeter.)

Exeter St Sidwells

St Sidwells

Sidefullan hiwisc 1050–73 Earle
parochia Sanctae Satavole in Exon 1199 FF, *Sanctı* (sic) *Sativole* 1269, *Sancte Sativole* t. Edw 1 Exon
St Sedewell 1434, *Seynt Sidewill fee* 1461 Pat, *Seynt Sidewelfe* 1441 *FF*

This parish takes its name from the virgin Saint *Sidefulle*, said to have been buried near Exeter[1]. Her name was probably a significant coinage from OE *sidu*, 'morality,' and *full*, hence 'virtuous one.' *f* was voiced to *v* and then by later popular etymology the final element of the name became *well*. (The change may have been largely phonetic, *v.* Introd. xxxv.) The *hiwisc* of the first reference (the *fee* of the later ones) probably denoted a piece of land dedicated to the service of the saint.

Exeter St Thomas

St Thomas 138 B 9

Kapellis...Sancti Thome 1209–15 HMC iv, 63, *ecclesia Sancti Thome* 1366 Exon, *parochia Sci Thomae ultra pontem Exon* 1562 *FF, Saynt Thomas Churche* 16th Oliver 104

In early documents the parish is more usually referred to by the name of Cowick, *v. infra* 438.

---

[1] *þonne resteþ sancta Sidefulla fæmne wiðutan Exanceastre* (c. 1000 Saints).

COWICK BARTON

(*on*) *cuic lande*, (*on*) *Cuike*, (*at*) *Cuicu* (sic) c. 1100 Earle, *Cuwic*
1235 Fees 561
Coic 1086 DB, *Cuic* c. 1140 BM, 1150–9 NGl 4, 27, *Cuick*
c. 1270 Gerv
Couwyk(*e*) 1269 Exon, 1284 *Ass*, *Couwykstrete* 1295 Ipm
Cowek 1283 *Ass*, *Cowyck* 1283 Exon

'Cow farm,' *v.* cu, wic. Cf. Quickbury (Ess), *Cuica* DB, *Cowik*
1234, *Cuwik* 1240 FF and Bulwick (Nth) *Bulewic* 1162 P, *-wich*
1166, 1184 P.

EXWICK is *Essoic* 1086 DB, *Exewyk*(*e*) 1244 Fees 1386, 1244 *Ass*,
1291 Tax. 'wic by the river Exe.'

HAYES (6″) is *La Hacghe* 1242 Fees 785, *Haghen* 1269 FF, *la
Hachen* 1275 RH, *la Heghen* 1291 Tax, 1322 Exon, *Heghen juxta
Exon*' 1301 *Ass*, *Heghes* 1291 Tax, 1355 BM, *The Heghes juxta
Couwyk* 1339 *Ass*, *Hegges* 1389 Exon. *v.* Hayne *supra* 129. This
name offers a good example of the interchange of the strong and
weak plural forms in ME.

HAMLYNS and PARKER'S HILL (both 6″) are to be associated with
the families of Thomas and John *Hamlyn* (1524, 1582 *SR*) and
Edmund *Parker* (1582 *SR*).

BARLEY HO is *Bereley* 1298 *Ass* (p), *Berlegh*(*e*) 1314 *Ass* (p), 1325
Lives, *Barlegh* 1504 Ipm. 'Barley clearing,' *v.* bere, leah. BOW-
HILL (6″) is *Bogehull* 1249 *Ass* (p), *Bouehill* 1312 FF. 'Curved
hill,' *v. supra* 37. HACCOMBE is *Haccombe Downs* c. 1576 HMC
Exeter. RED HILLS is *Red Hill* in 1765 D and is perhaps identical
with the spot called *la Rededowne* 1264 NGl 5, 45. The name
refers to the red soil here.

Gidleigh

GIDLEIGH 138 C 2

Geddelegæ 1158 RBE, *Gedelega* 1158, 1169 P
Giddeleia 1167 P *et freq* to 1324 Exon with variant spellings
Gydde- and *-legh*(*e*), *Giddeley al. Giddelith* 1270 Ipm
Gudeleghe 1284 Exon, *Guddeleg*(*h*) c. 1200 (15th) *Torre* (p),
1330 *FF*

'*Gydda*'s clearing,' *v.* leah. This pers. name is not on record but is apparently found in *gyddan dene* BCS 789 and in Gidding (Hu) (PN in *-ing* 88). Cf. also Gidcott *supra* 153.

CREABER is *Creubergh* 1238 *Ass*, *-burgh* 1330 *SR*, *Crewebergh* 1244 *Ass*, *-ber'* 1275 RH (all p), *Crewburgh* 1481 *Ct*. 'Crow hill,' *v.* beorg and Introd. xxxiii.

ENSWORTHY is *Avenysworthi* 1330 *SR*, *Avenesworth* 1340 *SR* (both p), *Answorthy* t. Hy 8 *FF*. The first element is doubtful. It may be the British pers. name *Afan* (Iolo MSS), *Avan* (NSB).

THULE (6″) is *Thuell* 1609 *FF*, and was the home of Henry de *la Thivele* (1249 *Ass*) and Richard *atte Thyvele* (1340 *SR*). This is the OE *þýfel*, 'tuft, clump,' cf. Rixdale *infra* 488.

BERRYDOWN, GREENAWAY (6″) and MOORTOWN were probably the homes of Simon de *Beridon* (1333 *SR*), Ralph de *Greneweyesfote*, i.e. 'green way's foot' (1244 *Ass*), and John *atte More* (1333 *SR*). The last is *Moretown* in 1536 (DA 33). *v.* burh, dun, mor. For *town*, *v. infra* 676.

Heavitree

HEAVITREE[1] 138 A 10

> *Hevetrowa* 1086 DB (Exon), *-trove* (Exch)
> (*on*) *Hefatriwe* c. 1130 Earle 259
> *Eueltrea* 1179 P, *Heveltre* 1286 Cl
> *Hevetre* 1242 Fees 791, 1280 Exon, 1303 FA, 1306 *FF*, *-trewe* 1284 *Deed*, 1314 Ipm, *-truwe* 1285 FA, 1314 Ipm, *-tru* 1286 *Ass*, 1308 Exon, 1346 FA
> *Hevedtre* 1270 Exon
> *Hevytre* 1345 Ipm, 1387 Exon, (*juxta Exon*) 1453 *FF*

This is a difficult name. If any stress is to be laid on the second form one should perhaps compare *hefancroft* (KCD 608) and note the late Devon pers. name John *Hevya* (1333 *SR*), inflexional *n* being commonly lost in the document in which the Anglo-Saxon form of Heavitree is found. Hence, '*Hefa*'s tree.' Alternatively we may perhaps take the name to be from OE *hēafod-trēow*, with a trace of the *d* surviving in late forms with *l* and *d*. If that is correct, the name may be interpreted in the same way as *hēafod-stocc* (BT Supplt *s.v.*), viz. a tree on which

---

[1] Now a suburb of Exeter.

the heads of criminals were placed. This is confirmed when we find that the gallows stood here once at Livery Dole *infra* (Oliver, *Ecclesiastical Antiquities* i, 46 n).

LIVERY DOLE (not on O.S.)

> *Luveredole* c. 1270 NGl 3, 122, 1276 NGl 5, 81
> *Lyverydole* 1465 NGl 3, 147, *Lyverdoll* 1531 HMC Exeter
> *Leverydole* 1519 NGl 3, 129, *Leweredole* n.d. HMC Exeter

The second element in this name is clearly OE dal, 'share of the common field.' The first element is perhaps the OE pers. name *Lēofhere*, the name of its one-time holder.

OLD MATFORD (6″) is *Madaworthi* 1245–57, *Madeworthy* 1280, 1348, 1352, *St Johns*[1], *Maydeworthy al. Madford* 1622 BM. '*Mada*'s farm,' cf. the same name *supra* 130. For the modern form *v.* Introd. xxxv. It may also have been influenced by the not far distant Matford in Exminster *infra* 496.

POLSLOE

> *Polesleuga, Polesleuia* 1086 DB (Exon), *Poleslewe* (Exch)
> *Polslewe* 1159 HMC iv, 49
> *Poleslawa* 1179, 1194 P, *Pollesslawe* 1238 *Ass*, Fees 1368
> *Poleslo* 1212 Fees 96, *Polslo* early Hy 3 BM, c. 1270 Gerv,
>   1274 Ipm, *Polslou* 1267 Exon, *Polsloghe* 1329 Exon
> *Polleshou* 1231 Pat

'*Poll*'s marsh,' *v.* Slew *supra* 28, with common confusion of the second element with hlaw, hlæw. This pers. name is apparently found also in Polesden and Pollingfold (Sr), *Pollesdene* 1279 QW, *Pollingfold* 1241 FF, and in Polesworth (PN Wa 95).

RINGWELL COTTAGES (6″) is *Ringeswille* 1269 FF, *Ryngeswelle* 1275 RH, *Ryngeswille Prodhomme* 1361 FF. '*Hring*'s spring,' *v.* wielle. John *Prodhome* held the manor in 1346 (FA).

ROLLESTONE (6″) is *Rokesdon near Hoperneland* 14th, *Rokysdon* 1389 St Johns, *Rolleston* or *Ruxton* c. 1550 Leland, *Ruxston* 1573 *Deeds Enrolled*. Either 'rook's down' or 'down of a man named *Hrōc*.' The modern form is clearly corrupt, having been influenced most likely by Rollstone in Upton Pyne *infra* 456, a few miles away.

---

[1] *Ex. inf.* Miss Lega-Weekes.

St James Church (6″) was on the site of the ancient monastery called *Jacobescherca* 1086 DB, *-circa* a. 1095, *-cyrca* a. 1122 *Exeter Book*[1].

Whipton is *Wipletona* 1086 DB, *Wippeton* 1341, *Whipeton* 1393 Lives, *Whippeton* 1461 Pat. The first element in this name is the pers. name *Wippa*, for which *v.* Whiphill (PN Sx 28). The DB form is probably an error. If correct, it points to a diminutive *Wipela*, with later loss of *l*.

Wonford

(*on*) *Wunforda* c. 1100 Earle 259, *Wnford* 1177 P, 1237 Fees
  612, *Wumford* 1249 *Ass*
Wenfort 1086 DB, *Winford* 1249 *Ass*
Wonford 1276 Ipm, *Wondeford* 1292 Pat, *Woneford* 1290 Ch,
(*juxta Exon*) 1305 *Ass*, *Wonfordspek*, *Wonford juxta Exon*
1370 *Ass*

Originally a stream-name, *v. supra* 10, *s.n.* Mincing Lake. *Spek* must refer to the (*E*)*spec* family, who held the not far-distant manor of Brampford *supra* 422.

Heath and Hill Bartons were the homes of Hugo *atte Hethe* and Hugo *atte Hille* (1333 *SR*). The former is *Hethdowne, Heath Close* (1616, 1694 *Deeds*).

Cholwell Cottages (6″) is *Chaldewelle* 1231–9 *Deed, Chalde-wellehay* c. 1305 HMC Exeter. 'Enclosure by the cold spring,' *v.* ceald, wielle, (ge)hæg. Mary Pole Head (6″) is *Marepoll* 1461 Pat. Probably 'boundary pool,' *v.* (ge)mære. It is on the parish boundary.

Hittisleigh

Hittisleigh 138 A 3

Hitenesleia 1086 DB, *Hittenessleghe* 1285 Exon
Hutteneslegh' 1238 *Ass et passim* to 1391 *FF, Utteneseghe* 1291
  Tax
Hettenysleghe 1351 Exon
Hyttyngeslegh 1433 Exon
Hitsley oth. Hittisleigh 1820 *Recov*

[1] *Ex inf.* Mrs Rose-Troup.

v. leah. Ekwall (*Studies* 9) points out that there is evidence for an OE pers. name *Hyht*. Cf. Hixon (St), *Huchtesdona* 1130 P, *Huyhtesdon* 1289 *Ass*, *Huttesdon* 1292 *Ass*. Cf. also *hihtesgehæg* (BCS 1106). *Hyhten* would be a regular *n*-derivative of this. Hence, '*Hyhten*'s leah.'

BEWSLEY is *Buueshele* 1321 *Ass* (p), 1333 *SR* (p). CREYFORD is *Creuford* 1333 *SR* (p). 'Crow ford,' *v.* Introd. xxxiii. DAVYLAND (6") is *Daviland al. Davidsland* 1719 *Recov*. *Davy* or *David* was probably its medieval owner. MIDLAKE (6") is *Medlak* 1238 *Ass*, *la Medlak*' 1242 Fees 774 (p), *Medelak* 1249 *Ass* (p). 'Meadow streamlet,' *v.* lacu. SWALLOWTREE is so spelt in 1765 D. TEIGN-HOLT (6") is *Teyngeholte* t. Ed 1 BM. *v.* holt. For the river Teign, *v. supra* 14. TRENNA (6") is *Trayne* 1727 *Recov*. WHITETHORN is *Whitethorn* or *Hittesley Mills* 1673 *Deed*.

Holcombe Burnell

HOLCOMBE BURNELL [houkəm] 138 B 7

> *Holecumba* 1086 DB *et freq* to 1370 IpmR with variant spellings -*comb*(*e*), -*cumb*(*e*)
> *Holecumbe Bernard* 1263–76 Exon, *Holecomb Burnell* 1370 IpmR, *Holcombe Bernard* 1440 IpmR

> *v.* holh, cumb. Ralph the son of *Bernard* held the manor in 1242 (Fees 779). The modern form is corrupt.

MATRIDGE is *Materugge* 1330 *SR* (p), -*rigge* 1333 *SR* (p), *Maderygge* 1493–1500 ECP 3, 497, *Madrigge* 1524 *SR*. '*Mætta*'s ridge,' *v.* hrycg and Martinhoe *supra* 65.

BILSDON is *Billesden* 1333 *SR* (p). '*Bil*'s valley,' *v.* denu. DOWN HO is *Downe* 1711, *Downhouse* 1713 *Recov*. FORD was the home of William *atte Forde* (1333 *SR*). KINGSFORD is *Kyngesford* 1270 *Ass* (p). This may be 'King's ford.' There is also a Kingswell *infra* 459, at the source of the stream on which Kingsford stands[1]. LONGDOWN is *Longdown End, Longdown Heath* 1675 Ogilby.

---

[1] In DB the manor of Holcombe belonged to Queen Matilda, having been in the possession of one Bristric TRE.

Huxham

HUXHAM 128 J 10

> *Hochessam* 1086 DB (Exon), *Hochesham* (Exch), *Hockesham*
> 1206 Montacute, 1255 Ipm, *Hokesham* 1212 Fees 96 *et freq*
> to 1316 Ipm, *Hoxam* 1234 Fees 396
> *Hoggesham* 1245 Ipm (p)
> *Hukkesham* 1265 Exon

> '*Hōc(c)*'s ham(m).'

BUSSELL'S FM is to be associated with the family of Thomas
Bussell (1680 Wills). RATSLOE is *Radeslo* 1244 *Ass* (p), 1249 FF,
la Radesslo 1287 *Ass*. 'At the red slough or miry place.' The
soil here is red.

Pinhoe

PINHOE ['pinhou] 138 A 11

> *Peonho* c. 1050 ASC *s.a.* 1001
> (*on*) *Pynnoc* c. 1120 Earle 259, *Pinnoc* 1086 DB
> *Pinho* 1216–27 *St Nicholas*, 1238 *Ass*, *Pynho* 1236 FF, 1269
> Exon, 1275 RH, 1307 Cl, 1324 Pat, *Pynhoo* 1344 Pat
> *Pynnow* 1390 Cl, *Pynn al. Pynnhooe* 1615 *Deed*

The form in the OE Chronicle suggests that this name is a
hybrid compound of the British word *pen*, 'head, top, end,' and
OE hoh, with a curious development of *pe(o)n* to *pin* otherwise
not paralleled. The final *c* is probably an AN spelling for *h*. The
relation to Pinhoe of Pinn Court and Pinwood (*v. infra* 444) and
Pinbrook in this parish is not clear. Pinn Court is right down in
the valley.

MONKERTON is *Monketon* 1420 *Ct*, *Mounkton* 1672 *Recov* and it
probably represents the virgate of land in Pinhoe held by the
monks of the abbey of Battle in 1086 (DB), cf. DA 44, 289. For
the medial *er*, *v.* Introd. xxxvi.

PILTON HO (6″) is *Pyle* 1370 *Ct*, *Pyleton* 1631 *Recov*, *Pulton* 1667
Recov, and was the home of Margery wid. Thomas *atte Pyle*
(1345 *Ass*). This is probably the OE word *pīl*, 'stake,' cf. Pilemoor *supra* 420, with later addition of *-ton*.

BLACKHORSE is so spelt in 1765 D. The hamlet takes its name from an inn so called. GOFFIN'S FM is probably to be associated with the *Coffin* family found in the neighbourhood in 1613 etc., (Wills). HARRINGTON FM is *Herrington* 1662 Polwhele 126, 1728 *Recov, Herriton* 1689, *Hereton* 1733 *Deed.* MILL LANE (6″), cf. *atte Mille* 1370 *Ct* (nom. loc.). PINN COURT is *Pynne* 1370 *Ct.* PINWOOD LANE (6″) is *Pynnewode, Pynnehowode* 1420 *Ct. v. supra* 443. REDHAYES is a modern house, built since 1890 (F. R.-T.). WOTTON COTTAGES (6″) is *Wotton* 1370 *Ct, Wottonmede* 1420 *Ct.* 'Farm by the wood,' *v.* wudu, tun.

Poltimore

POLTIMORE   128 J 11

> *Pontimora, Pultimora* 1086 DB
> *Pultemor(e)* 1219 *Ass et freq* to 1378 IpmR
> *Pultimor(e)* 1242 Fees 788, 1249, 1278, 1287 *Ass,* -ty- 1279 *Ass,* 1306 *FF*
> *Poltemor(e)* 1244 *Ass, Poltimor(e)* 1263 Ipm (p), 1275 RH, 1278 *Ass,* 1284 Misc, 1291 Tax, *Poltymar* 1314 Misc, *Polty-moor* 1408 *Ass*
> *Pyltemor(e)* 1275 Cl (p)
> *Poultemor* 1355 Exon, *Polton moor* 1675 Ogilby

The first element in this name would seem to be identical with that found in Poultney (Lei), DB *Pontenei*, 1292 Ch *Pultenei*, but the interpretation must remain doubtful. *v.* Addenda, Part ii, xiii.

BAMPFYLDE LODGE is *Benefeld* 1306 *Ass, Baumfeld* 1317 *Ass, Baun-* 1330 *SR*, 1346 *Ass, Ban-* 1346 FA (all p), *Baunfelde* 1432 *FF.* The second element is clearly feld. The first is probably bean.

CUTTON is *Cutetone, Cotetone* 1260 Exon, *Coteton* 1275 RH, 1285 FA, *Cotiton* 1341 Ipm. 'Cotta's farm,' *v.* tun. This *Cotta* may be the Olmer *cota*, who had a holding in Poltimore in DB (307 b). MOORLANE COTTAGES (6″), cf. *La More* 1270, 1278 *Ass. v.* mor.

Rewe

REWE 128 H 10

Reuwa 1086 DB

Rewe 1242 Fees 773 *et passim*, (*juxta Stok Canonicorum*) 1288 *Ass*, (*juxta Sulferton*) 1289 *Ass, Rewes* 1252–71 Ipm, 1279 Exon, *Rew oth. Row* 1750 *Recov*

v. ræw. The village extends along the main road for some way and the parish borders on Stoke Canon.

RUDWAY is *Radewei* 1086 DB, *la Redewei* 1238 *Ass* (p). 'Red road,' *v.* read, weg. The soil here is the deep red characteristic of this part of Devon.

UP EXE [ʌbəks] is *Olpessa* 1086 DB (Exon), *Ulpesse* (Exch), *Uphexe* 1238 *Ass*, *Uppe Esse* 1242 Fees 773, *Upexe juxta Rewe* 1346 *Ass*. It lies farther up the river than Nether Exe *infra* 566.

CARPENTER'S FM is to be associated with the family of Humfrey *Carpenter* (1624 Wills). There was a John *Carpenter* in Pinhoe in 1420 (*Ct*). HEAZILLE BARTON is *Hesele* 1270 *Ass*, *Hesel* 1326 Ipm. 'At the hazel.' LATCHMOOR GREEN (6″) is *Lechmore Green* 1739 *FF*. Cf. Lashbrook *supra* 132, and Letchmore Heath (Herts), *Lachemeresheth* 1321 *Ass*. MILLHAYES (6″), cf. John *atte Mulle* 1330 *SR*.

Sowton

SOWTON 138 A 11

Clis 1086 DB

Clist Fomicon 1242 Fees 779, *Clistfomyson* 13th Exon, *Clyst Fomecon, Fomechun* 1278 Exon, *Clist Fomizoun* 1299 Ipm *Southton* 1420 *Ct*, *Clyst S'ci Mich'is al. Sowton* 1535 VE

This was one of the numerous places named from its position by the river Clyst *supra* 3. It was distinguished by the name of the family of *Fomicum* (*Fomyson, Fomizoun*) first found in the parish in 1242 (Fees 779). The later name 'south farm' has reference perhaps to Monkerton to the north. Cf. Sowton *supra* 435. *St Michael* from the dedication of the church.

MOOR is *la More* c. 1280 Exon, *More* 1500 Ipm, *Moure al. Ryggedon* 1542 NGl 4, 169. *v.* mor. VENN FM (6″), cf. *la Fennbrigg'* 1420 *Ct*. *v.* fenn.

Spreyton

SPREYTON 128 J 2

> *Espreitona* 1086 DB (Exon), *Spreitone* (Exch), *Spreyton(e)*
> 1234 Fees 399, 1269 Exon, 1286 *Ass*, 1291 Tax, *Spreiton*
> 1238 *Ass*, 1242 Fees 785
> *Espretoñ'* 1169 P (p), *Spreton(e)* 1216 ClR, 1238 *Ass*, 1316
> Ipm
> *Sprayton* 1346 FA, 1355 Pat, 1377 *SR*, 1420 *Ass*
> 'Farm in the brushwood land,' *v.* tun, cf. Sprytown *supra* 208.

FALKEDON is *Falketon* 1270 *Ass*, 1378 IpmR. *v.* tun. The first element is probably identical with that of Faulkbourne (Ess), *Falcheburna* DB, *Falkeburn(a)* 1253 Ch and Falkenham (PN Sf 52). These names all point to the possibility of an OE *fealca*, presumably denoting the falcon. Skeat (*loc. cit.*) calls attention to the form *Fealcnaham* for Fawkham (K) in BCS 1132, i.e. 'homestead of (or frequented by) falcons,' cf. Birdham (PN Sx 80). If this is correct, light is thrown on the ultimate etymology of the word 'falcon.' OE *fealca*, OHG *falcho* and the Langobardic personal name *Falco* would all point to the ultimate Germanic origin of the bird-name[1].

HOLLYCOMBE is *on hurran cumbes heafod* 739 (11th) Crawf 1, *Hurracombe* 1615 FF. Possibly 'Hurra's valley,' *v.* cumb. *Hurra* is not on record but would be a regular pet form for OE *Hūn-rǣd*.

NORTH BEER is *Northbeere* 1683 Recov. *v.* bearu. BEGBEER is *Bykebeare* 1310 *Ass*, 1330, 1333 *SR* (p), *Bygbeare* 1484 DA 34. '*Bicca's* wood,' *v.* bearu and Abbots Bickington *supra* 124. BOWBEER is *Bobeare* 1518–29 ECP 5, 312. COMBE was the home of Alexander *atte Combe* 1333 *SR*. CROFT is *la Crofte juxta Spreyton* 1292 *Ass. v.* croft. DOWNHAYS is *Downe in Sprayton* 1504–15 ECP 4, 197. *v.* dun and Hayne *supra* 129. FUIDGE

---

[1] Since this was written Ekwall (*Studies* 23–4) has noted the p.n. *fealcnes ford* (BCS 576), suggesting a pers. name *Fealcen*, and the name *Uestorualcna*, *Westerfalc(n)a* in the Northumbrian genealogies. He suggests therefore that in Fawkham (K) we may have an OE pers. name *Fealcna*, with characteristic Kentish loss of inflexional genitival *n*. This probably does not affect the etymology of Falkedon or Faulkbourne. He points out, however, that Falkenham (Sf) is *Faltenham* in DB, 1291 Tax and 1331 BM. Forms with *c* and *k* are probably errors.

[fjuˑdʒ] is *La Fowych* 1289 *Ass*, *Fuge* or *Fuydge* or *Fuidge* 1767 *Recov. v.* Fuge *supra* 316. HEATH is *Hethe* 1517 *Recov.* NETHER-COTT is *Nethercote* t. Hy 8 *Star Chamber.* 'Lower cot(e).' RUG-ROAD is *Ruggerode* 1491 Ipm. This may be '*Hrucga*'s clearing,' *v.* rod and cf. Ruckham *supra* 380. ST CHERRIES is a corruption of *Sanctuary* (*-ies*)[1], cf. Centry *supra* 305. SPREYTONWOOD is *Sprayholt Wood* 1708 *Recov. v.* holt. WEEK is *Northewyk by Spreyton* 1327 Banco. *v.* wic. WOODHOUSE is *Woodhouse* 1709 *Recov.*

Stoke Canon

STOKE CANON[2] 128 J 10

Hrócastoc 938 BCS 723, *æt Stoctune* c. 970 BCS 1244, *æt Stoce* c. 1060 Earle, *Stocha* 1086 DB, *Stoke Canonicorum* 1281, 1288 *Ass*, *Stoke Canon* 1535 VE

The earlier name meant 'the rooks' stoc(c).' In 938 the manor was granted by Athelstan to Exeter monastery, whence the later name. Cf. Canonteign *supra* 430 and Canonbury (Mx).

---

[1] *Ex inf.* the late incumbent, the Rev. E. V. Freeman, from church records.

[2] The boundaries of the Stoke Canon charter are difficult to follow. The *sulford* is perhaps the ford on the Exe at the north-west corner of the parish. Thence it goes along the *herpoð* to the Culm. The present boundary here follows Green Lane, a continuation of the road which is called *herpoð* in the Crediton charter *supra* 402 n. No mention is made of the departure from that road, which takes the boundary round the south end of Rewe parish to the Culm. From the Culm the boundary goes due east to the 'long ford' and then south along a stream to *culum lace*. The stream is the backwater which here unites the two arms of the Culm. The boundary goes along it and then down the eastern arm of the Culm. From the *lacu* it goes up to the old *dic* and along the ditch to *ceaggan cumb* and thence to the king's *sloh* or marsh, when we have once more reached a *weg* or road. This must carry us round the western projection of Huxham parish. The bounds then go along the *weg* to an unidentified *mægenstan* and south to the junction of two roads, i.e. the crossroads by Drew's Clieve (6″). Thence along the 'northmost ridge-way' (the road down to Exeter) till it reaches the ridge, whence it follows the 'ridge' of high ground to the *eorð burh*, clearly the camp now marked on Stoke Hill, thence past the *brydena wyll*, 'brides' well,' possibly the spring near Chamber Copse (6″), to the Exe. Thence up the Exe to *scræwan leages lace*, probably the stream which comes down from *Lake* Bridge to the Exe. The land is then said to include *scræwan leage*, possibly the strip of land on the west side of the Exe which is here included in Stoke Canon. The next point is *æðelstanes hammes ford*. The ford cannot be identified but the hamm is almost certainly the hamm of land formed here by the great bend in the Exe. We finally come back to *sulford*. We cannot identify the four acres west of Exe which lay opposite *edferðes eald land*.

BRIDGE FM (6″) was the home of Hugo de *Ponte* (1301 Exon). BURROW FM was the home of Walter de *la Burghe* (ib.) and Walter *atte Burgh* (1330 *SR*). 'At the hill,' *v.* beorg. The farm may take its name from the long low range to the east. burh is also possible. OAKHAY BARTON is *Okehaye* 1630 *FF. v.* (ge)hæg. STOKE WOODS is *Stokewode* 1322 Exon.

South Tawton

SOUTH TAWTON 138 A 1

Tauetona 1086 DB. It is first called South (*Suth-*) in 1212 (Fees 980) to distinguish it from North Tawton *supra* 370. Further forms are without interest except *Suthtaunton* 1256 Pat, 1310 Cl, which may, however, be for *Tauuton*. 'Farm on the Taw river' (*supra* 14), *v.* tun.

ADDISCOTT

> *Ædrichescota* 1166 P, *-iscote* 1172 P, *Edrichescote* 1168 P, 1417 IpmR, *Aderichescote* 1212 Fees 98
> *Aielrischescote...in parochia de Sustautoñ* 1199 ChR, *Haylrichescote* 1210 RBE, *Eilrichescot'* 1228 Cl, *Aylrichecot* 1230 P
> *Atherigescote* 1238 *Ass*, *Atherscote* 1287 *Ass* (p)
> *Idrichescote* 1340 *SR*
> *Arscott al. Addiscott* 1658 DA 37

'*Æþelrīc*'s cot(e).'

ALLISON is *Allingeston* 1199, c. 1203 DA 33, *-don* 1249 *Ass*, *Alyngston al. Allersdon* 1558 DA 33. '*Ælling*'s farm,' *v.* tun. *Ælling* would be a patronymic derivative of OE *Ælla*.

EAST ASH is *Aissa* 1086 DB and was the home of Isaak de *Esshe* 1249 *Ass*.

CAWSAND BEACON (kɔsdən, kɔˑzən) is *the Hoga of Cossdoune* 1240 (15th) Dartmoor, *Costendoune* 1240 Buckfast, *Cosdon al. Cosson* 1608 Dartmoor, *Cawson-hill* 1797 Polwhele. There is not much to go upon here. We have perhaps as the first element a pers. name *Cost(a)* found also in Costessy (Nf), DB *Costeseia*, Cosford (Sa), *Costesford* BCS 22, and in a diminutive form in *Costices myln* (BCS 1076). Cf. OGer *Costica*, *Costilo* (Förstemann, PN 384). Hence, '*Cost(a)*'s hill.' *hoga* is a Latinised form of OE hoh.

COCKTREE is *Caketreu* 1248 FF, *-trewe* 1279 Ipm, *Kaketrewe* 1285 Ipm, *Kockestrewe* 1281 *Ass*, *Coketrewe* 1303 FA, *-trouwe* 1331 Ipm. Possibly '*Cac(c)a*'s tree,' cf. Cakeham PN Sx 88, but the vowel is difficult. Perhaps folk-etymology has affected this name.

DISHCOMBE is *Disserescumb* 1289 *Ass* (p), *Dys(s)heliscomb* 1333 *SR* (p), *Disshelliscombe* 1336 *Ass*, *-elys-* 1340 *SR* (p). '*Dīcel*'s valley,' *v.* cumb. For the pers. name, cf. Ditchling PN Sx 300.

ITTON is *Hedeton* 1244 *Ass* (p) *ȝydeton* c. 1262, *Yedeton* 1526 DA 33, 34, *Yetton* 1475 Pat. '*Geddi*'s farm,' *v.* tun.

JUSTMENT is *Agismont* (sic) *in parochia de Southtawton* 1713 Recov. *Justment, gistment*, 'piece of land of which the pasture or grazing is let,' is still a dialect word in D, *v.* NED *s.v.* Properly it is a Norman-French legal term, and more than one example of it is found in Devon farm-names. *v.* Introd. xxvii.

LIVATON is *Levi(n)tona* 1168 DA 35, *Estleueton* 1330 *SR* (p), *Lyveton* 1340 *SR* (p), *Levyton* 1546 *SR*. '*Lēofa*'s farm,' *v.* tun.

LOVATON is *Loueton* 1309, *Luffeton* 1327 DA 33, *Luffeton* 1330 *SR* (p). The first element is identical with that of Luffenham (R), *Lufenham* 1086 DB, *Suthluffenham* 1284 Ch, Luffenhall (Herts), *Luffenhale* c. 940 BCS 737, *Luffehale, Luvehale* 1181 St Pauls DB, *Luffenhale* 1243 *FF*, and Lowick (Nth), *Lofwyc* 12th Survey, *Luffewich* 1166 P, *-wyk* 1242 Fees. Cf. also Luffland *supra* 157, and the pers. name de *Loffegrave* (1327 *SR* Berks). All point to a pers. name *Luffa*.

NYMPH, EAST and WEST (6″) is *Nymet* c. 1262 DA 33, 1281 *Ass* (p), *Est Nympte* c. 1509, *East, West Nympe* c. 1570 DA 33. *Nymet* was originally the name of the river Yeo, near which the farms are situated. *v. supra* 348.

POWLESLAND is *Polesland, Polleslande* 1244 *Ass*, *Polislond* 1333 *SR* (p). '*Pol(l)*'s land.' Cf. Polsloe *supra* 440. 'Land of (or by) the pool' (*v.* pol) is also possible here, as the land is marshy.

SCARHILL CROSS may be associated with John de *Scoriawell* (1333 *SR*) and Robert de *Storiawall* (1337 DA 33). Cf. Roger *Scori* found in the parish in 1263 (DA 33). *v.* Addenda, Part ii, xiii.

SESSLAND is *Serichesland'* 1238 *Ass*, *Sercheslond(e)* 1330 *SR*, 1327 Banco (all p), *Sherselond* 1540 *Deeds Enrolled*, *Searsland* 1594 *Recov*, *Sesland al. Seresland* 1674 *Recov*. '*Sǣrīc's* land.' The name *Seric* occurs in DB as holder of Baccamoor manor in Plympton (TRE).

SPITLAR CROSS is *la Spitele* 1289 *Ass*, *atte Spitele* 1330 *SR* (both p), *Spitla* 1730 *Deed*, suggesting that an ancient hospital or leper house may have once existed here. For the final *r*, *v*. Introd. xxxv.

TRUNDLEBEER is *Trendelbere* 1249, 1336 *Ass*, *-biare* 1313 Exon (p), *-beare* 1342 Exon (p). The first element in this name is OE *trendel*, 'circle,' the second is **bearu** and the name probably refers to the small circular hill here.

WEEK, WYKE is *Wicha* 1158 P, *Wike* 1212 Fees 98, 1238 *Ass* (p), *Nordwyk* 1244 *Ass* (p), *Northwyk* 1333 *SR* (p), *Midleswyk* 1287 *Ass* (p), *Middelwyk* 1289 *Ass* (p), *Meddelwek* 1527 DA 37, *Este Weke* 1527 DA 37. *v.* **wic**. The present-day spellings of the farm-names are East, Middle and West *Week*, but North *Wyke*.

WICKINGTON is *Wykyndone* c. 1262, *Wykenton* 1509, *Wyckington* 1580 DA 34, *Wyggenton* 1581 DA 33, 34, *Wekington* 1618 *FF*. This may, as suggested by Professor Ekwall, be from OE *wicc(e)na-dun*, 'hill of the witches,' with *cc* remaining stopped before following *n*.

SOUTH ZEAL is *(la) Sele* 1167 P (p), 1302 Cl, 1316 Ipm, *Zele Tony* 1299 Ch, *Sele juxta Stikelepathe* 1322 *Ass*, *(juxta Troulegh)* 1345 *Ass*, *Southsele* 1544 DA 34. *v.* **sele**. Constancia de *Tony* held the manor of South Tawton in 1212 (Fees 98).

FORD (6″), THORN, WELL[1], and WOOD HO were the homes of Roger de *la Forde* (1289 *Ass*), William *atte Thorne* (1333 *SR*), Richard *atte Wille* (ib.), Roscelin de *Bosco* (1238 *Ass*) and Richard *atte Wode* (1333 *SR*).

BLACK STREET (6″) is *Blakenestrete* 1340 *SR* (p), *Blackestreate* 1595 DA 37. COLLYBEER is *Colebere* 1175 P (p), 1244 *Ass*. *v.* **bearu** and Collacott *supra* 50. COURSEBEER is *Curtesbere* 1299 *Ass*, *Cortesbear'* 1330 *SR* (both p). *v.* **bearu**. The first element

---

[1] *Wyll* 1546 *SR*.

is the pers. name *Curt* discussed under Curtisknowle *supra* 300.
CRAYDON is *Croydon* 1625 *Recov.* CULLAFORD is *Colleford* 1333
SR (p). '*Col(l)a*'s ford.' FROG MILL (6″) is *Frog mill, Froggymill*
t. Eliz DA 33. GOOSEFORD is *Goseford* 1249, 1254 *Ass* (p).
HENDICOTT is *ʒondecote* c. 1262 DA 34, *Yundecote* 1330 *SR*
(both p). 'The far cottages,' from their position in the parish,
v. cote and Youngcott *supra* 216. HOLLAND BARN (6″) is *Howland*
1661 *Recov. v.* holh. There is a slight hollow here. LANGDOWN
is *Langedon* 1249 *Ass* (p). 'Long hill,' *v.* dun. OLDITCH (6″) was
the home of Geoffrey *de Veteri fossato* 1263 DA 33, *de la Yolle-
deche* 1289 *Ass.* 'The old ditch.' There was a boundary ditch
of Dartmoor Forest here (*ex inf.* Miss Lega-Weekes). OXENHAM
is *Oxeneham* 1330 *SR* (p). *v.* ham(m). RAMSLEY is *Ramselay al.
Ramscliffe* 1683 *Recov. v.* clif. There is a steep slope here. TAW
GREEN is *Tawegreene* 1635 *Recov* and was probably the home of
William de *Tau* (1238 *Ass*). For the river-name, *v. supra* 14.
TORHILL is *Torhill* 1661 *Recov* and was probably the home of
Richard *atte Torre* (1333 *SR*). WHIDDON DOWN is *Whyddon
Doune* 1565 DA 33, *Whiddon Downe* 1661 *Recov.* Probably
'white hill,' *v.* dun. WOODLAND (6″) is so spelt in 1716 DA 34.
GREAT YOULDEN is *Ialdedune* 1244 *Ass* (p), *Oldedone* c. 1262 DA
34. 'Old hill,' *v.* dun. For a probable sense of 'old,' *v.* Addenda,
Part i, lviii.

Tedburn St Mary

TEDBURN ST MARY 138 A 6

> *Tettaborna* c. 1120 Earle 259, *Teteborna* 1086 DB
> *Tetteburn(e)* 1234 Fees 399, 1242 Fees 792, *Tettesburne* 1266
> *Ass, Sct. Marytedborne* 1577 Saxton

All forms have *e* except *Tytteburn' juxta Crydinton* 1294 *Ass.*
'*Tetta*'s stream,' *v.* burna, and cf. Ted and Titchberry *supra*
14, 76.

GREAT FAIRWOOD is *Feyrwod* 1244 *Ass, Fairewode* 1275 RH,
1285 FA, *Farewode* 1301 Ipm, 1303 FA, *Feirwod* 1346 FA,
Fayrewode 1333 *SR* (p). 'Beautiful wood,' *v.* fæger.

HACKWORTHY is *Hacheurde* 1086 DB, *Hakewrth* 1238 *Ass,* -worth'
1242 Fees 788, 1275 RH, -*worthy* 1316 FA, *Hackewrth*' 1242
Fees 786. '*Hac(c)a*'s worþig.' Cf. *haccan broc* BCS 801.

MELHUISH BARTON [meliʃ] is *Melewis* 1086 DB, *Melehiwiss* 1242 Fees 785 *et freq* to 1329 *Ass* with variant spellings *-hewis*, *-hywysh*. *v.* hiwisc. This may contain the element *mǣle*, 'variegated,' discussed under Meldon *supra* 203, or it may contain the pers. name *Mægla* or *Mǣla*, as suggested by Professor Ekwall.

RUBBY HAY is *Robysheye* 1330, *Robyngheie* 1333 *SR* (p), *Rubhay* 1461, *Rubehayes* 1482 IpmR. *v.* (ge)hæg. The first element is probably the name of an early owner.

TAPHOUSE is *la Tappehous* 1356 *Ass*. This is most probably an early example of the common term *taphouse* for an ale-house, first recorded in 1500 in NED. Taphouse is on an important main road and so is Taphouse in Braddock (Co), so spelt in 1532 (ECP). There are two inns at the cross-roads here.

UPCOTT is *Opecota* 1086 DB, *Uppecote* 1249 FF, (*juxta Tetteburne*) 1313 *Ass*. 'Higher cot(e),' *v.* uppe.

ALLER, BERRY, BROOK, COOMBE, MOOR PARK (6″), OAK FM and TOWN were probably the homes of John de *Aure* (1311 *Ass*) and William de *Alre* (1314 *Ass*), John *atte Byry* (1330 *SR*)—there is an old 'camp' here—Walter de *la Brok* (1311 *Ass*), Nicholas *atte Combe* (1333 *SR*), Walter *atte More* (1330 *SR*), Richard *atte Ok* (ib.), John *atte Toune* (ib.), In the *Toune* (1333 *SR*). *v.* alor, burh, cumb, mor, tun.

BLACKDOWN COTTAGE (6″) is so spelt 1743 *Recov*. BROOKDOWN PLANTATION (6″) is *Brokedon* 1464 Pat. *v.* dun. COLLEY HO (6″) is *Colehegh'* 1242 Fees 780 (p), *-heie* 1285 FA, *-haye* 1313 *Ass* (p), *Colheie* 1275 RH. *v.* (ge)hæg and Collacott *supra* 50. FLOYTE is *Floydway* 1717 *Recov*. Cf. Fludda *infra* 471. FRANKFORD is *Frankeford* 1313 *Ass* (p). '*Franca*'s ford.' HEMBEER is *Henbere* 1593 DA 26, *-beare* 1608 *FF*. Probably 'high wood.' *v.* heah, bearu. HILL, cf. *Hilhead* 1717 *Recov*. GREAT HUISH is *Hywisse* 1242 Fees 788, *Hewis* 1275 RH, *Hywyssh* 1303 FA. *v.* hiwisc. SPICERY (6″) is *Spicer* 1464 Pat. WESTWATER COTTAGE (6″) is *Westwaterlond* 1461 IpmR. 'West of the water.' WINDOUT is *Wyndowte* 1544 *Deed*, *Wyndoutehill* 1617 *FF*. WITHYCOMBE is *Wythycumb* 1249 *Ass*, *Wydecombe* 1329 *Ass*, *Wydi(a)comb* 1333 *SR* (all p), *Widecombe* 1376 IpmR. *v.* wiðig, cumb.

Throwleigh

THROWLEIGH [θruˑli] 138 B 1

Trula 1086 DB, *Trulegh* 1243 DA 33, 1256, 1286 *Ass*, *Thru-leg*(*h*) 1263 Ipm, 1285 FA, *Troulegh* 1335 *Ass*
Trowlegha 1236 Bracton, *Trowlee* 1243 DA 33
Truwelegh, Thruwelegh 1238 *Ass*
Throulegh' 1242 Fees 788 *et freq* to 1341 Ipm, (*juxta Gydde-legh*) 1296 *Ass*, *Throughly* 1631 Wills

v. leah. The first element is probably OE *þruh*, 'chest, coffin,' perhaps referring to one of the early burial grounds which lie so thickly over Dartmoor and are actually found in this parish. Similarly Duignan (PN St 152) notes the presence of many tumuli in the neighbourhood of Throwley (St).

MURCHINGTON is *Morcheston* 1330 *SR*, *Morcheton, Morchyngton* 1443 *Ct*, *Morecheneton* 1525 *Recov*, *Morchington* 1562 *FF*, *North Murchenton* 1638 *FF*. In the *SR* for 1340 Richard, Walter and Robert *Morch* were taxed under Throwleigh, and probably this family gave name to the place, which is thus of medieval origin, and an example of a very late use of connective ing. *v.* tun.

WONSON is *Wnston* 1238 *Ass*, *Woneston* 1244, 1254 *Ass*, *Wonstone* 1333 *SR*, *atte Wonston* 1374 *SR* (all p). The last form shows that the first element must be a descriptive epithet and not a pers. name. Possibly the name goes back to OE *æt wō(ga)n stāne*, 'at the crooked stone,' cf. Windbow *supra* 420, and Langstone close at hand.

ASH, FORDER, MILL FM (6″), NORTHDOWN (6″) and WAY were probably the homes of John de *Ayshe* (1333 *SR*), William *atte Forde* (1296 *Ass*), Walter *Attemulle* (1296 *Ass*), John *Binorthedon* i.e. 'north of the down' (1238 *Ass*), and Richard de *la Weye* (1281 *Ass*). *v.* æsc, dun, weg.

BLACKATON is *Blakedon* 1249, 1285 *Ass* (p). 'Dark hill,' *v.* blæc, dun. CLANNABOROUGH is *Clanaburgh* 1498 *Ct*, *Clannabor*, *Clannabour at Throwlegh* 1573 *DuCo*. 'Clean hill,' *v.* beorg and cf. Clanacombe *supra* 312. LANGSTONE is *Langeston* 1303 FA. 'Long stone.' No menhir exists here now. SHILSTONE is *Schelston* 1352 *SR* (p), *Shilston* 1417 *Ct*. *v.* Shilstone *supra* 433.

According to Crossing the moormen have removed any stones which may once have existed here. SHILSTON TOR is *Shelston Downe* 1558 DA 33. WALLANDHILL may be identical with *capella atte Wallen* 1332 Exon, *La Walle juxta Chaggeford* 1346 *FF, Wallon by Chageford* 1347 Ipm. Cf. Wallon *supra* 434. There are no walls here now.

Topsham

TOPSHAM [tɔpsəm] 138 C 11

> *Toppesham, æt Toppeshamme* 937 BCS 721[1], (*æt*) *Toppeshamme,* (*to*) *Toppes hamme,* (*of*) *toppes haṁ lande* 12th Earle *Topeshant* 1086 DB

The subsequent forms are of no interest except:

> *Thopesham* 1234 Cl, *Tapsam* 1359 *Ass, Toppyshamporte* 1405 Cl, *Opsham* 1480–3 ECP 2, 308, *Appisham al. Toppisham* 1588 HMC Exeter, *Topsham vulg. Apsum* 1675 Ogilby

'Topp's hamm.' For this pers. name, found also in *toppesoran*[2] (BCS 721) close at hand, *v.* Topleigh (PN Sx 99). For the loss of the initial consonant in some of the later spellings, *v. s.n.* æt.

COUNTESS WEAR takes its name from Isabella de Fortibus, *Countess* of Devon, daughter of Baldwin de Redvers, earl of Devon. She held the manor of Topsham and according to LGS (157) constructed the weir c. 1284 to injure the trade of the city of Exeter, she having been offended by the citizens of that place for some petty reason.

---

[1] Endorsed: *Toppeshammes boc* (10th), *Topesham* (11th).

[2] The boundaries of the Topsham Charter begin and end at *toppesoran*, at the junction of the Exe and the Clyst, the *ora* being probably the slope to the south of Mount Howe. The boundary goes up the Exe to the nearer *teampol*, a breeding pool, then up the Exe and leaving that river for a short time, along a small *lacu* or stream, back to the Exe. The boundary of Topsham from Tumbling Hills (6″) to Countess Wear follows to this day not the Exe but a side stream. Thence to the upper *teampol* and along the Exe to the old *herepæð*. The present boundary when it leaves the Exe makes its way straight to the Exeter-Topsham road, which must be an old one. The boundary goes along the *herepæð* (as it does to this day) to an unidentified *dyran treowe*. The boundary then goes south to a stream called *wynford*, the present Mincing Lake (*v. supra* 10), up that stream to *wyndelescumb* (there is a combe at the northern corner of the parish), up the combe to a 'pear tree,' thence along a *dic* to the *weg* or way, the present Ridon Lane, thence east along the *weg* to the *dice hirnan*, i.e. the cross-roads by Blue Bull Inn, and so along a *dic* to the Clyst. Topsham owned a yard-land at *æschyrst*, of which the boundaries are given, but they cannot at present be identified.

SEABROOK FM (6″) is *Seybrok* 1420 *MinAcct*, *Sea brooke* t. Jas 1 *Rental*. For the etymology of this name, *v.* Ekwall on Seabrook (PN Bk 97–8) and RN 284 *s.n.* Medesing. 'Slow stream.'

SEDGE (lost) is *la Segge* 13th *Torre*, *La Sege* 1276 Ipm, *Sege juxta Toppesham* 1378 IpmR, *Sege in Topsham* 1423 IpmR, *Seige* c. 1630 Risdon, *Sedge* 1631 *Recov*. Mrs Rose-Troup calls attention to the phrase *pro duobus lignis ducendis usque la Sege* in the Cathedral Fabric Rolls (1324) and suggests that this is the OFr *sege*, 'seat,' used here of the highest point on the river at which a load could be landed. This word appears in early ModEng as *sedge*. The nearest parallel for this sense given in the NED is 'ground on which a ship lies.'

WEAR HO is *Weyre* 1549 *AD*, *Were* 1611 *Recov*, *Weare* t. Jas 1 *Rental*, *Ware Mills* 1664 DKR 40, 119. *v. supra* 454.

BRICKNELLS (6″) is perhaps to be associated with the family of Thomas *Bricknoll* of Powderham (1571 *SR*). NEWCOURT BARTON is so spelt in 1667 *Recov*. NORTHBROOK PARK is *Northbrooke* t. Jas 1 *Rental*. RIDON LANE (6″) is *Ryden lane* t. Jas 1 *Rental*. Perhaps 'rye hill,' *v.* dun. TOPSHAM BRIDGE (6″) is *Topesham bridge* t. Jas 1 *Rental*. WHITEHILL LANE (6″) may be identical with *Whitewell* t. Jas 1 *Rental*.

Upton Pyne

UPTON PYNE 128 J 9

> *Opetone* 1264 Exon
> *Uppeton(e)* 1275 RH, (*Pyn*) 1283 Exon, 1297 Pat, 1316 *Ass*, *Uppen Pyne* 1624 HMC Exeter

'Higher farm,' perhaps with reference to Brampford *supra* 422. *v.* tun. Herbert de *Pyn* held the manor in the 13th cent. (1264 Exon, 1275 RH).

COWLEY, COWLEY BRIDGE, is *Cuneleghe* (sic) c. 1200 NGl 5, 20, *Couelegh(e)* 1237 Fees 613 *et freq* to 1389 with variant -*v*-, (*juxta Exon*) 1389 FF, *Covelegh Bridge* (sic) 1286 HMC Exeter, *Cowlegh Brygge* 1537 id. '*Cufa*'s leah.' Cf. Cowley (Bk, Mx, O).

PYNES is *mansion of Pyn* (1400 Exon) and derives its name from the family mentioned above.

ROLLSTONE (6″) is *Rollandeston'* 1242 Fees 785, 1316 *Ass*, *Roul-* 1284 FA, *Rolston* 1346 FA and is to be associated with *Rolandus* de Braunford Especc (1230 P). *v.* tun.

STEVENSTONE [stensən] is *Steveneston(e)* 1242 Fees 779, *Stevenys-ton juxta Uppeton Pyn* 1346 *Ass*. It was held by one *Steven* in 1166 (LN). *v.* tun.

MOXEY'S COPSE, PAGES DOWN and PEARCE'S FM (all 6″) are probably to be associated with the families of *Moxhey*, *Moxhay* (1582, etc. Wills), Adam *Page* (1333 *SR*) and Walter *Pers* (1330 *SR*).

GOSSIFORD (6″) is *Glosseford* 1657 HMC Exeter. JACKMOOR is *Chagmore* 1505 Ipm, *Jackmore* 1712 *Recov*. *v.* Chagford *supra* 424. LEY is *Leye* 1386 Exon. *v.* leah. MILL COTT (6″) is *Millcott* 1639 *FF*. *v.* cot(e). NETTACOTT is *Nettecot, Netecot* 1254 *Ass,* *Nattecote* 1329 *Ass* (all p). The first element may be the OE *nēat*, 'cattle,' cf. Netton *supra* 258. TURLAKE (6″) is *Terlake* 1765 D. This may be for ME *atter lake*, 'at the streamlet,' *v.* lacu, and cf. Tredown *supra* 146.

Whitestone

WHITESTONE [witsən] 138 A 8

> (*on*) *hwita stane* c. 1100 Earle 266, *Whitestan* 1238 *Ass*, *Whyteston* 1303 *Ass*, *Whytston* 1297 Pat
> *Witestan, Witestani* 1086 DB, *Witestan* 1219 FF, *Wittestone*, *Wytestane* 1263 Exon
> *Whiston* 1333 Pap

'At the white stone,' cf. Whitstone (Co), *Witestan* DB.

COPPERWALLS FM is *Coplewalle* 1323 *Ass* (p), 1330 *SR* (p). This is a difficult name. The second element would seem to be *weall* but there are no remains of such here. The first element may be the *copel* discussed under Copplestone *supra* 403 but the application of the term to the undiscovered wall must remain uncertain.

HALSFORDWOOD

> (*of*) *Halsforda* c. 1100 Earle 265, *Halsford, Halesford* 1275 RH, *Halesford* 1276 Ipm, *Halsford* 1285 FA, 1331 *FF*, *Halseford juxta Whyteston* 1303 FA
> *Halseord* 1274 RH

Probably 'ford by the neck of land,' with the element *heals* discussed in Addenda, Part i, lviii. There is a long ridge here between the Alphin and the Nadder streams.

NORWAY and SOUTHWAY appear as *Northway* (1698 *Recov*), *Southeway* (1469 *Ct*) and were the homes of Roger *Bynortheweye* and Ralph *Bysouthweye* (1344 *Rental*), i.e. north and south of the *way*, referring to the main road which passes between the two farms.

OLDRIDGE

> *Walderige* 1086 DB, *-rigge* 1204 FF, *-rug* 1269 Cur, *Waldrigge* 1269 FF
>
> *Wallerig'* 1242 Fees 785
>
> *Wolderigge* 1291 Tax, *Wollerigg* 1292 Ipm, *Wollerugge Cadiho* 1303 FA

The persistent medial *e* here as in Waldridge (PN Bk 160), *wealdan hrigc* in BCS 603, would suggest a pers. name *Wealda*. This is confirmed by the existence of a *wealdan cumb* in the near neighbourhood of the Devon place. *v. supra* 402 n. 1. The same pers. name is found in *wealding ford* in the Thorndon Hall charter. *v. supra* 296 n. 1. The manor was held by the heirs of Richard *Cadiho* in 1242 (Fees).

EAST and WEST ROWHORNE is *Rohorn(e)* 1275 RH, 1303 FA, 1330 SR (p), *La Rohorne* 1285 FA, *Rowehorn* 1378 *FF*, *Rughehorne* 1525 *AOMB*. *v.* ruh, horn. There is a spur of land here.

TRILLOW is *Trillawe* 1281 *Ass* (p), *Trillowe* 1336, 1339 *Ass* (p), *Trillouwe* 1339 *Ass*, *Trillewe* 1378 *FF*. The second element is hlaw. The first may be an old name of the Nadder Brook, *v. supra* 11 and cf. Ekwall RN 418.

TWISCOMBE is *Tywiscumb(e)* 1238 *Ass* (p), *Tywes-* 1244 *Ass* (p), 1294 *Ass*, *Tewescomb* 1301 *Ass* (p), *Tuwyscombe* 1325 Oliver 157 (p). This name resembles Tuesley (Sr), *Tiwesle* DB, which designated a clearing sacred to the Saxon god Tiw. It is very doubtful, however, if a heathen name of this type could be found in Devon. Alternatively we might take *Tiw* as a short form of such an OE pers. name as *Teoweald, Teowulf*.

VOGHAY (6″) is *focgan igeðas* 739 (11th) Crawf 1, *Voggeheyes*

c. 1340 HMC Exeter, *Foghaye* c. 1520 HMC Exeter, *Fogghey* 1575 BM. The first form, derived from the great Crediton charter, refers to the islets at the junction of the Exe and the Creedy. Voghay Fm is a quarter of a mile south-east, away from the river, and it is more likely that the two names contain the same first element than that the places concerned are actually identical, though from the point of view of form Voghay(s) might conceivably go back to *focgan igeðas*. More probably the second element in Voghay is OE (ge)hæg, 'enclosure.' For the first element we have, as Stevenson notes (*Crawford Charters*, p. 48), a choice between a possible OE *focga*, the ultimate source of *fog*, a term for aftermath and for coarse reeds[1], and a pers. name *Focga*. We get *focga* in *focgan crundel* (KCD 1309), but it is difficult to see how *focga* as a significant word could have anything to do with crundel. An aftermath on the tiny eyot in the Exe is also very unlikely, though reedy grass is possible. On the ground also of the difficulty of a genitival compound in the only two known examples of this word, one must incline to a pers. name. This, as Stevenson notes, receives some support from the phrase *focginga byras* (BCS 343), though that is not decisive. *Focga* would be a natural pet-form for such a name as *Folcgār*.

BRIDGE COTTAGE (6″), CLEAVE FM, COOMBE (6″), FORD FM, HILL FM, WAY FM and WOODHAY were probably the homes of Mathew *atte Brugge* (1339 *Ass*), John de *Northereclyve* (ib.), John Gardiner de *Combe* (ib.), Richard *atte Forde* 1469 *Ct*, Ric. *atte Hille* 1382 *Rental*, Nicholas *atte Weye* (1330 *SR*), and Walter *atte Wodehaye* (ib.). *v.* clif, cumb, weg, (ge)hæg.

DYMOND'S BRIDGE, LAKES COTTAGE and SLADES COTTAGE (all 6″) are probably to be associated with the families of William *Dyamond* (1333 *SR*), Hugo de *la Lake* (1238 *Ass*) and John *Slade* (1582 *SR*).

BONDHOUSE (6″) is so spelt in 1756 *Recov*. BOWLISH is *Bollishe* t. Jas 1 ECP. Possibly the name contains the word hiwisc, cf. Mowlish *infra* 500. HACKWORTHY is *Hakeworthy* 1284 *Ass*, 1333 *SR* (p). cf. Hackworthy *supra* 451. HARE is *Heyre* 1518–29 ECP

[1] That *fog* could be used in the South in some topographical sense is shown by the pers. name *del Fogge* found in Devon in 1260 (*Ass*).

5, 524. HEATH BARTON is *la Heth* 1275 RH, *La Hethe Sancte Marie* 1378 IpmR. HURSTON HO is *Hurtesthorn* 1344 Ct. 'Hart's thorn tree' or 'thorn tree of a man *Heort.*' KENT is *Lower Kent* 1743 *Recov.* KINGSWELL is *Kingeswell* 1249 *Ass.* NADDER FM (6") and NADDERWATER are *Nadder* 1244 *Ass* (p), *Naddre* 1378 *FF*, *Naderbrigge* 1481 *Ct.* Probably originally a stream-name, *v. supra* 11. PITT FM is *Pitt* 1733 *Deed.* POOLE FM is *Pool* 1765 D. WEST TOWN is *Westtown* 1481 *Ct* and is identical with the early manor of *Westecot(e)* 1226 FF, 1242 Fees 785. *v.* cot(e).

Ten Hide

NOTE. The following parishes form a detached area lying to the south of the Teign estuary. In DB the district contained thirteen manors of which the total hidage amounted to about ten hides. The whole area was therefore known as the 'Ten Hide,' and this was later, in the case of Combe and Stoke *infra* 460, corrupted to 'Teignhead' through the influence of the river-name.

Haccombe with Coombe

HACCOMBE (with COMBEINTEIGNHEAD) 138 H 9

Hacoma 1086 DB
Hakcumbe c. 1200 (15th) *Torre* (p), *Hakcome* 1323 Ipm (p)
Haccumbe 1238 *Ass* (p) *et passim* with variant spelling *-com(be)*
Heccham 1293 DA 50
Hakecombe 1509 DA 50

In view of the absence of any sign of an inflexional syllable the first element is perhaps OE *haca*, 'hook' (*v. s.n.* Hackpen *infra* 538), rather than a pers. name *Hacca. v.* cumb.

COMBEINTEIGNHEAD is *Comba* 1086 DB, *Combe, Cumbe in Tenhide* 1227 Ch, *Cumbe in Tynhide* 1259 Exon, 1277 *Ass*, *Comyngteynhede* 1417 Exon, *Comyng Tynid* t. Eliz ChancP, *Combyntynhedd* 1608 FF, *Combentinheade* 1635 *Recov.* 'The cumb in the Ten Hide area,' *v. supra.* For *Tenhide*, cf. Tinhead (W) in Mawer, *PN and History* 47.

BUCKLAND BARTON is *Bochelanda* 1086 DB, *Bocland* 1219 FF, *Barones Boclande* 1289 *Ass*, *Westerboclond juxta Niweton Abbatis* 1324 *Ass. v.* bocland. The place was associated with John and Richard *le Baron* in 1219 FF.

Milber Down is *Milburdoune* 13th *Torre*, *Milberdone* 1557, 1628 *FF*, 1566 DA 43. In the Torre Cartulary the ford in the valley below is referred to as *Milburnford*, i.e. 'millstream ford,' *v.* burna.

Netherton is *Nithereton* 1242 Fees 792, *Nythereton* 1269 FF. 'Lower farm,' *v.* neoðera, tun.

St Nicholas

St Nicholas 138 H 9/10

This is a modern parish-name, from the dedication of the church at Ringmore *infra*.

Ringmore is *Rumor* 1086 DB, *Redmor(e)* 1275 RH, 1285 FA, 1289 *FF*, *Reddemore* 1428 *Ct*, *Rydmor(e)* 1281 *Ass*, (*juxta Teynghmouth*) 1356 *Ass*, *Ridemor(e)* 1289 *Ass*, 1303 FA, *Ridmore* 1318 Ch, *Riddemore* 1424 IpmR, *Rydmer* 1428 FA. 'Cleared marshland,' *v.* Ringmore *supra* 283.

The Ness is *The Nesse* c. 1550 Leland. *v.* næs. The name refers to the prominent headland south of the estuary of the Teign. Shaldon is *Shaldon* t. Jas 1 ECP.

Stokeinteignhead

Stokeinteignhead [stoukəntini(d)] 138 H 9

Stoches 1086 DB, *Stokes* 1242 Fees 788
Stokes in Tynhide 1279 Exon, *Stok in Tynhyde* 1285 FA, *Stokeyntynhede* 1492 Ipm, *Stoken Teynhed* 1540 *Recov*, *Stokentynhedde al. Stoke next Tynhedde* t. Eliz ChancP, *Stockinge Tynid* t. Eliz ChancP

'The stoc(c) in the "Ten Hide" area', *v. supra* 459.

Gabwell is *Gabewell* 1228 FF, *-will'* 1242 Fees 788, *Houeregabewell* 1279 *Ass*, *Over Gabewelle* 1286 *FF*, *Nythere Gabewill* 1303 FA, *Gabbewill(e)* 1303 FA, *Overa-* 1414 *FF*, *-wyll* 1420 BM. We may perhaps compare Gapton (Sf), DB *Gabbetuna*, which would suggest for both names an OE pers. name *Gabba*, a correct pet-form for *Gārbeorht*, hence '*Gabba*'s spring,' *v.* wielle.

Maidencombe is *Medenecoma* 1086 DB, *-cumba* 1168 Oliver 137, *-cumbe* 1219 *Ass*, 1242 Fees 785, (*in Tynhyde*) 1283 *Ass*, (*juxta*

Teygnemuth) 1299 *Ass, Medencumb* 1303 FA, *Maiden(e)cumbe*
1228 FF, 1238 *Ass.* 'The maidens' valley,' *v.* **cumb** and Maidenford *supra* 26.

ROCOMBE

> *Racomba, Racoma, Racum* 1086 DB (Exon), *-cumbe, -chum*
> (Exch), *Racumbe* 1228 FF, 1242 Fees 788, *Overe-* 1277 *Ass*
> *Raucomb* 1275 RH, *Raucomb Cadyho* 1285 FA
> *Rowecumb* 1281 *Ass, Roucomb Hugh* 1285 FA, *Roucumbe Hughe*
> *juxta Stok in Tynhyde* 1313 *Ass*

'Roe-valley,' *v.* **ra, cumb.** Richard *Cadyho* held the manor
in 1242 (Fees 785). For later *Rowe* forms, cf. Rogate (PN Sx 38).

TEIGNHARVEY (6") is *Taigna* 1086 DB, *Teyng in Tynhide* 1285 FA,
Tenghervey 1288 *Ass, Teynghervy* 1334 *SR,* 1351 Ipm. The
identity of this *Hervey* is unknown.

CHARLECOMBE is *Cherlecumb'* 1242 Fees 790, *-comb(e)* 1303 FA,
1322 Misc, *Charlecombe* 1420 IpmR. *v.* **ceorl, cumb.** IVY TREE
COTTAGE (6") is *Yvitree* 1615 *Deed.*

Ogwell

EAST and WEST OGWELL [ougwel] 138 H 7

> *(to) woggan wylle* 956 (13th) BCS 952, *(oð) wocga willes (hafod)*,
> *(oþ) wogga will (lacu), (of) wocgga willes (heafde)* 10th BCS
> 1323
> *Oghawillæ, Oghawille, Woguwel, Wogewil* 1086 DB (Exon),
> *Wogwel* (Exch)
> *Wogewill'* 1242 Fees 779, *West-, Est-* 1242 Fees 791, *Est-*
> *woggewill* 1275 RH, *East-, Westwogewelle* 1278 Ipm, *Est-*
> *woghwill* 1285 FA, *Wogwell* 1675 Ogilby
> *Estwugwyll* 1244 *Ass, Wugewell* 1249 *Ass*
> *Estwogwille, Estwokewelle* 1258–72 Exon

According to Ekwall RN 308, '*Wocga*'s or *Wogga*'s spring,'
v. **wielle.**

HOLBEAM is *Holebem(a)* 1086 DB, 1242 Fees 788, *Holebyem* 1321
FF. 'Hollow tree,' *v.* **holh, beam** and cf. *le Holebemes* 13th
Canonsleigh.

BUTTERCOMBE MOOR COPSE (6″) is *Butercumbe* 1238 *Ass*. 'Valley with rich pasture,' *v.* cumb and cf. Buttercombe *supra* 40. CHERCOMBE is *Chyri-, Churycumb* 1244 *Ass, Churycumbe* 1294 *Ass* (p). *v.* Cherricombe *supra* 335. GREAT MARSH COPSE (6″) is *Marshe grove* 1550 *AOMB*. METLEY (6″) is *M(e)attelegh* 1370 *Ass* (p), 1424 Pat.

XX. TEIGNBRIDGE HUNDRED

Tenebr̄ 1159 P, *Teinebr'* 1179 P, *Teineber'* 1181 P, *Teinnebrig* 1212 Fees 98, *-brugg'* 1219 Fees 264
Teingnebrige 1187 P, *Teignebrigge* 1238 *Ass, Teygne-* 1278 *Ass*
Teynbrig 1244 *Ass, Teyngebrugg'* 1275 RH, *Teyngbrigge* 1359 Ipm

v. Teignbridge *infra* 480. The hundred was called *Taintona* in the Geld Roll (1084), from Kingsteignton *infra* 478.

Ashburton

ASHBURTON[1] [æʃbətən] 138 H/J 4

(*æt*) *æscburnan lande* 1008–12 Crawf 23
Essebretona 1086 DB
Aisbernatonam c. 1150 (14th) *Launceston, Aisbernetune* 13th Buckfast
Eispreton' 1185, *Esperton* 1187 P, *Aspernetune* 13th Buckfast, *Asperton(e)* 1238 *Ass et freq* to 1309 Ch, *Assheperton juxta Bukfast* 1304 *Ass, As(s)hperton* 1313 Ch, 1323 *Ass*, 1356 Ipm, *-purton* 1313 *Ass, Aysshpertone* 1356 Ipm, *-berton* 1483 IpmR

'Farm by the Ashburn stream,' *v. s.n.* Yeo *supra* 17.

---

[1] Earle (pp. 266 ff.) and Birch (No. 1323) print the *landscearu* of a place called *peadingtun*. No trace of that name has been found in later documents, but as the document concerns itself in the first place with the area now included in the parish of Ashburton we may deal with it here.
  The boundary begins at the junction of the *æscburne*, now the Yeo River *supra* 17 and the Dart. It then goes by the Dart to *wede burne*, i.e. the Webburn River *supra* 17, probably the western one. It goes up the Webburn to *wiþimor*, which is perhaps to be connected with Widdecombe in the Moor, just to the east. Thence to *cealfa dune* which again should probably be connected with Challacombe in Manaton *infra* 481. The *dun* must have been to the south of Challacombe, for the next point is *sufonstanas*, which is clearly to be identified with Soussons in Manaton. Close by is a stone circle

AUSEWELL is *Ausewell, Ausewellwode* 1553 Pat, *Aweswell* 1583 DKR 38, 202, *Apswell Rock* 1606 Dartmoor. The forms are too late for any certainty. If the last form is correct the meaning may have been 'aspen spring,' *v.* wielle.

BOWDLEY (6″) is *Bogedelegh* 1330, *Bogwodelegh* 1333 *SR* (p). 'Clearing by the curved wood,' *v.* leah and cf. Bowden *supra* 37.

which may actually be the 'seven stones.' From Soussons the boundary seems to make a big leap to *hyfan treow*, which is clearly to be identified with Heatree in Manaton *infra* 482. The *hord burh* or 'treasure fort' cannot now be identified. The *deor ford* was probably over Becky Brook. From *deor ford* the boundary goes to *langa stan*. There is a Langstone in Manaton, but this is a long way to the north-east and in view of the commonness of such a name, identity of name need not mean identity of object. The next point in the boundary is *eofede tor* and there is much to be said for identifying this with Haytor in the light of its early forms, *v. infra* 476. If so, the 'long stone' must be some unidentified rock or tor on the Moor. From Haytor the boundary goes over the 'high down' to a 'blind' or hidden well, thence to *writelan stan*, and from the stone to 'rough hill,' from the rough hill to the 'furze enclosure,' from there to the head of *wyrt cum*, and thence to the next point which we can definitely identify, viz. Ramshorn in Bickington. From Ramshorn it goes to *lulca stile*, which must be connected with Lurcombe in Bickington *infra* 466, as can be seen from the early forms of that name. Thence it goes to the head of *wice cum*, and so to the River Lemon, which it probably touches at Chipley. The boundary goes east along the Lemon till it joins Kester Brook, which is called *wocg(g)a will* in the Charter (*v.* Ogwell *supra* 461). It goes up that stream to its head and strikes the *weg* or road which still forms the southern boundary of Bickington. Thence west along the road to an unidentified great *dic*, thence to a spring at the top of the moor. This would seem to be the point marked 621 feet at the summit of the boundary, just by Combe Cross. From there it goes to *þa lace*, a little stream to the south-east, thence to an unidentified *sweliende*, and so to *yederes beorh*, which may be the hill (contour line 400 feet) at the top of a road which here forms the north boundary of Woodland. The road now goes downwards to the 'great lime-tree,' which must have been by the present Moorfoot Cross.

We cannot identify the *dyra snæd* or the three fords which follow, but they probably carry the bounds round the eastern corner of Woodland. Just here we have a ford called Pulsford (*v. infra* 525) and there must also have been one at Collacombe Bridge across the Am Brook. We do not know where *hildes ford* or *lege* were or *sole get*, but *Brynes cnolle* was probably the knoll (contour line 400 feet) near the south-west corner of Woodland parish. The boundary from here goes southwards to *puneces wurði*, following the Woodland boundary as it travels southwards. The present boundary now turns north-west and goes to the head of a combe, probably to be identified with the *hremnes cumb* of the charter. It goes down the combe to a little *riþ* and so to *æscburne* once again. The *riþ* is probably the stream which joins the Yeo at Chudleigh. Finally it goes down the Yeo to the point at which it started.

This area includes the whole of Ashburton parish. To the west and north it includes a large part of Widdecombe, Manaton and Ilsington, but it does not follow, so far as can be determined, the present boundaries of those parishes. To the east and south it would seem to follow the present boundaries more definitely and includes the parishes of Bickington and Woodland.

CHULEY CROSS is *Chiuelege* 1228 FF, *Chiuelegh juxta Asperton* 1299 *Ass*, *Chyvelegh(e)* 1301 Exon, (*juxta Asshperton*) 1323 *Ass*, *Cheuelegh, Cheyuelegh* 1322 *Ass*. 'Cifa's leah.' For this pers. name, not on actual record, *v.* Chevington (PN Wo 319) and cf. Chivenor *supra* 45.

DOLBEARE (6″) is *Dollebeare* 1333 *SR*, 1395–1419 Exon, 1422 *Ass*, -*ber* 1340 *SR* (all p). The first element in this name is probably the OE pers. name *Dola*, recorded in a Devon manumission (BCS 1247), hence 'Dola's grove,' *v.* bearu. Cf. also William *Dola* and Nicholas *Dolya* (1333 *SR*).

HALSHANGER [hɔˑsæŋər] is *Halshangre* 1244 *Ass*, 13th Buckfast (p), -*hanger* 1330 *Ass*, *Hallesangre* 1284 *Ass* (p). 'Hazel-wooded slope,' *v.* hæsl, hangra. The situation forbids our taking the first element as *heals*, 'neck, col.' Cf. Addenda, Part i, lviii.

WELSTOR is *Welestorre* 1281 *Ass* (p), *Welles-* c. 1326 Exon (p), *Welstorre* 1330, 1333 *SR* (p). 'Tor of (or by) the spring,' *v.* torr, wielle, and cf. Welsford *supra* 77. There is a spring here.

KNOWLE, MEAD, PITT FM (6″), REW and WAYE were the homes of John *atte Knolle* (1356 *Ass*), Bartholomew *atte Mede* (1327 Banco), de *Prato* (1281 *Ass*), John *atte Pytte* (1323 *Ass*), Maurice *atte Rewe* (1333 *SR*), and Joel de *la Waye* (1244 *Ass*). *v.* cnoll, mæd, pytt, ræw, weg.

ALSTON is *Alston* 1504 DA 56. ASHBURTON DOWN is *Aishberton Downe* 1641 *FF*. BLACKMOOR (6″) is *Blackmore* 1579 *Recov*. BORO' WOOD is *Boroughwod* 1553 Pat. *v.* beorg or burh. There is an ancient 'castle' here. BROWNSWELL is *Bruneswell* 1238 *Ass*, -*wyll* 1244 *Ass* (p). 'Brūn's spring,' *v.* wielle. BYLAND (6″) is *Bilond* 1604 DKR 38, 471, *the Bye* 1615 *DuCo*. This may be OE *byge*, 'curve, bend,' referring to the shape of the land here. CATON is *Cadetone* 1330 *SR* (p), *Kaeton al. Kadaton* 1539 Ct Wards. 'Cada's farm,' *v.* tun. DART BRIDGE is *Dertebrygge* 1356 *Ass*. DRUID is a modern house, late 18th cent. (F. R.-T.). FURZE-LEIGH is *Furslegh* 1304 *Ass*, 1461 IpmR. 'Furze clearing,' *v.* leah. GAGES (6″) is *Gades* 1413 IpmR. GOODSTONE is *Gotston* 1571 *SR*, *Goodstone oth. Gutson* 1792 *Recov*. HEADBOROUGH (6″) is *Hedbury* 1599, 1603 DA 28. HELE is *Hele* 1553 Pat. *v.* healh. HOOKS (6″) is *Hooke* 1788 *Recov*, and was the home of Mathew *atte Hoke* (1340 *SR*). *v.* hoc. HORSEHILL (6″) is *Horshoohill* 1553 Pat. LEMONFORD is *Limneford* 1244 *Ass.* 'Ford over the river Lemon,' *supra* 8. LENTHILL (6″) is *Leane Hill* 1567 DKR 38, 153. LURGECOMBE MILL (6″) is *Loryggecombe* 1504 DA 56, *mill called Lurge* 1553 DA 28. Cf. also *Lurge hyll* 1583 (ib.). OWLACOMBE FM (6″) is *Hulecomb* 1244 *Ass* (p), *Ulecumbe* 1244 *Ass.* 'Owl valley.' PITLEY (6″) is *Pytley* 1603 DA 28. PRIESTAFORD HO is *Prusteford(e)* 1330 *SR* (p), 1339, 1356 *Ass*, *Pristover* 1765 D. 'Priests' ford,' *v.* preost. REWLEA COTTAGES (6″) is *Reylecomb* 1330 *SR* (p), *Rewlacomb* 1583 DKR 38, 202. ROCKPARK CROSS (6″) is *Rookparke* 1636 *Recov.* RUSHLADE is *Ryshslade* 1333 *SR* (p). *v.* rysc, slæd. SUMMERHILL (6″) is *Sumerhill* 1238 *Ass* (p), *Somer-* 1330 *SR* (p). 'Hill used for summer pasturage.' WATER TURN (6″) is *Watertorne* 1553 Pat. The *turn* is presumably the cross-roads here. There is no water here but there is a small valley with a stream just to the south. WESTABROOK HO (6″) is *Westabrook* 1604 DKR 38, 471. WHIDDON is *Wheddoune* 1504 DA 56. YOL-LAND HILL is *la Yoldelonde* 1270 *Ass* (p), *Oldelond* 1330 *SR* (p), *Yollande Hill* 1603 DA 28. *v.* Addenda, Part i, lviii.

Bickington

BICKINGTON 138 H 6

> *Bechintona* 1107 (1300) Ch, *Bekynton* 1524 *SR*, *Bekenton* 1597 *Recov*
> *Buketon* 1219 *Ass* (p), 1228 FF, *Bukyngton* 1303, 1428 FA, (*by Ashperton*) 1356 Ipm, *-ynton* 1346 FA
> *Byketon* 1330 *SR*

'*Beocca*'s tun.' *v.* Abbots Bickington *supra* 124.

CHIPLEY is *Cheplegh* 1333 *SR* (p), *Chyplegh* 1505 Ipm, *Chipleigh* 1597 *Recov. v.* leah. The first element may be OE *cēap*, 'price,' cf. *ceaplond* (BCS 1020), which Middendorff (*s.v. ceap*) interprets as 'purchased land,' hence in this case, 'woodland clearing which has been bought.'

GALE is *la Gale* 1315 Exon, *atte Gale* 1330 *SR*, 1356 *Ass* (all p), *Gale* 1567 Pemb Surv. Cf. also Stephen *atte Gale* 1333 *SR* (Plympton). Professor Ekwall suggests that this is the OE plant-name gagel, 'bog-myrtle.'

LURCOMBE (6″) is *Lulcacumba* t. Hy 2 Oliver 135, *Lulkecum* 1276 *Ass* (p), *-combe* 1340 *SR*, *Lolkecombe* 1330 *SR*, *-cumbe* 1340 *SR*, *Lokkecumbe* 1228 FF, *Lorkecombe* 1291 Tax. This must be near the *lulca stile* mentioned in land boundaries in the neighbourhood (BCS 1323). In that charter final *n* is often dropped, so we may take this to be for *lulcan stile*. *Lulluc* is on record in a Devon charter (BCS 451). Here we have a weak form *Lull(u)ca*. Hence, '*Lulca*'s valley,' *v.* cumb.

RAMSHORN DOWN is (*on, of*) *rammes horn(e)* 10th BCS 1323, *Rameshorn* 1333 *SR* (p). As seen from Hay Tor the top of this hill curves in a manner strongly resembling a ram's horn (*ex inf.* Mrs Rose-Troup).

BURNE[1], COMBE[1], LEE and YEO[2] were the homes of Jacob de *la Borne* (1302 *Ass*), William de *Combe* (1330 *SR*), John *atter Leghe* (ib.), and Geoffrey de *la Yha* (1244 *Ass*). *v.* burna (there is a stream here), cumb, leah, and Yeo *supra* 17–18.

FARLACOMBE is *Verlecombe* 1330 *SR* (p), *Farlecombe, Farrelcombe* 1567 Pemb Surv. Perhaps 'bracken-clearing valley,' *v.* fearn, leah, cumb. HEREBERE is *Harebeare* 1324 *Ass* (p), *Herebere* 1567 Pemb Surv, *Hearebeare* 1626 *Recov*. *v.* bearu. The forms are not sufficient for any interpretation of the first element to be suggested. LOVELANE (6″) is *Love Lane* 1434 *FF*, *Livelan* 1530 *Recov*, *Loveland* 1646 *FF*. WRIGWELL is *Wygwyll mede* 1543–58 *Ct*, and is probably identical with *Wyggerewelle* 1317 *Ass* (p). Cf. the pers. name *Wiggere* in Devon c. 1100 (Earle 258).

Bovey Tracy

BOVEY TRACY[3] [bʌvi] 138 F 6

> *Buui* a. 1093 Earle 263[4]
> *Bovi* 1086 DB, (*in*) *Boveio* 1088 Totnes, *Bovy* 1219 Fees 264, 1274 Ipm, *Sutbovi* 1219 FF
> *Bovitracy* 1309 Exon, *Bovetracy* 1386, *Boven-* 1397 Cl, *Bovey-* 1401 Exon

---

[1] *Laborne, Combe* 1567 Pemb Súrv.
[2] *Middell Yeo* 1566 DA 43.
[3] In DB there is mention of a manor in this parish called *Brungarstona*. It is not found in subsequent records. The meaning is '*Brūngār*'s tun.'
[4] Printed *Buin*, corrected from the MS. by Professor Max Förster.

The village takes its name from the river on which it stands, *v. supra* 2. *South* to distinguish from North Bovey *infra* 470. *Tracy* from the family of that name who held the manor from the 13th cent. (1219 FF, Fees 264, etc.).

BRIMLEY is *Bromleg* 1285 *Ass*, *Lower Bremley* 1655 *Recov* and is very likely identical with (*æt*) *Bromleage* 956 BCS 952, a *hiwisc* belonging to Ipplepen. 'Broom clearing,' *v.* leah.

CROWNLEY is *Crundal, Crondal* 1281 *Ass, Croundel* 1330 *SR* (p), *atte Croundel* 1399 *Rental, Croundell, Crowdell* 1596 DCo NQ 9, 1, *Crowndell* 1722 *Recov. v.* crundel. There is more than one quarry in the immediate neighbourhood.

ELSFORD

> *Ailavesfort* 1086 DB (Exon), *Eilavesford* (Exch)
> *Alardeford* 1195 FF, *Aylardesford* 1326 Ipm, *Ayll-* 1326 Cl, *Haylerdesford* 1330 *SR* (p)
> *Alenesford* 1242 Fees 774
> *Aylesford* 1303 FA

The first element is clearly a pers. name but its form is doubtful. The first two forms suggest an unrecorded *Æþel-lāf* and the form *Alenesford* can best be taken as for *Alevesford* from the same name. Other forms point to *Æþelheard*. Possibly the ford was at different times in its history associated with different persons.

HAWKMOOR is *Hauocmora* 1086 DB, *Haukemor* 1399 *Rental. v.* mor.

INDIO is *Yondeyoe* 1544 LP, *Judeyo* (sic) 1547 Pat, *Indeho* 1765 D. '(Place) beyond the water,' *v.* Indicombe *supra* 35. The farm is directly opposite Bovey across the river.

LITTLE BOVEY is *Little Boui* 1195 FF, *parua Bouy juxta Bouy Tracy* 1303 *Ass*, and is probably identical with the DB manor of *Adonebovi*, which stands for '*Ofdune* or *Adoun* Bovy.' It is further down the stream.

PLUDDA (6″) is so spelt 1596 DCo NQ, 10, 1. This is the word *plud(d)*, 'pool, puddle, swampy surface of a field,' *v.* NED and EDD *s.v.* and cf. also Pludd *supra* 48, *Pludd park* 1561 *Rental*

(Whitchurch), and the surname *atte Plodde* in a Gloucestershire *SR* of 1327.

PULLABROOK is *Polebroc* 1086 DB, *-brok* 1333 *SR* (p), *Pollebrok* 1330 *SR* (p). The *ll* points to a pers. name *Polla* rather than the OE pol, 'pool.' Cf. Pulborough PN Sx 152.

RIDDAFORD WATER is *Crideford* 1219 *Ass*, 1333 *SR*, *Kryddeforth* 1399 *Rental* (all p), *Cridiford* 1596 DCo NQ 10, 1, 1785 *Recov*, *Reedaford* or *Redaford* 1737 *Recov*. The first element is probably the name of the stream here and must be identical with Creedy *supra* 4. In later times the name must have been associated by popular etymology with 'reed.'

SOLDRIDGE (6″) is *Solrugge* 1281 *Ass* (p), *Great Salrudge* 1596 DCo NQ 10, 1. The name may be identical with Solridge (Ha), *Solrigge* 1255, 1305 *FF*, 1327 *SR* (p). The first element is probably OE *sol*, 'mud, mire, wet place.' The second is hrycg, hence 'ridge by the miry place.'

STICKWICK (6″) is *Stekeweke* 1524 *SR*, *Stikeweeke* 1596 DCo NQ 10, 1. The forms are late but it may be that the first element is OE *sticca*, 'stick,' hence 'stick farm,' *v.* wic, though the exact sense must remain obscure. Cf. Stick Park in Winkleigh. Unfortunately we have no early forms for it.

WHISTLEWELL is *Whyslewylle* 1395–1419 Exon (p), *Whiselwill(e)* 1596 DCo NQ 10, 1, 1652 *FF*, *Whisselwell* 1667 *FF*. *v.* wielle. The name probably referred to a 'whistling' or noisy spring. According to Mr Watkin a stream rises here.

WOOLLEY is *Olueleia* 1086 DB (Exon), *Ulvelei* (Exch), *Wlueleia* 1195 FF, 1196 P, *-leg* 1219 *Ass*, *Wolvelegh* 1303 FA, *Wolflegh* 1242 Fees 774, *Wlveleyheye* 1326 Ipm. 'Wolves' wood or clearing,' *v.* leah. The final form shows addition of (ge)hæg.

YARNER is *Yarnour*, *Yarnouere* 1344 Pat, *Yerner* 1399 *Ct*, *Yarner*, *Yarner Wood*, *Yarner Downe* 1553 Pat. 'Eagle bank or slope,' *v.* earn, ofer.

FORDER and NORTHCOMBE (6″) were probably the homes of Robert de *la Forde* (1330 *SR*), and Richard de *Northecombe* (ib.).

ALLER (6″) is *Alre* 1238 *Ass*, *Allere*, *Alre*, *Aure* 1339 *Ass*. 'At the alder.' ATWAY (6″) is so spelt in 1765 D. 'At the way.' It is on

the main road. BOVEY BRIDGE (6″) is *pontem de Boui* 1244 *Ass.*
BRADLEY is *Bradelēg* 1219 *Ass.* 'Broad leah.' BULLATON is
Boleton 1244 *Ass*, 1330 *SR* (p). Probably 'bull farm,' *v.* tun.
CHALLABROOK (6″) is *Chorlebrooke* 1596 DCo NQ 10, 1. 'Brook
of the ceorls.' CHAPPLE (6″) is *Chappell* 1596 DCo NQ 10, 1.
COLEHAYS is *Colehouse* 1596 DCo NQ 10, 1. The modern form is
corrupt. COMBE is *atte Combe* (nom. loc.) 1399 *Rental. v.* cumb.
CULVERHOUSE COMBE (6″) is *Coluerhouse* 1330 *SR* (p). 'Dove
house,' *v.* culfre. DRAKE LANE (6″) is *Drakelane* 1399 *Ct.* The
first element is probably the name of the bird. DUNLEY Ho is
Dunlegh 1524 *SR* (p), *-ley* 1596 DCo NQ 10, 1. 'Hill clearing,'
v. dun, leah. HATHERLEIGH (6″) is *Hatherlegh* 1330 *SR* (p). *v.*
Hatherleigh *supra* 142. HEATHFIELD is *la Hethfeld* 1228 FF,
Bovihezfelde c. 1327 Exon, *Bovyhethfeld* early 15th ECP 1, 170.
'Waste land,' *v. supra* 265. HELE (6″) is *atte Hele* (nom. loc.)
1399 *Rental. v.* healh. JEWS BRIDGE is *ponti Iudeorum* 1406
Exon, *Jewysbrugge* 1421 Exon. KELLY is *Calwelegh* 1437, *North-
callewelegh* 1485 Wreyland. 'Bare clearing,' *v.* leah and cf.
Kellacott *supra* 179. KNOWLE is *Knolle* 1625 Wreyland. *v.*
cnoll. LANGALLER is *Longhalre* 1286 *Ass*, *Langealler* 1475 IpmR.
'The tall alder.' LUSCOMBE is *Loscomb* 1330, 1333 *SR* (p). *v.*
Luscombe *supra* 221. PARKE is *the Parke* 1596 DCo NQ 10, 1.
v. pearroc. PLUMLEY (6″) is *Plumlegh* 1333 *SR* (p). 'Plum-tree
clearing,' *v.* leah. SHAPTOR is *Shabbetorre* 1330, 1333 *SR* (p),
1345 *Ass. v.* Scobitor *infra* 528. SHEWTE (6″) is *la Shute* 1303
Ass, *atte Shuta* 1330, *atte Schute* 1333 *SR* (all p). *v.* Shute *supra*
184. SLADE is *atte Slade* (nom. loc.) 1399 *Rental. v.* slæd.
SOUTHBROOK is *Sudbroc*, 1219 *Ass* (p), *Southbroke* 1299 Ipm.
ULLACOMBE is *Oulecumbe* 13th Buckfast (p), *-comb* 1330, 1333 *SR*
(p), *Ullacombe next Yarner* 1553 Pat, *Owlacombe* 1582 *SR* (p).
'Owl valley,' *v.* cumb. WARMPIT COPSE (6″) is *Warmepitte* 1330
SR (p). 'Warm hollow,' cf. Warmacombe *supra* 295. WARWICKS
(6″) is *Walweeke*, *Wallwyke* 1596 DCo NQ 10, 1. WHITESTONE is
Whetistan 1238 *Ass* (p). Probably 'at the whetstone.' WIFFORD
is *Weyford* 1596 DCo NQ 10, 1. *v.* weg. WILLMEAD (6″) is
Wilmeade 1588 DA 28 (p). WOODLANDS (6″) is *Wodelond* 1399
Rental. WRAYLAND is *Wreyland* 1596 DCo NQ 10, 1, taking its
name from the river Wray *supra* 17. YEO COTTAGES (6″) is *Yeo*
1596 DCo NQ 10, 1. 'At the water,' *v.* Yeo *supra* 17–18.

North Bovey

NORTH BOVEY 138 D 4

Bovi 1086 DB, *Northebovy* 1199 FF

The place lies some miles further up the river than Bovey Tracy *supra* 466.

BEETOR is *Begatora* 1086 DB, *Byghetorre* 1333 *SR* (p), *Beeter al. Beetorr* 1732 *Recov*. The first element may be OE *byge*, 'bend, curve,' etc., referring to the circular hill here, but the forms are too scanty for certainty.

HOOKNEY [huknə]

Hokneton t. Hy 3 Dartmoor, 1275 RH, *Hokeneton* 1283 *Ass*, 1320 Ipm, *Hokenton* 1323 *Ass*
Hokene 1334 *SR*, *Hokyn* 1505 Dartmoor

The material is insufficient for any satisfactory suggestion.

KENDON (6") is *Kynedon* 13th *St Nicholas*, *Kingdon* t. Hy 3 Dartmoor, *Kyngdon* 1275 RH (p). Possibly 'king (or royal) hill' from cyning (or *cyne*) and dun. Close by are KING TOR and KING'S BARROW.

LETTAFORD is *Lottreford* 1244 *Ass*, -ter- 1308 Seld 17, *Lutterforde* 1390 IpmR, *Lotternaford* 1396 Cl, *Litterford* 1505 Dartmoor. The first element is the OE *hlūt(t)or*, 'clear, pure, bright.' It may be the old name of the stream here. Cf. Ludder Burn (PN La 200).

POTWORTHY (lost) is *Pot(t)eworthy* 1306 *Ass* (p), 1443 *Ct*, *Potworthey* 1654 *Deed*, *Potworthy al. Pottery* 1799 *Recov*. This may mean 'pot farm,' v. worþig, but a pers. name is also possible as first element. Cf. Potton, Potsgrove (PN BedsHu 106, 131).

SHAPLEY is *Essapla*, *Escapeleia* 1086 DB (Exon), *Scapelie* (Exch), *Sappeleg*' 1212, *Sapesleg*' 1219 Fees 98, 264, *Sheppelegha* 1230 Bracton. 'Sheep clearing,' v. sceap, leah.

ALLER and YARD were probably the homes of Walter de *Alre*, i.e. 'at the alder' and Robert *atte Yurd* (1333 *SR*). v. Yard *supra* 48.

BOWDA (6") is *Boghewode* 1330 *SR* (p), *Bowode* 1396 Cl. 'Curved or bow-shaped wood,' cf. Buda *supra* 96. BOWDEN (6") is *Bog-*

hedon 1330 *SR* (p). 'Curved hill,' *v. supra* 37. CLEAVE FM (6")
is *Cleve* 1571 *SR*. 'Steep slope,' *v.* clif. WEST COOMBE (6") is
Wester Comb 1562 *FF*. ELLACOMBE (6") is *Ellecomb* 1330, 1333
SR (p). '*Ella*'s valley' or 'elder tree valley,' *v.* ellen, cumb.
GRATNAR is *Grenetorre* 1333 *SR* (p), 1339 *Ass* (p). 'Green tor.'
GREENAWELL is *Greenwell al. Greenewell* 1663 *Recov.* HELE is
Heale 1654 *Deed. v. supra* 46. LANGDON is *Langedon* 1277 *Ass*
(p), *-dene* 1330, 1333 *SR* (p), *-done* 1364 IpmR. 'Long hill,' *v.*
dun. LUCKDON (6") is *Loketon* 1330, 1333 *SR* (p). *v.* tun. The
first element may be the OE loc(a) noted under Luckcroft
supra 128. MILLAWNS (6") is *Mullond* 1275 RH (p). 'Mill land.'
There is a mill near by. For the modern form, cf. Millawn (Co),
Middellond 1365 FF. SOUTHMEAD (6") is *Suthmede* 1244 *Ass.*
v. mæd. THORN is *Thorne Park* 1619 *Recov.* WORMHILL is
Wormhull 1325 *Ass* (p). The first element may be the OE *wyrm*,
'reptile, snake.'

Hennock

HENNOCK [henək] 138 E 7

> *Hainoc* 1086 DB (Exon), *Hanoch* (Exch)
> *Hanok* c. 1200 (13th) *Torre et freq* to 1450 *FF*, *-ek* 1306 Ipm
> *Henoc* 1234 Fees 396, *Henyk* c. 1540 CtRequests
> *Hynnok* 1238 *Ass*, *Hyanac* 1242 Fees 786
> *Heynok* 1281, 1286 *Ass*, *Heanok(e)* 1292 Ipm *et freq* to 1434
>   Exon, *Heannoke* 1450 Exon

Professor Ekwall suggests OE (*æt þǣre*) *hēan āc*, 'high' or 'tall
oak,' *v.* ac.

FLUDDA (6") is *la Flode* 14th Oliver 179, 1316 Pat, *Flode* 1291
Tax, *atte Flode* 1399 *Rental* (p). *v.* flode. The farm lies in a slight
valley in which is a streamlet normally dry. For the final vowel,
v. Introd. xxxvi.

HUXBEAR is *Hokesbere* 1295 Ipm, 1335 Ch, *Houkesbeare* 1372 Cl.
'*Hōc*'s wood' or possibly 'wood at the spur of land,' *v.* hoc,
bearu and cf. Huckham and Huxtable *supra* 56, 35.

CHUDLEIGH KNIGHTON is *Chenistetona* 1086 DB, *Knicheton* 1285
FA, *Knyghteton(e)* 1299 *Ass*, 1382 Exon, *Knyghton juxta Chud-
legh* 1464 IpmR, *Knytteton* 1305 Ipm, *Knyghton Hethfeld* 1488

AD iii, 1492 Ipm. *v.* cniht, tun. *Knyghton Hethfeld* is probably the area of waste land now called Knighton Heath. *v.* Heathfield *supra* 265. It is near Chudleigh *infra* 489.

WARMHILL

> *Wermehel(e)* 1086 DB, c. 1270 *Deed*, *-hale* 1330 *SR* (p)
> *Warmehull* 1219 *Ass*, *-hill* 1238 FF
> *Wormahull* 1333 *SR* (p)

'The warm hill,' *v.* hyll, with confusion at times with the common element healh.

MOORHOUSE (6″) and STONELANDS were probably the homes of Matilda *atte More* and John *de la Stone* (1330 *SR*). *v.* mor.

BEADON is *Beydon(e)* c. 1200 (15th) *Torre*, 1330 *SR* (p). '*Bǣga's* hill,' *v.* dun. BOTTOR is *Bodetorre* 1238 *Ass* (p), *Bottetorre* 1306 *Ass* (p), *Bottorre* 1330 *SR* (p), *Westbottore* 1414 *FF*. '*Botta's* torr' or *Boda's*. BOWDEN (6″) is *Boudon* 1238 *Ass* (p), *Boghedon(e)* 1331 *FF*, 1333 *SR* (p). 'Curved hill,' *v.* Bowden *supra* 37. CLAYPARKS (6″) is *la Cleye* c. 1200 (15th) *Torre*, *Claypark* 1664 *Recov*. CROCKHAM is *Crocomb* 1765 D. FURZELEIGH CROSS (6″) is *Fursley* 1823 *Recov*. 'Furze clearing,' *v.* leah. HAZELWOOD (6″) is *Halswood* 1783 *Recov*. *v.* Addenda, Part i, lviii. HUISH CROSS is *Hewis* 1238 *Ass* (p), *Hywys* 1286 *Ass*, (*juxta la Flode*) 14th Oliver 179. *v.* hiwisc. HYNER is *Hayner Mills* 1783 *Recov*. LONGLANDS (6″) is *Langland* 1685 *Recov*. LYNEHAM is *Lyncumbe* c. 1200 *Torre*, *Lineham* 1765 D. Possibly 'flax valley' or 'lime tree valley,' *v.* lin, lind, cumb. MARDON (6″) is *Mardon* 1545 *SR*. 'Boundary hill,' *v.* (ge)mære, dun. The farm lies by the parish boundary. PITT HO is *Pitt* 1712 *Recov*. POOLMILL BRIDGE, cf. *Polemyll Downe* 1564 *Deed*. RILEY is *Rilega* 1177 P, *Rilegh* 1238 *Ass* (p), 1330 *SR* (p). 'Rye clearing,' *v.* leah. STOKELAKE is so spelt in 1664 *Recov*. *v.* stocc, lacu. TOTTIFORD (6″) is *Toteworthi* 1333 *SR* (p). '*Totta's* farm,' *v.* worðig and Introd. xxxv.

Highweek (with Newton Abbot)

HIGHWEEK 138 H 7

> *Teyng(e)wike* c. 1200 (15th) *Torre*, *-wy(c)k* 1248 Ch, 1275 RH,
> *Teinngweke* 1224–44 Exon, *Teynguewike* 1331 Ch

Teinnewic c. 1200 Lay, *Teignewic* 1218 ClR, *Tennewick* 1219
  Fees 264, *Taynewyc* 1230 P, *Teynnewyk* 1281 *Ass*
Tengewyke 1238 FF, *-wike* 1247 Ch, *Tenggewyk al. Teyngwyk*
  1269 Ipm
Hegewyk c. 1270 QW, *Heghwyk* 1301 *Ass*, *Hegh Wyk* t. Ed 3
  Ass, *Tengweke al. Highweke* 1467 Pat, *Hywyke* 1493 Ipm,
  Hewyk 1675 Ogilby

v. wic. The place was originally distinguished by its position
near the river Teign (*supra* 14) and later by the adj. 'high' with
reference to the prominent hill on which it stands.

NEWTON ABBOT

Nova Villa late 12th Oliver, *la Novelevile in parte pertin' ad
  manerium de Teyngewyk* 1275 RH
Schireborne Nyweton c. 1200 (15th) *Torre, Nyweton Abbatis*
  1270, 1289 *Ass*, *Nyweton Abbots* 1338 Ipm, (*Abbas*) 1387 *FF
  villa de Nyweton Abbatis in parochia de Wolleburgh* 1419 Exon

'New farm,' *v.* tun. The place was granted to Torre Abbey by
William de Briwere in 1196 (Oliver). The meaning of *Schireburn*
is not known. Possibly it was an old name for the Aller
(*supra* 1). Part of the manor lay in the parish of Wolborough.

FORGES CROSS is *the Forchys* 1422 *Deed* and is so called from the
furcae or gallows of the Bussel family (MS. note by the late
Professor John Earle). Forches Cross is fairly common in Devon
as the name of cross-roads.

HOUGHTON is *Hugeton* 1238, 1244 *Ass*, *Huggeton* 1249 *Ass*,
Hugheton 1275 RH (all p). For a possible interpretation, *v.*
Houghton *supra* 267.

MAINBOW is *Maynbogh* c. 1200 (15th) *Torre, Meynbogh* 1244
Ass, *Maynbough* 13th Oliver 179, *la Maynbouhe* 13th Buckfast,
la Meynbogh 1301 *Ass* (p). This may be a compound of the British
word *maen*, 'stone' and OE *boga*, 'bow' (*v.* Bowden *supra* 37),
hence 'curve of land by the rock.' Or the first element may be
OE *mægen-* as in the compound Mainstone *supra* 228.

NEWTON BUSHEL (6″) is *Nyweton Busshel* 1329 *Ass*, (*Boischel*)
1359 Ipm, and represents the manor held by the family of
Busshel (1329 *Ass*), *Bussel* (1331 Ch), *Busshel* or *Boischel* (1359
Ipm).

RINGSLADE is *Ryngeslad* 1238 FF, *Ringe-* 1238 *Ass* (both p), *Ryngeslade juxta Heghwyk* 1301 *Ass*, *RYngheslade* 1330 *SR* (p). 'Circular valley,' *v.* hring, slæd.

ASH HILL (6″) is *Aysshehyll* 1524 *SR*. BERRY KNOWLES (6″) is *Biriknolle* 1318 *Ass* (p), 1330 *SR* (p). *v.* burh, cnoll. There is a well-marked hill here, but no traces of fortifications survive. BRADLEY MANOR is *Bradelegh* 1238 *Ass* (p), (*juxta Teynbrigg*') t. Ed 3 *Ass*. 'The wide clearing,' *v.* brad, leah. DARACOMBE is *Dodecumbe* 1238 *Ass* (p). '*Dodda*'s combe,' cf. Darracott *supra* 43. GREENHILL is *Grenewill* 1356 *Ass* (p). *v.* wielle. There is a spring here. HELE HO is *Heale* 1613 *Recov. v. supra* 46. LITTLE JOY is so spelt 1809 M. Cf. Little Comfort *supra* 40. MOOR FM (6″) is *More* c. 1620 Risdon. *v.* mor. MORLEY is *Morley* 1289 *Ass. v.* mor, leah. PERRY COTTAGES (6″) is *Perry* c. 1620 Risdon. 'At the peartree,' *v.* pyrige. SINGMORE COTTAGE (6″) is *Seynguemore* (sic) 1433 *FF. v.* Singmore *infra* 505.

Ideford

IDEFORD [idifəd] 138 F 8/9

> *Yudaforda* 1086 DB, *Yuddeford* 1275 RH, 1316 FA, 1440 Exon, *ȝuddeford(e)* 1309 Exon, *Yuddes-* 1276 RH, *Yudes-* 1346 FA
>
> *Ghudeforde* 1281 Ipm
>
> *Hiddeford* 1285 FA, *Idyforde* 1291 Tax, *Idde-* 1390 Exon, *Ideford* 1440 Exon
>
> *Giddeforde* 1315 Exon
>
> *Yeddeford(e)* 1353 *Ass*, 1356 Ipm, 1373 *FF*, *Yede-* 1441 Pat, Exon
>
> *Jyddeford* 1357 Ipm, *Yidde-* 1357 Cl
>
> *Edeforde* 1440 Exon, 1577 Saxton, *Edford* 1571 *SR*

The first element cannot be the OE pers. name *Gydda*, as the initial *g* would remain before OE *y*. Professor Ekwall suggests OE **Giedda*, a WS weak form corresponding to the recorded strong form *Geddi*.

HESTOW FM is *Historre* 1238 *Ass*, 1330 *SR*, *-tore* 1244 *Ass*, *Hystorre* 1333 *SR* (all p). *v.* torr. It is possible that this is a compound of OE *hīehst*, 'highest' and torr. Hestow stands near the top of a prominent hill. Cf. Winstow *infra* 480.

UNDERHAYS (6″) is so spelt in 1649 (*FF*). *v.* (ge)hæg. WELL was probably the home of John de *Fonte* (1333 *SR*).

Ilsington

ILSINGTON 138 G 5

Ilestintona 1086 DB (Exon), *Lestintone* (Exch)
Elstington 1186–91 Oliver 138, *Elstinton* 1262 Ipm, *Elsynton* 1393, *Elsinton* 1424 Pat
Ilstingtun c. 1200 Buckland *et freq* to 1342 Exon with variant spellings *Yl-*, *-yng-*, *-in-*, *-ton*, *Ilstinctona* 1282 Ch, *Hylstyncton* c. 1400 Exon

This is possibly from OE *Ielfstāningtūn*, an ingtun compound of the pers. name **Ielfstān*, a variant of the more common *Aelfstān* of the same type as that noted under Ilfracombe *supra* 46.

BAGTOR is *Bagathora* 1086 DB (Exon), *Bagetore* (Exch), *Baggetorre* 1220 Bracton *et freq* to 1333 *SR* (p), *Bagetorre* 1238 *Ass* (p), *Baghtorr(e)* 1275 RH, 1285 FA, *Baggatorre juxta Wydecumbe* 1329 *Ass*, '*Bacga*'s torr,' cf. Bagga Tor *supra* 232.

COLDEAST is *Choleyest* 1430 *DuCo*, *Coldyest* 1452 *MinAcct*, *-east* 1609 *DuCo*. This may be a compound of OE *ceald*, 'cold,' with dialectal *chold* in the first form and *east*, 'east,' with dialectal *yest* in some of the forms. No parallel for such a compound is known but the farm is in the east of the parish on land sloping down to the east.

COLESWORTHY is *Chauelesweye, Cawlesweye* c. 1200 (15th) *Torre* (p), *Caulesweye* 1330, 1333 *SR* (p), *Coleswey* 1566 DA 43, *Colswaye* 1726 *Recov*. '*Cāfel*'s weg.' This pers. name is not on record but *v.* Keyberry *supra* 524 and Colesworthy *infra* 563. The *worthy* is apparently a quite recent corruption.

CUSTREET (6″) is *Cor(r)yngestret(e)* 1306 *Ass* (p), 1330 *SR* (p), *Curryngestrete juxta Aynekesdon* 1310 *Ass*, *Curryngstrete* 1339 *Ass*, *Coristret* 1339 *Ass* (p), *Correstrete* 1342 Exon, *Custreete* or *Curstreete* 1624 *Deed*, and is perhaps to be associated with the family of William *Curre*, who was living here in 1339 (*Ass*). If so, we have another example of the late use of connective ing. Cf. Murchington *supra* 453.

GAVRICK COPSE is *Gaverick* in 1566 (DA 43), and was the home of Philip de *Gaverok* (1330 *SR*), *Bygaverok* (1333 *SR*). Possibly this was originally a stream-name, denoting the little brook which joins the Teign above Teigngrace. The root may be the British word corresponding to W *gafr*, 'goat.' For the *-oc*, *v.* Ekwall RN lxxviii.

HALFORD is *Halford* 1275 RH, 1285 FA. Perhaps 'ford by the healh or nook of land between two streams.' If so, we have a development of OE *healh* not usually found in this county. Cf. Hele *supra* 46.

HARTFORD FM (6″) is *Herpadforda* c. 1200 Buckland, *Herford* 1330 *SR* (p). *v.* herepæð, ford and cf. Harford *supra* 342.

HAYTOR is *Idetordoune* 1566 DA 43, *Ittor Doune* 1687 *Deed*, *Idetor* 1737 *Recov*, *Eator Down* 1762 *Recov*, *Itterdown* 1789 *Recov*. The modern form is corrupt and must have been influenced by the spellings of Haytor Hundred *infra* 504. Nothing can be done with the forms as they stand and the etymology is not made easier if we take the *eofede tor* of BCS 1323 to refer to this tor.

HORRIDGE is *Holerigge* 13th Oliver 175, *Holrig* 1242 Fees 790, *-rigge* 1303 FA, *-rugg(e)* 1316 FA, 1330 *SR* (p), *Haurig* 1242 Fees 792, *Horugg* 1275 RH (p). 'Hollow ridge,' the reference being to the hollow in the hillside at this point, *v.* holh, hrycg.

INGSDON

> *Ainechesdona* 1086 DB, *Aynekedon* 1228 FF, *Aynokesdon* 1285 FA, *-ek-* 1316 FA, 1317 *Ass*
> *Aylekesdon'* 1242 Fees 790
> *Anekesdon* 1244 *Ass*, 1244–62 Ipm, *Estanekesdon juxta Ilstyngton* 1294 *Ass*, *Aynkesdon* c. 1630 Pole
> *Enkedon* 1244–62 Ipm, *Enkesdon* 1428 FA
> *Henekesdon* 1251 Ch, *Nether Henkesdon* 1311 FF, *Netherehenekesdon* 1316 *Ass*

Dr Schram suggests an OE pers. name **Aegenoc*, a diminutive of one of the OE names in *Aegen-*. Hence, '*Aegenoc*'s hill,' *v.* dun.

LIVERTON

> *Levinton* 1227 Ch, *Leuetone* 1342 Exon, *Levaton* 1566 DA 43
> *Luueton* 1333 *SR* (p), 1339 *Ass* (p)
> *Lyueton* 1336, 1339 *Ass* (p), 1408 *Ass*

'*Lēofa*'s farm,' *v.* **tun.**

PINCHAFORD is *Puncheford* 1238 *Ass* (p), 1323 *Ass*, 1330 *SR* (p), *Poncheford* 1333 *SR* (p), *Pyncheford* 1566 DA 43. '*Puneca*'s ford.' This place-name probably contains in its weak form the same pers. name which is found in *puneces wurði* (BCS 1323); the site of that place is not known, but it was somewhere in this neighbourhood.

RORA is probably identical with *la Hore* 1230 P, 1238 *Ass*, *atte Hore* 1399 *Rental* (all p), representing ME *at ther ore*, *v.* **æt, ora.** The farm stands at the foot of a steep slope. For the final vowel, *v.* Introd. xxxvi.

SIGFORD and HIGHER SIGFORD are *Sigeforda* 1086 DB, *Sygeford'* 1242 Fees 788, *Sigge-* 1281 *Ass*, *Sygge-* 1356 Ipm, *Ouerasigeford* 1408 *Ass*. '*Sicga*'s ford.' The last reference is to 'Over' or 'Higher' Sigford.

STAPLEHILL

> *Estapeleia* 1086 DB (Exon), *Stapelie* (Exch)
> *Stapelhill(e)* 1242 Fees 788, 1303 FA, *Estera-* 1324 *FF*, *Est-*
> *stapilhille* 1339 *Ass*

'Hill marked by a post,' *v.* **stapol.** The DB form, if it belongs here, seems to be corrupt.

HILL FM, MILL CROSS, POOL FM, WESTABROOK and WOOD COTTAGES (all 6″) were probably the homes of Walter *atter Hille* (1330 *SR*), Richard *atte Mille* (1339 *Ass*), Stephen de *la Pole* (1317 *Ass*), Henry *Westabrok* (1374 *SR*) and William *atte Wode* (1333 *SR*).

BENEDICTS BRIDGE is probably to be associated with the family of Thomas *Benet* (1330 *SR*) and John *Bennett* (1612 *SR*). CLEAVE PLANTATION (6″) is *la Clyve* 1342 Exon. *v.* **clif.** COCKSLAND (6″) is *Cockeslond* 1322 *Ass*. *Cock* was probably the name of its medieval owner. HEMSWORTHY[1] is *Aylmersworth(y)* 1327 Banco,. 1340 *SR* (p), *Aylmesworthy* 1379 Fine (p), *Omsworthye* 1566 DA 43. '*Æþelmǣr's* worþig.' GREA TOR is *Greate Torre, Grettor bridge* 1566 DA 43. 'The great tor.' HOLBROOK (6″) is perhaps identical with *Halwyll browke* 1566 DA 43. 'Holy well.' HOLLOWCLEAVE COPSE (6″) is *Holclyf* 1533 *Recov. v.* holh, clif. HOLWELL TOR is *Holewyltorre* 1262 NGl 5, 44. *v.* holh, wielle,. torr. HONEYWELL (6″) is *Hunewyll* 1249 *Ass* (p), *Honewill* 1330 *SR* (p), *Honywyll* 1499 Ipm, *-well* 1566 DA 43. *v.* wielle. The spring was perhaps so named from the sweetness of its waters. OLD LAYS FM (6″) is possibly to be associated with Nicholas *atte Laghe* (1330 *SR*). LENDA is *la Lynde* 1238 *Ass* (p), *Lende* 1566 DA 43. 'At the limetree,' *v.* lind. For the final vowel, *v.* Introd. xxxvi. LOUNSTON is *Luueneston* 1238 *Ass* (p), *Loueuyston* 1330 *SR* (p), *Lounston* 1566 DA 43. *v.* tun. The first element is the pers. name *Lēofwine.* MIDDLECOTT is *Myddell Cott* 1566 DA 43. *v.* cot(e). MOUNTSLAND is *Mounteslond* 1400 Ct (p), *Mountsland* 1701 DKR 41, 201. Cf. Mounson *supra* 429. NARROWCOMBE is *Northcomb* 1330 *SR* (p), *Northacomb* 1752 *Recov. v.* cumb. RIPPON TOR is *Rippentorr* 1726 *Recov, Rippen Tor* 1827 G. SADDLE TOR is *Saddletor* c. 1620 Risdon and is so named from its shape. It seems to be identical with the *tor* called *Lether Torre* in a perambulation of 1566 (DA 43). Cf. Laughter Tor *supra* 195. SMALLACOMBE (6″) is *Smalecombe* 1342 Exon, *-la-* 1566 DA 43. 'Narrow valley,' *v.* cumb. STANCOMBE is *Stoncomb juxta Bukyngton* 1302 *Ass, Stoncombe in Ilsington* 1481 IpmR. SWINE DOWN (6″) must be near the spot called *Swynepath juxta Ilstyngton* 1322 *Ass.* WOODHOUSE is *Wodehouse* 1370 IpmR, *Wodehousdoune* 1501 ECP 4, 45.

Kingsteignton

KINGSTEIGNTON 138 G/H 8

> *Tegntun* c. 1050 ASC (*s.a.* 1001), *Teintona* 1086 DB, *Teyn-* 1224–44 Exon, 1242 Fees 782, 1252 Ch, *Teincton* 1212 Fees 98, *Teing-* 1224–44 Exon, 1242 Fees, *Teintone Regis* 1259 Exon, *Kingestentone, Kings Teyntune* 1274 Ipm, *Keyngesteyngton* 1394 *Ass, Kingstenton* 1628 DA 6, *Kings Staynton* 1675 Ogilby

---

[1] *Emsworthy* on 6″ map.

'Farm on the river Teign' (*supra* 14). *v.* tun. The manor was held by the king in 1086 (DB).

BELLAMARSH BARTON is *Beldemerse* 1242 Fees 791 (p), *Bealde-* 1285 FA, *Beallesmershe* 1276 *Ass*, *Beallemers* 1279 Ipm, *Bealde-mersh* 1345 *Ass*. '*Bealda*'s marsh,' cf. Belleigh *supra* 297.

GAPPAH is *Gatepada* 1086 DB, *-path(e)* 1242 Fees 791, 1279, 1331 Ipm, *Gadespad* 1230 P (p), *Gatespathe* 1285 Ipm, *Gappath* 1599 *Recov*, *Gappa* 1670 *FF*. 'Goats' path,' *v.* gat, pæþ.

HACKNEY is *piscar' in aqua de Teyng vocat' Haking* 1422 IpmR. *Haking*, found also in Hackney *infra* 506 and in *le Hakyng* t. Hy 8 *MinAcct* (South Pool), is clearly the obsolete word *haking* found in Carew's *Survey of Cornwall* 30 a, where it is used of a kind of fish-net employed in tidal waters. Ekwall (PN La 71) suggests that it is a derivative of OE *haca*, 'bolt.' The derivation of Hackney from *Haking* is obscure.

TWINYEO is *Betunia* 1086 DB, *Bitweneya* 1263 Ipm, *Betwynyo juxta Ilstington* 1303 *Ass*, *Twyneya* 1242 Fees 790, *Twynya* 1303 FA, *Twyneyo* 1311 Exon (p). 'Between the water(s),' cf. Tinney *supra* 163. The farm is situated in the fork where Bovey and Teign unite.

WARE BARTON is *la Were* 1277 *Ass*, *Burdouneswere* 1322 *Ass*, *Bourdoneswere* 1370 Exon. *v.* wer. The place was held by Robert *Bourdoun* in 1322 (*Ass* 189 m 14).

WHITEWAY BARTON is *Witeweia* 1086 DB, *Whiteweye* 1234 Fees 396, *Whyte-* 1238 *Ass*, 1242 Fees 790, *Whitweye* 1333 *SR* (p), *Whythaweye* 1335 *Ass* (p). Self-explanatory. The soil here is white clay.

BURNELLS and GILDONS (both 6″) are to be associated with the families of Hugh *Burnell* (1545 *SR*) and John *Gildene* (1333 *SR*).

ABBROOK is *Abbrok(e)* 1330 *SR* (p), 1335 *Ass* (p). '*Abba*'s brook.' BABCOMBE is *Babbecumb'* 1242 Fees 791, *-coumbe* 1305 Ipm, *Babecumbe* 1275 RH (p). '*Babba*'s valley,' *v.* cumb. BUCKLEY WOOD (6″) is *Bogheclyve* 1330 *SR* (p). 'Bow-shaped steep hill-side,' *v.* clif and cf. Bowden *supra* 37. DURLEY (6″) is *Dorlegh* 1330, *Durlegh* 1333 *SR* (p). *v.* deor, leah. FISHWICK (6″) is

Fishwyk 1330, *Fyshwyke* 1333 *SR* (p). 'Fish farm,' *v.* **wic**. It lies by the river Teign. GREEN HILL is *Grenehill(e)* 1330, 1333 *SR* (p). HONEYWELL (6″) is *Honewille* 1330 *SR* (p). *v.* Honeywell *supra* 478. PONSWINE (6″) is *Pawnswyn al. Potisfyn* 1558–79 ECP. PRESTON is *Prustaton* 1335 *Ass* (p), *Preston in decen. de Teyngton* 1356 *Ass*, *Pruston* 1620 *Recov*. 'Priests' farm,' *v.* **tun**. TEIGNBRIDGE HO is *Teyngebrugge* 1318 Pat, *Teyngbrigge* 1351 *Ass*, *Tyngbrygg* 1412 Exon. TORHILL COTTAGE (6″) is *Torrehill* 1592 *Recov* and was probably the home of Martin *atte Torre* (1330 *SR*). *v.* **torr**. WINSTOW COTTAGES (6″) is *Winesthorre* 1238 *Ass* (p). '*Wine*'s tor.' For the modern form, cf. Hestow, Downstow *supra* 474, 291. The spellings with *stow* for *stor* are due to the reduction of both these final syllables to *ster* in popular speech. Cf. Plaster Down *supra* 249.

Lustleigh

LUSTLEIGH 138 E 5

> *Leuestelegh'* 1242 Fees 793, 1327 Banco, *-leḡ* 1249 *Ass*, *Leuistelegh* 1276 Ipm
> *Luuesteleg(h)* 1276, 1277 Ipm, *Luuastelegge* 1282 *FF*
> *Lustelegh(e)* 1276 Ipm, 1282 Exon, *-leye* 1285 FA
> *Lisleigh* 1672 *FF*, *Listleigh al. Lustleigh* 1712, *Listleigh oth. Lustleigh oth. Lisley* 1749 *Recov*

The surname *Luvesta*, 'dearest one,' is found in Ermington in the *SR* for 1333. The place-name Lustleigh may be of late OE or ME formation and denote the clearing (*v.* leah) of a man so nicknamed. Professor Ekwall suggests an OE pers. name *Lēofgiest*.

FOXWORTHY (6″) is *Farkysworthi* 1330, *Vearkesworth* 1333 *SR* (p), *Ferkesworthy* 1399 *Ct* (p). '*Færoc*'s worþig.' This pers. name is not recorded, but might be a diminutive of an OE *Fær*-name.

MAPSTONE (6″) is *Mattepaneston* 1249 *Ass* (p), *Mappestone* 1330 *SR* (p). The first element may be the pers. name discussed under Martinhoe *supra* 65. The second part would seem to be identical with Panson *supra* 164, the reference being to the large block of granite, resembling a haystack, round which the road has to bend (*ex inf.* Mr H. R. Watkin).

PETHYBRIDGE (6″) is *Pidebrigg(e)* 1318 Pat, 1333 *SR, Pydebrugg'* 1330 *SR, Pythebrygge* 1443 *Ct* (all p). ‘*Pyd(d)a*’s bridge’ or ‘*Pidda*’s.’ Cf. *Pidborough* (PN Sx 13).

COMBE (6″), FURSDON and NARRAMORE were probably the homes of Thomas *atte Combe* (1318 Pat), John de *la Fursen* (1318 Pat) and Richard *atte Fursen* (1352 *SR*) (cf. Furze *supra* 415), and Reginald *Bynorthemore* (1318 Pat), i.e. ‘north of the moor,’ cf. Narraway *supra* 433.

BARNECOURT is *Barne Court* 1674 *Recov.* BOVEYCOMBE (6″) is *Bovycomb* 1330 *SR*(p). ‘Bovey valley,’ *supra* 2, *v.* cumb. CASELY is probably identical with *Carswillegh* 1330 *SR* (p), *Carslegh* 1413 Exon (p). ‘Cress-spring clearing,’ *v.* cærse, wielle, leah. SOUTH HARTON is *Hurton(e)* 1318 Pat, 1330, 1352 *SR* (all p). *v.* tun. The first element is OE *heort*, ‘hart.’ LUSTLEIGH CLEAVE is *Cleyfe* 1712 *Recov, Lesley Cleave* 1797 Polwhele. *v.* clif. There is a very steep descent here to the Teign. RUDGE (6″) is so spelt in 1694 *Recov. v.* hrycg. SANDUCK is *Sandhulke* 1333 *SR* (p), 1619 *Recov.* For the meaning, *v.* Hucken Tor *supra* 244.

Manaton

MANATON [mænətən] 138 E 4

Magnetona, Manitona 1086 DB

Maneton(e) 1234 Fees 399 *et freq* to 1443 Exon, *Parva Maneton'* 1242 Fees 786, *Magna Maneton juxta Northbovy* 1356 *Ass*

Parua Manneton 1238 *Ass, Manaton* 1348 Ipm

For the interpretation of this name, *v.* Manadon *supra* 246.

CANNA (6″) is *Canna* or *Cann East* 1771 *Recov*, and was the home of Andrew *atte Canne* (1374 *SR*). This would seem to be the OE *canne*, ‘can, cup,’ used in some topographical sense, but the name is very difficult. There is a Cann House in Tamerton (*v.* 243 *supra*), Cann Wood in Plympton, five Canna Parks and one Canny Park in Devon and it is frequent in field-names. Cf. also the pers. name *atte Canne* 1333 *SR* (W).

CHALLACOMBE COMMON is *Chaluecomb(e)* 1481 *Ct* (p), 1555 *DuCo, Chaluecombe* 1505 Dartmoor. ‘Calves’ valley,’ *v.* cumb. This must be very near the *cealfa dun* of BCS 1323.

CRIPDON DOWN is *Crepedon* 1238 *Ass* (p), *Crupedene* 1275 RH (p). The first element is probably the OE *crȳpe*, 'narrow passage, drain,' etc., discussed under Crypt (PN Sx 16).

EASDON is *Yernesdon* 1330, 1333 *SR* (p), *Yeresdon* 1384 *DuCo*, *in vasto de Yeresdon* 1384 *Ct*, *Yerson Downe* 1727 *Recov*. 'Eagle's hill,' *v.* earn, dun. Cf. Yes Tor *supra* 205.

GRIMSPOUND is a circular enclosure on the moor containing twenty-four hut circles belonging to the Bronze Age. No early references to the site have been found before Polwhele (1797), but there is no doubt that *Grim*, as in Grims Dyke (W), *grimes dic* in BCS 934, Grims Ditch (Herts), *Grymesdich* 1291 Ch, Grimes Dike (Mx), *Grim(m)esdich* 13th AD i, AD ii, *Grimesdich* 1289 AD ii, refers to the Devil and that the name is one of those instances where a large prehistoric work was associated by the Saxons with diabolic forces. Cf. IPN 161.

HEATHERCOMBE is *Heddercumb* 1244 *Ass*, *Hedercomḃ* 1330 *SR* (p), *Hathercombe* 1413 IpmR. *v.* Hatherleigh *supra* 142.

HEATREE [heitri·] is *(on, of) hyfan treow(e)* 10th BCS 1323, *Hevitree* c. 1620 Risdon. In OGer we have a series of names *Hufo, Huba, Huvika, Huvilo, Huffinc* which suggest a pers. name stem *Huf-*. We have also in England in the 12th cent. a Lincolnshire pers. name *Huf*, which suggests that the same stem was used in this country. *Hyfa* may be a mutated derivation of this stem *huf-*. Hence, '*Hyfa*'s tree,' *v.* treow.

HOUNDTOR is *Hundatora* 1086 DB, *Hundetorre* 1238 *Ass*, 1242 Fees 781, *Hounde-* 1438 BM. 'Hounds' or *Hunda*'s torr.' The animal name is apparently found in Hunton (Ha), *(in) Hundatune* BCS 629.

LANGSTONE is possibly *(on) langa stan* 10th BCS 1323, and is *Langhestan* 1086 DB. No menhir survives here now.

NEADON [neidən] is *Beneadona* 1086 DB (Exon), *Benedone* (Exch), *Nythedon* 1303 FA, *Bynythedon* 1333 *SR* (p). 'Beneath the down,' cf. Naithwood *supra* 181.

SOUSSONS is *Soueston* t. Hy 6 *Ct* (p), *North Souson* 1771 *Recov*, *South Stone Farm* 1809 M. The probable meaning is 'at the seven stones,' though no trace of such now remains. Cf. Zeaston *supra* 287. The place is to be identified with *(oð) sufen stanas*

(BCS 1323). In that charter the next boundary mark is *hyfan treow*, which is undoubtedly Heatree, some three miles NNE of Soussons.

BARRACOTT (6″) is *Bodecote* 1330 *SR* (p), 1331 Misc. '*Boda*'s cot(e).' For the modern form, cf. Arracott, Darracott *supra* 208, 43. BECKAFORD is *Bykeford* 1303 *Ass* (p), *Byka-* 1333 *SR* (p). '*Bic(c)a*'s ford.' BECKHAMS (6″) is probably to be associated with the family of William le Tosere de *Bukecoumbe* (1303 *Ass*). BLACK HILL is *Blackaball* 1566 DA 43. For *ball* = hill, *v. supra* 211. BLISSMOOR (6″) is *Blissmore* in 1622 *Recov*. BOWERMAN'S NOSE is so spelt in 1765 D. It is a rock on the moor, shaped like a man's profile. HAYNE (6″) was the home of Michael *atte Heghes* (1330), *atte Heghen* (1333 *SR*). *v.* Hayne *supra* 129. HAYNE DOWN is *Heighen-down* 1797 Polwhele and takes its name from the farm. HOLWELL (6″) is *Halghewill(e)* 1333 *SR* (p), *Ass* (p). 'Holy well.' HORSHAM (6″) is *Horsham* 1340 *SR* (p). Cf. Horsham *supra* 242. LEIGHON [li·ən] is *Leyne in parochia Mannedone* 1291 Tax, *atte Leaghyn* 1356 *Ass* (p). It is apparently the weak plural of OE leah. SOUTHCOTT is *Shucote, Scucote* 1330, *Southcote* 1333 *SR* (p). Probably 'south cot(e),' the earlier forms being corrupt. It lies due south of Manaton. VOGWELL is *Foghille* 1333 *SR* (p), *Fogwell* 1765 D. 'Hill with fog-pasture.' For the first element, *v.* Voghay *supra* 457. WINGSTONE is *Winkesdon* 1623 *Recov*.

Moretonhampstead

MORETONHAMPSTEAD 138 C/D 4

> *Morton(a)* 1086 DB *et freq* to 1291 Tax, (*subtus Dertemor*) 1270 *Ass*, (*juxta Northbovy*) 1345 *Ass, Morton Hampsted* 1493 Ipm, (*Hempstede*) 1514 *Ct, Mourtonhampstede* 1514 *Ct, Moreton al. Moreton Hampstead* 1692 *Recov*
>
> *Moureton in the More* 1446 *FF*

'Moor farm,' *v.* tun. It lies at the edge of Dartmoor. The reason for the later addition of *Hampstead* is not clear, especially as this element occurs nowhere else in the county.

ADDISCOTT (6″) is *Otiscote* 1333 *SR, Adescote* 1443 *Ct, Addescote* 1524 *SR, Adiscote* 1599 DA 28 (all p), *Allescott al. Liddiscott* 1636 *Recov*. Probably '*Æddi*'s cot(e),' the 14th cent. form being corrupt.

BRINNING is probably identical with *Brendon Parkes* or *Brandon Parkes* 1504 Ipm. For the etymology, *v.* Brendon *supra* 58, and for the phonetic development, cf. Brimley and Runnon *supra* 411, 144.

BUDLEIGH (6″) was the home of John *atte Bothele* (1330 *SR*) and Roger *atte Bothele* (1333 *SR*). This may be the OE *boðl*, 'building,' though that element has not hitherto been noted in South Country place-names. We have, further, Buddelhayes (*infra* 631), Buddlehay in Wiveliscombe (So), *Botheleheye* in 1327 *SR* (p), Buddle Oak in Halse (So), *atte Bothele* 1327 *SR* (p), and Buddle in Fordingbridge (Ha), *la Bothele* 1305 *Ass*.

LINSCOTT is *Luuescote* 1330, *Luuenescote* 1333, 1340 *SR* (all p). *v.* cot(e). The first element is probably *Lēofwine*, hence 'Leofwine's cot(e).'

LOWTON is *Lewendona* 1086 DB, *Lowedon Peverel* 1303 FA, *-done* 1423 IpmR, *Lughedon* 1346 FA, *Luedo(u)n* 1396 Cl, 1428 FA. This is probably the same hill-name as Lewdon in Thelbridge and Lewdon in Cheriton *supra* 396, 428. If the first form is correct, it would suggest the weak adjective *hlēowa*, rather than the noun *hlēow* as the first element of the compound. The farm lies below the top of a hill.

SLONCOMBE is *Slancomb(e)* 1160–2 DA 36, c. 1580 *Ct*, *-cumb* 1216 DA 36, *Sloucombe* 1209 DA 36, *Slan(n)acomb* c. 1450 *Ct*, *Slandcomb* c. 1580 *Ct*, *Slanokcombe* 1609 *Recov*. The first element is probably OE *slāna* (ME *slone*), gen. plural of *slāh*, 'sloe,' hence 'valley of the sloes.'

STEWARD is *Storygge* 1444 Pat (p), *Stoures, Stowrysshe al. Stowresshe* 1504 Ipm, *Steward al. Stewrish* 1721 *Recov*. The forms are too late and too inconsistent for any satisfactory etymology to be suggested.

WRAY BARTON is *Wereia* 1086 DB (Exon), *Wergi* (Exch), *Wreie* 1238 *Ass* (p), *Wrey(e)* 1292 Ipm (p), 1370 IpmR, (*juxta Morton*) 1314 *Ass*, *Wrey al. Wreycombe* 1467 Pat, *Wray* 1249 FF. *v.* Wray *supra* 17.

COOMBE FM (6″), HAYNE[1], MOORBARN (6″), and UPPACOTT were

---

[1] *Heghen* 1396 Cl, *Heyne* 1504 Ipm.

probably the homes of William *atte Combe* (1333 *SR*), Adam *atte Heghen* (ib.), Ralph *atte More* (ib.), and John de *Uppecote* (ib.). *v.* cumb, mor, cot(e), and cf. Hayne *supra* 129.

BOWDEN (6″) is *Bughadun* 12th *St Nicholas*, *Bowedon* 1384 *FF*, *Boghe-* 1415 *Ass*, *Bough-* 1496 Ipm. 'Curved, bow-shaped hill,' *v. supra* 37. BUTTERDON HILL is *Boterdoune* 1330 *SR* (p), *-don* 1415 *Ass. v.* Buttercombe *supra* 40. CLIFFORD FM is *Clyfford* 1330, 1333 *SR* (p). *v.* clif. COSSICK is *Coswick* 1809 M. CRANBROOK is *Cranbroc* 12th *St Nicholas*, *Parva Cranbrok* 1345 *Ass*, *Little*, *Gret Cranbroke* 1496 Ipm. 'Crane or heron brook.' DOCCOMBE is *Dockumb'* 1221–30 Fees 1443, *Doccombe* 1330, 1333 *SR*(p). Probably 'valley where dock grows,' *v.* cumb. HINGSTON DOWN is *Hengesdon* 1333 *SR* (p). 'Stallion hill,' *v.* hengest, dun and cf. Hingston Down (Co), *æt Hengestdune*, *æt Hengestes dune* ASC *s.a.* 835. HOLCOMBE is *Holecumbe* 1244 *Ass*. HOWTON is *Hugheton Sawte* 1285 FA, *Hugheton* 1333 *SR* (p), 1345, 1415 *Ass*, (*juxta Morton Cortenay*[1]) 1349 *FF. v.* Houghton *supra* 267. The identity of *Sawte* is unknown. LANGHILL (6″) is *Langehill* 1634 *Recov*. 'Long hill.' LEIGN is *Layne* 1571, 1582 *SR* and is probably of the same origin as Leighon *supra* 483. LEWDOWN'S FM (6″) is to be associated with the family of Robert de *Luwedon* (1333 *SR*). MEACOMBE is *Meacombe* 1588 DA 28 (p), *Mead-* 1657 *FF.* NORTHMOOR is *Northemore* 1568 *Recov.* PAFFORD (6″) is *Pafford* 1330 *SR* (p), 1415 *Ass.* Probably of the same origin as Parford *supra* 432. PEPPERDON is *Pypedenne* 1310 *Ass*, *Pippedene* 1333 *SR* (p), *Peppedon* 1727 *Recov.* '*Pippa's* valley,' *v.* denu. PINMOOR (6″) is *Pinmore* 1582 *SR.* SAINTHILL is *Sweynthull* 1333 *SR* (p). 'Swinged or over-worked hill,' *v.* Saint Hill *infra* 565 and Addenda, Part ii, xiv. WILLOWRAY (6″) is *Willaway al. Wallaway Wood al. Willaway Cliffe* 1609 *Recov*, and was the home of William *atte Wellewey* (1352 *SR*). 'Way or track past the spring,' *v.* wielle. The modern *r* is intrusive. WOOSTON is *Wlrichestona* 12th *St Nicholas*, *Worston* 1333 *SR*(p). '*Wulfrīc's* farm,' *v.* tun. YALWORTHY (6″) is *Yoldworthi* 1333 *SR* (p), *Yolworthie* 1582 *SR*, *Yalworthy* or *Yelworthy* 1761 *Recov.* 'The old worþig.' *v.* Addenda, Part i, lviii.

---

[1] I.e. Moretonhampstead; cf. 1346 (FA).

Teigngrace

TEIGNGRACE [tiŋ'greis] 138 G 7

Taigna 1086 DB
Tengue 1277 *Ass*, *Teng* 1292 Ipm
Teygne Bruere 1281 *Ass*, *Teynghebruer* 1352 Pat
Teyngegras 1331 Exon, *Teyngras* 1386 *Ass*, *Teyng Graas* 1391 FF, *Teyngcras* 1438 Exon, *Graseteyng* 1443 *Ct*, *Grace-* 1543 SR, *Tingrace* 1675 Ogilby

This manor on the Teign was first held by the family of (de la) *Bruere* (1277 *Ass*). It had passed by 1352 (Pat) to Geoffrey *Gras* who was no doubt related to 'John called *Gras*' (i.e. the fat one), a canon of the monastery of Torre (1351 Pat).

LEYGREEN is *Ley Commons* t. Eliz ChancP 3, and was the home of William *atter Leghe* 1333 SR. *v.* leah. STOVER HO is *Stover* 1723 *Recov*, *Stoford Lodge* 1765 D. Cf. Stowford *supra* 41.

XXI. EXMINSTER HUNDRED

Esseministra 1084 Geld Roll, *Exemenistr'* 1187 P
v. Exminster *infra* 496.

Ashcombe

ASHCOMBE 138 E 9

Aissecoma 1086 DB, *Aiscumb(e)* 1200 Seld 3, 1259 Exon
Ascumbe 1200 Cur, *Ashcombe* 1291 Tax

v. æsc, cumb.

CHARLWOOD FM (6″) is *Churlewode* 1330 SR (p). *v.* ceorl. GRAMMARCOMBE is *Grammercombe* 1827 G. Possibly we may compare Grammerby *supra* 221. LANGDON BARTON is *Langedon* 1334 *Ass* (p). 'Long hill,' *v.* dun. WOODHOUSE FM is *Wodehous* 1422 *Rental*, and was the home of Adam *de Bosco* (1267 *Ass*). WOODOFFICE COPSE (6″) is clearly a corruption of the more correct *Wood-ovis*. Cf. Woodovis *supra* 220.

Ashton

Ashton 138 D 7

> *Haiserston, Essestone* 1086 DB (Exon), *Aiserstone* (Exch),
> *Essereston* 1181 P
> *Asser(e)ston* 1244 *Ass*, 1263 Ipm, *Assher(e)ston(e)* 1275 Exon,
> 1297 Pat, 1356 Ipm
> *Aysherston* 1295 *Ass*, *Aysseriston* 1303 FA, *Aysscherstone* 1317
> Exon
> *Asschestone* 1374 Exon

'*Æschere*'s tun.'

George Teign Barton is *Teigna* 1086 DB, *Tegne Georg'* 1281 *Ass*, *Teyng S. Georgii* 1283 BM, (*Sc' Georgis*) 1334 SR, *Georgistenge* 1438 FF. For the River Teign, *v. supra* 14. There was once a chapelry here dedicated to St George.

Spara Bridge is so spelt in 1765 D. The NED *s.n. sparr* defines this as a 'light bridge for crossing broken arches, rivers with steep banks, etc.'

Combe (6″) and Penn (6″) were the homes of Ralph *In the Combe* (1333 *SR*), and Thomas *atte Penne* (1330 *SR*). *v.* cumb, penn.

Bramble is *Brumel* 1244 *Ass* (p), *Bremele* 1301 *Ass*, *Bremel* 1504 Ipm. *v.* bremel. Cowley is *Couelegh* 1333 SR (p). '*Cufa*'s leah,' cf. Cowley *supra* 455. Kiddens Plantation is *Kyddon* 1504 Ipm, *Kidden* 1654 FF. Rydon is *Rydon* 1333 SR (p). Probably 'rye hill,' *v.* dun.

Bishopsteignton

Bishopsteignton 138 G 9

> *Taintona* 1086 DB
> *Teigtune* (sic) 1133 Earle 260, *Teinton* c. 1150 (14th)
> *Launceston*, 1185 P, 1224 Pap, *Teyngton* 1245 Pap, *Teygtone
> Episcopi* 1262 Exon, *Teynton Bishops* 1341 Pat

'Farm on the Teign river' (*supra* 14), *v.* tun. The manor was held by the bishop of Exeter in 1086 (DB f. 117).

Cockhaven (6″) is *Cockfen, Cockven* t. Jas 1 *LRMB, Cockeven* 1589 *SR*, 1628 *FF, Cockhaven* 1809 M. This is probably OE *cocca fenn*, 'cocks' marsh,' the modern form showing the same corruption as in Horsehaven *supra* 380.

HUMBER is *Hundeberghe*, *-birgh* 1244 *Ass*, *-burgh* 1330 *Ass* (p), *Houndeburgh* 1330 *SR* (p), *Humber* 1589 *SR*, 1706 *Recov*. 'Hounds' hill' or '*Hunda*'s hill,' *v.* beorg. Cf. Hound Tor *supra* 198.

LUTON

> *Leueton* 1238 *Ass*
> *Lynynton* 1292 Ch
> *Luneueton* 1303 FA, *Lunaton* 1346 FA
> *Luton al. Louton al. Loveton al. Levaton* 1811 *Recov*

Either '*Lēofwynn*'s farm' with a feminine pers. name, or '*Lēofwine*'s farm' without genitival *s* in the compound, cf. *Loventor infra* 506. *Lynynton, Luneueton, Lunaton* would probably have been transcribed more correctly *Lyuyneton, Luveneton, Luueton*. The forms show that this cannot be the *Liwtun* of Alfred's Will (BCS 553) as suggested by Harmer (*English Historical Documents* 98).

RIXDALE is *Rixtiuele* 1244 *Ass*, *atte Rixthiuele* 1299 *Ass* (p), *Nytherryxstinele* (sic) 1303 FA, *Rixthyuele* 1330, 1333 *SR* (p), *Rixtivell* 1424 IpmR, *Rixteuyll, Ryxthyvell* 1436 BM, *Rixtell* 1725 *Recov*. This is a compound of OE rysc, 'rush,' and *þӯfel*, 'clump, tuft,' cf. *to þam riscðyfele* BCS 687.

SHARRACOMBE (6″) is *Shirrecombe* 1330, *Schurrecomb* 1333 *SR* (p). The forms vary too much for any certain etymology to be possible. Professor Ekwall suggests that the first element may be OE *scīrgerēfa*, 'sheriff,' cf. Shrewton (W) which is a compound of this word and appears as *Sherretone* in 1310.

BROOK COTTAGE (6″), COOMBE and CROSS HO (6″) were the homes of Walter *atte Broke* (1330 *SR*), Bartholomew de *Cumbe* (1244 *Ass*), and John Babbe of *Crosse* (1524 *SR*). *v.* cumb.

BUDDLEFORD FM (6″) is *Bodeleford* 1407 *FF*. Possibly we may compare Budleigh *supra* 484. COLE'S BARN (6″) is to be associated with the family of Walter *Cole* (1333 *SR*). LYNDRIDGE is *Linrigga* c. 1150 (14th) *Launceston*, *Lindrich* 1343 Cl, *Lyndrigg*

1356 Cl, *Lynderigge* 1535 VE. 'Limetree ridge,' cf. Lindridge (PN Wo 57). PARK FM (6″) is *Parke* 1599 *Recov.* RADWAY (6″) is *Radeweye* 1361, *-way* 1437 Exon. 'Red way.' SALTINGS (6″), cf. *Salternehay* 1361 Exon. From *saltern*, 'salt house,' *v.* ærn. There were formerly saltings here. SHUTE FM (6″) is *Shute* 1302 *Ass* (p), *Shutt* 1571 *SR. v.* Shute *supra* 184. VENN FM is *La Fenne* 1303 FA, *the Fen* t. Eliz ChancP. *v.* fenn. WESTERLAND COTTAGE (6″) is *Wisterland* 1671 *Recov.* WOLFSGROVE is *Wolysgrove* 1333 *SR* (p), *Wollesgrove* 1619, *Woolsgrove* 1716 *FF*, suggesting that the *f* is a quite late introduction.

Chudleigh

CHUDLEIGH 138 E/F 8

Ceddelegam c. 1150 (14th) *Launceston*, *Cedele* 1161 RBE
Cheddeleghe c. 1200 (15th) *Torre*, 1259 Exon, *Chedele(ghe)* 1236 Cl, 1244 *Ass*, 1263 Exon, *Chedley* 1456 Pat
Chuddeleghe c. 1200 (15th) *Torre*, 1281 *Ass et passim* to 1484 IpmR, *Chudele* 1379 Pat
Chideleghe 1249 *Ass et freq* to 1421 Pat with variant spelling *Chyde-*, *Chyddelegh* 1281 *Ass*, *Chidlegh* 1454 Pat, *-lay* 1577 Saxton, 1675 Ogilby

The first element in this name is probably a pers. name, though its date and form are uncertain. Cf. William *Chuda* in the 1333 *SR*. This may well derive from the OE *cēod(e)*, 'bag,' used as a nickname. It is possible, however, that the first element is that word itself, used in some topographical sense. Chudleigh lies on a hill in a hollow. Cf. Addenda, Part i, liv and Part ii, xiv, *s.n.* Chidham, and Ekwall, *Studies* 68–9.

GRIMSBURY (lost) is *Grendelbury* 1330 SR (p), *Grendelesbiry* 1333 SR (p), *Greenbury al. Grinsbury al. Grimsbury* 1779 *Recov.* This name, together with Greenscombe in Stoke Climsland (Co), *Gryndeliscombe* 1339 *MinAcct*, *Grendelliscomb* 1399 Ct, *Grendescombe* 1427 Pat and Gransmore *al.* Grimmesmore (Ess), *grendelsmere* 12th *Caen*[1], must be taken with *grendeles pytt* (BCS 1331) in Devon, *grendles mere* (BCS 677) in Wilts and *Grendelsmere* (BCS 1023) in Staffs. All alike seem to preserve the name of the monster *Grendel* of the Beowulf story. They are quite

---

[1] *Ex inf.* Mr P. H. Reaney.

distinct from the *grendel*-names dealt with by Zachrisson in the *Jespersen Miscellany* 39.

HARCOMBE is *Harecumbe* 1249 FF, 1281 *Ass* (p), *Harcumbesheved* 1281 *Ass*, *Harrecombe* 1365 IpmR, *Harcombe* 1370 *Ass*. 'Hare valley,' *v.* cumb.

LAWELL HO is referred to in the phrase *infra mansum suum de la Welle* 1329 Exon. *v.* wielle. For the coalescing of the French definite article with the noun, cf. Lifford PN Wo 355 and Leafield (O), *Feld* 1226 Sarum, *la Feld* 1240 Eynsham Cartulary, *Felda* 1316 FA. It was a manor of the Bishops of Exeter, hence perhaps the curious Anglo-Norman form.

RUGGADON is *Ruggeton* 1249 *Ass* (p) and probably contains as first element the pers. name *Hrucga* found in *hrucgan cumbes ford* (Crawf 1). The fact that there was a pers. name (de) *Roggecomb* in the 1333 *SR* for Chudleigh suggests that there may also have been a *hrucgan cumb* in that parish named after the same man as Ruggadon.

HAMLYNS and HOLMAN'S WOOD (both 6″) are probably to be associated with the families of Henry *Hamlyn* (1524 *SR*) and Richard *Holman* (1330 *SR*).

ASHWELL (6″) is *Aishwell* 1634 *Deed*, *-will* 1655 *Recov*. *v.* wielle. BIDDLECOMBE CROSS (6″) is *Byttelecomb* 1330 *SR* (p). 'Bit(t)ela's cumb,' cf. Bittleford *infra* 526. BRIDGELANDS (6″) is *lower Bridgland* 1634 *Deed*. BRIMLEY CORNER and STILE (6″) is *Bremele* 1314 *Ass* (p), *Bremley Stile* 1692 *Recov*. 'Bramble leah.' CATSHOLE (6″) is *Catteshole* 1330 *SR* (p), *Catshole* 1663 *Recov*. 'Hollow of the wild cat,' *v.* holh. COMBESHEAD is so spelt 1692 *Recov*. *v.* cumb. CRAMMERS is *Cranmere* 1330 *SR* (p). 'Heron pool,' *v.* mere. The *s* is probably pseudo-manorial. CROCOMBE BRIDGE is *Craccumbe* 1238 *Ass* (p), *Crockham* 1664 *Recov*. *v.* cumb, cf. Crackaway *supra* 40. DUNSCOMBE FM is *Donscomb* 1330 *SR* (p), *Donnescombe in Chuddelegh* 1484 IpmR. Probably 'Dunn's combe.' FARLEY (6″) is *Lutelfarlegh* 1249 FF. Probably 'bracken clearing,' *v.* fearn, leah. GREALY (6″) is *Grayley* 1634 *Deed*. Perhaps 'grey leah.' HEATHFIELD (6″) is *Heathfield Downe*, *Heathfield Lakes* 1693 Moulton. HEIGHTLEY (6″) is so spelt 1664 *Recov*. *v.* leah. MILESTONE CROSS is *Milestone* 1383 Exon. Four

roads meet here. OAKLANDS, cf. *atte Oke* 1394 *Ass* (nom. loc.).
OXENCOMBE is *Oxencombe* 1641 *Recov*, (*Higher*) 1669 *FF*. Self-
explanatory, *v.* cumb. RANSCOMBE is *Rammiscomb(e)* 1330 *SR*
(p), *-mes-* 1333 *SR* (p), 1351 *Ass*. 'Ram's valley,' *v.* cumb.
RATTYBALL WOOD (6″) is *Raddyball* 1634 *Deed*. Probably 'red
hill,' *v. supra* 211. ROWELL (6″) is *Rowehill* 1333 *SR* (p). 'Rough
hill,' *v.* ruh. TOWN MILLS (6″) is *the Towne Mills* 1634 *Deed*.
UGBROOKE HO is *Ugbro(o)ke* 1552 Wills, c. 1620 Risdon, 1653
Deed. '*Ucga*'s brook,' cf. Ugborough *supra* 284. UPCOTT is
Uppecote 1358 *FF*. 'Higher cote.' WADDON is *Wadden* 1249 *Ass*
(p), *-don* 1303 FA. Probably 'hill where woad grew,' *v.* dun.
WAPPERWELL (6″) is *Wappull Will* 1603 *Deed*, *Wapplewell* 1737
Recov. Cf. Wapplewell *supra* 251. WHITEWAY HO is *Whiteweye*
1330 *SR* (p).

East and West Dawlish

DAWLISH 138 F 11

Doflisc, on doflisc ford 1044 OS Facs ii, Exeter xii, *to dofolisces
landscore* 1069 OS Facs ii, Exeter xvi, (*æt*) *doflisc* 1050–73
Earle[1]

Douelis 1086 DB, 1253 Ch, *Douelis, Douelisford* c. 1200 HMC
iv, 59, *Dovelish* 1302 Cl

Duvelis 1148 HMC iv, 46, *Deulis* 1276 RH, *Deuelus by Teng-
mouth* 1418 Pat

Doulissh juxta Kenton 1323 *Ass*, *Doulesch* 1324 Fine, *-lech*
1324 Cl, *Doulyshford juxta Doulish* 1345 *Ass*

Daulysshford 1404 *Ass*, *Dawlysshe* 1483 *FF*, *-lisshe* 1468 Pat

Dawlish[2] takes its name from the stream (*supra* 5) on which
it stands.

---

[1] *Daflysch* in 15th cent. copy (*ex inf.* Professor Max Förster).
[2] In the first OS Facsimile we have a grant of land at Dawlish dated 1044.
As shown by Davidson (JAA 39, 292) it included Dawlish and East Teignmouth, formerly Holcombe (*v. infra* 493). The boundaries are as follows:
From the mouth of the Teign up along the estuary to *crampan steort*, clearly
the tongue of land now called 'The Point,' then past the 'salterns' or salt-houses
to the road on the west side of St Michael's church. The present boundary
runs thus and agrees with the charter in travelling north. We cannot identify
the *stræt*, the great *dic*, the 'blind' spring, the grey rock, the old *dic*, along
which it pursues its northward path. It crosses *sceota cumb*, perhaps the old
name for the north part of Holcombe. Thence along the old 'row' to the
'staples,' perhaps on the site of Holcombe Down Cross, thence along the
ridge to the sand-hollows. Here the present boundary follows the *stræt* to

CASTLE DYKE. The castle is to be identified with the *eorð birig*
of the Dawlish charter (*v. supra* 491). We may compare Arbury
(PN La 98) and Arbury Banks (Herts).

CHECKSTONE (6″)

> *Checston, Checkston* 1265 HMC Exeter
> *Litleham juxta Chekston* 1296 *Ass*
> *Lyttelham juxta Chikeston* 1371 *FF*, *villa de Chikeston* 1388
>   Seld 33
> *a ston called Orcheston now named Chikston* 1422 HMC Exeter
> *certain rocks which they call the Checkstones* 1586, *a rock called*
>   *Cheekston at the mouth of the river* 1599 DKR 38, 411

blacan penn, to *bradanmores heafdon* and to *eorðbirig* and then north along the
stræt to *stan beorg* and then down the *stræt* to Dawlish ford. The *heafdon* must
be the point marked 782 ft., the *eorðburh* is Castle Dyke, the *stanbeorg* may
be the tumulus just to the west of the boundary. The boundary here follows
the Port Way and runs down to Dawlish Water. From Dawlish Water we
go north along the *port stræt* (i.e. the Port Way) to the head of the *risc
slæd*. This must be the shallow valley at the head of which the bounds take
an eastward turn. They now go down stream to *cocc ford*, i.e. Cofford, and so
along the *fleot* to the Exe, the boundary following a little brook which enters
the Exe at Cockwood, thence down the Exe to where the *sciterlacu* (cf.
Shutterton *infra* 493) enters the Exe. After this there is a difficulty; the
present boundary runs along the seashore but in the charter it goes up to
the head of the *sciterlacu*, thence north to the old *dic* and straight on to the
red rock and so out along the sea.

If one goes up the *sciterlacu* to its head, one strikes the western boundary of
East Dawlish and it may be that the other points lie along the boundary of
East Dawlish which would then be almost entirely excluded from the grant.
There is a second charter (OS Facs ii, Exeter xvi) making a grant of land in
1069 at *Holacumb*. Davidson (*op. cit.* 299) shows that this refers to Holcombe in
East Dawlish. The boundaries from the start to the old *dic* agree with those
of Dawlish *supra*, though the points are not identical. They are *crampan-
steort, floraheafdo*, the road to the west of the church, *ferngara, dunnastan* and
the *dic*. They now turn east along the *dic* to 'the water' and north over 'the
water' to *þæs crohtes heafod*. The boundary of East Dawlish turns east at
Holcombe Down Cross and goes east along Holcombe Down Road (probably
the *dic*) and so north to Dawlish Water. It crosses the river and makes its
way to the head of the *sciterlacu* (*v. supra*). This may well be the *crohtes
heafod*, for it is clear that the compilers of these two charters used either
different boundary marks or different names for them. From here the boundary continues north to a small 'path' and so down to the *þwirs dic*, to the
bounds of Dawlish and thence to *arietes stan* on the shore. The present boundary follows a small path north-east from Langdon House and goes downhill
to the extreme north-east point of Dawlish parish, thence it follows the West
Dawlish boundary to the sea at Rockstone. This may be the site of the
arietes stan. It is clear that this second grant includes East Teignmouth and
East Dawlish parishes. It looks very much as if the other grant which covers
a larger area and included something of the same ground, covered East
Teignmouth and West Dawlish, except for its south-east corner. It may be,
however, an accident that the last fragment was not included.

The term is now used of a sandbank and rock at the mouth of the Exe. It is clear that this is not the original name of the rock itself. There was a *villa de Chikeston* in the middle ages, in the neighbourhood of Littleham. This *vill* may well have been somewhere on the site of the present Exmouth which, as the name of a town, is not ancient (*v. infra* 591). The 1422 reference suggests that the rock was originally called *Orcheston* and came to be named after the vill at a comparatively late date. The ultimate etymology of *Checston* and *Orcheston* must remain uncertain.

COFTON is *Coctone* 1282 Exon, *Cokton(e)* 1333 *SR* (p), 1356 *Ass*, 1386 Exon, *Cofton* 1289 Cl, *Coffeton al. Caughton* 1715 *Recov*. For this name, *v.* Cofford *infra* 500.

DUCKALLER (6″) is *Duckalre* 1277 *Ass* (p), *Dok(e)-* 1333 *SR* (p), 1422 *Rental*. 'Duck alder.' For other examples in the county of an animal name compounded with *alder*, cf. Bulealler, Hawkealter, Houndaller *infra* 562, 557, 548 and cf. also Foxearle (PN Sx 477).

HENSFORD is *Helmisford(e)* 1301 Exon, 1330, 1333 *SR* (all p), *Helmysford* 1428 *Deed*. '*Helm*'s ford.' For the pers. name, *v.* Helmsley (PN NRY 71).

HOLCOMBE is (*æt*) *holacumba* 1050–73 Earle, *Holacumbe* 1069 OS Facs ii, Exeter xvi, *Holcomma* 1086 DB. 'Hollow valley,' *v.* holh, cumb.

LIDWELL is *Lidewelle* 1380, *Lydeswyll* 1412, *Lydewylle* 1422 Exon. The first element may be the old name of the stream which rises here, *v.* wielle and cf. Lydford *supra* 191.

SECMATON (6″) is *Sakkemaneton, Sakemaneton* 1244 *Ass*, *Est-*, *Westsakematon* 1422 *Rental*. The name is identical with Seckington *supra* 358.

SHUTTERTON is *Schiterton* 1277 *Ass* (p), *Est Shitereton, West Sheterton* t. Hy 4 *Deed*. The first element is probably the old name of the streamlet here, referred to as *sciterlacu* in 1044 OS Facs ii, Exeter xii. See further RN 363.

SOUTHWOOD is (*æt*) *supwuda* 1050–73 Earle, *Southwode juxta Doulyssh* 1321 *Ass*.

ALLER FM[1] (6″), CLEVELAND[2], FORD FM (6″), GATEHOUSE and WESTON FM (6″) were the homes of William de *Alre* (1333 *SR*), Adam *atte Clyve* (ib.), Richard *atte Forde* (ib.), Eustace *atte Yate* (ib.), and John de *Weston* (ib.). *v.* alor, clif, geat, tun.

BOTCHELL FM is *Bouchehill* 1422 *Rental*, *Bochyll* 1514 *Ct.* BRANSCOMBE (6″) is perhaps identical with *Brumston* 1277 *Ass*, *Brounston* 1330 *SR* (p), 1422 *Rental*, 1514 *Ct.* '*Brūn*'s farm,' *v.* tun. COCKWOOD is *Est-, Westcokwode* 1514 *Ct. v.* Cofford *infra* 500. DAWLISH WARREN is *Warenna in Manerio de Douelis* c. 1280 Exon. This is a sandy spit of land projecting into the Exe estuary. EASTDON is *Est Doune* t. Hy 4 *Deed*, *Estdown* 1529 *Ct.* GREENWAY LANE (6″) is *Grenewey* t. Edw 1 *Deed*. LANGDON HO is *Langedun* 1244 *Ass* (p), *-done* 1282 Exon. 'Long hill,' *v.* dun. LUSCOMBE CASTLE is *Luscombe next Doulyssh* 1354 *Deed*. Cf. Luscombe *supra* 310. MIDDLEWOOD (6″) is *Middelwode* 1514 *Ct.* ORCHARD (6″) is so spelt in 1422 (*Rental*). RIXDALE is *Rixstyle* 1671 *Recov.* Without earlier forms certainty is impossible, but the name is probably identical with Rixdale *supra* 488. SMALLACOMBE FM is *Smalecomb* 1333 *SR* (p). 'Narrow valley,' *v.* cumb. SUMMERCOMBE WOOD (6″) is *Somerscombe* 1750 *Recov.* The meaning is probably 'summer-pasture valley.'

Doddiscombsleigh

DODDISCOMBSLEIGH [daskəmzliˑ] 138 C 7

Leuga 1086 DB, *Lega* 1263 Ipm, *Legh* 1303 FA
Leghe Gobol, Guobol, Gobolde c. 1260 Exon, *Gobaldeslegh* 1289 *Ass*
Leghe Peverel juxta Brideford 1313 *Ass*, (*juxta Cristowe*) 1361 *Ass*
Legh Dodescomb 1334 *SR, Dodyscombeleghe al. Leghe Peverel* 1375 Exon, *Dowiscombelegh al. Doddiscombleigh* 1480 IpmR, *Dascomley* 1628 DA 6

v. leah. The manorial history of the place is as follows. It was held by one *Godbold* in 1086 (DB) and by 1242 (DA 45) had passed to Hugh *Peveril*. Ralph de *Daddescumb* or *Doddescombe* held it twenty years later (c. 1260 Exon, 1263 Ipm), but in

---

[1] *Aller* 1422 *Rental*.   [2] *Cleve* 1422 *Rental*.

1303 (FA) it was held jointly by John de *Dodescomb* and Hugo de *Gubbewolt*, presumably a descendant of the DB tenant.

LOWLEY

> *Leualiga* 1086 DB (Exon), *Levelege* (Exch), *Leveleye* 1279 *Ass*
> *Loueleg'* 1279 *Ass, Luuelegh* 1377 BM
> *Lyvelegh* 1426 DA 33

'*Lēofa*'s clearing,' *v.* leah.

LAKE COTTAGE (6″), PERRY FM (6″) and WOODAH were probably the homes of Stephen de *Lake* (1249 FF), William *atte Pirie* (1333 *SR*), and Robert *atte Wode* (1330 *SR*). *v.* lacu, pyrige.

KINGSCOURT COTTAGES (6″) is *Kyngyscourte* 1486 *Deed.* MISLEIGH COPSE (6″) is *Misclyffe* 1672 *SR*. PITT FM (6″) is *la Putte* 1279 *Ass*. 'The hollow,' *v.* pytt. SEXTON'S CROSS is probably to be associated with the family of Richard *Sexton* of Kenn (1678 Wills). SHELDON is *Shildone* 1333 *SR* (p), *Schylden,* -*don* 1394 *Ass.* Probably a compound of scylf and dun, there being a steep slope here to the Teign. SHIPPEN (6″) is *Shipping al. Shippen* 1764 *Recov.* This is OE *scipen*, 'shippon, cow-shed.' SPANISHLAKE COTTAGE (6″) is *Eastpinishlake* 1672 *SR, Spynishlake* 1687 *FF, v.* lacu. The forms are too late for an interpretation of the first element to be suggested, but it is clear that the modern form is corrupt. WHITEMOOR is *Hwytemore* 1333 *SR* (p), *Whitmore* 1613 *Recov. v.* mor.

Dunchideock

DUNCHIDEOCK [dʌnʹtʃidik] 138 C 8

> *Donsedoc* 1086 DB
> *Dunsidioc(h')* 1187 P, 1219 *Ass*, -*ok* 1238 *Ass*, 1244 FF, -*oke*
>   1261 Exon, *Donsidioke* 1291 Tax
> *Dunchidyoc* 1291 Tax, -*yok* 1396 Pat, *Dunshydiok* 1297 Pat,
>   -*schidiock* 1308 Exon, *Dunschedyoke* 1425 Exon
> *Dounschidioke* 1328 Exon, *Douneschydiok* 1377 *SR*
> *Donshediok* 1370 *Ass*
> *Dunsherick* 1675 Ogilby

This is a British name, the elements answering to W *din* (**duno-*), 'fort, camp, castle,' and *coediog* (**kaitako*), 'woody, wooded,' from *coed* (**kaito-*), 'wood.' Cf. Ekwall, RN 77

ESRIDGE is *Estrigg'* 1244 *Ass*, *Easridge* 1620 *Recov.* 'East ridge.'
HORRELLS (6″) is to be associated with the family of Jacob de
Horwill (1330 *SR*). IDESTONE is possibly identical with *Edweyston*
1249 *Ass* (p). '*Ēadwīg*'s tun.' WEBBERTON CROSS is *Wibbeton(e)*
1304 *Ass* (p), 1333 *SR* (p), *Wybbeton* 1359 *Ass.* '*Wibba*'s tun.'

Exminster

EXMINSTER 138 C 10

> *æt Exanmynster* 880–5 (c. 1000) BCS 553, *Exemenistre* 1208 FF,
> *Exiministre* 1218 Pap, *Exemeinstre* 1274 Exon
> *Esseministra* 1086 DB
> *Exemystere* 1447 Exon, *Axmister* 1675 Ogilby, *Exminster al.*
> *Exmister* 1742 *Recov*

'mynster (i.e monastery) by the river Exe.'

BRENTON

> *Brenton* 1242 Fees 790 (p), 1304 Abbr
> *Brunton* 1263 Ipm
> *Breington* 1284 Pat, *Breyngton* 1286 SR (p), 1303 FA, 1333
> SR (p), *Breynton* 1346 FA

Professor Ekwall suggests OE *Brȳningatūn*, 'farm of *Brȳni*'s
people,' but no certainty is possible.

MATFORD Ho

> *Matforda* 1086 DB
> *Matheford* early 13th *St Nicholas*, *Mathforde* c. 1234 NGl 3,
> 190
> *Mat(te)ford'* 1242 Fees 785, 793, 1332 Ipm, *Mateforde* 1250
> NGl 2, 191
> *Matford* 1301 Ipm, (*Spek*) 1303 FA

Professor Ekwall suggests that this is a compound of OE
mægðe, 'mayweed,' or *mægða* (gen. pl.), 'maidens' and ford. For
'maidens' ford,' cf. Maidenford *supra* 26.

MILBURY FM (6″) is *Meleburi* 1330, *Melebiry*, *Melbury* 1333 *SR*
(p). *v.* burh. For the first element, *v. s.n.* Meldon *supra* 203.

PEAMORE Ho

> *Peumera* 1086 DB
> *Paumera* 1194 P, *Paumere* 1250 NGl 3, 191

Pyeumere c. 1234 NGl 3, 190
Peaumer(e) 1303 FA *et freq* to 1444 IpmR
Pewmar 1540 LP

The first element may be OE *pāwa, pēa,* 'peafowl,' the phonetic development being similar to that in Crebar Creacombe, *supra* 282–3. The second is **mere**. There is a pool here.

TOWSINGTON (6″) is *Tuz Seinzton* 1242 Fees 792, *Tuzseinteston, Tusseynston* 1246 FF, *Touceynston* 1301 Ipm, *Touseyneston* 1303 FA, 1324 Ipm, *Towsyngton* 1465 Pat. This place derives its name from the family of Lucas de *Tuz Seinz*, who held the manor in 1242 (Fees).

BLACKALL'S COPSE (6″), CROCKWELL'S FM (6″), HOOPER'S FM (6″), HOPPIN'S COTTAGE (6″), LUCCOMBS FM, POTTLES FM, SENTRY'S FM and YEO'S FM are probably to be associated with the families of Mary *Blackall* (1635 Wills), Anne *Crockwill* (1611 Wills), Henry *le hopere* (1330 *SR*), John *Hoppinge* (t. Jas 1 ECP), Adam de *Luecomb* (1330 *SR*), John *Potyll* (1524 *SR*), Simon *Saundre* (1330, 1333 *SR*) and Thomas *Yeo* (1628 Wills).

BOWHAY FM is *Bogheweye* 1238 *Ass*, 1275 RH, 1330 *SR* (all p), *Bogweye* 1370 Exon, *Bowaye* 1529–32 ECP 6, 196. 'Bent or curved way,' *v.* Bowden *supra* 37. CRABLAKE FM is so spelt 1809 M, and is possibly to be associated with the family of William *Crabbe* (1333 *SR*). *v.* lacu. HALL FM (6″) is *Hole* 1637 *Deed. v.* holh. KENBURY HO is *Kenebiri* 1083 St Nicholas, *-byry* 1313 Exon (p). 'burh by the river Kenn.' MARSHROW (6″) is *Marshbrowe* 1611, *Marshrowe* 1671 *Recov.* The *b* is probably a clerical error. The place lies in flat land by the Exe. WAYBROOK is *Way Brook* 1765 D. WRACOMBE (6″) is *Wracombe* 1286 *MinAcct* (p), 1542 *Deed, Wraccomb* 1589 *SR*.

Ide

IDE [iˑd] 138 B 9

(*æt*) *Ide* 1050–73 Earle, *Ida* 1086 DB, 1244 *Ass, Ide* 1291 Tax, (*Sancti Petri*) 1316 FA, (*juxta Exon'*) 1394 *Ass*
Ede 1511 Lives, 1577 Saxton, 1634 *FF, Eide* 1628 DA 6

This may be a stream-name, as suggested by Ekwall RN 208.

MARSHALL FM is *morces hille* 1050–73 Earle[1], *Morkishill* 1238 *Ass* (p), -*kes*- 1256 FF, *Morkeshull(e)* 1307 Cl (p), 1329 Exon (p), *Morxhill* 1535 VE, *Moxhill* 1620 Wills, *Marshall* 1682 *Recov*. '*Moroc*'s hill.' This is a well-evidenced Celtic pers. name, a derivative of *mor*, 'sea.' Cf. Branscombe *infra* 620.

DRAKE'S FM and HAYNES FM (both 6″) are probably to be associated with the families of William *Drake* (1524 *SR*) and John *Hayne* (t. Eliz ChancP).

FORDLAND FM (6″) is *La Forde* 1334 *Ass*, *Furde* 1486 Pat. HALSCOMBE is *Halescumb* 1238 FF, 1244 *Ass* (p), *Halscombe* 1291 Tax. *v*. Addenda, Part i, lviii. IDE BRIDGE (6″) is (*de*) *ponte de Ida* 1244 *Ass*. PERRIDGE HO is *Pirrigge* 1314, 1334 *Ass*, *Purigge* 1333 *SR* (all p). 'Pear-tree ridge,' *v*. pyrige. WHIDDON is *Wyteton* 1330 *SR* (p), *Whetton* 1524 *SR*. 'White farm' or '*Hwīta*'s farm,' *v*. tun.

Kenn

KENN 138 D 9

> *Chent* 1086 DB
> *Ken* 1167 P *et passim*

This place takes its name from the river on which it stands, *v. supra* 7.

CLAPHAM is *Clopton* 1330 *SR* (p), *Clapton*, *Clappeton* 1547 *Ct*, *Clapton* t. Ed 6 *Rental*. 'Farm by the stump(s) or stub(s),' *v*. tun. See further *s.n*. Clapton PN BedsHu 22. For the change of second element, cf. Popham *supra* 345.

LIPPER (lost) is *Higher Lipper* 1792 *Recov* and was the home of Richard *atte Lipe* (1330 *SR*) and Nicholas *atte Lype* (1333 *SR*). *v*. hlype and for the final *er*, *v*. Introd. xxxvi.

SPLATFORD FM is *Sprotford* 1333 *SR* (p), *Spratford* 1631 *Recov*. The first element is OE *sprot*, 'sprout, twig, peg,' used also of a coarse kind of rush. *v*. BT Supplt *s.v. sprott*. The term still survives in dialect.

---

[1] *Markeshyll* in a 15th cent. copy (*ex inf*. Professor Max Förster).

WHITCOMBE

Wethecumb 1249 *Ass* (p), *Wedecumbe* 1281 *Ass* (p)
Wetecomb 1330, *Whetecomb* 1333 *SR* (p)
Whitcomb 1376 IpmR

'Wheat-valley,' *v.* hwæte, cumb.

BAMFIELDS COTTAGES (6″), BROWN'S FM, LAMBERCROFTS (6″),
LYALLS, POPE'S COPSE (6″), PRIDHAM'S COTTAGES (6″), ROLLE-
STONES (6″), TOWELLS (6″) and TUCKER'S COTTAGE (6″) are
probably to be associated with the families of John *Bondfeild*
(1582 *SR*), Walter *Broun* (1330 *SR*), Peter *Lomecroft* (1333 *SR*)
and Michael *Lamacraft* (1582 *SR*), Thomas *Lyell* (1582 *SR*),
Thomas *Pope* (ib.), John *Pridman* and William *Pridam*
(ib.), Robert *Rolston* (ib.), Richard *Towill* (ib.) and Richard *le
Touker* (1330 *SR*).

BICKHAM HO is *Bikecumb* 1249 *Ass*, -*cume* 1249 FF, *Byccomb*
1333 *SR* (all p). '*Bic(c)a*'s cumb.' EMPTY (6″) is so spelt 1765 D.
HANNAFORD FM (6″) is *Hunaford* t. Ed 6 *Rental*. HILL FM was
the home of Adam de *la Hill* 1249 *Ass*. HOLLOWAY FM is *la
Holeweie* 1238 *Ass* (p), *Holewey* 1244 *Ass*, 1488 Ipm. 'Way or
path in the hollow,' *v.* holh, weg. KENNFORD is *Netherekeneford*
1298 *Ass*, *Keneford* 1300 Ch. 'Ford over the river Kenn' (*supra*
7). KERSWELL FM is *Carswille* 1330, 1333 *SR* (p). 'Cress
spring,' *v.* cærse, wielle. PENNYCOMBE FM is *Pennycombe* t. Ed 6
Rental, *Penecombe* 1588 CtRequests. Cf. Pynamead *supra* 378.
THORNTON FM is *Thorn(e)ton* 1249 *Ass* (p), 1298 BM. *v.* tun.
TREHILL is *Trehill al. Kennhouse* t. Jas 1 ECP. WOODLANDS is
la Wodelande 1244 *Ass*.

Kenton

KENTON 138 D 10/11

Chenton(a) 1086 DB, 1158 P, *Ken-* 1167 P, 1269 Exon, 1291
Tax
Kynton 1267 *Ass*, *Kin-* 1276 RH, *Chin-* 1321 Pap
Keynton beside Opsam 1546 Seld 6

'Farm on the Kenn river' (*supra* 7). *Opsam* is Topsham,
across the river, *v. supra* 454.

BABELS BRIDGE (6″) is *Baplesbridge* 1577 *Deed*, *Bayles Bridge* 1611 *Recov*, *Beapford Bridge* 1650 *Deed* and is probably to be associated with the family of Peter and William *Babl* (1650 *Deed*).

CHIVERSTONE FM is *Chevereston* 1284 *Ass* (p), 1292 *Ass*, 1340 Ipm, *Chiverston* 1406 IpmR. *v.* tun. Professor Ekwall and Professor Förster agree in suggesting that this may be OE *Cēolfriðestūn*, 'farm of one *Cēolfrið*,' *v.* tun.

COFFORD FM is *on cocc ford* 1044 OS Facs ii, Exeter xii, *Cokford* 1311 *FF*. This place and Cofton and Cockwood *supra* 493–4 may all take their name from the one stream on which they stand. For the possibility of *Cocc* as a stream-name, denoting the 'red' stream (Welsh *coch*), *v.* Ekwall RN 83.

HELWELL FM is *Hulewell* 1244 *Ass*, *Heylwille* 1249 *Ass*, *Hayle-wille* 1275 RH, 1330 *SR*, *Halywelle* 1279 *Ass* (all p). The forms are mutually inconsistent and no solution is possible.

MOWLISH FM

    Milehyuis 1086 DB (Exon), *Milchewis* (sic) (Exch)
    Mulehewis 1219 *Ass*, *-hiwis* 1219 FF
    Molehiwis 1242 Fees 793, *-hiwys* 1284 *Ass* (p)
    Moliwys 1249 *Ass* (p)
    Moulysse 1276 Ipm, *Moulys juxta Kentone* 1304 *Ass*, *Moulissh juxta Doulissh* 1324 *Ass*
    Moulehywissh, *Mouleshywhisshe* 1306 Ipm

v. hiwisc. The first element is apparently the gen. pl. of OE *mūl*, 'mule,' perhaps referring to a farm where these animals were kept. Cf. Moulton (Nth), *Multone* DB, *Muleton* 1163 P, 1229 Ch, *Multon* 1200 Cur.

OXTON HO is *Okeston* 1238 *Ass* (p), 1262 FF, *-tune* 1269 Ipm (p), *Ockeston* 1238 *Ass* (p), 1275 RH (p), *Oxtone* 1378 Exon. Possibly '*Ocg*'s farm' (*v.* tun), with unvoicing of *g* to *c* before *st*.

STARCROSS (village) is *Star Crosse* 1689 DKR 40, 455. In the absence of early spellings the etymology of this name must remain uncertain. Possibly we have reference to a cross of a particular shape. Cf. Handy Cross (PN Bk 202) and Hand Cross (PN Sx 278).

WILLSWORTHY is *Wyllesworth* 1244 *Ass* (p), 1275 RH (p), *Wileswurth* 1249 *Ass*, *Wylleworth* 1298 *Ass* (p). ' *Wil(l)*'s worþig.' This pers. name is not actually on record, but the weak form *Willa* is well evidenced. Cf. Willesden (Mx).

SAMPSON'S FM and THORNS COTTAGE (6") are to be associated with the families of Christopher *Sampson* and John *Thorne* (1582 *SR*).

OAK FM and SOUTHBROOK were probably the homes of Henry *atter Ok* (1330 *SR*), Walter *Bisudebrok* (1238 *Ass*) and Peter *Bysouthebrok* (1333 *SR*), i.e. south of the brook.

ASH FM is *Asse* 1244 *Ass* (p), *Ayssh* 1406 IpmR. COLLEYWELL BOTTOM is *Colewille* 1333 *SR* (p). *v.* wielle and Collacott *supra* 50. HAYDON COMMON is *Hayeton* 1244 *Ass*, *Heyton* 1330, *Hayton* 1333 *SR* (all p). Probably a compound of (ge)hæg and tun. KENWOOD is *Kenewode* 1275 RH (p), *Kynewode* 1330 *SR* (p). It is some way from the river Kenn. PITTSMOOR (6") is *Putesmor* 1330, *Puttesmor* 1333 *SR* (p). 'Marshy land in the pit or hollow,' *v.* mor. There is a little hollow here by the Kenn river. VENNBRIDGE FM is *Fenny brigge* c. 1327 Exon, *Venn* 1671 *Recov. v.* fenn. WITCOMBE (6") is *Wydecomb* 1334 *SR* (p). 'Wide cumb.'

Mamhead

MAMHEAD 138 E 10

Manneheva, Mammehetua 1086 DB (Exon), *Mammeheua* (Exch)

Mamiheuid 1238 *Ass*

Mammehavede 1242 Fees 786, 1260 Ipm, -*heuid* 1249 *Ass*, -*hevede* 1291 Tax, (*by Doulesch*) 1325 Ipm

This is no doubt a compound of OE *mamme*, 'teat' and heafod, referring to the shape of the prominent hill here.

ASHFORD (lost) is *Aiseforda* 1086 DB, *Asscheford* 1249 *Ass*, *Asheford juxta Mammehede* 1378 IpmR, *Aishford* 1721 *Recov*. Self-explanatory. The site is probably identical with that of NEW-HOUSE FM (6") according to Reichel (DA 45).

PORT WAY is referred to as (*andlang þære*) *port stræt* (1044 OS Facs ii, Exeter xii) in the boundaries of Dawlish. The Port Way is an ancient track leading across Little Haldon Hill. It is not the old Roman road, which was a few miles to the west, nor is it clear to what town it led (*v.* **port**).

GULLIFORD is *Colleford* 1333 *SR* (p), *Golyford* 1753 *Recov.* PITT FM was the home of Herbert de *la Putte* 1249 FF and Thomas *atte Pytte* 1333 *SR*. 'In the hollow,' *v.* **pytt**. WESTLEY FM is *Wistele* 1267 *Ass*, *Wyslegh* 1287 *Ass*, *Wyshlegh* 1330 *SR* (all p). 'Marsh clearing,' *v.* **wisc, leah**.

Powderham

POWDERHAM 138 D 11

> (*of*) *poldraham* (*lande*), *apoldraham* c. 1100 Earle 257
> *Poldreham* 1086 DB
> *Pouderham* 1219 *Ass*, 1259 Exon, 1303 FA, *-hame* 1257–71 Exon
> *Puderham* 1219 FF, *Pudrehame* 1238 *Ass*
> *Poudram* 1257–71 Exon, 1291 Tax

Powderham lies low by the Exe estuary and the surrounding country is flat and marshy. We may therefore take the first element to be the English cognate of MLG *polre, polder*, 'low-lying land reclaimed from the sea,' familiar in the Dutch *Polders*. Cf. Polders in Woodnesborough (K), *Poldre* 1232 Cl, *Polre(s)* 1246 Ch and PN Sx 561. The *a* in one of the earliest forms is no doubt a trace of the OE preposition *æt* wrongly attached to the name.

EXWELL BARTON is *Yerkeswill* 1219 FF (p), *Ekeswell* 1230 P (p), *-wille* 1319 Exon (p), 1392 IpmR, *Yekeswell juxta Powderham* 1292 *Ass*. There can be little doubt that the first form is corrupt (though it has been checked by the MS) and that this name is really OE *gēaces-wielle*, 'cuckoo's spring.'

BLACKHEATH FM, cf. *Blackland* 1753 *Recov.* DISCOMBES (6″) is to be associated with the family of William *Discombe* (1790 Wills). MELLANDS is *Myllond* 1497 Ipm and is to be associated with John *atte Mille* (t. Ed 3 *Ass*), who probably lived at Kenton Mill.

Shillingford

SHILLINGFORD 138 C 9

Esselingaforda, Selingeforda 1086 DB

Sullingford' 1234 Fees 399

Sillingeford' 1242 Fees 790, 1248 Ipm, *Schill-* 1244 *Ass*,
  Schylingford 1244 *Ass*, *Shillyngforde* 1291 Tax

Syllingesford 1267 *Ass*

Shyllyngesford, Abbodeshyllyngford 1281 *Ass*, *Schyllengeford*
  1303 FA

Cf. Shillingford (O), *Scillingeford* c. 1185 *Cartae Antiquae*,
Shillingford 1278 Cl, 1316 FA. Professor Ekwall would take
these names and also Shillinglee (Sx), differently explained
in PN Sx 106, as containing an OE pers. name *Sciella*. Cf.
further the OE pers. name *Scilling*. Part of the manor was
held by Torre *Abbey*.

Teignmouth

TEIGNMOUTH [tinməθ] 138 G/H 10

(*on*) *tenge muðan* 1044 OS Facs ii, Exeter xii

Teignemudan 1148 HMC iv, 46, *Teigemue* 1242 Fees 787

Tinemuth 1213 ClR, *Teingnemue* 1238 *Ass*, *Teingnemouth*
  1253 Ch

Taynguem̃ 1249 *Ass*

Tengemue 1276 RH, *Westeyngemouth* 1283 *Ass*, *Estengemuth*
  1284 *Ass*, *Teyngemwe Burgus* 1291 Tax

Tengmuth 1301 Ipm, *Tenegemue* 1330 Cl, *Yesteyngmouth* 1394
  Ass

Tingmouth 1675 Ogilby

'The mouth of the Teign river' *supra* 14. The earliest form
refers to the mouth of the river, not to the village.

GORWAY (6″) is *Goraway* 1737 *Recov* and was the home of Serlo
de *la Goore* (1284 *Ass*), de *la Gore* (1303 FA). *v.* **gara**.

Trusham

TRUSHAM [trisəm] 138 E 7

Trisma 1086 DB, 1370 Exon, *Trysma* 1377 *SR*, *Trisme* 1259
  Exon *et freq* to 1431 Exon with variant spelling *Trysme*
Trismel 1260–74 Exon

Tryssam 1535 VE

. *Trussham* 1540 Wills, *Trusham* 1577 Saxton, *Trusham al.*
Trisme 1630 *Recov*, *Tressham* c. 1630 Pole

This name may be a compound of the British *trev*, 'homestead, village,' and *isam* (Mod. Welsh *isaf*), 'lowest.' The place
is not in a low situation, but might have been so named in
distinction from other still higher settlements. If this is correct,
it is identical with Trevisa (Co). Professor Ekwall would take
the name to be a derivative of OE *trus*, 'brushwood.'

XXII. HAYTOR HUNDRED

Heithorn 1184, 1185 P
Heitor(r) 1187 P, 1219 Fees 265, *Heytore* 1238, 1249 *Ass*,
-*thorre* 1254 FF
Haytor 1242 Fees 767 *et freq* to 1298 *Ass* with variant spelling
-*torre*

The name seems to be a compound of (ge)hæg and torr, but
the site of the place is unknown and any interpretation of the
name impossible. It can have no connexion with Haytor in
Ilsington *supra* 476. In the Geld Roll (1084) the Hundred was
called *Carseuuilla* from Abbots- and Kingskerswell *infra* 514.

Abbotskerswell

ABBOTSKERSWELL 138 J 7

Cærswylle 956 (13th) BCS 952
Carsuella 1086 DB
Kareswill' 1242 Fees 769, *Karswill Abbatis* 1285 FA, *Abbotes-*
charswelle 1314 *Ass*, *Abbodescarswill* 1316 FA
Abbots Keswell 1675 Ogilby

'Cress spring,' *v.* cærse wielle. The manor was held in DB
by the abbot of Horton.

ALLER is *Alra* 1086 DB, *Aure* 1197 FF, 1242 Fees 790, *Overalre*
juxta Kynges Carswell 1333 *Ass*, *Awre* 1428 FA. 'At the alder,'
v. alor.

MADDACOMBE CROSS (6″) is *on mædercumbe* 956 (13th) BCS 952, *Madercombe* 1561 *FF.* 'Valley where madder grows,' *v.* cumb.

SINGMORE BARN (6″) is *Sengmore* 1317 *Ass* (p), *Seyngmor* 1333 *SR* (p), *Syngmore* 1420 HMC v. The first element may be that discussed under Saint Hill *infra* 565, when the whole name would mean 'burnt mor,' referring to land cleared by burning.

BROOMHILL (6″) is *Bromehyll Crosse* 1543–58 *Ct.* DIFFORD'S COPSE (6″) is perhaps identical with *Dypford myll* 1566 DA 43. 'Deep ford.' GOTEM LINHAY and GOTEMHILL (6″) is *Gotham* 1330, 1524 *SR* (p). Probably 'goat ham(m).' LANGFORD BRIDGE is *Langeford* 1338 Ipm. 'Long ford.' RYDON HILL is *Rydone* 1330 *SR* (p). 'Rye hill,' *v.* dun. WHIDDON is *Wetedene* 1333 *SR* (p). Probably 'wheat valley,' *v.* denu.

Berry Pomeroy

BERRY POMEROY 145 B 6/7

> *Beri* 1086 DB, 1242 Fees 769, *Berri* 1267 Ch, *Byry* 1275 Exon, *Bery* 1278 Ipm
> *Bury Pomerey* 1281 Ipm, (*juxta Toteneys*) 1294 *Ass*, *Burgh Pomeray* 1303 FA, *Biry Pomerey* 1347 Pat, *Byrypomeray* 1388 Exon, *Piry Pomeray* 1413 Pat

v. burh. This may refer to an ancient fortification on the site of which the medieval castle was built. Henry de *la Pomeraye* held the manor in 1242 (Fees 769).

AFTON [aˑtən] is *Afetona* 1086 DB, *Affeton* 1293 Fees 1311, 1297 Pat, 1394 *Ass.* '*Aeffa*'s farm,' *v.* tun. Cf. Afton (Wt), *Affetune* DB.

BOURTON is *Boureton* 1293 Fees 1310 (p), 1313 *Ass*, 1333 *SR* (p). This is probably from OE *būra-tūn*, 'farm of the peasants.' Cf. Burraton *supra* 272.

LONGCOMBE is *Comba* 1086 DB, *Lancombe* 1321 HMC iii, 344 (p), 1541 Recov, *Langcombe* 1463 Totnes, *Lancombe, Langcombe, Lancombedoune* 1553 Pat. 'Long valley,' *v.* cumb.

LOVENTOR

> Lovenetorna 1086 DB, Lovenestorr 1285 FA, Lovenetorre
> Arundel 1292 Ass, Lovingtorr or Lountor 1734 Recov
> Luvenetor(re) 1238 Ass, 1242 Fees 768, 795, (Arundel) 1303 FA

Either 'Lēofwine's torr,' with absence of genitival s, or as suggested by Professor Ekwall, Lēofwynn's, a feminine pers. name with OE genitive singular Lēofwynne, cf. Luton supra 488. John de Arundel held one part of the manor in 1242 (Fees 795).

TRUE STREET is Trustede Way 1268 Totnes, Trewestide 1442 HMC xv, App. 7, Trew Street t. Jas I ECP, Trustreet 1634 Recov. Probably a compound of OE treow, 'tree' and stede, later corrupted to street. Hence 'site marked by a tree.'

WEEKABOROUGH is Wykebergh 1305 Ass (p), Wekeborough 1567 PembSurv, Wickaborough 1827 G. This may be from OE wīcabeorg, 'hill of the farms,' though no such compound of wīc has hitherto been noted. Weekaborough has sometimes been identified with Wicganbeorg (ASC s.a. 851) where the men of Devon defeated the Danes. A battle in the neighbourhood of the estuary of the Dart is not unlikely but the identification is difficult on the formal side. The vowel development would be curious, though not impossible, and the change from voiced cg to unvoiced k would be very difficult to account for, unless folk-etymology has been at work under the influence of the common wīc (Devon week). We get a late change from g to k in Bickaton infra 509, in one of the early forms of Wigford supra 306 and in the pronunciation of Wiggaton infra 607 as [wikətən].

BROADMOOR COTTAGES (6″) is Brodemour 1497 Ipm. v. brad, mor. DENNIN'S LINHAY (6″) is to be associated with the family of William Dennyng (1545 SR). For linhay v. infra 592. FLEET MILL (6″) is Flute, Flute Mille 1497 Ipm. v. fleot. It is by the Dart. HACKNEY BARN (6″) is Le Hayken 1497 Ipm. Cf. Hackney supra 479. MOCKWOOD QUARRY (6″) is terram de Mokewode 1293 Fees 1308. Cf. Mockham supra 61. NETHERTON is Nytherton 1333 SR (p). 'Lower farm,' v. tun. RYPEN COPSE (6″) is le Rypen 1553 Pat. Probably 'rye enclosure,' v. penn. SANDLANE CROSS (6″), cf. Sonde yate 1497 Ipm. SHADRACK is Shadrick 1809 M. SOUTHFIELD WOOD (6″) is Southfeld 1553

Pat. WEEK was the home of Roger de *la Wik* (1249 *Ass*). *v.*
wic. WESTON is *Weston* 1242 Fees 768, 786, 1497 Ipm. 'West
farm,' *v.* tun.

Brixham

BRIXHAM 145 D 9/10

Briseham 1086 DB, 1143 Totnes, (*in*) *Brisehamme* 1088 ib.

Brixaham, Brixe- 1143 Totnes, *Brixham* 1242 Fees 769, 1246
Ipm, 1276 RH, *Ass et passim* from 14th cent.

Brikesham 1205 FF *et freq* to 1347 Cl, *Briges-* 1276 Cl,
Brikkes- 1285 Pat

Possibly '*Brioc*'s ham(m).' *v.* Brixton *supra* 249.

BOOHAY

Lid(d)ewige(s)ton, Ludewycheton c. 1200 (15th) *Torre*

Ledwycheton' 1242 Fees 767, *Lydewicheston* 1276 Ipm,
Lydewichetton juxta Kyngeswere 1298 *Ass, Ludewithestone*
1317 Exon

Bogheweye 1330 *SR* (p), 1365 Cl, *Bowehay* 1427 IpmR

Bowhay al. Lethewytston 1545 LP

v. tun. Professor Ekwall suggests that the first element is
connected with the name *Lidwiccas, Lioðwicas* used in the
ASC for the Bretons. That is an Anglicising of the adj. formed
from Latino-British *Letavia*, 'Brittany,' and found in the
Gaulish pers. name *Litavicos*. It would be used of a settler
from Brittany. The later name means 'curved way or track,'
v. Bowden *supra* 37. The road from here to Kingswear has
numerous slight turns and twists at this point. *v.* Addenda,
Part ii, xiv.

BROWNSTONE is *Bruneston'* 1242 Fees 767, *Broun-* 1303 FA, 1334
SR, Bromyston 1346 FA. '*Brūn*'s farm,' *v.* tun.

COLETON is *Coletona* 1086 DB, *Colet(h)on'* 1242 Fees 767, 1303
FA, *Colton* 1285 FA, *Coleton Fischacre* 1341 Ipm. '*Col(l)a*'s
farm,' *v.* tun. Egidius de *Fyssacre* held the manor in 1303 (FA).

KINGSTON is *Kyngeston Facy juxta Dertemuth* 1292 *Ass, Kyngeston juxta Brikesham* 1302 *Ass, Kyngeston Facy* 1306 Ipm. 'King's
farm,' but neither the royal owner nor the connexion of the
Facy family is known. *v.* tun.

Lupton Ho

Lochetona 1086 DB, *Loketon* 1285 FA, *Lokatone* 1293 *FF*,
  Logheton 1346 FA
Lughaton' 1242 Fees 769, *Lugheton(e)* 1242 Fees 795 *et freq*
  to 1323 Orig, *Luckton* 1409 Exon
'*Luh(h)a*'s farm,' *v.* tun. Cf. Loughtor *supra* 253.

Noss Cottage (6″), also Creek (6″) and Point is *Nesse Creeke*
c. 1550 Leland and was the home of John *atte Nasse* (1330 *SR*).
The name is identical with Noss Mayo *supra* 257. Here the
reference is to two spurs of land above the Dart estuary. *v.* næss.

Polhearn Fm (6″) is *Poleheron* 1581 *SR*. This is probably simply
the ordinary word 'pool' (*v.* pol), the second element being the
name of some unknown medieval tenant. Cf. Pool Anthony *infra*
544. The modern name has a somewhat Cornish look but no Celtic
word is known which would account for the second element.

Raddicombe is *Raftercumba* 1183 P (p), *Raftecumb* 1249 *Ass*,
Reftercumb(e) 1242 Fees 767, 796, 1244 *Ass* (p), *Reftercombe
juxta Clyfton Dertemouth* 1356 *Ass*. This seems to be a compound
of OE *ræfter*, 'rafter, beam,' and cumb, but the exact meaning is
not clear. Possibly the name referred to a valley where trees and
logs were cut up for building purposes.

Woodhuish [wudiʃ] is *Odehiwis* 1086 DB, *Wodehuwis'* 1196 Cur,
-hywis 1242 Fees 767, *-hywysch* 1301 Ipm, *Wudehiewis* 1198 FF,
Woodish 1779 *Recov.* *v.* wudu, hiwisc.

Berry Head is *Byri pointe* c. 1550 Leland. *v.* burh. There are old
earthworks here. Castor Fm (6″) is *Caster* 1621 *FF.* Chally-
croft Road (6″) is *Challycrofte* 1726 *Recov.* Chiseldon Hill
(6″) is *Chaseldone* (sic) 1347 HMC xv, 7, *Cheseldon* 1783 *Recov.*
'Gravel hill,' *v.* ceosol, dun. Croftland is *Crofte* 1365 Cl. *v.*
croft. Durl Head is *Derle Point* 1765 D. Furzeham[1] (6″) is
Fursham 1476 IpmR. *v.* fyrs, hamm. Guzzle Down is *Gosewille*
1333 *SR* (p), *Gosewyll Doune* 1529–32 ECP 6, 176. 'Goose
spring,' *v.* wielle. Hillhead was probably the home of William
del *Hille* (1276 *Ass*). Hoodown is *Ho in the manor of Brixham*

---

[1] Preserved in *Furzeham Road.*

1276 Ipm, *Hoo* 1303 FA, 1306 Ipm, (*juxta Brixham*) 1345 *Ass*, (*next Dertemouth*) 1391 *FF*, *Howdowne* 1709 *Recov*. *v*. hoh. NETHWAY HO is *Nythewaye* 1384 *FF*. Probably 'beneath the way.' SCABBACOMBE is *Schobecumb* c. 1250 *Deed*. '*Sceobba*'s valley,' *v*. cumb and cf. Scoble *supra* 327. For the initial *sk*, *v*. Introd. xxxv. SOUTHDOWN is *Sowdon* 1615 *Recov* and was the home of Lucy *Bysouthedon*, i.e. 'south of the down' (1333 *SR*). UPTON MANOR is *Uppeton juxta Brixham* 1289 *Ass*. 'Higher farm,' *v*. tun.

Broadhempston

BROADHEMPSTON 145 A 6

> *Hamistona* 1086 DB, *Hameston*' 1179 P (p), -*tune* 1219 *Ass*, *Ammeston* 1238 *Ass* (p)
>
> *Emmeston*' 1175 P, *Hemmeston(e)* 1220 FF, 1242 Fees 768, 795, 1244 *Ass*, 1281 Exon, (*Magna*) 1232 FF, *Hemeston* 1236–51 BM, *Hemestone majoris* 1266 Exon, *Hemeston Magna* 1337 Exon
>
> *Hemmiston Cauntelu* 1285 FA, *Hemmeston Cauntelou* 1315 *Ass* *Brodehempstone* 1362 Exon, *Hempstone Magna al. Brode-hempstone* 1422 Exon, *Hempston Cantelhoo al. Brodehampston* 1534 *Recov*

Professor Ekwall suggests (RN 195) that this is from OE *Hæmestūn*, '*Hæme*'s farm,' with a pers. name *Hæme*, connected with OE *Hæmgils* and the like. At that time no early forms were known for the Hems river on which Hempston stands. He took it to be a back-formation. Early forms have now been noted (*v. supra* 7). These may be taken as proof of the early date of the back-formation or we may, as Professor Ekwall would prefer, take it that the river was named after the same man as the farm and interpret it as *Hæme*'s 'ea' or stream. For *Broad*, *v. supra* 338. William de *Cantelupo* held the manor in 1242 (Fees 767).

BICKATON is *Biggeton* 1314 *Ass* (p), *Bygatone* 1333 *SR* (p), *Byggeton* 1382 *FF*. This place-name clearly contains the OE pers. name (or nickname) *Bicga* or *Bygga* found in the 11th cent. and fully discussed by Stevenson (*Crawford Charters* 149), or the adjective from which that nickname is derived, if, as seems probable, that name is to be identified with the adjective *big*, of which the etymology is at present unknown. The same pers. name (or adjective) is found in Bigfrith (Berks), *Bigefrithe* in 1247 (*Ass*), *Byggefrith* in 1284 (*Ass*).

FISHACRE is *Fishacre* 1210–12 RBE, *Fisacre* 1242 Fees 769, *Fisch-* 1260 Ipm, *Fissakere* 1265 Exon (all p), *Fissacre* 1276 Cl, *Fysshacre* 1359 *Ass*. The meaning of the compound is not very clear. It may have referred to a field for which dead fish were used as manure, or possibly to a field where fish were found after some inundation. The land here is low-lying.

PURCOMBE is *Porecumbe* 1219 *Ass*, *Porrecomb(e)* 1323 *Ass*, 1333 *SR* (all p), *-come* t.Ed 3 *Ass*. *v.* cumb. There is some evidence for a pers. name **Porra*, cf. Poringland (Nf), *Porringalanda, Porringelanda* 1086 DB, *Poringeland* 1225 Pat, *Porringlond* 1346 FA[1].

BOROUGH FM (6″), DOWN, FORDER GREEN, KNOWLE, LAKE (6″), and PITT (6″) were probably the homes of Richard *atte Burghe* (1330 *SR*), Richard *Bywestedon*, i.e. 'west of the down' (1333 *SR*), John *atte Forde* (1333 *SR*), Walter *atte Knolle* (ib.), Benedict de *la Lak* (1244 *Ass*), and Robert *Bythelake* (1333 *SR*), and John Barter *at Pitt* (1571 *SR*). *v.* beorg, cnoll, lacu, pytt.

BEASTON is *Bagiston* 1330, *Bachestone* 1333 *SR* (p). HALSWELL is *Halssewyll* 1543–58 *Ct*. 'Hazel spring,' *v.* wielle. LEE is *La Legh* 1238 *Ass*, *at Ley* 1571 *SR* (p). *v.* leah. OLD WALLS (6″) is *Oldwalls* 1699 *FF*. WAYTOWN is *Waytown* 1790 *Recov*. *v.* weg.

Churston Ferrers

CHURSTON FERRERS 145 D 9

   Cercitona 1086 DB (Exon), *Cercetone* (Exch)
   Cherchetun 1088 Totnes, *-ton* 1262 FF, 1303 FA, *Cherecheton*
     1243 FF
   Churchetun 1143 Totnes, *-ton* 1289 *Ass*, 1324 Ipm, 1346 FA,
     Churechetone 1242 Fees 767, *Churcheston* 1365 Cl, 1369 Pat
   Chircheton 1249 *Ass*, 1306 Ipm, *-ston* 1327 Cl
   Churcheton Ferers juxta Brixham 1345 *Ass*
   Chessen 1675 Ogilby

'Church farm', *v.* cyric(e), tun. Hugo de *Fereris* held the manor in 1303 (FA).

[1] *Ex inf.* Dr O. K. Schram.

GALMPTON [gamtən]

> *Galmentona* 1086 DB, *Galmetun* 1198 FF, *-ton* 1285 FA,
> (*juxta Bryxham*) 1299 *Ass*, (*juxta Wadeton*) 1309 Orig
> *Gaumethon'* 1242 Fees 768, *Gaumenton* 1249 *Ass*
> *Gamelton* 1279 Ipm, *Gampton* 1765 D

For the interpretation of this name, *v.* Galmpton *supra* 304.

ALSTON is *Elston al. Elson* 1779 *Recov.* BRIMHILL PLANTATION
is *Bromhille* 1409 *Deed.* 'Broom hill.' ELBERRY is possibly
identical with *Eleworthy* 1278 Totnes. '*Ella*'s worþig' or 'eldertree worþig,' cf. Butterberry *supra* 232. GREENWAY is *la Grenewey* 1328 Exon (p), *Grenewey* 1438 IpmR.

Cockington

COCKINGTON 145 A 8/9

> *Chochintona* 1086 DB (Exon), *Cochintone* (Exch)
> *Kokington* c. 1180 Oliver *et passim* with variant spellings *Cok-*,
> *-in-, -ing-, -yng-*

'*Cocca*'s farm,' *v.* ingtun and cf. Cocking (PN Sx 16) for the
pers. name.

CORBONS HEAD. In 1196 Roger de Cockington granted the
canons of Torre permission to quarry under the *tuyveldeclive*
in the part east of *Corvenasse*, i.e. Corbons Head (*Torre*).
The name must be a compound of OE *corfen*, past participle of
ceorfan, 'to cut, cut out, carve, etc.,' and næss, perhaps with
reference to the small detached rock here. *tuyveldeclive* must be
a compound of OE *twīfeald*, 'double,' and clif.

EDGINSWELL

> *Willa* 1086 DB, *Welles* 1238 FF
> *Wylle Egelf* 1281 *Ass*, *Wille Eggelf* 1285 FA
> *Eggeneswill(e)* 1292 *Ass*, 1378 IpmR, *-ys-* 1325 FF, 1334 SR,
> *-welle* 1343 FF
> *Eggreswelle juxta Whelberewe* 1294 *Ass*
> *Eggereswill* 1303 FA, *Eggereswille et non in Eggeneswille* 1325
> *Ass*, *Eggeryswill* 1316 FA, *-is-* 1423 IpmR

v. wielle. No trace has been found of the *Ecgwulf* who gave
rise to the earliest manorial addition. *Eggelfeswill* may have

become *Eggeleswill* and been dissimilated to *Eggeneswill* (cf. Edenbridge (K), earlier *Edulvesbregge*), and then with common confusion of *n* and *r* in the sequence *n...l*, forms in *Eggeres* may have arisen. It is clear from the specific distinction in the Assize Roll of 1325 that though *Eggereswille* was officially recognised as the correct form, the popular *Eggeneswille* ultimately survived. For *Whelberewe v.* Whilborough *infra* 515.

SHIPHAY COLLATON is *Coletona* 1086 DB, *-ne* 1301 Exon, *Collaton Shephay* 1697 FF. '*Col(l)a*'s farm,' *v.* tun. It is distinguished from the other Devon Collatons by its adjacency to Shiphay Ho *infra*.

CADEWELL HO (6″) is *Caddewell* 1238 FF. '*Cad(d)a*'s spring,' *v.* wielle. LIVERMEAD is *Lefremede, Levermede* c. 1200 (15th) *Torre, Levermede* 1317 Oliver, *-mead* 1438 IpmR. The first element is probably OE *lǣfer*, 'wild iris.' SHIPHAY HO is *Shepehay* 1541 Oliver 178. 'Sheep enclosure,' *v.* (ge)hæg.

Coffinswell

COFFINSWELL 138 J 8

> *Willa* 1086 DB, 1185 Buckland, *Welles* 1231 Cl, 1242 Fees 781, *Wille* t. Ed 1 Exon
> *Coffineswell* 1249 Ass, *Wylle Coffyn* 1281 Ass, *Wille Coffin* 1285 FA, *Coffynswille* 1301 Exon

v. wielle. Hugo *Coffin* held the manor in 1185 (Buckland).

DACCOMBE

> *Daccumba* 1177 P (p), *-cumb(e)* 1228 FF, 1242 Fees 781, *-combe* 1291 Tax, *Dakkumbe* 1280 Ass (p)
> *Doccuma* 1185 Buckland
> *Daggecumba* 1193 Oliver 95

This probably contains the same pers. name *Dæcca* as Dagenham (Ess), *Dæccanhaam* BCS 81. Hence '*Dæcca*'s valley.' *Dæcca* would be a shortened form of *Dǣdica*, a pet form of one of the OE names in *Dǣd*. Cf. *Dedic, Tadica* (Förstemann PN 387–8).

DREW'S FM (6″) is to be associated with the family of William *Dryw* (1333 SR). FOOTLAND (6″) is so spelt in 1727 (*Recov*).

Ipplepen

IPPLEPEN[1] 145 A 7

(*to*) *Ipelanpænne*, (*to*) *Iplanpenne*, *Iplanpen* 956 (13th) BCS 952
Iplepena 1086 DB, *Yppelpen* 1172 P, *Ip(p)elpenne* 1235 Cl,
1237 Fees 612
Hypelepenn' 1212 Fees 97, *Ippelepen(ne)* 1231 Ch, 1291 Tax,
Ypele- 1235 Fees 560, 1274 Exon, *Ipele-* 1242 Fees 768
Ippellapenne 1275 RH
Uppelpen 1383 Pat

'*Ip(p)ela*'s penn.' Cf. Ipplesborough PN Wo 319.

BATTLEFORD (6″) is *Bacheleford* 1086 DB, *Bakele-* 1242 Fees 790,
1330 *SR* (p), 1438 BM, (*juxta Ipelepenne*) 1304 *Ass*, *Bakeles-*
1304 *Ass*. '*Baccela*'s ford.' This pers. name is not on record,
but would be a regular *l*-derivative of OE *Bacca*.

COMBE FISHACRE is *Comba* 1086 DB, *Cumba* 1228 FF, *Come
Fishacre* 1285 FA. *v.* cumb. Martin de *Fisacre* held the manor
in 1228 (FF). Presumably he came from Fishacre *supra* 510.

DAINTON is (*to*) *Doddingtune*, (*æt*) *Doddintune* 956 (13th) BCS
952, *Dodinton(e)* 1249 *Ass*, 1275 FF, *Doyngton* 1558 Ct, *Doington*
1754 *Recov*, *Doington oth. Daington* 1797 *Recov*. '*Dodda*'s farm,'
v. ingtun.

DORNAFIELD is *Dornefeld* 1238 *Ass*, 1330 *SR* (both p). *v.* feld.
The first element seems to be some pre-English word, perhaps
that found in Dorchester and Dorset.

AMBROOK is *Ambrok* 1238 *Ass*, 1330 *SR* (both p), *-ock* 1427
IpmR. *v. s.n.* Amicombe *supra* 191. BELTOR CROSS and BILVER
COTTAGE (both 6″) are *Byltorre*, *Bylfford* 1543–58 *Ct*. Bow
GRANGE was the home of Henry *atte Bowe* 1298, 1321 *Ass*, *atte
Bogh* 1304 *Ass*. It takes its name from the bridge over the river
Hems here. BULLEIGH BARTON is *Bullegh* 1238 *Ass*, *Bolelegh*

---

[1] BCS 952 is a grant of 15½ hides at Ipplepen, Dainton (in Ipplepen) and
Abbotskerswell. The area is clearly a large one and the boundaries are
difficult to identify, for in proportion to the size of the area very few boundary
points are mentioned, the boundary more than once being indicated by the
unsatisfactory statement that it goes *on landscore*, i.e. along the boundary. We
can only be sure of Maddacombe in Abbotskerswell, and Ogwell, the latter
being referred to in the phrase *on herepath to woggan wylle*.

1330, 1333 *SR* (all p). 'Bull clearing,' *v.* leah. CASTLEFORD (6″) is *Castelford* 1543–58 *Ct.* Possibly there was once some ancient castle or camp here, though nothing now remains to be seen. MAITLANDS (6″) is *Metelond, Meytlond Grene* 1558 *Ct.* MUDGE'S LANE (6″) is to be associated with the family of Robert *Mudge* of Abbotskerswell (1545 *SR*). PRATOR COMMON (6″) is *Prator* 1748 *Recov.* WAYE BARTON was the home of Walter *atte Weye* 1333 *SR. v.* weg. YARNEFORD COTTAGE (6″), cf. *Yernaborough* c. 1550 *Ct.* 'Eagle ford and hill,' *v.* earn, beorg.

Little Hempston

LITTLE HEMPSTON 145 B 6

> *Hamistona* 1086 DB
> *Hemmeston'* 1242 Fees 769, (*Arundel*) 1285 FA, 1313 Ipm, (*Chatard*) 1303 FA, *Hemestone minor* 1264 Exon, *Parva Hemestone* 1284 Exon, *Little Hameston* 1297 Pat, *Little-hempstone* 1608 Wills
> *Hompston Arondell* 1390 Cl

v. Broadhempston *supra* 509. The manor was held by John de *Arundel* in 1242 (Fees 769). The identity of *Chatard* is unknown.

BUCKYETT is *Bokeyeth'* 1242 Fees 767 (p), *Bocyett* 1275 RH (p), *Bukyete* 1330 *SR* (p). 'Beech-tree gate,' *v.* boc, geat.

LILLISFORD is *Lilles-, Lullesford* 1438 BM, *Lullesforde* 1454 *FF*, '*Lull*'s ford.' Cf. *to lulles beorge* BCS 727. There is a LILLISPIT (6″) close by.

GATCOMBE Ho is *Gatecomb(e)* 1320 *Ass*, 1330 *SR* (both p). 'Goats' valley,' *v.* gat, cumb. PARKHILL (6″) was the home of Henry *atte Parke* 1330 *SR. v.* pearroc. PENN'S BARN (6″) is to be associated with the family of Roger *Penne* (1333 *SR*). UP-HEMPSTON is *Uphemston* 1652 *Recov.* It lies higher up the river Hems.

Kingskerswell

KINGSKERSWELL 138 J 8

> *Carsewilla* 1086 DB, *Carsuill* 1194 P, -*well* 1230 Ch, *Karswell* 1212 Fees 97, *Karswill Regis* 1285 FA

Cassewell 1158, 1159 P
Kyngescharsewell 1270 FF, *-karswelle* 1270 *Ass*
Kings Keswell 1675 Ogilby, *Kingscraswell* 1736 *FF*

'Cress spring,' *v.* **wielle**. The manor was held by King William in 1086 (DB).

ODICKNOLL FM (6″) is *Odeknoll(e)* 1292 *Ass*, 1343 *FF*, 1423 IpmR, *Odyknolle* 1378 IpmR. '*Odda*'s cnoll.' It may be noted that this place cannot be very far from the *Oddingtorre* of the Ipplepen Charter (*supra* 513 n.) and the same man probably gave name to both the tor and the knoll.

WHILBOROUGH[1]

Weghelburgh 1292 *Ass*, *Sutwhegelbergh* 1294 *Ass*
Whelberewe 1294 *Ass*, *South Welbergh* 1342 Inq aqd
Huwelburghe 1301 Exon

The first element is OE *hwēol*, 'wheel,' referring doubtless to the circular hills here. *v.* **beorg**.

MOLES CROSS is to be associated with the family of William *le Mol* (1300 Totnes). ORESTONE CROSS (6″). No early form has been noted but, as it is on the parish boundary, the analogy of Oar Stone *infra* 519 suggests that we have here OE *hārstān*, 'grey' or 'boundary stone,' *v.* **har, stan**.

Kingswear

KINGSWEAR 145 E 8

Kingeswere 1170–96 Totnes *et passim* to 1493 Ipm with
  variant spelling *Kynges-*, *Kingeswerr* 1200 ChR, *Kyngges-*
  were 1267 Exon, *Kynggiswere juxta Dertemouthe* 1340 *Ass*,
  Kyngesware 1445 Pat
Kynkeswere 1272 Misc

Self-explanatory. *v.* **wer**. Kingswear was originally a part of Brixham parish (*supra* 507) in which is also a Kingston. Since no manor in the parish was a royal one, either TRE or TRW, it is clear that the association of these two places with a king must go back to pre-Norman times.

---

[1] North and South Whilborough (6″).

Down End is *Downe, Downesend* c. 1550 Leland. Waterhead Brake is *Water Hed* c. 1550 Leland.

Marldon

Marldon 145 A/B 8

Mergheldon(e) 1307 Exon, 1308 Oliver 428
Merledone 1307, 1370 Exon
Mareldon 1524 *SR*

The forms are few and late, but presumably the first element is the OE *meargealle*, 'gentian,' referring to a hill where this plant grew, *v.* dun.

Aptor is *Uppetorr(e)* 1254 *Ass*, 1333 *SR* (p), *Apator, Apetor* 1443 *Ct* (p), *Apptorre* 1554 *Recov. v.* torr. The first element seems to be the OE *uppe*, 'up, above.' It lies above Marldon.

Hulstercombe (6″) is *lez Hustercombs, Hulssecombe, Hullescombe* 1567 Pemb Surv, *Hulstercombes* 1634 *Deed*. The first element is OE *heolstor*, 'hiding place,' cf. Hylters (PN Sx 49).

Stantor is *Stantora* 1166 RBE (p), *-torr* 1275 RH (p), 1436 BM, *Stontor(r)e* 1242 Fees 767. 'Stone hill,' *v.* torr. According to Mr Watkin there is no outcrop of stone here, but there may once, as he suggests, have been a monolith or sacred stone here.

Churscombe is *Chesecombe* 1567 Pemb Surv. Compton is *Cumpton* 1244 *Ass, Compton juxta Cokyngton* 1330 *Ass*. 'Valley farm,' *v.* cumb, tun. Comptonpool is *Qumtonpole* 1285, *Compton Pole* 1303 FA, *Coumptonpole* 1326 FF. A small stream rises here. Longpark Linhay (6″) is *Lange Parke* 1567 Pemb Surv. *v.* Linhayes *infra* 592. Moretor (lost) is *Moretoor* 1800 *Recov* and was the home of John de *Mortetorre* (1333 *SR*). *v. s.n.* Morthoe *supra* 52. Occombe is *Occombe* 1567 Pemb Surv, *Ockombe* 1626 *Recov*. Peter's Tenement (6″) is to be associated with the family of Thomas *Peter* (1333 *SR*). Ridgeway Hill (6″), cf. *lez Ridge* 1567 Pemb Surv. Singmore Ho (6″) is *Synge more* 1514 *Ct*, *Syngmoore* 1567 Pemb Surv. Cf. the same name *supra* 505. Smallwell Lane (6″) is *Smalwyll* 1567 Pemb Surv, *Smallawell* 1724 *Recov*. Stringland Lane (6″) is *Straungland* 1567 Pemb Surv. Westerland is *Wisterland* 1567 Pemb Surv, 1626 *Recov*, *Wester-* 1610 *Recov*. Widdicombe (6″) is *Wythycombe* 1554 *Recov*. 'Withy valley,' cf. the same name *infra* 526.

Paignton

PAIGNTON 145 B 8

Peinton(a) 1086 DB, 1159 Buckfast, 1238 *Ass*, -*thon* 1242
Fees 769, *Peyntone* 1265, 1274 Exon
Peinctun early 13th Totnes, *Peynctone* 1259 Exon
Painton' 1215 ClR, 1230 P, *Paynton* c. 1630 Risdon
Peington(e) 1267 Exon, 1291 Tax, 1316 FA, *Peyng-* 1307
Exon
Pynton 1285 FA, 1347 Ipm, *Pyngton* 1438 FF
Paington 1837 *Act*

'*Pǣga*'s farm,' *v.* ingtun. The usual 18th and early 19th cent.
spelling was *Paington*, the present spelling being substituted by
the Railway Company since 1850 (*ex inf.* Mr J. J. Alexander).

NOTE. COLLEY END is *Culverhey Strete*. 'Pigeon enclosure,' *v.*
culfre, (ge)hæg. FERNHAM ROAD perhaps corresponds to *lez Ferneham*.
v. fearn, hamm. FISHER STREET is *Fisherstreete*. GERSTON ROAD is *lez
Garston*. *v.* gærstun. KIRKHAM STREET perhaps derives from the
family of George *Kyrkeham* who held land in the parish in 1567. TOTNES
ROAD is called *Trewe streete*, 'tree street,' cf. True Street *supra* 506.
WELL STREET may be near the place called *atte Wille juxta Peyntone*
(1306 *FF*). *v.* wielle. WINNER STREET is *Wynerdestrete*. This must be
OE *wīngeard*, 'vineyard,' unless it takes its name from the common
Devon pers. name *Wynerd*. All the above spellings, unless otherwise
stated, are taken from the Pembroke Survey of 1567.

COLLATON ST MARY is *Coletone* 1261 Exon, *Coleton*(e) *Clavill*(e)
1285 FA, 1289 *FF*. '*Col*(*l*)*a*'s farm,' *v.* tun. There is no record
of the Claville family holding land in this part of the county.

GOODRINGTON [gɔrintən, gʌrintən]

Godrintona 1086 DB
Godrington 1199 FF, -*yng-* 1346 FA, *Godering-* 1242 Fees 767,
-*yng-* 1414 BM, *Godryngton* 1346 FA
Godelingthon' 1242 Fees 793, *Gothelyngton* 1316 FA, 1388
AD iii
Gutherington 1249 *Ass*
Gotherington 1276 Ipm, -*yng-* 1334 *SR*, 1414 BM
Gorrenton sands 1667 DA 16

'*Gōdhere*'s farm,' *v.* ingtun. Cf. Gotherington (PN Gl 73).

YALBERTON

> *Aleburne* 1242 Fees 767, 1254 FF, *Ala-* 1275 RH (p), *Hale-*
> 1285 FA, *Cnythesaleburne* 1282 *FF, Aleborne* 1309 Exon,
> *-bourn* 1313 *Ass, Allebourn(e)* 1346 FA, 1348 Ipm, *Albourne*
> 1347 Ipm
> *Yealborne* 1422 IpmR, *Ealbourne* 1436 BM, *Yarberton oth.*
> *Yalbourne* 1786 *Recov*

It is probable that this name has the same history as Enborne
River (Berks), which was OE *alorburna*, 'alder stream,' ME *Ale-*
burne, v. RN 148. For the later addition of *-ton,* cf. Harberton
supra 325. For *Cnythes-* it may be noted that one John *le Cnigth,*
the 'knight,' was a juror in Haytor Hundred in 1242 (Fees 767).

BARCOMBE HALL (6″) is *Barkhame* 1634 *Recov.* Possibly 'birch-
tree ham(m),' *v.* beorc. BLAGDON is *Blakedune* 1242 Fees 786 *et*
freq to 1436 BM with variant spelling *-don(e).* 'Dark hill,' *v.*
blæc, dun. BLATCHCOMBE LANE (6″) is *Blatchcombe* 1742 (*FF*).
CLAYLAND CROSS is *Cleyland* 1671 *Recov.* CLENNON HILL is
Clendon 1567 Pemb Surv, 1748 *Recov.* 'Clean hill,' i.e. one
cleared of undergrowth, etc., *v.* clæne, dun. HOLLICOMBE is
Holecomb c. 1200 (15th) *Torre* (p), 1333 *SR* (p). *v.* holh, cumb.
HOLLOWAY HILL COTTAGE (6″) is *Holleway hill, Holowayehill*
1567 Pemb Surv. HOOKHILLS is *Hook Kiln* 1809 M, 1827 G.
MAY'S POOL (6″) is perhaps identical with *Meremeade al. Mere-*
poole 1567 Pemb Surv. It is *Measpoole al. Mearspoole* 1642 *Deed.*
POLSHAM is *Pawlesham* 1567 Pemb Surv, *Polsham* 1664 DA 16.
Perhaps 'Paul's ham(m),' cf. Polson *supra* 190 and Polsham (So),
Paulesham 1065 KCD 816, *Poulesham* 1284 FF. PRESTON is *Preste-*
ton 1275 RH (p), *Pruston, Preston* 1567 Pemb Surv. 'Priests' farm,'
v. preost, tun. PRIMLEY HO is *Prymley, -leigh, Est Prymleigh*
1567 Pemb Surv. ROUNDHAM HEAD is *Rown(e)ham* 1567 Pemb
Surv, t. Jas 1 ECP 478. SHORTON [ʃəˑtən] is *Shiraton* 1567
Pemb Surv, *Shorton* 1672 DA 16, *Shereton al. Shorton* 1728
Recov. The etymology may be the same as that of Skerraton
supra 298. SMALLCOMBE CROSS (6″) is *Smalecombe al. Godrington*
Park 1558–79 ECP, *Smallacombe* 1609 *Recov.* 'Narrow valley,'
v. smæl, cumb. TWEENAWAYS CROSS (6″) is *Twyneweye, Twyne-*
wayes 1567 Pemb Surv. 'Between the ways,' cf. Twinyeo *supra*
479. WHITESTONE (6″) is *Whytestone, Litle Whitestoone* 1567
Pemb Surv.

St Mary Church

ST MARY CHURCH 145 A 10[1]

(æt) *Sce Maria circean* 1050–72 Earle, *Sc̃e Marie Cherche* 1086 DB, *Seintmarichurche* 1242 Fees 796

BABBACOMBE is *Babbecumbe* c. 1200 (15th) *Torre* (p), *Babbecombe* n.d. Oliver 175 (p), 1467 Pat, *Babbacombe* 1504–15 ECP 4, 143, *Babicomb* 1765 D. '*Babba*'s valley,' *v.* cumb. Cf. Babbacombe *supra* 85.

ILSHAM MANOR

> *Ilesam* 1086 DB (Exon), *Ilesham* (Exch), 13th Buckfast, *Hyles-* 1291 Tax, *Yles-* 1316 Pat (p)
> *Eylsham* n.d. Oliver 174
> *Ilsham* 1249 *Ass*, *Elsham* 1541 Oliver 178

The second element is ham. The first is possibly OE *igil, ïl*, 'hedgehog,' used as a pers. name.

THE QUINTA (6″) is *Quinta Parke* 1606, *Wester Quente* 1640 *FF*. There can be little doubt that this is an early example of the introduction into this country of the Spanish and Portuguese *quinta*, 'country house' or 'villa,' first recorded in NED *s.a.* 1777. Such a name in a coastal parish to which some Devon seaman had retired is not improbable.

APPAWAY (6″) is *Happerway Hill* 1763 *Deed*. BARTON is *Bertone* 1333 *SR* (p), 1414 *AddCh*, *Barton* 1566 DA 43. *v.* beretun. HOPE FM (6″) and HOPE'S NOSE are *Hope, Hope's Nose* 1765 D. Cf. Hope *supra* 308. OAR STONE (rock in sea) is *Horestane* c. 1550 Leland. 'Grey stone,' *v.* har. TOZER'S FM (6″) is to be associated with the family of John *Tosere* (1333 *SR*). WATCOMBE PARK is *Whatecomb* 1414 *AddCh*, *Whetecombe* 1438 IpmR. 'Wheat valley,' *v.* cumb. WESTHILL FM (6″) is *Westhill* 1598 *Recov*. WINDMILL HILL (6″), cf. *Windmylparke* 1580 *Depositions*.

---

[1] Now part of Torquay, not marked by name on the 1″ map.

Staverton

STAVERTON 145 A 5/6

(*æt*) *Stofordtune* 1050–72 Earle[1], *Stovretona* 1086 DB, *Stover-ton*(*a*) 1148 HMC iv, 46, 1345 *Ass*
Staverthon' 1242 Fees 769, *-ton* 1285 FA

The first part of this name is identical with Stowford from *Stanford* (*supra* 41). There seem to have been alternative later developments (i) with very early rounding of *a* to *o*, (ii) with shortening of *ā* to *ă*.

HALSWORTHY is *Haldeswurthy* 1249 *Ass* (p), *Holdesworthy* 1530 *Recov*, *Halsworthie* 1588 DA 28 (p). *v. s.n.* Holsworthy *supra* 146.

KINGSTON Ho is *Kineston*(*e*) 1204 Cur *et freq* to 1397 *FF* with variant spelling *Kynes-*, *Keneston* 1329 *Ass* (p), *Kynston* 1333 *SR* (p), 1340 *Ass*, *Kenyston* 1426 *FF*. '*Cyne*'s farm,' *v.* tun. Cf. Kingscombe (Co), *Kynescombe* 1284 *Ass*.

PRIDHAMSLEIGH is *Legh*(*Prod*(*h*)*omme*) 1281 *Visit*, 1291 Tax, *Prodomisle* 1500 Ipm, *Prodehomeslegh* 1529–32 ECP 6, 195, and takes its name from the family of *Prodhomme* of which John is mentioned in 1281 (*Visit*). *v.* leah.

SPARKWELL

spearcan wille 1050–72 Earle
Sperchewilla 1086 DB, *Sperkeswell'* 1204 Cur
Sparkewill' 1242 Fees 786, *Sparkawille juxta Hemston* 1364 *Ass*

This may be compared with Sparkwell *supra* 255 and Sparkford (So), *Spercheforde* DB, *Sparkeford* 1242 FF. The first element in these names is identical in form with OE *spearca*, 'spark,' but no connexion of sense seems possible and one can only suggest that the word *spearca* was early used as a pers. name of the nickname type. That the word might have some specific topographical sense, however, is suggested by the surname *atte Sperke* found in Dorset in 1333 (*SR*). Cf. also Sparkaton *supra* 231, and Sparkhayne *infra* 531.

---

[1] Professor Max Förster notes for us the form *Stafortun* in an 11th cent. copy of this document.

WOOLSTON GREEN is *Holveston* 1353 *Ass*, *Wolveston, Olveston* 1384 *Rental*, *Ulston* 1431, *Wolston* 1467 *Deed*, *Wolston greene* 1662 *Recov.* Perhaps '*Wulf*'s farm,' *v.* tun, but the early spellings without initial *w* point rather to the Scandinavian *Úlfr*.

COMBE, FURSDON[1], HOLE[2], HIGHER PENN[3] (6″), WARE[4], WASH[5] and WELL were probably the homes of Thomas de *Cumbe* (1281 *Visit*), Wm de *Fursdon* (ib.), Robert *atte Hole* (1384 *Rental*), Richard Rugge de *la Penne* (1238 *Ass*) and Johanna *atte Penne* (1330 *SR*), John *atte Were* (1281 *Visit*), Thomas *atte Waysshe* (1330 *SR*), and Benedictus *atte Welle* (1281 *Visit*). *v.* cumb, fyrs, dun, penn, wer, (ge)wæsc (there is a stream here), wielle.

ABHAM is *Obbeham* 1301 Exon (p), 1384 *Rental*, *Abhambrigge* 1514 *Ct.* '*Obba*'s ham(m).' For the pers. name, cf. PN Wo 283. BADDAFORD is *Badeforde* 1244 *Ass* (p), 1384 *Rental*. '*Bad(d)a*'s ford.' BARKINGDON (6″) is *Berkedon* 1279 *Ass*, 1330 *SR* (p), 1348 *FF* (p). 'Hill of the birches,' *v.* beorc. BEARA is *La Bere* 1228 FF and was the home of William *atte Beare* (1333 *SR*). *v.* bearu. BLACKLER is *Blacalr* 1219 *Ass*, *Blakalre* 1333 *SR* (p), *Blakoler* 1515–18 ECP 5, 74. 'Black alder.' BOW COTTAGE (6″) was the home of Henry *atte Boghe* (1333 *SR*). The name refers to a bridge over the Hems river here. BULLAND (6″) is *Boldelonde* 1384 *Rental*. BUMPSTON CROSS is *Bomyston* 1333 *SR* (p). CADDAFORD is *Caddewrthi* 1238 *Ass* (p). '*Cada*'s worþig,' *v.* Introd. xxxv. CROFT COTTAGES (6″) is *Croft* 1427 IpmR. *v.* croft. GULLAFORD is *Goldeford* 1333 *SR* (p). The first element is probably a plant-name, cf. Goldbridge (PN Sx 275). GULWELL (6″) is *Goltawill* 1325 *Ass* (p), *Goolewill* 1571 *SR*. The first element may be as in the preceding name. The places are, however, far apart. NETHERTON (6″) is *Nytherton* 1330 *SR* (p). 'Lower farm,' *v.* tun. PORT BRIDGE is *Portbrigpark* 1467 *Deed*. For *port, v. s.n.* Doggaport *supra* 95. RUGGADON (6″) is *Roggedon* 1384 *Rental*. *v.* Ruckham *supra* 380. STAVERTON BRIDGE is *Staverton Brygge* 1436 Exon and was the home of John Coole *to Bridge* 1576 *SR*. Cf. Two Bridges *supra* 197. STRETCHFORD is *Strichefort* 1161–84 Totnes, *Streccheford* 1333 *SR* (p), *Straccheford* 1514 *Ct. v.* Strashleigh

---

[1] *Firsdon* 1384 *Rental*.   [2] *Hole* 1588 DA 28.
[3] *Penne* 1384 *Rental*.   [4] *Weare* 1595 *AddCh.*
[5] *Washe* 1588 DA 28.

supra 273. TIDWELL (6″) is *atte Todiwill* 1281 *Visit, Todewylle* 1301 Exon (p), *Tudewille* 1330 *SR* (p). *v.* Tiddy Brook *supra* 14. WADDONS (6″) is *le Waddon yeate* 1514 *Ct*. Perhaps 'woad hill,' the *s* being pseudo-manorial. Cf. Waddon *supra* 491. WESTON (6″) is *Westeton* 1330 *SR* (p), 1423 IpmR. 'West farm,' *v.* tun.

Stoke Gabriel

STOKE GABRIEL 145 C 7

> *Stoke* 1307 Exon, *Stokegabriel* 1309 Exon, *Gabrielstok(e)* 1313 Exon (p), 1356 *Ass, Gabrielestoke* 1372 *FF*
> *Stoke Sancti Gabrielis* 1396, 1453 Exon

v. stoc(c). The place was distinguished from the other Devon Stokes by the dedication of the church to St Gabriel.

WADDETON is *Wadenton* 1199 FF, *Wadeton* 1285 FA, 1303 FA. 1309 Orig. Probably '*Wada*'s farm,' *v.* tun.

AISH is *Aishe* 1567 Pemb Surv. *v.* æsc. BYTER MILL (6″) is *Bittor, Byttor* 1567 Pemb Surv, *Boyter al. Byter* 1789 *Recov. v.* torr. CROWNLEY LANE (6″) may be identical with *Crundall* 1567 Pemb Surv. Cf. Crownley *supra* 467. There is a quarry near by. DUNCANNON is *Duncanon* 1765 D. PENN'S QUARRY (6″), cf. *Greatepenne, Litlepenne* 1567 Pemb Surv. *v.* penn. The *s* is probably pseudo-manorial. ROWES is to be associated with the family of William *Rowe* (1333 *SR*). SANDRIDGE PARK is *Sandrigge* 1238 *Ass, Sanderig* 1242 Fees 767, *Sandriche* 1374 Exon. LOWER WELL FM is *Welles* 1242 Fees 768, *Wills* t. Eliz ChancP. *v.* wielle.

Torbryan

TORBRYAN 138 J 6[1]

> *Torra* 1086 DB, *Torre* 1242 Fees 768, 786, *Torre Briane* 1238 *Ass*

v. torr. Wido de *Brione* is first mentioned in connexion with the place in 1238 (*Ass*), his name being spelt *Brionne* in 1242 (Fees).

COPPA DOLLA is *Coppadaller* 1660 *Recov*. 'At the pollarded alder,' *v.* coppede, alor. The present quaint spelling seems to be fairly modern.

[1] Part of the parish is in 145 A 6.

DENBURY

Devenaberia 1086 DB, *-bury* 1336 *Ass*

Devenebire 1228 FF, 1237 Cl, *-byr'* 1242 Fees 769, *-byri* 1278
Exon, *-byr* 1286, 1290 Ch, *-bire* 1291 Tax, *Defnebery* 1265
Exon

Devenesbir(i) 1285 FA, *-bury* 1415 *FF*

For this name, *v.* Introd. xiv, n. The burh is the earthwork
known as Denbury Camp.

KILLINCH is *Cavelynche* n.d. Oliver 104, *Keallynch* 1440 *FF*,
Calynche 1483 IpmR. '*Cāfa*'s hlinc.' Cf. Keybridge PN Wo
305 and Keyberry *infra* 524.

POOLE, WELL BARN (6") and YEATT were the homes of Margery
atte Pole (1333 *SR*), Stephen *atte Wille* (ib.), and William de
Yete (ib.). The last is *Yeate* 1544 *Ct.* *v.* pol, wielle, geat.

BREMRIDGE is *Bremmelrigg* 1244 *Ass*, *Brimbelrigge* 1276 *Ass*,
Bremelrigge 1427 IpmR. 'Bramble ridge.' BROADWAY (6") is so
spelt in 1715 *Recov.* COMBE COTTAGE (6") is *the Higher Comb*
1544 *Ct.* *v.* cumb. DOWN is *Downe* 1502 ECP 4, 248. DYER'S
WOOD (6") is to be associated with the family of Thomas *Dyer*
(1571 *SR*). HALWELL is *Hollwell mead* 1748 *Recov.* Probably
'spring in the hollow,' *v.* holh, wielle. HEATHFIELD is *Hethfild*
1544 *Ct.* 'Waste land,' *v. supra* 265. NORDON is *Northdowne*
1544 *Ct.* ORLEY COMMON is *Orleigh* 1715 *Recov.* *v.* leah. SHUTE
(6") is *Shute* 1749 *Recov.* *v. supra* 184. SIMPSON is *Sewenneston'*
1238 *Ass* (p), *Seuenestone* 1244 *Ass* (p), *Seeweneston* 1378 IpmR.
Probably '*Sigewine*'s farm,' *v.* tun. TORNEWTON is *Nywetone* 1330
SR (p), *Torr Newton* 1748 *Recov.* 'New farm,' *v.* tun. WOTTON
is *Wudeton, Wutton* 1249 *Ass, Wottone* 1333 *SR* (p). 'Farm by the
wood,' *v.* tun. WRENWELL (6") is *Warnewill* 1544 *Ct, Wranwill*
1701 *Recov.* wran is a Devon dialect form for *wren* (EDD).

Tormoham

TORMOHAM (TORQUAY) 145 A 9

Torra 1086 DB, *T(h)orre* 1233 Cl, 1238 *Ass*

Torre Brywere c. 1200 (15th) *Torre*, 1242 Fees 769, (*Bruwer*)
1238 *Ass, Torrebruere* 1291 Tax

Torre Moun 1279 Cl, *Torremohon* 1308 Exon (p), *Torremohun,*
Torre Mohoun 1331 Ipm

The torr was that under the southern side of which Torre Abbey was built. The manor first belonged to the *Briwere* family, but passed to that of *Mohun* on the marriage of Alicia, fourth daughter of William Briwere, to William de *Mohun* (1242 Fees 769, DA 40).

TORQUAY [tɔ·'ki·] is *Torrekay* 1591 *Deed* (J. J. A.), 'a small village called *Torkay*' 1668 DA 27, 'Fleete[1] otherwise *Torkey* within the parish of Tormohun,' 1670 ib., *Torkey* 1715 Moulton, *Tor Quay* 1765 D. An earlier reference to the place occurs perhaps in 1412, when a French ship laden with wine was seized and brought into Devon '*a un lieu appelle le Getee de Torrebaie*' (Seld 10). The name was applied at first to a quay or landing stage, perhaps built by the monks of Torre Abbey near by. The town, which covers the whole of the ancient parish of Tormoham, most of St Mary Church, and a part of Cockington, is chiefly of 19th cent. growth, though the reference above shows that a small settlement existed on the spot as early as 1668.

CHILSON (6″) is *Chilston* 1438 IpmR. TORRE ABBEY is *Thore* 1226 Pat, *Torr(e)* 1238 *Ass et passim. v. supra.* PETIT TOR is *Petitorre, Peritorre Pointes* 1550 Leland. TORWOOD GARDEN is *Torrewood* 1574 DKR 38, 188.

Wolborough

WOLBOROUGH 138 H 7

> *Olveberia* 1086 DB (Exon), *Ulveberie* (Exch)
> *Wulveberg* 1221 ClR, -*burg* 1223 ClR, *Wlueberue* 1228 FF, *Wolvebergh'* 1242 Fees 768
> *Wullebergh'* 1242 Fees 786, *Wolleburghe* 1291 Tax
> 'Wolves' hill,' *v.* beorg.

KEYBERRY PARK (6″) is *Kauebiri, Cawbiry* c. 1200 (15th) *Torre, Kauebire* 1238 FF, -*bur'* 1281 *Ass* (both p), *Cauebyri* 1256 FF, *Caybiry* 1336 *Ass* (p). '*Cāfa's* burh.' The burh may have been on the small round hill here, by the Aller stream.

CONITOR QUARRY (6″) is *Conytorre* 1388 Exon. *v.* torr. The first

---

[1] *v.* fleot. There is still a *Fleet Street* in Torquay where a small stream formerly entered the sea.

element is probably ME *coni, conin(g)*, 'rabbit.' FORD HO is
Forda 1238 *Ass, Ford juxta Nyweton* 1305 *Ass.*

Woodland

WOODLAND 138 J 5

Wodeland 1424 Exon, 1436 Pat, 1473 IpmR, *capella de Woodland* 1535 VE

Self-explanatory. The parish was originally a chapelry of
Ipplepen, and is thus rarely mentioned in early records.

PULSFORD is *Pollokysford* 1330, *-kes-* 1333 SR (p). '*Polloc*'s ford,'
v. Poulston *supra* 323.

BRAMBLEOAK CROSS (6″) is probably identical with *Bremel Crosse*
1543–58 *Ct.* CREEK BEACON may be associated with John de
Crekhulle 1330 *SR.* The first element may be Co *cruc*, 'barrow,'
'hill.' DIPWELL (6″) is *Depwyll* 1244 *Ass* (p). 'Deep spring,'
v. wielle. FURZE COTTAGE (6″) is *at Furse* 1543–58 *Ct.* LAKE (6″)
is *Lake* 1543–58 *Ct. v.* lacu. LEE is *Toleigh* 1709 *Recov. v.* leah.
To may have the sense of *at, v.* Two Bridges *supra* 197. LEVATON
is *Luuetone* 1330 *SR* (p), *Levaton* 1543–58 *Ct.* '*Lēofa*'s tun.'
ORLYCOMBE COTTAGES (6″) is *Orlecombe* 1333 *SR* (p). Possibly
'alder valley,' *v.* cumb and cf. Orleton PN Wo 67. TOR (6″) is
Torre 1238 *Ass* (p), *Torre grounde* 1558 *Ct. v.* torr. WELL was
the home of Ralph *atte Wille* 1330 *SR.* 'At the spring,' *v.* wielle.
WICKERIDGE HO is *Wykerig* 1543–58 *Ct.*

Buckland in the Moor

BUCKLAND IN THE MOOR[1] 138 H 3

Bochelanda 1086 DB, *Bocland*' 1242 Fees 768
Bokelaund in the More 1318 Ch, *Boklonde Inthemore* 1334 SR,
Bokelond in La More 1378 IpmR

v. bocland. This place is distinguished from the many other
Devon Bucklands by its situation on the borders of Dartmoor.

PUDSHAM is *Puttekesham* 1318 *Ass, Pottekysham* 1330, *-es-* 1333
SR (p), *Puttokisham* 1374 *SR* (p), *Northeputtysham* 1554 *Recov.*

---

[1] This parish and that of Widdecombe *infra* 526 form a detached area,
separated from the rest of the hundred by the parish of Ashburton in Teignbridge Hundred.

'*Puttoc*'s ham(m).' Alternatively the first element may be ME *puttock*, 'kite.'

BOWDEN (6″) is *Boghedoune* 1330 *SR* (p). 'Bow-shaped hill,' *v. supra* 37. CHALLAMOOR (6″) is *Choldemor*' 1374 *SR* (p). 'Cold moor,' *v.* cald, mor. RUDDYCLEAVE (6″) is *Radeclyve* c. 1200 (15th) *Torre, -clive* 1316 Pat, *Redeclyve* 1330 *SR* (p). 'Red clif.' SOUTHBROOK (6″) is *Suthbrok* c. 1200 (15th) *Torre*. STONE FM (6″) was the home of William *atte Stone* 1330 *SR*.

Widdecombe in the Moor

WIDDECOMBE IN THE MOOR 138 F 3

> *Widecumb(a)* t. Hy 1 (1270) Ch *et freq* to 1453 BM with variant spellings *Wyde-* and *-comb(e)*, *Wydecombe juxta Asshpirton* 1323 *Ass*
> *Whithecombe in the More* 1362 *Ass*
> *Wydecomb yn the More* 1461 BM, *Wydecombe in Mora* 1481 IpmR
> *Wedecomb yn the more* 1505 Ipm
> *Wythecomb* 1535 VE, *Withecomb* 1675 Ogilby
> *Widecombe oth. Withecombe in the Moor* 1784 *Recov*

> Either 'withy valley' or 'wide valley.' *v.* wiðig.

BITTLEFORD (6″) is (*æt*) *Bitelanwyrthe* 956 (13th) BCS 952, *Bitteleworthi, Bitelleworth*' 1277 *Ass, Byteleworthi* 1333 *SR* (p), *-thy* 1339 *Ass, Bittelford Yeat* 1587 Dartmoor. '*Bit(t)ela*'s worþig,' cf. Beechcombe *supra* 187. *Yeat* = 'gate' (*v.* geat), referring to one of the entrances to Dartmoor Forest.

BLACKSLADE DOWN is *Blakslade* 1544 DA 28. 'Dark valley,' *v.* blæc, slæd. The place has been identified with *Blackestac, -stach, Bacheslac* 1086 DB, but if this is correct the forms must be corrupt.

BONEHILL DOWN is *Bunhildowne* 1652 *Recov*. The first element may be simply the word *bone*, perhaps with some reference to the prehistoric burial grounds which are so thick on Dartmoor. Cf. Bunhill (London). The old local pronunciation survives in BUNHILL COTTAGE (6″) close by.

CATOR is *Cadatrea* 1167 P (p), *Chade-, Kadetrew* n.d. AD vi,

Cadetrewe 1270 *Ass*, *-truwe* 1313 AD vi, *-treo* 1371 Pat, *-tru* 1412 *Ct*, *Caddetreo* 1377 *Ct*, *Nythercatrew* 1481 *Ct*. 'Cada's tree,' v. treow.

CHITTLEFORD (6″) is *Chytilford* 1244 *Ass*, *Chitelford* 1303 DA 8, *Chetelford* 1443 *Ct* (all p). The first element is probably the OE *cietel*, 'kettle, cauldron,' the reference being to the rapid rushing stream here at the spot where there is now a bridge on the road from Dunstone to Chittleford.

DEWDON[1] (lost)

> *Depdona* 1086 DB
> *Dawedun* n.d. AD vi (p), *Deaudon* 1234 Fees 400, 1256 FF,
>   *-den* 1288 Cl, *Dyaudone* 1328 Exon, *Dewadone* 1387 Exon
> *Dendon* (sic) 1326 Cl, *Dewdon Down oth. Dewdon Ball* 1737
>   Recov

v. dun. The first element is the OE *dēaw*, 'dew,' and the name must have originally referred to a hill where the dew fell heavily. Cf. Dewcombe (Co), *Deaucumba* 1208–13 Fees (p). For the DB form, if it belongs here, cf. Pickwell *supra* 44.

DUNSTONE is *Dunestanetuna* 1086 DB, *Donston juxta Wydecomb* 1283 BM, *Dunstanestoune juxta Wydecumbe* 1311 *Ass*, *North-donston* 1453 BM. 'Dunstān's farm,' v. tun. Cf. the same name *supra* 261. There is, however, close at hand, a *Dunstone* Rock, so that the name may really be 'farm by the *dūnstān* or hill-rock' or 'by the grey rock' (OE *dunn*).

HAMEL DOWN [hæməldən] is *great waste called Hameldon* 1566 DA 43, *Hammeldon* 1652 Recov. The shape of the hill resembles a hog's back (F. R.-T.) and *hamel* must here have the sense of 'cut off.' v. hamel.

HATCHWELL is *Hatteshull* 1352 SR (p), *Hatteshill* 1478 Ct (p), *-hyll* 1550 DA 28. This may be a compound of OE *hæt*, 'hat,' and hyll, referring to a hill of a particular shape. Cf. Hat Hill (PN Sx 49). The modern form is corrupt.

LEUSDON is *Leweneston* t. Hy 3 Dartmoor, *Leuston* 1303 DA 8 (p). Probably 'Lēofwine's farm,' v. tun.

---

[1] Now merged in Blackslade Fm (*ex inf.* Mr H. R. Watkin).

NATSWORTHY MANOR

> *Noteswrde* 1086 DB, *Nottesworth'* 1242 Fees 768, 796, *-wrthy*
> 1299 Ipm, *-worth(y)* 1316 FA, *Notteworth(y)* 1303 FA,
> *Notesworthy* 1428 FA
> *Nattesworthy* 1571 *SR*

'*Hnott*'s worþig,' see further *s.n.* Natsley *supra* 58.

OLLSBRIM (6″) is *Oldesbrom* 1317 Pat (p), *Holesbrom* 1333 *SR* (p),
Ollesbrom 1344 Dartmoor, *Ollys-* 1544 *Deed*. The second element
is brom, here perhaps in the sense of 'piece of broom-covered
land.' The first element is obscure. It may be a ME pers.
name *Olde*.

PONSWORTHY

> *Pauntesford* 1281 *Ass* (p)
> *Pontesford(e)* 1347 *MinAcct* (p), *-tis-* 1374 *SR* (p), *Pountesford*
> 1524 *SR* (p)
> *Pamsforth* 1544 *Deeds Enrolled*
> *Ponceford* 1600 *SR, Pounsford al. Pounsworthy* 1674 *Recov*

This name is probably identical with Ponsford in Cullompton
infra 561. The first element is difficult; it may be the British
word equivalent to W *pant*, 'hollow.' Ponsworthy lies in a
hollow opening out of the West Webburn valley and Ponsford
in Cullompton is in a slight hollow. For the interchange of *ford*
and *worthy*, *v.* Introd. xxxv. See further Ekwall RN 319.

SCOBITOR (6″) is *Scabatora* 1086 DB, *Scobetorre* c. 1200 (15th)
Torre, Scobe- 1388 Exon, *Scobbetorre* 1219 *Ass, Skobbe-* 1452
MinAcct. '*Sceobba*'s torr.' Cf. Scoble, Scabbacombe *supra* 327,
509. For the initial *sk*, *v.* Introd. xxxv.

SPITCHWICK

> *Espicewita* 1086 DB (Exon), *Spicewite* (Exch), *Espiceuuic*
> 1100–3 (1332) Ch, t. Hy 2 (1387) Pat, *Espichewich* 1155–8
> (1332) Ch
> *Spikeswic* 1167 P (p), *Spikewyk* 1244 *Ass, Spicwyk* n.d. AD vi
> *Spichewiche* 1170–96 Totnes, *Spychewik'* 1242 Fees 768, *-wyke*
> 1283 Exon, *Spicheswich* 1305 Ipm, *Spycheswyk* 1306 Pat

This name is probably a compound of OE *spic*, 'bacon,' and

wic, hence 'bacon-farm.' Cf. Chiswick (Mx), Butterwick (Herts), Cowick *supra* 438.

YAR TOR is *Hurtetorre in vasto de Spychewyk* 1377 *Ct*, *Hurtetore Doune* 1385 *DuCo*, *Hartor land in Widecomb* 1578 *DuCo*. 'Harts' tor.'

LOWER AISH[1] (6"), LAKE[2] (6"), NORTHWAY, SOUTHWAY[3] (6"), LOWER TOWN[4] and LOWER UPPACOTT (6") were the homes of Richard de *Aysshe* (1371 Pat), William *atte Lake* (1333 *SR*), William *Bynorthewey* (1330 *SR*) and Walter *Bysoutheweye* (1333 *SR*), i.e. 'north and south of the way,' i.e. the road over the moor here, John *Inthetoune* (1333 *SR*), and Ralph de *Uppecote* (1330 *SR*). *v.* æsc, lacu, tun, cot(e).

BAGPARK is *Baggeparke* 1566 DA 43. Cf. Bagga Tor *supra* 232. BEL TOR is *Belletore* 1315 Inq aqd (p). Cf. Belstone *supra* 131. BLACKATON MANOR is *Blakedon* 1238 *Ass*, *Blacadun* 1249 FF, *Blackdon* 1570 *Ct*. 'Dark hill,' *v.* blæc, dun. BROADFORD (6") is *Brodford* 1525 *SR*. COOMBE (6") is *Combe juxta Vernhille* 1384 FF. *v.* cumb. CORNDON is *Corndon* 1303 DA 8, *Corendone* 13th Buckfast (both p), *Corindon* 1412 *Ct*. *v.* Corringdon *supra* 290. DOCKWELL (6") is *Doggeswell* 1807 *Recov*. FERNHILL (6") is *Vernhille* 1384 FF, *Fernehill* 1498 *Ct*. GRENDON is *Grenedone* 1313 AD vi (p), *Grendon* 1505 Dartmoor. 'Green hill,' *v.* dun. HANNAFORD is *Haneworthi* 1333 *SR*, -*thy* 1400, 1443 *Ct* (all p), *Hier Hanneworthy* 1554 *Recov*, *Hannaford* 1671 *Recov*. 'Hana's worþig,' cf. Hanworth (Mx). ISAFORD (6") is *Esaford* 1566 DA 43. KINGSHEAD (6") is *Kyngessette* 1333 *SR* (p), *Kingeshedd* 1670 FF. Cf. Kingsett *supra* 201. LANGWORTHY (6") is *Langeworthi* 1333 *SR* (p). 'The long worþig.' LEIGH TOR is *Leghetorr*' 1377 *Ct*, taking its name from a lost farm referred to as *Leye juxta Spikeswyke* (1298 FF). *v.* leah. LIZWELL is *Leysville* 1443 *Ct*, *Lesewill* 1543–58 *Ct*. *v.* læs, wielle. MEL TOR is *Molletor* 1443 *Ct*. PITTON (6") is *la Pitte* 1311 *Ass* (p), *la Pytton* 1342 Moulton, *atte Pytten* t. Hy 6 *Ct*, *Pyttinge* 1566 DA 43. *v.* Pitten *supra* 263. ROWBROOK (6") is *Robroke* 1291 Tax, *Rowbrookes* 1671 *Recov*. Probably 'roe brook,' *v.* ra. ROWDEN (6") is *Rowadoune ball* 1674

---

[1] *Higher, Lower Aishe* 1581 *SR*.
[2] *Lake* 1581 *SR*.
[3] *Southway* 1525 *SR*.
[4] *Towne* 1581 *SR*.

Recov. 'Rough hill,' *v.* dun. For *ball, v. supra* 211. SHALLOW-
FORD is *Sholeford* c. 1400 *Ct,* 1411 Dartmoor. SHERRIL is *Schire-
will* 1303 DA 8 (p), *Shyr-* t. Hy 6 *Ct, Sherwell* 1555 *DuCo.* 'Clear
spring,' *v.* scir, wielle. SOUTHCOMBE is *Southcumbe* 1313 AD vi
(p). STONE (6″) is *Atteston* 1566 DA 43 (nom. loc.), *Stone* 1652
Recov. SWEATON (6″) is *Sweton* 1544 *Deeds Enrolled.* Cf. Sutton
infra 550. LOWER TOR (6″) is *La Torre* 1249 *Ass, Torr* 1410
Moulton. TUNHILL (6″) is *Tonehill* 1253 Ipm (p), *Tunehill* 1254
Ass. UPHILL (6″) is *Uphill* t. Eliz ChancP, and was the home of
Lucas de *Uppehille* (1330 *SR*). VENTON is *Fenton* 1249 *Ass.*
'Farm in the marshy spot,' *v.* fenn, tun. WIND TOR may be
identical with *Wyndowne* 1674 *Recov.* Perhaps 'windy hill.'
WITTABURROW (6″) is *Whiteburghcomb* c. 1400 *Ct.* Probably
'white hill,' *v.* beorg.

XXIII. BAMPTON HUNDRED

Badentone 1084 Geld Roll, *Baunton* 1177 P, 1238 *Ass*
v. infra.

Bampton

BAMPTON[1] 128 A 11

Badentona, Baentona 1086 DB, *Baðentuna* c. 1090 (12th),
  Bathentona 1156 HMC Wells, *Bahentona* c. 1120 (12th)
  Bath, *Banton* c. 1156 (12th) Bath, 1238 *Ass, Baenton'* 1176,
  1183 P
Benton' 1183 P
Baunton 1221 FF *et freq* to 1368 BM, *Baunptone* 1274 Exon
Bamton 1253 Ipm, *Baumton* 1336 Ch

The forms make it clear that the first element in this name is
OE *bæð,* 'bath,' cf. Morebath *infra* 536, and Simonsbath (So),
Simonsbath, Simon's Bath c. 1550 Leland, *Symmonsbath* 1657
Exmoor. Ekwall (RN 27) would take the name to be from OE
Bæþhæmatūn, indicating a settlement of men from Morebath
infra 536, but settlement from Morebath on the hill to Bampton
in the valley seems unlikely and perhaps we should rather assume

[1] *Briton Street* in Bampton is *Brettyn streate* 1571 *Deed.*

that the *bæð* refers to a pool in the river at Bampton. Hence, 'farm of the dwellers by the pool.' Blomé (78) takes the name to be from OE *Baþumtun* and quotes the parallel of *Baðum tune* for Bath (*Baðum*) from ASC (*s.a.* 906). This form is, however, only found in the late 11th cent. MS D. The other MSS read *æt Baðum gerefa* and it may be suspected that D's *æt Baðum tune gerefa* is an error for *æt Baðum tungerefa*.

DIPFORD (6″) is *Deppaforda* 1086 DB (Exon), *Depeforde* (Exch), *Deopeforð* 12th Bath, *Depeford* 1238 *Ass* (p), *Dup(e)ford* 1303, 1346 FA. 'Deep ford.'

DRUIDSHAYNE (6″) is possibly identical with *Durantisheyes* (1310 Seld 22), a tenement in Bampton held by one William *Duraunt*. If so the modern form must be due in part to popular etymology as in Druidston (Pembrokeshire) for earlier *Dreweston*. For *hayne*, *v. supra* 129.

DUVALE BARTON is *Deuual* 1185 P, -*val(e)* 1239 FF, 1242 Fees 793, 1284, 1394 *Ass*, *Devale* 1284 *Ass*, *Dyeu*- 1356 FF, *Douwal* 1303 FA. This is probably a Celtic name, though it cannot refer to any stream, the place being on the Exe. The elements may correspond to the British *du*, 'black,' and *bâl*, 'peak, prominence,' referring to the curiously shaped hill here between the Exe and the Batherm.

LODFIN is *Lodefenne* 1288 *Ass*, 1333 *SR* (p), *Lodde*- 1317 *Ass* (p), *Lodfen* 1481 IpmR. For the first element, *v.* Ladford *supra* 108. The second element is OE fenn, 'fen, marshy spot.'

PETTON

 Peteton 12th Bath, *Petton* 1368 BM
 Patteton 1219 *Ass*, *Pate*- 1238 *Ass* (p), *Patton* t. Ed 1 BM,   *Pyaton* 1303 FA, *Patington* 1244 *Ass*
 Peadeton 1316 FA, *Peatton* 1368, 1504 BM

 '*P(e)atta*'s farm,' *v.* tun. Cf. Patcott *infra* 543.

SPARKHAYNE is *Sperkeheghe* 1311 *Ass* (p), *Spearkeheghes* 1356 *Ass*, *Sperkeheys* 1475–85 ECP 2, 205. The first element is probably the name of a medieval owner. Cf. Sparkaton *supra* 231, and Sparkhayes (So), *Sperkheys* 1419 Som Rec Soc 33, 168, to be associated with the family of Roger *Sperke* found in the parish in 1327 (*SR*).

RILL and WESTBROOK were the homes of Robert *atte Hille* (1333 *SR*) and John de *Westebrok* (1281 *Ass*). Cf. Rill *infra* 606.

BALL'S BARN (6″), BOWDENS (6″), DAYLES, POPES (6″) and WHITE'S COTTAGE (6″) are probably to be associated with the families of Henry *Ball* (1524 *SR*), John *Bawdyn* (ib.), John *Daly* (1333 *SR*), Nicholas *Pope* (1330 *SR*), and Nicholas *le Whita* (1333 *SR*).

ARTHUR'S HAYNE (6″) is *Higher Arterishain* 1772 *Recov. v.* Hayne *supra* 129. BREMRIDGE is *Bremeridge* 1549 Pat. Probably 'bramble ridge.' CUDMORE FM is *Cuddemore* 1238 *Ass* (p), *Code-* 1330 *SR* (p). '*Cudda*'s mor.' DODDISCOMBE is *Doddescumb*' 1242 Fees 793, *Duddescum* 1244 FF (p), *Dodiscomb* 1303 FA, *Dodes-combe* 1491 Ipm. '*Dodd*'s or *Dudd*'s combe.' FORD is *Lafford* 1281 *Ass* and was the home of Margery *atte Forde* (1333 *SR*). HAYNE BARTON is *la Heghes* 1333 *SR* (p), (*le*) *Hayne* 1432 BM, 1504 Ipm. *v.* Hayne *supra* 129. HOLCOMBE FM is *Hol(l)ecumbe* 1238 *Ass* (p), 1244 *Ass*, *-comb*' 1275 RH. 'Hollow combe,' *v.* holh. HONE is *la Hone* 1238 *Ass* (p). OE *hān*, 'boundary stone.' The place is near the parish boundary. LUTTRELL is *Lutterell* 1717 *Recov* and is probably identical with *Lutterwill* 1327 *Ass* (p). The first element will then be OE *hlūttor*, 'clear, bright,' the second wielle. NORTH DOWN WOOD (6″) is *Northdowne* 1549 Pat. PRIESTLAND COPSE (6″) is *le Pristes Lond* 1549 Pat. QUARTLEY is *Quarterley* 1827 G. RANSCOMBE is *Ramyscombe* 1549 Pat. SHIL-LINGFORD is *Sellingeford* 1179 P, *Shillyngford* 1333 *SR* (p). Cf. Shillingford *supra* 503. SNAILCOTT (6″) is *Snailcott* 1738 FF, *Snaylcok oth. Snailcott oth. Snaylcroft* 1825 *Recov*. SUNDER-LEIGH is *Synderdelegh* 1249 FF, i.e. 'separated or sundered clearing,' *v.* leah and cf. OE *syndrian*, 'to separate.' WATERHOUSE FM is so spelt 1714 *Recov*. WEEK COTTAGE (6″) is *Estwyk juxta Baunton* 1311 *Ass*. 'Dairy farm,' *v.* wic. WHITTENHAYS is *Wytheheies* 1330 *SR* (p). WONHAM HO is *Wonneham* 1330 *SR* (p). This may be '*Wunna*'s hamm,' *v.* Wonwell *supra* 279. The place lies in a bend of the River Exe. ZEAL FM is *Lasela* 12th Bath *v.* sele.

Clayhanger

CLAYHANGER 128 A 12

Clehangra 1086 DB, *-gre* 1291 Tax
Clahangre 1257 Pap
Cley(h)angre 1271, 1283 Exon
Clayheingre 1311 Pat, *-hangre* 1322 Cl

v. clæg, hangra. There is a slope here.

DONNINGSTONE MILL[1] (6″) is *Donicestona* 1086 DB, *Dun(n)inge-ston* 1228, 1238 FF, 1234 Fees 396, *Douneyngestone* 1291 Tax, *Donningeston* 1333 *SR* (p), *Donyng(ge)ston* 1408, 1432 BM, *Donston* 1420 BM. The place was held TRE by one *Donin* (Exch DB *Donninc*), which must be the OE pers. name *Dunning*. Hence, '*Dunning*'s farm,' *v.* tun.

CROSSE'S FM, FLEEDS FM (6″), HEARN'S FM, PERRY'S FM (6″) and POTTER'S FM are probably to be associated with the families of Robert de *la Crosse* (1330 *SR*), David *Fleed* (1730 Wills), William de *la Hurne* (1330 *SR*), Walter de *la Pirye* (ib.) and Henry *Potter* (1524 *SR*). In Crosse's, Hearn's and Perry's the *s* may be pseudo-manorial. *v.* hyrne, pyrig.

BERRY FM was the home of Walter *atte Berehaie* (1333 *SR*). 'Barley enclosure,' *v.* bere, (ge)hæg. BROCKHAM (6″) is *Broccombe* 1494 Ipm. 'Badger valley,' *v.* brocc. BULCOMBE is *Bolecumbe* 1281 *Ass*, *-comb* 1330 *SR* (p). 'Bull(s') valley,' *v.* cumb. HAND-LEY FM is *Honlegh* 1330 *SR* (p). 'Boundary stone clearing,' *v.* leah and cf. Hone *supra* 532. The farm is just by the county boundary. NORTH and SOUTH HELE are *Hele* 1303 FA, *Suth Hele* 1317 *FF*, *Northele* 1333 *SR* (p). *v.* healh. HOOKHAYS FM (6″) is *Hookey* or *Hookhay* 1800 Recov. NUTCOMBE FM is *Notcomb(e)* 1244 *Ass* (p), 1330 *SR* (p), 1334 *Ass*, *Nuthcomb* 1275 RH (p). 'Nut valley.'

Hockworthy

HOCKWORTHY 128 B 13

Hocoorda 1086 DB (Exon), *Hocheorde* (Exch)
Hockeworthy 12th *Canonsleigh et freq* to 1378 IpmR with variant spelling *Hokke-*, *Ockewrthy* 1282 Exon

---

[1] In DB there was a manor called *Alwinestona*, held with *Donicestona* by one *Alwin* (TRE). Cf. Alston *supra* 307.

'*Hocca*'s farm,' *v.* **worþig**. Cf. *on hoccan stige* BCS 1134 (Wo) and William *Hocke* and Roger *Hocca* 1308, 1311 Exon.

HOCKFORD WATERS is *Hochaorda* 1086 DB, *Hockeford* 13th *Canonsleigh*, *Hoke-* 1238 *Ass* (p), *Hoggeford* 1303 FA. '*Hocca*'s ford' with the same pers. name and probably the same man as in Hockworthy *supra.*

LEA BARTON is *Lega* 1086 DB, *Legh'* 1242 Fees 793, *Pouletteslegh* 1303 FA, *Poulettisleghe juxta Cleyhangre* 1339 *Ass*, *Leagh in Hokkeworthy* 1449 *FF. v.* leah. William *Poulet* held the manor in 1303 (FA).

LUCKLESS COTTAGE (6″) is to be associated with Vincent de *Louueclyve* (1281 *Ass*) and William de *Loueclyve* (1333 *SR*). '*Lēofa*'s steep hillside,' *v.* clif. The *s* is probably pseudo-manorial.

SLANTYCOMBE FM is *Slanycombe* 13th *Canonsleigh*, *Slanecumbe* 1281 *Ass* (p). OE *slānacumb*, 'valley of the sloe-trees,' *v.* slah, cumb. So similarly Wallenberg (StudNP 2, 92).

STALLENGE THORNE is (*æt*) *Stanlince* c. 1100 Earle, *Stanlinz* 1086 DB, *-lynche* 1316 FA, *Stonling* 1196 P 17, *Stallengethorne* 1680 *FF.* 'Rock hlinc.' The 'thorn' seems to be a late addition, cf. also Ekwall, PN in -*ing* 164.

TURNHAM is *Trewenham* 1377 Cl, 1378 IpmR, *Trounham* 1441 IpmR, *Tornam* 1482 IpmR. Probably, as Blomé suggests (82), this is a compound of ham(m) and *treowena*, a weak gen. pl. of treow, hence 'ham(m) marked by trees.' Weak inflexions in the plural are very common in Devon p.n.'s.

MORRELL'S FM, REDWOODS FM and STUCKLEYS (6″) are probably to be associated with the families of William *Morrell* (1684), Thomazine *Redwood* (1700) and George *Stucley* (1667 Wills).

HOLE FM was the home of Thomas de *la Hole* (1281 *Ass*). *v.* holh. STAPLE COURT FARM is *Staple* 1244 *Ass. v.* stapol. The *staple* must be the Staple Cross close at hand. WATERSLADE is *la Waterslade* c. 1200 *Canonsleigh. v.* slæd.

Holcombe Rogus

HOLCOMBE ROGUS 128 B 14

(*on*) *holancumbes land scare* 958 BCS 1027

Holecoma 1086 DB, *-cumbe* 1238 *Ass*, 1242 Fees 786, *Hole-combe Roges* 1281 *Ass*, *Holcombe Rogys* 1383 Exon, *Holecomb Regis* 1414 IpmR

'Hollow valley,' *v.* holh, cumb. In DB it was held by one *Rogo*; Simon, son of *Rogo*, gave Holcombe Church to Monta-cute Priory c. 1160 and Jordan fil. *Roges* held the manor in 1238 (*Ass*). For *land scare*, cf. Landskerry *supra* 215.

HIGHER BESLEY FM is *Beasselegh* 1330 *SR* (p), 1353 *Ass* (p), t. Ed 3 *Ass*, *Beselegh* 1482 IpmR. The first element is probably a pers. name *B(e)assa*, a pet-form of such a name as *Beadusige*. *v.* leah.

FENTON FM is *Fenneton in Holecombe Roges* 1449 *FF* and is probably identical with *Fenhamton* 1330, 1333 *SR* (p). *v.* fenn, (ham)tun.

KERSWELL FM is *Cressewalla* 1086 DB, *Carswille* 1330 *SR* (p). 'Cress spring,' *v.* cærse, wielle.

KYTTON BARTON is *Kytone* 1286 *FF*, 1330 *SR* (p), 1373, 1386 Exon, *Keton* 1416 Exon, *Kytone al. Keeton* 1670 *Recov*. The vowel here should clearly be long. *Kyton* is a compound of tun and *cȳ*, the nom. pl. of cu, 'cow.' Hence 'cows' farm.'

WISEBURROW FM is *Wiseburg* 1249 *Ass*, *Wysburgh* 1394 *Ass*. The forms are against a pers. name *Wīg*, as suggested by Blomé (82). Probably we have a pers. name *Wīsa*, cf. *Godrico Wisesune* (Dugd vi, 262) in a Lilleshall document. The second element is beorg.

BURROW FM, KNOWLE FM (6″), RULL COTTAGES (6″) and WAY TOWN (6″) were probably the homes of Anestas *atte Burghe* (1333 *SR*), Stephen de *la Cnolle* (1330 *SR*), Robert *atte Hulle* (1333 *SR*), and Walter *atte Weye* (ib.). *v.* beorg, cnoll and weg and cf. Rill *infra* 606 and *town infra* 676.

BRINSCOTT (6″) is *Brunescote* 1238 *Ass* (p). '*Brȳni*'s cot(e)' or '*Brūn*'s cot(e).' FORD is *La Forde* 1257 Montacute 180. FREA-

THINGCOTT FM is *Friechoth* 1330 *SR* (p), *Frethingcott* 1716 *Recov*. Probably '*Freði* or *Friði*'s cottages,' these names being on record, with ing as a connective element. LOWDWELLS is to be associated with the family of Richard *Ludwyll* (1524 *SR*) and Roger *Lowdwell* (1618 Wills). RAMSEY FM is so spelt 1623 *FF*. The second element may be eg or (ge)hæg. The farm lies near the Tone river. WHIPCOTT is *Webbechoth* 1330 *SR* (p), *Wybecotte* 1543 *SR* (p). '*Wibba*'s cot(e)' or 'the weaver's cot(e).'

Morebath

MOREBATH 119 J 10

> *Morbath(a)* 1086 DB *et passim* to 1316 FA with variant spelling -*bathe*, -*ba* 1179 P, 1291 Tax
> *Morpath* 1327 Pat
> *Murbath* 1675 Ogilby

There are chalybeate springs here, hence the use of the term *bath* (OE *bæþ*) (Blomé 82). The mor is the marshy land close at hand.

BURSTON is *Briteliston* 1330 *SR* (p), *Brytleston* 1346 *Ass*, *Borston* 1526 Wardens, and takes its name from *Britellus* de Amberes to whom the king granted the manor of Morebath in 1212 (Fees 97). Cf. Briston in Pillaton (Co), *Briteleston* 1200 FF.

LOYTON is *Loy(e)ton* 1330, 1333 *SR* (p), *Lawton* 1530, 1533 Wardens. Professor Ekwall suggests that we may have here the OE **hlīeg*, 'warmth, shelter,' postulated by Skeat (PN Sf 56) in explanation of Layham, earlier *Hligham*. The form *Loye-* would be a ME dialectal development.

WARMORE is *Weremore* 1249 *Ass*, (*juxta Bamton*) 1298 *Ass*, *Wermore* 1311 *Ass*. The first element is probably, as suggested by Blomé (83), the gen. pl. of OE wer, the place being by the Exe. The second element is mor, probably with reference to the flat marshy land just to the south. Hence 'marshy land near the fishing pools.' Wallenberg (StudNP 2, 92) notes that there is a *Wear* House on the other side of the Exe.

WILLISHAYES FM is *Willyngeshayes* 1346 *Ass*, and is to be associated with the family of Johanna *Wylling* (1330 *SR*). For *hayes*, *v. supra* 129.

Ashtown[1], Brockhole[2], Combeland[3], Court, Hayne[4], Hol-well[4], Moore[4] and Pool[4] were probably the homes of Reginald de *Esse* (1330 *SR*), Adam de *Brochol*, i.e. 'badger hole' (ib.), Richard de *Combe* (ib.), John *at Courte* (1526 Wardens), Robert *atte Heghen* (1340 *Ass*), Adam de *Halegwell*, i.e. 'holy well' (1249 *Ass*), Galfridus *atte More* (1333 *SR*), and William de *la Pole* (1330 *SR*). *v.* brocc, hol, cumb, mor, pol.

CHILTERN is *Chilthorn* 1740 *FF*, 1772 *Recov*, *Chiltern* 1765 D. EXEBRIDGE is *Exebrigge* 1256 FF, 1309 *FF*, *apud pontem de Exe* 1256 *Ass*. HAWKRIDGE (6″) is *Hauekrigg'* 1249 *Ass*, *Hockerige Downe* 1596 *Deed*. HUKELEY is *Hukley* 1524 *SR*, *Hucly Brige* 1531 Wardens, *Hewkley* 1765 D. KEENS is to be associated with the family of Lewes *Kene* (1610 *SR*). SURRIDGE is *Sowridge* 1546 *Rental*. Probably 'south ridge,' cf. Sowton *supra* 435. TIMEWELL is *Trymwyll, Tymwyll* 1524, *Tymwyll* 1541 *SR*.

Uffculme

UFFCULME [ʌfkəm] 128 D 14

>*Offecoma* 1086 DB, *Offeculum* 1227 Oliver 394, 1249 FF, *Ofculm* 1267 Ch, 1284 Exon, *Of Colmp* 1316 FA
>*Uffe Culum* 1175 P, *Uffekulum* 1216 ClR, *Uffeculum* 1238, 1249 *Ass*, *Huffeculm* 1248 Ipm

'*Uffa*'s farm on the Culm,' cf. Goodameavy *supra* 229.

BODMISCOMBE is *Bothemyscombe, Bothenescumb* 13th Buckland, *Bothemescumbe* 1275, 1281 *Ass*, *-coume* 1276 RH, *-hames-* 1275 *Ass*, *Bodemescombe* 1297 Buckland, *Bodmiscumb* n.d. (ib.). Probably '*Bōthelm*'s cumb.'

BRIDWELL is *Bredewylle* 1280 *Ass*, *Bridewille* 1288 *Ass*, 1333 *SR* (all p), *Brydewill* 1298 *Ass*, *Bridwildoun* 1499 Ipm. No certainty is possible as to the first element in this name. The forms are perhaps in favour of OE *brȳd*, 'bride,' rather than *bridd*, 'bird.' The reason for such a name must remain a matter of speculation. Equally ambiguous is *brydena wyll* (BCS 723,

---

[1] *Ashton* 1765 D.
[2] *Brokhole* 1526 Wardens.
[3] *Come* 1527 Wardens, *Combeland* 1731 *Recov*.
[4] *Hayne* 1527, *Hollwyll* 1573, *More, Pole* 1526 Wardens.

a Devon Charter), which may be 'birds' or brides' spring.'
Cf. Breadwick *supra* 49.

CRADDOCK is (*on*) *craducc* 938 BCS 724, *Cradok* 1249 FF, *Crad-docke* 1589 *SR*. This must originally have been the name of the small stream which flows into the Culm here. The valley is called *Cradocumbe* (1185), *Cratecombe* (12th) in the Buckland Cartulary. Ekwall (RN 101) considers that the name may have been elliptical for *Nant Caradoc* or the like (*nant*, 'valley, brook').

HACKPEN BARTON is (*on*) *hacapenn* 938 BCS 724, *Hakepen(ne)* 1249 FF, 1281 *Ass*, 1291 Tax. Hackpen Hill is a prominent hook-shaped hill and so is Hackpen Hill (W), earlier *hacan penn* (BCS 734). These names and Inkpen (Berks), earlier *Ingepenne* (BCS 678), suggest that British *penno-* (W, Co *pen*) 'head, top, end,' was adopted by the English as a hill-name. The first element is OE *haca*, 'hook,' used in the Wiltshire name in a genitival compound.

HURST (lost) is *Hurst* c. 1630 Pole and was the home of William *atte Hurste* (1330 *SR*). *v.* hyrst. The name is interesting as being the only example of this element found in Devon place-names which survived the Norman Conquest. According to Pole the place was situated 'neere unto Bradfyld' i.e. Bradfield *infra*.

PENSLADE (6″) is *Pynstoneslade* n.d. Oliver 228, c. 1200 (15th) *Canonsleigh*, 1329 Ch, *Pyntenneslade* 1287 *Ass*. The forms are definitely against association with *penny*, as suggested by Blomé (84), and the name must remain an unsolved problem.

SMITHINCOTT is *Smithenecota* 1223 Bracton, *-te* 1238 *Ass* (p), *Smythenecote juxta Ulfcolmp* 1306 *Ass*. *v.* Smithacott *supra* 93.

COCKS FM (6″), GILL'S FM (6″), OSMOND'S FM (6″), REED'S CROSS, RUGGSMOOR (6″) and SKINNERS FM are probably to be associated with the families of Drogo *Coke* (1543 *SR*), Henry *Gill* (1610 *SR*), George *Osmond* (ib.), William *Rede* (1543 *SR*), Henry *Rugge* (1610 *SR*), and William *Skynnere* (1333 *SR*).

BROOK DAIRY and CLEVE (both 6″) were the homes of William de la *Brok* (1238 *Ass*) and John atte *Clyve* (1330 *SR*). *v.* clif.

ASHILL is *As(s)hull* 1249 FF, 1346 *Ass*. BRADFIELD is *Bradefeld(e)*

1254 FF, (*juxta Ulfcolm*) (sic) 1338 *FF, Bradvyle* 1438 Exon.
'Wide open space,' *v.* brad, feld. FORD FM is *La Forde* 1322 *FF.*
FOXHILL FM is *Foggeshill* 1238, 1249 *Ass, -hulle* 1281 *Ass* (all
p), *-hull* 1322 *FF.* The first element must be the strong form of
the pers. name discussed under Voghay *supra* 457. GADDON HO
is *Gatton* 1249 *Ass* (p), *Gaddon* 1408, 1413 IpmR. 'Goat farm or
hill,' *v.* dun, tun. GOODLEIGH is *Godelegh* 1249 FF, 1281 *Ass* (p),
Goddeley 1275 RH (p), *Godelegh by Dunkeswill* 1496 Ipm. '*Gōda*'s
clearing' or 'good clearing,' *v.* leah. HAYN FM (6″) is *Hegh* 1249
FF. Cf. Hayne *supra* 129. NORTHCOTT is *North(e)cote* 1249
FF, 1330 *SR* (p). RULL HO is *Hylle* 1249 FF, *Hulle* 1281 *Ass,
Rill* t. Eliz *SR.* Clearly 'at the hill,' *v.* Rill *infra* 606. SOUTHILL
is *Suthewell* 1249 FF, *Sudwell* 1275 RH (p). There is a spring
here, so the second element is clearly **wielle**. STENHALL is
Stenenhalle 1242 Fees 782, *Stenihale* 1303, *Stenhall* 1346 FA.
'Stone hall,' cf. Stenhill *supra* 160. UMBROOK FM (6″) is *Wombrok*
1249 FF, 1330 *SR* (p), *Won-* 1337 Ipm, *Umbrooke* t. Jas 1 *SR.*
'(At the) crooked brook,' *v.* woh, broc. WOODROW FM is
Wodrowe 1524 *SR* (p), *Wood al. Woodrew* 1729 *Recov* and was
the home of John *atte Wode* (1330 *SR*). YONDERCOTT is *Yundecote* 1289 Cl, 1303 FA, *Yonde-* 1428 FA. *v.* Youngcott *supra*
216.

XXIV. TIVERTON HUNDRED

Tueruetone, Tuluertone, Tuuuertone 1084 Geld Roll
Tiverton 1184 P, 1219 Fees 264, *Twyverton* 1238 *Ass*

v. Tiverton *infra* 541.

Calverleigh

CALVERLEIGH[1] 128 D 9

Calodeleia 1086 DB

Calewudelega 1194 P *et passim* to 1535 VE with variant
spellings *Kal(e)-, Cal(e)-, -wod(e), -legh(e), Calwodelegh juxta
Tuuerton* 1345 *Ass, Caldwodeleghe* 1382 Exon

Chaldewodelegh 1340 Pat (p)

Calwoodley al. Calverley 1557 Deed, *Kawoodlegh nowe called
corruptlye Calverley* c. 1630 Pole

[1] A small parish now united with Loxbeare.

The first element is OE *calu*, 'bald, bare,' and the whole name would mean 'clearing (*v.* leah) by the bare wood.' For *w* > *v* cf. Introd. xxxv.

Huntsham

HUNTSHAM [hʌnsəm]   128 B 12

> *Honessam* 1086 DB (Exon), *Honesham* (Exch), 1242 Fees 775 *et freq* to 1316 FA, (*juxta Baunton*) 1323 *Ass*
> *Hunnesham* 1238 *Ass*, *Hunesham* 1297 Var, *Hunsam* 1543 SR

'*Hūn*'s ham(m).'

HILL and VENLAKE'S COTTAGE (6″) were probably the homes of Roger *atte Hulle* (1333 SR) and Adam de *Fenlake*, i.e. 'marshy streamlet' (ib.). *v.* fenn, lacu.

COBBACOMBE (6″) is *Cobbecumb(e)* 1269 FF (p), 1270 *Ass* (p), *-combe* 1407 FF. '*Cobba*'s combe.' PERROTT'S FM is probably to be associated with the family of John *Parratt* (Halberton) and John *Parrett* (Tiverton) 1620, 1717 Wills.

Loxbeare

LOXBEARE   128 C 9

> *Lochesbera* 1086 DB, *Lockesbere* 1205 FF *et freq* to 1326 Ipm with variant spellings *Lokkes-* and *-bear(e)*
> *Lokeberga* 1195 FF, *Lokkesberg* 1249 *Ass*

'*Locc*'s wood,' *v.* bearu, with later confusion of second elements.

CHURCHILL is *Chirchehill(e)* 1238 *Ass*, 1319 *FF*, *Cherchehill*, *Chyrchehil* 1244 *Ass*, *Churhull* (sic) 1330 SR (p). *v.* Addenda, Part i, lii *s.n.* Churchill.

LEIGH BARTON is *Lega* 1086 DB, *Legh(e)* 1242 Fees 789, 1281 *Ass* (p), 1345 *Ass*. *v.* leah.

SIDBOROUGH[1] is *Seggeburgh* 1338 FF, *-berwe* 1346 *Ass*. '*Secga*'s hill,' *v.* beorg.

HILL FM was the home of Roger *atte Hulle* (1333 SR). INGRAMS is probably to be associated with the family of George *Ingram* (1705 Wills).

---

[1] West Sidborough and East Sedborough (sic) on 6″ map.

Tiverton

TIVERTON[1] [tivətən] 128 D 10

(*æt*) *Twyfyrde* 880–5 (c. 1000) BCS 553
Tovretona 1086 DB, *Toverton* 1167 P, (*Parva*) 1171 P,
Tuuerton' 1165 P, *Thuverton* 1245 Ipm
Tuiverton 1141–55 France, *Tuenertone* (sic) 1166 RBE (p),
Litle Twiuerton 1168 P, *Twiverton* 1228 FF *et freq* to 1341
FF with variant spellings *Twy-*, *Tuy-*
Litle Twuuertona 1167 P
Tivertun 1219 Fees 264, *Tevreton* 1245 Cl, *Tevertone* 1263
Exon, *Tiverton al. Twyford Town* 1695 *Recov*

'Double ford,' *v.* twi-. The place is situated at the confluence
of the Loman and the Exe. Cf. Twerton (So). The manor of
Little Tiverton is now represented by WEST EXE (6″), *West Exa*
1504 Ipm, from its position across the river.

BINGWELL is *Binewall(e)* 1238, 1244 *Ass*, *Bynne-* 1275 RH,
Bingewell 1249 *Ass* (all p). There is nothing to confirm the otherwise plausible suggestion that this is from OE *binnanwealle*,
'within the wall,' cf. Benwell (PN NbDu 18).

BOLHAM is *Boleham* 1086 DB, *Bolleham* 1175 P (p), 1242 Fees
786, 1281 *Ass*, 1285 FA, *Balleham* 1279 Ipm, *Bolham* 1284 *Ass*.
'*Bol(l)a*'s ham(m).' For such a pers. name, *v.* Bolnhurst (PN
BedsHu 13) and *Bola* (Redin 85).

BRADLEY is *Bradeleia* 1086 DB, *Bradeleg* 1228 FF, *Netherebrade-
legh* 1238 *Ass*, *Estbradelegh* 1242 Fees 774. 'Wide clearing,' *v.*
brad, leah.

CHETTISCOMBE (tʃeskəm) is *Chetellescoma* 1086 DB, *Chetescumbe*
1281 *Ass*, *Chettiscome* 1285 FA, *Chettescoumbe* 1316 Ipm, *Ched-
dyscomb* 1428 FA. This may be 'cumb of the cietel or hollow'
(cf. Chittlehampton *supra* 338).

---

[1] BAMPTON ST is *Bawnton Streate* 1573, leading to Bampton, BARRING-
TON ST is *Barrington Streat* 1565, CASTLE ST is identical with *Frogestreet*
1583, FORE ST is probably identical with *Hygh Strete* 1563, NEWPORT
ST is *Neweport Strete* 1564, ST ANDREW ST is *Seynt Androwez Streate* 1571,
ST PETER ST is *Peteres strete* 1583 from the dedication of the parish church
All the above spellings are from *Deeds*.

CHEVITHORNE

> *Chevetorna, Chiveorna* 1086 DB
> *Chevethorn* 1198 FF *et freq* to 1285 FA, *Westcheve-*, *West-chevathorn* 1339 *Ass*
> *Chivethorn(e)* 1238 *Ass*, 1242 Fees 786, *Chyve-* 1316 FA
> *Chyfethorn* 1242 Fees 791, *Cheathorne* 1630 Westcote

'*Cifa*'s thorntree' or *Ceofa*'s, cf. Chivenor *supra* 45.

COLLIPRIEST is *Colliprist* (1643 *FF*) and is probably to be associated with the family of Roger *Coleprust* (1310 Exon). This surname may be an early parallel to the term *cole-prophet*, 'deceptive prophet,' which is recorded from More in the 16th cent. (*v.* NED *s.v.*).

COVE is *La Kove* 1242 Fees 789, *aqua de Cove* 1249 *Ass*, *La Cova* 1285 FA. The sense of cofa in p.n.'s is difficult to determine. The only recorded sense in OE is that of 'inner chamber' and the like, but in dialect the term shows a wide development of sense and is used of (1) a shed, (2) a deep pit or cave, (3) a recess in the side of a hill (NCy) and (4) a hollow. The last sense would perhaps suit best here as there is a well-marked hollow in the hills, but in North Cove, South Cove and Covehills (Sf), three independent places, and in Cove (Ha), there can be no question of any 'hollow,' and there the term may be used of a shed, building or the like. So also in Coven (St) we probably have a dat. pl. of the word in that same sense. *cofa* is found once in an Anglo-Saxon charter (BCS 948) in a land-mark called *mædena coua*, but the bounds of the charter have never satisfactorily been worked out and we must remain in ignorance as to whether these particular maidens lived in a hollow or in a building of some kind.

CRAZE LOMAN is *Lonmela* 1086 DB, *Lumeneclauill* 1238 *Ass*, *Lomene Clavile* 1285 FA, 1287 Misc, 1318 *FF*, *Clavylys Lomyn* 1456 IpmR. For the River Loman, *v. supra* 8. John de *Clavile* held the manor in 1284 (FA) and probably *Craze* is a corruption of *Clavile*'s through an intermediate form **Craviles* by dissimilation, cf. Halshayne *infra* 633.

FAIRBY is *Fayrebye* 1280 *Ass*, *la Fayreby* 1286 *Ass*, *Fayrebye juxta Magna Twyverton* 1310 *Ass*. 'Fair bend,' cf. Veraby *supra* 384. It is in a bend of the Exe.

GREAT GORNHAY is *Gormundeheye* 1249 *Ass* (p), 1287 *Ass*, *Gor(e)-mundes(h)eye* 1281 *Ass* (p), 1330 *SR* (p), *Gornhay al. Gormanshays* 1683 *Deed*, and is probably to be associated with the family of Robert *Goremund* (1287 *Ass* 1275 m. 18). *v.* Hayne *supra* 129.

GOTHAM is *Gotte(s)ham* 1281 *Ass*, *Gotham* 1298 *Ass*, 1330 *SR* (p), *Gootham* 1407 *FF*. Probably 'goats' ham(m).'

HENSLEIGH FM is *Hengsteleg* 1228 FF (p), 1249 *Ass* (p), *He(n)xtelegh* 1270 *Ass*, *Suthenstelegh* 1407 *FF*. 'Stallion clearing,' *v.* hengest, leah.

HUNTLAND is *Huntelande* 1173–5 (1329) Ch, *Huntilond* 1275 RH (p), *Huntalonde* 1315 Exon (p), *Hountelond* 1330 *SR* (p). 'Land of the huntsman' (OE *hunta*) or 'of the hunt' (ME *hunte*). Cf. Huntland (PN NbDu 121).

LURLEY is *Leverlegh'* 1242 Fees 789, 1303 FA, *Leveringeleg'* 1263 Ipm, *Luverlegh* 1285 FA, (*juxta Caluodelegh*) 1310 *Ass*, *Lurelegh* 1346 FA. Probably '*Lēofhere*'s leah' with sporadic connective *ing*. The other forms show omission of genitival *s*.

EAST and WEST MERE are *La Mere* 1242 Fees 789, 1295 Ipm, *Westmere* 1303 FA. There is no pool here but the place is by the parish boundary, so we have probably OE (ge)mære rather than mere.

MOGRIDGE is *Moggherigg* 1333 *SR* (p), *Moggerigge* 1351 *Ass* (p), *Moggarygge* 1394 *Ass* (p), *Mogridge* 1606 *FF*. '*Mogga*'s ridge,' cf. Mogworthy *supra* 390. Wallenberg (StudNP 2, 94) notes that John *Mogge* and Stephen *Mogg* were tenants in Devon in 1285 and 1346 respectively. Cf. also Richard *Mogge*, a juror in Tiverton Hundred in 1244 (*Ass*).

PATCOTT is *Petecota* 1086 DB, *Petecote* 1333 *SR* (p), *Pattecote* 1489 *Ct* (p), *Patcote* 1543 *SR*. '*P(e)atta*'s cot(e).' Cf. Petton *supra* 531.

PEADHILL

> *Pedehael* 1086 DB, *-hill* 1205 FF, 1285 FA
> *Padehill'* 1242 Fees 773, *Pyadihull* 1281 *Ass* (p), *Peadehull* 1326 Ipm, 1428 FA, *-hill* 1339 *Ass* (p), 1346 FA

Pidehull 1303 FA
Peadle 1642 *SR*
'*Peada*'s hill.'

PLAINFIELD is *Plenyffelde* 1330, *Pleyniffeld* 1333 *SR* (p). Professor Ekwall suggests the possibility of OE *plegenafeld*, 'open land of the games' or 'of the players.' Similarly *Plenythorne*, a field-name in Devon (1520), might denote a thornbush near to which country games took place.

POOL ANTHONY is *La Pole* 1242 Fees 789, *Pole Antony* 1316 Ipm. *Antonius* de *la Pole* held the manor in 1242.

TIDCOMBE is *Tidecumb* 1249 *Ass*, *Tydecumbe* 1260 Exon, *-combe* 1343 Exon, *Tittecumbe* 1520 BM. '*Tida*'s valley,' *v.* cumb.

EAST BARTON, BERRY, BROOMFIELD, CLEAVE COPSE (6″), COMBE, DEEPALLER (6″), FORD, HAYNE, HOLMEAD, HOLWELL, LONG-HAYNE PLANTATION (6″), MILL FM (6″), NORWOOD FM, SHORT-RIDGE HILL (6″), WAY[1] and WELL FM were probably the homes of Philip *atte Berton* (1330 *SR*), William *atte Biry* (ib.), John de *Bromfeld* (1318 Ipm), Richard de *Clyve* (1275 RH), Robert Avenel de *Cumbe* (1249 *Ass*), Thomas de *Dupalre*, i.e. 'at the deep (? tall) alder' (1330 *SR*), Andrew *atte Forde* (ib.), William de *Heghen* (1289 *Ass*), Walter de *Holemede* (1302 *Ass*), Gervas de *Holewill* (1244 *Ass*) and Alice de *Holewill* (1333 *SR*), William de *Langeheie* (1330 *SR*), William *atte Mille* (ib.), John de *North-wode* (1322 *Ass*), Richard de *Shorterugge* (1330 *SR*), Cecilia *atte Weye* (ib.), Walter *atte Wille* (1404 *Ass*). *v.* beretun, burh, feld, clif, deop, alor, holh, mæd, weg, wielle, and Hayne *supra* 129.

BUCKHAYES (6″)[2], CROSS'S TENEMENT (6″), DAYMOND'S HILL (6″), HARTNOLLS, MARWOODS, NEWTES HILL (6″), PALFREY'S BARTON, PALMERS[3], PASSMOREHAYES (6″)[4] and SPURWAYS were probably the homes of William *Bugge* (1333 *SR*), Geoffrey *de Cruce* (1275 RH), John *Dayman* (1589 *SR*), Nicholas *Hartnoll* (1616 Wills), Agnes *Marwood* (1678 Wills), *Newte* (t. Eliz Dunsford), Thomas *Palfree* (1696 Wills), Thomas *le Paumer* (1238 *Ass*) and Richard

---

[1] *Waye* 1605 *Depositions.*   [2] *Buckhayes* 1624 Dunsford.
[3] *Palmeryshayes juxta Teverton* 1464 *FF.*
[4] *Pasmerhayes* 1548 Pat, *Pasemoores Hayes* 1604 DKR 38, 479.

le Palmere (1284 FA), Walter *Passemer* (1238 *Ass*), and William *Spyreway* (1443 Pat).

ASHLEY is *A(i)ssheley* 1483, 1547 Pat. *v.* leah. BROOK (6″) is *La Broke* 1349 *FF* and was the home of William *atte Brok* (1340 Pat). COOMBUTLER is to be associated with the family of Thomas *Botiller* (1330 *SR*). COURT, cf. *Courtland in Tiverton* t. Jas 1 ECP. COYDON (COTTAGES) (6″) is so spelt in 1692 *Recov*. It may be identical with *Cordington* (1280 *Ass*). FARLEIGH is *Farlegh* 1492 Ipm. Probably 'bracken clearing,' *v.* fearn, leah. FIRE-BEACON is *Fyerbeken* 1571 *SR*. FROGWELL is *Froggewell* 1270 *Ass*, *Frogwell* 1423 *FF*. FULFORD is *Volevorde* 1310 *FF*, *Fole-* 1330 *SR* (p). 'Dirty ford' or 'foul ford,' *v.* ful. GATCOMBE COPSE (6″) is *Gattecomb* 1330 *SR* (p). 'Goats' valley.' GOGWELL is *Goggewelle* 1286 *MinAcct*. Cf. Gogland *supra* 380. HAYPARK (6″) is *Heyparke* 1683 *Recov*. HONE was the home of Henry *atte Hone* (1330 *SR*). *v.* Hone *supra* 532. It is not near the parish boundary but there may have been some stone here marking the boundary between two estates or manors. HONEYLAND is *Honie-land* 1249 *Ass*, *Honelonde* 1313 Exon (p). HORSDON HO (6″) is *Horsdoune* 1286 *MinAcct*. KNIGHTSHAYES COURT is *Knyghtene-heie* 1330, 1333 *SR* (p). Probably 'enclosure of the cnihts,' *v.* (ge)hæg and cf. Knightacott *supra* 115. LANDRAKE is so spelt 1721 *FF*. LEVERLAKE (6″) is *Lyverlake* 1423 *FF*. 'Rush streamlet,' *v.* læfer, lacu. LITTLE SILVER (6″) is so spelt 1621 *Recov*. *v. supra* 358. LOOSELEIGH (6″) is *Loosley* 1574 *Deed*. Cf. Looseleigh *supra* 243. MARLEY is *Morlegh* 1281 *Ass* (p), 1285, 1303 FA. *v.* mor, leah. MOORHAYES is *Morhay* 1310 *FF*, *Morehayes* 1424 *FF*. *v.* Hayne *supra* 129. NETHERCLEAVE is *Netherclyff* 1541 *SR*. Cf. the same name *supra* 339. The place is on a steep hillside. PILEYWELL is *Pilywell* 1598 Dunsford. PITT is *Pytt* 1547 Pat. PLUSHAYES is *Pleashays* 1719 Harding. PRESCOTT is *Prestecote* 1244 *Ass* (p), *Prustecote* 1286 *MinAcct*. 'Priests' cot(e).' RIX is *Rex* t. Jas 1 *SR*, *Ryxe* 1648 *FF*. Cf. also Roger *ate Rixe* 1302 Exon (Broadhembury). 'At the rush(es),' cf. Rixdale *supra* 488. ROLIPHANT'S FM is *Rollavands* 1792 Dunsford. SHOOLEYMOOR COTTAGE (6″) is *Shoolymore* 1654 *FF*, *Showle moor* 1694 *Recov*. SOUTHWOOD is *Suthwod'* 1242 Fees 789, *South(e)wode* 1330 *SR* (p), 1378 IpmR. WAYLAND is *Welland al. West Wayland al. Westwelland* 1700 *Recov.* WITHLEIGH is *Witheleg(h)* 1219 *Ass,* (*juxta Tuuerton*) 1316 *Ass, Wythelegh* 1330 *SR* (p). 'Withy clearing,' *v.* wiðig, leah. WORMSLAND is *Wolmerislonde* 1330 *SR* (p). '*Wulfmǣr*'s land.' YEARLSTONE is *Erleston* 1249 *Ass* (p), *Yorliston* 1330 *SR* (p). 'The earl's farm' or '*Eorl*'s farm,' *v.* tun. The Redvers, earls of Devon, held the manor of Tiverton from the 12th cent.

XXV. HALBERTON HUNDRED

Hal(s)bretona, Hasbtone 1084 Geld Roll
Hauberton' 1179, 1183 P, *Alberton* 1219 Fees 64
v. Halberton *infra* 548.

Burlescombe

BURLESCOMBE[1] [bəˑleskəm] 129 C 1
Berlescoma 1086 DB
Buroldescumba t. Hy 2 Oliver 135, *Bur(e)woldescumbe* 12th Canonsleigh, *-dis-* 1173–5 (1329) Ch, *Borwoldiscumbe* 1374 Exon
Burlescombe 1219 *Ass, -cumb(a)* 1249 FF, 1329 Ch, *Burliscoome* 1303 FA
Bordlescumb' 1242 Fees 780, *Berdlescume* c. 1270 Gerv, *Burdelescombe* 1291 Tax *et freq* to t. Ed 3 *Ass* with variant spelling *-lis-*
Burghelescomb 1275 RH
Bertlescomb 1296 Ipm

---

[1] BCS 1027 dealing with the grant of 2½ hides at *Aescford* and *Beohyll* has been identified by Ekwall (*Festgabe Karl Luick* 155 ff.) as referring to Ayshford in Burlescombe and Boehill in Sampford Peverel. He notes further that the land at one stage marches with Holcombe Rogus, when it follows *holancumbes landscare* and touches *ruvancnol*, which is Rocknell in Burlescombe, and at one stage runs along the *linor* stream, now called Lynor (*v. supra* 9). We have noted one further point which can be identified, viz. the second of the two examples of *holan broc*. This must be the source of the name Holbrook Fm in Burlescombe, just to the south of Rocknell. The full bounds of the area cannot now be traced, as they clearly do not correspond definitely with the bounds of any one or more modern parishes and the construction of the Grand Western Canal makes it impossible now to identify the *holan broc*.

Brodelyscom 1314 Ipm, *Bridelescoumbe* 1327 Ipm, *Brydlis-*, *Bredele-* 1350 Ipm, *Brudelescombe* 1356 *Ass*
Burlescom al. Buscombe al. Buddlescom 1586 *Deed*, *Burlescombe oth. Burscombe* 1793 *Recov*
'*Burgweald*'s cumb.'

APPLEDORE

Surapla 1086 DB, 1173–5 (1329) Ch, *-apple* 1173–5 (1329) Ch
Sureapeldor 1242 Fees 780, *Sourapeldare* (sic) 1285 FA, *Sourappeldore* 1303, *Surapeldore* 1428 FA, *South-appeldore* 1797 Polwhele
'Sour apple tree' (i.e. crab-apple), *v.* apuldor.

AYSHFORD (6″) is *Escford*, (*to*) *æscforda* 958 BCS 1027, *Ais(s)eford(a)* 1086 DB, *Essheford* 1238 *Ass* (p). 'Ashtree ford.'

CANONSLEIGH FM is *Leiga* 1086 DB, *Lega* 1173–5 (1329) Ch, *Leghe Canonicorum* 1282 Exon, *Canounleye* 1403 BM, *Monchenleya* 1416 Exon, *Canonslegh al. Mynchenlegh* 1433 Exon. *v.* leah. The abbey was founded here c. 1170, originally for canons, later for canonesses, *v.* myncen.

FENACRE FM is *Vennacre* 1086 DB (Exon), *Wennacre* (Exch), *Fen-* 1242 Fees 780. 'Marshy piece of cultivated land,' *v.* fenn.

GREAT FOSSEND (6″) is *Fosseyend(e) al. Frostend* 1546 LP, 1548 Pat. Here probably lived Robert *atte Fosse* (1330 *SR*). For 'foss' we may compare Voss *supra* 254, but no ditch or dike has been noted at Fossend.

HOLBROOK FM is (*to*) *holon broce*, (*to*) *holan broces* (*heafdun*) 958 BCS 1027, *Holebrok* 1238 *Ass*. 'Hollow brook.'

PUGHAM FM is *Pogeham* 12th (14th) *Canonsleigh*, 1324 Exon, 1330 *SR* (p), *Pugeham* 1249 *Ass*, *Pug(g)a-* 1173–5 (1329) Ch, *Pugge-* 1287 *Ass*. '*Pocga*'s ham(m),' cf. Pugsley *supra* 349.

ROCKNELL FM is (*on*) *ruwan cnol* 958 BCS 1027, *Ruchcnolle* 1173–5 (1329) Ch, *Roueknolle* c. 1200 *Canonsleigh*. 'Rough hilltop,' *v.* ruh, cnoll.

CROSSE'S FM (6″), MEAR'S FM (6″) and TRUMPS are probably to

be associated with the families of Robert *atte Crosse* (1340 *Ass*),
Richard *Meere* (1640 *SR*) and John *le Trompour* (1330 *SR*).

CHACKRELL (6″) is *boscum de Chakerell* 13th *Canonsleigh*. EAST-
BROOK is *Bihestebroch* 1173–5 (1329) Ch, *Biestebrock* 1330 Oliver
228, *Eastbrooke* 1642 *SR*. 'East of the brook.' EBEAR FM (6″) is
Haybeare 13th *Canonsleigh*. *v.* bearu. HOUNDALLER FM is *Hun-
daler* 12th *Canonsleigh*, *-alre* 1306, 1345 *Ass*, *Houndehaller* 1374
Exon (p). 'Hounds' aldertree or grove,' cf. Duckaller *supra* 493,
and Bulealler, Hawkealter *infra* 562, 557. HUNTLAND HILL (6″) is
Hountelonde 13th *Canonsleigh*, *Hontilonde* 1333 *SR* (p), *Huntland*
1548 Pat. Cf. Huntland *supra* 543. MOORHAYES FM (6″) was the
home of Roger *atte More* (1330 *SR*). *v.* mor and Hayne *supra*
129. SOUTHDOWN FM is *Bisouthedon* 1219 *Ass* (p), 1333 *SR* (p).
'South of the down.' VELHAY FM (6″) is *Valeheies* 1330 *SR* (p).
v. Hayne *supra* 129. WESTCOTT FM is *Westcota* 1173 (1329) Ch,
Westecote 1330 *SR* (p). WESTLEIGH is *Westlegh* c. 1200 (15th)
Canonsleigh. *v.* leah.

Halberton

HALBERTON 128 D 12

    Halsbreton(a) 1086 DB, 1389 IpmR

    Halberton(e) c. 1200 *Canonsleigh et passim*, *Alberton(e)* 1272
    Exon, 1346 FA

    Hauberton(a) c. 1200 *Canonsleigh*, 1247 Ch, *Haberton'* 1242
    Fees 789

    Abbreton 1296 Ipm, *Helberton* 1350 Pat, *Holberton* 1400
    Barum 2, 186, *Halperton* 1500 Ipm, *Haulberton* 1675
    Ogilby

This name may be a compound of the OE pers. name
Hāligbeorht and tun, with omission of genitival *s* (cf. Elburton
supra 256).

ASH THOMAS is *Aisa* 1086 DB, *Asshe juxta Halberton* 1339 *Ass*,
Esse Thomas juxta Moreston 1351 *Ass*. According to Pole (362)
the place was held by *Thomas de Esse* in 1238.

BRITHEM BOTTOM is *Brid(d)enbotm* 1238 *Ass*, *Bridenebotin* 1249
FF, *la Brudenebotme* 1267, 1270 *Ass*, *Brethem Bottome al. Brim-
bottome* 1689 *Recov*. 'Birds' valley,' from *bridd*, 'young bird'
and botm. 'Brides'' is also possible, cf. Bridwell *supra* 537.

BYCOTT FM (6″) is *Boyecote* c. 1200 *Canonsleigh* (p), 1340 *Ass*, *Boya-* 1339 *Ass* (p), *Boy-* 1462 IpmR, *By-* 1500 Ipm. For the first element, *v.* Bystock *infra* 600.

CURHAM is *Curreham* 1275 RH, *Corham* 1330 *SR*, *Correham* 1333 *SR* (all p). *v.* Curriton *supra* 395.

LEONARD FM and MOOR

> *Lannor* 1086 DB, *terra de Lanor* 1215 Ch
> *Lynor* 1196 Oliver 396 *et freq* to 1330 *SR* (p) with variant
>   spelling *Linor*, *Lynour* 1346 FA, *la more de Lynor* 14th
>   *Canonsleigh*, *Lenor Abbe* 1316 FA, *Lynermor* 1394 *Ass*,
>   *Leynor* 1545 LP, *Lynard Moore* 1661 *Recov*

From the river Lynor *supra* 9. *v.* Addenda, Part ii, xiv.

EAST and WEST MANLEY is *Magnelega*, *Manelia* 1086 DB, *Mane-lega* 1196 Oliver 396, *-legh* 1242 Fees 780, 1303 FA, 1330 *SR* (p), 1350 Ipm, *Manalegh* 1346 FA, *Estmanlegh* 1480 IpmR. 'Clearing belonging to the community,' *v.* leah and Manadon *supra* 246.

MOORSTONE BARTON is *Moriston'* 1242 Fees 780, *Moreneston* 1249 *Ass* (p), *Moreston* 1249 FF and probably represents the manor of *Linor* held by *Morin* in 1086 (DB f. 461 *b*).

MOUNTSTEPHEN HO. This place is to be connected with the family of *Mountestephene* or *Mountestevene* found in the parish in 1281, 1322 (*Ass*) and 1330 (*SR*). Whether the family was of local origin we cannot say. The place is on a hill. The form suggests that the name was coined in England and not in France.

MUXBERE (6″) is *Mochelesberia* 1086 DB, *Mukele(s)ber(e)* 1237 FF, 1242 Fees 780, *Mokesbear* 1285, *Mokelesbere* 1303 FA. '*Mucel*'s wood,' *v.* bearu.

OBURNFORD

> *Woberneford* 1242 Fees 780, *Woburn(e)ford* 1248 Ch, 1262
>   Ipm, *-borne-* 1346 FA
> *Wuberneford* 1244 *Ass*
> *Womberneford* 1303 FA, *Wumburneford* 1306 *Ass*
> *Waburneford* 1500 ECP 4, 51

Probably 'crooked stream ford,' *v.* woh, burna and Womberford *infra* 625. For loss of initial *w*, cf. Oatnell *supra* 207 and Odle *infra* 642.

SELLAKE

> *Selac* 1086 DB, *-lak* 1303 FA, *Sellak* 1346 FA
> *Seglak(e)* 1175 P (p), 1249 *Ass*, 1269 FF (p), *Seghlak'* 1242 Fees 786
> *Seilake* 1316 FA, (*juxta Halberton*) 1420 IpmR, *Seyllake juxta Halberton* 1338 *FF*

The first element is probably an unrecorded OE adjective *sǣge* connected with *sīgan*, 'to fall, move, drip,' cf. Ekwall RN 284 *s.n.* Medesing. The whole name would refer to a slowly moving or sluggish streamlet, *v.* lacu and cf. Seabrook *supra* 455.

SPRATFORD BRIDGE (6″) is *Stratford* 1584, *Stratford greene* 1629, *Spratford Green* 1725 *Recov.* This is possibly a compound of stræt and ford, but the main road is about three-quarters of a mile to the east. The bridge may have been so named by the people of Halberton, since it is situated between that village and the main road to Exeter. For Spratford Stream, *v. supra* 9 n. 2.

SUTTON is *Suetatona, Suettetona* 1086 DB, *Sweteton'* 1242 Fees 780, 1275 RH (p), *Sweton* 1291 (1408) Dartmoor, *Swytton* 1330 SR (p), *Swetton al. Sutton* 1728 *Recov.* 'Swēta's farm,' *v.* tun. The name *Sweta* is found in the county c. 1100 (Earle 256).

BATTENS FM, CATFORDS FM, CRUWYS FM[1], HITCHCOCKS FM, MUDDIFORDS FM, SWANDHAMS FM and WHITES (6″) are probably to be associated with the families of John *Batyn* (1524 *SR*), William *Catysford* (ib.), Roger *Crus* (1333 *SR*), Robert *Hitchcocke* (1640 *SR*), Ambrose *Mudford* (1589 *SR*), Adam de *Swyndon* (1333 *SR*) and Roger *le White* (ib.).

BURROW (6″), FORD[2], HERNE, LAKE FM[3], PITT FM, RHODE, TOWNSEND HO (6″), VENN[4] and YEO FM (6″) were probably the homes of Walter *atte Burghe* (1330 *SR*), William de *la Forde* (1244 *Ass*), Robert de *la Hurne* (1281 *Ass*), William *atte Lake*

---

[1] *Crewys hayes* 1706 *Recov, v.* Hayne *supra* 129.
[2] *Netherforde* 1609 *Recov.* [3] *Lake* 1533–8 ECP.
[4] *Fenne* 1382 *FF.*

(1330 *SR*), Reginald *atte Pitte* (ib.), Wido *atte Rode* (ib.) and William *at Roode* (1524 *SR*), Roger *atte Touneshende* (1333 *SR*), John de *la Fenne* (1244 *Ass*) and Walter de *la Yha* (ib.), i.e. 'at the water,' *v. supra* 17-18, also beorg, hyrne, lacu, pytt, rod, fenn.

BACKSWOOD is *Baclyswoodclyves* 1500 ECP 4, 51. CHAPEL (6″) is *Chappelknappe* 1548 Pat, *Chapell* 1609 *Recov. v.* cnæpp. CHORLAND FM is *Churland* 1631, *Chor-* 1665 *FF*. Possibly 'land of the churls,' *v.* ceorl. CROSSLAND, cf. *Crosse Parkes* 1672 *Recov.* CROWGREEN (6″) is *Washbrooke al. Crowgreene* 1686 *Recov.* The old alternative name must mean 'sheepwash brook,' *v.* (ge)wæsc. FIVE BRIDGES FM is *Fyffbrugge* 1438 *AddCh, Fivebridges* 1662 *FF*. There is only one bridge here, but the first bridge built consisted of *five* wooden arches[1]. GOOSEMOOR COTTAGES (6″) is *Goosemore* 1608 *Deed. v.* mor. NETHER MILL (6″) is *Nethermyll* 1518–29 ECP 5, 557. 'Lower mill.' REMBARTON FM (6″) is *Rumberdon* 1281 *Ass* (p), *Rymerdon* 1330 *SR* (p), *Rymberdon al. Rumerdon* 1548 Pat. The forms are insufficient for any etymology to be suggested. ROWRIDGE is *Wumberneford juxta Rouerigge* 1306 *Ass*. Perhaps identical with Rawridge *infra* 650. SECKERLEIGH is *Sekerlegh(e)* 1275 RH (p), 1330 *SR* (p), 1383 Exon. SHUTHANGER is *Shetehanger* 1321 *FF*, *Shitehangre* 1339 *Ass*, *Shute-* 1404 *Ass*, *Shyt-* 1417 *FF*. 'Slope in the corner of land,' as suggested by Blomé (101). The place is in an angle of the parish boundary line. Cf. Shute *supra* 184. SLOW FM is *La Slo* 1319 *FF*, *Sloo* 1574 *Deed*. 'Slough, mire,' cf. Slew *supra* 28. THURLESCOMBE is *Thrusselcombe* 1638 *Recov, Thriselcombe* 1714 DKR 41, 443. 'Thrush combe,' *v.* Thrushelton *supra* 210. WATTON FM is *Wadetone* 1166 RBE (p) *et freq* to 1321 *FF*, *Wadde-* 12th *Canonsleigh*. '*Wada*'s farm,' *v.* tun. WAY MILL is *La Weye* 1273 *FF*, *Waymill* t. Jas 1 *SR. v.* weg. WHITEDOWN COTTAGE (6″) is *Whitdowne* 1609 *Recov*.

Sampford Peverell

SAMPFORD PEVERELL 128 D 13

Sanford(a) 1086 DB, 1212 Fees 96, *Saunforde* 1210–12 RBE, 1244 *Ass*, *Sanfordepeverel* 1339 Exon
Saundford 1237 FF, 1300 Ipm, *Sampforde* 1291 Tax

[1] *Ex inf.* Mr E. J. Baker.

'Sandy ford' (over the Lynor). Matilda *Peverel* held the manor in 1152 (Montacute).

BOEHILL FM

Byohyll 958 BCS 1027, *Beohill* 1173–5 (1329) Ch, 1343 Ipm
Bihede (sic) 1086 DB
Buhill c. 1200 *Canonsleigh, Nitherebuhull juxta Saunford* 1292 *Ass*
Behille 1242 Fees 781, *-hull* 1329 *FF*
'Bee hill.'

PAULLET HILL is to be associated with the family of *Poulet* (1525 *SR*). PITT is *Pytt* 1597 *Recov.* There are two deep hollows here. RIDGE (6″) was the home of Dionis' *atte Rugge* (1330 *SR*).

Uplowman

UPLOWMAN 128 C 12

Oplomia, Oppaluma 1086 DB (Exon), *Oppelaume* (Exch)
Lomene, Lumene 1242 Fees 780, *Lomene* 1281 Exon, 1291 Tax, 1322 Misc, 1327 Ipm, *Lommene* 1350 Ipm
Lomene Ricardi 1285 FA, *Lomeneghe* 1291 Exon
Uplomene 1303 FA, *Richardeslomene* 1317 *Ass, Uppelomyn* 1489 Ipm

'Settlement up the river Loman' *supra* 8. The place was probably first so named by the people of Tiverton. *Ricardus* held the manor in 1242 (Fees).

CHIEFLOWMAN

Lonmina 1086 DB, *Childelumene* n.d. Montacute 173, *-lomene* c. 1200 *Canonsleigh, Chyldelomen* 1346 FA, *Chyldlomene* t. Ed 2 Oliver 232
Chillelomene 1281 *Ass*, 1310 *FF, -lumena* 1329 Ch, *Chillomene* 1316 FA
Chiffeloman 1548 Pat

The name must have referred to a part of the Loman valley held by 'cilds,' *v.* cild. The reason for the substitution of *Chiffe* or *Chief* for earlier *Child* is obscure. Possibly it marked the most important of the Lowman manors. Cf. Capheaton (PN NbDu 39), earlier *Cappitheton, Magna Heton* (from Latin *caput*).

COOMBE is *Coma, Couma* 1086 DB (Exon), *Come* (Exch), *Cumb'* 1242 Fees 780, *Cumbepeyn* 1344 Ipm. Roger filius *Pagani* held the manor in 1284 (FA).

KIDWELL LANE (6″) is *Cadewila* 1086 DB, *-will(e)* c. 1200 *Canonsleigh*, 1242 Fees 780, 1333 *SR* (p). '*Cada*'s spring,' *v.* wielle.

MURLEY is *Morleia* 1086 DB, *-legh'* 1242 Fees 780, 1330 *SR* (p). *v.* mor, leah.

SPALSBURY FM is *Spaltbery* 1482 IpmR, *-bury* 1528 *Recov, Spalbury* 1694 *Recov, Spalsbury* 1750 *FF.* The forms are too late for any certain suggestion.

WHITNAGE

Witenes 1086 DB

Wytenehc n.d. Oliver 228, *Witenech* c. 1200 *Canonsleigh, Whytenech'* 1242 Fees 780

Hwytenych 1316 FA, *Whitenich* 1340 *SR, Wytenishe* 1346 FA *Wythenynch* 1347 *FF*

'At the white oak,' cf. Bradninch *infra* 555.

HILL FM, STAPLEGATE (6″) and WOOD (6″) were probably the homes of Walter de *la Hille* (1275 RH), William de *Stapele* (1330 *SR*) and John *atte Wode* (ib.). *v.* stapol.

BEER is *la Bere* c. 1200 *Canonsleigh* (p), *Beare* c. 1480 ECP 2, 199. *v.* bearu. CHURLEYS COTTAGE (6″) is to be associated with the family of William *Churley* (1543 *SR*). COTT is *Cott* 1827 G. *v.* cot(e). GULMOOR (6″) is *Goldemor(e)* 13th *Canonsleigh*, 1330, 1333 *SR* (p), 1546 LP. *v.* Gullaford *supra* 521. NEDDYCOTT (6″) is *Nythecott al. Newcott* 1699 *Recov.* WIDHAYES FM is *Wydehayes* 1560 *Deed. v.* Hayne *supra* 129.

Willand

WILLAND 128 E 13

Willelanda 1086 DB, *-lande* 1238 *Ass, La Willelaund* 1285 FA *Wildelanda* 1155–8 (1334) Ch, (*la*) *Wyldelonde* 1244 *Ass et freq* to 1438 BM with variant spelling *Wilde-, Wildelonde Prior* 1316 FA

'Uncultivated land, waste land,' *v.* wild. The place belonged to Taunton Priory.

COOMBES FM and QUICK'S FM (both 6″) are probably to be associated with the families of Robert *Combe* (1610 *SR*) and Henry *Quyk* (1330 *SR*).

BURNREW is *Burne* 1438 *AddCh*, *Burnerewe* 1729 *Recov*. Probably 'row of dwellings by the burn' (i.e. the stream here). DEANHILL FM is *Deanehill* 1732 *Deed*. GERSTON FM is *Geston* or *Griston* 1586 *Deed*, *Geston* 1653 *FF*, 1732 *Deed*. *v.* gærstun. HARPITT (6″) is *Harepit* 1438 *AddCh*. VERBEER is *Verbeare* 1586 *Deed*, 1653 *FF*. *v.* bearu. WERE MILL FM is *atte Were* 1319 *Add Ch* (p), *Weare Mill* t. Jas 1 ECP. *v.* wer. The place is on the Culm river.

XXVI. HAYRIDGE HUNDRED

Harrigge 1181 P, 1244 *Ass*, 1318 Ipm, *Harigg(e)* 1238 *Ass*, 1275 RH
Haurege 1184 P, *Haurig'* 1249 *Ass*
Hairigg 1323 Ipm

In the Geld Roll this Hundred is called *Sulfertone* from Silverton *infra* 569. The forms are difficult and inconsistent. It has been suggested that the hundred-name should be associated with Whorridge in Bradninch *infra* 556 (Blomé 91), but it is difficult to see how the names can be connected. It is possible that both alike go back to OE *hār-hrycg*, 'grey' or 'boundary ridge,' but if so the two names have developed on entirely independent lines.

Bickleigh

BICKLEIGH 128 F 10

Bichelia 1086 DB, *Guicheleia* (sic) 1093 France
Biggelegh 1238 *Ass* (p)
Bikelegh 1238 *Ass*, (*juxta Tyverton*) 1298 *Ass*, *Bykeleghe juxta Tuvertone* 1302 *FF*

'*Bicca*'s clearing,' *v.* leah. Cf. Abbots Bickington *supra* 124.

CHITTERLEY

Chederlia 1086 DB (Exon), -*lea* 1187 P, *Chedderlegh* c. 1225 Buckland

Chiderlie 1086 DB (Exch), *Chiderlegh* 1283 *Ass* (p)

Chud(d)erlegh c. 1225 Buckland, 1332 Cl, 1333 *SR* (p), 1408 Exon

Blomé may be right in comparing Cheddar (So), *Ceodre* (BCS 553, 765, 1219) and *Ceoddrum* (acc.) (Vita Dunstani B., c. 13), *Ceoddor* (1068 Earle), but one can hardly suggest that this is a river-name, as Chitterley is on the Exe and it is extremely unlikely that Cheddar took its name from the tiny stream which flows into the Axe there, rather than from the cliffs and gorge. Professor Ekwall suggests that the word in both cases is an OE **cēodor*, a derivative of OE *cēod(e)*, 'bag.' Chitterley lies in a well-marked hollow. Cf. more fully Ekwall, *Studies* 68 ff.

BRITHAYES is probably to be associated with the family of Bat'mus *Brite* (1330 *SR*). BURNHAYES is *Burne* 1238 *Ass*, *Burnehayes* 1610 *FF*. 'The stream,' *v.* burna. For *hayes*, *v.* Hayne *supra* 129. EXELAND is *Exelaunde* 1244 *Ass* (p), *Exelond juxta Thorvertone* 1294 *FF*. 'Land by the river Exe.'

Bradninch

BRADNINCH [bræniʃ] 128 G 12

Bradenesa 1086 DB *et passim* to 1348 Exon with variant spellings -*esse*, -*eis*, -*eys*, -*es(s)h*, -*eysh*, *Brahanies* 1200 Cur, *Braheneis* 1221–30 Fees 1443, *Braeneis* 1223 Pat, *Braydeneys* 1227 Ch, *Braeles*, *Brayles* 1230 Cl, *Braneys* 1242 Fees 758, 1261 Exon, 1275 RH, *Braghenes* 1249 *Ass*

Bradenech(e) 1238 Cl, 1282 Pat, 1309, 1351 Ipm, 1389 IpmR, -*egg* 1272 Pat, -*heche* 1315 Exon

Brednes 1240 Cl

Bradenasse 1244 *Ass*, -*assh(e)* 1342 Cl, 1349 Exon, Pat, -*aysh* 1356 DuCo

Bradenych 1306 *Ass*, -*iche* 1330 Exon, -*ynge* 1380 Exon, -*ynch* 1404 *Ass*, *Bradenyng al. Bradenassch* 1395 Exon

Bradenage 1310 Exon, -*ach* 1313 Pat, 1318 Cl, -*ache* 1375 Exon

Brodninche 1584, *Brodnidge* 1588 Wills, -*niche* 1589 *SR*

'The broad or spreading ash,' *v.* brad, æsc, with some confusion with ac. Cf. Whitnage *supra* 553. The second *n* is intrusive and is never heard in pronunciation. Cf. Brandish Wood (Herts), *Brad(e)nache* t. Hy 3 AD iii (p), 1461 *St Pauls*, from brad and ac.

CASEBERRY (6″) is *Kiresbury* 1330, *Kersbury* 1333 *SR* (p), *Kesbury* 1422 *Ct*, *-berie* 1589 *SR*. The forms are too late for any certainty. Professor Ekwall and Dr Ritter agree in suggesting that the first element may be the genitive singular of OE *Cyrrēd* (on record) for earlier *Cynerǣd*. *v.* burh.

GINGERLAND [gindʒ-] is *Gengelond* 1330 *SR* (p), *Gyng(e)lond* 1415–30 *Ct*. The modern form is clearly the result of folk-etymology. The true first element may be the stream-name *Ginge* (Ekwall RN 172). This should give Mod. [gindʒ]. Wallenberg (StudNP 2, 92) suggests connexion with OE *genge*, 'privy' (Nb dial. *ging*, 'dung').

HELE is *Hiele* 1086 DB, *Hele* 1242 Fees 786, 793, 1285 FA, (*Payn*) 1303, 1346 FA, 1416 Exon. *v.* healh. For a possible connexion of the *Payn* family with this manor *v.* DA 42, 233.

NETHER STOUTHAIES (6″) is (*ate*) *Stoute* c. 1420 *Ct* (nom. loc.), *Stowtys* 1445 *Ct*, *Stowte* 1469 *Ct*. *v. s.n.* Brimpts *supra* 192.

TEDBRIDGE is *Tot(t)ebrugg′* 1330, 1333 *SR* (p), *-brigge* 1415–30 *Ct*, *Tettebrugg* 1382 Fine, *Tuttebrigge* 1468 *Ct*. '*Teotta*'s bridge.'

WHORRIDGE FM is *Horerugge, Horerigge, Horugge* 1445 *Ct*. 'Boundary ridge,' *v.* har. It is by the parish boundary.

BATHAIES (6″), CRANISHAIES (6″), FLESTERHAIES, NELEHAIES (6″), SHEVISHAIES (6″) and WISHAY (6″) [wizi] appear as *Batynheghes, Batyneslond* (c. 1420 *Ct*), *Craneshegges* (1445 *Ct*), *Flatisheys* (1468 *Ct*), *Neyllysheys* (1445 *Ct*), *Shereveheyes* (1415–30 *Ct*), *Shirvehay* (1468 *Ct*), and *Wyseheys* (1445 *Ct*) and are probably to be associated with the families of William *Batyn* (1423 Pat), Hillary *Cran* (1333 *SR*), Philip *Floitere* (1330 *SR*), *Flotter* (1333 *SR*), Adam *Neel* (ib.), Robert *Shurreve*, i.e. 'sheriff' (1330 *SR*), and Richard *Wyse* (ib.). For *haies, v. supra* 129.

BAGMORE is *Baggemore* 1249 *Ass* (p), 1445 *Ct*. '*Bacga*'s mor.'
BOWHILL FM is *Boghehull, Boghull* 1415–30 *Ct*. 'Curved hill,'

v. Bowden *supra* 37. CHAPELHAIES is *Chapelhay* 1469 *Ct* and was the home of Sampson *atte Chapele* (1333 *SR*). COOMBE (6″) is *Combe* 1346 *Rental.* CROSS COTTAGES (6″) is *atte Crosse* 1346 *Rental* (nom. loc.). DOWNHEAD is *Duneheved* 1238 *Ass, Dounehed* 1445 *Ct.* DOWNS is to be associated with the family of Richard *Doun* (1330 *SR*). FORDISHAIES is *Forde* 1445 *Ct.* GARLANDHAYES FM is *Garlond Hayse* 1544 *SR. v.* gara, land. The place is in a triangular projection of the parish. HALTHAIES (6″) is *Haltesheys* 1468 *Ct.* The first element is probably the name of a medieval owner. HAWKEALTER (sic) is *Hauekeallere* 1275 RH (p), *Haukealler* 1415–30 *Ct.* 'Hawk aldertree (or copse),' cf. Houndaller *supra* 548. LITTERBOURNE (6″) is *Littelborne* 1379 *MinAcct.* 'Little stream,' *v.* burna. MILLWAY (6″), cf. *Mildich* 1445 *Ct.* PACY-COMBE (6″) is *Paryscomb* 1469 *Ct.* PARK, PARKLANDS (6″) are *atte Parke, le Parkland* 1445 *Ct. v.* pearroc. QUANTISHAIES probably takes its name from the Devon family *Quant* found in this part of the county (though not actually in the parish) in the 17th cent. (Wills). RODE (6″), RODE MOORS, cf. *la Rodeweye* 1270 *Ass* (p). 'Path through cleared land,' *v.* rod. STOCKWELL (6″) is *Stokhill* 1543 *SR.* STOKEHOUSE (6″) is *Stochouse* 1333 *SR* (p). *v.* stoc(c). TRINITY is *Capella Sancte Trinitatis* 1389 Exon, *Trenite* 1445 *Ct* (p), *Trynete dene* 1468 *Ct.* WATERLETOWN (6″) is *Waterleystowne* 1505 *Ct.* WEEKE (6″), cf. *Wykelond* 1415–30, *Wekehous* 1468 *Ct. v.* wic. WESTBEAR (6″) is *Westbeare* 1333 *SR* (p), 1345 *Ass*, t. Hy 6 *Ct. v.* bearu. For *hayes* in the above names, *v. supra* 129.

Broadhembury

BROADHEMBURY 129 G 1/2

> *Hemberia, Hanberia, Hainberia* 1086 DB, *Heimberia* 1165 P
> *Hamberia* 1166 RBE (p) *et freq* to 1272 *Ass* with variant spellings *-biry, -byr, -ber, Hambiritone* 1259 Exon, *Hanbyre* 1223 FF
> *Hembiri* 1227 Ch, *-byria* 1233 Bracton, *-bir* 1244 *Ass, -byr'* 1249 *Ass*
> *Brodehembyri* 1273, *-biri* 1284 Exon, *-bire* 1291 Tax, *-bery* 1308 Ipm, *-buri* 1334 *SR*

'At the high burh,' *v.* heah, with very early assimilation of *nb* to *mb.* The reference is to Hembury Fort near by, the largest earthwork in Devon (VCH 585). *Broad* as opposed to Payhembury *infra* 566, cf. *supra* 426.

DULFORD is *Dylfytt* 1525 *AOMB*, *Delvett* 1540 Oliver 313. It may be that we have here an OE derivative *dylfet* from OE *delfan*, 'to dig,' of the same type as *græfet*, *stān-hīewet*, noted under Grevatt's (PN Sx 17). Hence, 'place hollowed out.' An old marl-pit is marked close at hand.

KERSWELL is *Carseuilla* 1086 DB (Exon), *-welle* (Exch), *Karswille* 1201 FF. 'Cress spring,' *v.* cærs, wielle.

LUTON is *Levinton* 1227 Ch, *Luyton* 1249 *Ass* (p), *Liuetone* 1269 FF, *Lynynton* (sic) 1309 Ipm. '*Lēofa*'s farm,' *v.* ingtun. Cf. Luton *supra* 488.

BAKER'S FM, BALL'S FM, BUTT'S PIT, MATTHEW'S FM and SKINNER'S FM (all 6″) are probably to be associated with the families of John *le Bakere* (1330 *SR*), William *Bole* (1524 *SR*), Humfrey *But* (1610 *SR*), Walter *Mathu* (1524 *SR*) and Thomas *le Skynnere* (1333 *SR*).

BLACK DOWN is *Blackdowne* 1631, 1700 *Recov*. BOWERWOOD (6″) may be identical with *Bowode* 1495 Oliver 395. There is no wood here now, but there is curved land, cf. Bowden *supra* 37. COLLITON is *Coleton* 1483 Oliver 395. *v.* Collacott *supra* 50. CRAMMER BARTON is *Cranemore* 1244 *Ass* (p), *Cranmor* 1333 *SR* (p). 'Heron-frequented marshy land,' *v.* cran, mor. CULVERHAYES (6″), cf. *Culverheyball* 16th Oliver 104. 'Dove (ge)hæg.' For *ball* = hill, *v. supra* 211. THE GRANGE is *Grange* 1250 FF, *le Grangewode*, *Grangemeed* 16th Oliver 104. HANGER FM was the home of Nicholas *de la Hangre* 1281 *Ass* and David *atte Hangre* 1330 *SR*. *v.* hangra. HEMBERCOMBE is so spelt 1718 *Recov*. HEMBURY FORT is *Hembury Ford* 1670, 1700 *Recov*, *Fort* 1672 *Recov*. *v. supra* 557. GREAT MOOR (6″) is *More* 1495 Oliver 395. *v.* mor. PITNEY FM is so spelt 1765 D and is possibly identical with *Pittigheyg* 1249 *Ass* (p), *Pittingheye* 1269 FF, *Pittyngeshecches* 1307 Ipm. For *hayes*, *v. supra* 129. The first element is probably the name of a medieval owner. ST ANDREW'S WOOD is *Seynte Andrewes Wode* 1547 Oliver 314. The parish church is dedicated to this saint. SOUTHWOOD (6″) is *Southwod*

1303 FA. STAFFORD BARTON is *Stoford* 1310 *Ass*, *Stofford* 1333 *SR* (p). *v.* Stowford *supra* 41. UPCOTT FM is *Opecote* 1249 FF. 'Higher cot(e).' WINDWHISTLE FM is so spelt 1833 *Recov*. Such a name would probably refer to an exposed situation.

Cadbury

CADBURY 128 G 9

> *Cadabiria* 1086 DB, *Cadeberia* 1093 France *et freq* to 1356 AD iv, with variant spellings *-biri*, *-byre*, *-bury* and *Kade-*, *Chadebery* 1263 Exon

'*Cada*'s burh.' There is an ancient 'camp' here, referred to as *Cadbury Castell* 1397 Fine, now CADBURY CASTLE.

BOWLEY is *Bovelia* 1086 DB, *-legh* 1485 Ipm, *Bogeleg'* 1212 Fees 96, 1224–44 Exon, *Boghelee* c. 1250 *St Nicholas*, *Boghaleg* 1279 Ipm. 'Curved leah,' *v.* Bowden *supra* 37.

CHAPELTOWN and HOLLOW COMBE (6″) were the homes of Dionis' *atte Chapele* (1330 *SR*) and John de *Holecomb* (ib.). The former is *la Chapell'* 1434 IpmR.

ENDICOTT is *Hundecote* 1281 *Ass* (p), *Indecott* 1498 Ipm. 'The far cottages' or 'beyond the cottages,' cf. Youngcott *supra* 216. FURSDON is *Fursdon(e)* c. 1200 *St Nicholas*, 1330 *SR* (p). 'Furze hill,' *v.* dun. HALLSHOT (6″) may be identical with *Halsholte* 1291 (1408) Dartmoor, *La Halsholt* 1317 Pat. Probably 'hazel wood,' *v.* hæsl, holt and Addenda, Part i, lviii. MONKLAND BARN (6″) is *Monckland* 1676 *Deed*, perhaps with reference to the monks of the monastery of Séez to whom the manors of Cadbury and Bowley were granted in 1093 (France). PITT FM is *Lower Pitt* 17th *Deed*. UPPINCOTT is *Uppecote* 1249 *Ass*, 1330 *SR* (p), *Uppingcott* 17th *Deed*. 'Upper cottages.'

Cadeleigh

CADELEIGH 128 F 9

> *Cadelia* 1086 DB *et freq* to 1334 Cl with variant spellings *-leye*, *-legh(e)*, *Little Cadelegh* 1301 Ipm
> *Caddeleḡ* 1238 *Ass*

'*Cada*'s leah,' probably from the same man who gave name to Cadbury *supra*. The parishes adjoin.

ASHILFORD is *Ashlefords* 17th *Deed* and is possibly to be associated with John de *Ashulle*, i.e. 'ash hill' (1281 *Ass*). BURN-BRIDGE (COTTAGES) (6″) is *Bourne Bridge* 17th *Deed*, referring to a bridge over the stream here called the *Burn*. *v.* burna. BUS-LAND (6″) is *Busselond* 1395 IpmR, *Busselandmeade* 1562 *FF*. CATLAKE is so spelt 1576 *Deed*. *v.* lacu. COOMBE (6″) is so spelt 17th *Deed*. DART COTTAGES (6″) is *Lower Dart* 17th *Deed*. *v.* Dart river *supra* 5. DUNSTER is *West Dunster* 17th *Deed*. Without earlier forms it is impossible to say if this is identical with Dunster (So)[1]. GOTHAM is so spelt 17th *Deed*. Cf. the same name *supra* 543. LOWER LANGLEY is *Langeleg*(*h*) 1242 Fees 761, 790, 1263 Ipm, 1281 *Ass* (p). 'Long clearing,' *v.* leah. MEAD-HAYES is *Medhay* 1395 IpmR, *Meadehayes* 1619 *FF*. 'Meadow enclosure,' *v.* mæd, (ge)hæg. RIDGE is *Rudge* 17th *Deed*. *v.* hrycg. YATE was the home of Richard *atte Yate* (1333 *SR*). *v.* geat. The reference here may be to the narrow way between the hills.

Cullompton

CULLOMPTON [kʌlmptən] 128 F 12

(*æt*) *Columtune* 880–5 (c. 1000) BCS 553, (*æt*) *Culumtune* a. 1097 Earle 257, *Culimtone* 1159 RBE
Colump 1086 DB (Exon), *Colum* (Exch)
Culminton 1163, *Col-* 1166 P, *Culmeton* 1257 Ch
Culumt(*on*) 1212 Fees 96, *Columton* 1230 Cl, *Columpton*(*e*) 1263 Ipm, 1291 Tax, *Culmpton* 1321 Pat
Columpton al. Colehampton, Columbton, Collupton vulg. Culliton 1675 Ogilby

'Farm on the Culm river (*supra* 4),' *v.* tun.

COLEBROOK is *Colebroc*(*a*) 1086 DB, 1175 P, -*brok* 1314 *Ass*, *Colbroke* 1390 Cl, 1488 BM. 'Cool brook' or '*Cola*'s brook.'

CRANKLAND FM is *Cronkelond* 1330 *SR* (p). This is perhaps from OE *cranuca land*, 'cranes' or herons' land,' as suggested by Blomé (93).

GROWEN FM [grɑuən] is *Gorweheghes* 1330, *Grouheghes* 1333 *SR* (p), *Growen, Growhayes* 1701 *Recov*. No certainty is possible

---

[1] Blomé's early form (92) refers to Dunster (So). There are EAST and WEST DUNSTER on the 6″ map.

with regard to the first element. The second shows the common variation between *hayes* and *hayne*, cf. Hayne *supra* 129. The *-en* is the reduced form of *hayne* in the colloquial pronunciation of the compound, cf. Cottarson *infra* 609.

HACKLAND FM is *Hakelond* 1281 *Ass* (p), 1283 *Ass*, 1333 *SR* (p), *Hakalond(e)* 1305 *Ass*, (*juxta Alre Peverel*) 1311 *Ass*. William (de) *Haka* was living here in 1305 and 1311 (*Ass*) and his family probably gave name to the place. His name may itself be descriptive, referring to the projecting tongue of land here. *v.* Hackpen *supra* 538.

HILLERSDON

> *Hillesdona* 1086 DB, *-don* 1291 (1408) Dartmoor
> *Hilderesdon* 1242 Fees 775, *Westhildresdon* 1249 *Ass*, *-dris-* 1249 *Ass*
> *Hilleresdon* 1249 *Ass*, *-dune* 1283 *Ass*
> *Hildenesdon* 1270 *Ass* (p)

Probably '*Hildhere*'s hill,' *v.* dun. This name is not on record but both elements are found in OE compound pers. names.

LANGFORD is *Langafort* 1086 DB (Exon), *Langeford* (Exch), *Langeford juxta Braneys* 1299 *Ass*. 'Long ford.'

PADBROOK FM is *Paddo(c)kesbroke* n.d. Montacute 179, *Pad(d)ekebrok'* 1242 Fees 789, 1279 *Ass*, 1333 *SR* (p), *Padokbrok* 1291 (1408) Dartmoor, *Patrokesbroke* 1377, IpmR, *Paddesbrooke* c. 1630 Pole. The first element is ME *paddok*, 'toad, frog,' as suggested by Blomé (93). There is a small stream here.

PONSFORD is *Pantesfort* 1086 DB, *Pauntesford(e)* 1242 Fees 786, 1276 Ipm, 1284 *Ass*, *Pontes-* 1249 FF, 1279 Ipm, 1303 FA. '*Pant*' may have been the name of the streamlet here, probably a British name corresponding to W *pant*, 'hollow.' Cf. Ponsworthy *supra* 528 and Pont (Ekwall RN 332).

POTTSHAYES FM is *Potteshayes* 1566 DA 43 and is probably to be associated with the family of Maurice 'dictum *Pottere*' (1333 Exon). For *hayes*, *v. supra* 129.

SHUTELAKE is *Shutelake* 1330 SR (p), *Shittelake* 1409 IpmR. 'Stream in the corner of land,' *v.* lacu and cf. Shute *supra* 184.

There are two farms of this name in the parish, but, as pointed out by Blomé (94), the references are probably to the western one, which is on a stream on the western boundary of the parish. The other place is not near a stream and may be a more modern name.

ANDREW'S FM, SHEPHERDS MOOR (6″) and TRUMPS FM (6″) are probably to be associated with the families of Robert *Andreu* (1333 *SR*), William *Shephurd* (ib.) and Robert and John *Trump(e)* (1524 *SR*).

COOMBE FM, MOOREHAYES, RULL FM and WOODCOCKS WELL were probably the homes of Herbert de *Cumbe* (1244 FF), Gervas *atte More* (1333 *SR*), John *atte Hulle* (ib.) and John *at Ryll* (1524 *SR*), and John de *Wodecokeswill* (1333 *SR*). *v.* mor, **wielle** and Rill *infra* 606.

BIRCHEN OAK is *Birchin Oak* 1738 *Recov.* BULEALLER is *Bulalre* 1238 *Ass* (p), *Bolalre, Bolhalr'* t. Ed 3 *Ass*, *Bolealler* 1535 VE. 'Bull-alder (clump),' cf. Houndaller *supra* 548. CHALDON FM (6″) is *Chalvedon* 1249 *Ass* (p), 1333 *SR* (p). 'Calves' down.' HALSEWOOD is *Halswode* 1399 IpmR. 'Hazel wood,' *v.* Addenda, Part i, lviii. HAYNE BARTON is *La Heghen* 1283 *Ass*, *Hays* t. Hy 8 *FF*, *Heyn* 1571 *SR*. *v.* Hayne *supra* 129. HAYWOOD FM is *Haywode* c. 1320 *St Nicholas*, (*juxta Colompton*) 1345 *Ass*. 'Enclosed wood,' *v.* (ge)hæg. KING'S MILLS is *Kyngesmill* 1291 (1408) Dartmoor. Cullompton was a royal manor as early as the time of King Alfred. KNOWLE is *la Cnolle* c. 1200 *St Nicholas* (p). *v.* cnoll. MUTTERTON is *Motterton* 1571 *SR*, *Mutterton* 1578 *Deed*, t. Jas 1 *SR*. NEWLAND FM is *Niweland* 1242 Fees 789. OWLACOMBE FM (6″) is *Owlecombe* 1531 Oliver 400, 1566 DA 43. 'Owls' combe.' PAULSLAND FM is *Pallislond* 1279 *Ass* (p), *Pallyslonde* 1330 *SR* (p). This may be '*Pælli*'s land' but the forms are too late for certainty. SHUFFHAYES FM (6″) is *Shafteshayes* 1410 IpmR. HIGHER UPTON FM is *Uppeton* c. 1250 *St Nicholas*, *Uppeton Weure* 1334 *SR*. 'Higher farm,' *v.* tun. It lies above the river Weaver *supra* 16. VENN is *Fenne juxta Kentelesbere* 1314 *Ass*, *Ven* t. Hy 8 *FF*. *v.* fenn. WESTCOTT is *Westcote* 1439 IpmR. 'West' perhaps in relation to Bulealler. WHEATCROFT FM is *Whitecroft* 1809 M. WHITEHEATHFIELD BARTON is *West Wyte-*

hedfeld 13th Montacute, *Whytehet(h)feld* 1238 *Ass*, 1263 Ipm.
For *heathfield*, *v. supra* 265. WOOD MILL (6″) is *Wodmyll* 1543
SR. Cf. *la Wode juxta Columpton* (1314 *Ass*).

Feniton

FENITON 129 H 1/2

> *Finatona* 1086 DB, *Finetuna* 1185 Buckland 238 *et passim* to
> 1476 IpmR, with variant spellings *Fyne-* and *-ton(e)*, *Vine-*
> *tone* 1309 Exon, *Vyneton Malherbe* 1333 Cl
> *Feneton* 1169 P, 1311 *Ass*, *Venyton* 1585 *Recov*, 1637 Wills
> *Fynyngtone* 1454 Exon, *Fenyngton* 1543 *SR*

'Farm by Vine Water' *supra* 15. Willelmus *Male Erbe* held
the manor in 1242.

COLESWORTHY is *Kauleswrth* 1219 *Ass et freq* to 1333 *SR* with
variant spellings *Caules-*, *-worth(i)*, *-thy*, *Cauelesworth* 1313, 1314
Ass. '*Cāfel*'s worþig.' The name *Cāfel* is probably a form blended
from the recorded *Cāfa* and *Cǣfel*.

CURSCOMBE FM is *Cochalescoma* 1086 DB, *Coklyscomb* 1333 *SR*
(p), *Cokelescombe* 1370 *Ass* (p). Blomé (94) suggests that this is
for OE *cocc-hēales cumb*, 'valley of the cock-frequented nook,'
but such a compound is not in itself very likely. Wallenberg
(StudNP 2, 93) compares *Coklescomb* in Kent with a similar run
of forms except for one *Cukelescumbe* and Cuckoldscombe and
Cuxton (K) with persistent *Cu-*. He suggests an OE *cucola*,
'cuckoo,' cf. Latin *cuculus*. We may note further Coscott
(Berks), *Cokelescote* 1316 FA, *Cokkelescote* 1454 AD vi, and
Corscombe *supra* 165. Most likely Curscombe and Coscott
(Berks), like Corscombe *supra*, contain a pers. name **Coccel*.

SHERWOOD FM is *Shirford(e)* 1333 *SR* (p), 1546 BM, (*in Fyneton*)
1473 *AD*, *Sherwood* c. 1630 Pole. 'Clear ford,' *v.* scir. For the
later form *v.* Introd. xxxv.

YELLINGHAM FM is *Elyngham* 1289 *Ass*, 1441, 1512 *FF*, 1461
IpmR, *Elynggeham* 1306 *Ass* (p). 'Ham(m) of *Ella*' or 'of *Ella*'s
people, *v.* ing.

COLESTOCKS is *Colstock* 1675 Ogilby, *Coldstock* 1765 D. The second element may be stocc. VINE GREEN (6″) is *Vinegreen* 1723 *FF*. *v.* Vine Water *supra* 15. WHITE'S COTTAGES (6″) is to be associated with the family of Richard *White* (1330 *SR*).

Kentisbeare

KENTISBEARE 128 F 14

Chentesbera 1086 DB, *Kentesbere* 1577 Saxton
Kentelesbar 1212–23 *St Nicholas et freq* to 1291 Tax with variant spellings -*be(a)re*, -*bire* 1252 FF, -*byare* 1270 *Ass*, *Kenteslebiere* (sic) 1308 Exon
Kanteleber 1219 *Ass*, *Kaentlesbyar* 1297 Pat

It seems unlikely that the first element here is the same as in Kentisbury *supra* 49. There is no circular hill here, for Kentisbeare lies low by a stream and, more important perhaps than this, there is a Kentis Moor *infra* 566 a mile to the south, with similar early forms, but no topographical feature in common. There is an OE pers. name *Centa* and we have OE compounds *Centwine* and *Centweald*. The neighbouring Kentisbeare and Kentis Moor may well have taken their name from a man *Cæntel* called by a diminutive form of the name *Centa*.

ALLER is *Alra*, *Avrra* 1086 DB (Exon), *Avra* (Exch), *Alre* c. 1200 *St Nicholas*, (*in marlera de*) 1249 *Ass*, *Haure Pev'el* 1275 RH, *Alre Peverel* 1352 Ipm. 'At the alder.' William *Peverell*' de Essex held the manor in 1212 (Fees 96).

ALLHALLOWS FM [ællenz] marks the site of the manor of Blackborough *infra*, held by the heirs of Hugo de Bollay in 1242 (Fees 791). The chapelry attached to this manor is referred to as *chapell called Allhallowes chapel* in 1546 (Oliver 476). This has been replaced by the modern *All Saints* church.

BLACKBOROUGH is *Blacheberia*, *Blac(h)aberga* 1086 DB (Exon), *Blackeberge* (Exch), *Blakeburgha* 1173–5 (1329) Ch, -*berg(he)* 1242 Fees 790, 1249 *Ass*, 1274 Exon, *Butyesblakeburgh juxta Kentelesbeara* 1302 *Ass*, *Blakeberghesboty* 1357 Pat. 'Black (dark) hill,' *v.* blæc, beorg. Radulfus *Buty* held one manor in 1242. The other manor is now Allhallows Fm *supra*.

BUTSON'S FM is *Botuston* c. 1200 *Canonsleigh*, *Botyston juxta*

Kentelesbere 1339 *Ass*, *Butson* 1610 *SR*. It was held c. 1200 by the same Radulf *Boty* who is mentioned under Blackborough.

KINGSFORD is *Chinnesfort* 1086 DB, *Kingesford(e)* 1238 *Ass* (p), *Kynges-* 1242 Fees 786, 1441 IpmR, *Kynge-* 1356 *Ass*. Self-explanatory, but the exact royal owner is unknown.

ORWAY FM

    Orrawia 1086 DB (Exon), *Orrewai* (Exch)

    Orwey c. 1200 *St Nicholas* (p) *et freq*, *Horweie* 1228 FF

    Orreweie 1238 *Ass* (p), *-wey* 1267 *Ass* (p), *Orewaye* 1244 *Ass*

This is a difficult name. Blomé (96) suggests a compound of OE ora and weg, 'road along the bank.' This may be correct, but early and persistent double *r* is against it. *Orra is a possible pers. name as a pet-form of *Ordric* or *Orric*.

PIRZWELL FM is *Pissewilla* 1086 DB (Exon), *-welle* (Exch), *-well* 1238 *Ass* (p), *Pisevill* 1198 FF, *-will(e)* 1201 FF, 1242 Fees 792, *Pysewell* 1244 *Ass*, *-weyll* 1285 FA, *Pyswille* 1361 *Ass*. 'Pea(se) spring,' i.e. by which pease grow. *v.* pise, wielle.

SAINT HILL FM is *Sengethill* 1249 *Ass*, *Seynketille* 1291 Tax, *Swengetille* 1314 *Ass* (p), *Sweynghithull* 1327 Banco, *Sweynthull* 1326 Ipm, *Seynthill*, *Seyntylmede* 1448 BM. The first two forms suggest a compound of OE *sænget, 'burned place' (*v.* Syntley PN Wo 36) and hyll. For the next two cf. Sainthill *supra* 545 and Addenda, Part ii, xiv.

SOWELL FM is *Souewella* 1223 Bracton (p), *Seuewell* 1244 *Ass*, *-wyll* 1329 Ch, *Soueuille* 1333 *SR* (p), *Sowyll* 1498 Ipm. This must be OE *seofon wiellan*, 'seven springs.' Cf. *on syfan wyllan* BCS 731 (Ha) and Sinwell (Gl), *Suvenwell* 1248 *Ass*. According to the Rev. E. S. Chalk there are several springs near here.

BALLYMAN'S FM, BISHOP'S FM (6″), GREEN'S FM (6″), PALMER'S LAND (6″) are probably to be associated with the families of William *Balleman* (1612 Wills), William *Bysshop* (1330 *SR*), Richard *Grene* (1524 *SR*), and Henry *Palmere* (1330 *SR*).

ALLECOMBE FM is *Aldithecumb* 1244 *Ass*. 'Combe of a woman named *Ealdgȳð.*' CROYLE is *Crowhill* 1763 Map[1]. HENLAND FM is *Hynelonde* 1311 *Ass* (p), 1316 Exon (p). 'Land of the monks.'

---

[1] *Ex inf.* the Rev. E. S. Chalk.

v. **higna.** The name may have reference to the neighbouring Kerswell (*supra* 558), a cell attached to Montacute (So). HOLLIS GREEN is *Holways* 1841 *TA*[1]. KENTIS MOOR is *Kentelesmore* c. 1200 *St Nicholas, Kentys-* 1445 *Ct, Kentmore* 1525 *AOMB.* *v.* Kentisbeare *supra* 564. According to Pole it was a tract of wet uncultivated ground, *v.* mor. MOORHAYNE COTTAGE (6″) is *Morehayes* t. Hy 8 *FF.* POOL FM was the home of William *atte Pole* (1330 *SR*). SANDFIELD FM is *Sandfyld* 1525 *AOMB. v.* feld. STOFORD WATER is *Stoford* 1305 BM. *v.* Stowford *supra* 41. WOODBARTON is *Woda* 1407 Exon. *v.* beretun. WRESSING is *Wressen* 1809 M.

Nether Exe

NETHER EXE 128 H 10

> *Niressa* 1086 DB, *Nitherexe* 1196 AC, 1214–23 *St Nicholas,* 1238 *Ass,* *Netherexe* 1238 *Ass,* 1269 Exon, *Nytheresse* 1242 Fees 773, *Nether Exe juxta Exon* 1295 *Ass, Nethereux* 1543 LP

'Settlement lower down the Exe' as opposed to Up Exe *supra* 445, higher up the stream. *v.* neoðera.

Payhembury

PAYHEMBURY 129 H 1

> *Hamberia* 1086 DB, *Haumbire* 1238 FF
> *Paihember* 1236 BM, *et freq* to 1422 IpmR with variant spellings *Pay(e)-, -bury, -biri, -byre*
> *Payhaumbir'* 1242 Fees 786, *Pahembury* 1272 Exon, *-byre* 1291 Tax, *Payembre* 1285 FA.

v. Broadhembury *supra* 557. The same earthwork is referred to in both names. The manor must at one time have been in the possession of a man named *Paie* (OE *Pǣga*). Cf. Goodameavy *supra* 229.

HIGHER and LOWER CHERITON are *Cherleton(a)* 1086 DB, 1242 Fees 782, 1330 *FF* (p), *Brodechurleton(e)* t. Ed 1 BM, 1346 FA, *-cherletone* 1301 BM, *Northere Churleton* t. Ed 1 BM, *Southere-churleton* 1356 *Ass. v.* ceorl, tun. For 'broad' in the sense of 'great,' cf. *supra* 426. *Higher* and *Lower* correspond respectively to *Southere* and *Northere* Cheriton.

[1] *Ex inf.* the Rev. E. S. Chalk.

TALE is *Tala* 1086 DB, *Tale* 1236 FF, 1269 BM, 1330 *SR* (p), (*Monachorum*) 1269 BM, *Talle* 1313 Ch, taking its name from the Tale river *supra* 13. The *monks* of Ford abbey once held the manor.

FLAY'S FM (6″) and HASKINS FM are probably to be associated with the families of John *Flay* (1524 *SR*) and Charity *Haskins* (1679 Wills).

MELTON[1], POUND HO (6″), RIDGE COTTAGES (6″) were probably the homes of Agnes *atte Milton* (1330 *SR*), Hugo *atte Pounde* (1333 *SR*), i.e. 'cattle enclosure,' and John *atte Rygge* (ib.). *v.* myln, tun, hrycg.

BEER FM is *La Beare* 1289 *FF*, (*atte*) 1330 *SR* (p), *Great, Lytell Beer Hyll* 16th Oliver 106. *v.* bearu. COKESPUTT (6″) is *Kokes-pitte* 1244 *Ass* (p), *Kockesputte* 1291 Tax, *Cockesput* 1378 IpmR. 'Cock's pit' or '*Cocc*'s pit.' CULVER HO (6″) is *Culverhouse* 1543 *SR*. 'Pigeon house.' LEYHILL is so spelt 1648 *FF*. MONKTON PARK COTTAGES (6″) is *Monketon* 1333 *SR* (p). 'Monks' farm,' *v.* tun and cf. *s.n.* Tale *supra*. MOUSE HOLE is *Moushole* 1586 *Recov.* Either 'mouse hollow' or 'mousehole,' a term of contempt, *v.* holh. RULL FM is *La Hille, Hill in Upton, Rull al. Rill* 1302–1491 BM, *Le Hull* 1378 IpmR. 'At the hill,' cf. Rill *infra* 606. SLADE HO (6″) is *Slade* 1576 *Deed. v.* slæd. UGGATON FM is *Uggaton(a)* 1196 Oliver 394, 1206 ChR, *Uggeton* 1215 Ch, 1289 *Ass*. '*Ucga*'s farm,' *v.* tun, cf. Ugborough *supra* 284. UPTON is *Uppeton* 1238 FF, 1278 *Ass*. 'Higher farm,' *v.* tun.

Plymtree

PLYMTREE 128 G 13

> *Plumtrei* 1086 DB, -*tre* c. 1200 *St Nicholas*, 1249 FF, -*treoue* c. 1200 *St Nicholas*, -*trewe* 1281 *Ass*, -*trowe* 1299 Pat, 1364 Cl
>
> *Plimtre* 1219 Fees 264, *Plym*- 1291 Tax
>
> *Plumptre* 1270 *Ass*, 1370 IpmR, *Plymptru* 1284 Exon, *Plimp-trough* 1301 Cl
>
> *Plemtre* 1285 FA, -*trewe* 1313 *Ass*

'Plumtree,' *v.* Plympton *supra* 251.

---

[1] *Milton* 1589 SR.

CLYST WILLIAM

> *Clist* 1086 DB, *Clistewelm* 1238 *Ass*, *Clist Ewelme* 1242 Fees
> 782, *Clistewilme* 1256 FF, 1270 *Ass*, 1275 RH (p)
> *Clyst Wylliam* 1501 Ipm

'Source of the river Clyst,' *v.* æwielm. The later form is due
to popular etymology.

WEAVER is *Wævere* c. 1100, *Wevere* c. 1200, 1241 *St Nicholas*,
1291 Tax, 1476 Oliver 125, *Overe-* 1345 *Ass*, *Wevre* 1244 *Ass*
(p), 1263 Exon (p), *Weffre* 1281 *Ass*, taking its name from the
river Weaver *supra* 16.

WOODBEER

> *Wideberia* 1086 DB, *Wydebir'* 1249 *Ass*, *-byer'* 1249 FF,
> *-bere* 1281 *Ass*, *Widiebar'* 1249 *Ass*, *Widebergh* 1249 FF,
> *Wydibere* 1285 FA
>
> *Wudeber'* 1231 Cl (p), *Wodebere* 1242 Fees 779, *Wudebir'* 1249
> *Ass*, *Wodiabeare* 1310 *Ass*, *Wodebyare* 1316 FA, *Wode-*
> *be(a)r(e)* 1330 *SR* (p), 1346 FA, 1350 Ipm, (*juxta Plem-*
> *trewe*) 1313 *Ass*

The forms are difficult. There has evidently been confusion
between wiðig, probably the original first element, and wudu.
v. bearu.

NORMAN'S GREEN, SANGUISHAYES FM[1] and TYES FM (6″) are
probably to be associated with the families of John *Norman*
(1244 *Ass*), William *Sangwin* (1238 *Ass*) and John *Tye* (1524 *SR*).

DANES MILL (6″) is *Danes Mills* t. Eliz ChancP. FORDMOOR is
Forde 1249 *Ass*, *Fordemoore* 1672 FF. GREENEND is so spelt
1650 Recov. HEARN FM (6″) is *Hurn* 1503 Ipm and was the home
of John de *la Hurne* 1231 Cl. *v.* hyrne. The farm lies in a corner
of the parish. PENCEPOOL FM (6″) is perhaps to be associated
with the family of John *atte Penne* (1333 *SR*), *Pencepool* being
for *Penn's Pool*.

---

[1] *Sanguinshays* 1672 *Recov*.

Sheldon

SHELDON 129 E 2

Sildenna 1086 DB (Exon), *Sildene* (Exch)
Schildene 1185 Buckland 283 *et passim* to 1543 *SR* with
variant spellings *Shil-*, *Schyl-*, *Scil-*
Shyeldone 1269 Exon, *Shil-* 1334 *SR*, 1336 *FF*, *Sheyldon*
1642 *SR*

This is probably a compound of scylf and denu with reference
to the very steeply shelving hillside here.

NORTHCOTT is *Northcote* 1486 Oliver 395. SLADE FM is *Slade*
1249 FF and was the home of Stephen *atte Slade* 1330 *SR*. *v.*
slæd. SOUTHCOTT is *Suthcot* 1238 FF. WESTCOTT FM is *Westcote* 1509 Oliver 395, *Westcotedoune* n.d. Buckland 253.

Silverton

SILVERTON 128 G 10

Sulfretona, Suffertona 1086 DB, *Sulferton(e)* 1281 *Ass*, 1310
Ass, 1317 *FF*, 1318 Ipm, *-fur-* 1310 *Ass*, 1358 *FF*
Seluerton 1179 P
Silfreton(e) 1246 Ipm, 1279 QW, *-ver-* 1249 *Ass*, 1285 FA,
-fer- 1275 RH, 1291 Tax, *Olde-*, *Nywesylferton* 1346 *Ass*,
Sylferton 1356 *Ass*

This name may, as suggested by Blomé (98), go back to an OE
syle-ford-tun, 'farm by the miry ford.' Alternatively the first
element may be a stream-name. Cf. Little Silver *supra* 358,
though this would leave the almost persistent medial *f* un-
explained. Cf., however, Alphington *supra* 422. There is a small
stream which rises near here and joins the Culm. *v.* Addenda,
Part ii, xiv.

BURN is *Borna* 1086 DB, *Burne* 1242 Fees 789, *Borne juxta
Sillerton* 1378 IpmR. 'The stream,' *v.* burna.

DORWEEKE is *Dorwik* c. 1250 St Nicholas, *Dorwyk juxta Sulfurton*
1310 *Ass*, *Dorweke*, *-wyke* 1336 BM. This may, as suggested by
Blomé (98), be from OE dor and wic, the dor referring to a
narrowing of the valley by Dorweeke.

GREENSLINCH

Grenneliza 1086 DB

Grenesling c. 1200 *St Nicholas* (p) *et freq* to 1326 Ipm with variant spellings *-linch(e)*, *-lench(e)*, *lynch(e)*, *Gereneslynch* 1279 *Ass*

Gryneslenche 1286 *Ass*, *Greyneslynch* 1351 *Ass*

Grenelinch 1303 FA

The second element here is hlinc. The first is apparently a late OE surname. *Grene* is found once in DB in Sussex (Redin 25).

MONK CULM (lost) is *Colunp* 1086 DB, *Moneke Culum* 1250 FF, 1281 *Ass*, *Moncolm* 1291 Tax, *Monkeholme* 1384 IpmR, *Monkerton oth. Monkculm* 1777 Recov. The manor belonged to Montacute Priory (So).

SILVERTON PARK corresponds to the old manor of *Combe Sackville* for which the forms are *Colum* 1086 DB, *Colm Reyngny* 1242 Fees 779, *Colmp Regny* 1303 FA, *Culum Sechevill* 1305 *Ass*, *Culm Regny juxta Silferton* 1306 *Ass*, *Sechevilescolump juxta Bradenych* 1374 *FF*. It was held by Robert de *Sicca Villa* in 1242 (Fees) and according to Polwhele (250) belonged earlier to one John *Reigny* (cf. Ashreigney *supra* 355). For the river Culm, *v. supra* 4.

YARD FM and YARD DOWNS are *Heierda* 1086 DB, *Yurdon* 1303, 1346 FA, 1378 IpmR, *Yerdene juxta Bradenech* 1305 FF, *Yerd* t. Eliz *SR*. *v.* Yard *supra* 48. The two places are some distance apart, the former being by the Culm, the latter on a hill, *v.* dun.

BRIDGE MILL (6″), COOMBE, FORD FM (6″), LEIGH BARTON, GREAT PITT FM (6″)[1], ROACH and WORTH were probably the homes of Margery widow of Nicholas de *la Brigge* (1304 *Ass*), Sibill de *la Cumbe* (1249 *Ass*), Richard de *la Forde* (1270 *Ass*), Richard *atte Leye* (1333 *SR*), Philip de *Pytt* (1543 *SR*), Jordan *atte Roche*, i.e. 'at the rock' (1321 *Ass*), and Henry *atte Werth* (1333 *SR*). *v.* leah, worþ.

DUNSMOOR is *Dunesmore* 1211 RBE (p), 1270 *Ass*, *Netherdonesmore* 1279 *Ass*, *Donnesmor* 1306 *Ass*. 'Dunn's mor.' HAYNE Ho

[1] *Pytt* 1541 *SR*.

is *Hayes* 1518–29 ECP, *Hayne* 1642 *SR*. *v*. Hayne *supra* 129.
KEENS is to be associated with the family of John *Kene* (1524 *SR*).
LAND FM is *la Lunde* 1242 Cl (p), 1244 *Ass* (p). *Lunde* is probably
an error for *lande* and we have to do with a strip of plough or
pasture land, *v. land* sb. 7 in NED. LIVINGSHAYES is *Levenshayes*
1674 *FF*, *Lavenshais* 1674 *Recov*. The surname *Levyng* is found
in Axminster Hundred in 1333 *SR*. MOORLAND is *Morelond*
1445 *Ct. v*. mor. PERRY is *Pirie* 1336 BM, *Perry* 1625 *Recov*.
'Peartree,' *v*. pyrige. RUFFWELL FM (6″) is *Ruffewell* 1670 *FF*.
STOCKWELL HO (6″) is *Stokewell oth. Stockhill* 1779 *Recov. v*.
stocc.

Talaton

TALATON [tælətən] 128 H 14

> *Taleton(a)* 1086 DB *et passim*
> *Talleton(e)* 1206 Montacute 171, 1238 *Ass*, *Talliton* 1587 Wills
> 'Farm on the Tale river' (*supra* 13).

ESCOT is *Estcote al. Hoga* 1227 Ch, *Esshecote* 1249 *Ass* (p),
Est(t)ecote 1287 *Ass*. 'East cot(e).' It lies on a hill (*v*. hoh) east
of Talaton.

LARKBEARE[1]

> *Lavrochebere, Laurochebera* 1086 DB (Exon), *Liurochebere*
> (Exch), *Laurekebare* 1237 FF, *Laverk'ber'* 1237 Cl, *Lauerke-*
> *beare* 1266–71 Ipm
> *Lever(e)keber* 1219, 1345 *Ass*, 1244 Orig, *Leverikber* 1238 Cl,
> *Lerkebere* 1303 FA
> *Loverkeber'* 1238 Cl
> *Larkpere* 1675 Ogilby
> 'Lark wood,' *v*. bearu.

HARRIS'S FM and MARK'S FM (both 6″) are probably to be associated with the family of George *Harris* (1640 *SR*) and Richard
Marke (1524 *SR*).

LASHBROOK FM is *Lashbrooke* 1803 *Recov*. Cf. Lashbrook *supra*
132. There is a small streamlet here. MOORHAYES FM (6″) is
Morehaies 1606 *FF. v*. mor and Hayne *supra* 129. TALEWATER

---

[1] Larkbeare (hamlet) is in Talaton, Larkbeare Court in Whimple.

is *Talewater* 1665 *Manor Roll, Tailwater Mill* 1809 M. *v. supra*
13. WESTCOTT is so spelt 1691 *Recov.*

Thorverton

THORVERTON 128 C 9

> *Thurfurton* n.d. Oliver 123, 1340 NGl 4, 11
> *Torverton* 1201 Cur, 1212 Fees 96, 1213 HMC iv, 60, *Thor-
> verton(e)* 1263 Exon, 1275 RH, 1278 Ipm
> *Turverton* 1216 HMC iv, 64, 1221–30 Fees 1443, *Thurverton(e)*
> 1238 *Ass*, 1278 Ipm, 1282 Exon, 1284 *FF*, 1299 *Ass*
> *Thulvertone* 1301 Exon
> *Tharverton* c. 1630 Pole, *Darvelton* 1675 Ogilby

The first element is probably, as suggested by Blomé (99),
the Scand pers. name *þurferþ*, the name being of late OE or post-
Conquest origin. For the absence of medial *s*, cf. Kennerleigh
supra 408.

CHILTON is *Childetun* 1242 Fees 96, *Chilleton* 1303 FA, 1318
Ipm, *Childeton Furneaux* 1332 Fine, *Childeton* 1335 Ipm. *v.*
cild, tun. It was held by Henry de *Fornell'* in 1242.

RADDON COURT is *Raddona, Reddona* 1086 DB, *Reddon* 1208 Cur,
Est Raddon 1326 Ipm, *Estraddon juxta Uppetone* 1349 *Ass.* 'Red
hill,' *v.* dun. It is the same hill as that referred to in West
Raddon *supra* 417, about a mile distant.

ADAM'S COTTAGES (6″), BROOKS (6″), BERRYSBRIDGE, PROWSES
and SNOW'S FM (6″) are to be associated with the families of
Richard *Adam* (1524 *SR*), Robert *Brooke* (ib.), John *Berry* (1610
SR), John *Prowse* (1524 *SR*) and *Snow*[1] (ib.).

LYNCH, NORTHDOWN WOOD (6″), PERRY, POOLE FM, RULL,
STONE, TERLEY and UPCOTT were probably the homes of Thomas
de *la Linche* (1301 Exon), Ricardus *bi Northdone*, i.e. 'north of
the down' (ib.), William *atte Purie* (1330 *SR*), Elyas de *la Pole*
(1301 *Ass*), Walter *atte Hulle* (1330 *SR*), Gregorius de *la Stone*
(1301 Exon), Robert de *la Leye* (1306 *Ass*) and Hugo de *Uppecote* (1244 *Ass*). *v.* hlinc, pyrige, leah and cf. Rill *infra* 606 and
Tredown *supra* 146. For Terley, cf. Thurleigh (PN BedsHu 47).
There must have been an alternative form *atter Leye* for the
family name.

[1] Christian name illegible.

BIDWELL is *Bidewille* 1301 Exon (p), *Bydewill* 1330 SR (p). Cf. Bidwell *supra* 410. DINNEFORD BRIDGE (6″) is *Durneford* 1281 *Ass*. 'Hidden ford,' *v.* dierne. DUNSALLER (6″) is *Dunneshalre* 1238 *Ass* (p). '*Dunn*'s alder.' FORD CROSS is *la Forde, aque de Fordlake* 1301 Exon. HEATHFIELD is *Hathfeld* 1249 *Deed*. RAT-CLIFFES (6″) is *Radeclyve in Thurfurton* n.d. Oliver 123, *Radeclyve* 1340 NGl 4, 11. 'Red steep slope,' *v.* clif. The *s* is pseudo-manorial. TRAYMILL FM (6″) is *Mulle* 1408 Exon, *Tremyll* 1525 *FF*, 1594 *Recov* and was the home of Richard *atte Mulle* (1333 SR). 'At the mill.' For the *Tray-, Tre-, v. s.n.* Tredown *supra* 146. WAY is *Atteweye* 1306 *Ass* (nom. loc.). YELLOWFORD is *Yaldeford* t. Ed 1 *Deed*, (*H*)*olleforde* 1301 Exon, *Yalleford* 1306 *Ass*, *Yoldeford* 1333 SR (all p). 'Old ford,' cf. Introd. xxxiii.

XXVII. CLISTON HUNDRED

Clistona 1084 Geld Roll
v. Broad Clyst *infra*.

Broad Clyst

BROAD CLYST 128 J 11

Glistun 11th ASC *s.a.* 1006, *Gliston'* 1237 Cl
Clistunes gildscipe 1072–1103 Earle 265, *Cliston*(*a*) 1086 DB,
  1212 Fees 98, 1273 Exon, 1291 Tax
Brodeclyste 1372 Exon, *Clyston al. Brodeclyst* 1413 Exon

'Farm on the Clyst' *supra* 3, *v.* tun. For *broad* in the sense of *great*, cf. *supra* 426.

ASHCLYST FM is *Clist* 1086 DB, *Esse Clist* 1223 *St Nicholas*, *Aysseclist* 1260 Exon, *Aysh-* 1399 *FF. v.* æsc. For the river-name, *v. supra* 3.

CHURCHILL FM is *montem de Cherchull* 1281 *Ass*, *Chircheshull* 1311 *FF*, *Churchull* 1330 SR (p), *v.* Churchill (PN Wo 106) and Addenda, Part i, lii, *s.n.* Churchill.

CLYST GERRED FM (6″) is *Clist* 1086 DB, 1198 FF, (*Girardi*) 1276 Ipm and derives from *Gerard*, son of Elias de *Clist*, who held the manor t. Ric 1 (1198 FF).

WEST CLYST, and MOSSHAYNE are *Clista* 1086 DB, *Clyst Moyses* 1263 FF, *Clist, Clyst Moys* 1285 FA, *Clyst moyes* 1548 HMC Exeter, *West Clist al. Clist Moyes* 1776 *Recov, Moshayne* 1827 G. This settlement on the river Clyst must have been distinguished by the name of its one time owner who has not, however, been traced. For Hayne, *v. supra* 129.

COLUMBJOHN is *Colum* 1086 DB, *Culum* 1234 Fees 396, 1244 *Ass, Colm* 1242 Fees 789, *Colump Johan* 1316 Ipm, *Culmejon* 1474 Pat and derives from one *Johannes de Culum* who held the manor in 1234 (Fees 396). The name would thus mean 'manor (of John) by the Culm river,' *v. supra* 4.

DOLBURY is *Dulleberi* 1201 FF, *Dollebyr'* 1294 *Ass* (both p), *Dolbury-Hill* 1630 Westcote. The first element is identical with that discussed under Dolbeare *supra* 464. The second is burh. There is an ancient camp here.

EVELEIGH (lost) is *Iueleia* 1086 DB, *Iveleg* 1259 FF, *Yvelegh* 1275 RH (p), *Yevelegh* 1378 IpmR, *Eveleigh* 1733 *FF.* 'Ífa's leah,' cf. Ivinghoe (PN Bk 96).

KILLERTON

> *Kildringthon'* 1242 Fees 777, -*drinton* 1275 RH, -*drynton* 1305 Ipm
> *Kelringtone* 1244 *Ass* (p)
> *Kylderinton* 1275 RH (p), -*ington* 1306 *Ass, Kylderton* 1281 *Ass, Kildrynton* 1305 Ipm
> *Kyllerinton* 1281 *Ass* (p), *Killerington* 1285 FA, *Kylryngton juxta Clyston* 1306 *Ass, Kilrington(e)* 1311 *FF,* 1327 Banco
> *Killerton* 1493 Ipm

Professor Ekwall suggests an OE pers. name with the same first element which is found in *Cweldgils.* That is an Anglian name and the WS form would have been *Cwyld-. Cwyldhere* is a possible compound-name which would meet the phonological requirements. *v.* ingtun.

LIDDINGTON (6″) is *Louttyngdon* 1543 *Deed, Lyttingdon* 1740 *FF* and was the home of Henry de *Luttyngton* (1330 *SR*). '*Lutta's* farm,' *v.* ingtun. For the pers. name, cf. Lutworthy *supra* 401.

LOXBROOK is *Lokesbrok* 1281 *Ass* (p), 1333 *SR* (p), *Lokysbroke* 1422 *Ass*. '*Locc*'s brook,' cf. Loxbeare, Loxhore *supra* 540, 63.

LYMBURY (6″) is *Limberi* 1201 FF (p), *-bire* 1238 *Ass* (p), *-bergh* 1244 *Ass*, *Lymbyr'* 1242 Fees 777, *-bury* 1305 Ipm, *Lymbyry juxta Cliston* 1346 *Ass*. *v*. burh. The first element may be lind, 'limetree.'

SOUTHBROOK is *Subbrok* 1228 FF, *Sudthbrok'* 1242 Fees 777, *Suthebrok* 1281 *Ass*, *Bysouthebrok* 1287 *Ass*, *Southbrok juxta Cliston* 1345 *Ass*. 'South of the brook.' The farm is south of the Whimple stream.

SOUTHWHIMPLE FM is *Suthwymple* 1242 Fees 777, *-pel* 1267 *Ass*, *-wymple* 1279 *Ass*, *Bysouthewympel* 1333 *SR* (p), *Southwympel juxta Hynetonclyst* 1339 *Ass*, *Bysouthwhympel* 1345 *Ass*. 'South of the Whimple,' *v*. Whimple *infra* 579.

HIGHER WILLYARDS is *la Wildeyerde* 1238 *Ass* (p), *atte Wilde-yurde* 1317 *Ass* (p), *la Willeherd'* 1249 *Ass* (p), *la Willehurde* 1275 RH (p), *Willeurd* 1330 Exon. The second element of this name is the word *yard* discussed *supra* 48. The whole name would refer to a wild or uncultivated area of land. Cf. Willand *supra* 553.

WITHY BRIDGE (6″) is *Wyebrigge* 1270 *Ass* (p), *Wyghebrigg(e)* 1289 *Ass* (p), 1292 *Ass*, *Wythybrigg*, *Whithbrigg* 1408 IpmR, *Wethybrygge* 1523 *Recov*. Probably 'withy bridge,' i.e. a bridge by which these grew, or 'causeway made with withies.' Cf. Rice Bridge (PN Sx 254).

CARPENTERS COTTAGES (6″), CHANNONS FM (6″), EASTONS FM (6″), GODFREY'S FM, GOULDS FM, HAYMANS FM (6″), JARMANS (6″) PAYNES FM (6″) and PRATTS FM (6″) are probably to be associated with the families of John *Carpunter* (1333 *SR*), William *Chanon* (1524 *SR*), John *Eston* (ib.), *Godfrey* (1660–1748, neighbouring parishes, Wills), William *Gould* (1668 Wills), John *Hayman* (1524 *SR*), Hugh *Jermyn* of Coomroye (1638 HMC Exeter), John *Payn* (1333 *SR*) and Robert *Pratt* (1524 *SR*).

BRIDGE HO (6″), BROOM HILL FM (6″), BURROWTON[1], FROGMORE

---

[1] *Boryton* 1546 *SR*.

Fm, Hay, Heathfield (6″), Hillhead (6″), Lake Ho and Trow Fm were probably the homes of William *atte Brigge* (1330 *SR*), Isabella de *Bromhull* (ib.), Lucas de *Boreton* (ib.), Richard de *Froggemere* (ib.), Roger de *la Haye* (1244 *Ass*), Robert *atte Hethfelde* (1330 *SR*), Geoffrey de *la Hulle* (1281 *Ass*), Roger de *la Lak'* (1275 RH) and Philip *atte Lake* (1330 *SR*), and Thomas *atte Triwe*, i.e. 'at the tree' (1407–10 *AddCh*). *v.* Burrington *supra* 246 and mere, (ge)hæg, lacu, and cf. Heathfield *supra* 265.

Bluehayes, Francis Court and Younghayes (6″) appear as *Bluehayes* 1765 D, *Fraunceys Court* 1493 Ipm, and *Yongheyes* 1476 Oliver 125, and are probably to be associated with the families of Elizabeth *Bluet* 1330 *SR* and John *Blwet* 1428 FA, John *Fraunceys* 1333 *SR*, and William *le Yonge* 1334 *St Nicholas*. For *hayes, v. supra* 129.

Beare is *Bere* 1234 Fees 396, 1242 Fees 777, *Beare* 1293 Ch, 1330 *SR* (p). *v.* bearu. Black Dog (hamlet) takes its name from a public-house of that name (F. R.-T.). Brockhill is *Brokhill(e)* 1242 Fees 777, 1285 FA, *-hull* 1315 Ipm, 1330 *SR* (p), *Brokehull* 1281 *Ass*. 'Badger hill,' *v.* brocc. Budlake is *Buddlelake* 1779 *Recov. v.* lacu. Burrow is *la Berghe* 1238 *Ass* (p), *La Burgh* 1287 *Ass*, *atte Burgh* 1330 *SR* (p). 'At the hill,' *v.* beorg. Chillacombe Fm is *Chelecombe* 1433–72 ECP 2, 155. Comberoy Fm is *Comb Roie* 1378 IpmR, *Combry al. Combrew al. East Eveleigh* 1735 *Recov*. Craniford Fm (6″) is *Craneford* 1242 Fees 777, 1287 *Ass*, 1324 *FF*. 'Crane or heron ford.' Farthings Fm is *Ferthyng* 1537 CtAugm. *v.* feorðung. The *s* is pseudo-manorial. Heath is *Clystheythe* 1566 *Deed*. Nether Holwells (6″) is *Hollewille* 1238 *Ass* (p), 1330 *SR* (p). 'Spring in the hollow,' *v.* holh, wielle. Horswell is *Horswill* 1238 *Ass*. Kerswell Ho is *Kereswell* 1281 *Ass* (p), *Carswelle* 1305 Ipm, *Karsville juxta Cliston* 1316 *Ass*. 'Cress spring,' *v.* cærse, wielle. Langacre (lost) is *Lang-, Longacre* 1249 *Ass*, *Langacre juxta Cliston* 1324 *Ass*, *Langacre* 1779 *Recov*. Self-explanatory, cf. Long Acre in London. Moor Cottages (6″) is *Mora* 1229 FF, *La More* 1270 *Ass*, 1311 *FF*. *v.* mor. Mooredge (6″) is *Murrage* 1779 *Recov*. The 18th cent. form represents a local pronunciation. Newhall is *Newall al. Newhall* 1704 *Recov*. Newlands is *Newlond Downe* 1537 CtAugm. Ratcliffes (6″) is *Radeclive in*

Clistun, Rateclive 13th *St Nicholas, Redeclyve* 1407–10 *AddCh* (p). 'Red clif.' The *s* is pseudo-manorial. RATTLECOTT WOOD (6″) is *Rattlecott* 1661 *FF. v.* cot(e). SAUNDERCROFT FM is *Sandecroft* 1281 *Ass. v.* sand, croft. For the *er, v.* Introd. xxxvi. SHERMOOR FM (6″) is *Shermore* 1707 *Recov.* SPRYDONCOTE is *Sprydon* 1504 NGl 3, 148, 1566 *Deed, Est Spreydon* 1542 NGl 3, 149, *Sprydon al. Spreadon* 1704 *Recov.* 'Brushwood hill,' *v.* Sprytown *supra* 208. The cote must be a modern addition. TILL-HOUSE FM (6″) derives according to Pole from a Robert *Till* (t. Hy 3), cf. also Robert *Tylle*, a juror in Cliston Hundred in 1428 (FA). WHITE DOWN COPSE is *Whittdowne* 1566 DA 43. WISHFORD FM, WISH MEADOW LANE (6″) are *Wysshemeade* 1566 *Deed, Wishford* 1827 G, and are to be associated with Michael de *Wesche* (1333 SR). *v.* wisc. There is low marshy land here by the Clyst.

Butterleigh

BUTTERLEIGH[1] 128 F 11

> *Buterleia* 1086 DB, *-lega* 1161–84 *St Nicholas, -lea* 1187 P
> *Boterleg(he)* 1251 Fees 1263, 1277 Exon, 1291 Tax, *Botere-* 1281 *Ass*
> *Butreslegh* 1262 FF

'Clearing with good pasture,' *v.* Buttercombe *supra* 40.

COOMBE was the home of Walter de *Cumbe* (1281 *Ass*). *v.* cumb.

Clyst Hydon

CLYST HYDON 128 H 13

> *Clist* 1086 DB, 1242 Fees 786, *Clyst Ydone* 1258–77 Exon, *Clisthydon* 1285 FA

For the river Clyst, *v. supra* 3. The manor was held by Ricardus de *Hidune* in 1242 (Fees 786).

AUNK

> *Hane, Hanca* 1086 DB (Exon), *Hanc* (Exch), 1201 Cur (p), *Ank(e)* 1229 Pat (p), 1249 *Ass*, 1346 FA
> *Ancha* 1175 P (p), *Aunk(e)* 1229 Pat (p), 1285 FA, 1407–10 BM
> *Annock* 1303 FA

[1] Detached part of Cliston Hundred.

Aunk lies on a low but well-marked spur of land between two branches of the Clyst, the eastern end of the spur being called *Ratclyffe*. The situation makes it difficult to believe that we have to do with a stream-name. The name may be Celtic and contain the same root as Gaulish *anc-os*, 'hook' (*v.* Holder *s.n.*). Possibly this was the old name of the hill on which Aunk stands.

Hoop Fm is *la Hope* 1238 *Ass*, *atte Hope* 1317 *Ass* (p). This may be OE *hōp*, 'hoop,' but the topographical reference is obscure.

Blampin Fm (6″), Courtney's Fm (6″) and Farrant's Hayes are to be associated with the families of Thomas *Blampyn*, i.e. 'white-bread' (1662 Wills), Hugo de *Courtenay* (1333 *SR*) and John *Feraunt* (ib.).

Marsh Fm, Pyle Bridge (6″) and Yarde Fm were the homes of William de *Marisco* (1238 *Ass*) and John *atte Mershe* (1330 *SR*), Sibilla *atte Pile* (1330 *SR*), John de *la Verge* (1238 *Ass*) and John *atte Yurd* (1330 *SR*). *v.* Pilemoor *supra* 420 and Yard *supra* 48.

Chelveshayes (6″) is *Cheluehaies* 1646 *Deed*. 'Calves' enclosure,' *v.* cealf, (ge)hæg. Little Silver is so spelt 1765 D. *v. supra* 358. Parradon Fm is *Pirydon* 1333 *SR* (p), *Purydon* 1423 IpmR, *Peridonhill* 1646 *Deed*. 'Peartree hill,' *v.* pyrige. Ratclyffe is *Redeclyve* 1330 *SR* (p). 'Red clif.' Roach Fm is *Roach* 1697 *Deed* and was the home of Robert *atte Roche* (1330 *SR*). This would seem to be the ME *roche*, 'rock.' There is no prominent rock here, but there is a small but well-marked hill just to the west. Woodhayes is *la Wode* 1359 *Ass*. For *hayes*, *v. supra* 129.

Clyst St Lawrence

Clyst St Lawrence 128 H 13

> *Clist* 1086 DB, (*Sancti Laurencii*) 1203 Cur, *Clyst Sancti Laurencii* 1291 Tax, *Clistlauraunz* 1319 Orig, *Clist Seint Laurenz* 1361 Cl

This settlement on the river Clyst (*supra* 3) was distinguished by the dedication of its church.

Scorlinch Fm is *Shorelenche* 1420 *Ct*. The name is probably identical with Sharland (Ha), *Schorlynche* 1277 *FF*. The first element is the word 'shore' discussed under Shoreham (PN Sx 246), hence 'steep hill.' The place is on a slope above the Clyst river. For initial *sc v*. Introd. xxxv.

CLAP MILL (6″) is *Clapmylle* 1476 Oliver 125, probably referring to a mill which had a 'clap' or 'clapper,' *v*. NED *s.v*. and cf. *Clapmella* in a Sussex fine of 1206. HITT'S FM is to be associated with the family of Michael *Hett* (1524 *SR*). UPTON FM is so spelt 1765 D. 'Higher farm,' *v*. tun. It lies above the church.

Whimple

WHIMPLE 128 J 13

> *Winpla* 1086 DB, *Winpol, Wunpol, Wimple* 1238 *Ass*
> *Wimpell* 1218 Pat, *Wympel* 1274 Ipm, 1291 Tax, *Wimpel* 1285 FA, *Wynpel Scē Marie* 1296 *FF*
> *Hwympel* 1292 Ipm, *Whympel* 1391 Exon

Whimple was originally a stream-name (*v*. Southwhimple *supra* 575), the name being a compound of the British words corresponding to W *gwyn*, 'white' and *pwll*, 'pool.' *v*. Ekwall RN 456. That this was so is made certain by the fact that there was a place called *Wympelwell in parochia de Taleton* (1281 *Ass* 1249 m 1), referring to the spot where the stream rises in Talaton parish.

BARNSHAYES is *Clystebarneville* 1482 IpmR, *Clyst Barnvyle* 1495 Ipm, *Clyst Barnefeld* 1542 CtRequests, *Barnheys, Bernheys* 1736 Recov, and is to be associated with the family of John de *Berneville* (1323 *FF*). *v*. Hayne *supra* 129.

COBDEN is *Cobbewimple* 1242 Fees 792, *Cobbe Wymple* 1301 Cl, *Cobwynepol* 1379 IpmR, *Cobeton* 1279 *Ass*, *Cobbeton(e)* 1285 FA, (*juxta Wynpel*) 1296 *FF*. The meaning is 'Cobba's farm on the Whimple stream,' *v*. tun. For another name of this type, cf. Goodameavy *supra* 229.

RUTTON FM is *Ruttenland* 1616, *Rytton* 1628, *Rutten* 1633, *Ritton* 1665 Deed. The forms are too late for certainty but it may well be that we have here land added to a weak plural of the OE word *ryt* discussed under Rutt *supra* 286.

STRETE RALEIGH is *Estreta* 1086 DB, *Streta* 1184 P, *Strete* 1242

Fees 763, 1292 Ch, (*Ralegh*) 1303 FA. *v.* stræt. The place lies by the old Roman road from Honiton to Exeter. Henry de *Ralegh*' held the manor in 1242 (Fees 763).

CROSS TOWN (6") is *Crostowne* 1628 *Deed*. For *town*, *v. infra* 676. FORDTON FM (6") is *Forton* 1675 *Recov*, 1692 *Deed*. It may be identical with the place called *Fordplace* in 1646 *Deed*. HOL-WAYS FM is to be associated with Ralph de *Holeweye* (1333 *SR*). *v.* holh, weg. The 's' is probably pseudo-manorial. KNOWLE CROSS was the home of William *atte Knolle* (1330 SR). *v.* cnoll. PERRITON FM (6") is *Peryton* 1632 *FF*. 'Peartree farm,' *v.* pyrige, tun. PITHAYES FM is *la Pitte* 1238 *Ass* (p), *Putheghs* 1330 *SR* (p). For *hayes*, *v. supra* 129. RULL FM is *Rull* 1662, *Rill* or *Hill Rew* 1676 *Deed*. 'At the hill,' cf. Rill *infra* 606. SLEWTON Ho (6") is *Slowe Towne* 1665 *Deed* and is to be associated with the family of Cecilia *atte Sloo*, i.e. 'at the slough or miry spot' (1333 *SR*). For *town, v. infra* 676. WELSHE'S FM (6") is to be associated with the family of William *Walsshe* (1547 *SR*). WOODHAYES is *Woodhaine* 1628 *Deed*. For *hayes, v. supra* 129. YELLAND'S is *Yolland* 1634, 1658, *Yelland* 1647 *Deed*. Cf. Addenda, Part i, lviii.

XXVIII. EAST BUDLEIGH HUNDRED

Budeleia 1084 Geld Roll, *Budelega* 1167, 1168 P, *Estbudlegh* 1383 IpmR
Buddelegh 1212 Fees 96, 1238 *Ass*, 1242 Fees 761
Bodeleg' 1245 Orig
v. Budleigh *infra* 582.

Aylesbeare

AYLESBEARE 138 B 13

Ailesberga 1086 DB (Exon), *Eilesberge* (Exch)
Aylesbere 1227 Ch, 1244 *Ass*, 1269 Exon, 1274 Ipm, *Ailes-* 1242 Fees 787, *Aylebere* 1254 Pat
Aylesbare 1230 FF, *-bear* 1274 Ipm
Aylesbyr 1239 Ch, *Ailesbur*' 1242 Cl
Aillesbere 1315 Pat, *Ayllesbeare* 1316 FA, 1385 Exon, *Elsbeare* 1697 *Deed*

'*Ægel*'s bearu,' cf. Aylesbury PN Bk 145.

ALLEN WOOD (lost) is *Alynwod* 1238 FF, *Aylinewode* 1242 Fees 782, *Aylingewude* 1262 FF, 1263 *AD* D 7725, *Aillenewode* 1341 Ipm, *Aylyng(e)wode* 1346, t. Edw 3 *Ass*, *Allen Wood* 1743 *FF*. 'Wood of *Ægel* or of his people,' *v.* ing. This must have been the same man who gave name to the parish.

BEAUTIPORT FM is *Beaudeport* 1341 *FF*, *Beaudeport* 1342 Fine (p), 1346 FA (p), *Bowtiport* 1602 *Recov*, *Beautiport al. Berriport* 1787 *Recov*. Professor Ekwall suggests that the first element may be an OE *bēawede, 'infested by gadflies.' Such a name would be a good parallel to such contemptuous *port*-names as Taddiport and Doggaport *supra* 111, 122, 95.

HOUNDBEARE FMS is *Hunteber(e)* 1219 *Ass et freq* to 1290 Ipm, *-berg* 1226 FF, *-beare* 1255 Misc, (*by Ailesbere*) 1341 Ipm. 'Huntsman's wood' or '*Hunta*'s wood,' *v.* bearu.

ROSAMONDSFORD is *Rosemundevord* 1313, 1314 *Ass*, *Rosmoundsforde* 1359 AD vi, *Rosemondesforde* 1377 Cl, *Rosemoundeford* 1452 *Ct*, *Rosemansford* 1740 *Recov*, and possibly takes its name from an ancestor of William *Rosemond* mentioned in 1501 (*Ct*).

WITHEN FM and WITHEN FURSE (6") are *la Wythye* 1289 *Ass*, *la Wytheghen* 1323 *Ass*, *atte Withien* 1346 *Ass* (all p), *Wytheneffurse* 1501 *Ct*. 'At the withies,' all the forms except the first representing the OE weak plural. *v.* wiðig.

JEANS, LEATS FM (both 6") and PERKIN'S VILLAGE are probably to be associated with the families of Thomas *Jeanes*, William *Leate* (1612 *SR*, 1582 *SR*) and Thomas *Perkins* of Clyst Honiton (1652 *Deed*).

NUTWALLS is *Nutwall* 1731, *Nutwalls* 1743 *FF*. RILL FM was probably the home of Richard *atte Hulle* (1333 *SR*). Cf. Rill *infra* 606. RINDLEHAYS is *Randleshayes* 1737 *FF*, and is possibly to be associated with the family noted under Randell's Green *infra* 591.

Bicton

BICTON 139 H 1

Bechatona 1086 DB

Buketon(e) 1228 FF *et passim* to 1330 Ipm, (*beside Budlegh*) 1495 Ipm, *Boketon* 1275 Pat, *Bugetone* 1280 Exon, *Buckton* 1285 FA

Bukenton 1260 Oliver 251, *Bukinton* 1281 Cl, -*yntone* 1291 Tax, *Bukyngton(e)* 1303 FA, 1348 Cl, 1374 Exon, (*juxta Otriton*) 1370 *Ass*

Byketon 1330 Pat, *Bicketon al. Buckton* 1616 *Deed*

'*Beocca*'s farm,' *v.* tun and cf. Abbots Bickington *supra* 124.

UPHAMS PLANTATION is to be associated with the family of Richard *Uphome* (1524 *SR*). He may have come from Upham in Farringdon *infra* 588.

YETTINGTON is *Yetematon', Yethemeton'* 1242 Fees 762, 787, *Yet(t)emeton(e)* 1260 Oliver 256, 1292 Ipm, *Yttematon* 1303 FA, *Yeadmeton* 1316 FA. This seems to be a triple compound of OE geat, hæme and tun, the whole meaning 'the farm of the settlers by the gate.' Cf. Cotmaton *infra* 598. The 'gate' may be the comparatively narrow part of the valley here on either side of which the hills recede.

East Budleigh

EAST BUDLEIGH 138 D 14

Bodeleia 1086 DB (Exon), -*lie* (Exch), *Estbodelegh* t. Ed 3 *Ass*, 1412 Pat, *Boddelegh(e)* 1291 Tax, 1364 *Ass*

Budelega 1125–9 France, *Buddele(ghe)* c. 1210–16 HMC iv, 64 *et freq* to 1269 Exon,

Buteleg 1219 *Ass*

Budleigh al. East Budleigh 1671 *Recov*

v. leah. The first element is probably OE *budda*, 'beetle,' used as a pers. name (*v.* Redin 74).

DALDITCH [deilitʃ]

Dalediz 1210 (1326) Pat, -*dich* 1238 *Ass et freq* to 1346 FA with variant spelling -*dych*, *Dalledich* 1219 *Ass* (p)

Dyalediche 1281 *Ass*, 1309 Exon (p), -*dech* 1441 IpmR

'*Dealla*'s ditch,' cf. Dolish *infra* 643.

HAYES BARTON is *Heghenpoer* 1281 *Ass*, *Heghes juxta Daledych* 1360 *FF*, *Poiersheghes* 1378 IpmR. For *hayes*, *v.* Hayne *supra* 129. Roger le *Poer* held the neighbouring manor of Yettington in Bicton in 1242 (Fees 761).

TIDWELL BARTON

> *Todewell* 1306 *Ass* (p) *et freq* to 1378 IpmR with variant spellings -*will*(*e*), *Toddewille* 1408 *Ass*, *Tottewyll* 1490 Ipm *Tudewille* 1323 *Ass*, -*welle* 1339 *Ass* (p), *Tudwyll* 1498 Ipm

Perhaps '*Tud*(*d*)*a*'s spring,' *v.* wielle. See, however, Tiddy Brook *supra* 14.

CROSS'S FM (6″) is to be associated with the family of John *Crosse* (1524 *SR*). KERSBROOK is *Karsbroch* 1210 (1326) Pat, *Carsbrok* 1330 *SR* (p), *Crasbrok* 1457 *Cl*. 'Cress brook,' *v.* cærse. LEEFORD is so spelt in 1810 *Recov*, and may be by the place called *la Lege* in 1210 (1326) Pat. *v.* leah. LILLAGE LANE (6″) is *Louelinch* 1323 *Ass*, *Lullinch* 1635 DA 24. '*Lēofa*'s hlinc.' POUND FM (6″) may have been the home of Roger *atte Pounfolde* (1333 *SR*). PUL-HAYES FM is *Poleheys* 1457 *Cl*, and was probably the home of William *atte Pole* (1330 *SR*). The pool (*v.* pol) may be the branch of the Otter estuary here. *v.* Hayne *supra* 129. SHORTWOOD COMMON is *Shortwood* t. Hy 8 *Star Chamber*. THORN MILL FM (6″) is *Thorne myll* 1501 *Deed*. WASHMOOR FM (6″) is *Wayshemore* 1333 *SR* (p). *v.* (ge)wæsc, mor. The place lies low by a stream. WHEATHILL PLANTATION (6″) is *Whitehill* 1666 *Recov*, 1722 *Deed*. The modern form is corrupt.

Budleigh Salterton

BUDLEIGH SALTERTON[1] 138 E 14

> *Saltre* 1210 (1326) Pat, *Salterne in the manor of Buddeleghe* 1405 *Deed*, *Saltern*(*e*) 1439 *FF*, 1540 LP, (*in parochia de Budlegh*) 1454 *FF*, *Salteryn* 1492 Ipm, *Saltern Haven* c. 1550 Leland
>
> *Salterton* 1667 *Recov*, *Budley Salterton* 1765 D

This is a modern town, which derives its name from the *salterns* or salt pans (*v.* ærn) which existed here by the mouth of the Otter at an early date.

[1] A modern parish formed from East Budleigh in 1895.

KNOWLE is (*ultra*) *Cnollam* 1210 (1326) Pat, *Knoll* 1540 LP, *Knolles* 1660, 1676 DA 24. *v.* cnoll. The plural form may have reference to Knowle and Little Knowle near by.

OTTERMOUTH (lost) is *Ot'mue* 1238, *Otryesmue* 1244 *Ass*, *Oterimouth* 1297 Cl, *port of Oterymouth* 1332 Misc, *Otyrmouth havyn* c. 1475 Wm Wo. *v.* Otter river *supra* 11.

Clyst Honiton

CLYST HONITON   138 A 11

    (*æt*) *Hina tune* c. 1100 Earle 262

    Hinetun 1219 FF, -*ton* 1276 Ipm, *Hynethon'* 1242 Fees 764, *Clysthynetone* 1281 *Ass*, 1291 Tax, 1330 Exon, *Hynetonisclyst* 1340 *Ass*, *Hyneton Clist* 1399 IpmR

    Honiton Clyst 1472, *Clist Honyton* 1652 *Deed*

v. higna, tun. The manor belonged to a religious community, viz. Exeter Cathedral. For the river Clyst, *v. supra* 3. The modern form of the name has been influenced by that of Honiton *infra* 639.

BRIGHTSTON (lost) is (*æt*) *brihtrices stane* 1050–73 Earle, *Bedricestan* 1086 DB, *Brichtrikeston, Brictrikestane* 1219 *Ass*, *Brythrycheston* 1262 FF, 1316 FA, *Brytricheston* 1303 FA, *Bryghtstane* 1394 *Ass*, *Bryghteston juxta Hyneton Clyst* 1399 IpmR. 'Beorhtrīc's stone.'

HOLBROOK FM is *Holebroc(a)* 1086 DB, 1228 FF, -*ok(e)* 1242 Fees 783, *Halebrok* 1242 Fees 763, *Holebrok juxta Clyst Epī* 1356 *Ass*. *v.* holh, broc.

TREASBEARE FM is *Bere* 1242 Fees 764, *Tresaurerbere* 1535 VE, *Tresbeare al. Tresorers Beare* 1558–79 ECP. *v.* bearu. The distinguishing first element is due to the fact that the manor formed the endowment of the *thesaurarius* or 'treasurer' of Exeter Cathedral (cf. 1535 VE).

AXHAYES FM (6″) is *Axeheye, -heys* 1452 Ct, *Axhayne* 1544 AD v, and is to be associated with the family of Henry de *Axe* (1333 *SR*). HAYES FM is perhaps the place called *Deneheyes in the parish of Honiton Clyst* 1472 *Deed, Denehayse* 1508 AD iii. *v.* denu. For *hayes, v.* Hayne *supra* 129. FAIR OAK FM is *La Fairok*

1292 Ch. MARLBOROUGH FM is *Malleburgh* 1314 *Ass*, *Malborough* 1827 G. Probably of the same origin as Malborough *supra* 307. WATERSLADE FM is *Waterslade* 1333 *SR* (p). *v.* slæd.

Clyst St George

CLYST ST GEORGE[1] 138 C 11

Clyst wicon 963 BCS 1103, (*of*) *Clistwike* 1072–1103 Earle 265, *Clisewic* 1086 DB, *Clistwich'* 1200 Cur, -*wike* 1259 Exon, 1291 Tax, *Clystwik Sc͞i Georgii* 1327 *Ass*, *Clyst Sancti Georgii* 1334 *SR*, *Seynt Georgeclist* 1390 *FF*, 1396 Pat

v. wic. For the river Clyst, *v. supra* 3.

POUND LIVING is *Poundleving* in 1765 (D). *living* is fairly common in minor names in Devon and must be used in the sense 'holding of land,' 'tenement' (*v.* NED *s.v. living* sb. 4 *b*). The *pound* may be the rent or value of the tenement.

BUSH HAYS FM is *Bushayes* 1655 *Deed* and is to be associated with the family of John de *la Bussey* (1228 FF). KENNIFORD FM is *Keneford* 1276 Exon (p), *Kentford* 1547 *FF*. MARSH BARTON

---

[1] BCS 1103 gives us the bounds of *Clystwicon*. In later days *Clystwike* is clearly to be identified with Clyst St George but the -*on* form in OE looks like a dative plural form and suggests that the land in question may be the present parishes of Clyst St Mary and Clyst St George. If so, we may start the boundaries at the Clyst at the north-west corner of Clyst St Mary and go up to the *ealdan dic*, perhaps the present Mill Leat, then on to the *stræt*, the old Exeter-Lyme Regis Roman road to *sicgan mores heafod* and so by the *ealdan dic* to *grendel*, i.e. Grindle Brook, and then along the *grendel* to the old ford. The parish boundary here keeps close to Grindle Brook and cuts it where a ford is still marked, just above Greendale Fm. We cannot hope to identify the *wiðig pytt* or *wiðig þyfel*. From there it goes to the *ealdan dic* and so to *grendel* again, to (? *of* for *oð*) the red cliff and thence to the blind spring and so to the 'clean splott' where it is travelling south. This carries us round the western projection of Clyst St Mary parish to the spot where the boundary of Clyst St George turns south, where there is still a boundary stone. It goes past a *stanbeorh* and then due west to the old *weg* or road. This is clearly the southern boundary of Clyst St George which goes due west and strikes the road from Clyst to Exmouth. From the old road it goes to the old thornbush and thence due west across the *mor* or marsh to the road or *weg* on the south side of the long *dic* and so to *grendel*. The boundary turns west just by Ebford and makes its way across marshy ground (cf. Marsh Barton) to the road from Topsham Bridge to the Clysts. The relation of the bounds of the charter to those of the present parishes is not very clear after this. As the Clyst is not mentioned, they must have run along a line east of that stream. They pass the *wiðig*-row (cf. Winslade close by, which may be for earlier *wiðigslæd*) and then once more strike the Grindle Brook, and so back to Clyst.

is *Mershe* 1334 *SR* and gave name to John de *Marisco* (1203 FF). Possibly it is the place called *Hunts marshes al. Saltemarshes* 1634 BM. PYTTE is *Pytte* 1525 *SR*.

Clyst St Mary

CLYST ST MARY 138 B 11

Clist(e) Sancte Marie 1242 Fees 763, 1291 Tax, 1344 Exon, *Seynt Mary Clyst* 1544 *Recov*

For the river Clyst, *v. supra* 3.

BISHOP'S CLYST is *æt clist, of*[1] *Clist land* 1050–73 Earle, *Clist(a)* 1086 DB, 1232 FF, 1242 Fees 774, *Clist Sechevill* 1267 Pat, *Clyst Episcopi* 1276 Exon, *Clyst Secthevylle* 1282 FF, *Bysshopus-clist* 1339 *Ass*. The manor was held by Ralph de *Sicca Villa* in 1242 (Fees 774), but in 1267 he was forced to sell it to the Bishop of Exeter to raise money for debts owing to the Jews (cf. Pat 1267).

GREENDALE

Grendel c. 1180 Oliver, 1276 Exon (p), 1314 *Ass*, 1454 Oliver
Grendale 1199 ChR, 1320 Exon
Grendil c. 1200 (15th) *Torre*, -*dyl* 1291 Tax
Grendulf c. 1200 (15th) *Torre*
Grindel 1238 *Ass* (p), 1275 RH, *Grindulle* 1316 Inq aqd -*dell* c. 1630 Pole
Grendelf 1286, 1296 *SR* (p)
Grendel Serla juxta Clist Scē Marie 1314 *Ass*
Greyndel 1330 *SR* (p)

v. Grindle Brook *supra* 6. The forms *Grendulf* and *Grendelf* are probably to be explained by association with OE (*ge*)*delf,* 'place hollowed out.' The identity of *Serla* is unknown.

CLYST ST MARY BRIDGE (6″) is (*ad*) *pontem de Clist* 1238 *Ass*. SHEPHERD'S FM is to be associated with the family of Roger *Shephurd* (1333 *SR*). WINSLADE HO is *Wydeslade* 1330 *SR* (p). 'The wide slæd' or 'the withy slæd', *v.* wiðig, cf. Winslade *supra* 107. See also *supra* 585 n. 1.

[1] Corrected from MS., not *ofer* as in Earle (F. R.-T.)

Colaton Raleigh

COLATON RALEIGH 139 G 1

(*of*) *Colatune,* (*of*) *Colatunes gildscipe* 1072–1103 Earle 265,
Coleton(*a*) 1086 DB *et passim,* (*Ralegh*) 1316 FA, 1395 Exon,
(*Rayleghe*) 1378 Exon, *Colyton Rawley* 1680 Wills
Colinton 1230 Ch, *Colletone* 1280 Exon

'*Cola*'s farm,' *v.* tun. Cf. Collacott *supra* 50. Wimundus de
Ralegh held the manor in 1242 (Fees 783).

DOTTON FM is *Dodinton* 1201 FF, 1238 *Ass, -ingthon'* 1242 Fees
763, *Dodeton* 1242 Fees 787, 1303 FA, *Dotetone* 1441 IpmR. This
is almost certainly the DB manor of *Otrit* (i.e. by the Otter)
which was held TRE by one *Dodo* (*Dode* Exch). Hence, '*Dodo*'s
or *Dode*'s farm,' *v.* ingtun.

DRUPE FM (6″) is *Thorp* 1388 IpmR, *Droope* 1679 *Recov,* and was
the home of William *atte Thrope* 1330 *SR.* This name is interesting as being the only example of OE þorp which has
been noted in Devon.

HAWKERLAND is *Haueker*(*e*)*sland* 1227 Ch, 1316 Ipm, *Haueker-
land* 1238 *Ass, Hauekareland'* 1242 Fees 793 and must take its
name from some early owner called (*le*) *Hauekere,* i.e. 'the
hawker' or 'falconer.'

STOWFORD

Stauford c. 1200 (15th) *Torre, Staford'* 1242 Fees 763, 782
Nitherstoford juxta Buketon 1311 *Ass, Nether Stofford* 1331
Orig
Stouford 1303 FA, 1330 *SR* (p), 1341 Ipm, *Netherstoweford*
1309 Orig, *Stoweford juxta Bukyngton* 1426 *FF*

v. Stowford *supra* 41.

FARRANTS FM, HARDYS FM and SCOTT'S COTTAGE (all 6″) are
probably to be associated with the families of Richard, William,
and John *Ferrant* (1524 *SR*), John *Hardy* (1647 Wills) and
Richard and John *Scott* (1524 *SR*).

BLACKBERRY FM is *Blakeburgh*(*e*) 1227 Ch (p), 1303 FA, 1333
SR (p), *-bergh'* 1242 Fees 762, 794, 1249 *Ass* (p). 'Black hill,'

v. beorg. KINGSTON is *Kingeston* 1227 Ch, 1249 *Ass* (p), *Kyng-*
1377 Cl, *Kyngston in parochia de Colaton Raylygh* 1563 *Deeds
Enrolled.* 'King's farm,' *v.* tun. Colaton was a royal manor in
1086 (DB f. 96 *b*). NAPS LANE (6″) is *Knapps* 1670 *Recov. v.*
cnæpp. OWLESHAYES FM is *Owlishayes* 1796 *Recov.* For *hayes,*
v. supra 129. STONEYFORD is *Stonyford* 1827 G. WINKLEY FM
(6″) is *Wynkelegh* c. 1200 (15th) *Torre* (p), 1333 *SR* (p). Probably '*Wineca*'s leah.'

Farringdon

FARRINGDON 138 B 12

> *Ferentona, Ferhendona* 1086 DB
> *Ferendon(e)* 1234 Fees 399, t. Ed 1 Exon, 1291 Tax
> *Ferndon* 1242 Fees 763, 790, 1303 FA, 1310–15 Ipm, 1313
>   *Ass,* (*by Aylesbeare*) 1327 Banco
> *Farndon(e)* 1310–15 Ipm, 1321, 1372 Exon, *Faryngdone* 1310–
>   15 Ipm, *Farindon* 1313 *Ass*
> *Ferringdon* 1502 Pat

'Bracken hill,' *v.* fearn, dun. For the development, cf.
Faringdon (Berks).

CREELY BARTON is *Crauelec* 1086 DB, *Crauleg* 1228 Ch, *Creulegh*
1242 Fees 763, *Croulegh(e)* 1291 Tax, 1325 Ipm, 1326 Cl, *Crow-
legh* c. 1630 Pole, *Clyst Crewelegh* 1303 FA. 'Crow leah,' *v.*
Introd. xxxiii. The place is actually on the Grindle Brook, a
tributary of the Clyst.

DENBOW FM is *Denbowe* 1700 *FF.* The name is probably to be
traced to John *Denbaude* and his wife, who were granted a
licence for a private oratory at their manor in *parochia de Faren-
done* in 1386 (Exon). The same family (*Denebaut, -baud*) held
manors in East Budleigh Hundred in 1346 (FA).

ELLIOTT'S FM, WALDRON'S FM and WARES FM (all 6″) are probably to be associated with the families of Walter *Eliot* (1330 *SR*),
Humfrey *Walrond* (1524 *SR*), and John *Ware* (1452 *Ct*).

HILL FM is *La Hille* 1242 Fees 763, *La Hulle* 1402 IpmR. SPAIN
FM is so spelt in 1739 *Recov.* UPHAM FM is *Uphome* 1545 *Deeds
Enrolled, Upholme* 1623 *Recov.* Probably 'upper ham.'

Gittisham

GITTISHAM [gitsəm] 139 D 2

Gidesam 1086 DB (Exon), *Gidesham* (Exch), 1249 *Ass et freq*
   to 1375 Exon, with variant spelling *Gyd-*, *Ghidesham* 1321
   Exon, *Gydsham* 1467 Pat
Giddesham 1238 *Ass*, 1242 Fees 762
Gitesham 1249 *Ass*, *Gitsame* 1545 LP, *Gitsam* 1675 Ogilby
'*Gyddi*'s hamm,' cf. Gidleigh *supra* 438.

GITTISHAM HILL is *Gydesham Mount* 1525 Oliver 395. It was
called *Bromdun* in 1061 (1227) in the land boundaries of Ottery
and was still alternatively known as *Broundon* in 1607 (DKR 38,
508) and 1667 (*Depositions*). The meaning was 'broom-covered
hill,' *v.* brom, dun.

RAPSHAYS FM (6″)

Oteri 1086 DB
Rappinghegh' 1242 Fees 793, *-yngsheye* 1301 Ipm
Rapelinghegh' 1242 Fees 762, *Rapelingheghes* 1289 *Ass*, *-ynge-*
   heghes 1334 *Ass*, *-yngheyes* 1350 Ipm
Raplyngheghen juxta Bukerel 1294 *Ass*, *Raplingesheyes* 1313
   Ass

The first element in this *hays*-name is probably, as is usual,
a surname belonging to the ME period. It may be suggested
that it is the OE *ræpling*, 'captive,' used first as a nickname, then
as a surname. *v.* Hayne *supra* 129.

HALL'S FM, QUICK'S PLANTATION (6″), SHERMAN'S FM and
TRUANCES (6″) are probably to be associated with the families of
Hall (1689, 1701, 1731 Wills), John *Quyk* (1452 *Ct*), Richard
Sherman of Ottery (1524 *SR*) and Richard *Trewant* of Ayles-
beare (1582 *SR*). *Truances* must be for *Trewant's's* with a second
genitival *s* added later.

BEER BARN (6″), COMBE HO and HAYNE FM were probably the
homes of Richard *atte Bere* (1333 *SR*), John de *Combe* (ib.) and
Walter de *la Heghen* (1311 *Ass*). *v.* bearu, cumb, and cf. Hayne
supra 129.

CATSHAYES is *Catteshegh'* 1242 Fees 786, *-heye* 1314 *Ass*, *Cattyshayes* 1529–32 ECP 6, 195. *v.* Hayne *supra* 129. The first element is probably a ME pers. name *Catt* rather than the animal. NAG'S HEAD FM (6″) is so spelt 1765 D, and was the name of a well-known inn on the old coaching road (F. R.-T.).

Harpford

HARPFORD 139 G 1

> *Harpeford* 1167, 1230 P, 1244 *Ass*, *-fort* 12th France, *Harepeford* 1242 Fees 764
>
> *Helpefort* (sic) 1173 France, *Herpeford* 1212 Fees 96 *et freq* to 1289 *Ass*, *Herpaforde* 1262 Exon, *Herpford* 1292 Ipm
>
> *Hawford* 1675 Ogilby

The first element is doubtless OE herepæð, referring to the old road which crosses the Otter just to the north of the Exeter-Lyme Regis road (DA 43, 262). Cf. Harford in Crediton *supra* 405 and Harpford (So), *Herpoðford* 904 BCS 610, 1065 KCD 816, *Herpeford* 1236 FF.

WHITE'S LINHAY and WINTER'S FM (both 6″) are probably to be associated with the families of Stephen *Whita* (1330 *SR*) and Robert *Wynter* (1333 *SR*). For Linhay *v. infra* 592.

BOWD is *Boghewode* 1281 Exon, 1330 *SR* (p), *Boghwode* 1289 *Ass* (p), *Bowewode* 1345 *Ass*, *Bowood* 1566 DA 43. 'Curved wood,' *v.* Bowden *supra* 37. BURROW is *Burgh* 1566 DA 43, and was the home of William *atte Burghe* 1333 *SR*. *v.* beorg. HARPFORD BRIDGE is (*sub*) *ponte de Herpeford* 1259 Oliver 257. STOWFORD is *Stoweford(e)* 1281 Exon, 1396 Cl, *Stoford juxta Otery* 1294 *Ass*, *Stoufford* 1500 Ipm, *Stovord* 1566 DA 43. *v.* Stowford *supra* 41. WOOLCOMBES (6″) is *Wolcombe* 1566 DA 43. Perhaps 'wolves' cumb,' cf. Woolacombe *supra* 54.

Littleham

LITTLEHAM (with EXMOUTH)[1] 138 E 13

> (*to*) *Lytlanhamme* 1042 (13th) KCD 1332, *Litt(e)leham* 1242 Fees 764, 1291 Tax
>
> *Liteham* 1086 DB

---

[1] KCD 1332 gives us the boundaries of Littleham. These start at Exmouth and then go north to *Lydewicnæsse*, which must be the promontory now called The Point (*v.* næss). None of the other boundary marks can be identified with any modern names but the area covered probably coincides with that of the present parish of Littleham. *v.* Addenda, Part ii, xiv.

Further forms are unnecessary. The place was distinguished as *juxta Chekston* (1296 *Ass*), *Brodeham* (1340 *Ass*), *Exemuthe* (1346 *Ass*), *Wodebury* (1350 Orig), *Chikeston* (1371 *FF*) and as *Littelham Abbatis* (1316 FA). 'At the little ham(m).' *v*. Bradham *infra* 600. The abbot of Sherborne held the manor in 1086 (DB).

EXMOUTH is *Exanmuða* c. 1025 (*s.a.* 1001) ASC, (*on*) *Exanmuðan* 1042 (13th) KCD 1332, (*of*) *Examuða* 1072–1103 Earle 265. Further forms are unnecessary, but it may be mentioned that most of the early records of the name refer to the mouth of the river Exe and not to the town of Exmouth, which is of much later origin.

LIVERTON is *Luueretune* 1260 BM, *Loverton* 1270 *Ass*, *Leverton* 1301 Ipm, *Lyverton* 1440 *Cl*. Probably 'Lēofwaru's farm,' *v*. tun.

BROADWAY FM (6″) is *Broadwayes* 1714 DKR 41, 451. BULL HILL is *Bullhill* 1714 DKR 41, 451. This is the name of a sandbank in the Exe estuary, and may be descriptive of its shape. MAER FM (with THE MAER) was the home of Richard *atte Mere* (1333 *SR*). This is OE mere, descriptive of marshy ground rather than (ge)mære, since the farm is not near the parish boundary. MOUNTAIN FM is (*ad*) *Montanam* 1210 (1326) Pat and may have been so named because it is situated on high ground, *v*. Addenda, Part ii, xiv. ORCOMBE is *Orecombe* 1656 *FF*, *High Land of Orcomb* 1765 D. QUINTANCE (6″) is *Quyntynes* c. 1590 *CtRequests*, probably deriving from a former owner *Quintin*. RANDELL'S GREEN (6″) is to be associated with the family of John *Rondulf* (1330 *SR*). In 1452 (*Ct*) and 1524 (*SR*) the surname appears in the parish as *Rondell(e)*. SPRATTSHAYES is *Spratts hayes* 1683 *FF* and probably derives from some medieval owner. For *hayes*, *v. supra* 129. WEST DOWN FM is *Westdowne* 1667 *Recov*.

Lympstone

LYMPSTONE 138 D 12

Leuestona 1086 DB, *Leueston* 1249 *Ass*, 1285 FA
Lemineston 1219 *Ass*, *Lymeneston* 1254 *Ass*, 1336 Cl, *Limeneston(e)* 1291 Tax, 1336 Ipm, 1377 *SR*, -*nys*- 1308, 1347 Exon, -*nis*- 1388 Seld 32

Leveneston 1238 *Ass*, 1242 Fees 764, 1321 Ipm, 1369 *FF*,
   1386 *Ass*, 1397 Pat, (*Wodebury juxta*) 1322 *Ass*, *Leveny-*
   ston(e) 1308–14 Exon, 1356 *Ass*
Lewenestune 1268 Ipm
Luveneston(e) 1275 RH, 1301 Misc, 1308–14 Exon, 1316 FA,
   1328 Exon, 1334 *SR*
Limestone 1434 Exon, *Leningston now called Limpston* c. 1630
   Pole, *Lympstone al. Lymson* 1726 *Recov*

This is a difficult name. Ekwall (RN 245), with fewer forms,
suggested that it contained a British place-name parallel to the
Gaulish *Lemonum*, but it is difficult to see how, if we start from
a first element in *Lem-*, we can get all the later forms with *Leu-*,
Lev-, *Luv-* side by side with *Lem-*, *Lim-*. If we start with an OE
Lēofwinestun, all the early forms except the second series given
above can readily be explained. With regard to that series it may
well be that OE *Lēofwinestun* developed with nasal assimilation
forms *Lem(e)neston*, *Lim(e)neston* (cf. the history of OE *efn* and
hræfn becoming *emn* and *hremn*). See also Limscott *supra* 134.

Linhayes Fm (6″) is *Lennehays* 1501 *Ct*. This is the word *linhay*
(local *linney*), 'shed or open building,' 'farm building for cattle
or provender,' *v.* NED and EDD *s.v.*. The word is in common
use in Devon with the above meanings.

Coombe Fm, Sowden and Thorn Fm (6″) were probably the
homes of Godwin de *Cumbe* (1219 *Ass*), Herlewyn *Bysouthedon*,
i.e. 'south of the down' (1330 *SR*), and William *atte Thorne* (ib.).
The second is *Southdon* in 1429 (IpmR).

Backenhays (6″) is *Backynghay* 1356 *Ass*, *Backynheys* 1501 *Ct*.
Potter's Fm (6″) is to be associated with the family of Robert
Potter (1452 *Ct*). Watton Fm (6″) is *Wottone* 1330 *SR* (p).
Probably 'farm by the wood,' *v.* wudu, tun.

Newton Poppleford

Newton Poppleford 139 G 1

Poplesford 1226 ClR, 1274 Ipm, *Popelford* 1257 Pat, 1259
   Oliver 257, 1285 FA, *-leford* 1306 *Ass*
Neweton Popilford 1305 *Ass*, *Nyweton Popelesford* 1341 Cl,
   Nywatone Popelaforde 1380 Exon, *Newton Popler* 1675
   Ogilby

The first element is OE *papol(stan)*, *popel(stan)*, 'pebble,' from the round stones, known as 'Budleigh pobbles,' found here. 'Newton' (*v.* tun) seems to be a later addition and it is not clear in relation to what place it was 'new.'

GOOSEMOOR is *Goosemore* 1622 *FF*. *v.* mor. LANGSFORD FM (6″) is *Langeford* 1330 *SR* (p), *Langsford* 1770 *Recov*. 'Long ford.' The *s* is probably a late insertion. NEWTON POPPLEFORD BRIDGE (6″) is *Nyutonbrigge* 1452 *Ct*. PARSONS FM (6″) is to be associated with the family of Philip *Person* (1330 *SR*).

Otterton

OTTERTON 139 H I

> *Otritona* 1086 DB, *-ne* 1156 France, *-nia* 1254 BM, *-toune* 1329 Ipm
>
> *Otrinton(am)* 1157 France, *-tun* 1210–16 HMC iv, 64, *Hotrintone* 1272 Exon
>
> *Otteritune* c. 1200 (15th) *Torre*
>
> *Oterinton* 1235 Fees 56, *-ingthon'* 1242 Fees 764, *Ottrintone* 1261 Exon, *Otringtone* 1291 Tax
>
> *Oterytone* 1261 Exon, *Otreytone* 1284 Exon, *Ottryton Monachorum* 1321 *Ass*, (*Otriton*) 1325 *Ass*
>
> *Auterton* 1577 Saxton

'Farm by the river Otter' (*supra* 11), *v.* tun. For the *-in(g)*-forms, cf. Tavistock *supra* 217. *Monachorum* refers to the monks of Otterton priory.

BREADON LANE (6″) is *Bre(i)don(e)* c. 1260 Oliver 252, 257, 1330 *SR* (p). This name may be a hybrid one containing the Celtic *bre*, 'hill' and OE dun. Cf. Brill (PN Bk 118).

HETHERLAND (lost) is *Lahedreland* 1205 France, *Hetherland* 1242 Fees 764, *Hederlonde* 1260 Oliver 256, 1291 Tax, *Hedderlond* 1303 FA, *Hetherlond* 1487 Ipm. For the interpretation, *v.* Hatherleigh *supra* 142.

PINN is *Penna* 1254, 1325 *Ass*, *atte Pynne* 1330 *SR*, *Punne* 1336, 1339 *Ass* (all p), *Pynne* 1481 *FF*. This is probably the word found in Pinhoe *supra* 443, though the spellings with *u* suggest later confusion with OE *pynd*, 'enclosure' (*v.* Piend *supra* 151). The name would refer to the conspicuous hill called Pinn Beacon.

MAUNDER'S HILL, PAVER'S FM (6″) and SMITH'S FM (6″) are probably to be associated with the families of Joseph *Maunder* (1730 Wills), James *Paver* (1786 Wills) and William *le Smyth* (1330 *SR*).

CATSON HILL is *Kattesden* 1196, c. 1280 Oliver 258. Probably '(wild) cat's valley,' *v.* denu. HOUGHTON is so spelt in 1540 LP. *v.* hoh, tun. There is a slight spur of land here. MUTTER'S MOOR. The surname *Mutter* has been noted in Devon documents but not nearer than Cotleigh (1524 *SR*). NORTHMOSTOWN is *North-myston* 1480 *Ct*, *Normeston* 1540 LP. 'Northernmost farm,' *v.* tun. It is situated at the extreme north of the parish. OTTERTON BRIDGE (6″) is *Otertonbrugge* 1480 *Ct*. PASSAFORD is *Paseford* 1330 *SR* (p), *Passeford* 1478 *Ct*. '*Passa*'s ford,' cf. Passaford *supra* 144. PITSON FM is *Pytteston* 1483 *Ct*, *Pytston* 1523 *Ct*. The first element is probably a pers. name, cf. Pitsworthy *supra* 207. RADWAY LANE (6″) is *Radewey(e)* 1237 Oliver 257, 1309 *FF* (p). 'Red way,' referring to the red soil here. SOUTH FM is identical with *Slough Farm* 1809 M, 1827 G. The farm is situated at the extreme south end of the parish and probably the name has been changed. STANTYWAY (6″) is *Northestynteway* c. 1520 *Ct*. Probably 'stony way,' cf. Stentaford *supra* 249.

Rockbeare

ROCKBEARE 138 A 12

> *Rochebera, Rocebera* 1086 DB (Exon), *Rochebere* (Exch)
> *Rokeber(e)* 1196 AC, 1242 Fees 763, 1260 BM, 1261 Exon,
>   *-bear(e)* 1261 Exon, 1275 RH, 1316 FA, (*juxta Aylesbeare*)
>   1322 *FF*, *-byar* 1316 FA, *Rokkebeare* 1452 *Ct*

'Rook wood,' *v.* hroc, bearu. To this day there is a strip of woodland by Rockbeare House called 'The Rookery' (6″).

REW FM (6″), SOUTHWOOD FM and WOODHOUSE FM (6″) were probably the homes of William de *Rewe* (1330 *SR*), Adam *Bisouthwode*, i.e. 'south of the wood' (1333 *SR*) and Peter *atte Wode* (ib.). The first is *Rewe* 1412 (*Deed*), 1553 (*Deeds En-rolled*). *v.* ræw.

ALLERCOMBE is *Allacombe Doune* 1670, *Allicombe* 1773 *Recov.* FORD FM is *La Forde* 1303 FA. GRIBBLE LANE (6″), cf. *the*

Gribble parke 1602 *Deed. v.* Gribbleford *supra* 143. MARSH GREEN is *Mershe juxta Huntebeare* 1420 *FF*, *Mershe Bawdyn* 1491 Ipm, representing the manor of Rockbeare held by *Baldwin* the sheriff in DB. PALMER'S FM (6″) is to be associated with the family of Richard *Palmer* (1333 *SR*). UPCOTT is *Uppecote* 1249 *Ass* (p), 1378 IpmR, 'higher cot(e).' WESTCOTT HO is *Westecote* 1330 *SR* (p). *West* perhaps with reference to Marsh Green.

Salcombe Regis

SALCOMBE REGIS 139 G 3

> (*æt*) *sealt cumbe* 1050–72 Earle, *Saltecumba* 1175 P, *-be* 1219 *Ass*, *Saltcumbe* 1258, 1275 Exon, *-combe* 1291 Tax, (*juxta Sidemouth*) 1320 *Ass*
> *Selcoma* 1086 DB
> *Salcombe Regis* 1717 *Recov*

'Salt valley,' cf. Salcombe *supra* 311. The manor belonged to the Dean and Chapter of Exeter from the time of the earliest records. It is said to have been granted to them by Aethelstan, but even if this is true it can hardly account for the addition of *Regis* which does not seem to appear before the 18th cent. *v.* Addenda, Part ii, xiv.

CHELSON is *Chevelest(on)* c. 1154 HMC iv, 47, 1249, 1278 *Ass*, *Chevelestun*, *Chevestun* c. 1175 HMC iv, 52, *Chevilstone* 1301 Exon, *Chiveleston* 1278 *Ass*. The name is identical with Chivelstone *supra* 319.

DUNSCOMBE is *Dunscomb* 1249 *Ass* (p), *Donescumbe*, *Donscumbe* 1301 Exon, *Dunsecombe* 1330 Exon. Probably '*Dunn*'s combe,' *v.* cumb.

TROW is *Trowe* 1282 DCo NQ 3, 47 and was the home of Agnes *atte Trewe* and John *atte Trewen* (1333 *SR*). 'At the tree(s),' the last form representing the weak plural, *v. supra* 130.

GRIGGS, ORLEIGH'S HILL and SKINNER'S FM (6″) are probably to be associated with the families of Henry *Grygge* (1524 *SR*), William *Orley* (1780 Wills) and Richard *Skynner* (1333 *SR*).

KNOWLE and SLADE HO were the homes of Adam de *la Cnolle* (1282 DCo NQ 3, 47) and Juliana *atte Slade* (1333 *SR*). *v.* cnoll, slæd. The former is *le Knolle* 1420 *Ct*.

MILLTOWN LANE (6") is *Mill Towne* 1689 *Recov.*

Sidbury

SIDBURY 139 F 3

(æt) *sydebirig* 1050–72 Earle, *Sideberi(a)* 1086 DB, c. 1150 *St Nicholas* (p), 1303 FA, *Sydebiry* 1262 BM, *-bury* 1316 FA *Side-, Syde-* are the regular forms except for *Siddebir* 1238 *Ass*, *Sudebiry* 1305 *FF*, *Sytebury* 1377 *SR*, *Sedebury* 1394 DCo NQ 3, 47

'burh by the river Sid' (*supra* 12). The burh is the earthwork known as Sidbury Castle.

BUCKLEY FM is *Bougcleve* 1301, *Bohe clyve* 1307 Exon, *Bowclyve* 1369 *Rental.* It is a compound of OE *boga*, 'bow' and clif, referring to the steep curved hill here.

BUCKTON is *Buckadun* c. 1200 HMC iv, 58, *Bukedune* t. Ed 1 Exon, *Buccadone* 1280 DCo NQ 3, 47 (p). 'Bucks' hill' or '*Bucca*'s hill,' *v.* dun.

BURSCOMBE is *Berrdescumbes heafod* 1061 (1227) *Ottery*, *Bridescombe* 1333 *SR* (p), *Bordescombe* 1369 *Rental*, *Burdescombe* 1394 *Ct* (p). Probably '*Beornrǣd*'s combe,' as suggested by Dr Schram. Cf. *Cerred* for *Cǣnrǣd* in DB.

EBDON FM is *Ylbedon* (sic) 1280 DCo NQ 3, 47, *Ybbedon* 1501 *Ct*, *Ebbedon* c. 1510 *Ct*, *Ibbe-, Ybbedon* 1524 *SR* (all p). '*Ibba*'s hill,' *v.* dun. The *lb* in the earliest form is probably an error. Cf. *on ibbanhyrst* BCS 208.

HATWAY HILL and COTTAGE (6") is *Hitteweye* 1301, 1308 Exon, 1330 *SR*, *Huttewye* 1330 Exon (all p) and is possibly to be associated with the family of William *Huytte* (1260 DA 7, 204).

MANSTON FM is *Manneston(e)* 1278 *Ass* (p), 1280 DCo NQ 3, 47, 1281 *Ass* (p), *Manston(e)* 1307 Exon (p), 1495 Ipm. '*Mann*'s tun.'

MINCOMBE FM is *Myncome* 1313 Exon, *Myncomb* 1325 *Ass*, 1330 *SR* (all p). Possibly the first element is the old name of the stream here—one of the upper branches of the Sid. Cf. Mine (Ekwall RN 293). Professor Ekwall suggests OE *minte*, hence 'mint-valley.' No certainty is possible.

PLYFORD FM is *Plefford* 1330, *Pleyforde* 1333 *SR* (p), 1369 *Rental*. 'Play ford,' *v.* plega. Possibly this referred to a spot where young animals such as otters disported themselves. Cf. Playford (St), *Plegeforda* DB.

RONCOMBE FM is *Roncombe* 1369 *Rental*, 1394 DCo NQ 3, 47, *Roncomb al. Runckcombe* 1564 BM. The head of the valley is on the parish boundary and the first part of the combe runs parallel to its course. The first element may therefore be the OE *rān*, 'strip or boundary,' discussed under Rhon Hill (PN Bk 55). Cf. *rancumb* BCS 724, a Devon charter.

SWEETCOMBE is *Swetecumb* 1249 *Ass* (p), *Suetecumbe* 1302 Exon. This may mean 'sweet valley,' *v.* cumb, with reference to its fertility or the excellence of the pasture. Cf. Sweetlands *infra* 650, and *Sweterigge, Sweteford* 13th *Canonsleigh*. But possibly the name is to be associated with the family of Thomas *Suette* or *Suete*, who was living in the parish in 1260 (DA 8).

SYNDERBOROUGH (6″) is *Synderburge* 1262 FF, *Sylderburthge* 1262 BM. This seems to be a compound of OE *sinder*, 'cinder, dross, slag,' and beorh, cf. Syndercombe (So), *Sindercome* DB, *Syndrecumbe* 1284 FA. The meaning of such a compound in this context is not clear.

BERNARD'S FM and CLAPPS HILL (6″) are to be associated with the families of Thomas *Barnarde* (1612 *SR*) and Roger *Clappe* (1333 *SR*).

BROOK FM is *la Broke* 1283 *Ass* (p), *Broke* 1350 IpmR. CORE HILL is *Corehill* 1595 *Deed*. COTFORD HO is *Coteforde* t. Ed 1 Exon (p), *Cotteford(e)* 1311 BM, 1394 DCo NQ 3, 47. '*Cotta's* ford.' FILCOMBE FM is *Filcumbe* 1301 Exon (p). Possibly we may compare Philham *supra* 79. FURZE HILL FM (6″) is *Forshill* 1244 *Ass* (p). HARCOMBE is *Haracumb'* c. 1200 HMC iv, 58, *Harecumbe juxta Sidemuth* 1340 *Ass*. 'Hare cumb.' KNAPP FM is *la Cnappe* 1280 DCo NQ 3, 47, *la Knappe in manerio de Sydebir'* t. Ed 3 *Ass. v.* cnæpp. LINCOMBE FM is *Lincumbe* 1280 DCo NQ 3, 47, *Northlyncumbe* 1301 Exon (both p). *v.* Addenda, Part i, lviii. PACCOMBE is *Pecombe* 1369 *Rental*. PIN HILL FM is *la Pynne* 1301 Exon, *Pynne* 1333 *SR* (both p). Cf. Pinn *supra* 593. SAND BARTON is *Sande, Sonde* c. 1175 HMC

iv, 52 (p), *Saunde* 1394 DCo NQ 3, 47, *Oversonde* 1418 Exon.
SANDCOMBE is so spelt in 1630 Westcote. SIDFORD is *Sydeford*
1283, 1299, 1316 *Ass*. 'Ford over the Sid' (*supra* 12). SNOD-
BROOK (6″) is *Snodbrocke* 1576 *Deed*, 1652 *Recov*. STARCOMBE
FM is *Sturcombe* 1763 *Recov*. The first element is probably OE
stēor, 'steer, bullock.' VOGGIS HILL FM is *Voggeshill* 1621 *Deed*.
Cf. Foxhill *supra* 539. WOLVERSLEIGH FM is *Wlvislegh* 1244 *Ass*
(p), *Wlves-* 1270 *Ass*, *Wolves-* 1407 *FF*. 'Clearing of the wolf'
or more likely 'of a man named *Wulf*,' *v*. leah. WOOTON COT-
TAGE (6″) is *Wotton juxta Sydebere* 1277 *FF*. 'Farm by the wood,'
v. tun.

Sidmouth

SIDMOUTH 139 G/H 2

   (*of*) *Sidemuða* 1072–1103 Earle 265
Sedemuda 1086 DB, *Seduine* 1156 France (error for -*mue*)

   Further forms are without interest except that the first ele-
ment is *Sede-* 1238 *Ass*, 1400 Cl, *Site-* 1311 Pat, *Cyde-* 1322 Cl,
Sude- 1342 Cl. Otherwise it is almost invariably *Side-* or *Syde-*.
'Mouth of the river Sid' (*supra* 12).

ASHERTON (6″) is *Ascerton* 1260 DA 8, 204, *Asterestone* 1316,
1317 *Ass*, *Asserton* 1420 BM, 1466 *FF*. Probably '*Æschere*'s
tun.'

BULVERTON is *Boluortone* 1260 DA 8, 204 (p), *Bolferton* 1330 *SR*
(p), *Bulverton* c. 1520, 1523 *Ct*, *Bulverton hyll* 1525 *AOMB*.
There is no ford near, so the otherwise plausible 'bull-ford-farm'
seems impossible. There are OE names *Buleferð*, *Bultfrið*, which,
from a form *Buleferðingtun* or *Bultfriðingtun*, might give rise to
a later *Boluortuna*.

COTMATON [kɔt'meitən] (6″) is *Cottemetone* 1260 DA 8, 204,
Cottamaton 1333 *SR* (p), *Cottington* 1789 Camden, and is possibly
a triple compound of cot(e), hæme and tun. Cf. Yettington
supra 582. The interpretation of a name *Cothæmatun* is difficult
but it might denote the farm of some settlers from cottages
elsewhere.

PEAK HILL is *Peke* 1260 DA 8, 204 (p), *Pykehille* 1501 *Ct*, *Peek-
hill* 1724 *Recov*. This is the OE *pēac* discussed under Peek *supra*
152. There is a prominent hill here.

Woolbrook is *Ulebrok* 1244 *Ass* (p), *Ullebrocke* 1272 Oliver 258, *-ok* 1324 *Ass*, 1350 Ipm. The ME forms with *ll* favour a pers. name *Ulla* rather than OE *ūle*, 'owl,' cf. *Ullan crypel* BCS 624.

Avishayes (6″) is *Avelishayes* 1424 IpmR. For *hayes*, *v. supra* 129. The first element is probably the name of some medieval owner, cf. the surname *Avenel* found in Tiverton in 1244 (*Ass*), and Avishayes in Chaffcombe (So) *Avenelesheyghes* 1419 FF. Bickwell Fm (6″) is *Bekewelle* 1260 DA 8, 204 (p), *Buckwyll* 1525 *AOMB*. Probably '*Beocca*'s spring,' *v.* wielle, cf. Abbots Bickington *supra* 124. Boughmore (6″) is *Bogmore* 1267 Oliver 259, *Boghemore* 1351 *Ass*. 'Curved mor,' *v.* Bowden and Bommertown *supra* 37, 343.

Venn Ottery

Venn Ottery 139 F 1

Fenotri 1158 P, 1259 Oliver 257, 1269 Exon
Fenoteri 1212 Fees 95, *Fenhoterhy* 1299 Ipm, *Fennotery juxta Herpeford* 1346 *Ass*
Venawtrie 1606 *Deed*, *Autery* 1675 Ogilby

The name must have originally referred to some marshy land by or near the Otter (*supra* 11). *v.* fenn.

Elwill Dairy (6″) was the home of Richard de *Ellewille* (1333 SR). The site is so close to the southern *ellenford* of the Ottery charter (*v. infra* 603 n.) that we are probably right in assuming that the ford was on the wielle or stream and that both alike take their names from an ellen or elder tree. *v.* Addenda, Part ii, xiv.

Naplease Goyle (6″) must be near the spot referred to as *Knapdoune* in 1307 (Ipm), *v.* cnæpp. 'Goyle' must be the dialect word *goyle*, 'a deep trench or ravine' (*v.* NED *s.v.*). It is a fairly common element in south-east Devon place-names, though no example has been met with in early records. This is probably the same as the words *gole*, *gool*, *gull*, 'stream, gully, chasm,' referred by the NED to OFr *gole*, *goule*, 'throat,' found in Goole (PN SWY 148) and in *la Goule* (1347 Ipm) in Mudford Tracy (So).

Hoppings Fm (6″) is to be associated with the family of John *Hoppyng* of Colaton (1524 *SR*). Lynch Head (6″) is *the Lynche*

1566 DA 43. *v.* hlinc. SOUTHERTON is *Sowthetoune, Sowth Fenottery* 1566 DA 43. It lies south of Venn Ottery, *v.* tun.

Withycombe Raleigh

WITHYCOMBE RALEIGH   138 E 12

> *Widecoma* 1086 DB, *-cumbe* 1238 *Ass, Wydecome* 1273 BM, *-comb(e)* 1281 *Ass,* 1303 FA, *Widecombe Ralegh* 1465 IpmR
> *Wydicumb'* 1242 Fees 763
> *Wythycomb̃* 1334 *SR, -thi-* 1334 *SR, Withy-* 1340 *SR, Wythe-* 1377 *SR,* 1440 *Cl, Withecombralegh* 1527 *Recov.*

'Withy valley,' cf. Widdecombe *supra* 526. The manor was held by Walter de *Clavile* in DB (f. 112 *b*) but had passed to the *Ralegh* family by 1303 (FA).

BRADHAM FM (6″) is *Bradeham* 1167, 1172 P, c. 1210–16 HMC iv, 64, *(Regis)* 1176 P, *(in Widecumb)* 1212 *St Nicholas, Bradenham* 1230 P, *Brodeham* 1275 RH *(juxta Lytelham)* 1327 *Ass.* 'Wide' or 'large ham(m).' This was originally a *royal* manor till 1205, when it was granted by King John to St Nicholas priory, Exeter. 'Broad' in contrast to the adjacent Littleham.

BYSTOCK is *Boystok(e)* 1242 Fees 783, 1244 *Ass* (p), 1269 Exon, 1291 Tax, 1440 *Cl, -ock* 1303 FA, *Buystok* 1400 Pat. *Boy*-names have already been dealt with *s.n.* Boycott (PN Wo 304), where it is suggested that these names may contain early examples of the word *boy*, which hitherto has not been noted before c. 1300 as a significant word. To the names there given we may add Boyton (Co), DB *Boietune,* and *Boiemulna,* the old name of Iffley Mill (O), found in *Cartae Antiquae* c. 1185.

HULHAM

> *Haldeham* 1219 FF (p)
> *Holeham* 1219, 1254 *Ass* (p), *Hollehamme* 1244 *Ass*
> *Holdeham* 1262 Ipm, *Holdham* 1324 Ipm, 1377 IpmR
> *Hulham al. Holdham* c. 1630 Pole

This is a difficult name. It may be a compound of the OE adjective *heald,* 'sloping,' and hamm, hence 'sloping enclosure,' i.e. on sloping ground.

PRATTSHIDE (lost) is *Pratteshithe* c. 1250 NGl 5, 40, *-heth* 1268

NGl 5, 45, -*hide* 1287 NGl 5, 83, (*in parochia de Wydecombe*) 1329 Exon, *Pratsyde near Exmouth* 1327 NGl 5, 122, *Prattishedd* 1542 HMC Exeter. '*Pratt*'s landing place,' *v.* hyð. The name may well be of ME origin. For *Pratt* as a pers. name, cf. *s.n.* Page Hill (PN Bk 46).

LOVERING FM and SYMONDS'S FM (both 6″) are probably to be associated with the families of John *Loveryng* (1524 *SR*) and John *Symon* (1582 *SR*).

ASH FM (6″) is *Assch* 1397 IpmR. LACKINGTON FM (6″) is *Lokynton* 1330, *Lokyngton* 1333 *SR* (p). Probably '*Locca*'s farm,' *v.* ingtun. MARPOOL is *Merpol* 1331 Orig, *Marepole* 1562 *FF*. 'Boundary pool,' *v.* (ge)mære. The place is on the boundary between Withycombe and Littleham parishes. GREAT WOOD (6″) is *Wode* 1524 *SR*.

Woodbury

WOODBURY 138 C 12

(*on*) *Wudebirig*, (*on*) *Wudeburg*(*e*) *lande* 1072–1103 Earle 264, 265
Wodeberia 1086 DB, -*byr*(*e*) 1242 Fees 782, 1286 Ch, -*biri* 1268 Ipm
Wudeberi 1175 P, *Wdebir'* 1212 Fees
Wddebir' 1205 France
Further forms are without interest except: *Wadbury* 1465 Pat.

v. wudu, burh. The name was probably first applied to the ancient 'castle' on the common here, round which there is still much woodland.

EBFORD is *Ebworthy in the parish of Wadbury* 1465 Pat, *Ebworthie* 1525 AOMB, *Ebbeford* c. 1630 Pole. '*Ebba*'s worþig.' The modern form may have been influenced by the fact that the Clyst here is fordable at ebb tide.

NUTWELL COURT is *Hnutwille* 1072–1103 Earle 265, *Noteswilla* 1086 DB, *Notewell*(*a*) 1167 P, 1285 FA, 1301 Ipm, *Nothoella* 1173 France, *Nottewill* 1301 Ipm, *Nutewill'* 1242 Fees 764, -*well* 1301 Ipm. 'Nut spring,' i.e. one near which these grew. *v.* wielle.

PILEHAYES FM is *la Pyle* 1306 Ass, (*in Woodbury*) 1351 Deed, atte

Peyle 1330 *SR* (p). This must be the ME *pile*, 'pile, stake,' in some sense. Cf. Pilemoor *supra* 420. For *hayes*, *v.* Hayne *supra* 129.

POSTLAKE FM is *Potteslak(e)* 1249 *Ass*, 1333 *SR* (both p), *Poteslake* 1374 IpmR. '*Pott*'s streamlet,' *v.* lacu. Cf. Postlip (Gl), *Poteslepe* DB.

WITHYHAYES (6″) is *Wetherisheighes in Wodberye* 1408 IpmR and is probably to be associated with the family of Alexander *Wither* (1238 *Ass*). *v.* Hayne *supra* 129.

WOODBURY SALTERTON is *Salterton* 1306 *Ass*, 1374 IpmR, 1413 *FF*. This cannot be 'saltern town' (cf. Budleigh Salterton *supra* 583) for the place is inland on a stream, above high water mark. It may be 'salters' farm' from OE *sealtere*, 'salter, salt worker.'

BASS FM, BOND'S LANE, BROWN'S FM, COOK'S FM, DANIEL'S CORNER, HALL'S COPSE and WEBBER'S FM (all 6″) are probably to be associated with the families of John *Basse* (1333 *SR*), John *Bonde* (1524 *SR*), William *Broun* (1330 *SR*), Raffe *Cooke* (1524 *SR*), Richard *Danyel* (1330 *SR*), Henry de *Halle* (ib.) and John and Thomas *Webber* (1524 *SR*).

BRIDGE FM and COOMBE FM (both 6″) were the homes of Emeric' *atte Brugge* and John de *Combe* (1333 *SR*). *v.* cumb. The second is *Combe* 1357 Cl.

BAGMORES FM is *Baghemore* c. 1200 (15th) *Torre*, *Bagmore* 1525 *AOMB*. *v.* Bagtor *supra* 475. The *s* is pseudo-manorial. CANNONWALLS FM is *Cannonwall* 1809 M. CLAYHILL FM (6″) is *Cleyhulle* 1330 *SR* (p), *Clayhill* 1714 DKR 41, 457. EXTON is *Exton'* 1242 Fees 763, 1305 Ipm, *Exeton* 1244 *Ass*. 'Farm by the Exe' (*supra* 5), *v.* tun. FORD FM is *La Ford* 1242 Fees 763, atte *Forde* 1327 Banco (p). GULLIFORD is *Goldeford juxta Wodebury* 1311 *Ass*. *v.* Gullaford *supra* 521. HEATHFIELD FM is *Hethfelde* 1330, (*atte*) 1333 *SR* (p). 'Waste land,' *v.* Heathfield *supra* 265. HOGSBROOK FM is *Hoggesbrok, Hokes-* c. 1200 (15th) *Torre*, *Hoggesbroc* 1256 FF, -*brok* 1330 *SR* (p). 'Hog's brook' or more likely 'brook of a man named *Hocg*,' cf. Hoggeston (PN Bk 67). ROCKHAM WOOD (6″) is *Rotcombe wood* 1525 *AOMB*. RUSHMOOR FM is *Rushmore* 1701 DKR 41, 190. RYDON FM is *Rydon mede*,

Broderydon 1525 *AOMB*. 'Rye hill,' *v*. dun. SUMMERLANDS (6"),
cf. *Somerhyll* 1525 *AOMB*. The names would refer to land occu-
pied as summer pasture. WOODMANTON is *Wodemetton* 1452 *Ct*,
Woodmanton 1525 *AOMB*. 'Woodman farm,' *v*. tun.

XXIX. OTTERY ST MARY HUNDRED

Otri 1084 Geld Roll, *Scē Marie Otery* 1238 *Ass*

v. infra. The hundred contains only the parish of Ottery
St Mary.

Ottery St Mary

OTTERY ST MARY   139 E 1

Otrig land 1061 (1227) *Ottery*[1], (*æt*) *Oteri* a. 1100 Earle,
Otri 1086 DB, c. 1145 France, (*Sancti* (sic) *Marie*) 1291
Tax, *Oteri* 1190 France, *Sca Maria de Otery* 1207 PatR,
Otry 1241 *Cur*, *Otery Sancte Marie* 1242 Fees 763, *ecclesie
Ottri Sancte Marie* 1269 Exon, *Otreg St Mary* 1275 Cl,
Otrei 1361 Pat

Autre Sct Maries 1577 Saxton, *Autrey*, *Austrey St Mary* 1675
Ogilby

The settlement takes its name from the river on which it
stands (*supra* 11) and was further distinguished by the dedication of the church.

[1] In the Chapter Library at Canterbury there is a 13th cent. facsimile copy
of an 11th cent. charter granting *Otrig land* to the Church of St Mary at
Rouen. The charter is mentioned in the HMC Report on the muniments at
Canterbury. Mrs Rose-Troup has had it photographed and placed at our
disposal, together with much helpful comment. The boundaries are as
follows: From *strætgeat*, probably the present Straightway Head (close to
Straitgate Fm, actually preserving the name) to *tælenford*. It must here follow
the old Roman Exeter-Honiton road till it crosses the Tale close to the present
Taleford. Thence up the Tale to the 'blind spring,' presumably the point
where the present boundary leaves the Tale and takes a sharp turn eastwards.
Thence to *dene beorg*, i.e. the barrow (by the railway) which gives name to
fields called Denbury, thence to *hæðfeld mere*, still surviving as Heathfield
Brake, a field close by, thence to *finan*, i.e. Vine Water (*v. supra* 15) and
thence to *otrig*, i.e. the river Otter. (There may have been some slight change
in the boundaries here, for one does not actually touch Vine Water now,
though it is very close at hand.) From the Otter the boundary goes to
strætford, probably a ford at the point where the Roman road crosses the
Otter, thence to the middle of *bromdun*, i.e. presumably Gittisham Hill,
thence along the *hoan* (sic) *weg*, i.e. the hollow way, to the 'red flood,' and

ALFINGTON is *Alfinton* 1244 *Ass*, *-yngton* 1382 Oliver 279, *Affington* 1381 *Rental*. Probably '*Ælfa*'s farm,' *v.* ingtun. Cf. Alphington *supra* 422.

BELBURY CASTLE (old camp) is *bigulfesburh* in 1061 (1227) Ottery. The *g* is quite clear in the MS, but *ig* may possibly be for *ī*. If so the first element would seem to be the well-known OE pers. name *Beowulf*, cf. the spelling *biuulf* in LVD and the survival of the name as *Bowulf* in Devon in the 12th cent. (1195 P). The burh refers to an ancient camp here.

CADHAY HO is *Cadehegh* 1238 *Ass*, *-heye* 1309 Exon, *-heie* 1330 *SR* (all p), and is probably to be associated with the family of William *Cadey* (1249 *Ass*). '*Cada*'s enclosure,' *v.* (ge)hæg.

CHETTISHOLT (lost) is *cetesholt* 1061 (1227) *Ottery*, *Chettisholt* 1390 *Ct*, *Chettisholde* t. Eliz *LRMB* 191, *Chetisholte* 1612 (F.R.-T.). The name is interesting as being a compound of the type noted under Breadon *supra* 593, consisting in this case of the British word *cet* (W *coed*), 'wood' and OE holt, though one has the curious phenomenon of the first element being given genitival form.

thence south along the down to the *wyrtrum* as far as *wicgincland*. Here the present boundary goes along Landscore Lane (*v. s.n.* Landskerry *supra* 215) to Westgate Hill and then follows an old ridge road which continues south past Wiggaton (a name clearly to be associated with *wicgincland*, *v. infra* 607). Thence the boundary goes to *wæcces treow* (clearly to be associated with Waxway Fm *infra* 606, just to the west of the present boundary), the 'tree' having perhaps been replaced as a boundary mark by the present White Cross. The next point is *berrdescumbes heafod*, i.e. Hollow Head Cross at the head of the valley which gives its name to Burscombe in Sidbury *supra* 596. Thence it goes to *leofan dune*, the present Beacon Hill, and so southward to *cetes holt*, still recorded in 1612 as *Chettisholt*, i.e. the present Harpford Wood. Thence to the Otter, striking it at the *borstenan clife*. Thence it goes to the 'pinfold' and to the southern *ellen ford*. The present boundary here crosses the Otter and makes its way with several bends to the *hricweg*, probably the low ridge road which goes up past Metcombe. The next points *apolder treu*, *stanford* and *rægen ðornas* cannot now be identified but when the boundary goes from the last-named spot north to the *hearpað* we are clearly at Tipton Cross on the Roman road. The last stretch carries us along that road to *strætgeat*. The *geat* may possibly be the depression between the hills in the neighbourhood of Pitfield Fm.

The charter ends by defining the boundary between *wicgincland* and *otrigland*. *Wicgincland* is probably the south part of the present parish of Ottery. The points cannot be identified with certainty, except that *bigulfes beorh* is almost certainly Belbury Castle (*v. supra*).

CHINWAY HILL[1] is *Cheyneway* 1506, *Chyneway* 1573 *Ct*, *Chyne-waydowne* 1548 Moulton, *Chinneway* 1607 *Depositions*, *Chenyway* 1668, *Cheenway* 1670 *Rental*. The Chineway is the road which runs across the ridge here, and we may possibly have as the first element the word *chine* (OFr *eschine*) denoting 'spine, backbone.' Mrs Rose-Troup notes that the road goes to Gittisham and that that Manor was held (TRE) by one *Chinias, Chenias*. The history of that pers. name is unknown; it probably had a hard *k* but it may be that it represents a name with initial *Ch*.

CLAPPERENTALE FM is *Clobbere Thale juxta Fyneton* 1302 *Ass*, *Clobern Tale* 1381 *Rental, Clopernetale* 1573 *Deed*. The second element in this name is clearly that of the river Tale (*v. supra* 13) on which it stands. Presumably, as is so often the case in Devon, the various farms on its banks bore names distinctive of their owners or occupiers. This may point to some family nick-named the 'clubbers' from their fondness for using the club or cudgel. The *n* would be from the weak plural form. Later the name was clearly affected by the well-known *clapper*-bridge (cf. also Clap Mill *supra* 579).

FAIRMILE is *le faire mile* c. 1425 *Add*[2]. The name was probably given to an especially good stretch of the main Exeter road here in the days when even these were little more than muddy tracks. Cf. Fairmile (Sr), a part of the Portsmouth road near Cobham.

FLUXTON is *Flokeston(e)* 1270 *Ass*, 1291 Tax, 1308 Oliver 428, 1311 Pat, *Folkeston* 1289 *Ass* (p). As the name is only attested from post-Conquest times we may have a ME name *Floke*, of Anglo-Scandinavian origin, from ON *Flóki*.

HEATHFIELD BRAKE (local) is *hæðfeld mere* 1061 (1227) *Ottery*, *Hethfeldmere* 1339 *Ass, Heathfeld meare* 1612 (F. R.-T.). 'Waste land,' *v.* Heathfield *supra* 265. *me(a)re* is probably the OE (ge)mære, the place being on the parish boundary.

KNIGHTSTONE FM is *Cnitteston* 1238 *Ass* (p), *Knyghtiston* 1330

---

[1] Most of the early spellings for this name have been supplied by Mrs Rose-Troup.

[2] *Ex inf.* Mrs Rose-Troup.

SR (p), *Knythestone* 1378 Exon, deriving probably from the family of *le Knight* found in the parish in 1275 (*ex inf.* Mrs Rose-Troup).

LANCERCOMBE FM and LANE (6″) is *Lancercomb* 1333 *SR* (p) and is to be associated with *landscorhege, landscorebroc* in the boundaries between Ottery and Wiggaton in 1061 (*Ottery*). This is the OE *landscearu, landscoru,* 'boundary, landmark.' Cf. Landskerry *supra* 215.

RILL FM is *la Hulle* 1286 Misc (p), *Hill* 1382 Oliver 279, *Rylle* 1590 *Ct, Ryll al. Hyll* t. Eliz *LRMB* 191, *Rill oth. Trehill* 1763 *Recov.* 'At the hill,' *v.* æt and cf. River (PN Sx 123).

SALSTON HO is *Salveston* 1243 *Ass* (p), 1382 Oliver 279, 1524 *SR, Salfyniston* 1333 *SR* (p), and is to be associated with the family of Jordan *Saluin* (1281 *Ass*). Hence, '*Salvin*'s farm,' *v.* tun.

STRAITGATE FM is *Strætgeat* 1061 (1227) *Ottery, Stretyate* 1333 *SR* (p), *Streatyeat* 1612 (F. R.-T.). *v.* stræt, geat. The farm lies by the Roman road to Exeter. For the *geat, v. supra* 603 n.

TALEFORD is *tælen ford* 1061 (1227) *Ottery, Taleford* 1330 *SR* (p), 1612 (F. R.-T.), 'ford over the river Tale' (*supra* 13).

TIPHILL is *Tuphill(e)* 1381 *Rental,* 1448 *Bailiffs Acct, Tiphill* 1448 (ib.), *Tippehill, Brodetippehill* 1452 (ib.), *Typpehill* 1518–29 ECP 5, 538. *v.* Addenda, Part ii, xiv.

TIPTON ST JOHNS is *Tipton* 1381 *Rental, Tippeton* 1413 Oliver 278, 280, *Tuppeton* 1382 Oliver 279. These two somewhat difficult names should perhaps be taken together. Tipton lies low on a feeder of the Otter and probably contains the pers. name *Tippa,* found in various names (*v.* Tipnoak PN Sx 214). Tiphill is on comparatively high ground and *Tuphill* is probably for 'At uphill.' *Tuphill* would readily be transformed to *Tiphill* and it is probable that the influence of the not very distant *Tuphill* gave rise to such a form as *Tuppeton* for *Tipton,* while *Tipton* itself may have influenced some of the forms of *Tiphill.*

WAXWAY HO is *Wakeswey* 1249 *Ass, Wackesweye* 1322 *Ass* (both p), *Wakkesway* 1438 Oliver and must have been near the place called *Wacces treow* in the land boundaries of Ottery in 1061 (*Ottery*). '*Wæcc*'s way and tree,' *v.* **weg**. Cf. Waxwell (Mx) *Wakeswelle* 1235 *Ass*.

WIGGATON [wikətən] is *Wigaton* 1281 *Ass*, *Wygeton* 1289 *Ass*, *Wyggeton* 1333 *SR* (both p), *Wigeton* 1382 Oliver 279 and must have been by the land called *wigincland* in 1061 (1227) *Ottery*. '*Wicga*'s farm and land,' *v.* **tun, ing**.

WONSCOMBE HILL (local) is *Wonnyngescomb* 1330, 1333 *SR* (p), *Wynscomb* 1382 Oliver 279, *Wonyscumb* 1443 *Ct* (F. R.-T.). We may perhaps compare Wonwell *supra* 279.

BULLS FM (6″), HALL'S FM (6″), PUTT'S FM, SKINNER'S ASH FM (6″) and WOODS FM are probably to be associated with the families of Serlo *Bolle* (1330 *SR*), Walter *Halle* (1524 *SR*), Joane *Putt* (1712 Wills), John *Skynner* (1525 *AOMB*) and Alice *atte Wode* (1330 *SR*).

COOMBE[1], HAYNE BARTON, PITT FM[1], SLADE FM, THORNE FM and WARE FM were probably the homes of Henry de *Come* (1330 *SR*), Agnes *atte Heigheis* (ib.), *atte Heghen* (1333 *SR*), Geoffrey *atte Pitte* (1330 *SR*), Isabella *atte Slade* (ib.), Roger de *la Thorn* (1249 *Ass*) and William *atte Were* (1330 *SR*). *v.* **cumb, pytt, slæd, wer**, and cf. Hayne *supra* 129.

ASH FM is *Essche* 1238 *Ass* (p), *Asshe juxta Fyneton* 1324 *Ass*, *Aysshe* 1330 *SR* (p). BISHOP'S COURT is *Bishopps Court* 1657 *Recov*. The residence of the bishops of Exeter, who held the manor of Fluxton in Ottery. BLACKLAKE FM is *Blakelake* 1238 *Ass* (p). 'Dark streamlet,' *v.* **lacu**. BRADLEGH (6″) is *Bradlegh* 1449 *Bailiffs Acct*, t. Eliz *LRMB*. 'Wide clearing,' *v.* **brad, leah**. BREACHES (6″) is *la Breche* 1379 *Ct. v.* **bræc**. BRICKHOUSE FM is so spelt 1726 *Recov*. BURCOMBE FM is *Borecoumbe* 1305 Ipm, *Borcome* 1330 *SR* (p), 1381 *Rental*. Probably 'cumb by the burh.' There are two near here. BURROW HILL FM is *Burgh* 1382 Oliver 279, and was the home of Ralph *atte Burghe* (1330 *SR*). *v.* **beorg**. EAST HILL HO, WEST HILL COURT (6″) are so spelt 1691 *Recov*. FARWELL FM (6″) is probably to be associated with Richard *Farewell* 1486–1515 ECP 3, 135. It is *Farwells* c. 1660

---

[1] *Comb, Pitte*, 1382 Oliver 279.

Manor Roll. FENNY BRIDGES is *Saint Annes Bridge al. Fynee Bridge* 1553 *Deed. v.* Vine *supra* 15. GOSFORD is *Goseford* 1249 *Ass* (p), *Gosford* 1330 *SR* (p). ' Goose ford.' HOLCOMBE BARTON is *Holecumbe* 1244 *Ass* (p), *Holecombe juxta Gydesham* 1322 *Ass. v.* holh, cumb. METCOMBE is *Metcumbe* 1281 *Ass, Mettecumbe* 1381 *Rental, Met(te)comb(e)* 1382 Oliver 279. *v.* cumb. RAX-HAYES FM is *Rackehay* 1442 *Bailiffs Acct.* The first element may be the word *rack* discussed under Rack Street *supra* 23, but see Addenda, Part ii, x. RIDGWAY FM (6″) is *Rigewaye* 1389 *Ct, Rudgewaye* 1546, 1572 *Ct. v.* hrycg, weg. The road is locally still so named. GREAT and LITTLE (6″) WELL FMS are *Northwell* 1619 *Recov, Southwell* or *Greatwell* 1748 *Recov, Littlewell* 1677 *Recov.* At one must have lived John *atte Wille* (1330 *SR*). *v.* wielle. WOODFORD is *Wodeford in parochia Otery ƀe Marie* 1408 *Ass.*

XXX. HEMYOCK HUNDRED

Hamiohc, Hamioth 1084 Geld Roll
Hemioch 1187 P, *-iok* 1238 *Ass, -yok* 1249 *Ass*
Himeoc c. 1190 Buckland 291

v. Hemyock *infra* 616.

Awliscombe

AWLISCOMBE 129 G/H 2

Aulescoma 1086 DB *et freq* to 1535 VE with variant spelling *-cumb(e), Awelescumb'* 1221–30 Fees 1443, *Aullescombe* 1316 Ipm, *Auliscombe* 1339 *Ass*
Aurescumbe 1203 Cur
Houelescumb 1285 FA, *Ouliscomb(e)* 1303 FA, 1322 *Ass, Oules-* 1351 Orig, 1356 Ipm, *Owlyscombe* 1393 Exon, *Overaouliscombe juxta Honyton* 1394 *Ass*
Alscombe 1541 SR, *Aulscombe al. Alliscombe* 1706 *Recov*

Blomé (85) is doubtless right in identifying the first element in this name with the gen. of OE *āwel*, ' awl, hook, fork,' and the reference must be to some topographical feature which distinguishes the combe. Blomé takes it to refer to the triple fork of the river a mile from Awliscombe. It is more doubtful if he is correct in thinking that the river itself (now the Wolf) was actually called *Awel*. The frequent forms with *Ou-*, *Ow-* make any connexion with OE æwiell (StudNP 2, 92) unlikely.

COTTARSON FM is *Cotterilleshayes* 1622 *FF*, *Cotterallishayes* or *Cotterson* 1816 *Recov*, *Cottershaies al. Cottershene al. Cotterson* 1836 *Deed*. Final *-on* is a reduction of *hayne*. For *hayne* and *hayes*, *v. supra* 129. The first element is the pers. name *Coterel*, found in East Devon in the 13th and 14th cents. (*v. supra* 411).

GODFORD CROSS is *Codefort* 1206 ClR, *Godeford* 1227 Ch *et freq* to 1465 BM, *Goddeford* 1285 FA, (*juxta Aulescomb*) 1304 *Ass*. '*Gōda*'s ford.'

IVEDON HO (6″) is *Evedon* 1228 Cl, 1316 FA, *Ivedon* 1228 FF (p), 1244 *Ass*, *Yvedon* 1242 Fees 792, *Yevedon* 1303, 1428 FA. Probably from OE *Eofandūn*, 'hill of one *Eofa*,' a weak form of the recorded pers. name *Eof*.

WARINGSTONE or WESTON is *Weringeston(e)* 1227 Ch, 1282 *FF*, 1289 *Ass*, 1290 Ch, *Waringgeston* 1238 *Ass*, *Wyringeston* 1270 *Ass*, *Wetheringston* 1249 *Ass* and possibly takes its name from *Warin* who held a manor in *Oteri* of William (i.e. William Capra) in DB. Hence, 'Warin's or Waring's farm,' *v. tun*.

BENNETTSHAYES[1], BIRDS FM (6″), HAMLIN'S PARK (6″) and HUNTHAYS[2] are probably to be associated with the families of William *Benet* (1330 *SR*), Richard *Beard* (1333 *SR*), John *Hamelyn* (1330 *SR*) and William *Honte* (ib.).

MARLCOMBE (6″) is *Marlecumbe* 1227 Oliver, 1242 Fees 780, 1274 *Ass. v.* Malborough *supra* 307. RIDGEWAY FM was the home of Robert de *Rigweye* 1330 *SR*. SMALLICOMBE (6″) is *Smalecumbe* 1244 *Ass* (p), *-comb* 1303 FA. 'Narrow valley,' *v.* smæl, cumb. WADHAYS is *Wadehegh* 1238 *Ass* (p), *-heghen* 1285 *Ass*, *Wade-heyes juxta Aulscombe* 1310 *Ass*, *Wadeheghes* 1339 *Ass*. '*Wada*'s farm.' *v.* Hayne *supra* 129. WOLVERSTONE is *Wolveston* 1262 FF, 1293 Cl, 1350 Ipm, *Wuluyston* 1465 BM. '*Wulf*'s farm,' *v. tun*.

---

[1] *Bennettshayes* 1700 *Recov.*
[2] *Hunthayse* 1524 *SR.*

Buckerell

Buckerell 129 H 2

> *Bucherel* 1165 P, *Bukerell* 1221–30 Fees 1443 *et passim* with variant spellings *-el, -elle*
> *Bokerel* c. 1200 HMC iv, 59 *et freq* to 1316 FA with variant spelling *-elle*

This is a difficult name and it is impossible to tell whether it is more than a coincidence that we have parallels for the ending of this name in Chackrell *supra* 548, in Cheverell (W), DB *Chevrel*, 1249 Ipm *Chyverel*, Chickerell (Do), 1332 *SR Chikerel*, and Keveral (Co), 1299 FF *Keverel*.

Avenhayes (6″) is so spelt 1765 D. Colhayes is *Coleheia* 1238 *Ass* (p), *-hey* 1285 FA, *-heghen* 1346 FA, *-house* 1339 *Ass* (p). According to Pole this was granted by a de Pomeray to 'one *Cole* his cooke.' *v.* Hayne *supra* 129. Combehayes Fm was the home of Walter de *la Cumbe* (1310 *Ass*). Deerpark is *Deereparke*(*s*) 1663, 1669 *Recov*, formerly a 'chace' (Polwhele). Sowton is *Sutheton juxta Fineton* 1298 *Ass*, (*juxta Feneton*) 1311 *Ass*. 'South farm,' *v.* tun. It lies south-west of Buckerell. Splatts (6″) is to be associated with the family of John and William *Splat* (1524 *SR*). Treaslake (6″) is *Treslake* 1694 *FF. v.* lacu.

Clayhidon

Clayhidon 129 C 3

> *Hidona* 1086 DB *et freq* to 1428 FA with variant spellings *Hy-* and *-don*(*e*), (*juxta Hemyok*) 1304 *Ass*
> *Cleyhidon* 1485 Ct, *Cle-* 1495 Oliver 395, 1598 *Recov, Hydon al. Clehydon* 1539 CtWards

Possibly, as suggested by Blomé (86), from OE *hīeg-dun*, 'hay hill.' According to Polwhele the parish is remarkable for its clay.

Bolham Water is *Boleham* 1086 DB, 1227 Oliver 396, *Bolham* 1228 FF, 1346 FA, *Bolle-* 1215 Ch, 1242 Fees 786, 1256 FF, *Bollam* 1290 Ch. '*Bol*(*l*)*a*'s ham(m),' cf. *supra* 541.

Hole is *Holna* 1086 DB and gave name to William de *Holne* (1333 *SR*). The name is identical with Holne *supra* 301, 'at the holly.'

NEWCOTT FM

Nonicote 1242 Fees 786
Noningecot 1285 FA, *Nonyncote* 1299 *Ass*, 1346 FA, *Nonyng-cote* 1327 Banco, *Nonigncote juxta Hidon* 1299 *Ass*, *Nunnyng-cote* 1377 Cl
Nonycote 1303 FA, 1408 BM
Newcoote 1566 DA 43

Probably '*Nunna*'s cot(e)' or 'cot(e) of *Nunna*'s people,' v. ing. The development is without parallel and must have been influenced at a late stage by the adjective 'new.'

BATTEN'S FM, BELLETT'S FM (6″), CALLER'S FM (6″), CORDWENT'S FM (6″), DUNSGREEN FM, GARLANDHAYES[1], HOLMES HILL, JENNINGS' FM (6″), LOCKYER'S FM (6″), PALMER'S FM, SEARLES (6″), SHACKLES CROSS (6″), SHEPHERD'S FM (6″), SMITH'S FM, TROAKE'S FM (6″), TROOD'S COTTAGE (6″) and VALENTINE'S FM are probably to be associated with the families of *Batten* 1823, Robert *Bellett* 1810 (Hemyock ParReg), John *Calwe* (1330 *SR*), Thomas *Cordewente* (1615 Wills), Robert *Dunn* of Broadhembury (1670 Wills), John *Garlaund* (1333 *SR*), Simon *Home* (1330 *SR*), Roger *Jennynge* of Dunkeswell (1587 Wills), John *Lockyear* (1774 Wills), Roger *le Palmere* (1319 *AddCh*), John *Searle* of Hemyock (1613 Wills), Edward *Shackell* (1586 Wills), Henry *Shepherde* (1525 *SR*), John *Smith* (1660 Wills), John *Troke* (1548 Wills), John *Trod* (1333 *SR*) and Thomas *Valentine* (1699 Wills).

HEAZLE FM and WILTOWN were the homes of William *atte Hesele*, i.e. 'at the hazel' (1330 *SR*) and Richard Garlaund *atte Wille* (ib.). *v.* **wielle.** For *town v. infra* 676.

APPLEHAYES (6″) is *Aplynshayes* 1566 DA 43. Cf. Aplin's Fm *infra* 627 for this family name. For *hayes, v. supra* 129. BRIDGE HO (6″) is *Birchouse* 1765 D. FORCHES CORNER (6″), cf. Forges Cross *supra* 473. GLADHAYES FM is *Clodeheis* 1330 *SR* (p). GOLLICK PARK (6″) is *Gollakecoote* 1566 DA 43. *v.* lacu. *coote* is probably for *cott*, cf. the spelling of Newcott *supra* in the same document. GOTLEIGH MOOR is *Goteleye* 1274 *FF*. 'Goats' leah.' GRADDAGE FM (6″) is *Greatediche* 1566 DA 43 and was the home of William *atte Graddich* (1330 *SR*).

[1] *Garlandshayes* 1640 *Recov.*

Probably 'great ditch,' *v.* dic. HIDEWOOD LANE (6") is *Huyde-wood* 1566 DA 43. LILLYCOMBE FM (6") is *Lyllecombe* 1566 DA 43. LONGHAM FM (6") is *Langham* 1543 *CtAugm. v.* ham(m). MIDDLETON BARTON is *Middelton* 1244 *Ass.* 'Middle tun.' RIDGEWOOD FM (6") is *Rugewood* 16th Oliver, *Riggewode* 1521 *Recov.*

Culmstock

CULMSTOCK[1] 129 D 1

> *Culumstocc* 938 BCS 724, *Culumstok* 1244 *Ass*, *Cullumstok* 1249 *Ass*
> (*æt*) *culmstoke* 1050–73 Earle, *Culmestocha* 1086 DB
> *Columbstoke* 1675 Ogilby

'stoc(c) on the river Culm' *supra* 4.

CULLIFORD FM is (*on*) *culumford* 938 BCS 724, *Coliford* 1330 *SR* (p). 'Ford over the Culm.'

HENBOROUGH FM is *Hintebergh* 1238 *Ass* (p), *Hunde-* 1244 *Ass*

---

[1] The boundaries of the Culmstock charter (BCS 724) start from *hacapenn* (i.e. Hackpen) and go forward down to *secgwyll* and thence to *craduc* (cf. Craddock House) and along that stream to *culumford* (i.e. Culliford). The exact point of Hackpen Hill at which the bounds start is difficult to determine but since at the end of the charter they run due west along the edge to *haca-penn*, it may probably be placed in the neighbourhood of Park Fm. Craddock stands on a small stream, presumably *craduc*, but as the present boundary only goes near the house and never actually follows the stream, there must have been some adjustment of boundaries since Anglo-Saxon times. From Culliford it goes past unidentified *thornewell* and *bridewell* to the single oak, and thence along a *herpoð* to the middle of *heanhangra*. The unidentified points record the angles in the boundary here, the *herpoð* is the Tiverton-Taunton road along which the boundary runs for a time. It then passes Henegar and leads on to White Ball Hill, the *hwitan beorg* which comes next in the charter. Thence it makes its way direct to *fengel*. This is probably a stream-name (cf. Fingle *supra* 432), the present West Welsford brook. We cannot identify the old *geweorc*, *byrichangra* and *gyrantorr* which form the next boundary points, but the *hwyrfel* which follows is the circular hill (cf. The Whorl PN NRY 177) crowned by Black Down Common, where four parishes meet. After passing a thornbush the boundary goes east to *peon mynet*. The only eastward turn in the boundaries is a south-eastern one across Black Down Common to the end of a well-marked hill. This may well be *peon mynet*, 'end of the hill.' After that it goes straight to a *lacu* down to the Culm and from the Culm to an old *lacu* and then to Burgheard's *worþig* or farm. The two *lacu*'s are probably backwaters of the Culm just by where the present parish boundary crosses it. Thence we go straight to *rancumb*, i.e. probably 'boundary *cumb*' (cf. PN Bk 55 *s.n.* Rhon Hill), which may be the present Owlerscombe near the SE corner of the parish, and so west to Hackpen (as noted above).

(p), *Indeburgh* 1249 *Ass* (p), *Hyndeburgh* 1281 *Ass* (p), *-bergh* 1301 *Ass*. Possibly 'behind the hill,' *v.* beorg. There is a hill between this place and Culmstock village.

HENEGAR is (*on*) *heanhangran* 938 BCS 724, *Hanangre* 1249 *Ass* (p), *Henehangere* 1281 *Ass* (p), *Heanhangre* 1302 *Ass*. 'High slope,' *v.* heah, hangra.

NICHOLASHAYNE is *Nycolesheghe* 1305 *FF*, *Nicholeshaine* 1612 *Recov*, *Nicholson* 1814 ParReg and perhaps takes its name from an ancestor of *Nicholas* in the More who was living in the parish in 1373 (*Ct*).

WHITE BALL HILL is *Whitball* 1675 Ogilby and is identical with (*on*) *hwitan beorh* in the land boundaries of Culmstock (938 BCS 724). For *ball*, *v. supra* 211. 'White may refer to the white clay pockets in the greensand here' (*ex inf.* Rev. E. S. Chalk).

BARTLETT'S FM, BENSHAYNE FM[1], LIPPINGCOTTS, OSMOND'S FM, PURCHAS FM, QUANT'S FM, SOUTHWOODS FM (all 6″) and TUCKER'S FM are probably to be associated with the families of John *Bartlat* (1524 *SR*), John *Benet* (1301 Exon), Thomazine *Lippingcott* (1637 Wills), Thomas *Osmound* (1330 *SR*), Roger *Pochet* (1373 *Ct*), John *Quant* (1640 *SR*), John *Southwood* of Hemyock (1549 Wills) and Radulphus *Toukere* (1333 *SR*).

BOWHAYES FM, FURZE HO (6″), MOOREND (6″), SOUTHEY[2], UPCOTT[3], WOODGATE[4] and WOODHAYNE[5] (6″) were the homes of John de *Bogheweye*, i.e. 'curved way' (1330 *SR*), *v. supra* 37, Henry de *Forse* (1301 Exon), Nicholas in *the More* (1373 *Ct*), Sarra *Bysoutheya*, i.e. 'south of the water' (1330 *SR*), *v.* Yeo *supra* 17–18, Roger de *Uppecote* (ib.), Richard de *Wodeyete* (ib.) and Michael *atte Wode* (ib.). *v.* Hayne *supra* 129.

ALMSHAYNE FM is probably identical with *Almanisheghe* t. Ed 2 Exon (p), *Almysheghys* 1411 Exon, the first element being the ME surname *Almayne*. AXON FM is probably identical with *Iackesheghen* 1304 *Ass* (p). This name also contains as first ele-

---

[1] *Beneshayne oth. Bennettshaies* 1770 *Recov*.
[2] *Southey* 1484 IpmR.
[3] *Uppecote* 1373 *Ct*.
[4] *Wodyate* t. Hy 8 *SR*.
[5] *Woodhayn* 1524 *SR*, *Wodeheyghs* 1538–44 ECP 8, 58.

ment the name of a medieval owner, *v.* Hayne *supra* 129. HIGH-
FIELDS (6″) is *Hyefyld* 1524 *SR.* MAIDEN DOWN is *Maydendowne*
1661 *Recov.* MILLMOOR is *Mylmor* 1524 *SR, Milnemore* 1525 *SR.*
NORTH END is *Northend(e)* 1524 *SR,* t. Hy 8 *SR.* PRESCOTT is
Prestecote 1238 *Ass* (p), 1370 Exon, *Pruste-* 1339 *Ass* (p). 'Priests'
cot(e).'

Dunkeswell

DUNKESWELL 129 F 3

Doduceswilla 1086 DB (Exon), *Doducheswelle* (Exch)
Danekewell 1198 FF, *Dunekewill'*, *-kys-* 1221–30 Fees 1443,
   -well 1227 Ch, 1238 *Ass, Donekewelle* 1242, 1269 Exon
Dunekeswell(a) 1219 *Ass,* 1223 Bracton, 1233 Cl, 1238, 1278
   Ass
Dunkeswell 1234 Fees 399
Donecwell 1265 Pat, *Donekyswille* 1291 Tax
Donkewell, Dunkewell 1269 Exon

The first element is identical with that of Denes Brook (RN
119), which Ekwall takes to be either the OE pers. name *Dunnoc,*
a pet-form of OE *Dunn* or possibly the common noun *dunnock,*
'hedge-sparrow,' found in Devon (EDD). He suggests as a
further possible etymology a British derivative of the adjective
for 'dark' found in W *dwn,* Irish *donn.*

BOWERHAYES FM is *Bowrehays* n.d. Oliver 104, *Bureheghe* 1196
Oliver 394, 1206 ClR, 1215 Ch, *Borhaye* 1291 Tax. *v.* bur. For
hayes, v. supra 129.

BYWOOD FM is *Biuda* 1086 DB, *By-, Biwode* 1196 Oliver 394,
Biuuode 1285 FA, *Bywode* 1290 Cl, 1291 Tax. 'By the wood.'
There is still a wood just by the farm.

HOOKEDRISE is *Hokederis* 1215 Ch, (*La*) 1281 *Ass* (p), 1285 FA,
Hokederys 1292 *Ass, Hockedrys* 1346 FA. This name, as suggested
by Blomé (88), probably goes back to OE (*æt þæm*) *hōcedan
hrīsan,* 'bent piece of land covered with brushwood,' with the
derivative *hrīse,* 'brushwood,' from hris, suggested by Zachrisson
(*Englische Studien* 62, 96). The 'hook' may be the twist in the
direction of the valley at this point. The Rev. E. S. Chalk notes
a local pronunciation [rukəraiz]. This may go back to a ME
at ther hokedrise, cf. Rill *supra* 606.

ROUGH GREY BOTTOM is *Ruffegereihey* 1253 Buckland, *Ruffe-greihega* 13th Buckland, *Ruffegreydowne* 16th Oliver 105, *Roughe-grey Comon* 1550 *AOMB*. In 1253 (Buckland) Eleanor *Ruffere-gerey* held land here, so that we probably have here an example of the ME *hay* added to a pers. name, a common type of place-name in East Devon. *v.* Hayne *supra* 129.

SOUTHAYES FM was the home of Roger de *Suthheye* (1281 *Ass*) and William *Southeghen* (1333 *SR*). *v.* Hayne *supra* 129.

WOLFORD FM

> *Wlforthe* 1196 Oliver 396, 1206 ClR
>
> *Wilforcherch* 1205 ChR, *Wlferechirch'* 1215 ChR, *Wulfere-therth* (sic) 1227 Oliver, *Wulferchirche* 1237 Cl, *Wlfercherch'* 1290 Ch
>
> *Wullforde churche* 1496 Oliver 395, *Woolford Church* 1783 *Recov*
>
> *Wolverchirche Downe* 1545 *CtAugm*, *Woolverchurch Downe* 1709 *Recov*

The earliest form gives us a simple name for this place, viz. 'wolf-ford,' later expanded to 'wolf-ford church.' According to Polwhele "the name of Wolford church is sunk in that of Wolford Lodge. Near the house was anciently a chapel or church of which the walls partly remain."

MANSELLS (6″) and MUSGROVE'S FM are probably to be associated with the families of Cristofer *Mannsell* (1621 Wills) and *Mus-grove* (1809 Hemyock ParReg).

ABBEY WOOD (6″) is *Abby Wood* 1670 *Deed* with reference to Dunkeswell Abbey. BEANCROFT (6″) is *Beyn Crofts* 1539 Oliver 394. *v.* croft. CLEVE COPSE (6″) is *Middle Cliefe* 1670 *Deed*. *v.* clif. HUTSHAYES is *Hutteheies* 1330 *SR* (p), *Hutshaies* t. Eliz *LRMB* 191. *v.* Hayne *supra* 129. KNAP (6″) is probably iden-tical with *Bantescnapp* 1206 ChR. *v.* cnæpp. PARK, cf. *Parke-felde* 16th Oliver 105. PENN COPSE (6″) is *Olde parke al. Penn Wood* 1550 *AOMB*. *v.* penn. STEART COPSE (6″) is *Sterte* t. Eliz *LRMB* 191. *v.* steort. There is a tongue of land here between two valleys. STENTWOOD is *Stenetew(u)de* 1196, 1227 Oliver 394, *-wide* 1215 Ch, *Steyntewode* 1290 Ch, 1291 Tax. 'Stony wood,' cf. Stentaford *supra* 249. Trott's Down Moors (6″) is *Trotosdowne* 16th Oliver 104. *Trott* is a common surname near by (*ex inf.* Rev. E. S. Chalk). West Hill is probably identical with *Westdowne* 16th Oliver 105.

Hemyock

Hemyock [hemik] 129 D 2/3

Hamihoc 1086 DB, 1197 Cur, *Hamioc* 1204 Cur
Hemioch 1194 P, *-hoc* 1228 FF, *-yok*(*e*) 1244 *Ass*, 1267 Exon,
-ioc 1267 Exon, *-yoc* 1285 Ipm, *Hemmiac* 1212 Fees 98
Hymiok 1260 *Bridgewater Corporation MSS*

This, as suggested by Blomé (88), is probably a stream-name originally, going back to a British *Samiāco*. This is no doubt a derivative of *samo-* (W *haf*), 'summer,' and the name may have been given to a never-dry brook. Cf. such English names as Summerbrook, -well, etc.

Alexanderhayes is *Alysandreshayes* 1423, *Alexandreshayes* 1451 IpmR and is to be associated with the family of William *Alexander* (1244 *Ass*) and Thomas *Alysandre* (1333 SR). For *hayes, v. supra* 129.

Culm Davy is *Comba* 1086 DB, *Northcumbe* 1198 FF, *Cumb'* 1242 Fees 775, *Cumbe Wydeworth* 1281 *Ass*, *Combe Davi* 1285 FA, *Columbdavid* 1577 Saxton. *v.* cumb. William de *Wideword* (i.e. of Widworthy *infra* 632) held the manor in 1198 and *David* de *Wydeworth'* in 1242 (Fees). The modern spelling has been influenced by the river Culm near by.

Culm Pyne Barton is *Colun* 1086 DB, *Culum* 1242 Fees 786, *Colmp Herbert* 1285 FA, *Colmpyn* 1303 FA, named from its position by the river Culm. *Herbert* de *Pynu* held the manor in 1242.

Gorwell Fm is *Gorwilla* 1086 DB, *Gorewella* 1281 *Ass* (p), *-wille* 1318 FF. 'Dirty spring,' *v.* gor, wielle.

Mackham is *Madecomb* 1330, 1333 *SR* (p), *-come* 1349 *Ass* (p), *Matcombe* 1538–44 ECP 8, 11. Probably '*Mada*'s combe,' *v.* Madworthy *supra* 130. *Mada* would be a pet form of OE pers. names in *Mǣð-*, in this case probably *Mǣþhere*, judging by the early spelling of Madford *infra* 618. The two places are about a mile apart and may take their names from the same man. For the modern form of the name, cf. Stockham, Rockham *supra* 399, 602.

MOUNTSHAYNE FM (6″) is *Maundeuillesheghs* 1330 *SR* (p), *Maundesheghes* 1359 *Ass*, *Mounsheyes* 1566 DA 43 and is to be associated with the family of Robert de *Maundevill* mentioned in connexion with Awliscombe in 1299 (*Ass*). *v.* Hayne *supra* 129.

PEN CROSS is *Penn, Pen Cross* 1718 DKR 41, 543 and was the home of Elias *atte Penne* (1330 *SR*) and Richard *at Pen* (1524 *SR*). Blomé (89) would identify this with the *peon mynet* of BCS 724 in the land boundaries of Culmstock, but as has been shown *supra* 612 n. the two sites cannot be the same. We may have here the British *pen*, 'head, top,' as in Pinn *supra* 593, or else the OE penn, 'enclosure.'

SIMONS BURROW is *Simundesbergha* c. 1190 Buckland 291, *Symoundisburgh* 1360 FF, *Symondesborough Corner* 1566 DA 43. '*Sigemund*'s hill,' *v.* beorg. Cf. Symondsbury (Do), *Simondesberga* 1086 DB.

BROWNING'S FM, BUNCOMBE'S COTTAGE (6″), CHURCHILLS (6″), CLEMENT'S FM, CROCKER'S FM, ELLIS'S FM (6″), GOODALL'S FM (6″), HARTNELL'S FM (6″), JEWELL'S FM, LEMON'S HILL[1], LUGG'S COTTAGES (6″), PIKE'S COTTAGES (6″), POTTER'S FM and TOO-GOOD'S COTTAGES (6″) are probably to be associated with the families of William *Browninge* (1610 *SR*), Thomas *Bunkombe* (1699 Wills), John *Churchyll* (1524 *SR*), John and William *Clements* (1814, 1817 ParReg), Radulphus *le Crokker* (1330 *SR*), John *Ellis* (1657 ParReg), John *Goodhale* (1524 *SR*), John *Hartknoll, Hortknoll* (ib.), *Jewell, Juel* (1672, etc. ParReg), Margaret *Lemon* and Thomas *Leaman* (1633, 1636 Wills), *Lugg* (1692, etc. ParReg), *Pike* (1636, etc. ParReg), John *Pottere* (1333 *SR*), and William *Toogood* of Luppitt (1583 Wills).

BLACKALLER FM, BURROW HILL FM[2], COOMBESHEAD FM, HILL FM, MOORHAYES FM (6″), PITT FM and THORN BAR (sic) were probably the homes of Walter de *Blakeallre* (1244 *Ass*), Robert

---

[1] *Lemans Hill* 1811 ParReg.
[2] *Borowhill* 1605 Recov.

atte Burgh (1333 *SR*), Walter de *Cumbesheved* (1244 *Ass*), Richard *atte Hulle* (1340 *Ass*), John *atte More* (1333 *SR*), Robert de *la Putte* (1244 *Ass*) and William *atte Thorne* (1333 *SR*). *v.* alor, beorg, mor, pytt.

ASHCULM is *Aysshcomb* 1330 *SR* (p), *Aishecombe* 1566 DA 43. 'Ashtree combe.' The modern spelling has been influenced by that of the river Culm. CASTLE HILL, cf. *Castell Mote* 1566 DA 43. There is a medieval castle here. COLLINSHAYNE (6″) is *Collinshayes* 1752 *FF*, containing the pers. name *Colin* and the element *hayes* discussed *supra* 129. COMBE HILL is *Culmehill* 1605 *Recov.* 'Hill by the river Culm.' CONIGAR FM (6″) is *Cunniger* 1667 ParReg. This is ME *coneygarth*, 'rabbit warren.' CULMBRIDGE FM (6″) is *Columbrugg* 1281 *Ass*, *-brigge* 1304 *Ass*. DEEPSELLICK FM (6″) is *Deepsellacke* 1624 *FF*. Possibly we may compare Sellake *supra* 550. HACKPEN HILL is *Hackependowne* 1605 *Recov. v.* Hackpen *supra* 538. HOLCOMBE HO (6″) is *Holcombe Wood* 1566 DA 43. 'Hollow valley,' *v.* holh, cumb. HURCOMBE (6″) is *Hertecombe* 1330 *SR* (p). 'Harts' valley.' *v.* heort. MADFORD is *Madresford* 1281 *Ass*, *Madeford* 1400 Pat, *Mudford* 1635 *Recov.* Probably '*Mæþhere*'s ford,' *v.* Mackham *supra* 616. MILLHAYES is *Millesheghes* 1330 *SR* (p), *Myllehayes* 1566 DA 43 and is to be associated with Robert *atte Mulle* (1333 *SR*). NEWTON FM (6″) is *Newton* 1566 DA 43. OXENPARK FM is *Oxenparke Wood* 1566 DA 43. POUNDS HO (6″) is *the Pounde* 1566 DA 43. SHUTTLETON FM is *Sheteldoune* 1566 DA 43, *Shittledon* 1583 *Deed*. The first element may be OE *scytel*, 'dung,' or, less probably, the same as in Sheepstor *supra* 238. TEDBURROW FM (6″) is *Tedborough* 1566 DA 43. WESTOWN is *Weston* 1566 DA 43. 'West farm.' WINDSOR FM is *Wynsore* t. Eliz ChancP. *v. s.n.* Winsor *supra* 262.

Churchstanton

CHURCHSTANTON[1] 129 D 4

> *Estantona* 1086 DB (Exon), *Stantone* (Exch) *et freq* to 1291 Tax with variant spellings *Staun-*, *-tone*
> *Cheristontone* 1258–79 Exon, *Chery Sta(u)nton* 1282 Exon, 1285 Ch, *Chery and Staunton* 1285 Ch, *Cherystanton* 1338 Ipm

[1] Transferred to Somerset in 1896.

Churista(u)ntone 1258–79 Exon, 1312–16 Exon, *Churestanton*
1391 Cl
Chiriestaunton 1346 Pat
Churestaunton al. Churchestaunton 1512 *FF*

v. stan, tun. The first element is difficult. The forms are
hardly consistent with OE cyric, 'barrow,' or cyrice, 'church,'
and if the first element was, as is probable, added to distinguish
it from Whitestanton it can hardly be 'church,' as both villages
have churches. Perhaps the most likely interpretation is to take
it to be OE *ciris, cyrs*, ME *chiri, cheri*, 'cherry,' the place having
been noted for its cherries. It is clear that confusion with the
common *church* would arise early. That, and the influence of
initial *ch*, would account for the occasional *u*-forms. For such a
name cf. Cherryhinton (C).

BURNWORTHY is *Brene-, Bernewrth* 1238 *Ass* (p), *Burneworthi*
1330, 1333 *SR* (p). Perhaps '*Beorna*'s farm,' *v.* worðig, cf.
Burrington *supra* 362.

CHURCHINGFORD is *Suthchurchamford* 1386 *AddCh, Churcham-
ford* 1499 Ipm. This name must be a triple compound of cirice,
ham(m), and ford, the last referring to a passage over the Otter
here. There are the remains of an ancient church here, now part
of a farm building.

ACOMBE is *Accumbe* 1297 Buckland (p). Perhaps 'oak combe.'
BAGBEAR'S FM (6″) is *Baggebeare* 1330 *SR* (p), 1386 *AddCh,
Baggebereslane* 1386 *AddCh*. '*Bacga*'s wood,' *v.* bearu. Cf. the
same name *supra* 111. BEERHILL FM (6″) was probably the home
of John *atte Beare* (1333 *SR*). *v.* bearu. BISCOMBE is *Byscombys
clyff* 1525 *AOMB*. BRIMLEY HILL is *Bromlegh* 1238 *Ass* (p),
1330 *SR* (p), *Brymley, Bremleigh* 1566 DA 43. 'Broom clearing,'
v. leah. CLIVEHAYES FM is *la Clive* 1155–8 (1334) Ch. *v.* clif.
There is a steep hillside here. COURT'S FM, cf. Johan *a Corte*
(1525 *SR*). MUNTY FM may be connected with John *a Mount*
(1525 *SR*), the *y* being possibly a reduced form of *hey* (*v.* Hayne
supra 129). PAY FM must have been the home of Thomas Roger
a Pay (1525 *SR*). This may be associated with the pers. name
Paieheghs found in the parish in the 1330 *SR*. RING DOWN is
Ringdowne 1685 *Recov*. There is a circular hill here. SOUTHEY FM

is *Southehay more* 1525 *AOMB*. *v.* Hayne *supra* 129. It is at the south end of the parish. STAPLEY is so spelt in 1699 *Recov*. *v.* leah. TRICKEY is *Trikeheie* 1238 *Ass* (p). VENN FM is *Fenne* 1541 *SR*, *Venne* 1685 *Recov*. 'Marsh,' *v.* fenn.

XXXI. COLYTON HUNDRED

Culintona 1084 Geld Roll, *Colinton* 1167, 1168 P, *Culi(n)ton hundredo* 1175, 1183 P
Colmintona 1172 P

v. Colyton *infra* 621.

Beer

BEER 139 G 5/6

Bera 1086 DB, *Bere* 1242 Fees, 1275 RH, 1291 Tax
Beare 1303 FA, 1337 *SR*

v. bearu.

BOVEY HO is *Bouy* 1270 FF (p), *Bovegh* 1438 Exon. As there is no stream here, the name may be of manorial origin deriving from a man who came from Bovey *supra* 466.

Branscombe

BRANSCOMBE 139 G 4/5

(*æt*) *Branecescumbe* 880–5 (c. 1000) BCS 553, (*æt*) *brances cumbe* 1050–72 Earle
Branchescoma 1086 DB, *-coumbe* 1306 Ipm, *Brankescumb(e)* 1219 FF, 1310 Cl (p), *-kys-* 1297 Pat (p), *-om-* 1428 Exon
Brangescumbe 1238 *Ass*
Brankelescombe 1328 Exon
Brannescumbe 1342 Pat (p), *Braunscombe* 1376 Pat (p), 1408 *FF*, *Braynescombe* 1466 *FF*, *Brawnyscombe* 1525 *AOMB*

'*Branoc*'s cumb.' *Branoc* is a well-evidenced old Celtic pers. name, a derivative of *bran*, 'crow.' It should be noted, however, that *branoc* is also found as a place-name. Cf. *branok* (BCS 472) in a Somersetshire charter.

GAY'S FM, MARGELL'S HILL (6″)[1], SNELL'S PIT (6″), STOCKHAM'S HILL (6″) and STRANGMAN'S COVE (6″) are probably to be associated with the families of *Gay* (1686, etc. ParReg), *Marcle*, *Marckell, Markel* (1680, etc. ParReg), *Snell* (18th ParReg), John *Stottcombe* (1524 *SR*) and *Strangman* (1699, etc. ParReg).

HOLE, PIT COPPICE (6″), WESTON and WOODHEAD[2] were probably the homes of Ralph de *la Hole* (1249 *Ass*) and Thomas *Attahole* (1307 Exon), John fil. William *atte Putte* (1320 *Ass*), John de *Westone* (1307 Exon), Luke de *Bosco* (1280 DCo NQ 3, 47), and Lucas *Attawode* (1307 Exon). *v.* holh, pytt, tun.

BALDASH COPPICE (6″) is *Bald Ash Copse* 1797 ParReg. BARNELLS may be identical with *Bernhill* 1506 *Rental*, i.e. 'barn hill,' the *s* being pseudo-manorial. BERRY BARTON is *la Biry* 1301 Exon, *Bery* 1535 VE. The burh is the camp just to the south of the farm. BICKHAM (6″) is *Bykcomb* 1495 *FF*. Cf. Bickham *supra* 304. BRIMCLOSE HILL (6″) is *Browme close* 1525 *AOMB*. Perhaps 'broom close or field.' BULSTONE is *Bulston* 1506 *Rental*. CULVERHOLE (6″) is *Colverwill* 1330 *SR* (p). 'Dove spring,' *v.* culfre, wielle. EDGE BARTON is *(la) Egge* 1374, 1385 Exon. *v.* ecg. The place is on a steep hillside. ELVERWAY FM is *Elverway* 1792 ParReg. LITTLECOMBE BARN (6″) is *Lutelcumba* 1238 *Ass* (p), *Littel Combe* 1420 *FF*. LUGSMOOR LANE (6″) is *Luggysmore* 1525 *AOMB*, deriving probably from the family of *Lugg* which occurs in Colyton in 1330 (*SR*). ROCKENHAYNE is possibly to be associated with the family of John *Rocke* (1307 Exon). For *hayne*, *v. supra* 129. STREET was the home of William *atte Strete* (1333 *SR*). *v.* stræt. This cannot here refer to any Roman road. WATERCOMBE (6″) is *Watercombe* 1327 Banco. *v.* cumb.

Colyton

COLYTON 139 E 6

Culinton(am) 946 (12th) Laws
Colitona, Culitona 1086 DB
Culinton(a) 1086 BM, c. 1150 (14th) *Launceston*, 1159 P *et freq* to 1229 Pat, *Cullingthon'* c. 1225 HMC iv
Culigtun, Culitun 1193–1205 HMC iv, *Kuleton* 1219 *Ass*, *Culliton* 1356 *Ass*

---

[1] *Markel's Hill* 1801 ParReg.   [2] So spelt in 1797 (ParReg).

Colintun 1219 Fees, *-ton* 1220 Bracton, 1230 Ch, *Colyton*
1292 Cl

Coulitone 1237–74 Exon, *Cooliton* 1590 DCo NQ 4, 143

'Farm by the Coly river' *supra* 3, *v.* tun. For the *in(g)*
forms, *v.* Tavistock *supra* 217.

COLYFORD is *Culyford* 1244 *Ass*, 1263 Misc, *Culi-* 1274 Ipm,
Culliford 1356 *Ass*, 1675 Ogilby, *Coleford* 1275 RH, *Coliford
Burgus* 1495 BM, *Colyvert* 1538–44 ECP 8, 134. 'Ford over the
Coly river.'

COWNALLS LINHAY (6″) is *Cownell* 1597 *Recov*, *Counwell* 1649
ParReg. This is probably from OE *cūna-wielle*, 'cows' spring,'
the *s* being pseudo-manorial. The adjacent COWNHAYNE is
Couhayne 1591 ParReg. The name perhaps means 'cow enclosures,' *v. supra* 129. The second *n* is doubtless due to the
influence of the neighbouring Cownalls. Cf. Linhayes *supra* 592.

FARWOOD BARTON

Forohoda 1086 DB (Exon), *Forhode* (Exch)

Forwud' 1186–90 HMC iv, *Forewod(e)* 1199 FF, 1242 Fees
773, *-wde* 1275 RH

The meaning would have been 'before (in front of) the wood,'
but there is little or no woodland left in this part now.

GATCOMBE is *Gatcumba* 1086 DB, *Gatecumb(a)* 1175 P, 1242
Fees 791, 1281 *Ass*, *Gotecomb* 1282 Cl, *Catcombe* 1574 BM.
'Goats' valley,' i.e. where they were pastured. *v.* gat, cumb.
Cf. Gatcombe (Wt), *Gatecome* DB.

HOLYFORD FM is (*on*) *horegan ford* 1005 (12th) KCD 1301, *Horry-
ford* 1573, *Horriford* 1587 ParReg, 1809 M. 'Dirty ford,' *v.* horh.
The *l* must be quite recent.

PURLBRIDGE CROSS (6″) is *Puddelbridge* 1544, *Puddle-* 1549,
Pourl-, *Purle-* 1590, *Purrle-* 1623, *Porell-* 1650, *Pudel-* 1677
ParReg, and gave name to Richard de *Purlebrugge* (1330 *SR*).
The earliest form suggests that the place takes its name from a
bridge over a small stream called *Purle*. For the possibility of
such a stream-name, cf. *s.n.* Prill in RN 333. Some of the later
forms show the influence of folk-etymology in the attempt to
christen a very tiny stream.

STAFFORD is (*on nyðeran*) *Stanford* 1005 (12th) KCD 1301, *Estaforda* 1086 DB (Exon), *Staford* (Exch), *Stoford* 1306 *Ass* (p), *Stouford* 1330 *SR* (p). *v.* Stowford (*supra* 41). 'Nether' or 'lower' perhaps in contrast to the next ford up stream, now known as Holyford *supra* 622.

YARDBURY FM

> *Yhurdebur* 1279 *Ass*, *Yurdebury* 1420 BM
> *Yerdebiry* 1289 *FF*, *Yerdburye* 1408 IpmR, *Yeardebury* 1493 Ipm

v. burh. The first element is OE *gierd*, *gyrd*, 'rod, stick,' and the whole name may be for *gierda-burh*, 'fortified enclosure made with some form of wooden stakes.'

KNOWLE[1] (6″) and SLADE[1] were probably the homes of Cristina *atte Knolle* (1330 *SR*) and John in *the Slade* (1333 *SR*). *v.* cnoll, slæd.

COLE'S MILL, FRANKLIN'S COTTAGE, HAMLYN'S TANNERY, PHILLIPS MOOR, POPES CROSS, TURLING'S FM and WHITE'S FM (all 6″) are probably to be associated with the families of Walter *Cole* (1330 *SR*), John *Franckelyn* (1524 *SR*), Richard *Hamlyn* (1582 *SR*), Robert *Phelyppe* (1524 *SR*), Alicia *Pope* (1539 *AddCh*), John *Trullyng* (1524 *SR*) and Andreas and Johanna *Turlyng* (1539 *AddCh*), and Henry *White* (1524 *SR*).

BARRITSHAYES, BOLSHAYNE, BONEHAYNE, CADHAYNE (6″), COTTS-HAYNE COTTAGES (6″), DOWNHAYNE, FREAKHAYNE (6″), HOOPER-HAYNE, LOUTSHAYNE, LUGSHAYNE, PARKHAYNE, TRITCHAYNE (and TRITCHMARSH) appear as *Baretesheghes* 1306 *Ass*, *Barrasayes* 1585 ParReg, *Boltishayne* 1575 BM, *Bore(n)hayn(e)* 1539 *AddCh*, *Bornehayne* 1547 LP, *Cadeheghs* 1316 *Ass* (p), *Cadhayne* 1682 *Recov*, *Cowchehayne* 1539 *AddCh*, (*al. Cotchehayne*) 17th ParReg, *Dounheghs* 1330 *SR* (p), *Frekehayne* 1539 *AddCh*, *Hoberhayn* 1576 *Depositions*, *Howberhaine* or *Hooperhaine* 1741 *Recov*, *Lowdesayne* 1550 ParReg, *Lugsayne* 1572 (ib.), *Perkhayne* 1611 *Recov*, *Trycchehayne* 1539 *AddCh*, *Trutchmarshe* 1621 ParReg and are probably to be associated with the families of Walter *Baret* (1330 *SR*), William *Bolty* (ib.), Cristina *Bor* (ib.), John

---

[1] *Knoll* 1549, *Slade* 1525 *SR*.

Cada (1244 *Ass*), Robert *Couche* (ib.), Thomas de *la Doune* (1301 Exon), William *Vreke* (1330 *SR*), Ralph *Hobere* (ib.), Raynold *Lowde* (1541 ParReg), Robert *Lugge* (1524 *SR*), William de *Parco* (1330 *SR*), and John *Tricche* (1330 *SR*). For the meaning of *hayne* in these names, *v. supra* 129.

AXE BRIDGE is *Axebrig* 1228 FF. BLAMPHAYNE is *Blamphain* 1605 ParReg and is possibly to be associated with the *Blampyn* family (*supra* 578). COLCOMBE is *Col(e)combe* 1325 Misc, 1371 Exon, 1425 BM. *v.* Collacott *supra* 50. CROOKHAM is *Crocome* 1579, 1582 ParReg. ELM FM (6″) is *Elme* 1616 ParReg. GITTS-HAYNE is *Gytshayne* 1567 DCo NQ 4, 143. HAMBERHAYNE is *Hambrayne* 1538, *Ambershayes* 1614 ParReg. HAPPERHAYNE DAIRY (6″) is *Hapreheys* 1333 *SR* (p), *Haperhayn* 1547 LP. These three names probably derive from medieval owners, not traced. HEATHAYNE is *Heathehegh* 1330 *SR* (p), *Heathen* 1708 *Recov.* HORNSHAYNE is *Hornysheies* 1333 *SR* (p). *Horn* was probably a medieval owner. KINGSDON is *Kyngesdon* 1539 *AddCh*, -*downe* 1547 LP. Colyton was a royal manor in DB. LILLYLAKE (6″) is *Lyllye* 1636 ParReg. NUNFORD DAIRY is *Nonneford* 1333 *SR* (p), *Noneford* 1420 BM. 'Nunna's ford,' cf. Nunningham (PN Sx 481) or 'nuns' ford.' cf. Newcott *supra* 611. PAREHAYNE is *Pearren* 1539, *Peerhain* 1606 ParReg. RIDGWAY is so spelt 1636 *Recov.* ROAD GREEN is *Roodegreene* 1539 *AddCh*. ROCKERHAYNE is *Rawkerayne* 1539, 1550 ParReg, *Rokerhayne* 1586 *Recov.* SHIP-HAY FM (6″) is *Shepehay* 1539 *AddCh*. 'Sheep enclosure,' *v.* (ge)hæg. STREATHAYNE is *Strethegh* 1330 *SR* (p), -*heyne* 1504–15 ECP 4, 287. *v.* stræt. There is, however, only a small road here. SUDDON'S FM (6″) is *Suddens* 1674 *Deed.* SWANS NEST (6″) is *Swannesnest* 1608 *Recov.* Cf. Crowsnest *supra* 213. TYE LANE (6″) is *Taylane* 1616 ParReg. UMBORNE is *Winburn* 1281 *Ass* (p), *Wimborne* 1547 LP, *Umborne* 1558–79 ECP. *v. supra* 15. WADDEN is *Waddon* 1330 *SR* (p), 1539 *AddCh*. Perhaps 'woad hill,' *v.* dun. WATCHCOMBE is *Werdescumbe* 1238 *Ass*, *Wa(t)che-combe* 1539 BM, 1547 LP. Possibly '*Weard*'s valley,' *v.* cumb. WHITWELL is *Witewell* 1236 BM, *Whyte-* 1285 FA, *Whitewell juxta Colyton* 1294 *Ass.* 'White spring,' *v.* wielle. WILLHAYNE is *Wilhays* 1539 *AddCh*, -*hayne* 1612 *SR*. For -*hayes*, -*hayne* in all the above names, *v.* Hayne *supra* 129.

Cotleigh

COTLEIGH 139 C 5

Coteleia 1086 DB, *-legh* 1238 *Ass*
Cotteleg(he) 1195–1205 HMC iv, 1238 *Ass*, 1242 Fees 795,
1249 *Ass*, 1291 Tax, *-le(ye)* 1219 FF, 1321 Ipm
Cuttelegh 1449 *FF*
Southcotlegh 1492 Ipm

'*Cotta*'s clearing,' *v.* leah. The double *t* is against our taking
OE cote as the first element. Cf. Cottingham (Nth), PN in
-ing 143.

WOMBERFORD (lost)

Wiborda 1086 DB (Exon), *-burde* (Exch)
Winburnford' 1204 Cur, *Winborneford* 1237 Fees 612, *Wym-
burneford* 1244 *Ass*, *-berne-* 1394 *Ass*, *Wmbernefort* 1238 *Ass*
Wamberneford' 1242 Fees
Wunberneford 1244 *Ass*, *Wuberneford* 1244 Fees, *Woburneford*
1263 Ipm, 1294 *FF*, *Wonburneford* 1270 Ch, *Wobrenford*
1296 Ipm, *Womborneford by Cottele* 1321 Ipm, *Wombern-
ford* c. 1630 Pole

'Ford over the Umborne stream' *supra* 15.

HILLS FM (6″) and HOMESLEIGH GREEN are probably to be
associated with the families of John and William *Hyll* (1524 *SR*),
and John *Holme* of Cotleigh (1395 Pat).

BOWOOD FM is *Boghewode* 1333 *SR* (p). 'Curved wood,' *v.*
Bowden *supra* 37. WEST MILLHAYES COTTAGES (6″) is *Mill-
heghes* 1382 HMC xv App 7. For *hayes*, *v. supra* 129. SOUTH-
COTE FM is *Southcote* 1330 *SR* (p). *v.* cot(e). It lies south of
Cotleigh. SOUTH WOOD FM (6″) was probably the home of John
atte Wode (1330 *SR*).

Farway

FARWAY 139 E 4

Fareweia 1086 DB, t. Hy 2 Oliver 135 *et passim* to 1346 FA
with variant spellings *-weie, -weye, (juxta Honeton)* 1322 *Ass*
Fayrewaye juxta Colyton 1294 *Ass, Fayreweys* 1316 FA
Farweye 1297 Pat

The name is a compound of OE *faru*, 'way, going,' and **weg**, perhaps signifying a frequently used track.

DEVENISH PIT FM is *Devenische* 1381 BM, deriving probably from the family of Simon *Devenyshe* (1330 *SR*), *Doveneych* (1346 FA), who held half a fee in Farway in 1346.

HOLNEST is *Holnest* 1244 *Ass*, *-nyst* 1333 *SR* (both p). This is probably a compound of OE *holegn* and *nest*, 'nest,' hence 'nest in a holly tree.' For similar farm-names, cf. Crowneast (PN Wo 91).

POLTIMORE FM is *Pultimore* 1417 *FF*, *Poltymore in the parish of Farewey* 1449 *FF*. A John de *Poltimor* was living in the parish in 1330 (*SR*), deriving his name probably from Poltimore *supra* 444. *v.* Addenda, Part ii, xiii.

WHITLEY FM is *Wittelega* 1175 P, *Wyte-* 1173–5 (1329) Ch, *Whittelegh* 1238 *Ass*, *Whyteł* 1277 *Ass*, *Widelegh juxta Farwey* 1392 IpmR, *Whitelegh* 1417 *FF*. 'White leah.'

WIDCOMBE FM is *Widecumba* 1173–5 (1329) Ch, *Wydecumb* 1275 RH, 1285 FA, *Wydecome Hylioun juxta Honeton* 1319 *Ass*. 'Wide valley,' *v.* cumb. The *Hylioun* family have not been noted in association with the place in early records.

YALCOMBE (lost) is *Yallethecumbe* 1281 *Ass* (p), *Yaldecombe* 1417 *FF*, *Yalcombe juxta Farewaye* 1449 *FF*. 'Valley of a woman called *Ealdgӯð* or *Ealhgӯð*,' *v.* cumb. *Ialdgið* occurs in Devon c. 1100 (Earle 262).

EASTFIELD COTTAGES and THORN FM (both 6″) were probably the homes of John *Biestefeld*, i.e. 'east of the feld' (1292 *Ass*) and Richard *atte Thorne* (1330 *SR*).

APPLEDORE FM is *Attenappeldore* 1294 *Ass* (p), *Appuldore* 1518–29 ECP. 'At the apple tree.' BLACKLEY DOWN (6″) is *Blakeleyg* 1384 *FF*, *-leghe* 1408 IpmR. *v.* blæc, leah. BOYCOMBE FM is *Boycumb* 1278 *Ass* (p), *-combe* 1330 *SR* (p), 1377 BM, *Bwaye-comb* 1564 BM. *v.* Bystock *supra* 600. *Bway* represents the Devon pronunciation of *boy*. BRIMLEY FM (6″) is *Bromlegh* 1249 *Ass* (p), (*juxta Farweye*) 1292 *Ass*. 'Broom clearing,' *v.* leah. GOLEACRE FM is *Golleacre* 1597 Recov, *Goldacre* 1639 DCo NQ

8, 260. 'Field with yellow flowers,' *v.* æcer and cf. Gullaford
supra 521. LAMBROOK FM (6″) is *Lambroke* 1574 *Deed.* 'Lamb
brook' or 'loam brook,' cf. Lamerton *supra* 149. NETHERTON
HALL is *Nitheraton* 1173–5 (1329) Ch, *Nitherton* 1238 *Ass*,
Nythetone 1291 Tax. 'Lower farm,' *v.* tun. It lies low by the
Coly river. SALLICOMBE COTTAGE (6″) is *Sallacombe* 1516 *AddCh*,
Sallar- 1550 Pat. Possibly 'valley of the willows,' *v.* sealh, cumb.
STOWEY (6″) is so spelt c. 1300 *Canonsleigh.* Perhaps 'stone way,'
cf. Stowford *supra* 41.

Monkton

MONKTON 139 C 4

> *Muneketon* 1244 FF, *Monekatone* 1279 Ipm, -*eke*- 1279, 1325
> Ipm, *Monekedon* 1283 Pat
> *Monketon* 1284 FA, 1330 Exon, (*juxta Honyton*) 1455 *FF*,
> *Munkton* t. Ed 1 IpmR

'Monks' farm,' *v.* tun. The parish was formerly a chapelry of
Colyton which was royal demesne TRE (DB). The connexion
of the place with monks must, therefore, as in the case of
Monk Okehampton *supra* 153, go back to some early period of
Anglo-Saxon history.

SPILCOMBE COPSE is *Spillecumbe* 1238 *Ass* (p), -*comb* 1378 IpmR,
Speliacumb 1276 Ipm, *Spelecomb(e)* 1423 IpmR, (*juxta Honyton*)
1356 *Ass.* The first element may perhaps be associated with OE
spilian, 'to play,' ME *spile*, 'sport, play,' the whole name meaning
'valley where sports or games were held' or 'where animals disported themselves.' Cf. Plyford *supra* 597.

APLIN'S FM is to be associated with the family of Elias *Aplin* of
Honiton (1670 Wills). MONKTON DOWN is *Moneketondowne*
1479 *Ct.* NORTHWOOD FM is *Northwod* 1469 *Ct.* This must be
in relation to Honiton, for it is to the south of Monkton. TOVE-
HAYNE FM (6″) is *Tovyesheys* 1455 *FF.* It was then held by one
John *Tovy.* Cf. Hayne *supra* 129.

Northleigh

NORTHLEIGH [nɔ·rliˑ] 139 E 4

Lega 1086 DB, *Legh* 1228 FF
Northleghe 1291 Tax, (*juxta Honeton*) 1314 *Ass*, *Norley* 1555 Recov

Both this place and Southleigh *infra* 631 were called simply *Lega* in DB (*v.* leah), being later distinguished according to their position.

BUCKNOLE FM is *Bubecnolle* 13th *Canonsleigh*, *Bobeknolle* 1330 *Ass* (p), *Bobbeknoll* 1370 *Ass*. '*Bubba*'s cnoll.' For the modern form, cf. Bigknowle PN Sx 464.

CHILCOMBE is probably identical with *Churlecombe* 1303 *FF*. *v.* ceorl, cumb. Cf. Chilbrook in Roche (Co), *Churlebroke* 1309 *MinAcct*, *Chorlebrok* 1385 *Ct*.

SMALLICOMBE is *Hesmalacoma* 1086 DB (Exon), *Smelecome* (Exch), *Smalecumb*' 1242 Fees. 'Narrow valley,' *v.* smæl, cumb.

TRICOMBE is *Tricumbe* 1335 *AddCh*, *Trycomb* 1420 BM. Cf. Trecott *supra* 166.

CLODE'S COTTAGES and COLLINS'S FM (both 6″) are probably to be associated with the families of John *atte Cloude* (1330 *SR*) and Symon *Colyns* (1524 *SR*). The latter is *Collins Tenement* in 1694 (DKR 41). *Cloude* is from OE *clūd*, 'rock.'

Offwell

OFFWELL 139 D 4

Offawilla 1086 DB, *Offewell*(*e*) 1219 *Ass*, 1263 Exon, 1284 FA, -*wyll* 1244 *Ass*, *Offewille juxta Honeton* 1315 *Ass*
Uffewell 1238 *Ass*, -*will*(*e*) 1242 Fees 785, 1291 Tax, 1303 FA, -*wyll* 1244 *Ass*

Forms with initial *o* and *u* are almost equally frequent, but the balance appears to be slightly in favour of the *o* ones. Hence '*Offa*'s spring,' *v.* wielle.

CHEESEWAY ASH (6″) is *Chiseweye* 1316 *FF*, 1330 *SR* (p), *Cheseway* 1449 *FF*, *Chesewaydoune* 1481 *Ct*. The first element may be OE cis, 'gravel.' Hence, 'gravelly way or track.'

COLWELL BARTON is *Colewilla* 1086 DB, *-wille* 1242 Fees 785, 1292 Ipm, *-well* 1283 *Ass*, *Colewelle juxta Honytone* 1312 Seld 32, *Collewille* 14th Buckland.

CULBEER (6″) is *Collabera* 1086 DB (Exon), *Collebere* (Exch), *Collebare* 13th AD i, *Colebere* 1281 *Ass* (p), *Coulebeare* t. Ed 3 *Ass* (p), *Culbeer* 1822 Lysons. These two names may mean '*Col(l)a*'s spring and wood,' *v.* wielle, bearu, but it is possible that the first element in both cases may be a river Coly as in Colyton *supra* 621. The places are actually on a small tributary now called Offwell Brook, but this may earlier have been known also as Coly. Cf. Ekwall RN 91.

GLANVILL FM is *Clanefeld(a)* 1173–5 (1329) Ch, c. 1200 *Canonsleigh*, *-felde* 1322 *Ass* (p), 1333 *SR* (p). 'Clean open space,' *v.* clæne, feld. Cf. Clanville in Alford (So), *Clanefeld*' 1219 Fees 262.

WILMINGTON is *Willelmatoma*, *Wilelmitona* 1086 DB, *Wilhamtyn* 1332 AD ii, *Wyllampton* 1389 AD i, *Willem'ton* 1391 AD vi. '*Wilhelm*'s farm,' *v.* ingtun.

APLIN'S COMMON is probably to be associated with the family noted *supra* 627. CLEAVE is *Laclive* 13th AD i, *atte Clive* 1316 Ipm (p). *v.* clif. There is a steep descent here.

Seaton

SEATON 139 G 6

    (i) *æt Fleote*[1] 1005 (12th) KCD 1301, *Fluta* 1086 DB

    (ii) *Seton(e)* 1238 *Ass et passim*, (*juxta Coliford*) 1310 *Ass*, *Seetone* 1445 Exon, *Seton-havyn* 1478 Wm Wo

'Farm by the sea,' *v.* tun. The earliest name of the place has reference to its position by the estuary of the Axe (*v.* fleot). There

---

[1] This form is derived from a charter granting one hide of land at *Fleote* (dat.). (Cf. DA 17, 193 ff.) The place is by the sea, by a river *Axan*, and on these grounds alone one might suspect that the place referred to was Seaton, the DB manor of *Flute*. Examination of the bounds of the land, though not without difficulties, makes the identification certain. It should be premised that the old parish of Seaton included the present parish of Beer. The bounds start from the sea and go up to *scypcumb* and thence southwards to *bydelæcer*. This *æcer* must be by the angle south-east of Bovey House, the first point where the bounds make any southward turn. The *cumb* is perhaps the little valley south-east of Higher Barn (6″). From *bydelæcer* it goes to the *slæd*

was a place called *Fleete Hill* in the parish as late as 1704 *(Deed)*. Cf. also *le Flete de Seton* (1325 Misc).

COUCHILL FM is *Cocheswill* 1330, *Cocheriswill* 1333 *SR* (p). The first element looks like a pers. name, probably of ME origin. *v.* wielle.

HAREPATH is *(on) herpoð* 1005 (12th) KCD 1301, *la Herepathe* 1270 FF (p), *Herpathe* 1282 *FF*. *v.* herepæð. The place lies on the old Roman road from Exeter to Lyme Regis.

Shute

SHUTE 139 D 6

Schieta 1194–1206 HMC iv, 13th Exon
S(c)hete 1228 FF *et freq* to 1465 Pat, *La Shete* 1242 Fees 787, *Shete juxta Culitone* 1318 *FF*
Suthe 1269 Exon, *S(c)hute* 1301 Exon, 1456 Pat, *-ta* 1330 Exon, *Shoote* 1602 ParReg

v. Shute *supra* 184.

WHITFORD is *Witefort* 1086 DB, *-ford* 1167 P, *Witte-* 1172 P, *Whytford* 1228 FF, *Wyteford, Whyteford* 1242 Fees 782, *Wytheford* 1377 IpmR, *Wheteford* 1428 FA. 'White ford.'

BAKERS, COLHAYNE, PERHAM'S GREEN (6″) and WORHAM'S FM are probably to be associated with the families of William *Bakere* (1333 *SR*), John *Cole* (1249 *Ass*), Robert and Thomas *Peryen, Perryen* (1525 *AOMB*), and John *Warham* of Cotleigh (1705 Wills). For *hayne, v. supra* 129.

south of *dyrnanleage*, thence direct to *berhamme*, then up *berham* south to the ridge-way. The intervening points cannot be identified, but the south-ward turn must be the sharp bend in the northern boundary of the parish which brings one down to the old Exeter-Lyme Regis road. From here the boundaries are very obscure, they are said to go north up the *readan weg*, along the ridge to *bitun liege*, thence direct along the road to *crymelhamme* and up the *dic* to the *herpoð*. Here we are on safe ground again for this is the Roman road (previously called 'ridgeway') which to this day leads to Hare-path Fm. From the *herpoð* it goes to *cumbeorges heafod* and down the *cumbeorg* to *horegan ford*. This is clearly the present boundary, as it runs from the Roman road down a valley to Holyford, earlier *Horyford*. Thence it goes down stream to lower *Stanford*, the present Stafford. After that it goes north to *litegan hlosstede* and thence by *hreodmæde lace* to the Axe and so back to the sea. As the present boundary goes south-east, it is difficult to interpret this part of the bounds, but it is clear that the *hreodmæde lace* is the streamlet now called Stafford Brook which runs into the Axe.

KILHAYNE COPPICE (6″), LEXHAYNE and MOORCOX appear as *Kylinghegh* (1330 *SR*), *Leggesheghes* (1375 *FF*), *Lexhaine* (1643 ParReg), *Morecokisheygh* (1332 AD ii) and *More Cokkysheyghes* (1389 AD i), and are probably to be associated with the families of John *Culyng* (1330 *SR*), John *Leg'* (ib.), and Mathew *Morcok* (1244 *Ass*). For *hayne*, *v. supra* 129.

BLACKGATE (6″) is *Blakeyate* 1547 LP. *v.* geat. HADDON is *Haddon* 1330 *SR* (p), *Haddun hyll* 1525 *AOMB*. Probably 'heath hill,' *v.* hæþ, dun. HAMPTON is *Hampton* 1244 *Ass* (p), *Heaunton* 1277 *Ass* (p), *Hampton, Hehampton* 1481 Pat. 'High farm,' *v.* heah, tun. NORTHDOWN (6″) is *Northdowne* 1647 *Recov.* PACEHAYNE (6″) is *Paniotesheighes* 1408, *Panyetesheghes* 1426 IpmR, *Pavysheyse* 1525 *AOMB*. Probably *n* is a transcription error for *u*, the first element being the ME surname *Paviot*. PAINTER'S CROSS (6″) is *Peingtours* 1408 IpmR, *Paynters* 1525 *AOMB*. SHALFORD (6″) is so spelt 1748 *Recov*. Probably 'shallow ford.' SHUTE HILL is *Shutehill* 1647 *Recov*. SMITER'S PIT is *Smiters pitte* 1672 *SR*. *v.* pytt. SOLWAY'S COTTAGES (6″) is probably identical with *Solowgh pytte* 1525 *AOMB*. *v.* pytt. *Solowgh* might answer to OE *sulh*, 'furrow.' WOODHAYNE FM was the home of William *atte Wode* (1330 *SR*).

Southleigh

SOUTHLEIGH [sɑuli] 139 F 5
> *Lega* 1086 DB, *Suthlege* 1228 FF, *-legh* 1242 Fees 792, *South-leghe* 1291 Tax, *Sowley* 1555 *Recov*
> *v.* Northleigh *supra* 628.

BORCOMBE is *Borcombe* 1238 FF, *-cumb', -come* 1242 Fees 791, *Bourcombe* 1325 Pat. This is probably a compound of OE burh and cumb, 'valley marked by a burh.' An earthwork is marked on the map close by.

BUDDELHAYES is *Bothelehegh* 1330, *Bothelheys* 1333 *SR* (p), *Budleshaies* 1647 *FF*. *v.* Budleigh *supra* 484. For *hayes*, *v.* Hayne *supra* 129.

RADISH PLANTATION is *Reddix* 1086 DB (Exon), *Redic* (Exch), *Radich* 1280 DCo NQ 3, 47 (p), *Raddych, Radich* 1292 Ipm, *Radersh* 1327 Banco, *Raddish* 1792 *Recov*. 'Red ditch,' *v.* dic.

TOTTISKAY (6″) is *Tottekesweye* 1330 *SR* (p). '*Tottec*'s way,' *v.* weg. This pers. name is not on record, but would be a regular diminutive of OE *Totta*.

WISCOMBE PARK is *Wiscumb(e)* 1156 France, *Wysse-* 1244 FF, *Wys-* 1262 FF, *Wyshcombe* 1327 Banco, *Wyshecombe* 1330 *FF*, *Whyscombe* 1384 *FF*, *Wichecombe* 1388 Cl. *v.* wisce, cumb. The place lies low near a stream.

JOBBLESHAYES COTTAGES (6″), MORGANHAYES and POOKHAYNE (6″) are probably to be associated with the families of Henry *Jobyn* (1330 *SR*), Henry *Morgan* (1244 *Ass*), and John *Pouke* (ib.). The second is *Morganshayes* (1617 *FF*). For *hayes, v. supra* 129.

BLACKBURY CASTLE is *Blacke downe* 1525 *AOMB*. There is an ancient camp here. LOVEHAYNE is *Luuehegh* 1330 *SR* (p), *Lovayne* or *Loven* 1803 *Recov.* '*Lēofa*'s enclosure,' *v. supra* 129. MOORPLASH is so spelt 1809 M. *v.* mor, plæsc. RAKEWAY HEAD BRIDGE (6″) is *le Racke* 1547 LP, *v.* Raxhayes *supra* 608. SCRUEL BARTON is *Skryvell* 1280 *FF*, *Scrivell* c. 1630 Pole. STOCKHAM is probably identical with *Stok juxta Sudlegh* 1299 *Ass, Stokkes in Southele* 1449 *FF. v.* stocc. The modern form perhaps represents the old weak pl. Cf. *supra* 130. WEEKHAYNE is *Whetheghes* 1262 FF, *Wheathayne* 1618 *FF*. 'Wheat farm,' *v. supra* 129. WHITMOOR is *Whitemor* 1330 *SR* (p). *v.* mor.

Widworthy

WIDWORTHY 139 D 5

> *Wideworda* 1086 DB, *Wideworthe* 13th AD i (p) *et freq* to 1290
>   Ch with variant spellings *Wyde-, -wrth, -worthy* 1316 FA
> *Wyddeworth* 1297 Pat, *Wytheworthy* 1408 Exon

v. worðig. The first element may be OE *wīd*, 'wide,' but since names in *-worthy* contain as a rule a pers. name as first element, it is perhaps more likely that this is the OE pers. name *Wīda* (Redin).

SUTTON BARTON is *Sutuna* 1086 DB, *Sutton* 1219 FF, (*juxta Colyton*) 1296 *Ass, Sotton Lucy* 1363 IpmR. 'South farm,'*v.* tun. It lies south of Widworthy. Galfridus de *Lucy* held the manor in 1285 (FA).

COOKSHAYS, HALSHAYNE and LUCEHAYNE (6") appear as *Cockeshaie* 1219 FF, *Cockishaye* 1321 Exon, *Hauellesheghes* 1383 Cl, *Hawelesheghyn* 1468 Ct, *Lucehayne* 1570 *Deed* and are probably to be associated with the families of Richard *le Cok* (1330 *SR*), William *de Hauuille*, a juror in Axminster Hundred in 1238 (*Ass*), and Galfridus de *Lucy* (*v. supra* 632). For *hayne, v. supra* 129.

RULL is *the Ryll* early 16th *CtRequests*. Probably 'at the hill,' cf. Rill *supra* 606. SLADE is so spelt 1809 M. *v.* slæd. STOCKERS is to be associated with the family of John *Stocker* (1584 Wills).

XXXII. AXMINSTER HUNDRED

Axeministra 1084 Geld Roll, *Axemenistre* 1167, 1168 P
Æxemenistre 1179 P

v. Axminster *infra*. In early times there was also a Hundred of Axmouth, which included the four parishes of Axmouth, Combpyne, Musbury and Rousdon. It appears as *Axemuda* 1084 Geld Roll, *Axemue* 1156 France, *Axemude* 1181 P, etc, *v. infra* 636.

Axminster

AXMINSTER[1] 139 D 7/8

Ascanmynster c. 900 ASC Ā (*s.a.* 755), *Axanmynster* 1120 ASC
Aixeministra, Aexeministra, Alseministra 1086 DB (Exon), *Axeminstre* (Exch), *Axeministre* 1212 Fees 97
Asseminister 1233 Pap
Further forms are without interest except: *Exeminstre*[2] 1263 Pat, *Axemyster* 1421 Exon

'The mynster by the river Axe' *supra* 2.

BEVER GRANGE is *Bewer, Bever* 14th *Newnham*, 1324–38 Oliver 359, 364, *Bewer* 1511 Oliver 366. This is probably a Norman-

---

[1] For *Fore Street* in Axminster, cf. William *de Forstrete* (1316 *Ass*). The chief street in some Devon and Cornwall towns is often so called, where elsewhere in England we should find *High Street*.
[2] 'on the confines of Dorset and Devon'.

French name identical with Belvoir (Lei), 'beautiful view,' perhaps bestowed by the nuns of Newenham Abbey. The place on a hillside with a wide prospect to the west and south.

CUTHAYS is *Cuittehege* 1219 FF, *Coteheie* 1246, 1304 Oliver 359, 363, *-heye* 1334 Pat. This is probably a compound of OE cot(e) and (ge)hæg, the earliest form being corrupt.

NEWENHAM ABBEY is *Nyweham, Nywenham* 13th *Newnham,* 1264 Exon, *Newham* 1276 Ch, *Newenham* 1406 BM. 'Newhamm.' In DB the manor was known as *Alraforda,* 'alder ford.' *v.* alor. At some time between DB and the founding of the Abbey in 1246 the name was changed to Newenham.

SART FM (6") is *Sarte* 1809 M. We may compare Richard *atte Serte* 1365 (Crondal Records, Hants) and *le Serte* 15th (VCH Herts II, 298), *terra vocata Seart* (1538 *LRMB*), medieval field-names in Herts. This may be AFr *assart,* OFr *essart,* 'clearing in a forest,' 'piece of forest land converted into arable by grubbing up trees and brushwood.' There was no forest here in the legal sense, but the district was well wooded. For other names of this type, *v.* Introd. xxvii.

SMALLRIDGE is *Esmaurige, Esmarige* 1086 DB (Exon), *Smarige* (Exch), *Smalrigg(e)* 1200 Cur, *-rugge* 1279 Ipm, *Smalerig'* 1242 Fees 791. 'Narrow ridge,' *v.* smæl.

STAMMERY COTTAGES (6") and HILL are *Huverastamerlege* t. Hy 2 HMC Var 1, *Stamerligh, -legh* 1246 Oliver 363, *-legh* 1281 Ass, *-leygh* 1511 Oliver 366. This is probably a compound of stan, (ge)mære, and leah, the place lying on the parish boundary. *Huver* is for *uver,* i.e. over or upper.

TRILL is *Trill* 1173 (1329) Ch, 1285 FA, *Tril* n.d. AD iv (p), 1242 Fees 785, 1248 FF, 13th *Newnham, Tryl* 1242 Fees 791 (p). Ekwall (RN 418) takes this to be a stream-name identical with Tirle (Gl), *Tyrl* 780, 769–85 BCS 236, 246.

WEYCROFT

Wigacrosta, Willecrosta 1086 DB (Exon), *Wigegroste* (Exch), *Wigecroft* 1238 Ass, *Wiggecroft* 1238 FF
Wicroft(e) 1242 Fees 791, *Wy-* 1285 FA, 1324 Ipm, 1417 EEW, *Weecraft* 1675 Ogilby

Wytecroft 1256 *Ass*
Wydecroft 1256 *Ass*, 1377 BM, (*juxta Axeminstre*) 1307 *FF*
Probably '*Wīga*'s croft,' the later forms being corrupt.

WYKE GREEN is *Wicca* 1086 DB (Exon), *Wiche* (Exch), *Wyk'*
1242 Fees 788, *la Wyke* 1249 *Ass* (p). *v.* wic. For the modern
form, *v.* Introd. xxxiv.

BALLS FM[1], CHUBB'S FM, COLES'S FM, DUMMETT'S MEAD (6"),
KING'S FM (6"), PINNEYWOOD FM, RAYMOND'S HILL and
TUCKER'S MEAD (6") are probably to be associated with the
families of John *Bal* (1247 Misc), Alice *Chubbs* (1545 Wills),
John *Cole* (1330 *SR*), William *Dumet* (1635 Wills), Adam *le
Kyng* (1286 *SR*), John *Pynye* (1524 *SR*) and Robert *Pinney* (1581
ParReg), Arthur *Raymond* (1672 *SR*) and John *Tucker* of Ax-
mouth (1677 Wills).

FAWNSMOOR (6"), HUNTHAY FM and PAYNE'S PLACE (6") appear
as *Fawnes more* 1550 *AOMB*, *Hunteheighes* 1322, 1339 *Ass* (p),
Hunthayes t. Eliz ChancP, *Paynes place* 1550 *AOMB* and are
probably to be associated with the families of Richard *Fawne* of
Axmouth (1622, 1674 Wills), Adam *Hunte* (1238 *Ass*) and
William *Payn* (ib.).

BAGLEY HILL (6") is *Bakelegh* 1281 *Ass* (p), *Bakeleye* 1327 *SR*
(p), *Baggley* 1683 *Recov.* Perhaps '*Bacca*'s leah.' Cf. Baccamoor
supra 252. CASTLE HILL FM (6") is *le Castelhull* 1456 AD iv and
was probably the home of Nicholas de *Castell* (1228 FF).
CLOAKHAM is *Clocombe* 1366 DA 9, *Clocumbe woode* 1550
AOMB. This name, as Professor Ekwall suggests, may be a
compound of OE cloh, 'ravine,' and cumb. FROGWELL FM (6")
is *Frogewell* 1720 *Recov.* FURZLEY HO is *Fursligh* 1324–38 Oliver
364, *Furseleygh* 1511 Oliver 366. *v.* fyrs, leah. HORSLEARS is *the
Horselese* 14th *Newnham.* 'Horse pasture,' *v.* læs. Cf. Oxenlears
infra 641. MILLBROOK is so spelt 1755 *Recov.* SLYMLAKES is
Slymelake 1541 *CtAugm.* 'Muddy stream,' *v.* lacu and cf. Slimeford *supra* 224. SECTOR is *Secters woode* 1550 *AOMB.* SISTER-
HOOD FM is *Sisterwood* 1720 *Recov.* SYMONDS DOWN is *Symonde
downe* 1550 *AOMB.* TOLCIS FM is *Tolresheghes* 1346 Inq aqd,
Tolshaies 1606 ParReg. *v.* Hayne *supra* 129. The first element is

---

[1] *Ballis heighes* 1408 IpmR, *v.* Hayne *supra* 129.

a ME surname such as *Toller*. UNDERCLEAVE FM is *Underclyve* 1333 *SR* (p). 'Below the hillside,' *v.* clif. UPHAY FM is *Huppehaie* 1238 *Ass* (p), *Uppehey(e)* 1302 *FF*, 1374 Exon, *-heies* 1408 Exon. 'Upper enclosure,' *v.* Hayne *supra* 129. WESTWATER is so spelt 1589 *Deeds Enrolled*. WILLHAY FM (6″) is *Willehey* 1456 AD iv. 'Enclosure by the spring,' *v.* wielle, (ge)hæg. WOODHOUSE FM is *Wodehouse* t. Ed 6 *Rental*. YETLANDS FM is *la Gheata* 1167 P (p), *la Gate* 1238 *Ass* (p), 1260 Oliver 367, ʒeate 14th *Newnham, Yeatlands* 1760 *Recov. v.* geat.

Axmouth

AXMOUTH 139 F 6

(æt) *Axanmuðan* 880–5 (c. 1000) BCS 553, *Axamuða* 1046 E (c. 1120) ASC
Alsemuda 1086 DB
Axemud 1142–55, *-mue* 1201 France, *-muth* 1249 *Ass*, *-muwe* 1269 Exon

'At the mouth of the River Axe' (*supra* 2). The village is actually about one mile distant from the sea, but the estuary is known to have silted up.

BINDON is *Bendon* 1238 *Ass* (p), *Benedon* 1311 Seld 26 (p), *Bynedone* 1314 Ipm. Possibly 'hill where beans grow,' *v.* bean, dun. OE *bēonadūn*, 'hill of the bees,' is also possible.

BOSHILL is *Bostelwaye* t. Ed 6 *Rental, Bosthill* 1718 *Recov*, and was the home of Richard *atte Bostall* (1330 *SR*). *v.* burhsteall. There is a steep ascent here.

BRUCKLAND is *Brochelanda* 1086 DB, *Broclanda* 1156 France (p) *et freq* to 1330 *SR* with variant spellings *Brok-* and *-laund(e)*, *-lond(e), Brokelond* 1403 BM. The modern form favours OE broc rather than brocc. There is a stream here.

CHARTON is *Cherletona, Cheletona* 1086 DB, *Churletune* 1272 Ipm, *-ton* 1340, 1377 *SR, Chareleton* 1462 Pat. *v.* ceorl, tun.

STEDCOMBE HO is *Estotacoma* 1086 DB (Exon), *Stotecoma* (Exch), *Stot(te)cumb* 1285 FA, *-combe* 1377, 1392 Cl, *Stutecombe* 1374 IpmR, *Stodecomb* 1377 IpmR, *Stuttecomb(e)* 1420 IpmR, c. 1630 Pole. 'Bullocks' valley,' *v.* stott, cumb.

CROCKER'S PIT, DIGGENS MOOR, LEGGETT'S LANE and SQUIRE'S
LANE (all 6″) are probably to be associated with the families of
Alicia *Crocker* (1330 *SR*), Richard *Dykun* (1282 *FF*), Symond
Legat (1333 *SR*) and Alice *Squyer* (1333 *SR*).

HIGHER BARN (6″) is *Barnehays* t. Ed 6 *Rental*. BULMOOR is
Bulemore 1244 *Ass*, *Bole-* 1282 *FF*, 1330 *SR* (all p), *Bulmere* 1483
Rental. 'Bull marsh,' *v.* mor. CRABHAYNE is *Crabbehayne* t. Ed 6
Rental and is to be associated with the family of Henry *Crabbe*
(1333 *SR*). *v.* Hayne *supra* 129. DOWLANDS is *Downelande*
1680 *Deeds Enrolled*. HAVEN FM (6″) is *le Haven* 1483 *Rental*.
The 'haven' is Axmouth Harbour. HAWKSDOWN HILL is
Hawkdon t. Hy 8 *SR*, t. Ed 6 *Rental*. *v.* dun. HAY FM was the
home of Henry *atte Heḡh* 1333 *SR*. *v.* (ge)hæg. PINHAY is
Pynnehegh 1299 *AddCh* (p), *Pinnehegh* 1333 *SR* (p), *Pynneheye*
1359 *Ass*, *Pynhay* 1406 BM. This may be a compound of OE
pynd and (ge)hæg, cf. Piend *supra* 151. WHITLANDS, cf. *White-
clyff*, *Whitteclyfesyate* 1483 *Rental*. We are on the chalk here.

Combpyne

COMBPYNE 139 F 7

> *Coma* 1086 DB
> *Cumba Ricardi Coffin* 1175 P, *Cumb(e) Coffin* 1249 *Ass*, 1313
> Exon
> *Combpyn* 1377 *SR*, *Combepyn* 1387 Exon, *Combepeyne* 1462
> Pat, *Compine* 1675 Ogilby

v. cumb. The manor was first held by the *Cof(f)in* family
(1175 P), but the family of *Pyn* were already associated with
the place in 1270 (FF) and Sir Thomas de *Pyn* was patron of the
church in 1278 (Exon).

EDGE HILL is *Eggehyll* 1525 *AOMB*. LIDYATES BARN (6″) is
Leyde yate 1525 *AOMB* and was the home of John *atte Lideyete*
(1330 *SR*). *v.* hlidgeat. MILL COTTAGE (6″) was the home of
Philip *atte Mille* (1356 *Ass*).

Combe Raleigh

COMBE RALEIGH 139 C 3

> *Cumb(a)* 1237 Cl, 1242 Fees 793, *la Cumbe* 1300 Orig
> *Cumbe Sancti Nicholai* 1260 Exon
> *Cumb of Matthew of Baunton* 1279 Ipm, *Combe Banton* 1285
>   FA, *Comb Mathei* 1303 FA, *Combebampton* or *Cumber-*
>   *bampton* 1331 Ipm
> *Combe juxta Honytone* 1348 Exon
> *Comberalegh* 1383 Cl, *Combralegh* 1480 IpmR

v. cumb. The manor was held by Matheus de *Banton* (i.e. Bampton) in 1242 (Fees) but Henry de *Ralegh* held land here in 1292 (Ch). It was further distinguished by the dedication of the church to St Nicholas and by its position near Honiton.

CROOK is *Cruke* 1244 *Ass* (p), *Crouk* 1330 *SR* (p), *Crook* 1571 *SR*. It is the British word *cruc*, 'hill, barrow,' with reference to Crook Hill just above the farm. See further under Crooke *supra* 371.

ELLISHAYES FM is *Alysheys* 1420 BM, *Elishays* 1547 *Deeds Enrolled*. According to Pole (132) it was 'auncient land of *Elyas* de Churchill.' A Roger *Elys* was living here in 1333 (*SR*) and already in 1244 (*Ass*) there is mention of Nicholas fil. *Elye* de Cruke i.e. Crook *supra*.

CARPENTER'S HILL, HUTCHINGHAYES and SCOTCHAYES PLANTA-TION (6″) are probably to be associated with the families of Robert *Carpenter* (1643 Wills), John *Huchyn* (1481 *Ct*) and Gregory *Hutchin* (1587 Wills), and John *Scot* (1353 DA 9). The last is *Skottysheghys* (1468 *Ct*). *v.* Hayne *supra* 129.

ALLER (6″) is *Aller* 1629 *SR*. *v.* alor. STONEHAYES was probably the home of Thomas *atte Stone* (1330 *SR*). WOODHAYNE FM is *Woodheys* c. 1620 Risdon, *-heyne* 1724 *Recov*.

Dalwood

DALWOOD[1] [daləd] 139 C 6

> *Dalewude* 1195 P, 1205, 1207 ClR, *-wde* 1212 Fees, *-uuode* 1231 Cl

[1] Formerly a detached part of Dorset, transferred to Devon in 1832.

Dalwde 1201 Cur *et freq* to 1344 Ch with variant spellings
-*wude*, -*wod(e)*
Dallad, Dalad 1545 Colyton ParReg

'Valley wood,' *v*. dæl. There is little or no woodland here now.

CARTER'S FM, HUTCHINS BARTON and SHEPPARDS KNAP (all 6″)
are probably to be associated with the family of Nicholas *Carter*,
John *Houchyn* and William *Shepherd* (1525 *SR*).

BRAYS FM is probably identical with *Braysheys* 1426 IpmR, the
first element being perhaps the name of a medieval owner. For
the second *v*. Hayne *supra* 129. COMBEHEAD FM is *Coombeshead*
1809 M. HILL FM (6″) was the home of John in *the Hulle* (1327
SR). LEA is *Lye* 1351 Inq aqd. *v*. leah.

Honiton

HONITON [hʌnitən] 139 C 3

Honeton(a) 1086 DB *et freq* to 1289 *Ass, Honaton* 1302 *Ass*
Huneton 1210 FF *et freq* to 1247–51 Ch, (*al. Honniton*) 1254
Ipm, *Hunetune, Hunatone* 1258 Exon
Hunyton 1238 FF, 1268 *Ass*, *Huni-* 1244 Ipm, 1257 Ch, 1275
RH
Honniton 1244 Ipm, *Honiton* 1251 Ch, *Honyton(e)* 1260
Exon, 1275 RH, 1289 *Ass*
Hunnatone 1259 Exon, *Hunyton* 1577 Saxton
Honinton, Honnigton 1270 *Ass, Honyngton* 1293, 1297 Pat,
Honynton 1413 Exon

The numerous early forms with medial *e* and *in* for *ing* favour
the interpretation '*Hūna*'s farm' rather than 'honey farm,' *v*.
ing, tun.

BATTISHORNE [bætshɔˑrn] (6″) is *Battesthorne* 1238 *Ass* (p), *Batthes-*
torn 1253 Ipm, *Batesthorn* 1254 Ipm, 1373 *FF, Badesthorn'* 1255
Ipm, *Bettesthorn* 1361 Ipm. '*Bætti*'s thorntree,' cf. Battishill
supra 177.

BLANNICOMBE is *Blanecumbe* 1238 *Ass* (p) *et freq* to 1330 *SR* (p)
with variant spelling -*comb(e)*, *Blanycombe* 1560 AD vi. The
forms are insufficient for any certain conclusion. We should
perhaps compare Blandford (Do), DB *Bleneforde, Blaneforde*,
1201 BM *Bleineford*. This latter may be from OE *blǣgnaford*,

'ford of the gudgeon.' Professor Ekwall suggests the possibility of OE *blǣgna ēa cumb*, 'valley of the gudgeon stream.' Professor Max Förster suggests that the first part of Blannicombe may contain a British word corresponding to Welsh *blaen*, 'point, end, top.' The place is near the top of a narrow valley.

HALE FM is *Hale* 1238 *Ass*, *la Hele* 1249 *Ass*, *atte Hale* 1313 *Ass*, 1330 *SR*, *atte Heale* 1345 *Ass* (all p), *la Hale in the manor of Honeton* 14th AD iv. *v.* healh and cf. Hele *supra* 46.

CHENEY'S FM (6″), GARDENERS FM, GRIGG'S MILLS (6″), LIVERMORE'S FM and LOWMANS FM are probably to be associated with the families of Thomas *Cheney* (1726 Wills), Thomas *Gardner* (1634 Wills), Nicholas *Grigge* (1330 *SR*), Richard *Levermore* (1445 *FF*) and George *Lowman* (1582 *SR*).

GOBSORE is *Coppeshore* 1238 *Ass* (p). HEATHFIELD FM is *le zethfeld* 1406 Exon, *Hathfeld* 1629 *SR*. 'Waste land,' *v. supra* 265. HOLYSHUTE (6″) is *Holy Shutt Cott* 1797 *Deed*. *v.* Shute *supra* 184. LANGFORD BRIDGE is *Langeford* 1286 *MinAcct*. The bridge must have replaced an ancient 'long ford.' MIDDLEHILLS FM (6″) is *Middilhill* 1238 *Ass* (p). NORTHCOTE is *North(e)cote* 1238 *Ass* (p). *v.* cot(e). ROWLEY FM is *Roulegh* 1330 *SR* (p). 'Rough clearing,' *v.* ruh, leah. STOUT FM (6″) is *Stute* 1244 *Ass* (p), *la Stute* 1249 *Ass* (p). For the interpretation, *v. s.n.* Brimpts *supra* 192. SWINESLOOSE FM. The second element is probably the Devon dialect *looze*, 'pig-sty,' *v.* hlose.

Kilmington

KILMINGTON 139 D 7

> *Chienemetona* 1086 DB (Exon), *Chenemetone* (Exch)
> *Kelmeton(e)* 1219, 1238 *Ass*, 1221 Pat, *Kelminton* 1271 Ipm, -myn- 1281 *Ass*
> *Kilminton juxta Axeministre* 1296 *Ass*
> *Kulmyngton* 1346 FA, 1359 *Ass*

'*Cænhelm*'s farm,' *v.* ingtun. Cf. Kilmeston (Ha), *Cenelmestune, Chenelmestune* 961 BCS 1077.

DULSHAYES is *Dowylleshay* 1376 Exon, *Deuyllesheghes* 1393 *FF*, *Douilesheighes* 1408 IpmR, *Dawlyshays* 1544 *Deeds Enrolled*, *Dovilshays now Dulcis* 1765 D. The name, according to Pole, derives from a Sir Thomas *Dovile* to whom the place was granted t. Ed 3. Margery *Douyll* was living here in 1330 (*SR*).

NOWER FM is *Nore* 1384 *FF*, *Nower* 1425 Oliver 33 and was the home of Laurence *atte Nore* (1333 *SR*). 'At the slope or edge,' *v.* æt, ora, and cf. Nore Hill (PN Sx 70). The place is on a steep hillside.

STUDHAYES

> *Stedeheis, Stedehegh* 13th *Newnham, Stedeheis* 1246 Oliver 363
> *Studehays, Studhays* 1425 Oliver 33
> *Stedeheygh* 1511 Oliver 366

The forms are difficult to reconcile. The first element may be OE *stēda*, 'steed, stallion,' hence 'stallion enclosures,' *v.* (ge)hæg. Later the name seems to have been altered deliberately to *studhays*, under the influence of OE *stōd*, 'stud,' of allied significance.

GAMMONS HILL and RUGGS FM (6″) are to be associated with the families of Cristofer *Gammon* (1606 Wills) and John *Rugg* of Axminster (1671 Wills). The former is *Gammonshill* in 1698 (*Recov*).

CLIFTHORN (6″) is *Clisthorne* 1713 DA 48. CORYTON PARK is *Coriton* 1333 *SR* (p). 'Farm by the Corrie Brook' (*supra* 3), *v.* tun. FORDHAYES is *La Ford* 1256 FF, *Fordeheghs* 1330 *SR* (p). For *hayes, v. supra* 129. GORE LANE (6″) is probably identical with *Moons Goare* 1713 DA 48. *v.* gara. The first element may be the family name noted under Mohun's Ottery *infra* 642. MARSH FM is *Moorhays* or *Marsh* 1752 Recov. *v.* mor. OXEN-LEARS is *Oxen lees* 1525 AOMB. 'Oxen pasture,' *v.* læs. Cf. Horslears 635 *supra*. SUMMERLEAZE (6″) is *Somerlease* 1633 FF. 'Summer pasture land.' VEALHAYES is *Ve(a)lhayes* 1589 SR, 1694 FF and is to be associated with the family of Roger *Vele* (1330 *SR*). For *hayes, v. supra* 129.

Luppitt

LUPPITT 139 A 3/4

> *Lovapit* 1086 DB, *Loweputte* 1257 Pap, *Louepette* 1267 Exon, *Lovepute* 1267 Abbr, -*pytte* 1291 Tax, -*pitte* 1303 FA, *Loveputt nowe called Luppitt* c. 1630 Pole

Luuepuet 1175 P, *-pit* 1238 *Ass*, *-putte* 1334 Pat
Lippitt 1767 *Recov*

'*Lufa*'s pit or hollow.'

DUMPDON HILL [dʌmdən] is *Dumpton* 1690 *FF*. In 1344 it was called *Ryngburghe* (Exon 1344). 'Circular hill,' *v.* hring, beorg.

GREENWAY FM is *Grenoweia* 1086 DB, *Greneweye juxta Honeton* 1316 Orig, 1339 *Ass. v.* weg.

MOHUN'S OTTERY [muˑnzˈɔtəri]

> *Otri* 1086 DB, *Otery* 1242 Fees 793, (*Flandrensis*) 1247 Misc,
>   *Ottery Flemeng'* 1279 QW
> *Otermoun* 1285 FA, *Oteri Mohoun* 1297 Ipm
> *Mounesotery* 1453 Pat, *Moonsotery* 1630 Recov

v. Otter river *supra* 11. The manor was held by the *Mohun* family from 1242 (Fees), a part belonging to the family of William le *Flemmeng* in 1244 (*Ass*), called William *Flandr'*, in 1219 (FF).

ODLE is *Wodhulle* 1278, 1281 *Ass*, *-hille* 1333 *SR* (all p), *Odehill*, *Wodehill* 1469 *Ct*. Probably 'woad hill,' cf. Odell PN BedsHu 34. For the modern form, cf. Oatnell *supra* 207.

SHAPCOMBE (6″)

> *Escobecoma, Scobacoma* 1086 DB (Exon), *Cobecume* (Exch),
>   *Sobbecumb*(*e*) 1196 Oliver 394, 1206 ClR, 1215 Ch, 1244 *Ass*
> *Schabecumbe* 1238 *Ass, Schabbecumbe* 1278 *Ass, Shabbecombe*
>   1330 *SR* (p)
> *Shapcombe* n.d. Oliver 104

'*Sceobba*'s valley,' *v.* cumb and cf. Scoble *supra* 327.

SHARCOMBE FM (6″) is *Shorecumbe* 1245 FF, *-comb* 1520 *Ct*. The first element is probably the word *shore*, 'steep slope, declivity,' discussed in PN Sx 246 *s.n.* Shoreham. The place is in a small combe below a steep hillside.

SPURTHAM FM is *Spyrthamme* 1420 *MinAcct*. The first element is clearly the word *spirt*, 'jet of liquid,' found also in Spurt Street (PN Bk 138), cf. also *Spertlond* 1525 *AOMB* (Colyton). The second element is hamm. A stream runs through the farm here to the Otter.

BRADDICKSKNAP HILL[1], GOULD'S DAIRY (6"), LAMBERT'S COTTAGE (6"), MOUNTSTEPHEN'S FM (6"), SNOOK'S COTTAGE (6") and WHIPPIN'S COTTAGE (6") are probably to be associated with the families of John *Braddicke* (1687 Wills), Robert *Gould* (1563 *Rental*), John *Lambard* (t. Eliz ChancP), John *Mounsteven* (1525 *SR*), Jane *Snocke* (1685 Wills) and John *Wyppyng* (1330 *SR*).

BARN FM (6"), PIT FM (6"), WICK[2], WOODHAYES FM and YARD[3] FM were probably the homes of Richard de *la Berne* (1238 *Ass*), John *atte Pitte* (1330 *SR*), John de *la Wyke* (1278 *Ass*), William *atte Wode* (1333 *SR*), William de *la Verge* (1238 *Ass*) and Henry *atte Yurd* (1339 *Ass*). *v.* bern, pytt, wic, and cf. Yard *supra* 48.

CALHAYES, GULLYHAYES and GULLYLANE FMS, MESHAYES (6"), PALMERHAYES FM (6") and ROLLSHAYES FM appear as *Cawlehayes* (1620 *FF*), *Gullyheys*, *Golylane* (1520 *Ct*), *Maysheys* (1520 *Ct*), *Palmerisheys* (ib.) and *Rolshayes* (1733 *FF*), and are to be associated with the families of William *Calwe*, i.e. 'the bald' (1330 *SR*), Nicholas *Golye* (1333 *SR*), John *May* (1563 *Rental*), John *le Palmer* (1312 Seld 32), and Samuel *Roll* of Cotleigh (1672 *SR*). For *hayes*, *v. supra* 129.

BARNFIELD FM (6") is *Barnfild* 1469 *Ct*. BEACON is *Bekyn* 1469 *Ct*. The hamlet stands high. BLACKENFIELDS FM (6") is *Blakerynfilde* 1520 *Ct*. COMBESHEAD is *Combeshead* 1767 *Recov*. DOLISH FM is *Daledich* 1360 *Ass*, *Daledyche in parochia de Louepitte* 1377 Exon. Cf. Dalditch *supra* 582. FORD FM (6") is *la Forde infra villam de Daldyche* 1394 *Ass*. HALSDON HO is *Hallysdon* 1554 *CtRequests*. HARTRIDGE is *Hurtrugg(e)* 1321 Cl (p), 1330 *SR* (p), *Hurterygge* 1469, 1479 *Ct*. 'Hart ridge.' HENCE MOOR is *Hensmore*, *Hengismore* 1520 *Ct*, *Hinxmore* 1715 *Recov*. 'Stallion moor,' cf. Henscott *supra* 132. HONEYWELL (6") is *Honywell* 1690 *FF*. 'Spring with sweet water,' cf. Honeywell *supra* 478. MOORLAND FM (6") is *Morelond* 1469 *Ct*. *v.* mor. OVERDAY FM is *Averday*, *Overdeymore* 1520 *Ct*. PULSHAYES is *Pulleshayes* 1656

---

[1] *v.* cnæpp. [2] *Southweke* c. 1520 *Ct*.
[3] *La Yerd, La Yurd* 1346, 1347 Ipm.

Recov, Polishayes 1674 *FF.* SHAUGH FM is *Shagh, Sheagh, Shave* 1520 *Ct* and was the home of Peter *atte Schagh* (1333 *SR*). *v.* sceaga and Introd. xxxv. SHELF FM is *Shelffe* 1558 *Recov, Shelf* 1617 *Recov. v.* scylf. The farm is on a steep slope. SHELVIN is *Shelven* 1809 M, 1827 G. SMITHENHAYES FM (6″) is *Smythynhays* 1520 *Ct* and was perhaps the home of Ralph *atte Smythe* (1370 *Ass*). 'At the smithy,' cf. Smitha *supra* 386. WHITE'S PLOT (6″) is *Whytsplatt* 1520 *Ct.* 'The white splott,' *v.* Splatt *supra* 137. WINDGATE FM is *Wingate* 1809 M. Cf. Wingate *supra* 63, 145. WINDSOR FM is *Wynsore* 1520 *Ct.* Cf. Winsor *supra* 262. WITCOMBE FM (6″) is *Wydecombe* 1278 *Ass* (p). 'Wide valley.'

Membury

MEMBURY 139 C 7

> *Maaberia* (sic), *Manberia* 1086 DB, *Manbire* 1238 *Ass*
> *Membiri* t. Hy 2 HMC Var 1 (p) *et freq* to 1428 FA with variant spellings *-byr', -byri, -bery, Estmembyr'* 1242 Fees 792, *Membri* 1233 Pap
> *Mumbiri* 1185 P
> *Menbure* 1238 *Ass, -byri* 1279 *Ass, Estmenbire* 1238, 1244 *Ass, -byr'* 1270 *Ass*
> *Menebury* 1327 Cl
> *Estmeynbur'* 1270 *Ass, Westmeymbir'* 1313 Misc, *Meymbury* 1333 Cl, *Estmynbyry* 1270 *Ass*

This is probably a hybrid name, the first element being a British word corresponding to W *maen*, Co *maen, men*, 'stone,' and the second the OE burh, referring to the ancient 'castle' here. Cf. Mayne (Do).

CASEHAYES (6″) is *Capieheghes* 1303 FA, *Capihegh* 1346 FA and is to be associated with the family of John *Capy* who held the manor of Membury in 1242 (Fees 788). For *hayes, v. supra* 129.

CHALLENGER FM [tʃælɪŋgə] is *Chelhangre* n.d. AD iv, *Chalhangre* 1330 *SR* (p), 1340 *Ass, Chalangre* 1408 IpmR, *Chaldanger* c. 1630 Pole. 'Cold slope,' *v.* cald, hangra.

CRAWLEY[1] is *Craulaueie* t. Hy 2 HMC Var 1, *Cralleweye* 1333

---

[1] Formerly a detached part of Chardstock parish (Do).

SR (p). This may, as suggested by Professor Ekwall, be a triple compound *crāwe-hlāw-weg*, 'road to crow-hill.'

DENEWORTHY (lost) is *Deneord* 1086 DB and gave name to William de *Deneworthi* (1330 *SR*). This may be 'valley farm,' *v.* denu, worþ(ig), but there are not enough forms to go on.

ROKEHAY FM (6") was the home of Ralph *atte Rokehegh* (1333 *SR*). The preposition and article shows that the first element must be descriptive. The name may represent a ME *atter okehay*, 'at the oak enclosure or farm,' *v.* æt, (ge)hæg.

GAPPER'S FM (6"), GILLETT'S FM[1], GOODMANS, GOSLINS FM (6"), HARE'S FM[1], LUGG'S FM, POMEROY'S HILL (6") and STEVENS FM (6") are probably to be associated with the families of Robert *Gappath*[2] (1612 *SR*), William *Gillet* 1741 WillsDo, William *Godman* (1330 *SR*), William *Goscelyn*[3] (1330 *SR*), John *Hares* 1678 WillsDo, Robert *Lugge* (1556 *AOMB*), Robert de *Pomeray* (1330 *SR*) and Richard *Stephene*[4] (1330 *SR*).

FORD FM, LAND FM, LEA HILL FM (6") and THORN FM (6") were the homes of Henry de *la Forde* (1238 *Ass*), William *atte Londe* (1333 *SR*), Edith de *Legh* (ib.), and John *atte Thorne* (ib.). *v.* leah and cf. Land Fm *supra* 571.

STOTEHAYES (6") and TREBBLEHAYES are to be associated with the families of Robert *Stote* (1330 *SR*) and John *Trobbel* (ib.) or *Thurbel* (1333 *SR*). The latter is *Thurbelhegh* 1333 *SR* (p). For *hayes*, *v. supra* 129.

BECKFORD FM (6") is *Bykeford* 1408 IpmR. Probably '*Bic(c)a*'s ford.' BEWLEY DOWN is *Bewly Down* 1783 *Recov.* BRINSCOMBE FM is *Brunnescumbe* 1316 *FF*, *Brounscombe* 1414 Cl. '*Brūn*'s cumb.' CASTLE CROSS and HO (6"), cf. *Castelorchard* 1414 IpmR. The reference is to Membury Castle *supra* 644. FURLEY is *Furlegh* 1330 *SR* (p). *v.* leah. GODWORTHY FM (6") is *Gode-worthi* 1333 *SR* (p). '*Gōda*'s worþig.' HADDON HILL is *Hath-done* n.d. AD iv. 'Heath hill,' *v.* hæþ, dun. HASLAND FM is

---

[1] Formerly in a detached part of Chardstock parish (Do).
[2] His family must have come from Gappah *supra* 479.
[3] Elizabeth *Gosling* was living in the parish in 1668 (Wills).
[4] Robert *Stephyn* was living in the parish in 1612 (*SR*).

Haselonde 1330 *SR* (p), 'hazel land.' HAVELAND is *Haverlond*
1330 *SR* (p), *Havyland* 1666 *FF*. The first element is OE
hæfer, 'he-goat.' HOOKHILL FM (6″) was the home of John
atte Hokhole 1330 *SR*. *v*. hoc, holh, perhaps referring to a little
hollow in the spur of land here. OSMORE FM is *Osmore* 1333 *SR*
(p), 1672 *SR*. ROCK is so spelt 1809 M. The soil is chalky rock
here (Polwhele). WATERHOUSE FM was perhaps the home of
William *de Aqua* (1242 Fees). YARTY FM is *Yerty* 1299 *Ass*,
1330 *SR* (both p), *Yearty* 1406 *MinAcct*, deriving from the river
supra 17. YARTYFORD is *Yearteford* t. Hy 8 *Ct*.

Musbury

MUSBURY 139 E 7

> *Musberia* 1086 DB, -*biria* 1166 RBE (p), -*biri* 1219 Fees 264,
> 1260–6 Exon, -*byre* 1250 FF, -*bery* 1260–6 Exon
> *Museburi* 1204 Exon, -*biri(a)* 1222 Bracton, 1274 Ipm, 1285
> FA, *Mussebur'* 1281 *Ass*
> *Mosebiri* 1274 Ipm, -*byry* 13th *Newnham*, 1285 FA, -*bery*
> c. 1280 QW, 1377 IpmR, -*bury* 1289 *Ass*
> *Mousebur'* 1281 *Ass*, -*byry* 1291 Tax, -*burgh* 1356 *Ass*, *Mous-*
> *bery* late 13th BM, 1303 FA

The second element is burh referring to the ancient 'camp'
here. The first is simply the OE *mūs*, 'mouse,' perhaps used in
the compound to describe a deserted spot, *v*. IPN 149. Cf.
similarly Carloggas (Co), from *caer*, 'fort, camp,' and *loggos*,
'mice' (W *llygad*), and Mouseberry *supra* 402.

FORD (lost) is *Forda* 1086 DB, (*la*) *Forde* 1242 Fees 785, c. 1630
Pole, *Forde juxta Trill* 1378 IpmR. The ford must have been
over the Trill stream *supra* 634.

DRAKE'S FM, HOOPER'S MOOR LINHAY and KNIGHT'S FM (all
6″) are probably to be associated with the families of John and
Thomas *Drake* (t. Eliz ChancP 1), Tristram *Hoper* (1546 *SR*)
and Robert *Knight* (1709 Wills). *v*. Linhayes *supra* 592.

ASHE HO is *Asshe* 1289 *Ass* (p), 1461 IpmR, *Ayssh(e)* 1387 Exon,
1497 Ipm, *Ashe Mill* t. Eliz ChancP 1. DOATSHAYNE FM is
Dodesaine 1672 *SR*. *Dod(e)* was probably a medieval owner.

HARTGROVE FM is *Hargrave* 1292 Misc, *Haregrove* 15th *Newnham.* Probably 'boundary grove,' *v.* har, graf, the farm lying on the parish boundary. MAIDENHAYNE is so spelt 1765 D. MILLANDS (6″) is *Milland* 1672 *SR.* WARLAKE is *Werlake* 1324 *FF.* 'Weir stream,' *v.* wer, lacu. WHITFORD ROAD (6″) is *Witeford* 1238 *Ass* (p). 'White ford.' WOOD COTTAGES (6″) was the home of Richard *atte Wode* 1330 *SR.*

Rousdon

ROUSDON [rauzdən] 139 F 7

> *Dona* 1086 DB, *Dune* 1156 France *et freq* to 1248 Ipm, *la Dune* 1267 *Ass, Doune* 1303 FA
>
> *Rawesdon* 1285 FA, *Doune Rauf(e)* 1334, 1340 *SR, Doune Rafe* 1480 IpmR, *Downraff* 1498 Ipm
>
> *Rowston in Axmouth* 1529–32 ECP 6, 35, *Rowston al. Downe Ralfe* 1670 *Recov, Rowsedown* 1739 Camden

v. dun. The distinctive first element derives from the family of *Ralph* (*Radulfus*), first mentioned in connexion with the manor in 1156 (France) and thereafter frequently till 1303 (FA).

Stockland

STOCKLAND[1] 139 B 6

> *Stokelonde* 939 (late copy) BCS 739
>
> *Stocland* 998 KCD 701, *Stocland* 1202 Abbr *et freq* with variant spellings *Stok-, -lond(e), -laund(e)*
>
> *Stokeland* 1212 Fees, 1310 Inq aqd

'Land covered with stocks or stumps,' *v.* stoc(c).

BUCEHAYES is possibly identical with the place called *Bordesheye* in 1238 (*Ass*) and to be associated with the family of Gervas *Borde* (1244 *Ass*). *v.* (ge)hæg.

CORRIE and CORRYMOOR FMS are *Cory* 1244 *Ass, Corye* 1606 *Recov, Corrymoor* 1809 M, taking their names from the Corrie Brook *supra* 3.

HAM and HAYNE FM[2] were the homes of Reginald *atte Hamme* (1342 NI) and John *atte Heygh* (1333 SR). *v.* hamm and Hayne *supra* 129.

---

[1] Formerly a detached part of Dorset, transferred to Devon in 1832.
[2] *Hayne* 1606 *Recov.*

CLEAVE FM is *Cleeves* 1702 *Recov. v.* clif. CRANDONS FM, CRANDONS CROSS and COPSE (6″) are to be associated with the family of Laurence de *Crandon* (1288 *Ass*). FORD is *Ford* 1606 *Recov.* HEATHSTOCK is *Haystocke* 1606 *Recov. v.* stoc(c). HORNER is *Esthorner* 1547 *SR*, *East Harner* 1606 *Recov.* The second element is possibly ora, cf. Yarner *supra* 468. HORNS-HAYES is *Hornshay* 1547 *SR*. The first element is probably the name of a medieval owner. LAKE (6″) is so spelt in 1606 *Recov. v.* lacu. MILLHAYES is *Milleheghys* 1479 *Ct*. PENNY HILL FM (6″) is *Penyhyll* 1547 *SR*. Cf. Pynamead *supra* 378. POPE-HAYNE (6″) is probably to be associated with the family of Richard *Pape* (1244 *Ass*). RODWAY FM is so spelt in 1606 *Recov.*

Thorncombe

THORNCOMBE[1] 139 B 10

Tornecoma 1086 DB, *-cumb(a)* c. 1140 BM, t. John Abbr
Thorn(e)cumbe 1228 FF, t. Ed 1 QW

'Thorn valley,' *v.* cumb.

FORD ABBEY is *Ford(a)* 1136 (1340) Oliver 342 *et passim* with variant spellings *-de*, *-d*. The ford was over the Axe. In the foundation charter (Oliver 342) it is stated that the site was then called *Hartescath*, 'sed nunc Forda dicitur.' *v.* heorot, sceaga.

SPEARHAY (6″) is *Sperehegh* 1356 BM, *-hey* 1437 FF, 1439 IpmR and is to be associated with the family of Richard *Spere* (c. 1300 *AddCh*).

BEERHALL FM is *la Bere* 1281 *Ass* (p), *La Bere, Bera* t. Ed 1 BM, *Berehalle* 1377 FF. *v.* bearu. BROOM, cf. *Bromehyll* 1540 Oliver. COGAN'S FM is to be associated with the family of John *Coggan* (1578 ParReg). ELMORE FM is so spelt in 1606 FF. HEWOOD is *Haywood* 1668 *Recov.* 'Enclosed wood,' *v.* (ge)hæg. HOLDITCH COURT is *Holedich(e)* t. John Abbr, 1219 FF, 1247 Misc, *Auledge* 1765 D. SADBORROW is *Scateberge* 1291 Tax, *Satteburgh* 1396 DA 10. SYNDERFORD is *Sinderford* 1723 FF. Cf. Synderborough *supra* 597. VEMBURY (6″) is *Venbury* 1330 SR, *Fenbury* 1333 SR (p). *v.* fenn, burh. The place lies low near a stream. WESTFORD FM is *Westforde* 1291 Tax.

[1] Transferred to Dorset in 1844.

Uplyme

UPLYME 139 E/F 8/9

Lim 1086 DB, *Lym* 1284 Exon, *Uplim* 1238 *Ass*, *Huplym* 1254 Abbr, *Up Lym* 1282 BM, *Uplym juxta Nytherlym* 1310 *Ass*

'Up the river Lim' (*supra* 8), the name having been probably first given by dwellers at Lyme Regis at the mouth of the river.

CANNINGTON FM is *Canyton* 1282 BM, *Canyngton* 1333 *SR* (p), 1538 *MinAcct.* '*Can(n)a*'s farm,' *v.* ingtun. Cf. Cannings (W), PN in -*ing* 69, and Cannington and Canworthy *supra* 399, 390.

YAWL is *Yale* 1238 *Ass*, *Yall* 1809 M. It is probably the W *ial*, 'fertile region,' found also in the stream-names Deverill and Fonthill (W) (*v.* Ekwall RN 124, 161). It may here have been the name of the valley now known as Yawl Bottom.

HODDER'S CORNER and LANE and HORSEMAN'S HILL (both 6") are probably to be associated with the families of Roger *Hodder* (1612 *SR*) and Richard *Steere alias Horsman* (1598 Wills).

CARSWELL FM is *Carswelle* 1281 *Ass*, -*wille* 1284 *Ass*, 1333 *SR* (all p). 'Cress spring,' *v.* cærse, wielle. CATHOLE FM (6") is so spelt 1809 M. HARCOMBE BOTTOM is *Hertecomb* 1538 *MinAcct.* 'Hart valley,' *v.* cumb. HILL FM is *la Hille* 1238 *Ass* (p). HOLCOMBE is *Holecumb* 1281 *Ass* (p), -*comb* 1330 *SR* (p). *v.* holh, cumb. HOOK FM is *Hook* 1536 *MinAcct. v.* hoc. It lies below a spur of land. RHODE HILL is *Rode* 1536 *MinAcct. v.* rod. ROCOMBE BOTTOM is *Rocombeslane* 1538 *MinAcct.* 'Roe cumb.' SHAPWICK GRANGE is *Sapewica* 1167 P (p), -*wyk* 1281 *Ass* (p), *Shepwyk* 1249 FF, *Schapewyk* 1267 *Ass*. 'Sheep farm,' *v.* wic. VENLAKE (6") was the home of Peter *atte Fenlake* 1333 *SR*. 'Marshy streamlet,' *v.* fenn, lacu. WARE is *Ware* 1670, *Were al. Weare* 1690 *Recov.* WOODHOUSE is *Wodehouse* 1538 *MinAcct.*

Upottery

UPOTTERY 139 A 4

> *Upoteri* 1005 KCD 714, 1291 Tax, *Uppeoteri* 1301 Exon
> *Otri* 1086 DB, *Uppoteri* 1200 Cur, *Uppotori* 1201 Abbr,
>   *Upottri* 1270 Exon, *Upotery juxta Honyton* 1298 *Ass*,
>   *Upotray* 1403–16 Exon
> *Oppoteri* 1200 Seld 3, *Opotery* 1330–5 BM
> *Upautre* 1577 Saxton, *Upawtrey* 1598 *Recov*

'Settlement up the river Otter' (*supra* 11). The name was probably given first by people living further down the stream.

CHARLESHAYES FM (6″) is *Chaveleshegh* 1270, 1278 *Ass*, *-hayes* 1366 *FF*, and is to be associated with the family of Ralph *Chavel*, who was living here in 1270 (*Ass*). v. Hayne *supra* 129.

LUXTON is *Luggestone* 1313 *Ass* (p), *Loggeston* t. Ed 3 *Ass*, 1420 BM. The first element is probably a ME pers. name *Lugg*. Cf. Luxton *supra* 373.

RAWRIDGE

> *Rouerige, Rourige* 1086 DB
> *Roveruge* 1191 France *et freq* to 1421 IpmR with variant
>   spellings *Roue-, rigg(e), -rygge, -righ, -regge*
> *Raurygge* 1360 Ipm

The first element may be an adjective allied to OE *hrēof*, 'rough, scabby,' perhaps denoting an area much overgrown with bushes or shrubs. Cf. *of hrofan hricge* (KCD 655). For the possibility of such a form, cf. NED *s.v. rove* sb 1.

SWEETLANDS FM is *Sweteland* 1197 P (p), *Suueteland* 1247 Misc (p), *Swetelond(e)* 1306 *Ass*, t. Ed 3 *Ass* (p). The name perhaps denoted an area of great fertility. Cf. Sweetcombe *supra* 597.

TWISGATES FM is *Twystgett* 1386 Add, *Twistgate* 1789 Camden. 'Twist' may have the sense of 'flat part of a hinge fastened on a door or gate,' the first given for that word in the NED, the whole word describing some particular kind of gate.

BAXTER'S FM, COOKS MOOR (6″) and SPARKE'S FM (6″) are probably to be associated with the families of Humfrey *Baggister*

(1582 *SR*), William *Cooke* (1612 *SR*) and Hawis' *Sperke* (1330 *SR*).

CLEVE FM (6″), HIGHLEY FM (6″), HILL COTTAGE (6″), UNDER-DOWN FM and YARD FM (6″) were probably the homes of William *atte Clyve* (1330 *SR*), John de *Heghlegh* (1333 *SR*), William *atte Hille* (1360 Ipm) and Thomas *sub Monte* (1301 Exon), and Henry *atte Yurd* (1333 *SR*). *v.* clif, leah, and cf. Yard *supra* 48.

BUCKESHAYES (6″), COCKHAYES, HUGGINSHAYES[1] and MOON-HAYES[2] are probably to be associated with the families of Nicholas *Bucke* of Yarcombe (1546 *SR*), William *Cooke* (1612 *SR*), John *Hugyns* (t. Hy 8 *Ct*) and the *Mohun* family who gave name to Mohun's Ottery *supra* 642. For *hayes*, *v. supra* 129.

ALLER FM is *Allerhill* 1732 *Recov.* 'At the alder.' *v.* alor.
BEACON HILL is *Beacon Hills al. Bickins Hills* 1713 DKR 41,406.
CHAPELHAYES is *la Chapele juxta Upotery* 1314 *Ass.* CRINHAYES (6″) is *Greenehayes* 1589 *Deed.* DOWNELMS COTTAGE (6″) is *Downelmes* 1697 *Deed.* FAIR OAK FM is *Fayrooke* 1390 Cl, *Fayreoke* 1422 IpmR. Cf. Faroak (So), *Fayrok* 1316 FA. GORDHAYES FM (6″) is *Gorehayes* c. 1630 Pole. If the *d* is a late insertion—and the local pronunciation ignores it—the first element may be ME *gore*, 'corner of land,' *v.* gara. HOLEMORE FM is *Hoemoor* 1765 D, 1809 M. As there is a spur of land here it may be that the present spelling is corrupt, *v.* hoh. PHILLISHAYES is *Fylysheys* 1420 BM. The first element is probably the name of a medieval owner. PRESTON FM is *Preston* 1399 IpmR, c. 1630 Pole. 'Priests' farm,' *v.* tun. SLOUGH Lane (6″) is *atte Sloo* 1353 DA 9 (nom. loc.). Cf. Slew *supra* 28. SMEATHARPE is *Smith Harp* 1765 D. SUMMERHAYES is *Somerhayes* 1713 DKR 41, 406. ULLCOMBE is *Ullecumbe* 1290 Ch, *Oulacombe* 13th *Newnham*, *Oulecome* 1366 FF. 'Owl valley,' *v.* cumb.

Yarcombe

YARCOMBE 139 A 6

Erticoma 1086 DB (Exon), *Herticome* (Exch)
Ertincumb(e) 1155 France, *Erticumb(e)* 1175 (p), 1249 *Ass*, *-cum'* 1278 *Ass*, *Herti-* 1249 *Ass*

---

[1] *Huggleshayes* 1571 Wills, probably a clerical error.
[2] *Moonehayes* 1700 *Recov.*

Hertecumbe 1267 *Ass*, -*combe* 1291 Tax, *Ertecumbe* 1277 Exon (p)
Artecumbe 1269 Exon, *Yartecumbe* 1278 *Ass*, -*combe* t. Ed 1 QW, *Yartescombe* t. Ed 1 QW, *Yeartecombe* 1373 Exon
Zertecombe 1330 Ipm, *Yorkham* 1648 *FF*
'The valley of the river Yarty' (*supra* 17), *v.* cumb.

DENNINGTON (6″) is *Doniton(a)* 1086 DB, 1234 Oliver 258, *Donnington* c. 1260 Oliver 258, *North Dinynton* 1312 *FF*, *Donyngton, Denyngton, Dynyngton* 1406 *MinAcct*, *Den*- t. Hy 6 *Ct*, *Dyn*- 1485 *Ct*. '*Dunn(a)*'s farm,' *v.* ingtun.

ELSCOMBE FM (6″) is *Yellyscumb* 1445 Rental, *Yelescomb, Elles-comb, Ayllescomb, Yeallescomb* t. Hy 6 *Ct*. Cf. Yealscombe in Exford (So), *Yelescumb* 1155–8 (1334) Ch, *Eylescombe* 1327 *SR* (p). Probably '*Ægel*'s valley,' cf. Elston *supra* 407, with occasional inorganic *y*.

KNIGHTSHAYNE FM is *Knitteheie* 1238 *Ass*, *Knytesheye* 1267 *Ass* (p), *Knyghteshegh* 1333 *SR* (p), -*heighes* t. Hy 6 *Ct*. This may mean 'knights' enclosure,' *v.* cniht, but possibly the place derives from an ancestor of Thomas *Knyghte*, who was living in the parish t. Hy 8 (*Ct*).

PANSHAYNE FM (6″) is *Paynshay* 1420 BM, *Paynysheyes* 1445 Rental, *Paynesheys* 1472–85 *Ct*. According to Pole it was granted to a William *Payne* in 1260. A Thomas *Payn* appears in the *SR* for 1330.

KNAPP FM[1], LYE, MOORHAYNE[1], STOUT FM[1] and WATERHAYNE[1] were probably the homes of Agnes *atte Knappe* (1330 *SR*), Cristina *atter Leghe* (1333 *SR*), Ivo *atte More* (ib.), Henry *atte Stoute* (1330 *SR*) and John *atte Watere* (ib.). *v.* cnæpp, leah, mor, and cf. Brimpts *supra* 192.

LIVEHAYNE FM and SHEAFHAYNE HO appear as *Leveheghes* t. Hy 6 *Ct*, *Shenehegh* (sic) 1331 Cl, *Sheseheghes* (sic) 1391 IpmR, *Schef-hegh* 1445 Rental, *Shevehayne al. Shefhayne* 1583 Recov and are probably to be associated with the families of William *Leve* (1333 *SR*) and Henry *Sheve* (1330 *SR*).

---

[1] *Cnappemore, Moreheys, Stoute, Waterheys,* t. Hy 6 *Ct*.

COBURN'S FM, KEAT'S MILL, MANNING'S COMMON, MUTTER'S WOOD (6") and NORTHAM'S FM are probably to be associated with the families of Isabella *Colbrone* (1546 *SR*), Thomas *Keate* of Stockland (1525 *SR*), William *Mannyng* (1612 *SR*), Abraham *Mutter* (1707 Wills) and John *Northam* (1619 Wills).

BIRCH OAK FM is *La Birche* 1219 FF, *Byrches* 1312 *FF*, *Burches juxta Yertecombe* 1317 *Ass*. The 'Oak' must be a recent addition. BLACKHAYES FM is *Blakehayesyete* 1525 *Ct. v.* geat. BRIMLEY (6") is *Bremelegh* t. Hy 6, t. Hy 8 *Ct*. 'Bramble clearing,' *v.* leah. BROADLEY FM is *Bradele(gh)* 1278 *Ass* (p), t. Hy 6 *Ct*. 'Wide clearing.' CHAFFHAY FM is *Chelfehay* 1445 *Rental*, *Chalvehay* 1480 *Ct*. 'Calves' enclosure,' *v.* cealf, (ge)hæg. CLIFFHAYNE FM is *Clyfheys* t. Hy 6 *Ct. v.* clif. CORNHILL (6") is *Cornehyll* t. Hy 6 *Ct*. Cf. *Cornepyke* t. Hy 8 *Ct*, also in the parish. See Cornwood and Peek *supra* 268, 152. CROAKHAM FM (6") is *Croucombe* 1330 *SR* (p), *Crowcomb*, t. Hy 6 *Ct*. 'Crow valley.' HAY FM is *Heye* t. Hy 6 *Ct. v.* (ge)hæg. LITTLE DOWN (6") is *Lyteldone* t. Hy 8 *Ct*. MARSH is *Le Mersch in Ertecomb* 1307 *AD*. MOORPIT DAIRY is *Morepitte* t. Hy 8 *Ct. v.* mor. PETERHAYES FM is *Petresheghe* 1333 Exon, *Petersheys* t. Hy 6 *Ct*, and was so called because it belonged to the church of St *Peter* at Exeter. PITHAYNE FM is *Pytteheys* t. Hy 6 *Ct*. ROSEHAYNE FM is *Rowysheys* 1445 *Rental*, *Ravysheys* 1467 *Ct*. The first element is a pers. name, perhaps *Ralph*. Cf. Rose Ash *supra* 391. STOCKHOUSE COTTAGE (6") is *Stokhous* 1465 *Ct. v.* stoc(c). UNDERDOWN FM is *Underdon* 1467 *Ct*. 'Below the hill,' *v.* dun. WILLIAMBEER FM (6") is *Wyllyngbere* 1330 *SR* (p), *Williamesbeare* c. 1480 *Ct*. Cf. Willingcott *supra* 42. The later form must be due to popular etymology, *v.* bearu.

For *hayes*, *hayne* in all these names, *v. supra* 129.

NOTE. The following two parishes were formerly in Dorset. They were transferred from Dorset to Devon by Local Government Board Order in 1896; they have not been assigned to any hundred in that county.

Chardstock

CHARDSTOCK 139 B 8

> Cerdestoche 1086 DB, t. Hy 2 HMC Var 1, -stok(e) 1166 RBE
> et freq to 1297 Pat, Cherdestoke 1199 Cur, FineR
> Chardestock 1278 Abbr
> Churche Stoke 1577 Saxton, Cherstocke 1584 Deeds Enrolled

'The stoc(c) belonging to Chard' (So). This name appears as Cerdren in 1065 (KCD 816), Cerdre DB, Cerde, Cherde in subsequent records.

ALSTON is Alwoldestone, Alewoldestone 1201, Alwollestone 1202 Macray. 'Ælfweald's farm,' v. tun. Cf. Alewaldestun KCD 1298 and Alvaston (Db), Alewaldestune DB.

BOWDITCH is Buudihc 13th AD vi (p), Bouedich 1315 FF (p), 1349 Harl, -dych 1317 Harl. Probably 'above the ditch.'

COAXDEN HALL is Cochesdene t. Hy 2 HMC Var 1, Cockesden(e) 1201 Macray, 1342 NI (all p), Cockesden 1562 Recov. 'Cocc's valley' or possibly 'valley of the (wood)cock,' v. denu.

TYTHERLEIGH

> Tiderlege t. Hy 2 HMC Var 1, -legh 1342 NI (p), Tyderlegh
> 1247 BM, -ley 1431 FA
> Tuderlege 1201 Macray, -lee 1280 Ass, -legh 1317 Harl, 1333
> SR (p)
> Tidderleg(a) c. 1227 Macray, 1251 Ch, Tydderley 1581 FF

This name is repeated in Tytherley (Ha), DB Tiderlege, Tederlege, 1218 FF Tuderleg. Professor Ekwall suggests that this may be the OE adjective tīedre, 'fragile, weak,' applied to leah in its original sense 'woodland.' Hence, 'thin woodland.' In Tytherton (W) DB Tedrintone, 1291 Tax Tuderyngton we may have the same adjective used as a pers. name of the nickname type.

WOONTON FM is Wlmintuna t. Hy 2 HMC Var 1, Wulmintone 1201 Macray (p), -myngton 1502 BM, Wolmyngton 1316 FF (p), -ing- 1333 SR (p), 1347 BM. This is probably from OE Wulfhelmingtūn, 'Wulfhelm's farm,' v. ingtun.

AXE FM·was the home of Henry de Axe (1342 NI). For the river name, v. supra 2. BATTLEFORD FM (6″) is Bakelford 1333 SR,

1342 NI (both p), *Bakilford* 1544 DCo NQ 8, 123. Cf. Battleford *supra* 513. COLSTON FM (6″) is *Coltesthorn* 1342 NI (p). 'The colt's thorntree' or '*Colt*'s thorntree,' *v.* Culsworthy *supra* 125. COTLEY is *Cottelegh* n.d. AD vi, 1317 BM, -*lege* 1201 Macray (p). Cf. Cotleigh *supra* 625. EGG MOOR (6″) is *Eggemore* t. Hy 2 HMC Var 1. FARWAY MARSH is *Farneie* (sic) t. Hy 2 HMC Var 1, *Farewey* 1333 *SR* (p). *v.* Farway *supra* 625. The *n* is probably an error for *w*. FORDWATER is *Ford* 1647 BM. HOOK is *la hoche* t. Hy 2 HMC Var 1, *la Hok* 1201 Macray. *v.* hoc. There is a spur of land just to the south of the hamlet. HUNTLEY BARN (6″) is *Huntelege* t. Hy 2 HMC Var 1, *Huntley* 1558–79 ECP. Probably 'hunter's clearing,' *v.* leah. KNIGHT'S FM is to be associated with the family of Robert *Knight* (1711 WillsDo). LODGE FM is *Lodge, Cherdestokelodge* t. Hy 7 Ipm. MILLWAY (6″), cf. *Mulnehale, Milnehale* 1201 Macray. *v.* healh. PARKS COTTAGE (6″) was the home of William de *la Parroke* 1317 *Harl. v.* pearroc. RIDGE is *la Rigge* t. Hy 2 HMC Var 1. *v.* hrycg. TWIST is *la Twyste* 1280 *Ass* (p). *v.* Twist *supra* 233. There is a turn in the valley here.

Hawkchurch

HAWKCHURCH 139 C 9

> *Hauekescherich* 1201 Macray, -*cherch*(*e*) 1214 Macray, 1218 FF (all p)
> *Hauekx* 1235 (14th) *Cerne Cartulary*[1]
> *Avekechirche* 1262 Pap, -*church* 1291 Tax, 1342 NI
> *Hauekecherche* 1292 Pap, -*churche* 1311 *Ass*
> *Hauk*(*e*)*chirche* 1297 Cl, Pat, 1318 Ch, -*churche* 1408 *Ass*

The first element is the OE *heafoc*, 'hawk,' probably here used as a pers. name.

LAMBERT'S CASTLE is *Lambart's Castell* in 1732 (Coker, *Survey of Dorset*), and is probably to be associated with the family of *Lumbard* (1575–1681), *Lumbert* (1592) ParReg. It is an ancient 'camp' on the borders of Devon and Dorset.

PHILLEYHOLME MILL (6″) is *Finelegh* 1280 *Ass*, *Fyn*(*e*)*leye* 1288 *Ass*, *Fynle*(*gh*) 1327, 1333 *SR*, *Philyholme* 1525 *SR*. *v.* leah. The first element is possibly the OE *fin*, 'heap, pile,' cf. Findon (PN Sx 197).

[1] *Ex inf.* Mr A. Fägersten.

TILLWORTH is *Elleworth(e)* 1327 *SR*, 1344 DA 9 (both p). '*Ella's* worþ.' For the initial *t*, *v*. æt.

TUDHAY is *Thudeheye* 1244 *Ass*, *Tuddeheygh* 1511 Oliver 366 and is possibly to be associated with the family of Alexander *Tudde* (1247 Misc). There was also a Walter *Tudde* in the parish in 1392 (Pat).

BERRY FM (6″), CASTLE¹, NORTHAY and WOODHOUSE FM were the homes of Roger *atte Bury* (1327 *SR*), Cosin *atte Castele* (ib.), John de *Northeheye* (1280 *Ass*) and Thomas *atte Wode* (1327 *SR*). *v.* burh, (ge)hæg.

BARCOMBE (6″) is *Borcombe* 1327 *SR* (p). Cf. Burcombe *supra* 607. BERRY FM is close at hand and may be the burh of Barcombe. BINGLEY FM (6″) is so spelt 1655 *FF*. BRIMLEY is *Bramlegh* 1327 *SR* (p). Perhaps 'bramble clearing,' *v.* brame, leah. GRIGHAY FM is *Griggehegh* 1333 *SR* (p), perhaps deriving from an ancestor of Margaret *Grig* found in the parish in 1666 (ParReg). HAWKMOOR is *Haukemore* 1327 *SR* (p). LANGMOOR FM (6″) is *Langmore Common* 1748 *Deed*. PIERCY FM (6″) is to be associated with John de *Percy* (1327 Banco). POUND is so spelt 1809 M. WADBROOK is *Watebrok* 1392 Pat. WESTHAY is *Westhegh* 1327 *SR* (p). *v.* Hayne *supra* 129.

¹ *land in atte Castell in Haukechurch* 1449 FF.

THE ELEMENTS, APART FROM PERSONAL NAMES, FOUND IN DEVON PLACE-NAMES

This list confines itself for the most part to elements used in the second part of place-names or in uncompounded place-names. Under each element the examples are arranged in three categories, (a) those in which the first element is a significant word and not a pers. name, (b) those in which the first element is a pers. name, (c) those in which the character of the first element is uncertain. Where no statement is made it may be assumed that the examples belong to type (a). Elements which are not dealt with in the *Chief Elements used in English Place-Names* are distinguished by an (n) after them. The list omits a few of the minor names which appear to be of late origin.

ac Oak (4), Rook, Bradridge, Fair Oak (3), Hennock, Hoaroak, Monkey Oak, Whitnage.

æcer Fen-, Fish-, Gole-, Good-, Half-, *Long*-, Tinacre.

æps Apps, Tapps.

ærn Crockern Tor, Crockernwell, Hooperne, Quither, Salterton.

æsc Aish (3), Ash(e) (23), Arscott, Bradninch, Cholash, Seven Ash, (b) Bales Ash, Radnidge.

æwielm Clyst William.

alor Alder, Aller (14), Blackalder, Blackaller, Blackler, Bulealler, Coppa Dolla, Deepaller, Duckaller, Hawkealter, Houndaller, Longaller, (b) Dunsaller, Wizaller.

anstig Anstey (2).

apulder Appledore (5), Applethorn Slade.

bæc (c) Brinsabatch.

bæþ (n) Bathe, Bampton, Morebath.

ball ME (n) Hemerdon Ball, Millball, Rattyball, Thrushelball.

beacen (n) Beacon (2), Firebeacon (2).

beam Beam, Holbeam, Quickbeam.

bearu Beara (15), Beare (3), Beer (10), Beera (8), Beere, Bere, Berry, Beerhall, Birchenbeer, Bowbeer, Bugbear, Butterbeare, Cherubeer, Crebar, Crebor, Harrowbeer, Hembeer, Houndbeare, Huckworthy, Kellybeare, Langabear, Langabeer, Larkbeare (2), Loosebeare, Ogbear, Rockbeare, Rookabear, Rookbear(e) (2), Shebbear, Sheepsbyre, *Shillibeer*, Stockbeare, Treasbere, Trundlebeer, Welsbere, Westbear, Whitebear, Woodbeer, (b) 21, (c) 10.

begeondan (n) Endicott, Hendicott, Henwood, Incott, Indic-knowle, Indicleave, Indicombe, Indicott, Indio, Yendacott, Yendamore, Yondercott, Yonderlake, Yondhill, Youngcott.

behindan (n) Hemborough, Hindharton.

beniþan (n) Naithwood, Neadon, Nethercleave (2), Nethway.

beorg Borough (10), Burrough (2), Burrow (13), Burrowton, Blackberry, Blackborough, Broomborough, Clannaborough (2), Cornborough, Creaber, Ernsborough, Hanna-, Hem-, Henborough, Henderbarrow, Humber, Kern-, Owla-, Ro-(3), Saddle-, Sed-, Stan-, Synder-, Thu-, Under-, Weeka-, Whilborough, White Barrow, Witta-, Wolborough, (b) 11, (c) 2.

beretun Barton (5).

berewic Barwick.

bern Barn(e) (6), Canonbarn.

betweonan (n) Tinhay, Tinney, Twinyeo, Tweenaways.

bierce Birch (8), Burch. **biercen** Birchenbeer.

bocland Buckland (14).

boga (n) Bow (4), Beaumead, Belland, Bolland, Bommertown, Boode, Boohay, Boughmore, Bowbeer, Bowd, Bowda, Bow-den (18), Bowdin, Bowdley, Bowerthy, Bowerwood, Bowhay (2), Bowhill (2), Bowley, Bowood, Buckleigh, -ley (2), Buda (2), Bude (2), Holbeton, Main-, Windbow.

*bors (n) Boasley

botm Brithem Bottom.

boðl (?) Buddelhayes, Buddelswick, Budleigh.

bræc Breaches, Bratton (2).

brand (n) Braunder.

bremel Bramble.

broc Brook (11), Bell-, Bir-, Blackabrook, Brim Brook, Challa-, Cherry-, Cranbrook, *Denebroc*, East-, Easter- Fulla- (2), Hol-(3), Horn-, Horse-, Hurra-, Kersbrook, Kester Brook, Lam-, Lash- (3), Long- (4), Lud- (2), Mill-, North-, O-, Pad-, Rattle-, Row-, Sea-, Sho- (2), Small- (2), South- (4), Um-brook, Walla Brook (2), Westa- (2), West-, Withy-, Wood-brook, (b) 7, (c) 13.

brocc-hol Brockhole.

brom Broom, Black(a)broom (2), (b) Ollsbrim.

brycg Bridge (22), Deer Bridge, Dunnabridge, Five Bridges, Horra-, Hurl-, Ivybridge, Jews Bridge, Kingsbridge, Lee Mill Bridge, Little-, Lyd-, Purlbridge, Stockenbridge, Trow-bridge, Two Bridges, Vennbridge, Withy Bridge, Yeolm-bridge, (b) 5, (c) 2.

bur (n) 'peasant.' Bourton, Bowrish, Burraton (2), Burrington, Burrowton.

bur Bower, Bowerhayes, Birbrook.

burh Berry (12), Berrydown, Berry Knowles, Bury (2), Ashbury (2), Bleg-, Bolberry, Broadbury, Broadhembury, Brownberry, Butterbury, Clubworthy, Countis-, Cran-, Den-, Frog-, Halfs-, Hals-, Hem- (3), Ken-, Kentis-, Lym-, Mam-, Mel- (2), Mem-, Mil-, Modbury (2), Mouseberry, Mus-, Payhem-, Pos-, Sid-, Stad-, Stan-, Thorn- (2), Vem-, Wood-bury (2), Wrinkleberry, Yardbury, Youlaberry, (b) 23, (c) 5.

burhsteall Boshill.

burland (n) Bowerland.

burna Bourna, Burn(e) (7), Ashburton, Lamerton, Dean Burn, Englebourne, Ex-, Har-bourne, Lisburne, Litterbourne, Obornford, Sherberton, Shortburn, Umborne, Washbourne, Webburn, *Womberford*, Woodburn, (b) Tedburn, (c) Littabourne, Yalberton.

busc (n) Buskin.

butere Butterbeare, -berry, -bury, -combe (2), -don (2), -ford (2), Butter Hill, Butterleigh, -moor.

byden (n) Bennah, Betham, Bidna.

byge (n) Brambleby, Fair-, Grammar-, Hucca-, Tre-, Vera-by, Beetor, By-cott, -land. **bysc** Bushton.

ceald Chalhanger, Challa-combe, -moor, Challenger, Cholash, Chollacott, Cholwell (3), Coldacott.

canne ME (n) Cann (2), Canna, Cannamore (?).

catt Cathole, Catlake, Catshole, Catson Hill, Catstor.

*ceagga (n) Chagford, Chasty, Jackmoor.

ceaster Exeter, (b) Scobchester. **ceode** (n) Chudleigh (?).

ceodor (n) Chitterley (?).

ceorl Challabrook, Charlacott, Charlcombe, Charleton, Charlwood, Charton, Cheriton, Chilcombe, Chorland.

chapel ME (n) Chapel (5), Chapple (6), Whitechapel.

cild Chelsdon, Chieflowman, Chilley, Chillaton, Chilton.

cilfor (n) Chilverton.

ciric(e) Charford, Chercombe, Cheristow, Cheriton (3), Cherricombe, Cherrybrook, Cherubeer, Churchill (4), Churchstow, Churston Ferrers, St Mary Church, Whitchurch, Wolford, (c) Hawkchurch, Honeychurch.

cis Cheesway Ash.

clam (n) Clampitt (2).

clawu (n) Claw (2), Clawford, Claw Moor, Clawton.

clif Cleave (22), Cle(e)ve (3), Cleveland, Cliffhayne, Brimley, Buckleigh, Buckley (2), Gratleigh, Hollowcleave, Honey Cliff, Indicleave, Lucy Cleave, Maddacleave, Minnicleave, Monkleigh, Nethercleave (2), Ratclyffe, Ratcliffes (2), Rowcliffe, Ruddycleave, Rutleigh, Sittycleave, Turtley, Undercleave, Whitecleave, (b) 3, (c) 4.

clop (n) Clapham.
cnæpp Knap(p) (8), Naplease, Filk Knapp.
cnafa (n) Knathorn, Knaworthy.
cniht Knightacott (2), Knightshayes, Knighton (3).
cnoll Knowle (22), Berry Knowles, Hartnoll, Indicknowle, Kidknowle, Mary Knowle, Nattonhole, Rocknell, Whitnole, Yarninknowle, (b) 5, (c) 1.
*cnyll (n) Kneela, Oatnell.
cofa Cove.
coppede Coppa Dolla.
corn Corndon (2), Cornhill, -wood, -worthy, Corringdon.
cot(e) Caute, Cott (3), Cotton (2), Cotmaton, Courtlands, Cutland, Arra-, Ars- (2), By- (2), Charla-, Cholla-, Clay-, Colda-, Easta- (8), East- (3), Endicott, Escot, *Freemancott*, Hardi-, Harra-, Helles-, Hendi-, Hens-, Herdi-, His-, Honey-, Horsa-, Iddle-, In-, Indi-, Kella-, Kers- (2), Kitcott, Kittitoe, Knighta- (2), Lamma-, Lyd-, Middle- (10), Mill-, Narra- (10), Nether- (12), Netta-, Newacott, Newcourt, Northcote (5), North- (6), Nut-, Over-, Pres- (3), Presta- (2), Priesta- (3), Priest-, Prista-, Sanna-, Shap-, Sit-, Sletch-, Smitha- (2) Smithin-, Smyna-, Southa- (2), Southcott (11), Southcote, Spe-, Spre-, Tre-, Up- (39), Uppa- (3), Uppin-, Westa- (14), West- (13), Whit-, Withe-, Wooda-, Yenda-, Yonder-, Youngcott, (b) 114, (c) 35.
cran Cranbrook, -bury, Crandford, Cranford (2), Craneham, Crammer, Crammers, Cranscombe.
crawe Crawthorne, Craythorne, Creaber, Creacombe (2), -lake, Crebar, -ber, -bor, Creely, Crelake, Creyford, Croakham, Crowden, Crowsnest, Crow Tor.
croft Croft (8), Ashcroft, Bean-, Broad-, Downey-, Fox-, Hay-, Honey-croft, Luckcroft, Saunder-, Wheat-, White-, Wood-croft, (b) Weycroft.
cros ME Cross (8), Crossmoor, Torcross, Whitecross, (b) Nuns Cross
crundel Crowndale, Crownley (2).
crype (n) Cripdon, Crip Tor.
cumb Co(o)mbe (80), Culm Davy, Ashcombe (2), Ashculm, Assy-, Awlis-, Bar-, Bau-, Billa-, Blanni-, Bor-, Bovey-, Bow-, Boy-, Bramble-, Brimble-, Brocks-, Bul-, Bur- (3), Butter- (2), Challa- (3), Charle-, Cher-, Cherri-, Chettis-, Chil-, Clana-, Clani-combe, Cloakham, Cranna-, Crans-, Crea-combe (2), Croakham, Crocombe, Crookham, Darna-, Dean- (2), Doc-, Dras-, Earls-, Easta-, East- (2), Farla-, Fil-, Fox-, Gat- (4), Glass-combe, Goat Combe, Grina-, Hac-, Hals-, Har- (3), Hather-, Hay-, Heather-, High-, Hoc-, Hol-

(8), Hole-, Holla- (5), Holli-, Hollo-, Hollowcombe (3), Hollow
Combe, Horscombe, Huckham (2), Hulster-, Hur-, Indi-,
Indis-, Irish-, Knighton-, Lanna-, Lancer-, Land-, Lange-
combe, Lank Combe, Lar- (2), Lin- (4), Little- (2), Long-
Luscombe (5), Lyneham, Madda-, Maiden-, Met-, Middle-,
Mill-, Min-, Michel-, Molly-, Mor(e)- (2), Mothe-, Narrow-,
North-combe (2), North Combe, Nut- (4), Orly-, Owla- (3),
Oxen-, Parra-, Penny-, Pres-, Priest-, Raddi-, Rat-, Ro- (2),
Ron-, Rosen-, Sal- (2), Shar-, Sharra-, Sherra-, Shorta- (5),
Slanty-, Slo-, Slon-, Small(a)- (8), Smalli- (2), South- (4),
Spil-, Sprea-, Staddi-, Staddis-, Stan- (3), Star-, Sted-combe,
Stockham, Sunder-, Swanny-, Sweet-, Swin- (3), Teign-,
Thorn-, Throw-, Thurles-, Thyna-, Tory-, Tri-combe, Truck-
ham, Ull-, Ulla-, Varra-, Vinni-, Viza-, War- (2), Warmma-,
Wat-, Water- (2), Wel-, Well-, West- (2), Westa-combe, West
Coombe, Wheta-, Whit-, Wid-, Widda-, Widdi- (2), Wide-,
Wil-, Wis-, Wit- (2), Withi-, Withy- (2), Wood-, Wool-,
Woola-, Wres-, Yar-, Yarna-, Yarni-, Yarns- (2), Yolla-,
Youngcombe, (b) 80, (c) 52.

cwead (n) Quither, Quoditch.

dæl Greendale (?).

dæl (n) 'part.' Fardel.

dal Livery Dole.

denu Dean (6), Ashton, Catson Hill, Grendon, Lendon,
Markadon, Sheldon, Whiddon, (b) 3, (c) 2.

dic Bowditch, Ditchett, Dyke, Graddage, Holditch (2), Hurlditch, Mansditch, Olditch, Radish, Youlditch, (b) Dalditch,
Dolish.

dræg Drayford, Dreyton.

dun Down (23), Tredown (3), Dowlands, Anderton, Barkingdon, Barndown, Beardo(w)n (2), Berridon, Berry Down,
Berrydown, Bin-, Blacka-don, Blackdown (2), Black Down
(2), Blackaton (2), Blackerton, Blagaton, Blagdon (5), Blow-
den, Bowden (19), Bowdin, Braddon (2), Breadon, Brendon
(6), Brinning, Brookdown, Bur- (2), Butter- (2), Chal-,
Chisel-don, Chollaton, Churndon, Clayhidon, Clever-, Corn-
(2), Corring-, Craydon, Crowden, *Dew-*, Duer-, Dur-don,
Eas-, East-don, Eastdown (3), Eastontown, Farring-, Fox-,
Furs- (4), Glen-, Grad-don, Gratton, Greadon, Greendown
(3), Grendon (3), Had- (2), Hal-, Hals-don, Hamel Down,
Haredon, Hatherton, Haukadon, Hawkdon, Hawksdown,
Hay-, Hea- (2), Hed- (3), Hegga-, Hemer-, Hen-don, Hiller-
ton, Hingston Down, Holla-, Horn-, Hors-, Hunting-, Ken-,
King-, Kings-don, Lamerton, Langaton, Langdon (9),
Langdown, Lee Downs, Lewdon, Lewdown, Litchardon,

Lords Down, Lowton, Mana-, Mar- (2), Marl-, Med-, Mel-
(2), Mil-, Natta-, Nea-don (2), Nodden, Norden, Nordon,
Northdown (2), Norton, Parra-, Rad-don (2), Ratherton,
Riddon, Rightadown, Risdon (2), Rosedown, Rowden (9),
Ruston, Rydon (3), Seldon, Sheldon, Shilliton, Shuttleton,
Skerraton, Smalldon, Smeardon, Snapdown, Snowdon (2),
Southdown (6), Sowden (2), Sprydoncote, Stabdon, Staddon
(6), Stadson, Stall-, Stan-, Staple-don, Starraton, Steeperton,
Stocka-, Suddon (2), Swillaton, Swindon, Swineham, Swing-
don, Thorndon (4), -down, Thornham, Tordown, Underdown (2), Vearndon, Voaden, Wadden, Wad- (2), Waldon,
Westdown, Wheel-, Whid-don (3), Whitchurch Down,
Whitedown, Wither-, Woola-don, Worden, Youlden (3), -don
(3), (b) 43, (c) 11.
*dylfet (n) Dulford.
ea Yeo (21), Indio, Southey, Tinhay, Tinney, Twinyeo.
earn Easdon, Ernesettle, Ernsborough, Irishcombe, Yarnacombe, Yarnaford, Yarner (2), Yarnicombe, Yarninknowle,
Yarnscombe (2), Yes Tor.
ears (n) Landcross.
ecg Edge Barton.
efese Woodovis.
eg Babney.
emnet (n) Emmett.
ende Bridgend, Foss-, Green-, Hays-, Land's-end, Lands End,
North End, Northend, Townsend (2).
ersc Dux, Field Irish, Gawlish, Hillashmoor, Radge.
fæsten Buckfast.
falod Foldhay, Statfold.
*fealca (n) Falkadon.
feld Bampfylde, Barnfield, Blackenfields, Brad-, Broom-field,
Coarsewell, Dorna-, East-field, Forcewell, Glanvill, Heathfield (12), Heathfowl, Highfields, Marshall, Merafield, Merri-
(7), Merry-field, Merrivale, Plain-, Sand-, South-, Wash-,
Wed-, White- (4), Whiteheath-, Wide-field, Worswell, (c) 1.
felg (n) Velly.
fenn Venn (33), Vembury, Bradavin, Brindifield, Bullaven,
Cockhaven, Gorlofen, Gorvin, Gorwyn, Greenoven, Greno-
fen, Grenoven, Hawson, Horsehaven, Meravin, Redmonsford,
Warne, Withywind, (b) 7, (c) 2. **feo(h) (n)** Fuge, Fuidge.
feorðung Farthing Park, Farthings Fm.
flære (n) Flear.
fleot (a) Cofflete, Fleet Mill, Flete, Shortaflete, Warfleet, (b) 1,
(c) 1.
flod Flood, Floyte, Fludda, Laployd.

ford Ford (49), Forda (5), Forder (7), Fordmoor, Alder-, Aller-, Ash- (3), Aysh-, Bea-ford, Bellever, Brada-, Brad- (3), Bradi- (2), Bramp-, Bray-, Brid-, Broad-, Broada-, Broade-, Broom-, Brush-, Bur-, Burn-ford, Burver, Butter- (2), Castle-, Chag-ford, Chalk Ford, Char-, Chittle-, Claw-, Clif- (3), Cof-, Coly-, Cran(d)- (3), Crani-, Crey-, Culli-, Dept-ford (3), Difford's Copse, Dinne-, Dip-ford (2), Dippermill, -town, Dipt-, Dorna- (2), Dray-, Ef- (5), Far-, Father-, Ful- (4), Fulla- (4), Gal-, Ginga-, Goose-, Gos-, Gulla-, Gulli-, Hake-, Hal- (2), Hals-, Han(d)s-ford (3), Harbertonford, Har- (4), Harbourne-, Harp-, Hart-, Hay-, Hen-, Hena-, Hence-, Herna-, High-, Hollo-, Holly-, Holy-, Horse-, *Hunt*-, Hux-, Ken-, Kers- (2), King- (2), Kings-ford (2), Lambert (3), Lang- (8), Langa- (3), Langs-, Lap-, Lee-, Lemon-, Ley-, Litta-, Long-, Lyd-, Maiden-, Mat-, Mil- (4), Oak-, Oborn-, Paf-, Par-, Ply-, Pons-ford, Ponsworthy, Popple-, Priestaford, Pulsworthy, Racken-, Rad- (2), Raddi-, Red- (2), Redmons-, Ridda-, Riddi-, Rush-, *Ruther*-, Rux-, Samp- (3), Sand- (2), Shalla- (2), Shallow- (2), Sher-ford (2), Sherwood, Shilling- (2), Shutta-, Sid-, Sil-, Slime-, Splat-, Sprat-, Staf- (3), Staple-ford, Staverton, Stenta-, Stoli-ford, Stover, Stow- (12), Stretcha-, Tale-, Waga-, *Wal*-, Wamp-, Wash-, Wels-, Whit-, Wif-, Wins-, Withy-, *Womber*-, Won-, Wood- (4), Yarty-, Yellow-, Yeo-ford, (b) 49, (c) 27.

foss ME (n) Fossend, Voss, Forcewell.

furlang Furlong (2), Longfurlong.

fyrs Furze (11), Fursdon (3), Furzedown, Heiffers.

gærstun Garston (2), Gerston (2).

gafol (n) Galford, Gawlish.

*gafolmann (n) Galmington, Galmpton (2), Gammaton.

gagel Gale.

gara Gara Bridge, Gorway.

geard Duryard.

geat Yate, Yeat, Yeatt, Yetland(s) (2), Yettington, Blackgate, Boreat, Buckyett, Ditchett, Horsyeat, Moorgate, Portgate, Straitgate, Tolchmoor Gate, Twisgates, Warracott, Wingate, Withygate, Woodgate, Worthygate, (b) Curtlake.

(ge)hæg Hay (8), Hayes (3), Hayne (22), Haysend, Berry, Black-, Bower-, Buddle-, Burnhayes, Chaffhay, Chapelhaies, Cliff-, Cown-hayne, Cruwyshaye, Culver-, Cut-hay(e)s, Downhayne (2), Downhays, Elley, Foldhay, Ford-, Gord-, Green-hayes, Heathayne, Linhayes, Longhayne, Marshay, Meadhay, Meadhayes, Millhayes (3), Moorhay, Moorhayes (3), -hayne (2), Northay, Nymphayes, Oakhay, Parkhayne, Penhay, Pinhay, Pithayes, -hayne, Pulhayes, Raddy, Raxhayes, Roke-, Ship-hay (2), Smithenhays, Smith Hayne, Southayes, Stockey, Streathayne, Summerhayes, Tuckenhay, Underhayes, Uphay, Venhay, Weekhayne, Westhay, Widhayes, Willhay, Willhayne, Woodhay, -hayes, -hayne (3), (b) 109, (c) 22.

(ge)læt (n) Leat.

(ge)refa (n) Reveton, Rifton, Rivaton, Riverton.

(ge)wæsc Wash, Washbourne, -field, -ford, -moor, Westcombe.

gierd (n) Yard(e) (11), Westyard, Willyards, (b) Dodyard.

gogge ME (n) Gogland, Gogwell. goule ME (n) Naplease Goyle.

gribble ME (n) Gribble, Gribble Lane, Gribbleford.

greot Girt, Gourt.

graf(a) Grove (3), Grawley, Bla-, Harra-, Hart-grove, (b) 3, (c) 1.

grype (n) Hollowgreep.

haca (n) Hackland, Hackpen, Hakeford, Haycroft.

hæcc Hacche, Hatch (2), Hatchland, Hatch Moor, Hatchwood.

hæfen Haven.

hæme Chittlehampton, Cotmaton, Yettington.

hæsel Heazle, Heazille. hætt (n) Hatchwell.

hæþ Heath (10), Heddon.

haga Billany. haking ME (n) Hackney (2).

heals (n) Halse (2), Halsbury, -combe, -don, -ford, -hanger, -inger. See however Addenda, Part i, lviii.

ham(m) Ham (10), Hampit, Bar-, Birc- (2), Brad-, Bramble-, Broom-, Chelf-, Co-, Crane-, Fern- (3), Fill-, Furs-, Furze-, Gnat-ham, Gotem, Got- (2), Hend-ham, Hollam, Hors- (2), Hul-, Hux-, Lang- (2), Leigh-, Little- (2), Long- (3), Loose-, Lyne-, Morwell-, New(e)n- (3), Nort-, Od-ham, Odam, Oxen-, Park-, Phil-, Powder-, Pul-, Rams-, Round-ham, Saltram, Sharp-, Sheep-, Side-, Smyt-, Spur-, Spurt-, Stoken-, Stud-, Syde, Syden- (2), Turn-, Up-, Vive-, Whit-, Yap-ham, (b) 33, (c) 10.

hamtun Fenton, Han(d)sford (3) (?).

han (n) Hone (2), Handley.

hangra Hanger (2), Chalhanger, Challenger, Clayhanger, Cleaveanger, Halsanger, Halsinger, Henegar, Mullingar, Shut-, Small-, Spar-, Wool-hanger, (c) 3.

hassuc Hask, Haske.

heafod Head, Bull-, Co(o)mbes- (7), Dean-, Down-head, Erme Head, Lake- (2), Mam-, Moors-head, Nadrid, Pillhead, Plym Head, Willandhead, Yealm Head.

healh Hale, Heal(e) (7), Hele (19), Bozomzeal, Black Hall, Cripple, Kithill, Worthele, (b) Pethill, Pithill, (c) Bewsley.

heall Hall (2), Blackhall, Stenhall, Stenhill, Stiniel, Woodhall, (b) Burnshall, Vealeholme.

hengest Henceford, Hence Moor, Hens-cott, -leigh, Henstridge, Hingston Down, Hiscott.

heolstor (n) Hulstercombe.

heordewic Hardwick, Herdwick (2), Hurdwick.

herepæþ Harepath (3), Halford, Harford (2), Harpford.

higid Budshead, Combe, Stokeinteignhead.

hiwisc Hewish, Huish (6), Bowrish, Bucks, Gorhuish, Great Huish, Langage, Melhuish, Mowlish, Quoditch, Woodhuish.

hlæw (a) Crawley, (c) Trillow.

hleow (n) Lewdon (2), Leeford.

hlidgeat Lidyates Barn. *hlieg (n) Layton.

hlinc Lynch (3), Fairlinch, Marledge, Portledge, Prustledge, Puslinch, Scorlinch, Stallenge, (b) 4.

hlype *Lipper*, Cudlipptown, Poflet.

hoc Hook(e) (6), Hooks, Hookmoor, -way (2), Hoccombe, Huck-ham (2), -land, Hugglepit, Huxhill, Huxtable, (c) Shell-hook.

hod (n) Hood.

hoh Hoe (2), Hooe, Hoodown, Croyde Hoe, Dunterue, Lamer-hooe, Morthoe, Trentishoe, (b) Martinhoe.

holca (n) Hucken Tor, Sandick, Sanduck.

holegn Hole, Holne, Hollam.

holh Hall (2), Hole (31), Holeland, Holyeat, Addlehole, Cats-, Fox- (2), Hartshole, Hookhill, Horrell, Houndle, Mouse- (2), Owl-, Puts-hole, Witchells, (b) 3.

holt Chettisholt, Chittlehamholt, Hallshott, Spreyton Wood, Teignholt.

hop Hope.

hop (n) Hoop.

horn Cornborough, Horn-brook, -don, -er, Ramshorn, Row-horne.

hos (n) Hawson.

hraca (n) Rake.

hreod Reed, Rhude.

***hrise** (n) Hookedrise.

hrycg Ridge (5), Rudge (3), Ash- (4), Blackridge, Bremlidge, Brem- (6), Broad- (3), Bur- (2), Cold-, Cole- (2), Cor-, Dene-, Dor-, Dro-, Dun-, Dund-, Hart-, Hawk(e)-(4), Henst-, High-, Hold-, Hor- (6), Lang-, Lock-, Lynd-, Mar-, North-, Oak-, Part- (2), Per-, Ram-, Raw-, Sand-, Sheep-, Short- (4), Small- (2), Sold-, Sort-, Sticke-, Stucke-, Stor- (2), Stur-,

Sur-, *Tork-*, Vale-, Whor-, Withe-, Wool-, Yeathe-ridge, (b) 10, (c) 7.

hus Beare House, Broom-, Cale-, Culver-house (2), Down- (2), New- (2), Park-, Stock-, Stoke-, Stone-, Tap-, Vole-, Water-, White-, Wood-house (6), (b) Moonhouse, (c) 3.

hwetstan Whit(e)stone (2).

hwyrfel Hurlditch, Wheeldon, Worden.

hyll Hill (33), Rhyll, Rill (4), Rull (7), Ashill (2), Barrall(s), Boars-, Boe-hill, Bossellpark, Bowhill (2), Breazle, Brim-, Brock-, Broom- (2), Bull-hill, Cantrell, Churc- (3), Clay-, Cock-, Corn-, Crow-, Deer-hill, Dipple, Dural, Fern-hill (4), Furzehill, Furze Hill, Greenhill, Hatchwell, Houndall, Hux-, Kings-, Lang-hill, Metherall (2), Odle, Peek-, Pen-hill, Pizwell, Prawle, Rowell, Ryall, Sainthill (2), Southill, South Hill, Staple-, Summer-, Tip-, Tre-, Trey-, Up-hill (2), Vogwell, Warm-, Worm-hill, (b) 16, (c) 7.

*****hylte** (n) Emlett.

hyrne Hearn, Herne (2), Hernaford, Herner, Horne. **hyrst** *Hurst.*

hyð (a) Hyde, (b) *Prattshide.*

ing(a) (a) Shillingford (2), (b) 19. **ing(a)ham** Yellingham.

ingtun (b) 40, (c) Flitton.

lache ME Lashbrook (3), Latchmoor.

lacu Lake (20), Lakes, Black-, Cat-, Cho-, Cox-, Cre-, Crea-, Dark-lake, Dead Lake, Dry Lake, Eastlake, Fish Lake, Goat-, Hart-, Hay-, Hock-lake, Hollick, Horra-, Horse-, Horswill-, Lever-, Mid-lake, Mincing Lake, Red Lake, Red- lake (2), Sellake, Shutelake, Slymlakes, Smal- (2), Spire-, Stan-lake, Tongue Lake, Town-, Tur-, Vel-, Ven- (2), Ven- lakes, War-, Wed-, West- (2), Yonder-lake, (b) Lovelake, Postlake, (c) 15.

læs (a) Horselears, Oxenlears, Summerlease, (c) Batelease.

land Land (2), Bank-, Beat-, Bel-, Birch-, Black-land (2), -lands (2), Bol-, Boy-, Brook-, Bruck-, Bul- (2), Cart-, Chor-, Click-land, Courtlands, Crank-, Cut-, Dow-land, -lands, Down-, Exe-, Feather-, Frog-, Furze- (2), Gar-, Ginger-, Gog-, Green-, Grey-, Hack-, Hart-, Has-, Hatch-, Hather-, Have-, Hea-, Hen-, *Hether-*, High-, Hol- (5), Honey-, Huck-, Hunt- (2), Kings-, Lake-, Lap-, Leach-, Long-, Love-, Mar-, Med-land (2), Mellands, Millawns, Mol- (2), Monk-, Moor- (2), New-land (8), -lands (2), Penny-, Pil-, Pit-, Port-, Press-, Puck-, Run-, Shar-, Shil-, Sol-, Spur-, Stock-, Sutter-land, Sweetlands, Thorn-, Tongue-, Tree-, Tuff-, Wad-, Wag-, Wal-, War-, Water-, Way-, Wel-, Wester-, Wheat- (2), Wid-, Wil-, Wist-, Wix-, Wol-, Wood (12), Wray-, Yal-, Yel- (7), Yellow-, Yol-land (3), -lands, Yetland, (b) 33, (c) 29.

landscearu (n) Lancercombe, Landskerry, Langsford.

lane, lanu Lana, Lane (4), Laneland, Trelana, Drake Lane, Lovelane, (b) Acland.

leah Lea (2), Lee (11), Leigh (27), Ley (13), Lye, Leighon, Leigh Tor, Leyland, Treleigh, Ashleigh (2), -ley (2), Barley, Beenleigh, Benley, Blackley, Boas-, Bowd-, Bow-ley, Brad-legh, -leigh, -ley (4), Bray-, Brem-, Bright- (2), Brim- (5), Broad-ley (4), Buckfastleigh, Bul-, Bur-leigh, Burley, Butter-, Calver-, Canons-leigh, Casely, Chawleigh, Chil-, Chip-ley, Coxleigh, Creely, Dun-, Dur-ley, Eastleigh, Far-leigh (2), -ley (3), Filleigh, Fish-leigh, -ley (2), Furley, Furzeleigh (2), Furzeley, Gatherley, Gotleigh, Grawley, Grealy, Handleigh, Hart-leigh, -ley, Hatherleigh (2), Heasley, Hensleigh, High-leigh, -ley (2), Kelly, Kitley, Lang-leigh, -ley (5), Lightleigh, Loose-leigh, -ley, Manley, Marley (2), Monkleigh, Moreleigh, Mor-, Mur-, Mut-ley, Northleigh (2), Nut-, Oak-, Ow-ley, Philleyholme, Pit-, Plum-, Rad-ley, Raleigh (2), Rane-, Rashleigh, Ri-, Rock-, Row-ley (3), Rumleigh, Satterleigh, Shapley (2), Shep-leigh, Ship-, Shute-, Slo-ley, Snydles, Sorley, Southerley, Southleigh, Stammery, Stock-leigh (4), -ley, Stokeley, Stood-leigh (2), -ley, Strash-, Sunder-leigh, Terley, Thongs-, Throw-leigh, Toat-, Town-ley, Tyther-, Umber-leigh, Var-ley, -leys, Wark-, War-, Warm-leigh, Welles-ley, West-leigh (2), -ley, Whidley, Willes-, White-leigh, -ley (3), -ly (4), Whit-leigh, -ley (3), With-, Wood-leigh (2), -ley (2), Wool-leigh, -ley (2), Yarmley, (b) 63, (c) 17.

leap (n) Lapford.

lic-tun (n) Litchaton, Litchdon.

lind Lenda, Lyndridge.

lobb (n) Lobb (2), Labdon, Lobhill, Lopwell.

mæd Mead (3), Meads, Meddon, Metcombe, Beaumead, Broad-, Hard-, Hol-, Liver-, Manna-, Oxen-, Pyna-, South-, Yellow-mead (2), (b) Broomsmead, (c) 3.

mægden (n) Maidencombe, Maiden Down, Maidenford, Meddon St.

mægen (n) Mainbow (?), Mainstone (?).

mæle (n) Melbury (2), Meldon, Melhuish (?), Milbury.

(ge)mæne (n) Mana Butts, Mana-don, -ton, Manley, Manna-mead.

(ge)mænscipe (n) Mansditch.

mæþ (n) Meeth, Meethe.

mearc Marchweeke, Markadon, Markstone.

meos Muze.

mere Maer, Maire, Mere, Marland, Merton, Cranmere, Crammer, Frog-mire, -more (5), Hemerdon, Homer, Pea-more, (b) 2.

mersc Marsh (11), Longmarsh, (b) Bellamarsh, (c) 3.
milgemet (n) Milemead.
mire ME Yendamore.
mor Moor (37), Moore, Moor-acre, -end, -lane, -water, Morebath, -leigh, -ton, Mor-combe, -well, Blakemore, Bommertown, Boughmore, Brent Moor, Broadmoor (6), Buckfast
Moor, Bulkamore, Bull-, Challa-, Cox-moor, Cranmer, Dart-,
Fulla-, Goose- (2), Gul-moor, Hawkmoor (2), Hence Moor,
Hole- (2), Holla-, Hook-, Kings-, Loose-, Mill-, Monks-moor,
Narramore, Northmoor, Penn Moor, Pile-, Pitts-moor,
Port-, Ring-more (2), -moor, Singmore (3), Southmoor,
Trundlemore, Wardmoor, Warmore, Washmoor, Weeks-
in-the-Moor, White- (3), Whit-moor, Withymore, (b) 8,
(c) 9.
mountaine ME (n) Mountain Fm.
muþa Aune-, Ax-, Dart-, Ex-, Lyn-, Plym-, Sid-, Teign-,
Water-, Wid-mouth, Mothecombe, (c) Portlemouth.
myln Mill (6), Frog Mill, Kings Mill, Nether Mill, Shilla Mill,
Traymill, Tuckingmill.
myncen Minchendown, Mincing Lake.
mynster Ax-, Ex-minster.
næss (a) The Ness, Noss (2), Corbons Head, *Hardness*,
(b) Totnes.
nest (n) Crowsnest, Holnest, Swans Nest.
ofer Yarner.
ofes(e) (n) Ovis, Woodoffice.
ora (a) Horner, Nower, Rora, Yarner, (b) 8, (c) Gobsore.
orceard Orchard (4).
pæð Gappah, Smythapark, Sticklepath (2), Parford.
panne (n) Mapstone, Mis Tor Pan, Panson.
papol (n) Poppleford.
peac (n) Peek (2), Peak Hill, Peek Hill.
pearroc OE or parke ME Park (9), Parke, Park-ham, -land,
-wood, Parracombe, Down-, Oxen-, Sandy-park, Partridge (2).
penn (a) Penn (2), Pen Cross, Penn's Quarry, Hack-, Hecka-,
Ry-pen, (b) Ipplepen.
pil (n) Pilehayes, Pilemoor, Piley Lane, Pilliven, Pilton, Pyle
Bridge.
plega Durpley, Plyford.
plegstow Plaistow.
pludd ME (n) Pludd, Pludda.
pol Pool (14), Poole (5), Polhearn, Pulhayes, Pulrew, Addle-,
Barn-, Black-pool (3), Marpool, Mary Pole, Withypool,
(c) 2.
*polra (n) Powderham.

port (a) Port (2), Port Bridge, Portgate (2), Portland, Portmore, Port Way, Beauti-, Dogga-, New-, Olda-, Tad(d)i-port (3), Yellowford, (b) Bigport, Diggaport (c) 1.

preost Prescombe, Priestcombe, Prescott (3), Presta- (2), Priesta- (2), Priest-, Priesta-, Prista-cott, Priestaford, Priestland, Prustledge, Preston (10), Pruston.

puca Puckland.

pucel (n) Putshole.

pyll Pill (4), Pillhead, -mouth, Pilton, Pilland, Lophill.

pynd (n) Piend (2).

pyrige Perry (4), Parradon, Perriton.

pytt Pit (2), Pitt (20), Pytte, Pit-hayes, -hayne, -land, -lands, Pitten, Pitton (2), Bullapit, Clampitt (2), Cokesputt, Fallapit, Harpitt, Huggle-, Merri-, Moor-, Muddipit, Riddy Pit, Warmpit, (b) Luppitt, (c) 3.

quay, kay ME (n) Torquay.

ræden (n) Walreddon.

ræw Reeve, Rew(e) (5), Coombrew, Cumerew, Cumery, Hildrew, Millrow, Whiterow, Woodrow (3).

ridde ME Ringmoor, -more (2).

roche ME (n) Roach (2).

rock(e) ME (n) Rock.

rod Rhode (2), Road. rum Rumleigh.

rynel (n) Runland.

rysc Rix, Rixdale.

ryt (n) Collard, Rutt.

sæge (n) Seabrook, Sellake.

sæte Holset, Kingseat, Kingsett, Kingshead.

sacuman (n) Secmaton, Seckington.

sand Sand Barton.

sceaga (a) Shaugh (2), Huntshaw, (c) Grabbishaw.

sceap-wæsc Sheepwash (2).

sciete (n) Shewte, Shute (6), Shutelake, -ley, Shuthanger, Shuttaford, -moor, Watershute.

scipen (n) Shippen, Shipping.

scylf Shelf, Sheldon, Shillingford, Shilliton.

*scylfstan (n) Shilstone (7). scytel (n) Shettleton. scyttels (n) Sheepsbyre, Sheepstor.

sealtærn (n) Saltren, Salterton.

sege ME (n) Sedge. sele Zeal (6).

setl (n) Ernesettle.

shore ME (n) Score, Scur, Scorlinch, Sharcombe.

side Lamside.

slæd Slade (18), Addislade, Applethorn Slade, Blackslade, Bury Slade, Green-, Ring-slade, Rushlade, Water- (2), Wid-, Win-slade (4), (c) 3.

slæp Slapton.

slim (n) Slimeford, Slymlakes.

sloh (n) Slew (5), Sloo, Slough, Slow, Slewton, Horrislew, Pinslow, Polsloe, Ratsloe, (b) Tilleslow.

smiþþe (n) Smitha, Smithaleigh, Smithenhayes.

snæp (n) Snape, Snapper, Snapdown.

sound(e) ME The Sound.

spitel (n) ME Spitlar, Spittle.

splott (n) Splatt, White's Plott.

spræg (n) Spreacombe, Sprecott, Spreyton, Sprydoncote, Sprytown, Spurway, Oaksberry, Ratsbury.

stæniht (n) Stentaford, Stentwood, Stantyway.

stan Stone (22), Stone-hayes, -land, -lands, Bel-, Black-stone, Blaxton, Boreston, Brad-, Bullhorn-, Cold-, Copple- (2), Great-, Halmp-stone, Halsdon, Hard-, Hare-stone, Hingston, Hold-, Hore-stone (2), Hurston, Langstone (3), Launceston, Long-, Main- (2), Map-, Mark-stone, Milestone, Millsome, Orestone, Panson, Ritson, Shilstone (7), Smithson (2), Smythstone, Soussons, Swain-, Thirl-, Thurle-, Trim-, White-stone (3), Wilson, Wonson, Youlston, Yowlestone, Zeaston, (b) 8, (c) 1.

stapol Stable Green, Staple (3), Staple-don, -ford, -gate, -hill, -ton, Huxtable, Instaple, (b) Barnstaple.

stede True Street.

steort Start, Start Point, Steart (3), Stert (2), Holy Street, Ramsterland.

stig Chasty.

stigel Henstill.

stoc(c) Stock (2), Stocken, Stoke (8), Stokenham, By-, Chard-, Culm-, Hal-, Heath-, Plym-, Tavi-, Taw-stock, (b) Frithel-stock, Revelstoke, (c) Colestocks.

stoccen Stockenbridge.

stow Cheristow, Christow, Churchstow, Virginstow, Halstow and six compounds with a saint's name, (b) *Grendsetowe*.

stræt Street, Strete (2), Spratford, Straitgate, Streathayne, (c) 4.

strecche ME (n) Stretch Down, Stretchacott, Stretchford, Strashleigh.

strod Strode, Stourton.

stut (n) (a) Stout (2), Stouthayes, Southill, Brimpts, (c) Win-stout.

stybbe (n) Stibb (2), Stippadon.

sure (n) Sewer.

swan Sannacott, Swannaton (2).

swylle (n) Swilly, Swillaton.

tealt(e) (n) Tealta (?).

tiedre (n) Tytherleigh.

torr Tor(r)(e) (16), Tor-cross, -dean, -down, -hill(2), -land, Ap-, Ashel-, Bee-tor, Bel Tor, Berra Tor, Black Tor (3), Brat Tor, Brousen-, Buc-, Cats-tor, Clay Tor, Coni-, Crip-tor, Crockern Tor, Crow Tor, Crowthers Hill, Fox Tor, Fur Tor, Furze Tor, Gratnar, Grea Tor, Gutter, Harter, Hartland and Hawks Tor, Haytor Hd, Hen, Hollow, and Holwell Tor, Houndtor, Hound, Hucken, Laughter, Leather, Leigh, Mill, Mis, Nat, and Rough Tor, Router, Saddle Tor, Shap-, Sharpi-, Sheeps-tor, Stanterton, Stan-, Wels-tor, Wild Tor, Wotter, Yar and Yes Tor, (b) 10, (c) 15.

trendel (n) Trendwell, Trentishoe, Trundle-beer, -moor, Row-trundle.

treow Tree, Trew (2), Trow (2), True, Train(e) (2), Trayne, Trewyn, Treeland, Trowbridge, Ivy-, Lang-, Plym-tree, Rattery, Rowtry, Youltree, (b) 8, (c) 1.

trog Truckham.

tuffe ME (n) Toft, Tuffland.

tun Town (5), Town-house, -lake, -leigh, -ridden, Aller-, Ashbur-, Ave-, Bamp-, Bicker-, Bour-ton, Bowden, Bower-, Boy-, Brat-ton (2), Bridgetown, Bulla-, Burra-, Burring-, Burrow-, Bush-, Charle-, Char-, Cheri- (4), Ches-, Chilla-, Chil-, Chilver-, Chip-, Chittlehamp-, Churs-ton, Clapham, Clarks-, Claw-, Clif-, Clis-ton (3), Broad Clyst, Cocking-, Cof-, Coly-, Comp- (2), Cory- (2), Cotma-ton, Crabaton, Credi-, Cullomp-, Darting-, Doc-, Dol-, Down-ton, Downtown, Drewsteign-, Drey-, Dunter-, Easting-, Eas- (3), Erming-, Ex-ton, Falkedon, Feni-, Fen- (2), Fisher-, Flit-, Folla-, Ford-ton, Gaddon, Galmington, Galmpton (2), Gammaton, Gnat-, Grat- (2), Hamp-, Harber-, Harra-ton, Hartland, Har-ton (2), Haydon, Hean- (5), Her-, Highamp-, Holbe-, Honi-, Clyst Honi-, Hor-, Hough-, Ken-, Kings- (4), Kingshean-, Knigh- (3), Knights-, Kyt-ton, Labdon, Lamer-, Lidda-, Lif-, Litcha-ton, Litchdon, Loyton, Lyn-, Mana-ton, Martin, Mel-, Mer-, Middle-, Mil-ton (3), Milltown, Minchendown, Misdon, Mol-, Monker-, Monk-ton (2), Moretonhampstead, Nether- (7), Net-, New-ton (12), Newtown, Tornewton, Northmostown, Nor- (5), Nut-, Nymp- (2), Okehamp- (2), Orche-, Otter-, Over-, Perri-, Pil-, Pinna-, Pit-, Plymp-, Pres- (10), Prior-, Prus-, Reve-, Rif-, Riva-, River-, Saun-, Scotting-, Sea-, Secking-, Secma-, Shor-, Shutter-, Silver-, Slap-, Smeming-, Sour-, Souther-ton, Southtown, Sowton (4), Sowtontown, Sprey-, Stan-, Staple-, Staver-ton, Stippadon, Stocka-, Stour-, Sut- (4), Swanna- (2), Tala-, Tamer-,

Tavi-, Taw- (3), Teign- (2), Temple-, That-, Thorn-, Thrushel-, Titter-, Tiver-, Torring- (3), Turching-, Up- (10), Uppa- (3), Upper- (2), U-, Ven- (7), Vin-, Wat-, Westman-, Wes-ton (7), Westown, Whiddon, Woodbury Salterton, Woodman-, Woo-, Woot- (2), Wot- (5), Wraf-, Wranga-, Yealmp-ton, Yearlstone, Yella-, Yetting-ton, (b) 230, including some 60 definitely of post-Conquest origin, (c) 50.

tunsteall Townstal.

twicene (n) Twitchen (8), Tuchenor, Turchington, (b) Ben-twitchen.   twi- Tiverton.

twist ME (n) Twist (2), Twisgates.

þel Theale.

þelbrycg Thelbridge (3). *þoccere (n) Doggaport.

þorn Thorn(e) (21), Craw-, Cray-, Harra-, Harrow-thorn(e), Holdstrong, Kna-, Lap- (2), Lop-thorne, Western, (b) 6, (c) 3.

þorp Drupe.

þring (n) Thriverton, Dringwell.

þruh (n) Throwcombe, Throwleigh. *þryscele (n) Thrushelton, Thurlescombe.

þyfel (n) Thule, Rixdale.

þyrre (n) Turtley.

wætergefeal (n) Watervale.

waroð (n) Ward (3).

warren (n) ME Dawlish Warren.

waite ME (n) White.

wealh *Walford*, Walla Brook, Walland, Wallover, Walreddon.

weall (a) Wallen, Wallon, Wallandhill, Warfleet, Copperwalls, (c) 4.

weg Way(e) (17), Wayhead, -moor, Whey, Wifford, Boohay, Bowhay (2), Cheeseway, Chineway, Cracka-, Far-, Green-(3), Greena-, Hollo- (3), Hook- (2), Narra-, Neth-, North-(2), Nor-, Olda-, Rad- (2), Redda-, Ridg-, Ridge- (2), Road-, Rod-, Rud-, South- (3), Spur-, Stanty-way, Stowey, Tweena-ways, Whiteway (2), Willowray, Yelloways, (b) 5, (c) 3.

weorf (n) Warracott.

wer Ware (4), Weare (2), Were, Warcombe, -land, -more, Kingswear, Little Weir, Lewer.

wic Week(e) (27), Weeks, Wick (2), Wyke (2), Breadwick, Broomage, Buddleswick, Cholwich, Cowick, Dorweeke, Exwick, Fishwick, Fuge, Fuidge, Marchweeke, Middlewick, Shapwick, Southweek, Spitchwick, Stickwick, Westweek, (b) 2 compounds with a saint's name and 2 with that of a medieval holder, (c) 3.

wice Weach, Witchells.

wielle (a) Well (18), Lawell, Will, Willhayne, Willing, Wiltown, Wales, Walla Brook, Welcombe, Wellcombe, Welsbere, Welsford, Welstor, Wilcombe, Willesleigh, Woolhanger, Ash- (3), Black-, Blake-well (4), -will, Blind- (2), Brad-, Brid-, Brindi-, Broad-, Burn-, Cars- (2), Chol-well (4), Churchill, Crockern-well, Culverhole, Culver-, Dip-, Dock-, Dring-, El-well, Elwill, Exwell, Frog- (3), Gog-, Gold-, Goose-well, Gorrell, Gor- (2), Green-, Greena-well, Guzzle, Hals- (2), Hal-well (3), Halwill (2), Hart-, Has- (2), Hen-, Hol- (12), Hole-well, Holwill, Honey- (5), Hors- (2), Horse-well, Horsewells, Hor-, Kers- (10), Kings- (2), Lady-, Lang-, Lid-, Liz-well, Lobhill, Mead- (3), Mor-, Nuck-, Nut-well, Oakhill, Oakwell, Okewill, Pirz-, Pye-, Sand-, Sel-well, Sherril(l) (2), Sherwell (2), Shirwell, Sommerwell, Southill, Sowell, Spark- (2), Spire-well, Stare-hole, Summer-, Trend-well, Tuell, Vel-, Whistle-, Whit-, Wide-well (2), Willandhead, Woodcocks Well, Woodmans-well, Woodville, Wool-, Wren-well, (b) 29, (c) 32.

wincel Wrinkleberry.

*****winn** (n) Umborne, *Womberford*.

wisce Westley, Westworthy, Wiscombe, Wish-ford, -meadow.

wiðig Widey, Withen.

worþ(ig) Worth (3), Wortha, Worthy (2), Worthele, Worthy-gate, Bowerthy, Butterbury, Clat-, Cur-, E-, Fern- (2), High- (2), Hol-worthy, Honeyford, Lang- (2), Lark-, Middle-, Mux-worthy, Neopardy, Nettleford, Sil-, Small-, Stit-worthy, Thornery, Thornworthy, Wallaford, Wallover, West-, Wid-, Wrang-, Yal-worthy, (b) 126, (c) 20.

worðign (a) Worden (4), Wordens Cottage, Wortham (2), Worthen, Brad-, Vir-worthy, (b) Badg-, Rad-worthy.

wrang (n) Wrangaton, Wrangworthy.

wraþu (n) Wrafton.

wudu (a) Wood (24), Wooda (6), Woodah, Woodhead, Woods, Boode, Bowd, Bowda, Bowdley, Bowood (2), Buda (3), Bude (2), Bowerwood, Broad- (2), By-wood, Calverleigh, Charl-, Corn-, Dal-, East- (3), Fair-, Far-, Halse-wood, Harraton, Har-, Hatch-, Hay-, Hen-, He-, Hey-, Hide-, Hor- (2), Ken-, Lea-, Len-, Mar-, Middle- (2), Naith-, North- (4), Nor- (2), Park-, Ridge-, Shell-, Sher-, South- (6), Stent-wood, Stoke Woods, Westwood (3), (b) Wonwood, (c) 4.

wulf Wolborough, Woolacombe, Wooladon (2), Woolley (3), Woolwell.

NORSE, FRENCH AND CELTIC NAMES

Norse. Lundy.

French. Bever, Estrayer, Justment, Meshaw, Purps, Sart, Straypark (2), Viza, Vizacombe. Most of these are Anglo-Norman legal terms rather than place-names in the strict sense.

Celtic. (*a*) Purely Celtic names: Aunk, Bodgate (?), Camel's Head, Carley, Charles, Clovelly (?), Creek (?), Crook, Crooke, Crowdy (?), Dunchideock, Duvale, Gavrick (?), Kelly, Landkey, Maindea, Morchard (2), Penquit, Penrose, Petherwin, Pin (?), Pinn (?), Treable, Trebick, Trellick, Trusham (?), Whimple, Yawl. Of these, Gavrick possibly, and Whimple almost certainly, were originally stream-names.

(*b*) Celtic compounds to which an English second element was later added: Breazle, Dunterton.

(*c*) Hybrid names: Breadon, *Chettisholt*, Mainstone (?) (2), Penhill, Pinhoe. Cartland (?), Churndon (?), Clickland (?), Coarsewell (?), Countisbury, Crackaway (?), Dolton, Dowland (?), Kentisbury, Kernborough (?), Mainbow (?), Membury, Minnicleave (?), Penn Moor, Portledge (?), Portlemouth, Rosedown. The first six are tautological compounds.

NOTES ON THE DISTRIBUTION OF THESE ELEMENTS

A few notes on the distribution of certain p.n. elements may be given, but as the comparative material for other counties is not (except in a few cases) complete as yet, the remarks can to some extent be only tentative.

bearu in the forms *Beara, Beare, Beer*(*e*), etc., is very common in Devon (as common as **wudu**), and one of its most characteristic place-name elements. Over 100 examples are found in early documents. The same element, with similar phonological development, but in far less frequent use, is found in Somerset, Dorset, and East Cornwall.

beretun in the form *barton* is very common on the present-day map, when added to a place-name, e.g. Hayes Barton, but is hardly a place-name (*v.* EPN *s.v.*). Only five places called Barton pure and simple have been noted.

bocland. There are fourteen examples of this and it is worthy of notice that nine of these are names of parishes.

broc and **burna** are the commonest terms for small streams, broc as a rule denoting something much smaller than burna. It is to be noted that the more intensively we study the place-names of Devon the more in proportion are the broc-names that come to light.

burh in its dative form *bury*, *berry* is a very common element in Devon place-names. A small number, but a larger proportion than usual, can definitely be associated with still existing 'castles,' 'camps,' 'earthworks.'

cot(e), tun, worð, worðig, and worðign. The distribution of these elements is of particular interest in Devon. cot(e) names markedly predominate in the Hundreds of Braunton, Fremington, Shebbear and Black Torrington, there being more cot(e) names than there are tun and worðig ones. In Shirwell and in Lifton (the latter being the southernmost of these Hundreds) the proportion is fairly even, except that the cotes predominate in North Lifton Hundred. One should note specially thick groups of *cot*-names in Fremington (7), Tawstock (9) and North Petherwin (12). cot(e) is very rare in the south and south-east. Tavistock and Teignbridge Hundreds contain five each, the Hundreds of Roborough, Plympton, Ermington, Stanborough, Coleridge, Haytor, and Exminster only contain three between them. East of the Exe ten Hundreds contain only some thirty, of which seventeen are in Bampton and Hayridge. The north-eastern Hundreds of South Molton, North Tawton, Witheridge, Crediton, and West Budleigh, occupying a midway position, contain some ninety-seven examples each of cot(e) and tun. Wonford Hundred, the most southerly of the group, contains eleven *cotts* and thirty-four *tons*, the *cotts* being chiefly in the parishes in the north-west of the Hundred. On the whole it may be said that *cot*-names are found chiefly in the north, north-west, north-east and centre of the county, and it is natural, therefore, to find that names in cot(e) are rare in Dorset but common in north-east Cornwall and the Exmoor district of Somerset. That the cot(e) names were given to comparatively unimportant settlements is shown by their rarity in parish and in manor-names and by the fact that, of some 300 examples compounded with a descriptive element, some 140 are compounded with *north*, *south*, *east*, *west*, *up*, *nether* and *middle*.

It is impossible safely to distinguish between worð and worðig, and the examples of worðign are too few to call for separate consideration. Taking, therefore, these elements together, their great home would seem to be Hartland Hundred and the adjacent part of Black Torrington Hundred. In this area these elements are commoner than either cot(e) or tun. The Hundreds of Lifton, Roborough and, further to the east, Witheridge contain a good number. After these the distribution is fairly even, except for the Hundreds east of the Exe which contain only some ten between them. To some extent the distribution of worð(ig) names corresponds with that of cot(e) ones, except that we have a few scattered *worthy*-names in the South Hams district, where *cot(t)*-names are entirely absent. *Worthy*-names are common in West Somerset and some ten examples have been noted in Cornwall, but none in Dorset.

tun is naturally comparatively rare in those Hundreds where cot(e) is specially strong. It is exceeded by worð(ig) only in the Hundreds of Hartland and Black Torrington. It takes the place of cot(e) and worð(ig) in those Hundreds which have just been noted as containing few examples of these elements and is itself comparatively rare in the extreme south-east, in part no doubt because of the extreme frequency of the *hayes, hayne* names in this area (*v. infra* 677).

It may be noted that while there are several DB manors in tun, and a few in cot(e), which contain the name of the holder either TRE or TRW, there are no similar examples of worð(ig), and while there is abundant evidence for tun as a living suffix throughout the ME period, new formations with cot(e) and worð(ig) are very rare.

A word may be added in conclusion with regard to the common appearance of *town* in Devon farm-names such as *Town Farm* (frequent), *Southtown, Townsend*, etc. These are nearly all found in the immediate neighbourhood of some village or hamlet, in some cases actually inside the village in question.

A further point to note is the frequent addition of *town*, (*a*) to some already existing uncompounded place-name, e.g. *Wood-, Way-, Yeotown*, etc., and more rarely to a compound name, e.g. *Cudlipptown, Sowtontown supra* 232, 233, (*b*) to the name of some late owner, e.g. *Caseytown, Prowtytown, Rubbytown supra* 248, 219. This latter type seems to be confined to West Devon. In the east of the county *town* gives way to *hayes* or *hayne* in such compounds (*v. infra* 677).

cumb is, except for tun, the commonest of all elements found in Devon. Some 470 examples have been recorded. Of these roughly 80 are uncompounded. Some 250 are compounded with a first element of a descriptive character and some 80 with a pers. name. The only other counties in which its frequency is anything like so great are Dorset and Somerset. Devon goes with these two counties in making comparatively rare use of the alternative word denu to denote a valley.

ea is a common term for a stream in Devon and some twenty examples of its occurrence in the form *Yeo* in later days have been

noted. There is no parallel for this elsewhere, only three examples
having been noted in Somerset and one in Cornwall. It is to
be noted that it never assumes the form *Rea* or *Ray* which it does
so commonly elsewhere, presumably because the development
of initial *y* effectively prevented any running on of the *r* in ME
at ther ee.

eald. The use of this descriptive element seems to be a
characteristic Devon feature, especially in its very frequent
application to land (12) and to dun (5). The exact sense is not
certain, but it goes back to OE times. Cf. *edferðes ealdland* in
the Stoke Canon charter *supra* 447, and *hyples ealdland* 976 O.S.
Facs, Part II, Exeter vii. A few similar examples of eald have
been noted in Cornwall but none in Somerset and Dorset.
See further Addenda, Part I, lviii.

eg is practically unknown in Devon and is not found in Cornwall. This may be due in part to the comparative rarity of low-
lying marshland in Devon and East Cornwall.

feld is not very common and, except for one doubtful example,
it is always compounded with a descriptive element. Of the
forty-six examples thirteen are compounded with *heath*, ten with
merry, denoting 'pleasant,' and five with *white*. *Merryfield* is also
fairly common in Cornwall and eight of the Devon examples are
to be found in West Devon.

(ge)hæg in the forms *hay*, *hayes*, and *hayne* is a characteristic
Devon element found in some 250 names that we have noted,
chiefly, though by no means exclusively, in the south-east of the
county. It is also common in West Somerset and in the Marsh-
wood Vale district of Dorset, but is rare in East Cornwall. This
agrees well with its distribution in Devon. When used alone, or
in composition with a descriptive element, *hay* is fairly common.
Compounded with a pers. name, generally that of a medieval
owner, the plural forms *hayes* and *hayne* are more common.
Of the 250 examples noted roughly one-half are to be found in
the three easternmost Hundreds, viz. Hemyock, Colyton, and
Axminster. Twenty-three are found in the parish of Colyton
alone, the adjacent parishes of Upottery, Yarcombe, and Luppitt
contribute some thirty, and there are twelve in Bradninch parish.

gierd. This element, denoting a measure of land (*v.* Yard
supra 48), has not hitherto been noted in the volumes of the
Survey. Elsewhere it has been noted in that part of Somerset
which adjoins North and East Devon. One example has been
noted in East Cornwall and one in Dorset.

ham and hamm. These two elements are always difficult to
distinguish unless we have either an OE form, when as a rule the
two words are kept apart, or the name is uncompounded, when

hamm (the only one of the two ever thus used) nearly always appears in its ME forms as *hamme*. It should be noted that many of these uncompounded *hamm*-names appear as *Hama* in DB, but later evidence makes the true facts clear. It should be noted that there is no example in pre-Conquest Devon material of a name ending in ham, and that while cot(e), tun and leah are still used in the time of DB for the formation of fresh names, there is no evidence for such a use of either ham or hamm in DB. It is therefore exceedingly doubtful whether we are justified in postulating any common use of ham in the county. This perhaps receives some confirmation from the entire absence of hamstede and the very doubtful presence of hamtun-names.

If we examine the sites of all the places which either certainly or possibly contain hamm we find that a very large proportion are definitely away from streams, only a few lie by streams, while a still smaller number lie within well-marked river-bends. This makes it clear that in the vast majority of cases hamm in Devon can only mean 'enclosure.' It is very doubtful if it ever has the sense 'river-meadow' which has sometimes been assigned to that term. How far the places which naturally lie in a hamm or bend in a stream owe the second element in their name to mere chance, or how far the names actually record their position, we have no means of determining.

hamstede is not on record in any Devon name for which we have early documentary evidence, though one or two *Hampsteads* are to be found on the present-day map. For Moreton-hampstead *v. supra* 483.

hamtun is curiously absent from Devon place-names, except for its possible occurrence in the thrice-repeated Han(d)sford *supra* 355 and in Fenton. We have three examples of *hǣmatun* in Chittlehampton, Cotmaton and Yettington *supra* 338, 598, 582, with a possible further example in Bampton.

healh. This element is very common. In the uncompounded form *Hele, Heale* it is of frequent occurrence in the county, far more common than the corresponding form *Hale* in other parts of England. Two examples have, however, been noted in Cornwall and five in West Somerset. Compounds with healh as the final element are exceedingly rare in Devon, thus reversing the position found in the rest of England, where compound names in healh are far more common than uncompounded ones.

hiwisc. Devon is distinctively a south-western county in the frequency of this element in its place-names.

hyrst, which is very rare in the south-west (only three examples have been noted in Somerset), has only been noted thrice in Devon, first in a place (now lost) in the east of the county and further in the compounds *æschyrst* in an Anglo-Saxon charter belonging to Topsham (*v. supra* 454) and *stanhyrst* in the Thorndon Hall charter (*v. supra* 296 n.).

lacu, denoting a small stream, is specially common in Devon.

land is fairly common, as it is in Somerset, Dorset, and East Cornwall.

leah is very common, as was to be expected in a county which has always been well wooded. There are some fifty examples of it in the uncompounded form. In compound place-names a descriptive first element is more common than a pers. name.

ora is fairly common but ofer is only found once.

pytt is a characteristic Devon element and is fairly common also in East Cornwall and West Somerset. It would seem at times to be used simply as a name for a hollow, especially for a deep recess in a hillside.

ræw, generally in the form *rew*, is another characteristic Devon element. Some dozen examples have been noted, including two from Anglo-Saxon charters, viz. *widig ræwe* (963) and *ealdan ræwe* (1044).

stan. There are a large number of early stan-names in Devon. So far as they represent a distinctive rock or some boundary mark or the like it is but rarely that we can identify the object on the present-day landscape. There have been identified a *scylfstan*, denoting a cromlech, literally 'shelf-stone,' a *longstone* or 'menhir,' two examples of *þyrelstan*, i.e. one a 'holed stone,' the other a rock with a hole in it, a *Saddle Stone*, so called from its shape, and *Belstone*, an old bell-shaped logan rock.

stede. The only early example of this element is to be found in True Street from OE *trēow-stede*, 'tree site.'

stow. This element is rather more common than usual in Devon and is equally common in Cornwall. It has sacred associations in all the examples other than *Grendestow* (*v. supra* 111).

þorp. One example has been noted and that in the east of the county. It is also rare in Somerset, but is fairly common in Dorset and Wiltshire.

torr, as was to be expected, is notably common in Devon, but outside Dartmoor it is, with one exception, found only in the south of the county. It is fairly common in Cornwall but is only once found as a first element in a Celtic compound.

tun. *v. supra* 675–6.

twicene is fairly common in the north of the county, some dozen examples of its use having been noted. Two examples have been noted in Cornwall and one in West Somerset. The common use of cross-roads as giving rise to place-names has its parallel in the similar frequent Devon use of **weg** *infra* 680.

weald is unknown in the county.

weg is common in Devon to an extent not observed elsewhere.

wic is fairly common, especially in the uncompounded form *week*. This form occurs also in West Somerset but only one example has been noted in Cornwall. Occasionally in Devon we have the palatalised form *wich* but only two examples of the form *wyke* have been noted. It is doubtful if the element is ever found compounded with a pers. name.

worð, worðig, worðign. *v. supra* 675–6.

The commonest terms for a hill are beorg, cnæpp, cnoll, cnyll, dun, hoh and hrycg, while clif is very common with reference to the steep slope of a hill. There are some 330 dun-names and some 130 hyll-names; beorg accounts for some 70 hills and hrycg for some 100. hoh is not common and hlæw is very rare.

The commonest terms denoting marshland and the like are fenn, mersc, mor and sloh; mor and fenn are much the commonest.

It is also of interest to note the types of place-name element commonly found in (*a*) Domesday manors, (*b*) those Domesday manors which were destined to give their names to parishes. There are some 900 Domesday manors. Of these 149 end in tun, 35 in worð, worðig and worðign, 27 in ham(m), 24 in burh, 17 in cot(e) and 12 in wic. There are 13 examples of bocland—there are only 14 in the whole county—and 16 of hiwisc. There are 13 examples of land, 13 of stoc(c) and 81 of leah. Sixty-two manors take their name from river- or stream-names, but the same river-name may be applied to several manors, e.g. there are eight Ottery manors. Apart from the river-names there are some nine Celtic manor names.

Of the parishes, some 50 are not found in Domesday. Of the remainder (about 400), some 100 contain tun, 17 burh, 11 each stoc(c) and worð(ig), 3 each cot(e) and wic, 15 ham(m), and some 10 are of Celtic origin.

PERSONAL NAMES COMPOUNDED IN DEVON PLACE-NAMES

Names not found in independent use are marked with a single asterisk if their existence can be inferred from evidence other than that of the particular place-name in question. Such names may be regarded as hardly less certain than those which have no asterisk. Those for which no such evidence can be found are marked with a double star. Only those names are included which may be supposed to have been in use at the time of the Norman Conquest.

(A) CELTIC.

Afan (Ensworthy), *Branoc* (Branscombe), *Brioc* (Brixham, Brixton), *Cadoc* (Kigbear), *Caradoc* (Crosscombe), (?) *Cast* (Kersworthy), *Ebell* (Treable), *Gall* (Galsworthy), *Galloc* (Galsham), *Gwiroc* (Wrixhill), *Maeloc* (Trellick), *Moroc* (Marshall), *Piroc* (Prixford), *Was(s)o* (Was Tor).

(B) ANGLO-SAXON.

Abba (Abbrook), *Acca* (Accott, Acland), *Ædda* (Addistone), *Æddi* (Addiscott), *Æffa* (Affaland, Affeton, Afton), *Ægel* (Aylesbeare, Aylescott, Ayleston, Elscombe, Elston (2)), *Ægela* (Ellacott), *Ægenoc* (Ingsdon), *Ælfa* (Alfington, Alphington, West Alvington), *Ælfbeorht* (Alston (2)), *Ælfgār* (Ilkerton (?)), *Ælfgiefu* (f) (Allacott (?)), *Ælfgȳþ* (f) (Aldercott, Allacott (?)), *Ælfheard* (Alfardisworthy, Alfordon, Alscott, Arlington), *Ælfhelm* (Bere Alston, Yealmpstone), *Ælfmǣr* (Almiston), *Ælfmund* (Elmscott), *Ælfrēd* (Alverdiscott (?)), Ilfracombe), *Ælfstān* (Ilsington), *Ælfweald* (Alston), *Ælfweard* (Alverdiscott (?)), *Ælfwine* (Alston), *Ælfwynn* (f) (Alwington), *Æl(l)a* (Allaleigh, East Allington, Elwell, Yellingham), *Ælli* (Allisland), *Ælling* (Allison), *Æscbeorn* (Ashprington), *Æscel* (Ashelford), *Æschere* (Asherton, Ashton), *Æscmund* (Ashmansworthy), *Ætta* (Atworthy), *Æþelbeorht* (Elburton), *Æþelheard* (Elsford (?)), *Æþelhere* (Atherington (?)), *Æþellāf* (Elsford (?)), *Æþelmǣr* (Emsworthy), *Æþelnōþ* (Alston), *Æþelrīc* (Addiscott, Easton (?)), *Afa* (Blackawton (?)), *Babba* (Babbacombe (2), Babbadon, Babcombe, Babeny, Babington, Bableigh (2), Batcombe), *Bacca* (Baccamoor, Bagton, Beccott), *Baccela* (Battleford (2)), *Bacga* (Backstone, Badgworthy (?), Bagbear, Bagbeare, Bagborough, Bagga Tor, Bagley, Bagmore (2), Bagton, Bagtor), *Bad(d)a* (Badcott, Baddaford, Badworthy (2), Barnacott, Bason (?), Batson, Batworthy), *Bǣde* (Beeson), *Bǣga, Bēaga* (Beadon, Beaworthy, Bentwitchen), *Bǣgel* (Belsford), *Bǣgloc* (Bealy Court), *Bǣrela* (Barleycombe), *Bǣtti* (Batson, Batsworthy, Battishill, Battishorne), *Bana* (Bannawell (?)), *Bata* (Batton), *Battoc* (Battisborough), *Beadeca* (Backway), *B(e)adoc* (Baxworthy), *Beaduhelm* (Bamson), *Bealda* (Bellamarsh, Belleigh), *Bealdhere, Bealdrēd* (Barlington), *Bealdmund* (Beamsworthy), *Bearda* (Barnacott, Barnstaple), *B(e)assa* (Besley), *Bella* (Belliver), *Beocca* (Bickington, High Bickington, Bickwell, Bicton), *Beonna* (Binneford), *Beorhtel* (Brexworthy), *Beorhtla* (Brightlycott), *Beorhtrīc* (Brightston, Brixton (2)), *Beorhtsige* (Buzzacott (?)), *Beorhtstān* (Brixton),

Beorhtwine(Briscott's, Brisworthy, Burscott), *Beorn(a)* (Banbury, Burrington), *Beornheard* (Burnshall), *Beornlāf* (Burlestone), *Beornrǣd* (Burscombe), *Beornweard* (Buscombe (?)), *Bēowulf* (Belbury), *Bic(c)a*(Badgworthy(?)), Beckadon, Beckaford, Beckett, Beckford, Beckwell, Begbeer, Bickell, Bickenbridge, Bickford, Bickingcott (?), Bickham (5), Abbots Bickington, Bickleigh (2), Bicknor, Bickwill, Bigadon, Bigbrook, Bigbury, Bigport), *Bicga* (Bickaton (?)), **Bid(d)a* (Bidlake (?)), *Bill (Bilsdon, Bilsford), *Billa (Billacott, Billany, Billhole (2)), **Bit(t)a* (Bickleigh, Biddacott, Bitbeare, Biteford, Bittadon, Bitworthy), **Bit(t)ela* (Biddlecombe, Bittleford), *Bittel (Beechcombe), *Blaca* (Blackworthy), *Blæcca* (Blatchford), *Blæcci (-*a*) (Blachford, Blatchborough, Blatchworthy), *Blæcman* (Blackmoor Combe), *Blið-mǣr (Blinsham), *Bobba* (Bucknole), *Boda* (Barracott, Bodgate (?), Bodley), *Bodwine* (Bodstone), *Bol(l)a* (Bolham (2), Bondleigh (?)), *Bott (Butsford), *Botta* (Bottor), *Bōthelm* (Bodmiscombe), *Brand* (Bransgrove, Braundsworthy), *Bridd* (Birdsham), *Brōcheard (Broxham), *Brūn* (Branscombe, Brinscombe, Brinscott (?), Broomscott, Brownsham, Brownsland, Brownston, Brownstone (2), Brownswell (2)), *Brūnweard (Brownstone), *Brȳni* (Brenton (?), Brinscott (2), Brinson, Brinsworthy), *Bubba* (Bibbear, Bucknole), *Bucca* (Buckton (?)), *Bucga* (m), *Bucge* (f) (Budbrook), *Buga* (Bugford (?)), *Bulca (Bulkamore (?), Bulkworthy), *Buleferð* (Bulverton (?)), *Bultfrið* (Bulverton (?)), *Bunta (Benton), *Burgweald* (Burlescombe), *Butta (Buttery, Butland), *Bȳda* (Bideford), *Bynna* (Binworthy), **Cac(c)a* (Cocktree), *Cada* (Cadbury(2), Caddaford, Caddiford, Caddywell, Cadeleigh, Cadewell, Cadham, Cadhay, Cadleigh, Cadworthy, Caton, Cator, Kidwell), *Cadeca (Catkill, Kigbeare), *Cæntel (Kentisbeare, Kentis Moor), *Cærda (Cardwell), *Cāfa (Keyberry, Killinch), *Cāfel (Colesworthy (2)), *Calusige (Caulston), *Camme* (Campscott), *Can(n)a* (Cannamore (?), Cannington (2), Canworthy), *Ceadela (Chaddlehanger (?), Chaddlewood, Cheldon, Chillington), **Ceaffa (Chaffcombe), *Ceatta* (Chapner, Chattafin), *Cemmi (Chimsworthy), *Cēngiefu* (f) (Kennacott (?)), *Cēoca* (Cheglinch), *Ceofel (Chelson, Chivelstone (?)), *Cēol* (Chilsworthy), *Cēolfrið* (Chiverstone), *Cēolmund* (Chulmleigh), *Cēomma (Chumhill), *Cicca (Chichacott), *Ciccel (Chittleburn), *Cifa (Chevithorne, Chivenor, Chuley), *Cilla* (Chilton), *Cnafa (Knathorn, Knaworthy), *Cobba (Cabbacott, Cobbacombe, Cobbaton, Cobberton, Cobden (2), Cobley (2)), *Cocc* (Coaxden (?), Coxlake (?), Coxleigh (?), Coxmoor (?), Coxwall (?), Coxwell (?)), *Cocca (Cockington, Cookworthy), *Coccel (Corscombe (?), Curscombe (?)), *Codda (Cawdron, Codden, Coyton), *Cǣna* (Kennacott, Keynedon), *Cǣnhelm* (Kilmington), *Cogga (Cogworthy),

*Col(l)a (Colaton, Colebrook (?), Colebrooke (?), Coleton, Collabear, Collacott (4), Collacotts, Collaton, Colmer, Cullaford, Culleigh (?)), *Colt (Colston, Culsworthy), *Coppa (Capton (?)), *Costa (Cawsand (?)), Cotta (Cotford, Cotleigh, Cotley (2), Cotterbury, Cutteridge, Cutton, Cutwellwalls), *Cottela (Cuttleford), *Cuca (Cookbury), Cud(d)a (Coddiford, Cudlipptown, Cudmoor, Cudworthy, Kiddicott), Cufa (Cowley (2)), *Cula (Collacombe, Cullacott), Culling (Collingsdown), *Curt (Coursebeer, Curtisknowle), *Cwyldhere (Killerton), *Cybbi (Kipscombe (?)), *Cycca (Kitchadon), Cyd(d)a (Kedworthy, Kidland), *Cyl(l)a (Kellaton, Kilbury, Killatree, Kilworthy), *Cylli (Kilson), Cym(m)a (Kemacott, Kempthorne, Kimbland, Kimworthy), Cyna (Kennel (?)), Cyne (Kingscott, Kingston, Kingstree), Cynegiefu (f) (Kennacott (?)), Cynemann (Kernstone), Cynered (Caseberry), Cynewaru (f) (Kennerland (?)), Cyneweald (Killington), Cyneweard (Kennerland (?), Kennerleigh), *Cyppi (Kipscombe (?)), *Cypping (Kipscott), Cyrred (Caseberry), *Cyrtla (Curtlake), *Cȳta (Kittitoe), *Dæcca (Daccombe), Dealla (Dalditch, Delley, Delworthy), Deneweald (Densdon, Densham), *Dīcel (Dishcombe), Diga (Dydon (?)), *Docca (Dockworthy, Docton (?)), *Dodd (Dittiscombe, Doddiscombe, Dodscott), Dodda (Dadland, Dadworthy, Dainton, Daracombe, Darracott (3), Dodbrooke, Doddridge, Dodyard, Dotton), *Dod(d)el (Dittisham), Dola (Dolbeare, Dolbury), Dudda (Diddywell, Didwell, Didworthy (2), Dotheridge, Dudland), Dunn (Dunsaller, Dunscombe (2), Dunsford, Dunsland (2), Dunsley, Dunsmoor), Dunna (Dennington, Dennithorne, Dinworthy, Dunwell), *Dunneca (Dundridge (?)), Dunnewine (Dunsdon), Dunning (Donningstone), *Dunnoc (Dunkeswell (?)), *Dunstān (Dunstone (3)), *Dunt (Downstow), Dycga (Diggaport), *Dydda (Didham), *Dyddi (Dittisham), *Dynna (Dennington, Dinnaton), Dynni (Dunsbear, Dunscombe (2)), Dȳra (Derrill, Derriton (2), Derworthy), *Eabba (Yabbacombe), *Ēad (?) (Yadsworthy, Yeatson), Ēad(d)a (Adworthy, Edworthy, Yardworthy, Yedbury), Ēadburg (f) (Ebberleigh), Ēadhere (Atherington (?)), Ēadhild (f) (Ilton), Ēadmǣr (Edmeston), Ēadric (Iddlecott), Ēadwīg (Iddesleigh, Idestone), *Eagga (Yagland (?)), Ealdgȳþ (f) (Allecombe, Yalcombe), Ēama (Yeomadon), Ēana (Yennadon), *Earrīc (Axworthy), Ebba (Ebford), Ecca (Eckworthy, Egg Buckland, Eggworthy), Ecga (Adjavin, Edgcumbe, Edgeworthy, Eggbear (2)), Ecgbeald (Ebsworthy), *Ecgela (Eagle Down (?)), *Ecgen (Eggesford), *Ecghere (Eddistone), Ecgi (Edgeley), Ecgmund (Exmansworthy), Ella (Elberry (?), Ellicombe (?), Elwell (?), Tilworth, Yellingham, Yelverton (?)), Elli (Eyles barrow), *Eofa (Ivedon), *Eppa (Efford (?)), **Essa (Essworthy),

Et(t)a (Ettiford), **Fadda* (Vaddicott), **Fæccela* (Vaglefield), ***Færoc* (Foxworthy), **Fætta* (Fatacott), *Fitela* (Fiddlecott), **Flita* (Flitton (?)), **Focga* (Foghanger (?), Voghay (?)), **Fola* (Fowley), *Franca* (Frankaborough, Frankford, Frankhill, Frankland (?)), **Fremma* (Fremington), **Freði, Friði* (Freathingcott, Frittiscombe), **Friesa* (Frizenham), **Friþulāc* (Frithelstock), **Fucga* (Vognacott), *Fugel* (Fullingcott (?), Voulsdon, Vulscombe (?)), **Gabba* (Gabwell), ***Garoc(a)* (Gortleigh (?)), *Geagga* (Yagland (?)), **Gēana* (Ingleigh), *Geddi* (Ideston, Itton), *Gefwine* (Yanston), ***Geoloc* (Youlstone), **Gerla* (Garliford), **Giedda* (Ideford), **Gnæt* (Natson), *Gōda* (Godcott, Godford, Godworthy, Goodameavy, Goodamoor, Goodleigh (2), Gutton), *Gōde* (Godsworthy, Guscott (2), Guscotts), *Gōdgiefu* (f) (Goodcott), *Gōdhere* (Goodrington, Gurrington), *Gōdwine* (Gunnacott), *Golda* (Goldworthy), *Goldwine* (Goutsford), *Grēne* (Greenslinch (?)), **Gropa* (Gratton (?)), **Guppa* (Guphill), **Gydda* (Gidcott, Gidleigh, Gidley), **Gyddi* (Gittisham), **Gylli* (Gil(l)scott (2)), **Hac(c)a* (Hackworthy (2), Hakeford (?), Haycroft (?)), *Hæcga* (Hagginton), **Hæcgi* (Haxter, Haxton), **Hæfer* (Azores), **Hæme* (Broadhempston (?)), **Hagol* (Holsome), *Hāligbeorht* (Halberton (?)), *Hana* (Hannaford (?), Honicknowle (?)), **Haneca* (Hankford, Honicknowle (?)), *H(e)adda* (Haddacott, Heaton), *Hēahmund* (Hensley), *Hēahstān* (Hexworthy), **Heald* (Halsworthy, Holsworthy, Holdstrong), **Hearda* (Hardicott), *Heardwine* (Harding's Leigh), *Helm* (Hensford), **Heort* (Berrynarbor, Hurscott, Hurston (?)), *Heremōd, Heremund* (Hamsworthy), *Hererēd* (Hardisworthy), *Hereweald* (Hazard), *Heorowulf, Herewulf* (Harlston, Hursdon), **Hersa* (Hescott, Hessacott (?)), **Hiddel* (Headson), *Hiddi* (Heddiswell), **Hildegār* (Ilkerton (?)), *Hildhere* (Hillersdon), **Hlūd* (Lodgeworthy), ***Hluppa* (Lupridge), **Hnott* (Natsley, Natson, Natsworthy, Nottiston), **Hnotta* (Natcott, Nattadon (?), Noddon (?), Nutton (?)), **Hōc* (Huxbeare, Huxham), *Hocca* (Hockworthy), **Hocg* (Hogsbrook (?)), **Hodd* (Oldiscleave), **Hodel* (Huddisford), **Hoppa* (Hopworthy (?)), **Hring* (Ringwell), **Hringa* (Ringcombe), **Hringstān* (Ruston (?)), **Hrōc* (Ruxford (?)), *Hrōda, *Hrōþa* (Radnidge), ***Hrucga* (Ruckham, Ruggadon, Ruggaton, Rugroad), *Hucc* (Huxton), **Hud(d)* (Hudscott, Hudson), **Hudd, *Hutt* (Hutswell), *Hud(d)a* (Hudley), **Hudela* (Hurdlecombe), ***Huga, **Huhha* (Hewton (?), Howton, Houghton (?) (2)), *Hūn* (Hunscott, Hunsdon, Huntsham, Huntshaw (?)), *Hūna* (Holland, Honeycroft (?), Honiton, Hunnacott), **Hund* (Houndscombe (?), Hunstone (?)), **Hunda* (Houndle (?), Hound Tor (?), Humber (?)), *Hūneman* (Holmacott), *Hūngār* (Hungerscombe), **Hunta* (Houndbeare (?), Huntacott (?)), ***Hurra* (Hollycombe),

Hwīt (Whitsleigh), *Hwītuc* (Whiteoxen, Whitsford), **Hyfa* (Heatree), ***Hytten* (Hittisleigh), *Ibba* (Ebdon), *Ifa* (*Eveleigh*) **Illa* (Elworthy), *Imma* (Embridge (?)), **Incla* (Incledon (?)), **Ingflǣd* (Incledon (?)), **Inghild* (Incledon), **Inna* (Ennaton), **Ip(p)ela* (Ipplepen), **Leodwiht* (Boohay), *Lēof* (Luson), *Lēofa* (Levaton, Leworthy (3), Lillage, Livaton, Liverton, Loveacott, Lovehayne, Lovelake, Lowery, Lowley, Loworthy, Lowton, Luckless, Luton), *Lēofa, Lufa* (Lovaton), *Lēofede* (Lidstone (?)), *Lēofgiest* (Lustleigh (?)), *Lēofgӯþ* (f) (Lidstone (?)), Lydacott, Lydcott), *Lēofhere* (Lurley), **Lēofosta* (Lustleigh (?)), *Lēofwaru* (Liverton), *Lēofweard* (Lewersland), *Lēofwine* (Leusdon, Lims-cott, Linscott, Lounston, Loventor (?), Lympstone), *Lēofwynn* (f) (Loventor (?)), *Lil* (Liscombe, Lyshwell), *Lilla* (Lilly Brook), **Lippa* (Libbear), *Locc* (Loxbeare, Loxbrook, Loxhore), *Locc(a)* (Lackington), **Lodd* (Loddiswell), *Lod(d)a* (Ladford, Lodfin), **Loppa* (Luppingcott), **Luc(c)a* (Luckworthy), *Luda* (Lutton (?)), Lydacott), *Lufa* (Luppitt), **Luf(f)a* (Lovaton, Luffland), *Lufu* (f) (Lovacott), ***Lugga* (Lugworthy), *Luh(h)a* (Loughtor, Luckett, Luffincott, Lupton), *Lulca* (Lurcombe), *Lull* (Lillisford), **Lutt* (Lutson), **Lutt(a)* (Liddington, Lutton, Lutworthy), **Luttoc* (Lutsford), **Mad(d)a* (Mackham, Maddaford, Madford, Mad-worthy, Matford), *Mǣgla*, **Mǣla* (Melhuish (?)), *Mǣr(e)la* (Malborough, Marlborough, Marlcombe, Marlwell), *Mǣðhere* (Madford), **Mǣtta* (Martinhoe, Matcott, Matridge, Mettaford), **Mǣtti* (Mattiscombe), **Manec* (Monkswell), *Mann* (Manston), *Man(n)a* (Manacott, Manworthy), **Meall* (Malston), *Milla* (Millaton), *Moc(c)a* (Mockham, Mockwood, Muckford, Muck-worthy (?)), **Mōda* (Muddiford), **Mogga* (Mogridge, Mog-worthy), *Mol(l)* (Molescombe), **Molla* (Mullacott), *Muc(c)a* (Muckwell (?), Muckworthy, Muffworthy), *Mucel* (Muxbere), *Nunna* (Newcott, Nunford), ***Obba* (Abham), *Ocg* (Oxton), *Odda* (Adworthy, Odicknoll, Oddicombe, Ottery, Woodington), *Offa* (Offwell), *Ordlāf* (Orswell), **Orra* (Orway (?)), *Pada* (Padley), **Pæcca* (Patchacott), **Pæcci* (Paschoe, Patchill), **Pæcga* (Peagham), *Pǣga* (Paignton), **Pætti* (Padson, Patchole, Patsford), **Palling* (Palstone), *Passa* (Parswell, Passaford (2)), *Peada* (Pavington, Peadhill), **Pearta* (Particliffe), **P(e)at(t)a* (Paddon, Patcott, Pattacott, Petticombe, Petton), **Picca* (Pixton), **Pidda* (Pedley), **Piddic* (Pickwell), **Pīla* (Pennicknold, Pilemoor (?), Pillistreet (?), Pilliven (?)), *Pinca* (Pinkworthy (2), Pinnacle), **Pinna* (Pennaton, Pennicott), **Pippa* (Peppercombe, Pepperdon, Pippacott), *Pleghelm* (Butlass), ***Pocg* (Pugsley), ***Pocga* (Pug-ham), *Podd(a)* (Puddicombe, Pudhanger, Pudson), *Pohha* (Poflet, Poughill), **Poll* (Polsloe, Powlesland), **Polloc* (Poulston, Puls-ford), **Poppa* (Popham), ***Porra* (Purcombe), *Port* (Porsham),

Porta (Portontown, Portworthy), *Possa* (Posbury (?)), *Pott* (Postlake), *Potta* (Pottington, Potworthy (?)), *Pubba* (Pupers Hill), *Pud(d)a* (Potheridge, Puddaven), *Pulla* (Pullabrook, Pulworthy), *Pun(n)a* (Pomphlett), *Puneca* (Pinchaford, Puncherdon), *Putt* (Putsborough), *Putta* (Pitford (?), Puddington, Putford (2)), *Puttoc* (Pudsham (?)), *Pyd(d)a* (Pethill, Pethybridge, Pithill), *Pyttel* (Pittsworthy), *Rǣda, Rēada* (Radworthy), *Rægna* (Runnage), **Riddela* (Riddlecombe (?)), *Ruddoc* (Redstone), *Rum* (Rumsham), *Sǣbeorht* (Sepscott), *Sǣrīc* (Sessland), *Sǣwine* (Swimbridge), *Sc(e)obba* (Scabbacombe, Scobchester, Scobitor, Scoble, Shapcombe, Shaptor), *Scot* (Shaftsborough, Shutscombe), *Scyld* (Shelfin), *Seaxa* (Saxworthy, Sessacott), *Secca* (Seccombe (2)), *Secga* (Sidborough), *Sicga* (Seckington, Sigdon, Sigford), *Sigemund* (Simons Burrow, Simonsham), *Sigeweard* (Nun's Cross), *Sigewine* (Simpson (2), Zempson), *Stūfa* (Stewdon), *Stīþweard* (Stidston), *Strecca* (Strashleigh (?), Stretchford (?), Stretchacott (?)), *Stūf* (Stowsdon), *Sucga* (Sugworthy), *Sutta* (Sutcombe), *Sweorda* (Swaddicott), *Swēta* (Sutton), *Swēt(e)* (Sweetstone), *Tada* (Tadworthy (?)), *Tǣcca* (Tackbear), *Tæppa* (Tapeley), *Tāta* (Tadworthy (?)), *Teotta* (Tedbridge), *Tetta* (Tedburn, Tetcott, Titwell), *Tetti* (Titchberry), *Tibba* (Tibridge, Tippacott), *Tid(d)a* (Tidcombe, Tideford, Tidicombe), *Tīdheard* (Tidderson), *Tigga* (Tigley), *Tilla* (Tillerton (?)), *Tippa* (Tipton), *Tiw* (Twiscombe (?)), *Topp* (Topsham), **Tossa* (Tosberry), *Tott* (Tatson, Tattiscombe), *Tot(t)a* (Toatley, Totleigh, Totnes, Tottiford), *Tottec* (Tottiskay), *Tucc* (Tuxton), *Tud(d)a* (Tythecott), *Tud(d)a* (Tidlake (?), Tidwell (?)), *Tulla* (Tilleslow), *Tun(n)a* (Tennacott, Tennaton), *Tūneman* (Trimswell), *Twicca* (Twigbear), *Ucga* (Ugborough, Uggaton, Ugworthy), *Uffa* (Uffculme), *Waca* (Wakeham), *Wada* (Waddeton, Waddicombe (?), Wadham (?), Wadhays, Watton, Weddicott), *Wade* (Wadstray), *Wadel* (Waddlestone), *Wǣcc* (Waxway), *Wǣga* (Wembury (?)), *Wǣrbeorht* (Wapsworthy, Warbrightsleigh), *Wǣrmōd* (Warnscombe (?)), *Wǣrmund* (Warmscombe), *Want* (Wansley), *Warin(g)* (Waringstone), *Wealda* (Oldridge), *Wealh* (Walson), *Weard* (Wargery, Watchcombe (?)), *Wemma* (Hummacott, Wembworthy), *Wibba* (Webberton, Webbery (2), Webland, Whipcott (?)), *Wicga* (Wigdon, Wigford, Wiggadon, Wiggaton, Wigham, Wigmoor), *Wifel* (Willingcott, Willsworthy, Winswell), *Wīga* (Weycroft, Willey), *Wīgferð* (Wiverton), *Wīgheard* (Wizaller), *Wīghere* (Worswell (?)), *Wīglāf* (Willestrew), *Wīgmund* (Wembsworthy, Whympston), *Wihtlāc* (Whitlocksworthy), *Wilburh* (f) (Wilburton), *Wilhelm* (Wilmington), *Wil(l)* (Willsworthy), *Willa* (Woollaton), *Wilmǣr* (Wilsham), *Windel* (Windsor (2), Winsor),

Wine (Winscombe, Winscott (5), Winsdon, Winsham, Winsland, Winston, Winstow), **Wineca* (Winkleigh (?), Winkley), *Winemǣr* (Wilminstone), **Wippa* (Whipton), **Wīsa* (Wiseburrow), **Wlanca* (Flankwell), ***Wogga* (Ogwell), ***Wringa* (Wringworthy (?)), *Wuduman* (Bearscombe), *Wulf* (Wolversleigh (?), Wolverstone, Woolston (?), Woolstone), *Wulfgār* (Wilson), *Wulfgiefu* (f) (Woolaton), *Wulfheard* (Woolfardisworthy (2), Woolscott), *Wulfhelm* (Woonton, Wormsworthy (?)), *Wulfhere* (Wolford, Worlington), *Wulfmǣr* (Whelmstone, Woolsgrove, Wormsland), *Wulfnōþ* (Wollacott), *Wulfrēd* (Werrington, Worlington, Wormsworthy (?)), *Wulfrīc* (Wooston, Worston), *Wulfsige* (Woolstone), **Wun(n)a* (Wonham, Wonnacott, Wonwell, Wonwood), **Wyrci* (Wrixhill (?)).

(C) ANGLO-SCANDINAVIAN.

Cnut (Knowstone), *Colswegen* (Colscott), *Eilaf* (Aylescott (?)), *Farman* (Farmstone), *Floke* (Fluxton), *Frǣna* (Crinacott (?)), *Grim* (Grims Grove, Grimston), *Griñd* (Grindsworthy), *Grip* (Gripstone), *Gunner, Gunwerd* (Gunstone (?)), *Hrǣfn* (Ramsland, Ramsterland, Ranscombe, Rimpstone), *In(e)war* (Inwardleigh), *Ðorward* (Drewstone), *Ður* (Dorseley), *þurferþ* (Thorverton), *Ulf* (Oldstone, Woolston, (?)).

(D) CONTINENTAL.

Heremann (Hampson), *Lollaerd* (Loosedon), *Prant* (Praunsley), *Serlo* (Serstone), *Walo* (Walson), *Wigod* (Wixon).

FEUDAL AND MANORIAL NAMES

Manorial owner's name added or suffixed. Ashreigney, Ash Thomas, Ashwater, Aveton Giffard, Beer Charter and Ferrers, Berrynarbor, Berry Pomeroy, Bovey Tracy, Brampford Speke, Bratton Clovelly and Fleming, Bridgerule, Broadwood Kelly and Widger, Buckland Brewer, Filleigh and Tout-Saints, Cheriton Fitzpaine, Churston Ferrers, Clyst Gerred and Hydon, Colaton Raleigh, Columbjohn, Combelancey, Combpyne, Combe Fishacre, Martin, Raleigh, Royal and Walter, Coombutler, Culm Davy and Pyne, Dart Raffe, Down Thomas, Heanton Punchardon and Satchville, Holcombe Burnell and Rogus, Lewtrenchard, Milton Damarel, Newton Bushel, Ferrers and Tracy, Noss Mayo, Nymet Rowland and Tracy, Pool Anthony, Sampford Courtenay, Peverel and Spiney, Stockleigh English and Pomeroy, Stoke Damarel, Fleming and Rivers, Strete Raleigh, Sydenham Damarel, Tamerton Foliot, Teigngrace, Teignharvey, Torbryan, Tormoham, Upton Hellions and Pyne, Washford Pyne, Weare Gifford, Weston Peverel, Withycombe Raleigh, Woodterrill.

Manorial holder's name prefixed: Bosomzeal, Caffins Heanton, Challonsleigh, Cobham Week, Coffinswell, Craze Loman, Cruwys Morchard, Doddiscombesleigh, Drewsteignton, Edginswell (?), Grimpstonleigh, Jews Hollacombe, Julians Putford, Mohun's Ottery, Nichol's Nymet, Pridhamsleigh, Revelstoke, Rose Ash, Rousdon, Spence Combe, Spriddlescombe, Stilesweek, Swim-bridge (?), Vealeholme, Woolfin.

Other feudal names are used sporadically, e.g. Knowstone Beaupel, Pouletteslegh.

Other manorial or attributive additions: Abbots Bickington, Abbotskerswell, Abbotsham, Milton and Newton Abbot; Bishops Clyst, Bishops Nympton, Tawton and Teignton, Cheriton and Morchard Bishop; Stoke Canon, Canonsleigh, Canonteign; Countess Wear; Plympton Erle; Kingsheanton, Kingskerswell, King's Nympton, Kingsteignton, Salcombe Regis (?), Queen Dart; Monkey Oak, Monk Okehampton, Buckland and Zeal Monachorum; Dean Prior; Treasbeare. In addition to these we have in Devon a considerable number of places in which the name is a compound of *tun* or, more rarely, some other element, and the sometime holder, tenant or occupier. Examples of these names of a definitely manorial type have been noted by Tait in IPN 131 ff. These and other examples of which many are likely also to be manorial are as follows: Brousentor, Bunson, Burston (2), Butson, Button, Cadditon, Champson, Chenson, Chubston, Colleton, Colston, Corstone, Crockadon, Drewston(e) (3), Faunstone, Fluxton, Frenchstone, Gambuston, Goveton, Grilstone, Grimstone, Hampson (?), Harpson, Hearson, Johnstone, Jurston, Knightstone, Lixton, Lovistone, Luxton (2), Moorstone, Mounson (?), Murchington, Penson, Penstone, Rapson, Rawstone, Rol(l)stone (3), Salston, Sexton, Shearston (?), Simpson (?), Stevenstone (2), Towsington, Vielstone, Waddington, Waringstone.

Post-Conquest pers. names compounded with other second elements are: Baron's Wood, Bickleighscombe, Bolterscombe, Bountisthorne, Bowringsleigh, Burnshall (?), Chambercombe, Custreet (?), Ditsworthy (?), Doggetsbeer, Fowelscombe, Frenchbeer, Gracesford (?), Grasscott, *Grendestow*, Gulworthy, Hexworthy, Moonhouse, Norsworthy (?), Partridge Walls (?), Prowtworthy, Pusehill, Rabscott, Rosamondsford, Swaddledown, Trowlesworthy, eight examples with *town*, ten with *land* and about 100 with *hayes* or *hayne*.

Names of the type Smith's Farm, Norman's Green are not so common in Devon as in the east of England, and the vast majority of such names are to be found in the east and south-east of the county. In a few cases the possessive *s* is omitted, e.g. Austin, Collipriest, Denbow, Devenish Pit, Dira, Durrant, Dury, Lillicrapp, Marshall, Norris, Paullet Hill, Poltimore (in Farway) and Trenchard.

FIELD AND OTHER MINOR NAMES

In collecting material for the interpretation of place-names (i.e. those found on the O.S. maps) a good deal of material has been gathered in the form of field and other minor names. It is impossible to deal with these exhaustively because they are too numerous and many are without interest, whilst interpretation is often impossible without a succession of forms.

An analysis of the more interesting of these elements follows, with illustrations of their use. Those elements which have been fully illustrated in the major place-names are for the most part left unnoticed.

ac. Broadridge and Whitnage show the palatalised dative form *ǣc*. Cf. *to þære ænlipan æc* (10th) in a Devon Charter and the plural form *on eahta æc* (8th) in another Devon Charter.

æcer. *Halfacre* and *Tinacre* have their parallel among field-names in *Nyenakerland* (13th), *Longacre* has its parallel in *Smalaker* (1566), *Fenacre* in *Lakeacre* (1465), *Medacre* (1238), *Goodacre* in *Goseacre* (1422). To the *reeve* must have belonged *Reveacre* (1448), while *Caines æcer* (8th) is presumably a very early nickname for some land on which a curse had fallen.

ærn. To the known compounds of **ærn** may now be added *croccærn* for a place where pots were made, *cweadærn* (*v.* Quither) and *shyterne* (1299).

æsc. *Murdreneaysshe* (1420) must be for 'murderers' ash,' with weak genitive plural, and refer to some medieval crime. *Stroutasshe* (1565) must similarly refer to some forgotten quarrel (OE *strūt*).

ball (ME) denoting a rounded hill is very common on the present-day map and is found in numerous minor names. It has not been noted earlier than 1429 when we have *le North-*, *Southball*.

broc. A few interesting compounds are *ælbroc* (1031), 'eel brook,' *risc-* and *secg-broc*, named from 'rush' and 'sedge,' *Boghebrok* (1311) from the curves in its course and *Ludebrok* from its 'loud' babbling.

burh. *Hordburh* (11th) must refer to some old camp where buried treasure had been found or was traditionally suspected.

croft is a common field-name element.

furlang is found in such compounds as *Mersforlang, Boterforlang* (13th), containing mersc and butere, and *Almerysforlang* (1445) named after one *Almer* or *Ælfmær*.

(ge)hæg is as common among minor unidentified names as in those still surviving on the map.

haga seems to be unknown, except for one reference in an Anglo-Saxon Charter.

hamm is fairly common. It can form late compounds such as *Nycoleshamme* (13th), *Cademanneshamm* (1238), *Constabeleshamm* (1286).

hlinc is fairly common in minor Devon place-names, identified and unidentified. It is usually qualified by some descriptive element such as 'cold,' 'good,' 'white,' 'clean.'

hryding is notably absent from Devon field-names.

læs is fairly common. *Somerlese* (1346), *Newelese* (1485), *Shipcroftles* (15th), *Blakkelees* (1525) are characteristic compounds.

land. This as usual is very common among field-names. *Hedlonde* (1259) and *Forelond* (1525) are to be associated with the common field strips. *Bromelond* (1355), *Rixlond* (1430) from *rysc*, 'rush' and *Haslond* (13th) are named from their characteristic vegetation, *Wlveslond, Falkelonde* (13th), *Scheppelond* (1525), *Larkeland* (1611) from bird or beast, *la Sladlonde* (1210) (*v.* slæd), *Wyllislond* (1244) (*v.* wielle), *Tungeland* (1546), *Spertlond* (cf. Spurtham *supra* 642) from characteristic topographical features, *la Neplonde* (1292) (OE *næp*, 'neep,' 'turnip'), *Benlond* (1427) from the crops, *Prestelond* (1259), *Chapmanneslond* (1254), *Colmanneslond* (1423), *Reveland* (1567) from their owners or those associated with them in some way. *Blowelond* (1378) (*v.* blaw) was 'bleak,' 'exposed,' *Chalkelond* (1482), *Radelond* (1472) (*v.* read), *Blakelond* (1427) have reference to the soil.

landscearu (cf. Landskerry *supra* 215). Further examples are found in *la Landshore* (1278), *la Landiscore* (1546), *Landscore* (1697).

lanu. *Cartlane* (1370), *Durkelane* (1479), i.e. 'dark lane,' and *Cherelane* (1509), i.e. a lane with a *chere* or *chare* or 'turn' in it, are worthy of note.

mæd is very common. As one might expect it is often associated with such terms as wer and fleot (*Weremede, Flutemede* 13th), plæsc (*Playsshemede* 15th), rysc (*Russemede* 1483), hamm (*Hammede* 1465).

mor is common. *Thacchemore* (1520) was clearly a place where reeds were cut for thatching.

myln. We may note *Walkemyll* (13th), 'fulling-mill,' carrying that compound a good deal further back than the NED.

pearroc is common for a small enclosure as in *Penparke* (1497), *Fursepark* (1509), *Menepark* (1691) (cf. Manadon *supra* 246), *Sperraparke* (16th), the last doubtless having reference to its being closed by a spær, i.e. a balk or pole.

pol. *teampol* (937), 'fish-breeding pool,' may be noted.

pytt. *wulfpytt* (739), *frogpytt* (963), *Bulpyt* (1547) may be noted.

sceaga is very rarely found. We may note *alrscaga* (739), 'alder shaw.'

slæd is very common both in identified and in unidentified names.

splott. Further examples of this word (*v.* Splatt *supra* 137) are to be found in *la Morsplot* (13th), *Woldsplott* (1210), *le Splott* (1525).

stan. Interesting compound-names are (*on*) *writelan stan* (11th) which may refer to some sharp pointed stone, (*þone*) *dunnan stan*, 'the grey stone,' *la Restingstone* (1291) and *Sheldestane* (1325), apparently a shield-shaped stone.

steort is fairly common among the minor names (identified and unidentified) in Devon. In a county containing so much broken ground, 'tails' of land are likely to be frequent.

torr. Among minor names may be noted *la Clovenetorre* (1291), and *Hameletorre* (1197) containing the rare OE *hamel*, cf. Hamel Down *supra* 527.

trendel is fairly common in Devon place and minor names. In addition to those noticed *supra* 671 we have *trendelham* (1484) from hamm, *trendelhou* (13th), a circular hoh or hill. The most interesting *trendel* name is perhaps Rowtrundle, 'rough circle,' applied to an ancient hut-circle (*v. supra* 245).

weg is fairly common. We may note *cyric wege* (1031), *Meneweye* (1368) (*v.* Manadon *supra* 246), *Kystilmere Waye* (14th), *Kystemereway* (1427) apparently containing the same first element as Kismeldon *supra* 161.

Among the other minor names of interest we may note: *eorðgeberst* (739), referring to some landslide or gap in the ground, cf. Theobald Street (Herts), *Titeberste* DB, -*burst* t. Ric 1 Ch, -*berst* 1204 Cur, etc., till *Tybur strete* 1501 ECP. Also *la Causee* (13th), 'the causeway,' *la Funteyne* (13th), *Murysele* (1448), 'pleasant hall,' *Thomasbeate* (1465), cf. Beatland *supra* 258.

Names compounded with OE *puca*, 'goblin,' are not as common as in Sussex. We may note, however, *Poukemede* (13th), *Pokemore* (1463), *Pokepytte* (1473) and *Pokemershe* (c. 1500).

PERSONAL NAMES IN FIELD AND OTHER MINOR NAMES

Ælfgōd (*Algodesworthi* 1339), Ælfstān (*Alstanyssete* 1430), Æscwulf (*æsculfes weorðig* 930), Æþelmǣr (*Aylmeresmore* 1244, *Almerysforlang* 1445), Beocca (*beoccan bricge* 962), Beornheard (*Bernardesmora* 1086), Beornwynn (f) (*beornwynne treow* 739), Blæcmann (*Blakemanneshassoc* 1219), Brūnwold (*brunwoldes treow* 739), Brȳni (*brynes cnolle* 11th), Bucge (*bucgan ford* 739), Burhgeard (*burhgeardes worðig* 938), Cædmon (*Cademannesham* 1238), Cēolferð (*Celvertesberia* 1086), Codda (*Coddelake* 1464), Colman (*Colmanneslond* 1423), Colswegen (Anglo-Scand.) (*Colsweineston* 1195), Cudda (*Cuddan cnoll* 930), Cyneferð (*Cyneferðes broc* 930), Cyneweard (*Kinewardeburge* 1228, *Kyne-wardesbergh* 1242), Deneweald (*denewaldes stan* 845), Dodda (*doddan hrycg* 739), Ēadmǣr (*Edemerescumbe* 1279, *Edmerescomb* 1286), Ēadswið (f) (*edswyðe torre* 1031), Ēadweard (*Edwardeslegh* 1249), Eald (*Aldeswrthi* 1238), Ealdrēd (*Aldredescote* 1256), Ecghere (*Egeresford* 1547), Ēadman (*Yedmanston* 1333), Fitela (*Vitelecote* 1303, *Vyttelecote* 1346), Franca (*francan cumb* 739), Friðustān (*fryðestanes dic* 976), Godman (*Godmaneswill* 1288), Godwine (*Godwinesdon* 1262), Hild (*hildeslege, hildesford* 11th), Hūnburh (f) (*hunburgefleot* 845), Lēofa (*leofan dune* 1061), Lēofgȳð (f) (*Lyuedecumb* 1244), Lēofric (*Levricestone, Lieuriche-stona* 1086), Lēofsige (*Luuesispitte* 13th), Lēofwine (*Louenesalre* (13th)), Luca (*lucan weorðig* 930), Luh(h)a (*Luhan treow* 739), Lulla (*Lulleworthy* 1403), Mann (*on manning ford* 962), (*Mannes-ford* 1242), Odda (*Oddingtorre* 956), Ordrīc (*Ordrychescrofte* 1293), *Pinnoc (*Pynnokeshele* 13th, *Pynnokyshulle* 1330), Putta (*puttan stapul* 739), Sicga (*sicgan mores heafod* 963), Swiðrēd (*switheredes stan* 956), Unna (*unnan beorg* 739), Wealda (*wealding forda* 962, *Wealdan cumbe* 739), Wilmund (*Wilemundesburga* 13th), Wulfweard (*Oluardesdone, Ulwardesdone* 1086), Wyngifu (f) (*wungyfe fordan* 937).

OFr or Continental. Bertram (*Bertramesheyghes* 1255), Colin (*Colynesheys* 1479), Flambert (*Flamberdeswyke* 1394), Geoffrey (*Geffreyeshulle* 13th), Gilbert (*Gylbertesheys* 1420), Grand (*Grandescombe* 1259), Hamelin (*Hamelyneshayes* 1483), Hamon (*Hamondyswode* 1476), Hubert (*Hoberdesmulle* 13th, *Huburds-cliffe* 1285), Margery (f) (*Margeryheyes* 1483), Nicol (*Nycoles-hamme* 13th), Rendel (*Rendelesheys* 1427), Reinfrid (*Rynfreyes-land, Reymfreyeslond* 1277, 1289), Roger (*Rogersdone* 1280), Russel (*Russeleston* 1330), Talbot (*Talbottswyke* 1500), Vincent (*Vincentisheghes* 1348), Wadekin (*Wadekynsmore* 1411).

INDEX

OF PLACE-NAMES IN DEVON

The primary reference to a place is marked by the use of clarendon type.

In the case of certain names repeating themselves many times in Devon, e.g. Ash, Cleave, Hill, Stone, Upcott, Yeo, no attempt has been made to distinguish in what parish they are. Users of the Index desiring to identify any particular example of these names should look up the reference to the parish in which the place is found and this will enable them readily to determine on what page to look for the reference for the minor name which they are seeking; e.g. the reference for Bremridge in Atherington (358) may be picked out from the others by noting that Atherington is dealt with on p. 357.

de la Lynch.

INDEX

OF PLACE-NAMES IN COUNTIES OTHER THAN DEVON

References to place-names in Bk, Beds, Hu, Wo, NRY, Sx, are not included, as these have been fully dealt with in the volumes already issued upon the names of those counties.

CAMBRIDGE: PRINTED BY W. LEWIS, M.A., AT THE UNIVERSITY PRESS